◆ ARBITRATION ADVOCACY ◆
Second Edition

NITA Practical Guide Series

◆ARBITRATION ADVOCACY◆
Second Edition

JOHN W. COOLEY with Steven Lubet

© 1997, 2003 by the National Institute for Trial Advocacy
PRINTED IN THE UNITED SATES OF AMERICA
ALL RIGHTS RESERVED
No part of this work may be reproduced or transmitted in any form or by any means, electronic or mechanical, including photocopying and recording, or by any information storage or retrieval system without the prior written approval of the National Institute for Trial Advocacy unless such copying is expressly permitted by federal copyright law. Address inquiries to:
Reproduction Permission
National Institute for Trial Advocacy
53550 Generations Dr
South Bend, IN 46635
(800) 225-6482,   Fax (574) 271-8375   www.nita.org

Cooley, John W. with Steven Lubet, *Arbitration Advocacy, Second Edition* (NITA, 1997, 2003).

ISBN 978-1-55681-799-1

Library of Congress Cataloging-in-Publication Data
Cooley, John W., 1943–
    Arbitration advocacy / John W. Cooley with Steven Lubet.--2nd ed.
        p. cm. -- (NITA practical guide series)
    Includes index.
    ISBN 1-55681-799-1 (alk. paper)
        1. Arbitration and award--United States. I. Lubet, Steven. II. Title. III. Series.
    KF9085.C643 2003
    347.73'9--dc22   2003066500

 Wolters Kluwer

Official co-publisher of NITA.
WKLegaledu.com/NITA

◆ABOUT THE AUTHORS ◆

◆ JOHN W. COOLEY ◆John W. Cooley is a former United States Magistrate, Assistant United States Attorney, Senior Staff Attorney for the United States Court of Appeals for the Seventh Circuit, and a litigation partner in a Chicago law firm. He is a Fellow of the Chartered Institute of Arbitrators, London, England, of the American Bar Foundation, and of the International Academy of Mediators. He is the current Chair of the Mediation Committee of the American Bar Association (ABA) Section of Dispute Resolution.

In private practice in the Chicago area, he is a founding member of Judicial Dispute Resolution, Inc. (JDR). He has served as a Special Master for federal judges and as an arbitrator and mediator in a wide variety of complex, multi-million dollar commercial disputes, both domestic and international in character.

An Adjunct Professor of Law at Northwestern University School of Law, he teaches a course in negotiation and mediation. In addition, he is the principal designer and instructor of a new Mediation Advocacy cybercourse that was developed by Northern Illinois University in cooperation with the ABA's Section of Dispute Resolution. He is the author of *The Mediator's Handbook (Advanced Practice Guide for Civil Litigation)* (NITA, 2000); *Mediation Advocacy* (NITA, 1996 and the Second Edition, 2002), *Arbitration Advocacy* (NITA, 1997 and this Second Edition, 2003, co-authored by Northwestern University Law Professor Steven Lubet), *The Arbitrator's Handbook* (NITA, 1998), and more than fifty articles on litigation, judicial, and ADR topics. The first editions of *Arbitration Advocacy* and *Mediation Advocacy* have also been published in the Portuguese language by the University of Brasilia in Brazil.

Mr. Cooley is a Vietnam War veteran, a graduate of the United States Military Academy at West Point, and the University of Notre Dame Law School. He received a year of his legal training in international and comparative law at the Notre Dame Law School Centre for Legal Studies in London, England.

◆ STEVEN LUBET ◆Steven Lubet is a Professor of Law at Northwestern University. As Director of the Law School's Program on Advocacy and Professionalism, he teaches courses on Legal Ethics, Trial Advocacy, Pretrial Litigation, and Negotiation. In addition to over fifty books and articles on legal ethics and litigation, he has published widely in the areas of international criminal law and dispute resolution. Professor Lubet is the author of *Modern Trial Advocacy* (NITA, 2001), which has also been published in Canadian and Israeli editions. Professor Lubet is co-author of *Judicial Conduct and Ethics* (Lexis, 2000), which has been called the nation's leading authority on judicial ethics. Professor Lubet's other books include *Nothing But The Truth: Why Trial*

Lawyers Don't, Can't and Shouldn't Have to Tell the Whole Truth (NYU Press, 2001), as well as *Exercises and Problems in Professional Responsibility* (NITA) and *Problems and Materials in Evidence and Trial Advocacy* (NITA), both co-authored with Northwestern University School of Law Professors Robert Burns and Thomas Geraghty. In conjunction with the National Institute for Trial Advocacy, he has organized litigation programs in the United States, the United Kingdom, Canada, Israel, New Zealand, Australia, Singapore, and Hong Kong.

FOR JOHN AND CHRISTINA—
AND IN LOVING MEMORY OF MARIA
◆J. W. C.

TO ROBERT BURNS, MY COLLEAGUE, TEACHER, GUIDE, AND
FRIEND
◆S. L.

◆CONTENTS ◆

◆CHAPTER FOUR◆

Preparing for the Arbitration Hearing 95

◆CHAPTER FIVE ◆

Advocacy During the Arbitration Hearing   107

✦ CHAPTER SIX ✦

Post-hearing Advocacy 239

◆CHAPTER SEVEN ◆
Description of the Hybrid Processes   249

◆CHAPTER EIGHT ◆
Effective Advocacy in Cyberarbitration   271

◆ APPENDICES ◆

✦PREFACE✦

The Ever-Expanding Artistic Role of the Effective Advocate

Advocates—effective ones anyway—are artists and scientists, whether they wish to be or not. We can't help it. As lawyers, we are initially trained in the science of advocacy—thinking and reasoning—and we generally find a level of comfort there because the results of analytical thinking are relatively objective, predictable, stable, and secure. This is not necessarily true of the art of advocacy—the intuitive-creative aspects—because it is more subjective, ambiguous, less predictable, and risky. It is more risky because it requires us to use our imagination—to see things not only as they are but as they could be and to attempt to do things in ways we have never tried before.

In addition to being guided by the intuitive-analytical model of the effective advocate, we have developed this book using what might be called a "pracademic" approach—taking care to create, throughout, a judicious blend of practice and theory. Moreover, we explain arbitration advocacy with several audiences in mind. First, we have written for Alternative Dispute Resolution (ADR) practitioners—advocates representing clients who have either opted, or who have been mandated, to have their disputes resolved through an ADR process. Organized into eight chapters and an appendix section of arbitration checklists, forms, and rules, the book provides a full range of features to help the arbitration advocate represent his or her client competently and efficiently. Chapter 1 introduces uninitiated advocates to the two principal ADR processes—arbitration and mediation—and provides basic information regarding the nature of the two processes and their advantages and disadvantages in relation to the court adjudication process. Chapters 2 through 6 provide useful information and practice tips for advocates regarding every stage of representation in the arbitration process. Each of these chapters has a related checklist in the appendices detailing key actions to take at critical stages of the arbitration process. Chapter 7 addresses the hybrid ADR processes (mini-trial, summary jury trial, etc.) and describes successful applications. Chapter 8, a new chapter in this second edition, addresses the topic of effective advocacy in cyberarbitration. The appendices also contain sample arbitration forms and rules and a listing of ADR providers, organized geographically, together with a listing of nonprofit organizations which study and promote the use of ADR.

One chapter of the book deserves special mention. Sections 5.4 through 5.11 of chapter 5—concerning advocacy during the arbitration hearing—are adapted from Steve Lubet's book, *Modern Trial Advocacy*, (NITA, 2001). That chapter presents, in an abbreviated, reader-friendly format, many of the useful trial advocacy principles directly applicable to an arbitration hearing. Space limitations prevent inclusion of the in-depth explanations and the many helpful examples contained in the Lubet trial advocacy book. Chapter 5 cross-references the Lubet book so you can quickly find those explanations and examples.

The second audience we have written for consists of the organizers of and participants in continuing legal education (CLE) programs around the country. The step-by-step approach, analyses of critical process and advocacy issues, and the succinct presentations of useful information in chart form, make it an ideal teaching tool for arbitration seminars.

A third audience we have geared this publication to is the teachers and students of law school courses on arbitration advocacy. At this writing, there are very few, if any, law student textbooks providing detailed "hands on" instruction on effective representation of clients in arbitration. This book seeks to fill that gap in ADR literature currently available for law school instruction.

Finally, ADR neutrals—especially arbitrators—may indeed find this book quite useful. In particular, chapter 5 on effective advocacy in arbitration sessions may provide arbitrators insight on how the advocates appearing before them can most effectively present information and bring the dispute to closure.

In conclusion, we would like to make a few observations about the style and architecture of this book. At our editor's good suggestion, we have made every effort to use a personable and personalized writing style, as if we were having a face-to-face conversation with you. We hope you find this style to be friendly and engaging as intended. With regard to format, you will encounter what some of you will believe is somewhat unusual for a law-related publication. At various (we think) appropriate locations throughout several chapters, you will happen onto anecdotes—some funny, some not; some about famous people; some about ordinary people. We have done this for several reasons. First, anecdotes can enliven and invigorate instructional passages which would otherwise be hortatory and didactic. Second, we consider anecdotes to be the "origin of all teaching," helping readers not only understand the teaching points, but also remember when and how to apply them later in practice. Third, CLE and law school instructors can use the anecdotes as teaching devices in ADR advocacy seminars and courses. Additionally, advocates can use them (particularly the ones appearing in chapter 4) to explain to their clients the "dos and don'ts" of client conduct during arbitration hearings.

We sincerely hope this book will significantly enhance the quality of arbitration advocacy, both nationally and internationally, for many years to come.

John W. Cooley
Steven Lubet
1997, 2003

✦ACKNOWLEDGMENTS ✦
OF JOHN W. COOLEY

I am grateful for the people, both lawyers and nonlawyers, who taught me much about problem solving, lawyering, and life and who, unwittingly, have shaped the content of this book. The list would be endless, but I particularly want to recognize: Angela Cooley, Joan Kottemann, Judge Thomas Fairchild, Collins Fitzpatrick, Judge Michael Mason, Howard Stone, Antoinette Saunders, Terry Tierney, John Buccheri, Michael Siegel, David McGuire, Lynn Gaffigan, John Huston, Nancy Peace, Jim Alfini, Leonard Schrager, Stephen Goldberg, Jeanne Brett, Lynn Cohn, Jamie Carey, Jim Faught, Tom Haney, Mitchel and Pam Byrne, Tom and Perlita Campbell, Jordan Margolis, Ray and Joyce Zeiss, Nancy and Bob Doyle, Nina Appel, Richard Salem, Jim Sullivan, Jim Bailey, Gino DiVito, Erwin Katz, Douglas Johnson (my "Beast Barracks" squad leader at West Point), Todd and Betty Musburger, Judge Morton Denlow, Dennis Coll, Judy and Bob Holstein, Bonnie and Neal Rubin, Bill O'Laughlin, Ron and Sarah Basso, Jeffrey Rogers, Dan Murray, Thomas Strubbe, Art and Sheila Kriemelman, Judge Marvin Aspen, Petronio Muniz and Keila Porto, Judge Frank McGarr, Bill Quinlan, Cheryl Niro, Paul and Diane Schultz, Tom Croak, David Hopkins, Tom Geraghty, Bob Burns, Paul Lisnek, Mark Schoenfield, and of course, my co-author, Steve Lubet. I also extend special thanks to my NITA editor, Ann Jacobson, who congenially attended to the details of integrating and finalizing this second edition.

Special acknowledgment is extended to my recently deceased wife, Maria, and to my children, John and Christina.

✦ACKNOWLEDGMENTS ✦
OF STEVEN LUBET

I am grateful for the support of a great academic institution: the Northwestern University School of Law. In particular, I am indebted to two fine colleagues, Bob Burns and Tom Geraghty, and to two supportive deans, Robert Bennett and David Van Zandt.

◆ CHAPTER ONE ◆

General Description of Arbitration in the ADR Context

In my Travels I once saw a Sign call'd The Two Men at Law; One of them was painted on one Side, in a melancholy Posture, all in Rags, with this Scroll, 'I have lost my cause.' The other was drawn capering for Joy, on the other Side, with these Words, 'I have gain'd my Suit'; but he was stark naked.

—Benjamin Franklin

In the last decade of the twentieth century, the legal profession has experienced vast changes. Not insignificant among them is a growing interest among advocates in the use of alternatives to traditional court litigation to resolve their clients' disputes more efficiently and economically, with less risk and better results. In the days of Benjamin Franklin, as suggested by the opening quotation, no alternatives to the traditional judicial process existed. Lawyers took their cases to court, subjected themselves to a seemingly interminable, self-torturing ordeal, with the worst-case potential of subjecting their clients to lifelong poverty. Fortunately for today's advocates, there are alternatives. We can learn about and apply new and innovative methods for resolving disputes when the court process does not appear to provide the best procedural alternative to satisfy our clients' emotional, economic, and psychological needs and interests.

Among the many dispute resolution alternatives available to us today, the most prominent are arbitration and mediation. Although this book principally focuses on arbitration, it is instructive to view it initially in the context of other dispute resolution processes, particularly mediation. A companion book, *Mediation Advocacy, Second Edition* (NITA, 2002), provides in-depth treatment of the mediation process and the art and science of mediation advocacy. This chapter will discuss several topics necessary to developing a working knowledge of both processes. We will define arbitration and mediation and view them in the context of other dispute resolution mechanisms; consider the differences between the two processes; compare the relative advantages and disadvantages of court litigation, arbitration, and mediation; and gain an understanding of the distinctions between mandatory and voluntary arbitration and mediation. In addition, we will become familiar with the three basic steps to initiating alternative dispute resolution—choosing which process to use, persuading opposing counsel to participate, and selecting the appropriate provider of dispute resolution services.

1.1   Overview of the Processes

Arbitration and mediation are two principal processes in a broad spectrum of means for resolving disputes, collectively called alternative dispute resolution or ADR.[1] Arbitration may be defined as a process in which one or more neutrals (a disinterested third party) render a decision after hearing arguments and reviewing evidence. Mediation, on the other hand, may be defined as a process in which a neutral assists the disputants in reaching a voluntary settlement of their differences through an agreement that defines their future behavior. The essential distinction between the two processes lies in who makes the resolution decision for the parties. In arbitration, the parties relinquish their decision-making right to the neutral who makes a decision for them. By preagreement, the neutral's decision is either binding or nonbinding. If binding, the neutral's decision is final and the winning party may enforce it against the losing party. If nonbinding, the neutral's decision is advisory in aid of settlement. In mediation, the parties participate in a joint decision-making process and make the decision themselves.

It may be helpful to view the two processes in the context of the ADR spectrum shown in the chart that follows:

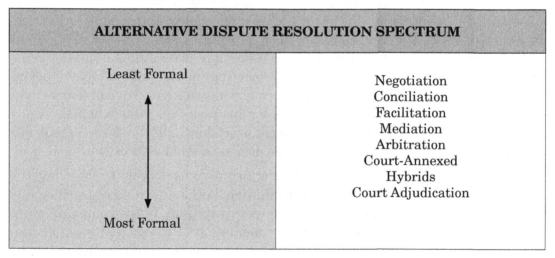

ALTERNATIVE DISPUTE RESOLUTION SPECTRUM

Least Formal

Most Formal

Negotiation
Conciliation
Facilitation
Mediation
Arbitration
Court-Annexed
Hybrids
Court Adjudication

We can view the ADR spectrum graphically as extending from the least formal process on the top of the chart, pure negotiation, to the most formal process on the bottom, court adjudication. Pure negotiation, a process familiar to all advocates, is the only process in the spectrum in which the parties and counsel

---

1. See generally, Stephen B. Goldberg, Frank E. A. Sander, and Nancy H. Rogers, *Dispute Resolution: Negotiation, Mediation, and Other Processes* (Little, Brown and Company, 1992); Leonard L. Riskin and James E. Westbrook, *Dispute Resolution and Lawyers* (West Publishing Co., 1987).

engage without the assistance of a neutral. Many times, however, it serves as an ancillary dispute resolution mechanism to other processes in the spectrum. In the next process, conciliation, the neutral's goal is to assist in reducing tensions, clarifying issues, and getting the parties to communicate. In essence, it is the process of "getting the parties to the table" and inducing their active involvement in solving their problem. Moving down the chart, facilitation is the process in which a neutral functions as a process expert to facilitate communication and to help design the process structure for resolving the dispute.

Ordinarily, a facilitator deals only with procedures and does not become involved in the substance of the dispute. Mediation and arbitration, already defined, combine in the process called med-arb. In med-arb, by preagreement of the parties, the neutral first conducts a mediation to settle the entire dispute or part of it, after which the neutral arbitrates any unresolved issues. The same neutral may perform the role of mediator and arbitrator, or different neutrals may serve in those roles. Court-annexed or mandatory arbitration is a form of nonbinding arbitration administered by court systems. Hybrid processes are specially designed to meet the procedural needs of particular kinds of disputes. Hybrids that have, in recent years, become recognized methods of ADR include the mini-trial, summary jury trial, simulated juries, and expert panels. Chapter 7 describes these and other hybrid processes. The most formal and final of the dispute resolution processes is, of course, court adjudication. It is always a viable alternative to the other ADR processes, and in some instances it may be the most advantageous alternative to best protect and serve your client's interests.

1.2   Important Differences Between Arbitration and Mediation

As previously noted, the most basic difference between arbitration and mediation is that arbitration involves a decision by the intervening third party (or neutral) after an evidentiary hearing, while mediation does not. Another way to distinguish arbitration and mediation is to compare the neutral's mental functions under each process. In arbitration the neutral uses primarily "left brain" or "rational" mental processes—analytical, mathematical, logical, technical, and administrative. In mediation the neutral additionally employs "right brain" or "creative" mental processes—conceptual, intuitive, artistic, holistic, symbolic, and emotional. Furthermore, an arbitrator deals largely with the *objective*, whereas a mediator deals primarily with the *subjective*. The arbitrator is typically a passive participant whose role is to determine right or wrong. The mediator by contrast, is generally an active participant who attempts to move the parties to reconciliation and agreement, regardless of who or what is right or wrong.

Because the mediator's role involves instinctive reactions, intuition, keen interpersonal skills, and sensitivity to subtle psychological and behavioral indicators, in addition to the application of logic and rational thinking, some people find it much more difficult to perform effectively than the role of the arbitrator.

Besides the distinctions outlined above, the two processes also differ in that they are typically employed to resolve two different types of disputes. Parties generally use mediation where they reasonably believe they can reach an agreement with the assistance of a disinterested third party. Mediation is also used when parties will have an ongoing relationship after resolution of the conflict. On the other hand, parties generally use arbitration under two conditions: no reasonable likelihood of a negotiated settlement exists, and the relationship between the parties will not continue after they have resolved the dispute. If the parties use the two processes in sequence, mediation normally occurs first, and if it is unsuccessful, the parties resort to arbitration. Viewed in terms of the judicial process, arbitration is comparable to a trial, and mediation is akin to a judicial settlement conference.

Although mediation and arbitration differ substantially, they both have the underlying structure of a decision-making process. The following chart depicts the interrelationship of their various stages. Section 2.1 discusses the stages of arbitration in more detail.

STAGES OF MEDIATION AND ARBITRATION	
MEDIATION PROCESS	*ARBITRATION PROCESS*
Initiation	Initiation
Preparation	Preparation
Introduction	Prehearing conference
Problem statement Problem clarification	Hearing
Generation and evaluation of alternatives Selection of alternatives	Decision making
Agreement	Award

1.3 Relative Advantages and Disadvantages of Arbitration, Mediation, and Court Adjudication

Most trial advocates are well aware of the advantages and disadvantages of litigation culminating in a court adjudication. They are not always as knowledgeable, however, as to the advantages and disadvantages of arbitration and mediation and how to assess them in relation to court adjudication. This section describes the advantages and disadvantages of these three processes by analyzing the nature of the forum, the nature of the procedures, and cost.

1.3.1 Relative advantages of the processes

With regard to the nature of the forum, court adjudication occurs in a public forum where judges are randomly assigned cases to supervise and decide and are held accountable for their decisions. Both mediation and arbitration are nonpublic, a trait advantageous to the resolution of certain types of disputes where the parties desire privacy of both the proceedings and the outcome. Furthermore, in both mediation and arbitration, by mutual agreement the parties select qualified neutrals, who sometimes have specific expertise relevant to the dispute. Also, in arbitration, but more so in mediation, the parties usually have significant control over the resolution process. Representation by counsel is advisable but not necessary in some instances.

As to the nature of the procedures, in the court adjudication process the procedures are highly structured and institutionalized, typified by detailed rules and numerous compliance mechanisms. Rules of evidence enhance the reliability of proof of claims and defenses. Court adjudication yields results that are appealable and ultimately final and binding and enforceable, making absolute closure a real possibility. In disputes not requiring these types of stringent procedures, mediation and arbitration offer certain measurable advantages. Arbitration, while having some of the evidential and procedural regularity of court adjudication, is conducted in a less formal and less rigorous setting, thereby enhancing the potential for a more expeditious resolution. Applying legal and equitable norms and creating remedies often tailor-made to the situation, arbitrators issue decisions as awards that can be enforced through the judicial process, bringing finality to the conflict.

Some disputes are best resolved in settings having few, if any, procedural restraints. With respect to those disputes, the mediation process offers several advantages. With its minimal procedural requirements, mediation provides an unlimited opportunity for the parties to exercise flexibility in communicating their underlying concerns and priorities regarding the dispute. It can educate the parties on potential alternative solutions, empower them to improve and strengthen their relationship in future interactions, and stimulate them to explore and to reach creative solutions affording mutual gain and a high rate of compliance.

As to the cost of the process, court adjudication is publicly funded—tax dollars pay the cost of the judges' services and other court administrative services. In mediation and arbitration, the parties usually share the expense of the neutrals' fees and certain administrative costs. Depending on the nature of a particular dispute, however, the fees and costs associated with the mediation and arbitration process are normally much less than those associated with a case that traverses the course of the court adjudication process.

1.3.2   Relative disadvantages of the processes

Each of the three processes also has disadvantages. With respect to the nature of the forum, the proceedings of the complex court adjudication process routinely mystify parties, who usually need to be represented by legal counsel. Moreover, a judge randomly assigned to hear a particular case may not have the necessary substantive or technical expertise to appreciate fully the intricacies of legal counsel's arguments. Also, the crush of court caseloads sometimes results in substantial delay in processing individual cases. Parties often find that the court adjudicative process significantly disrupts their personal lives over long periods of time and ultimately produces a result that leaves them even more polarized than they were when they began the process.

Arbitration and mediation similarly have forum disadvantages. Private arbitration lacks quality control since the arbitrators are independently selected in individual cases and are not generally accountable to any supervisory authority. In mediation, the neutrals have little power or authority over the parties and certainly no power to impose unwanted outcomes on them. Consequently, one or more parties can significantly influence settlements in some situations by the power they possess and exercise behind the scenes. Moreover, in mediation there is no application or development of public standards.

As to procedural disadvantages of the court adjudication process, a limited range of possible remedies exists and because of the rigidity of the procedural structure compromise is difficult. Arbitration, a process becoming increasingly encumbered by "legalization," has its own drawbacks, which include the lack of public norms, the lack of binding precedent, insufficient opportunity for full discovery, relaxed rules of evidence, usually no written reasons for decisions, no uniformity of decisions, and usually no opportunity for appeal. Similarly, mediation has several procedural disadvantages: no real due process safeguards exist, participation by the parties cannot be compelled by subpoena or otherwise, access to information may be severely constricted, and outcomes need not be principled. Closure to mediated outcomes is weak in the sense that they are nonbinding and unenforceable, except as provided by relevant contract law.

Finally, as to costs, the public substantially funds the administration of the court adjudication process. In many situations, however, it can be extremely expensive to use because the cumbersome discovery process and delays sometimes cause huge investments in attorneys' time and therefore increased attorneys' fees. Some complex arbitration hearings can spread over weeks and months, costing the parties much more than they had initially projected. Unsuccessful pre-adjudication or pre-arbitration mediations can also add somewhat to the overall cost of securing closure of a dispute.

For quick reference, the charts that follow present the advantages and disadvantages of the three processes.

ADVANTAGES OF THE PROCESSES		
COURT ADJUDICATION	*ARBITRATION*	*MEDIATION*
Public forum	Privacy	Privacy
Neutrals are accountable	Parties control forum	Parties control forum
Already institutionalized	Expertise	Parties select neutrals
Rules of evidence	Parties select neutrals	Reflects concerns and priorities of disputes
Announces and applies public norms	Written procedures	Flexible
Precedent	Expeditious	Process educates disputants
Deterrence	Choice of applicable norms	Addresses underlying problem
Uniformity	Tailors remedy to situation	Often results in creative solutions
Independence	Enforceability	High rate of compliance
Decision appealable	Relatively inexpensive	Relatively inexpensive
Binding/closure		
Enforceability		
Publicly funded		

DISADVANTAGES OF THE PROCESSES		
COURT ADJUDICATION	*ARBITRATION*	*MEDIATION*
No control over selection of judges	Lack of quality control	Neutrals have no power to impose settlement
Lack of special substantive or technical expertise	Neutrals unaccountable	No power to compel participation
Requires lawyers	Becoming increasingly encumbered by legalization	Limited access to information
Mystifying	Relaxed rules of evidence	No due process safeguards
Delay	Limited or no discovery	
Time consuming	No public norms	Powerful party can influence outcome
Polarizes, disruptive	No precedent	Weak closure
Compromise difficult	No uniformity	Not binding
Limited range of remedies	Usually no written reasons for decision	Lacks enforceability
Expensive	Usually no appeal	No application/ development of public standards
		Outcome need not be principled

1.4   Mandatory Versus Voluntary Arbitration and Mediation

Traditionally, arbitration and mediation have been voluntary in the sense that the parties agree, either before or after the dispute arises, to submit it to one or both resolution methods. However, in recent years there has been an increasing trend toward the creation of statutes and court rules providing for mandatory (also called court-annexed) arbitration and mediation both as a means of easing the backlog of cases and as an attempt to reduce the amount of time and money parties spend to resolve their disputes. The rules governing these programs vary significantly from jurisdiction to jurisdiction, and you should take care to apprise yourself of the specific requirements of the jurisdiction in which you are representing a client. For example, with respect to mandatory mediation, some jurisdictions require that parties submit all cases of a particular type to mediation as a prerequisite to litigating in the system. Some rules permit defendants to waive the mediation requirement, others do not. In some jurisdictions, the mediations are facilitative, in others, evaluative. In some states, judges can independently determine whether a case should be submitted to one of any number of ADR processes for treatment, and in others, rules require neutrals to report back to judges on settlement progress. Some mandatory ADR programs require the parties to share the cost of the neutral, while others appoint the neutrals and pay them a nominal session fee. Some mandatory arbitration programs impose penalties, in the form of court costs and fees, on parties who reject the mandatory arbitration award, go to trial, and fare worse than they did in the arbitration proceeding.

Many people criticize these programs for their coercive nature, pressuring parties who are sometimes unrepresented into forgoing substantial due process rights they would otherwise enjoy in the traditional trial proceeding. However, because a growing number of courts consider early settlement of cases to be in the parties' and the courts' best interests, the courts are likely to expand rather than shrink their use of mandatory arbitration and mediation.

1.5   Initiating the Processes

How you initiate the arbitration and mediation processes will depend on the particular circumstances. If you are proceeding in a court that has a mandatory ADR program, the court will notify you of the date that it has scheduled your case for a mediation conference or an arbitration hearing, as appropriate. If your client's dispute arises out of a contract and the contract contains a mediation and/or arbitration clause, then the terms of that clause determine the steps to initiate the appropriate ADR process. If the contract clause contains no specific guidance, or if the dispute is one not based in contract, then you will have wide latitude in initiating the appropriate ADR process. But you must negotiate several hurdles before you can accomplish initiation: you must: (1) tentatively decide which process would be most appropriate for your dispute; (2) convince opposing counsel that the process you are suggesting is the appropriate one; and (3) with your opposing counsel, jointly decide on the provider of neutral services that you will engage.

1.5.1   Choosing between mediation and arbitration

Assuming you have narrowed your options to mediation and arbitration for use in resolving your dispute, you should consider several important criteria in choosing between them. (Section 2.4 discusses additional criteria.) If the parties to the dispute will have future dealings with each other and want to preserve a continuing relationship, mediation is indicated. On the other hand, if the parties do not need or desire to have future dealings, or if they have repeatedly acted in bad faith and have become hostile toward each other, it may be better to choose arbitration. If one party is considerably more powerful than the other, the party with lesser power may benefit from the fairness-determining aspects of arbitration. If one or more parties need to avoid a win-lose decision—a published opinion, for example, which might enforce undesirable rights and/or duties into the future—mediation is the favored choice. Large corporate clients, for example, that are engaged as defendants in a high volume of low-dollar disputes, where there is also a premium on speed of decision, privacy, and closure, may be well advised to opt for arbitration over mediation. If, in a particular dispute, your client has no clear legal entitlement, you are probably better advised to use mediation so that you can concentrate on favorable facts in the process or end the process at any point you think appropriate. A case having multiple parties and/or multiple issues may be better suited for mediation than arbitration because a greater opportunity for beneficial trade-offs exists in such a facilitated bargaining process. If a fair resolution of the dispute requires that certain witnesses be compelled to be present, then you clearly should choose arbitration over mediation. The following chart organizes and highlights some of these important criteria to consider when choosing between mediation and arbitration.

IMPORTANT CRITERIA FOR SELECTING BETWEEN MEDIATION AND ARBITRATION	
MEDIATION	*ARBITRATION*
Desire to preserve continuing relations	Need to offset power imbalance
Emphasis on future dealings	Need for decision on past events
Need to avoid win-lose decision	High volume of disputes
Disputants desire total control of process	Need to compel participation
Dispute has multiple parties and issues	Premium on speed and privacy
Absence of clear legal entitlement	Premium on closure

1.5.2   Persuading opposing counsel to participate

After you have tentatively selected mediation or arbitration and have convinced yourself of the wisdom of your choice, you must then convince your opposing counsel that your choice of process is a reasonable one. This is not always easy. Lawyers who have never used or been involved in an arbitration, for example, are reluctant to use it for the first time. This is just human nature. If they have never experienced it, they feel unknowledgeable and therefore uncomfortable about recommending it to their clients. What if their clients ask questions about the process? Those lawyers will inevitably be embarrassed when unable to provide their clients with an explanation. Or worse yet, they may provide information that is incomplete, inaccurate, or derogatory of the arbitration process altogether.

If confronted with the situation of an opposing counsel who is uneducated in ADR, you might try the following. Agree to meet with him or her to explain your experiences with arbitration, for example, and answer any questions counsel may have. Or, offer to provide a videotape of an arbitration of the type of dispute in which you are engaged. Many videotapes available through law school libraries and other sources are quite instructive on the arbitration process. Viewing the video may be enough to quell counsel's jitters. Another option may be even better: you can contact the dispute resolution organization that you propose to engage to administer the arbitration and have one of its case managers call your opposing counsel. Case managers spend a great deal of their time explaining ADR processes to lawyers, and they can probably easily answer your opposing counsel's questions about arbitration.

1.5.3   Selecting the appropriate type of neutral services

Currently many sole practitioners and even law firms offer ADR services. You can obtain background information on these lawyer-providers from ADR directories available in most law school libraries. In addition, by one estimate nearly 400 nonprofit and for-profit organizations across the United States specialize in providing ADR services.

For your convenience, Appendix K lists various dispute resolution organizations.

◆ CHAPTER TWO ◆

Preliminary Pre-Arbitration Considerations

We cannot freely and wisely choose the right way for ourselves
unless we know both good and evil.
—*Helen Keller*

Arbitration has had a long history in this country, going back to procedures carried over into the Colonies from mercantile England. George Washington put an arbitration clause in his last will and testament to resolve disputes among his heirs. Abraham Lincoln urged lawyers to keep their clients out of court and arbitrated many controversies, including a boundary dispute between two farmers.[1] Today we use arbitration to resolve a broad range of disputes in various industries and in myriad areas of law. This chapter addresses specific considerations when initiating the use of arbitration. We will explore the stages of the arbitration process and differences in the application of the arbitration process depending on the area of the law involved. We will also discuss drafting agreements to arbitrate, selecting cases for arbitration, choosing the appropriate arbitration panel, considering bifurcation and other procedural alternatives, choosing site inspections and audiovisual aids, and deciding whether to mediate first. These preliminary pre-arbitration considerations involve important choices that you need to take seriously to best represent your client's interests. As the opening quote suggests, to make these important choices wisely, you must be able to distinguish between good and bad, between effective and ineffective, between efficient and inefficient, between economical and uneconomical.

What makes these choices very difficult sometimes is that the rules for choosing will change depending on the particular circumstances. Winston Churchill once brilliantly made this point about choosing the correct rules for choosing. Though he was talking about the folly of never deviating from rigid rules of grammar, he could just as easily have been referring to any rules of choice, including those applicable to the arbitration process. It seems that an editor once had the temerity to correct a Churchillian sentence on the ground that he should not have ended the sentence with a preposition. In a devilish mood, Churchill scribbled a note of his own in the margin next to the editor's changes, and sent the manuscript back. The note read: "This is the sort of English up with which I will not put."[2]

---

1. *See* John W. Cooley, *Arbitration vs. Mediation—Explaining the Differences,* 69 Judicature 263, 264 (February–March, 1986).
2. Anecdote adapted from Clifton Fadiman, ed., *The Little Brown Book of Anecdotes* 124 (Little, Brown and Company, 1985).

Churchill's point was simple, yet powerful. Even the most revered and time-honored rules must give way to situational needs and common sense. This same principle applies in making initial choices in arbitration. What is a good choice in one situation may be a very bad choice in another depending on the nature of the dispute; the nature of the applicable law; and the identity of the parties, counsel, and the arbitrator(s). In making these initial choices as advocates we draw heavily on our inner functions as artist and scientist, and in particular, as architect. Good structural design begins with good initial choices. The purpose of this chapter is to help you make the right initial choices about the architecture of arbitration regardless of the circumstances of the dispute.[3]

2.1   Stages of the Arbitration Process

The arbitration process normally consists of six stages: initiation, preparation, prehearing conferences, hearing, decision making, and award.[4] We discuss these stages briefly in this section and in more detail in succeeding chapters.

2.1.1   Initiation

There are three principal ways to initiate an arbitration proceeding: by a submission; by a "demand" or "notice" pursuant to a pre-dispute agreement; and in the case of a court-annexed proceeding, by court rule or court order.

Parties use initiation by submission where there is no prior agreement to arbitrate. First, both parties need to decide whether other parties need to be involved in the arbitration and whether the entire dispute is appropriate for arbitration. If the entire dispute should not be arbitrated, you must, at some point, decide with your opposing counsel what aspects of the dispute will be arbitrated. Next, the parties must decide whether the arbitration will be administered by an agency or will be non-administered. You can choose an arbitrator, for example, from a panel of a national dispute resolution organization, from a panel of a community center that deals in alternative dispute resolution, or you and opposing counsel can agree to use an independent arbitrator.

If the arbitration is administered, the dispute resolution organization may schedule an administrative conference to coordinate the exchange of information, and to consider other matters that will expedite the arbitration process. If the arbitration is non-administered, the parties must decide how they will split up the administrative functions. Eventually, all parties to the dispute must sign the submission. It normally, at a minimum, names the arbitrator(s) or method of appointment and describes the arbitrator's authority, the procedure to be used

---

3. For additional guidance, *see* Martin Domke, *Domke on Commercial Arbitration* (Revised Edition) (Clark Boardman Callaghan, 1995).
4. Cooley, *supra* note1 at 264–66.

at the hearing, a statement of the matter in dispute, the amount of money in controversy, and the remedy sought.

As you can see, initiating arbitration by submission is very difficult because it requires parties already in dispute to cooperate in designing a process and procedures, choosing the neutrals, and administering the process. Because it is unrealistic to expect parties who are emotionally at odds to cooperate in this way, many advocates avert these problems by incorporating an arbitration clause into a contract, which locks in these parameters before the fact. This provides a vehicle through which arbitration can automatically be initiated by "demand" or "notice" as next described.

Where parties have agreed by virtue of a clause in a contract to arbitrate disputes arising out of the contract, one party may initiate arbitration unilaterally by serving upon the other party or parties a written "demand" or "notice" to arbitrate under the terms of that clause. When demanding arbitration pursuant to a contract clause, you should send a copy of the demand to the administering agency if the arbitration is being administered. You should also be careful to comply with all the procedural requirements in the arbitration clause to avoid losing arbitration rights on any issues. An opposing party may submit an answer to a demand. However, an answer is ordinarily not required, and a claim usually will be assumed to be denied in the absence of an answer. The demand and answer, if filed, will be read by the arbitrator prior to the beginning of the hearing and will often frame his or her decision, so you should set out the issues of the dispute as completely as possible.[5]

In court-annexed arbitration, the court initiates arbitration by order or rule. Such mandatory arbitration is usually nonbinding, unless the parties agree otherwise. Depending on the particular court-annexed system, an arbitrator or panel of arbitrators is chosen by the parties or is appointed by the judge or court administrator to preside for the arbitration process.

2.1.2 Preparation

As counsel you must fully understand and thoroughly prepare your case for arbitration as if you were proceeding to trial. Depending on the case's nature, prehearing discovery may be necessary and the arbitrator normally determines its permissible extent. The goals of simplicity and utility in arbitration often weigh against extensive discovery. During the preparation period, counsel often enter into fact stipulations where possible. Ordinarily, in court-annexed arbitration, no discovery is permitted after the arbitration panel is assigned, though much discovery may have occurred before the panel assignment while the case was pending on the court's docket.

---

5. *See* sections 3.1 and 3.2 infra for more detailed information on drafting an arbitration demand and answer.

2.1.3   Prehearing

A preliminary hearing (or prehearing conference) is usually held in more complex arbitration cases. The arbitrator conducts this hearing to clarify any pre-arbitration issues; discuss scheduling matters which would tend to expedite the arbitration process; and to handle any procedural, discovery, or evidentiary issues. At this hearing, you can make any necessary motions or objections which can either be ruled upon during the hearing or scheduled for briefing. All pertinent communication should take place at the preliminary hearing, because in arbitration, unlike mediation, no ex parte conversations between the arbitrator and a party or a party's counsel are permitted.

2.1.4   Hearing

Parties may waive oral hearing and have the dispute determined on the basis of documents only, but this is rarely done. In virtually all cases, an arbitrator conducts an evidentiary-type hearing. Because arbitration is a private proceeding, the hearing is not open to the public, but all persons having a direct interest in the case are normally entitled to attend. Other persons may attend by agreement of the parties and with the arbitrator's permission. When a necessary party fails to appear in person or through counsel, the arbitrator may enter a default award against that party.

A formal written record of the hearing is not usually necessary, and the use of a court reporter is the exception rather than the general practice. A party requiring an interpreter has the duty to arrange for one. Witnesses appearing at the hearing are normally required to speak under oath.

Counsel for the parties customarily make an opening statement designed to acquaint the arbitrator with each party's view of what the dispute is about and what the party expects to prove by the evidence. Occasionally, a respondent may opt to make an opening statement immediately prior to presenting initial evidence.

Counsel for the complaining party normally presents his or her evidence first, and counsel for the parties may introduce any evidence they choose, subject to procedural, fairness, relevance, and materiality objections. Unless otherwise agreed, counsel ordinarily need not comply with the strict rules of evidence, though the arbitrator may rely on principles underlying those rules for guidance when ruling on objections to evidence. You should be aware, however, that certain court-annexed arbitration programs require that evidentiary rules be applied to some, if not all, the evidence sought to be introduced. Unlike the court setting, the arbitrator may direct that evidence be introduced which has not been previously advanced by either party. When authorized by rule or by law, the arbitrator may also subpoena witnesses or documents upon his or her own initiative or by request of counsel. In the appropriate case, an arbitrator may exercise the right to inspect the particular premises, accident location, or construction site in question.

2.1.5 Decision making

When the issues are not complex, an arbitrator may render a decision immediately after the hearing ends and normally no later than thirty days from the hearing's closing date. However, when there are multiple arbitrators and the case has several issues, the more usual procedure is for the arbitrators to take the case under advisement, sometimes direct post-hearing memoranda to be filed, meet later to thoroughly discuss the issues in the case, reach their decision, and commit it to writing. In very complex cases, these tasks may occur over several weeks.

2.1.6 Award

The arbitrator's decision is rendered in the form of an award. It may be given orally, but more commonly it is in written form and signed by all of the arbitrators. Awards are normally short, definite, and final as to all matters under submission. Occasionally, particularly in labor cases, they are accompanied by a short, well-reasoned opinion. Depending on the parties' pre-arbitration agreement, the award will be binding or nonbinding. If binding, it will be judicially enforceable and, to some extent, reviewable. In court-annexed arbitration, the award is usually nonbinding, and if either party rejects it, the parties proceed to a trial *de novo* in court.

2.2 Application of Arbitration to Various Types of Disputes

Arbitration may be used in a variety of dispute settings in various practice areas. This section describes some of the considerations in using arbitration in several of these dispute settings and practice areas.

2.2.1 Business disputes

Business contracts and business agreements increasingly incorporate arbitration or more general ADR clauses. One of the advantages of including arbitration clauses in such contracts and of arbitrating commercial disputes is the opportunity it allows counsel to choose their neutral decision makers. Arbitrators who are knowledgeable about the specific industry will understand technical terms and subtle nuances of the dispute which might otherwise escape a jury or a judge who have no experience in the particular business field in question.

For example, technology disputes bring their own unique problems. These disputes often involve multiple parties and contain a number of difficult technical or scientific issues to comprehend and decide. Decisions in such disputes also may impact a variety of other businesses, including publishing, cable, entertainment, telecommunications, and manufacturing. Arbitration can provide a useful, tailored mechanism to resolve these intricate problems and save parties both time and expense.

Another group of business disputes particularly well suited for arbitration is that which produces a high volume of small to mid-size claims. A principal type of dispute falling into this category is the consumer complaint. The Better Business Bureau and other organizations have been very successful for years in administering arbitration programs which handle and resolve large volumes of such disputes efficiently and cost effectively.

2.2.2   Construction disputes

Nearly without exception, business disputes of all types are amenable to resolution through arbitration. One category of business dispute—the construction claim—warrants separate consideration here because it is particularly suited to arbitration (or arbitration after attempted mediation). Construction disputes are characteristically technically complex, involve a unique vocabulary, and require the testimony of numerous experts. Often, the number of documents associated with these disputes is formidable, but in the arbitration proceeding, discovery can usually be effected voluntarily and much more quickly than it could be if the case were to be litigated in court. Also, because the arbitration procedure is less formal and more flexible than a court proceeding, the arbitrators can accommodate the schedules of parties and witnesses more easily, take witnesses out of turn, and design the process to meet the sometimes unusual needs of the particular dispute and of the disputants.

2.2.3   Employment disputes

Since the 1940s, apart from negotiation, arbitration has been the leading mechanism for resolving labor disputes involving unionized workers. In recent years, parties have increasingly used both arbitration and mediation in resolving employment disputes not involving collective bargaining issues. For example, you can use arbitration in disputes which pit a nonunion employee against an employer. These disputes include alleged discrimination based on race, sex, religion, sexual orientation, and physical and mental disabilities. They also include disputes which arise out of the terms and conditions of employment as contained in an employment contract. These contractual disputes sometimes concern wages, promotion, termination, benefits, covenants not to compete, confidentiality clauses, and scope of function. In many of these situations, parties use arbitration after mediation proves unsuccessful.

2.2.4   Insurance disputes

Arbitration has been used for many years to resolve all types of disputes that arise from insurance policies. These disputes can involve disagreements between insurance companies and their policyholders; between two or more insurance companies over liability; and between a third-party claimant and an insurance company over that claimant's right to be reimbursed under another person's policy. Personal injury, medical malpractice, legal malpractice, and property damage claims are just a few of the many types of cases that fall into this insurance dispute category. Other types of insurance-related claims that are routinely arbitrated include: workers' compensation; title insurance; toxic tort and other environmental claims; architectural and engineering professional negligence claims; and flood, earthquake, and other natural disaster claims.

2.2.5   Securities disputes

The securities industry has used arbitration since the early 1800s. Within the industry there are ten self-regulatory organizations (SROs) that administer arbitrations and provide arbitrators for disputes. In the past, many arbitration clauses in securities contracts mandated that arbitration be administered by the SROs. However, due to customer complaints, many clauses now include a choice among several dispute resolution organizations to administer the arbitration proceedings should a dispute arise.

Because of increased overcrowding of the court system and of several opinions by the United States Supreme Court removing any barriers to resolving securities cases through arbitration, the use of arbitration has increased dramatically in this practice area during the last decade.

If you represent an investor in a securities case, and the dispute arises under an investment agreement containing an arbitration clause, the arbitration must take place in the forum dictated by the clause. You should note that each arbitration forum has specific rules describing what information must be in a claim, the amount of filing fees that will be charged, and how notification must be made to the other party. You should carefully read the rules of the pertinent arbitration forum before proceeding.

2.2.6   Real estate disputes

In the last decade, the use of ADR, including arbitration, has expanded in the real estate industry. The disputants' desire to save time and money and to preserve confidentiality is driving this increased use. Types of real estate disputes commonly submitted to mediation and arbitration for resolution include: home purchase and sale agreements, listing agreements, leases, real estate partnerships and joint ventures, and real estate valuation. It is important to note that ADR may not always satisfy the needs of parties to real estate contracts, particularly as those contracts pertain to foreclosure; enforcement of a deed of trust, mortgage, or land contract; and mechanics' liens, all of which are more appropriately suited for resolution by judicial means. Thus, advocates who draft buy/sell agreements should seriously consider excluding from arbitration these and other related procedures and remedies which the court system is better equipped to handle.

2.2.7 Family disputes

Because of the sheer number of disputes involving family laws, the courts and parties are increasingly turning to private dispute resolution organizations for administrative relief. Before beginning the arbitration process, both sides sign an arbitration agreement that sets out the issues to be arbitrated, names of the arbitrators, and the parties' understanding that the arbitrators' decision will be binding. Although mediation is normally the preferred process in family disputes—particularly with respect to custody and visitation issues—arbitration is often quite helpful with respect to property division issues where mediation has been ineffective and the parties desire a speedy, economical resolution. Many divorce settlement agreements include arbitration clauses to settle any post-divorce disputes. This helps minimize the possibility that one party will attempt to harass the other through a prolonged court battle. The mere presence of such arbitration clause in a divorce decree encourages the parties to negotiate settlement of post-decree disputes rather than to submit them to the uncertainty of decision by a neutral arbitrator.

2.2.8 Health care disputes

Although the health care industries have been slow to use ADR processes for resolving disputes, ADR, and particularly arbitration, is quite well suited for the types of conflicts that arise in those industries. The industries define a broad spectrum of potential ADR users, including hospitals, physicians, health insurers, medical equipment manufacturers and distributors, pharmaceutical companies, nursing homes, various managed care and health maintenance organizations, dental clinics, independent laboratories, etc. Arbitration and other ADR processes have been used successfully to resolve disputes between health care institutions and providers, intellectual property disputes, disputes between insurers and subscribers, and contract disputes between medical product manufacturers and medical providers.

2.2.9 Government disputes

In recent years, both state and federal governments have been incorporating public and private dispute resolution into their systems of doing business. The Administrative Conference of the United States, a federal agency that researches and monitors federal agency procedures, has been the vanguard in this trend toward the expanded use of ADR methods to resolve disputes in which an agency of the federal government is a party. The Administrative Conference sponsors educational workshops on ADR and wants to implement dispute resolution programs in every agency of the federal government. By 1994, twenty-four federal agencies had signed pledges to review existing contract disputes and to consider settling them with out-of-court dispute resolution procedures. Thus, in any situation in which your client has a civil contract dispute with the federal government, you should consider arbitration as one of the possible means for resolving it.

2.2.10 International disputes

Arbitration has been the preferred method for settling international disputes for decades. Companies doing business internationally routinely include arbitration or other ADR-type clauses in their contracts to avoid problems that can arise when dealing with a foreign legal system. Also, many foreign companies feel more comfortable with the arbitration process than they do with litigation. Parties can choose non-administered arbitration, but pursuing international arbitration through an organization has several advantages, including the fact that these organizations have well-established rules and lists of highly qualified individuals to act as arbitrators. Besides the American Arbitration Association, JAMS, and the International Chamber of Commerce, other organizations that administer international arbitration include the United Nations Commission on International Trade Relations and Law, the International Bar Association, the International Centre for Settlement of Investment Disputes, and the World Intellectual Property Organization, which offers many arbitration services.

A recurring challenge for the advocate in initiating international arbitration is agreeing with the opponents on a site to hold the arbitration proceedings. It is best to choose a neutral location where professional and technical support are available. It is also important to consider how politically stable the area is, how local laws might affect the enforcement of the arbitration clause, and the degree of difficulty in enforcing an arbitral award once obtained. Other important challenges include determining where the other party's assets are held and whether the host jurisdiction adheres to the New York Convention on the Recognition and Enforcement of Foreign Arbitral Awards.

2.3 Drafting the Arbitration Agreement

There are essentially two types of arbitration agreements: (1) a future dispute arbitration agreement, normally called an "arbitration clause," which is contained in a broader contract (for goods, services, etc.) between the parties and which anticipates arbitration procedures to follow should a dispute arise under that broader contract; and (2) a present-dispute arbitration agreement, called a "submission agreement," which counsel for the parties craft when the parties desire to arbitrate a dispute, but where there is no pre-existing contract clause. In either type of agreement, the parties may provide that a dispute resolution organization administer the arbitration. You can use a submission agreement to initiate an arbitration either before commencing litigation or after a lawsuit has been filed, but before trial. Occasionally, when a dispute arises and counsel deems that the "arbitration clause" inadequately addresses the situation's needs, they supplement the arbitration clause by entering into a submission agreement.

There are at least two schools of thought about how detailed the first type of arbitration agreement—the arbitration clause—should be. Some lawyers draft the arbitration clause in an abbreviated format, indicating the parties' desire to arbitrate any and all contract disputes, designating a dispute resolution organization, adopting its procedural rules, and choosing the jurisdiction whose laws are to govern the legal issues. Any specific technical or procedural issues are worked out later, should a dispute arise. Other lawyers draft the arbitration clause to be as detailed as possible to minimize the amount of attorney time involved in getting an eventual dispute to an arbitration hearing and receiving a timely decision by an arbitration panel. The most suitable drafting solution probably falls somewhere in the middle. Each contract, each set of contracting parties, and each set of lawyers, presents a unique configuration of possibilities you must carefully analyze in deciding the appropriate arbitration clause. Do not believe that simple, familiar language will satisfy every situation. Consider the example of legendary musicians Benny Goodman and Jimmy Dorsey who shared a flat in the early stages of their careers. Both played the clarinet and the saxophone, so there was fierce competition when any job came up. Rather than share the work equally, they agreed to operate on the simple rule that whoever answered the telephone first got the job. This agreement worked fine for awhile until one day the old stand-type telephone jingled and both lunged for it. As Goodman later reminisced: "Jimmy got the mouthpiece of the phone and accepted the date. But I had the receiver and knew where the job was."[6]

In this section, we will explore the types of provisions to consider for inclusion in a submission agreement and an expanded arbitration clause.[7] Sample arbitration clauses appear infra in Appendix F.

---

6. Anecdote adapted from Fadiman, *supra* note 3 at 249.

7. *See generally* Branton & Lovett, *Alternative Dispute Resolution* (Vol. 10) 2–61 to 2–63 (Knowles Publishing, Inc. 1995); Whitmore Gray, *Drafting the Dispute Resolution Clause*, in Richard J. Medalie (Ed.), *Commercial Arbitration for the 1990s* 150–52 (ABA, 1991).

2.3.1 Intent to arbitrate

When you draft an arbitration clause, you must communicate unequivocally the circumstances under which the parties intend to arbitrate any dispute between them. Most arbitration clauses allow the parties equal access to arbitration—that is, each party has a separate right to invoke arbitration and no party has a right to sue the other in court over disputes the agreement defines as arbitrable. Some arbitration clauses reserve to one party (usually the drafter of the agreement) the option to sue in court. Presumably, such agreements are enforceable if the parties to the arbitration agreement had equal bargaining power when they entered into the agreement. However, if there is a bargaining power imbalance, as in the situation of a Fortune 500© Company and an individual consumer, a court may find the consumer's obligation to arbitrate to be unenforceable either because of duress or misunderstanding.

2.3.2 Disputes arbitrable

Typically, future-dispute arbitration clauses contain language committing the parties to arbitrate "any controversy or claim arising out of or relating to this contract." One would think that such broad language would include all possible disputes between the contracting parties within its sweep. This is not always so. Enterprising, creative lawyers who want to litigate in court always seem to find ways to argue that a particular dispute does not "arise out of or relate to" the contract in question. The present dispute, they might argue, arises out of a separate contract, not having an arbitration clause; or the dispute relates to a *service* related to the purchase of products and therefore not to the product sales contract containing an arbitration clause. Thus, when drafting a future-dispute arbitration clause by which you want all disputes arbitrated, anticipate many future possibilities. Also, take care to review other contracts between the parties and even reference them, as necessary, in the clause so there is no confusion about what kinds of disputes the parties intend to arbitrate.

On the other hand, there may be particular disputes that are apt to arise during the contract's term that the parties agree should not be arbitrated, but rather should be litigated in court. For example, as pointed out in section 2.2.6, supra, certain types of real estate disputes must be carved out of an agreement to arbitrate, particularly those relating to foreclosures and enforcement of mortgages, liens, etc. Also, in service contracts or joint ventures where there are increased risks of personal injuries, consider excluding from the arbitration clause's coverage any dispute regarding compensation for a contract-related injury. The principal point is that the more effort you expend at the drafting stage to explain the parties' understanding of the disputes that are arbitrable under the contract, the less time you will spend later, arguing before the arbitrators or in court before a judge, which of the claimant's issues are arbitrable and which are not.

2.3.3 Joinder of claims or parties

In drafting an arbitration clause or a submission agreement, give some thought to the question of joinder of claims or parties. If you are drafting a submission agreement, the parties may already have claims pending in litigation that, although not technically arising out of the same contract, are related to an ongoing business arrangement and would more efficiently be resolved in a single forum. In such case, you might consider discussing with your opposing counsel the possibility of resolving those claims, along with others arising out of the contract, in arbitration.

As to arbitration clauses, if you are representing a guarantor of a contract, and the parties to the underlying transaction agree to arbitrate any future disputes, you need to make clear in any contract in which the guarantor is a signatory that he or she does or does not agree to arbitrate any claim arising out of his or her status as guarantor. Perhaps you represent a corporate client that routinely enters into numerous contracts with members of the public (e.g., investment broker) and that may be a future target of multiple lawsuits by separate plaintiffs or even a class action. If so, give serious thought to including in each contract's arbitration clause a provision clearly stating your client does not agree in advance to either a consolidated arbitration procedure or a class-action arbitration procedure, whether or not the rules of the pre-selected arbitration forum provide for such proceedings.

2.3.4 Designation of dispute resolution organization

Whether you are drafting an arbitration clause or a submission agreement, give serious consideration to designating a dispute resolution organization to administer the arbitration process. Obviously, one factor in choosing a particular dispute resolution organization is determining which has on its roster the neutral or neutrals who have the experience and expertise pertinent to your dispute and to the legal, technical, and business issues, as appropriate. We discuss factors you may want to consider in selecting an appropriate dispute resolution organization or arbitration forum in section 2.6.1, *infra*.

2.3.5 Location of arbitration

If the parties to an arbitration agreement are located in different parts of the country or of the world, the location of the arbitration hearing may become an important drafting consideration. If not dealt with clearly in an arbitration clause, location can develop into a major issue particularly if an inconvenienced party believes that the suggested location does not appropriately take into account its logistical and economic limitations. Usually, by pre-selecting a particular office of a dispute resolution organization to administer the arbitration, the parties by implication are agreeing to the arbitration's location. Office selection may also determine the region in which that particular organization's affiliated arbitrators live and perform their neutral services. Thus, if you are choosing a dispute resolution firm in advance, take into account where it likely would be most convenient for all the parties and witnesses, etc., to attend an arbitration hearing should a future dispute arise—in addition to where your preferred neutrals work and reside. If you are not naming a dispute resolution organization to administer the arbitration process, it is all the more important that you include in the arbitration clause an agreed location for holding an arbitration. If after the dispute arises, you and opposing counsel realize that the preselected location is inconvenient, then you can agree to change the location.

2.3.6   Procedure to initiate arbitration

If you pre-select a dispute resolution organization to administer the arbitration process and adopt its procedural rules, those rules will dictate how and when an aggrieved party can initiate an arbitration. Nonetheless, it is a good idea to include in the arbitration clause the details of that organization's procedure for initiating arbitration. This has several benefits. First, it saves you the trouble of locating the organization's rules if you need to initiate arbitration in an emergency, or if you need to advise the client of the procedure when access to the rules is inconvenient—e.g., on the holidays, weekend, or while you are on vacation. Second, should a dispute arise, it provides a basis for posturing in your efforts to negotiate an early resolution. You can direct your opposing counsel's attention to the arbitration provision and quote chapter and verse how and when you will initiate the arbitration process should you both be unsuccessful in resolving the dispute consensually. Finally, if a dispute arises in which your client has, in your view, breached the contract but his anger precludes him from acknowledging it, you can review the arbitration initiation procedure in the clause and use it as leverage to coax him back to the reality of the advantages of a negotiated solution over the more expensive arbitrated one.

2.3.7   Pre-arbitration ADR

Before you draft any arbitration agreement, discuss with your client the possible advantages of including pre-arbitration methods of dispute resolution, particularly mediation. Mediation-first arbitration clauses are becoming more popular because of their proven cost benefits. Usually, after just a few hours of mediation, counsel and parties can determine whether a mediated resolution is possible, whether the mediation should continue, or whether the parties are irreversibly deadlocked and arbitration should proceed. Usually parties attempt mediation before investing the time and money to have their counsel prepare for an arbitration hearing.

2.3.8 Time limits

The typical arbitration clause contains a time limit within which a party must initiate arbitration. Usually, the period is thirty days and is measured from the date the parties reach an impasse in their negotiations to resolve a dispute. Some arbitration agreements—particularly submission agreements—contain a provision setting time limits for each of the parties to present their case. This type of provision attempts to set some reasonable limit on the length, and therefore the cost, of the entire arbitration process. This is very important when multiple parties are involved. Arbitration agreements may also specify the time period within which the arbitration panel is to render its decision. Ordinarily, this period is thirty days after the close of the evidence. In especially complex cases, longer periods are specified.

2.3.9 Arbitrator selection procedures

If the arbitration agreement designates a dispute resolution organization, unless specified otherwise, that organization's procedures will govern the selection of arbitrators. However, where the arbitration is administered by the disputants, it is very important to spell out in detail the method of selecting the arbitrators. You should specify the number of arbitrators to be appointed, and you should also include a procedure for selecting arbitrators where the parties are unable to agree. A common method is to have each party select one arbitrator and then to have those two arbitrators mutually select a third, or "neutral", arbitrator. Some agreements designate the arbitrator or arbitrators by name. Also, if the arbitrators must have special qualifications, specify them in the agreement. Section 2.6, infra, covers arbitrator selection in more detail.

2.3.10 Scope of arbitrator's authority and jurisdiction

Another important aspect of any arbitration agreement is the parties' written understanding of the arbitrator's authority and jurisdiction. For example, what action will the arbitrator be authorized to take if a respondent or his counsel fails to appear at a hearing or if a claimant fails to prosecute? Some dispute resolution organizations have specific rules to guide arbitrators in such instances, but if your arbitration is to be nonadministered, you should draft clear provisions to cover these eventualities. Also, if you want to limit the arbitrator's jurisdiction—for example, no subject matter jurisdiction to hear or decide punitive damage claims or claims related to matters pending before a judge for decision—you should carefully describe those limitations in the arbitration agreement.

2.3.11 Pleadings and discovery

Normally, rules of dispute resolution organizations let the arbitrator specify the nature and type of pleadings and discovery that will be permissible in arbitration proceedings. However, if your arbitration agreement specifies permissible pleadings and the nature and scope of discovery, the arbitrators must honor that agreement. Thus, in the arbitration agreement, you can specify whether the parties desire fact or notice pleading for the claim, and you can agree as to the required detail for the answer or possible counterclaim.

Usually, discovery is minimized in arbitration. Nonetheless, if you believe that contract disputes will require more discovery than is normally permitted in arbitration, you and counsel for the other side can agree in advance to the form and extent of discovery which each party might initiate. For example, you might agree in advance to a limited number of interrogatories, requests to produce, and depositions of a specified length. You might also agree to procedures governing discovery related to experts and their reports. Although it is very tempting, you should think long and hard before you simply adopt the federal discovery rules for the typical arbitrated dispute. This could prove to be unnecessarily costly and burdensome to your client and turn into a situation where a discovery tail is wagging a small dog of a dispute.

2.3.12 Confidentiality

In arbitration clauses, particularly in submission agreements, there may be good reason to include a confidentiality provision. For example, if the dispute involves sensitive business, technological, or financial information, you may want to draft specific prohibitory provisions, with associated automatic sanctions, preventing the disclosure of information exchanged in or introduced during the arbitration proceeding. You may also wish to require the return of all such confidential information to the producing party at the end of the arbitration proceeding.

2.3.13 Evidence

Although rules of evidence do apply in some court-annexed arbitration programs, they do not customarily apply in private arbitration. In the type of arbitration that is the subject of an arbitration agreement, hearsay evidence is usually admissible, and other types of evidence that are ordinarily excluded in a court of law may be deemed admissible in arbitration, with the arbitrators' caveat that they "will give the evidence the weight they deem appropriate." The perceived advantage, of course, of not having rules of evidence apply in private arbitration is that the number of evidence objections and related lawyer squabbling is greatly minimized, making the proceedings more efficient overall. Even when no evidence rules apply, counsel will still make objections regarding the evidence's relevance or materiality, but the arbitrators can normally rule on these objections very quickly without the need for extensive argument by counsel. The disadvantage of proceeding without rules of evidence is that your opponent may introduce information that has no foundation in fact, is unauthenticated, and that may be very prejudicial to your case. You should ask arbitrators to reject this type of evidence in your closing argument.

In drafting an arbitration agreement, consider whether you want the rules of evidence to apply to all the evidence in the case or to certain types of evidence. Realize that if you agree, for example, to have the Federal Rules of Evidence apply in the arbitration proceeding, the arbitrators you choose should know how to make appropriate evidentiary rulings based on them. A panel of scientific experts, without a member who is a lawyer, may have difficulty applying evidentiary rules. Thus, if you do decide to propose that an arbitration agreement contain a provision requiring evidentiary rules to apply to arbitration evidence, you should also propose that at least one of the panel arbitrators be a present or former litigator or former judge.

2.3.14   Court reporter

In many arbitrations it is not necessary to have a court reporter make a record of the proceedings. However, in certain circumstances, it may be advantageous to have a record of the proceedings. For example, in a complex case where the hearing will extend over several days or weeks, and post-hearing briefs will be filed, normally the parties will agree to hire a court reporter and share the cost. A transcript of the hearing will be indispensable in preparing post-hearing briefs. If the parties do not agree, one side can arrange for the court reporter and pay all costs. You may also want to use a court reporter when one or more witnesses who will be testifying under oath in the arbitration proceeding are also testifying in a court case involving the same subject matter. While arbitration proceedings are considered confidential, witnesses who testify in court can be impeached by any prior statement made under oath, even if made in an arbitration proceeding.

Thus, when you draft an arbitration agreement, consider including a provision allowing the parties an option to hire a court reporter to record the proceedings.

2.3.15   Nature, effect, and enforceability of award

In an arbitration agreement it is also important to specify the nature, effect, and enforceability of an award or awards issued by an arbitration panel. The parties should agree as to whether they desire the customary short award without a statement of reasons or whether they desire the award to incorporate a reasoned opinion.

Realize that if you opt for the reasoned opinion, there will be a basis to challenge the award by way of a motion for reconsideration. This may be fine if you are the one who wants to do the challenging, but if it is your opponents who are unhappy with the arbitrators' reasoning, their motions for reconsideration may extend the proceedings, cause additional costly briefing, and delay the award's enforcement. In the rare case, the opinion may even provide the basis for a court challenge on the grounds that the arbitrators exceeded their authority or jurisdiction or that the award was manifestly unjust—whether or not there is actual merit to such challenges. Thus, under such circumstances, the award's enforceability would be even further delayed.

When you draft an arbitration agreement, you should also consider whether to give the arbitrators the authority to issue partial awards. For example, in certain cases, it may be crucial that your client obtain a preliminary award directing a respondent to protect or preserve certain assets. In construction situations, you may want to allow for the opportunity to request the arbitrators to order that construction of a building continue. Or in a commercial situation, you may want the option of requesting, even before the arbitration hearing, that the arbitrators direct a manufacturer to continue shipping products to a distributor. Depending on your client's needs, these considerations deserve your very close attention in the arbitration agreement drafting stage.

With respect to the award's enforceability, the agreement should make clear when the award will be enforceable. Normally, an award is not enforceable until it is confirmed in court. However, if some other time better suits the parties' needs, state this explicitly in the agreement.

2.3.16 Appeal procedures

In recent years, certain dispute resolution organizations have added to their ADR rules provisions allowing parties to pre-select a second panel of arbitrators to hear any appeals from the first arbitration panel's decision. You normally use this appellate procedure in cases involving huge damage claims where the stakes are so high that the parties are unwilling to risk having a single arbitration panel issue an unchallengeable binding award. If you are involved in such a case, you may want to consider proposing an appeal procedure, whether or not a dispute resolution organization will administer the arbitration.

2.3.17 Designation of law to govern the arbitration agreement

It is quite important to specify in the arbitration agreement the jurisdiction whose law is to govern the agreement. This can pose a very knotty problem which sometimes warrants substantial thought. If you are drafting an arbitration clause, realize that the jurisdiction whose law governs the arbitration agreement may differ from the jurisdiction whose law controls all or some of the legal issues in the underlying contract. For example, a state's law of contract may govern several of the legal issues arising out of a contract for goods and services, but because interstate commerce is involved, the Federal Arbitration Act may govern some of the procedural and even substantive issues related to the arbitration and the arbitration clause itself. These drafting problems become even more thorny when one or more of the parties are incorporated or reside in foreign countries. Sometimes you will need to do substantial legal research before you will be able to satisfy yourself that the arbitration clause which you are drafting best satisfies your client's interests regarding choice of law.

2.3.18 Court to have jurisdiction to enforce agreement and award

Also keep in mind that the jurisdiction whose law governs the underlying contract may be different than the one whose law will govern or will be convenient for controlling the proceedings or enforcing an award. Because the parties' circumstances may change significantly—even to the extent of relocation or reincorporation of companies—between the time that the arbitration clause becomes effective and the time that a dispute arises, you should normally make the language of such provision as broad as possible, permitting the filing of such motions or the enforcing of awards "in any court having jurisdiction" at the pertinent time.

2.3.19 Payment of arbitration fees and expenses

If your arbitration clause pre-selects a dispute resolution organization, your client will be obligated to pay the organization's administrative costs and the arbitrator fees. In some organizations, the fee amount varies depending upon the number of parties to the dispute and the claim's complexity. It is customary that the parties each pay an equal share of the arbitrators' fees. Also, arbitrators, in rendering their award, often require that the losing party pay the winning party's administrative costs.

2.4   Selecting Cases for Arbitration

2.4.1   Favorable situational indications for arbitration

Obviously, the most accurate indicator of the suitability of a case for arbitration is when parties and counsel agree to arbitrate to achieve a prompt resolution of their conflict. In the scheme of natural human interaction, however, such situations only arise occasionally. Because of lawyers' natural tendency to resolve disputes in court rather than arbitrate, cost-minded lawyers often include arbitration clauses in transactional contracts they draft for their clients. Such clauses, as discussed in the preceding section, can set the stage for a less combative and quicker method of resolving disputes and indicate the parties' desire to resolve their differences privately. Where no arbitration clause governs the selection of a dispute resolution process, and a complaint has not been filed in court, sometimes you can base a suggestion to arbitrate on the fact that the dispute qualifies for compulsory arbitration under local court rule. Depending on the nature of the dispute, the relative costs, and the condition of the court docket, private arbitration might be indicated as a resolution process instead of having to resort to a beleaguered, unresponsive court system.

Other situational factors related to the nature of a case's facts and law may weigh in favor of proceeding to arbitration. For example, if legal issues predominate over factual issues, arbitration is normally indicated over mediation. Where legal issues exist, lawyers tend to be more positional and therefore mediation may be less effective. In arbitration, however, you can select arbitrators who can deal directly with the legal issues and decide them based on the application of legal principles and case precedent. Also, if sufficient discovery has occurred in a case while pending on the court's docket, a case may be appropriate for arbitration. In such situations, the lawyers have taken all their necessary discovery—an opportunity probably not available to them had they proceeded to arbitration initially. Yet, fully informed, they can go to arbitration and take advantage of its speed and reduced expense. Essentially, they can have their cake and eat it too. Finally, arbitration is indicated for a case in which testimony or documents need to be compelled by subpoena or a case in which the parties have radically differing appraisals of the case's facts and of the applicable law.

Arbitration can be ideal for those cases where the parties desire confidentiality, where a substantial power imbalance exists, where the parties have a history of dealing in bad faith, or where the parties have deadlocked after mediation. It is also most useful in situations where the parties will not have to maintain a relationship after the dispute's resolution. Finally, with respect to finality and precedent considerations, arbitration is indicated where either the parties wish to avoid establishing a judicial precedent, they wish to establish an arbitration precedent to guide their future conduct, or they need an immediate decision to protect the interests of a third party or the public.

2.4.2 Unfavorable situational indications for arbitration

A situation unsuitable for arbitration would be where a disputant, because of physical or mental disabilities, cannot effectively represent his or her best interests and will not be represented by counsel at the arbitration sessions. Such a dispute is probably best resolved in court, where a judge can appoint counsel or an appropriate representative, guardian, etc., and where the person will have available the full panoply of due process rights. Another fairly obvious situation not suitable for arbitration would be where your case is pending before a judge who is mutually acceptable to the parties and who could hear and decide the case sooner than you could select arbitrators and hold an arbitration hearing.

Other cases not suitable for arbitration would include those where a party is seeking an unusual remedy or creative resolution that is not available in arbitration, where the neutral's decision will require monitoring, or where the best resolution can result only if the neutral has access to confidential information not disclosable to the other side. Some cases have pivotal, emotional aspects that are best presented to and considered by a jury. Those types of cases are ordinarily unsuitable for arbitration. Also unsuitable for arbitration are those cases where the stakes are too high to risk a binding unappealable award or where judicial precedent is needed to explain the application of a new or rarely construed statute.

2.5   Indicator Guide for Selecting Cases for Arbitration

2.5.1   Favorable indicators chart

The following guide lists some situational indicators favorable to an arbitrated resolution of a dispute. The presence of only one of these indicators (and the absence of any unfavorable indicators) may be sufficient to trigger scheduling of an arbitration.

FAVORABLE INDICATORS FOR ARBITRATION	
Parties and counsel agree to participate in the arbitration process and desire a prompt resolution	Parties will not have to maintain a direct or indirect relationship after resolution of a dispute
Pre-agreement exists to arbitrate disputes arising out of an underlying contract	Parties want to minimize litigation costs
An immediate decision by a third-party neutral is needed to protect the interests of a disputant or the public	Parties wish to avoid establishing a judicial precedent, or they wish to establish an arbitration precedent that will guide their future conduct
Legal issues predominate over factual issues	A significant power imbalance exists between parties
Sufficient discovery has occurred or information has been developed to permit counsel to present their clients' claims and defenses cogently	Parties are still deadlocked after an attempted negotiated and/or mediated settlement
Parties have a history of acting in bad faith in negotiations	Information (testimony or documents) in the possession of third parties is crucial to a claim or defense, and the third parties will not provide the information unless subpoenaed
Dispute qualifies for compulsory arbitration under local court rules	Parties have dramatically differing appraisals of the case's facts and of the applicable law
Parties want the matter settled confidentially	

2.5.2   Unfavorable indicators chart

The following guide lists some of the situational indicators unfavorable to the use of arbitration. The presence of one of these indicators could be a sufficient basis to decline using arbitration to resolve a particular dispute.

UNFAVORABLE INDICATORS FOR ARBITRATION	
A party cannot effectively represent its best interests and will not be represented by counsel at the arbitration sessions	A party seeks an unusual remedy or creative resolution that is not available in arbitration
The resolution will require monitoring	Major constitutional issues are involved
The best resolution requires disclosure of information to the decision maker, but such information cannot be disclosed to the other side	Substantial formal discovery is needed to provide a party with the information necessary to support a claim or defense
Stakes are too high to risk a binding unappealable award	A judicial precedent is needed to explain application of a new or rarely construed statute
Case has some pivotal emotional aspects that would best be presented to and considered by a jury	Case is currently pending in court before a judge who is mutually acceptable to the parties and who could hear and decide the case sooner than arbitration could begin

2.6   Choosing the Appropriate Arbitration Forum and Panel

When you select an arbitration panel, you and your opposing counsel will be required to agree to: (1) an arbitration forum; (2) the number of arbitrators who will serve on your panel; and (3) the individual(s) who will serve as your arbitrator(s). The considerations related to these three topics are discussed *infra*.

2.6.1   Choosing the appropriate arbitration forum

If you and your opposing counsel decide not to administer the arbitration process yourselves, depending on the nature of the dispute, you may have several alternative arbitration forums, both nonprofit and for profit, from which to choose. Some of these alternatives follow.[8]

2.6.1.1   Court-annexed arbitration programs

Many local jurisdictions have ADR programs which provide for arbitration of certain kinds of disputes. Some programs require all cases of a certain type to be arbitrated or mediated. Others give the judges discretion to determine which

---

8. *See generally,* George P. Haldeman, *Alternative Dispute Resolution in Personal Injury Cases,* chapter 3 (Clark Boardman Callaghan, 1993).

are suitable for a particular dispute resolution process and to direct counsel to participate in it. In some of these programs, the only out-of-pocket expenses for using the arbitration services are the filing fees and other routine court costs. In other programs, the parties pay for the neutral's services. While many of these programs provide for nonbinding arbitration with an assessment to the party who rejects an arbitration award, you and opposing counsel can circumvent these potential additional costs by having your clients agree in advance to be bound by the arbitrators' decision. Thus, if you decide to arbitrate your dispute, you may want to investigate whether any court-annexed programs can provide inexpensive administrative support services of which you can take advantage.

You should be aware, however, that there may be disadvantages to using the court-annexed arbitration forum. First, in many of the court-annexed programs, the arbitrators are lawyers who are appointed randomly to serve on panels, and the users have no control over who will be their arbitrators, except where there are grounds for disqualification based on bias or conflict of interest. In addition, in most of the court-annexed programs, the parties do not control the proceedings. The court normally sets the hearing's time and place and there is no guarantee of confidentiality of the proceedings or of the award.

2.6.1.2   State or local government arbitration programs

If you do a little investigation, you may find that your state, county, or city government has an ADR program providing arbitration services. In recent years, it has become common for governmental agencies to sponsor dispute resolution training and related services. The ADR services usually focus on high-volume low-stakes dispute areas, including landlord-tenant, neighborhood, minor criminal, consumer, etc. However, some governmental programs extend their mediation and arbitration services to employment discrimination disputes which can often be quite costly if resolved through traditional court adjudication.

2.6.1.3   Bar Association arbitration programs

Some bar associations have ADR programs which offer arbitration services. Normally, because of volunteer attorney support, disputing parties can access these services at minimal expense. Parties usually have more control over the arbitration process than in the court-annexed programs, and the association's staff or volunteers handle administrative details.

2.6.1.4   Nonprofit ADR organizations

Many nonprofit organizations offer ADR services and administer arbitration programs. Examples are the American Arbitration Association (AAA), the Center for Public Resources, and the Better Business Bureau. These organizations vary drastically in the costs they charge for use of their services. If you decide to go this route, carefully analyze and compare the costs and fees charged for your particular type of dispute.

2.6.1.5   For-profit organizations

Many for-profit or "private" dispute resolution organizations offer arbitration services, some on a national basis, some regionally or locally. Some specialize in certain types of disputes; others service a wide range of disputes. Some have only attorneys on their panel of neutrals; others have attorneys and retired judges. Standard fees and costs vary from one company to another, and some companies will negotiate costs and fees depending on the case's size. If you and opposing counsel decide to use a private ADR firm to administer your arbitration, it may be a good idea to shop around to compare prices.[9]

2.6.2   Deciding on the number of arbitrators

The selection of the arbitrator(s) may be the most important aspect of the entire arbitration process. In most cases, a single arbitrator will satisfy your needs; in other cases—particularly those which are complex and which require both legal and technical expertise—multiple arbitrators will be needed.

If you and your opposing counsel decide not to use a dispute resolution organization, you should set time limits for selecting an arbitration panel to prevent one party from unduly delaying a case. If together you cannot agree on an arbitrator panel, a court may have to appoint the arbitrators for you. In such situations, courts attempt to follow the criteria specified by the parties if possible.

2.6.2.1   Single arbitrator panel

There are several advantages to having a single arbitrator. A single arbitrator can normally render a decision more quickly than if several arbitrators have to review all the evidence, conduct a post-hearing conference, and jointly reach a decision. With a single arbitrator there are usually fewer scheduling delays and there is obviously less cost. Also, it will be easier to choose a single arbitrator who fits your case's expertise and qualifications needs, rather than trying to find several arbitrators who are all well qualified, available, and willing to serve on a panel. Furthermore, the proceedings will run more efficiently because you will deal with only one person. However, there can also be some disadvantages. One arbitrator might not have all the required qualifications, where a panel of several arbitrators can cover all contingencies. Also, if a case deals with more than one area of law, you could have experts in several areas. It would be nearly impossible to have the same kind of coverage with one person.

---

9. *See* Appendix K for a listing of nonprofit and private ADR organizations.

If the case is administered, the organization will usually submit a list of arbitrators' names to each party who will then strike off a certain allowed number of names of arbitrators they do not want, and note the rest in order of preference. The organization will then appoint an arbitrator based on the parties' choices from the remaining names. If the parties can't agree on an arbitrator, the organization will appoint one. The parties can also use the strike method until only one person is left on the list. However, this can create problems where one side will get its choice because it was last to strike, and the other party may be unhappy with this choice. That is why it is often easier to use an arbitration organization that has an abbreviated approved list of neutrals whose qualifications are widely known, rather than having to research the background of the arbitrator candidates and then use the strike-off mechanism, which on occasion can produce a disappointing result for one or more parties.

As pointed out in section 2.3, supra, the option to have the arbitration administered can be included in the arbitration clause, or it can be specified later when you and the opposing counsel decide to arbitrate, independent of a clause. If you mutually decide not to have the arbitration administered, you can, usually for a modest service charge, still receive a list of arbitrators from an organization, such as AAA, from which you can make a selection. If a contract submits the parties to an organization that no longer exists, then you or your opponent can choose another one, or a court can substitute an appropriate organization.

You and the opposing counsel can also agree in a future-dispute arbitration clause to have one specific person act as arbitrator, such as a well-known expert in your client's business field. However, there are risks associated with this technique. If the arbitrator is unable to serve, lengthy, costly, and unnecessary disputes can arise over the issue of who will fill the vacancy. It is also problematic to specify arbitrator attributes in an arbitrator clause, because if made too narrow, it can become difficult or impossible to find someone who meets the specific qualifications. This tactic can also be used by the opposing party to delay the case.

2.6.2.2   Multiple arbitrator panels

Most multiple arbitrator panels consist of three arbitrators. You can choose panels in several ways. Each party can pick an arbitrator and those two arbitrators can pick a third (sometimes called an "umpire"). If the two arbitrators can't decide on the third, an organization can pick a neutral third person to serve on the panel. The organization can also pick three neutrals from their list of qualified arbitrators. They can tailor their choices to your particular needs and specifications, while streamlining the process by choosing the arbitrators for the parties. You can also choose the panel through the strike method used to choose a single arbitrator. A court can also appoint multiple arbitrators to a panel, and a party can request the court to appoint arbitrators as well.

Some of your clients may want to opt for the umpire system of arbitrator selection because they like the idea of having a "friend" on the panel. However, as you are probably well aware, even the friendliest of arbitrators must abide by the procedural rules and the arbitrator ethical norms. And, sometimes, in an attempt to overcompensate for the built-in appearance of bias, the arbitrator appointed by the party tends to be harsher to the appointing party than the arbitrator appointed by the opposing side. You should make your client aware of this phenomenon before he or she agrees to use the umpire system of arbitrator selection. While the umpire system is still widely used in international arbitrations, in other arbitration situations fully neutral panels are much more common. Because of the increasingly perceived advantages of impartial decision makers and the fact that the umpire system can often lead to delay if one party refuses to cooperate, the umpire system is being used much less frequently.

2.6.3 Choosing individuals to serve as arbitrators

Whether an arbitrator is selected or appointed by a party, an organization, the court, or other arbitrators, the most important attribute for an arbitrator to possess is impartiality. Other attributes an arbitrator should possess include patience, intelligence, common sense, the ability to make a decision with an open mind, and the firmness to control the proceedings. Although some arbitrators are lawyers, many arbitrators are chosen from different business fields based on their professional experience. Regardless of an arbitrator's background, however, all should be trained in the arbitration process.

An arbitrator need not be trained in every minute aspect of law. In fact, many effective arbitrators are not lawyers and have no legal training whatsoever. Functionally, it is much more important that an arbitrator is reasonable, flexible, and willing to conduct the proceeding so as to achieve a fair outcome. An effective arbitrator is actively involved in the management of the dispute before him or her. An arbitrator who sits on the sidelines and lets two parties fight it out does not qualify as an effective arbitrator.

When choosing an arbitrator, you should screen potential candidates as carefully as possible to determine their experience, level of education, and personality. If you are selecting an arbitrator from a list provided by a dispute resolution organization, you will normally be provided a brief curriculum vitae for each potential arbitrator. If the arbitrator is a lawyer, you can often research his or her background further through Martindale-Hubbell or Lexis. You can also ask the administering organization for more information about particular arbitrators. Sometimes, the best sources for investigating potential arbitrators' suitability are friends and professional associates who may know of the arbitrators' suitability from previous cases or by reputation in particular fields. You can occasionally greatly minimize your work in selecting an arbitrator by calling a few people you know. Do not underestimate the value of other advocates' experience with particular arbitrators in making your selection.

It was Aristotle who once said, "[T]he arbitrator looks to what is equitable, the judge to what is law."[10] This statement is true of many arbitrators even today. You should take this fact into account when choosing arbitrators. If you have a situation where the equities are in your favor, but your position on the law is weak, then search out an arbitrator who will decide on a more equitable basis. Conversely, if you have a strong case on the law, you would want to identify and select an arbitrator who has a reputation for taking a more legalistic approach to decision making in arbitration.

Thus, you must realize that the attributes you will be looking for in an arbitrator may vary dramatically depending on the particular dispute. If a dispute is highly technical, you will probably want an arbitrator who is well versed in the particular technical or scientific area in issue. If complex legal issues predominate in your dispute, and if more than one area of law is involved in a dispute, you may want your panel of experts to include one or more arbitrators particularly competent in the pertinent areas of law.

However, you should exercise care in these selection situations. Sometimes an expert can be so focused on one area that he or she might miss other aspects of the dispute or bring assumptions to the dispute which could color the outcome. In many disputes, a well-rounded arbitrator with a wide base of experience will be more than qualified to settle a dispute.

Also, if you are unsure of what attributes you are looking for, are unable to obtain advice from others, or are unsure about which of several candidates you should select, you may be wise in letting an organization pick an arbitrator for you. Many case administrators have years of experience in working with arbitrators in the administrative phases of cases, know how other parties and counsel have evaluated arbitrators' service, and can pick someone who is well qualified to decide your particular dispute.

But if you do relinquish your right to choose your panel, do not blame the organization if the arbitration's result is not as good as you would have wanted. No one can guarantee how an arbitrator will rule in any case. Your perception of what is fair may be much different from that of the arbitrator. The only measure that the organization has to determine a particular arbitrator's effectiveness is user evaluations. If the organization appoints an effective arbitrator and you are unhappy with the result, the chances are good that any effective arbitrator you would have selected would have arrived at a similar, if not identical, result. Mistakes in judging talent routinely occur. It is said that when a young Fred Astaire

---

10. Aristotle, as quoted in, M. Frances McNamara, *2,000 Famous Legal Quotations* 31 (Aqueduct Books, 1967).

went to Hollywood and submitted himself for the usual screen test, the studio evaluator jotted for the record, "Can't act. Slightly bald. Can dance a little." [11] Of course, Astaire, whose partnership with Ginger Rogers produced a series of films that charmed the world, exhibited such masterful footwork that both Balanchine and Nureyev later were to describe him as the world's greatest dancer.

Finally, but certainly not least in importance in your selection process, is consideration of the ethics of your arbitrator candidates. Arbitrators are held to a Code of Ethics which defines the ethical limits of what they can and cannot do in performing their function.[12] An arbitrator must keep confidential everything told to him or her during the arbitration proceeding. He or she must also keep confidential the nature of any award given. An arbitrator must uphold the integrity and fairness of the arbitration process and must disclose any interest or relationship which could lead to partiality or bias. An arbitrator is further required to avoid any appearance of impropriety and to conduct proceedings fairly and diligently, ultimately rendering decisions in a just, independent, and deliberate manner. Any arbitrator you select should be able to comply, at a minimum, with these prescribed norms of ethical conduct and other norms described in section 2.12.

One important postscript here is that even after you select an arbitration panel, your job may not be completely finished. Arbitrators may be disqualified from serving on a particular arbitration panel for a variety of reasons. Disqualifications can occur on your motion or on the arbitrator's own motion. For example, you or the opposing counsel may have had past dealings with the arbitrator, or the arbitrator may have been employed in the past in a position which would give the appearance of having interests conflicting with those of your client or the interests of the other party. Arbitrators are required to disclose potential conflicts of interests, and if there is any doubt, they normally recuse themselves, concluding that it is better to err on the side of caution rather than to have an award later overturned on grounds of prejudice or bias. Arbitrators can also recuse themselves if the time frame for the proceedings is incompatible with their schedule, or if he or she does not feel qualified enough to handle a particular dispute. A financial interest in any particular dispute is also a ground for disqualification of an arbitrator.

2.7   Attorney Ethics

Codes of professional conduct for lawyers vary from state to state, and although a few states still follow variations of the American Bar Association's Model Code of Professional Responsibility, many have adopted the more

---

11. Anecdote adapted from Fadiman, supra note 2 at 24.
12. The Code of Ethics for Arbitrators in Commercial Disputes—Revised 2004 is contained in Appendix I.

recent ABA Model Rules of Professional Conduct (Model Rules). The discussion that follows addresses the lawyer's ethical duties in an advisory and advocate role in an adjudicative process, such as arbitration, and includes references to the 2003 Edition of the Model Rules. This discussion is divided into subsections related to lawyers' duties to the client, to the tribunal, and to opposing parties, opposing counsel, and third parties. Readers are cautioned that the following discussion is merely an overview of the Model Rules, and for guidance in a specific situation, they should consult the text of the Model Rules.

2.7.1 Duties to client

2.7.1.1 Competence and allocation of authority between client and lawyer

A lawyer is required to provide competent representation to the client. Competent representation means that the lawyer is required to have the legal knowledge, skill, thoroughness, and preparation reasonably necessary for the specific representation undertaken. (MR 1.1). The client normally has the ultimate authority to determine the purposes to be served by the legal representation, within limits imposed by law and by the lawyer's professional obligations. (MR 1.2). A lawyer may limit the scope of representation if the limitation is reasonable under the specific circumstances and the client gives informed consent.

2.7.1.2 Diligence and communication

A lawyer must proceed with reasonable diligence and promptness in representing a client. This requires a lawyer to control his or her workload so that each matter can be handled competently. (MR 1.3). A lawyer must keep the client reasonably informed about the status of the matter, and must explain a matter to the extent necessary to permit the client to make informed decisions regarding the representation. (MR 1.4).

2.7.1.3 Confidentiality of information

In general, a lawyer must not reveal information relating to the representation of a client unless the client gives informed consent or unless the disclosure is impliedly authorized to carry out the representation. There are several exceptions to this rule, however. A lawyer may reveal information relating to the representation of a client where the disclosure is reasonably necessary to: avoid reasonably certain death or substantial bodily harm; secure legal advice about the lawyer's compliance with the Model Rules; establish a claim or defense on behalf of the lawyer in a controversy between the lawyer and the client; comply with other law or court order. (MR 1.6). Many states have adopted broader exceptions that allow disclosure to prevent non-life threatening crimes or to rectify civil fraud.

2.7.1.4   Conflicts of interest

A lawyer must not represent a client if the representation involves a concurrent conflict of interest. Such conflict of interest exists if the representation of one client will be directly adverse to another client or if the representation of one or more clients will be materially limited by the lawyer's responsibilities to another client, a former client, or a third person, or by a personal interest of the lawyer. Notwithstanding the existence of a concurrent conflict of interest, a lawyer may represent a client if: the lawyer reasonably believes that he or she will be able to provide competent and diligent representation to each affected client; the representation is not prohibited by law; the representation does not involve the assertion of a claim by one client against another client represented by the lawyer in the same litigation or other proceeding before a tribunal; and each affected client gives written informed consent. (MR 1.7; 1.8). The rules concerning concurrent conflicts of interest have extensive comments and they should be consulted if an apparent, concurrent conflict of interest arises. The Model Rules have requirements regarding other types of conflicts of interest that relate to: representation adverse to a former client (MR 1.7(b)); lawyers who are associated in a firm or who have terminated an association with a firm (MR 1.10); lawyers who are former and concurrent government officers and employees (MR 1.11); and lawyers who are former judges, or who serve as arbitrators, mediators, or other third-party neutrals. (MR 1.12). Under Model Rule 1.12, in general, a lawyer may not represent anyone in connection with a matter in which the lawyer participated personally and substantially as a judge or other adjudicative officer or law clerk to such a person or as an arbitrator, mediator, or other third-party neutral, unless all parties to the proceeding give written informed consent. Unless qualifying for an exception to the provisions of Model Rule 1.12, no lawyer from a disqualified lawyer's firm may knowingly undertake or continue representation in a matter. The Rule also prohibits a lawyer from negotiating for employment with any person who is involved as a party or as lawyer for a party in a matter in which the lawyer is participating personally and substantially as a judge or other adjudicative officer or an arbitrator, mediator, or other third party neutral.

2.7.1.5   Organization as client

A lawyer employed or retained by an organization represents the organization acting through its authorized constituents. (MR 1.13). Under this rule, a lawyer has special duties if he or she knows that an officer, employee, or other person associated with the organization is engaged in an action, intends to act, or refuses to act in a matter related to the representation that is in violation of a legal obligation to the organization, or a violation likely to result in substantial injury to the organization. Subject to certain conflict of interest prohibitions of Model Rule 1.7, a lawyer representing an organization may also represent any of its directors, officers, employees, members, shareholders or other constituents.

2.7.1.6   Client with diminished capacity

When a lawyer reasonably believes that the client has diminished capacity, is at risk of substantial physical, financial or other harm unless action is taken and cannot adequately act in the client's own interest, the lawyer may take protective action, including consulting with individuals or entities that have the ability to take action to protect the client, and in certain cases, seeking the appointment of a guardian *ad litem*, conservator or guardian. Information relating to the representation of such client is protected from disclosure, except that the lawyer is impliedly authorized to reveal information about the client, only to the extent reasonably necessary to protect the client's interest. (MR 1.14).

2.7.1.7   Declining or terminating representation

A lawyer may not represent a client, and must withdraw from representation of a client where: the representation will result in a violation of the Model Rules; the lawyer's physical or mental condition materially impairs the lawyer's ability to represent the client; or the lawyer is discharged. Upon termination of representation, a lawyer must take appropriate steps to protect a client's interests, such as giving reasonable notice to the client, allowing time for employment of other counsel, surrendering papers and property to which the client is entitled, and refunding any advance payment of fee or expense that has not been earned or incurred. (MR 1.16).

2.7.1.8   Lawyer as advisor

A lawyer must exercise independent professional judgment and render candid advice on behalf of a client. In rendering advice, a lawyer may refer not only to law, but to other considerations such as moral, economic, social, and political factors that may be relevant to the client's situation. (MR 2.1).

2.7.2   Duties to tribunal

2.7.2.1   Meritorious claims and contentions

The Model Rules define a tribunal as "a court, an arbitrator in a binding arbitration proceeding, or a legislative body, administrative agency or other body acting in an adjudicative capacity." Quite simply, a lawyer may not bring or defend a proceeding, or assert or controvert an issue before a tribunal, unless there is a basis in law and fact for doing so that is not frivolous, which includes a good faith argument for an extension, modification or reversal of existing law. A lawyer has a duty not to abuse legal procedure. (MR 3.1).

2.7.2.2   Expediting litigation

A lawyer must make reasonable efforts to expedite litigation consistent with the interests of the client. Acquiring financial or other benefit from otherwise improper delay in litigation is not a legitimate interest of the client. (MR 3.2).

2.7.2.3   Candor toward the tribunal

A lawyer may not knowingly make a false statement of fact or law to a tribunal or fail to correct a false statement of material fact or law previously made to the tribunal by the lawyer. Furthermore, a lawyer may not knowingly fail to disclose to the tribunal legal authority in the controlling jurisdiction known to the lawyer to be directly adverse to the position of the client and not disclosed by opposing counsel. Also, a lawyer may not knowingly offer evidence that the lawyer knows to be false. A lawyer who represents a client in an adjudicative proceeding and who knows that a client or person intends to engage, is engaging or has engaged in criminal or fraudulent conduct related to the proceeding shall take reasonable remedial measures, including, if necessary, disclosure to the tribunal. (MR 3.3).

2.7.2.4   Impartiality and decorum of the tribunal

Many forms of improper influence of proceedings before tribunals are proscribed by the Model Rules. For example, Model Rule 3.5 prohibits a lawyer from influencing a judge, juror, prospective juror, or other official by means prohibited by law or from engaging in conduct intended to disrupt a tribunal. Furthermore, it prohibits a lawyer from communicating ex parte with such a person during the proceeding unless authorized to do so by law or court order. Additionally, a lawyer may not communicate with a juror or prospective juror even after discharge of the jury if: (1) the communication is prohibited by law or court order; (2) the juror has made known to the lawyer a desire not to communicate; or (3) the communication involves misrepresentation, coercion, duress or harassment.

2.7.2.5   Lawyer as witness

A lawyer may not act as an advocate at a trial in which the lawyer is likely to be a necessary witness. (MR 3.7). Exceptions to this rule are that the lawyer may testify in the proceeding if: the testimony relates to an uncontested issue; it relates to the nature and value of legal services rendered in the case; or disqualification of the lawyer would work a substantial hardship on the client. A lawyer may act as advocate in a trial in which another lawyer in the lawyer's firm is likely to be called as a witness unless the lawyer is specifically prohibited from testifying by other Model Rules.

2.7.2.6   Unauthorized practice of law

A lawyer may not practice law in a jurisdiction in violation of the regulation of the legal profession in that jurisdiction, or assist another in doing so. Arbitration advocates should pay careful attention to this Model Rule. Some states have laws prohibiting lawyers not licensed in their particular jurisdictions from representing clients in arbitrations conducted in those jurisdictions. These prohibitions also extend in some states to paralegals who assist lawyers serving as advocates in arbitrations. (MR 5.5). Lawyers may be subject to the disciplinary authority of more than one jurisdiction for the same conduct. (MR 8.5).

2.7.2.7   Misconduct

A lawyer may not violate or attempt to violate the Model Rules, knowingly assist or induce another to do so, or do so through the acts of another. Furthermore, a lawyer may not commit a criminal act that reflects adversely on the lawyer's honesty, trustworthiness or fitness as a lawyer in other respects; engage in conduct involving dishonesty, fraud, deceit or misrepresentation; engage in conduct that is prejudicial to the administration of justice; state or imply an ability to influence improperly a government agency or official or to achieve results by means that violate the Model Rules or other law; or knowingly assist a judge or judicial officer in conduct that is a violation of applicable rules of judicial conduct or other law. (MR 8.4).

2.7.3   Duties to opposing parties and counsel and third persons

2.7.3.1   Fairness to opposing party and counsel

Fair competition in an adversary proceeding contemplates prohibitions against destruction or concealment of evidence, improperly influencing witnesses, obstructive tactics in discovery procedure, and the like. Under Model Rule 3.4, a lawyer may not unlawfully obstruct another party's access to evidence, nor may a lawyer unlawfully alter, destroy, or conceal a document or other material having potential evidentiary value, or counsel or assist another person to do so. Further more, a lawyer may not falsify evidence, counsel or assist a witness to testify falsely, or offer a witness an inducement that is prohibited by law. A lawyer may not knowingly disobey a tribunal's rules, except in a situation where the lawyer can assert that no valid obligation exists. In a pretrial procedure, a lawyer may not make a frivolous discovery request or fail to make reasonably diligent effort to comply with a legally proper discovery request by an opposing party. At trial, a lawyer may not allude to any matter that the lawyer does not reasonably believe is relevant or that will not be supported by admissible evidence, assert personal knowledge of facts in issue (except when properly testifying as a witness), state a personal opinion as to the justness of a cause, the credibility of a witness, the culpability of a civil litigant, or the guilt or innocence of the accused. Finally, a lawyer may not request a person, other than a client, to refrain from voluntarily giving relevant information to another party unless: (1) that person is a relative or an employee or other agent of a client; and (2) the lawyer reasonably believes that the person's interests will not be adversely affected by refraining from giving such information.

2.7.3.2   Truthfulness in statements to others

A lawyer generally has no affirmative duty to inform an opposing party of relevant facts, but a lawyer is deemed to be engaging in a misrepresentation if he or she incorporates or affirms a statement of another person that the lawyer knows is false. Improper misrepresentation also arises in situations where a lawyer provides partially true by misleading statements or omissions that are the equivalent of affirmative false statements. Specifically, Model Rule 4.1 prohibits a lawyer, in the course of representing a client, from knowingly making a false statement of material fact or law to a third person and from failing to disclose a material fact when disclosure is necessary to avoid assisting a criminal or fraudulent act by a client unless such disclosure is prohibited by another Model Rule. Whether a particular statement of a lawyer should be regarded as one of fact depends on the circumstances in which the statement is made. For example, under generally accepted conventions in negotiation, certain types of statements ordinarily are not taken as statements of material fact. Examples of these types of statements made during the course of a negotiation are: estimates of price or value placed on the subject of a transaction; a party's intentions as to an acceptable settlement of a claim; and the existence of an undisclosed principal except where nondisclosure of the principal would constitute fraud.

2.7.3.3   Communication with person represented by counsel

Under Model Rule 4.2, a lawyer representing a client may not communicate about the subject matter of the representation with a person the lawyer knows to be represented by another lawyer in the matter, unless the lawyer has the consent of the other lawyer or is authorized to engage in the communication by law or court order. This rule applies even though the person represented by another lawyer initiates or consents to the communication. The rule requires a lawyer to immediately terminate a conversation with such represented person as soon as the lawyer learns that person is represented by another lawyer. There are exceptions to this rule, however. The rule does not preclude a lawyer from communicating with a represented person, or an employee or agent of such person, concerning matters outside the representation. Thus, the existence of a controversy between a government agency and a private party, or between two corporations, does not prohibit a lawyer for either party from communicating with nonlawyer representatives of the other regarding a separate matter. Nor does the rule prohibit a lawyer from communicating with a represented person who is seeking advice from a lawyer who is not otherwise representing a client in the matter. And most importantly, a lawyer may not engage in a communication prohibited by the rule through the acts of another person. The rule, however, does not prohibit parties to a matter from communicating with each other, and a lawyer is not prohibited from advising a client concerning such communication. A lawyer who is uncertain whether a particular communication is precluded by the rule may seek a court order regarding the ethical propriety of the proposed communication.

2.7.3.4 Dealing with unrepresented person and prospective clients

Model Rule 4.3 addresses the circumstances in which a lawyer may communicate with an unrepresented person and it distinguishes between situations involving unrepresented persons whose interests may be adverse to those of the lawyer's client and those in which the person's interests are not in conflict with those of the client. When representing a client and when dealing with an unrepresented person, a lawyer may neither state nor imply that the lawyer is disinterested. When the lawyer knows or reasonably should know that the unrepresented person misunderstands the lawyer's role in the matter, the lawyer must make reasonable efforts to correct the misunderstanding. A lawyer may not give legal advice to an unrepresented person, other than the advice to obtain counsel, where the lawyer knows or reasonably should know that the interests of such person are or have a reasonable possibility of being in conflict with those of his client. The rule does not prohibit a lawyer from negotiating the terms of a transaction or settlement with an unrepresented person so long as the lawyer has explained that he or she represents an adverse party and is not representing the person. The lawyer may explain to such person the terms on which the lawyer's client will enter into an agreement or settle a matter, prepare documents for the person's signature, and explain the lawyer's own view of the meaning of the document or the lawyer's view of the underlying obligations. It is wise for the lawyer to advise the unrepresented person to seek legal review of the documents before signing them.

Model Rule 7.3 addresses a lawyer's communications with a particular type of unrepresented person—a prospective client. Under that rule, generally a lawyer may not by in-person, live telephone, or real-time electronic contact solicit professional employment from a prospective client when a significant motive for the lawyer's doing so is the lawyer's pecuniary gain. Exceptions to this general rule include situations where the person contacted is a lawyer, or has a family, close personal, or prior professional relationship with the contacting lawyer.

Similarly a lawyer may not solicit professional employment from a prospective client if that prospective client has made known to the lawyer a desire not to be solicited; or if the solicitation involves coercion, duress, or harassment. Written, recorded, or electronic communication from a prospective client known to be in need of legal services in a particular matter must include the words "Advertising Material" on the outside envelope, if any, and at the beginning and ending of any recorded or electronic communication, unless the intended recipients are members of the excepted categories of persons identified immediately above in this paragraph. Exceptions to this rule apply to a lawyer who participates with a prepaid or group legal service plan operated by an organization not owned or directed by the lawyer that uses in-person or telephone contact to solicit memberships or subscriptions for the plan from persons who are not known to need legal services in a particular matter covered by the plan.

2.7.3.5   Respect for rights of third persons

Model Rule 4.4 addresses the ethical restrictions on methods of obtaining evidence from third persons and unwarranted intrusions into privileged relationships, such as the lawyer-client relationship. Under that rule, when representing a client, a lawyer may not use means that have no substantial purpose other than to embarrass, delay, or burden a third person, or use methods of obtaining evidence that violate the legal rights of such a person. Furthermore, a lawyer who receives a document relating to the representation of another lawyer's client and knows or reasonably should know that the document was inadvertently sent shall promptly notify the sender.

2.8   Considering Procedural Alternatives

Assuming that a dispute has arisen and arbitration is going forward, either by virtue of an arbitration clause or by a negotiated submission agreement, you should carefully consider whether there are procedural alternatives available to help make the arbitration hearing process more efficient, less time consuming, and less expensive. Depending on the dispute's nature and the parties involved, you may want to consider, very early in the preliminary planning process, the usefulness of: (1) videotaped or telephone testimony; (2) bifurcated hearing; (3) consolidation of claims; (4) phasing the arbitration; or (5) a class-action procedure.[13]

---

13. *See generally,* Ian R. MacNeil, Richard E. Speidel, and Thomas J. Stipanowich, *Federal Arbitration Law,* (Vol II) §18.9 (Little, Brown and Company, 1995); C. Edward Fletcher, *Arbitrating Securities Disputes* §9.2[2] (Practicing Law Institute, 1990); Medalie, *supra note* 7 at 63; Domke, *supra* note 3, at 413–415.

2.8.1   Videotaped or telephone testimony

In cases where the testimony of witnesses or experts will be unavailable at the arbitration hearing, by agreement with opposing counsel you may be able to have the testimony—both direct and cross examination—videotaped in advance and then played back at the hearing. The disadvantage of this procedural alternative, obviously, is that the arbitrators cannot question the videotaped witness. A remedy for this is to have the videotaped witness available on speaker phone after the videotape is shown so that he or she can answer the arbitrators' questions should there be any. Also, where witnesses for whatever reason are unable at the last minute to be present for the hearing, by agreement of counsel and approval of the arbitrators, they may be able to testify by speaker phone.

2.8.2   Bifurcation

You should consider whether it makes sense to ask the arbitrators to bifurcate the hearing into two parts. In the initial part, the parties would present their respective evidence on the liability issues. After hearing the evidence and counsels' arguments on liability, the arbitrators would recess to decide the liability issues and then return and announce their decision. If they determined there was no liability on the part of any respondent, they would enter an award to that effect and the hearing would be adjourned. If they determined liability as to one or more of the respondents, then the hearing would proceed as to the damage issues in relation to only those respondents. This procedure can be very effective in reducing a hearing's length in the appropriate case.

However, in many situations, it is very difficult for counsel to separate evidence related to liability from that related to damages. Thus, they tend to err on the side of inclusiveness, so that where the apportionment of a witness's testimony is unclear, counsel normally attempt to introduce all of the testimony under a liability label. Also, where certain witnesses' testimony can clearly be apportioned between liability and damage issues, witnesses might have to testify once in the liability portion and then return to testify again in the damage portion. This can greatly inconvenience witnesses and cause considerable expense to the parties. In short, bifurcation is probably best suited to cases in which the damage evidence is in the form of the testimony of expert witnesses who need not be called to testify on liability issues.

2.8.3   Consolidation of claims

When at least one party is common to separate disputes, there may be several reasons why you might propose that claims be consolidated for arbitration before the same arbitration panel. These include: (1) reducing the risk of conflicting arbitration awards; (2) reducing the expense to the parties; and (3) minimizing the time spent by parties and witnesses in providing testimony. And, depending on the circumstances, there may be very good reasons to object to consolidation if your opposing counsel favors it. For example, if your respondent client has a minor dispute with the common party, but that common party has a number of disputes with a respondent third party, your client would not be happy about paying your fees to observe the other two parties battle out their dispute before the arbitrators. Also, your client may not want to be tainted by what the arbitrators may perceive as much more egregious conduct committed by the third party. If parties cannot agree to consolidation, the party desiring it may file an action in court to compel it. Although courts are not uniform in their decisions, it is safe to say that where the issues to be resolved are substantially the same and no party will be prejudiced by consolidation, courts will usually order arbitrations to be consolidated.

2.8.4   Phasing the arbitration

Phasing the arbitration is a combination of consolidation and bifurcation. It can be quite useful in complex multi-party arbitrations. In this procedure, after several cases are consolidated for hearing, the arbitrators divide the proceedings into three parts: (1) determining the liability of the various parties; (2) awarding damages and interest; and (3) allocating arbitration costs among the parties. The key to this procedure's success is the arbitrators' subdivision of the first part of the proceedings dealing with liability determinations into "phases." The hearings can be phased so that the principal parties present their cases in the first phase against each other. These may involve both claims and counterclaims. The second phase can consist of the hearings of the multiple-respondent claims against each other, and the third and fourth phases can consist of hearing the claims of a third group of claimants against the parties already described and the third group's claims against each other. Although this procedure seems quite complicated when described in words, as applied it actually expedites the procedure. What actually occurs is that the arbitrators' decisions in the first liability phase of part one have a direct impact on issues that were to be raised by the parties who would subsequently be presenting their liability claims and defenses. As the arbitrators decide these issues, those parties learn how the arbitrators would most likely rule on similar claims or defenses should they present them in their cases. This causes a streamlining of the subsequent cases, the dropping of certain claims by some parties, and even settlement of many of the claims.

2.8.5   Class-action procedure

Some disputes may be amenable to application of a class-action procedure. If the number of potential plaintiffs is known and finite and the potential damages reasonably predictable, a respondent or respondents in arbitration may agree to such procedure. However, in many multiple-claimant situations, several arbitrations may be pending, but the class-action procedure will require that notice be issued to individuals who have no present formal claim against respondents, but who may have such a claim. This could expose respondents to the possibility of defending themselves before a single arbitration panel having authority to impose an award of an unknown high value, and without the right to an appeal. Respondents, faced with such a prospect, will normally oppose the class-action procedure, opting instead to take their chances in separate arbitrations before different panels. Nonetheless, it is possible that, despite a respondent's objection, a court may order class-wide arbitration if an arbitration clause can be construed to authorize it and/or if such class arbitration procedure is authorized by state law.

2.9   Considering Site Inspection and Audiovisual Aids

In some arbitrations, your preparations have to begin far in advance of the arbitration hearing—sometimes even before you select the arbitrators in the case. Two prime examples are preparations for cases which may involve site inspections by the arbitrators and cases which require a long lead-time to prepare presentational aids.

Site inspections are most common in construction and accident cases—particularly catastrophic accidents. The use of exhibits and audiovisual aids are important to the effective presentation of any case, but they are particularly important in cases where proof requires the demonstration of the condition of physical objects as they were at the time of or immediately before or after a particular event.

In the appropriate case, you or one of your associates should visit the pertinent site as soon after the event as possible. You should arrange for photographs to be taken, and if applicable, for accident reconstruction experts to examine the site and prepare their reports. And if relevant, you should also investigate to see if there are any available photographs of the site taken before the pertinent event occurred. If you determine that a model or mock-up of the site would be useful during the arbitration hearing, you should make the necessary arrangements to have them built or fabricated so they will be available at the arbitration hearing. Remember, arbitrations often proceed to hearing faster than court cases ordinarily do. The lead time for preparations for an arbitration may therefore be much shorter.

If you determine that the effective presentation of your case will require the arbitrators to make an on-site visit, you should visit the site in advance and think through how you wish to conduct the arbitrators' visit. You will also want to consider how the parties and the arbitrator will travel to the site and if any travel costs are involved. In the rare situation involving multiple clients and a site far distant from the arbitration's location, you may even have to arrange for bus transportation in advance of the visit. Sometimes the testimony of witnesses is taken on site. If this is the situation in your case, you may have to arrange for the presence of a stenographer.

With the arbitrators' permission, you may also want to arrange for photographs of the site to be taken during the arbitrators' site visit for use later when you resume the hearing. Photographs will not only preserve the scene as the arbitrators saw it, but they will also serve as a valuable visual aid for you in demonstrating to the arbitrators a view of the site which either they did not see or saw but did not appreciate the relevance at the time. Thus, during the site inspection, photographs should be taken from several angles to get a total perspective. Depending on the case, you may want to engage the services of a professional photographer to do this. It is also often helpful to have both black and white and color exposures. Most photographs are enlarged to 8 by 10 inches so that they can be easily reviewed during the arbitration proceedings.

2.10 Selecting Expert Witnesses

Your consideration of what kinds of experts you will need for your case should begin very early in your arbitration preparations. In arbitration, expert opinions are necessary where the matter in question is highly technical and only a person with specialized skills will be able to clarify the issue for an arbitrator. Expert testimony is almost always necessary where your opponent intends to call an expert to testify.

If you determine that experts are necessary, it is usually not prudent to arrange for multiple experts to testify on the same technical issue. Rarely does cumulative expert evidence provide any tactical advantage. In fact, it can be dangerous to your case because a skilled cross examiner can draw out conflicts in your experts' separate testimony.

In selecting an expert witness, you may wish to consider the following criteria.

Qualifications
   ➢ Does the expert have the right kind of background to testify on the issues in the arbitration?
   ➢ Is the expert well qualified and knowledgeable in the relevant subject area?

Professionalism
   ➢ Is the expert a person of integrity?
   ➢ Does the expert's physical appearance exude confidence?
   ➢ Does the expert "look" professional?
   ➢ Does the expert speak with authority?

Communication

> ➤ Can the expert boil down complicated processes to easily understood language?

> ➤ Can the expert create readily understandable analogies or illustrative examples?

Personality

> ➤ Does the expert articulate his or her thoughts well?

> ➤ Have you had an opportunity to observe the expert testify previously?

> ➤ Would you believe the experts opinion?

When selecting an expert, you should exercise both insight and caution. Your expert must be measured, reliable, and careful. He or she must be able to explain his or her positions without rambling or exaggeration. Your expert must know when to speak and when to stop speaking.

In choosing an expert, we might profit from the example provided many years ago by Marshall Field II. It is said that when Field was a small child, he displayed some of the insight and caution that made his grandfather become known as the greatest merchant prince in America. Being left alone in a hotel lobby for a half an hour, young Marshall approached an old lady and asked her if she could crack pecans. "No dear," replied the old lady. "I lost all my teeth years ago."

"Then," said the young Field extending both hands full of pecans, "please hold these while I go and get some more."[14]

2.11 Considering Whether to Mediate First

Even if your arbitration clause does not provide for mediation before resorting to arbitration, you may want to consider that option very seriously when a dispute arises under your contract. You should also consider the mediation-first option when you and your opposing counsel negotiate the provisions of a submission agreement. You can resolve many cases which would require days or even weeks of arbitration in a few hours with the help of a skillful mediator. Actually, there is much benefit and very little risk of harm in trying mediation first. Even if a successful mediation were to last a full day, your client would come out far ahead cost-wise in paying your fees and half of a mediator's fees compared to what it would cost were you to spend a day or two or more in preparing for the arbitration, much less the time spent at the arbitration hearing itself. Besides, even if the mediation process did not resolve the dispute, it might result in

---

14. Jacob M. Braude, *Speaker's and Toastmasters Handbook of Anecdotes By and About Famous Personalities*, 70 (Prentice-Hall, Inc., 1971).

the informal disclosure of information which may obviate the need to take any discovery for the subsequent arbitration. Mediation might also be beneficial in draining anger and hostility from the dispute, permitting the arbitration to proceed more efficiently and thereby guaranteeing a less costly arbitration. In most dispute situations where an attempt at a negotiated resolution fails, mediation should be your next choice of process.

2.12 Arbitrator Ethics

In this chapter, we have discussed considerations to take into account when selecting an arbitrator. In this section, we wish to review briefly the ethical code which governs the conduct of arbitrators. It is important for you to be familiar with the ethical restraints on arbitrator behavior so that you will know when it is appropriate for an arbitrator to disqualify or recuse himself or herself from a case, for you to file a motion for recusal, or for you to file a post-hearing court challenge to the award should you not become aware of the ethical problem until after the hearing.

The Code of Ethics for Arbitrators in Commercial Disputes—Revised 2004 (Code),[15] prepared jointly by a special committee of the American Arbitration Association (AAA) and a Task Force of the American Bar Association (ABA), consists of ethical guidelines for may types of arbitration, but it does not apply to labor arbitration, which is generally conducted under the Code of Professional Responsibility for Arbitrators of Labor-Management Disputes. It addresses ethical norms applying to arbitrators whether they are: selected or designated by the parties or other individuals as "neutrals"; or appointed by the parties, acting alone, and then those two party-appointed arbitrators select a neutral arbitrator. In the discussion which follows, we will address the ethical norms which apply specifically and separately to neutral arbitrators and party-appointed arbitrators.[16] It should be emphasized that party-appointed arbitrators are of two types: (1) neutral and (2) "Canon X arbitrators," defined as arbitrators who by agreement or understanding of the parties may be predisposed toward the party who appointed them, but in all other respects, are obligated to act in good faith and with integrity and fairness.

---

15. A copy of this Code is included in the Appendix I. The version described here and appearing in Appendix I is the one approved by the American Arbitration Association in September, 2003. At this writing, this version of the Code is scheduled to be considered for approval by the House of Delegates of the American Bar Association in February, 2004.
16. The ethical considerations relating to arbitrators appointed by one party appear in Canons IX and X of the Code of Ethics for Arbitrators in Commercial Disputes—Revised 2004.

2.12.1 Canon I—Integrity and fairness of process

Canon I of the Code provides: An arbitrator should uphold the integrity and fairness of the arbitration process.

Neutral arbitrators. An arbitrator has a responsibility not only to the parties, but also to the arbitration process itself. An arbitrator must observe high standards of conduct so that the integrity and fairness of the process will be preserved. Thus, an arbitrator should recognize a responsibility to the public, to the parties whose rights will be decided, and to all other participants in the proceeding.

A person should accept appointment as an arbitrator only if fully satisfied that he or she: (1) can serve impartially; (2) can serve independently from the parties, potential witnesses, and the other arbitrators; (3) is competent to serve; (4) can be available to commence the arbitration in accordance with the requirements of the proceeding; and (5) is able to devote the time and attention to its completion that the parties are reasonably entitled to expect. Arbitrators should conduct themselves in a way that is fair to all parties and should not be swayed by outside pressure, public clamor, and fear of criticism or self-interest. They must avoid conduct and statements that give the appearance of partiality toward or against any party. Arbitrators must also act within the parameters of the authority given them by the agreement of the parties, but arbitrators are not required ethically to comply with any agreement, procedures or rules that are unlawful or that, in the arbitrator's judgment, would be inconsistent with the Code. Arbitrators should not withdraw or abandon an appointment unless compelled to do so by unanticipated circumstances that would render it impossible or impracticable to continue. Arbitrators who are compelled to withdraw prior to the completion of an arbitration should take reasonable steps to protect the interests of the parties in the arbitration, including return of evidentiary materials and the protection of confidentiality.

Party-appointed arbitrators. A party-appointed arbitrator has an obligation under Canon IX to ascertain, as early as possible but not later than the first meeting of the arbitrators and parties, whether the parties have agreed that the party-appointed arbitrators will serve as neutrals or whether they shall be subject to Canon X, and to provide a timely report of their conclusions to the parties and other arbitrators. In making this determination, party-appointed arbitrators should review the agreement of the parties, the applicable rules and any applicable law bearing upon arbitrator neutrality. In reviewing the agreement of the parties, party-appointed arbitrators should consult any relevant express terms of the written or oral arbitration agreement. It may also be appropriate for them to inquire into agreements that have not been expressly set forth, but which may be implied from an established course of dealings of the parties or well-recognized custom and usage in their trade or profession. Where party-appointed arbitrators conclude that the parties intended for the party-appointed arbitrators not to serve as neutrals, after making their report as just described, they may act as provided in Canon X unless or until a different determination of their status is made by the parties, any administering institution or the arbitral panel. In addition, until party-appointed arbitrators conclude that the party-appointed arbitrators were not intended by the parties to serve as neutrals, or if the party-appointed arbitrators are unable to form a reasonable belief of their status from the foregoing sources and no decision in this regard has yet been made by the parties, any administering institution, or the arbitral panel, they should observe all of the obligations of neutral arbitrators set forth in the Code. Party-appointed arbitrators not governed by Canon X must observe all of the obligations of Canons I through VIII unless otherwise required by agreement of the parties, any applicable rules, or applicable law.

"Canon X Arbitrators" must observe all of the obligations of Canon I subject only to the following provisions: (1) they may, by agreement or understanding of all participants, be predisposed toward the party who appointed them but in all other respects they are obligated to act in good faith and with integrity and fairness. For example, Canon X arbitrators should not engage in delaying tactics or harassment of any party or witness and should not knowingly make untrue or misleading statements to the other arbitrators. The provisions of subparagraphs B (1), B (2), and paragraphs C and D of Canon I, insofar as they relate to partiality, relationships, and interests are not applicable to Canon X arbitrators.

2.12.2   Canon II–Disclosure of bias or conflicts of interest

Canon II of the Code provides: An arbitrator should disclose any interest or relationship likely to affect impartiality or which might create an appearance of partiality or bias.

Neutral arbitrators. Persons who are requested to serve as arbitrators must, before accepting, make a reasonable effort to inform themselves of any pertinent interests or relationships, and disclose: (1) any known direct or indirect financial or personal interest in the outcome of the arbitration; (2) any known existing or past financial, business, professional or personal relationships which might reasonably affect impartiality or lack of independence in the eyes of any of the parties; (3) the nature and extent of any prior knowledge they may have of the dispute; and (4) any other matters, relationships, or interests which they are obligated to disclose by the agreement of the parties, the rules or practices of an institution, or applicable law regulating arbitrator disclosure. This obligation to disclose pertinent interests or relationships is a continuing duty and any doubt as to whether or not disclosure is to be made should be resolved in favor of disclosure. Disclosure is normally made to all parties unless the parties' agreement, the law, or rules direct otherwise. After the arbitrator's disclosure, if the parties desire that the person serve as the arbitrator, that person may properly serve.

If all parties request an arbitrator to withdraw, the arbitrator must do so. If less than all the parties request that the arbitrator withdraw because of alleged partiality, the arbitrator must withdraw unless: (1) an agreement of the parties, or arbitration rules agreed to by the parties, or applicable law establishes procedures for determining challenges to arbitrators, in which case those procedures should be followed; or (2) in the absence of applicable procedures, if the arbitrator, after carefully considering the matter, determines that the reason for the challenge is not substantial, and that he or she can nevertheless act and decide the case impartially and fairly.

If compliance by a prospective arbitrator with any provision of the Code would require disclosure of confidential or privileged information, the prospective arbitrator should either:

1. secure the consent to the disclosure from the person who furnished the information or the holder of the privilege; or

2. withdraw.

Party-appointed arbitrators. Canon X arbitrators have the obligation under Canon II to disclose to all parties, and to the other arbitrators, all interests and relationships which Canon II requires disclosed. They are not obliged to withdraw under Canon II for alleged partiality if requested to do so by a party or parties who did not appoint them.

2.12.3 Canon III—No improper communications with parties

Canon III of the Code provides: An arbitrator should avoid impropriety or the appearance of impropriety in communicating with parties.

Neutral arbitrators. If the parties have entered into an arbitration agreement and it contains procedures regarding communications between the arbitrator(s) and the parties, those procedures govern. If the arbitration agreement does not have a provision regarding communications between arbitrators and parties, the following procedures apply.

An arbitrator or prospective arbitrator should not discuss a proceeding with any party in the absence of any other party, except in any of the following circumstances:

Prospective arbitrator. When the appointment of a prospective arbitrator is being considered, the prospective arbitrator:

1. may ask about the identities of the parties, counsel, or witnesses and the general nature of the case; and

2. may respond to inquiries from a party or its counsel designed to determine his or her suitability and availability for the appointment. In any such dialogue, the prospective arbitrator may receive information from a party or its counsel disclosing the general nature of the dispute but should not permit them to discuss the merits of the case.

3. Unless otherwise provided in Canon III, in applicable arbitration rules or in an agreement of the parties, whenever an arbitrator communicates in writing with one party, the arbitrator should at the same time send a copy of the communication to every other party, and whenever the arbitrator receives any written communication concerning the case from one party which has not already been sent to every other party, the arbitrator should send or cause it to be sent to the other parties.

4. Discussions may be had with a party concerning such logistical matters as setting the time and place of hearings or making other arrangements for the conduct of the proceedings. However, the arbitrator should promptly inform each other party of the discussion and should not make any final determination concerning the matter discussed before giving each absent party an opportunity to express the party's views.

5. If a party fails to be present at a hearing after having been given due notice, or if all parties expressly consent, the arbitrator may discuss the case with any party who is present.

Party-appointed arbitrators. In an arbitration in which the two party-appointed arbitrators are expected to appoint the third arbitrator, each party-appointed arbitrator may consult with the party who appointed the arbitrator concerning the choice of the third arbitrator. In addition:

1. In an arbitration involving party-appointed arbitrators, each party-appointed arbitrator may consult with the party who appointed the arbitrator concerning arrangements for any compensation to be

paid to the party-appointed arbitrator. Submission of routine written requests for payment of compensation and expenses in accordance with such arrangements and written communications pertaining solely to such requests need not be sent to the other party.

2. In an arbitration involving party-appointed arbitrators, each party-appointed arbitrator may consult with the party who appointed the arbitrator concerning the status of the arbitrator (*i.e.*, neutral or non-neutral).

Canon X requires Canon X arbitrators to observe all of the obligations of Canon III, subject only to the following provisions:

1. Like neutral party-appointed arbitrators, Canon X arbitrators may consult with the party who appointed them to the extent permitted in paragraph B of Canon III (See Appendix I);

2. Canon X arbitrators shall, at the earliest practicable time, disclose to the other arbitrators and to the parties whether or not they intend to communicate with their appointing parties. If they have disclosed the intention to engage in such communications, they may thereafter communicate with their appointing parties concerning any other aspect of the case, except as provided in paragraph 3 below.

3. If such communication occurred prior to the time they were appointed as arbitrators, or prior to the first hearing or other meeting of the parties with the arbitrators, the Canon X arbitrator should, at or before the first hearing or meeting of the arbitrators with the parties, disclose the fact that such communication has taken place. In complying with this requirement, it is sufficient that there be disclosure of the fact that such communication has occurred without disclosing the content of the communication. A single timely disclosure of the Canon X arbitrator's intention to participate in such communications in the future is sufficient;

Canon X arbitrators may not at any time during the arbitration:

    a. disclose any deliberations by the arbitrators on any matter or issue submitted to them for decision;

    b. communicate with the parties that appointed them concerning any matter or issue taken under consideration by the panel after the record is closed or such matter or issue has been submitted for decision; or

c. disclose any final decision or interim decision in advance of the time that it is disclosed to all parties.

5. Unless otherwise agreed by the arbitrators and the parties, a Canon X arbitrator may not communicate orally with the neutral arbitrator concerning any matter or issue arising or expected to arise in the arbitration in the absence of the other Canon X arbitrator. If a Canon X arbitrator communicates in writing with the neutral arbitrator, he or she shall simultaneously provide a copy of the written communication to the other Canon X arbitrator;

6. When Canon X arbitrators communicate orally with the parties that appointed them concerning any matter on which communication is permitted under the Code, they are not obligated to disclose the contents of such oral communications to any other party or arbitrator; and

7. When Canon X arbitrators communicate in writing with the party who appointed them concerning any matter on which communication is permitted under the Code, they are not required to send copies of any such written communication to any other party or arbitrator.

2.12.4   Canon IV—Fairness and diligence

Canon IV of the Code provides: An arbitrator should conduct the proceedings fairly and diligently.

Neutral arbitrators. An arbitrator should conduct the proceedings in an even-handed manner. The arbitrator should be patient and courteous to the parties, their representatives, and the witnesses and should encourage similar conduct by all participants. In addition:

1. The arbitrator should afford to all parties the right to be heard and due notice of the time and place of any hearing. The arbitrator should allow each party a fair opportunity to present its evidence and arguments.

2. The arbitrator should not deny any party the opportunity to be represented by counsel or by any other person chosen by the party.

3. If a party fails to appear after due notice, the arbitrator should proceed with the arbitration when authorized to do so, but only after receiving assurance that appropriate notice has been given to the absent party.

4. When the arbitrator determines that more information than has been presented by the parties is required to decide the case, it is not improper for the arbitrator to ask questions, call witnesses, and request documents or other evidence, including expert testimony.

5. Although it is not improper for an arbitrator to suggest to the parties that they discuss the possibility of settlement or the use of mediation, or other dispute resolution processes, an arbitrator should not exert pressure on any party to settle or to utilize other dispute resolution processes. An arbitrator should not be present or otherwise participate in settlement discussions or act as a mediator unless requested to do so by all parties.

6. Co-arbitrators should afford each other full opportunity to participate in all aspects of the proceedings. Code provision is not intended to preclude one arbitrator from acting in limited circumstances (e.g., ruling on discovery issues) where authorized by the agreement of the parties, applicable rules or law, nor does it preclude a majority of the arbitrators from proceeding with any aspect of the arbitration if an arbitrator is unable or unwilling to participate and such action is authorized by the agreement of the parties or applicable rules or law.

Party-appointed arbitrators. Canon X arbitrators must observe all of the obligations of Canon IV .

2.12.5 Canon V—Just, independent, and deliberate decision making

Canon V of the Code provides: An arbitrator should make decisions in a just, independent and deliberate manner.

Neutral arbitrators. The arbitrator should, after careful deliberation, decide all issues submitted for determination. An arbitrator should decide no other issues. In addition:

1. An arbitrator should decide all matters justly, exercising independent judgment, and should not permit outside pressure to affect the decision.

2. An arbitrator should not delegate the duty to decide to any other person.

3. In the event that all parties agree upon a settlement of issues in dispute and request the arbitrator to embody that agreement in an award, the arbitrator may do so, but is not required to do so unless satisfied with the propriety of the terms of settlement. Whenever an arbitrator embodies a settlement by the parties in an award, the arbitrator should state in the award that it is based on an agreement of the parties.

Party-appointed arbitrators. Party-appointed arbitrators must observe all of the obligations of Canon V except that they are permitted to be predisposed toward deciding in favor of the party who appointed them.

2.12.6   Canon VI—Trust and confidentiality

Canon VI of the Code provides: An arbitrator should be faithful to the relationship of trust and confidentiality inherent in that office.

Neutral arbitrators. An arbitrator is in a relationship of trust to the parties and should not, at any time, use confidential information acquired during the arbitration proceeding to gain personal advantage or advantage for others, or to affect adversely the interest of another. In addition:

1. The arbitrator should keep confidential all matters relating to the arbitration proceedings and decision. An arbitrator may obtain help from an associate, a research assistant or other persons in connection with reaching his or her decision if the arbitrator informs the parties of the use of such assistance and such persons agree to be bound by the provisions of Canon VI.

2. It is not proper at any time for an arbitrator to inform anyone of any decision in advance of the time it is given to all parties. In a proceeding in which there is more than one arbitrator, it is not proper at any time for an arbitrator to inform anyone about the substance of the deliberations of the arbitrators. After an arbitration award has been made, it is not proper for an arbitrator to assist in proceedings to enforce or challenge the award.

3. Unless the parties so request, an arbitrator should not appoint himself or herself to a separate office related to the subject matter of the dispute, such as receiver or trustee, nor should a panel of arbitrators appoint one of their number to such an office.

Party-appointed arbitrators. Cannon X arbitrators must observe all of the obligations of Canon VI.

2.12.7 Canon VII—Integrity and fairness in arrangements for compensation and expense reimbursement

Canon VII of the Code provides: An arbitrator should adhere to standards of integrity and fairness when making arrangements for compensation and reimbursement of expenses.

Neutral arbitrators. Arbitrators who are to be compensated for their services or reimbursed for their expenses shall adhere to standards of integrity and fairness in making arrangements for such payments. In addition:

Certain practices relating to payments are generally recognized as tending to preserve the integrity and fairness of the arbitration process. These practices include:

a. Before the arbitrator finally accepts appointment, the basis of payment, including any cancellation fee, compensation in the event of withdrawal and compensation for study and preparation time, and all other charges, should be established. Except for arrangements for the compensation of party-appointed arbitrators, all parties should be informed in writing of the terms established.

b. In proceedings conducted under the rules or administration of an institution that is available to assist in making arrangements for payments, communication related to compensation should be made through the institution. In proceedings where no institution has been engaged by the parties to administer the arbitration, any communication with arbitrators (other than party appointed arbitrators) concerning payments should be in the presence of all parties; and

c. Arbitrators should not, absent extraordinary circumstances, request increases in the basis of their compensation during the course of a proceeding.

Party-appointed arbitrators. Canon X arbitrators should observe all of the obligations of Canon VII.

2.12.8   Canon VIII—Truthful and accurate advertising

Canon VIII of the Code provides: An arbitrator may engage in advertising or promotion of arbitral services which is truthful and accurate.

Neutral arbitrators. Advertising or promotion of an individual's willingness or availability to serve as an arbitrator must be accurate and unlikely to mislead. Any statements about the quality of the arbitrator's work or the success of the arbitrator's practice must be truthful. In addition:

1.   Advertising and promotion must not imply any willingness to accept an appointment otherwise than in accordance with the Code.

2. Canon VIII does not preclude an arbitrator from printing, publishing, or disseminating advertisements conforming to these standards in any electronic or print medium, from making personal presentations to prospective users of arbitral services conforming to such standards or from responding to inquiries concerning the arbitrator's availability, qualifications, experience, or fee arrangements.

Party-appointed arbitrators. Canon X arbitrators should observe all of the obligations of Canon VIII.

2.12.9   Canon IX—Party-appointed arbitrators' duty to determine and to disclose their status

Canon IX of the Code provides: Arbitrators appointed by **one party have a duty to determine and disclose their status and to comply with this Code, except as exempted by Canon X.**

Party-appointed arbitrators. Canon IX pertains to party-appointed arbitrators and imposes certain duties on them relating to determination, disclosure, and compliance of their neutral or non-neutral status. Explained in more detail:

1.   In some types of arbitration in which there are three arbitrators, it is customary for each party, acting alone, to appoint one arbitrator. The third arbitrator is then appointed by agreement either of the parties or of the two arbitrators, or failing such agreement, by an independent institution or individual. In tripartite arbitrations

to which the Code applies, all three arbitrators are presumed to be neutral and are expected to observe the same standards as the third arbitrator.

2. Notwithstanding this presumption, there are certain types of tri-partite arbitration in which it is expected by all parties that the two arbitrators appointed by the parties may be predisposed toward the party appointing them. Those arbitrators, referred to in the Code as "Canon X arbitrators," are not to be held to the standards of neutrality and independence applicable to other arbitrators. Canon X describes the special ethical obligations of party-appointed arbitrators who are not expected to meet the standard of neutrality.

3. Specific requirements imposed on party-appointed arbitrators are stated above under the heading "Party-appointed arbitrators" in the discussion related to Canon I.

4. Canon X arbitrators must observe all of the obligations of Canon IX.

2.12.10 Canon X—Exemptions for non-neutral party-appointed arbitrators

Canon X of the Code provides: Exemptions for arbitrators appointed by one party who are not subject to rules of neutrality.

Party-appointed arbitrators. Canon X applies only to party-appointed arbitrators who are not subject to the rules of neutrality. Their obligations under the Code are described above in relation to each of the Canons I through IX.

2.13 Lawyer Serving As Third-Party Neutral

In the last decade, alternative dispute resolution has come to be a substantial and important aspect of our public and private systems for resolving disputes. Apart from advocating on behalf of clients in arbitration, lawyers now often serve as arbitrators, either individually, or as members of three-arbitrator panels. It should be noted that the role of arbitrator (and other third-party neutral functions) is not unique to lawyers. Non-lawyers can also serve as arbitrators and as other third party neutrals. When lawyers and non-lawyers serve in the neutral role, they may be subject to court rules or other laws that apply to third-party neutrals generally. Lawyer-neutrals, however, may also be subject to lawyer-specific court rules and rules of professional conduct. One such rule of professional conduct was added by the American Bar Association in recent years to the Model Rules of Professional Conduct in order to help clarify and distinguish a lawyer's duties in a neutral role versus duties owed when serving in an advocate role. That rule, Model Rule 2.4, defines a lawyer's service in a neutral role as occurring "when the lawyer assists two or more persons who are not clients of the lawyer to reach resolution of a dispute or other matter that has arisen between them." It further provides that service as a third-party neutral "may include service as an arbitrator, a mediator or in such other capacity as will enable the lawyer to assist the parties to resolve the matter." (MR 2.4 (a)). When serving as a third-party neutral, a lawyer has two important initial duties to perform with respect to parties. The lawyer-neutral must first inform unrepresented parties that he or she is not representing them. Second, when a lawyer-neutral knows or reasonably should know that a party does not understand the lawyer-neutral's role in the matter, he or she must explain the difference between a lawyer's role as a third-party neutral and a lawyer's role as one who represents a client. (MR 2.4(b)).

Lawyers who serve, personally and substantially, as third-party neutrals subsequently may be asked to serve as a lawyer representing a client in the same matter. Generally speaking, the ABA Model Rules of Professional Conduct forbid such representation unless all of the parties to the proceedings give their informed consent, confirmed in writing. (MR 1.12(a)). Other laws or codes of ethics governing third party neutrals may impose more stringent standards of personal or imputed disqualification in such situation. The conflicts of a lawyer who is personally disqualified under MR 1.12(a) will be imputed to other lawyers in a law firm unless: (1) the disqualified lawyer is timely screened from any participation in the matter and is apportioned no part of the fee generated by the firm's representation; and, (2) the firm provides the parties prompt written notice to the parties and any appropriate tribunal to enable them to determine compliance with the provisions of MR 1.12. (MR 1.12(c)).

It is common these days for lawyers to represent clients in some matters and to serve as third-party neutrals in others. This broadening of the lawyer's role requires lawyers to be especially vigilant of the ethical requirements imposed by the requirements of each role.

Lawyers who represent clients in alternative dispute resolution processes are typically governed by the Model Rules of Professional Conduct. Those ethical requirements are addressed above in this chapter in section 2.7. When advocating on behalf of a client before a tribunal, as in binding arbitration, the lawyer's duty of candor is governed by MR 3.3. Otherwise, a lawyer's duty of candor toward both the third-party neutral and other parties is governed by MR 4.1.

2.14 Civility Guidelines

In 1998, the American Bar Association's Litigation Section issued a set of Guidelines for Litigation Conduct to address what it viewed as a decline in professionalism and civility among lawyers.[17] Modeled on the Standards of Professional Conduct adopted by the United States Court of Appeals for the Seventh Circuit, the ABA Section of Litigation's Guidelines are purely aspirational and are not used as a basis for liability or discipline. You should draw these Guidelines to the attention of other arbitration advocates, as necessary, when inappropriate or unprofessional behavior of lawyers tends to threaten the intended purpose, the integrity, or the character of the arbitration process. Guidelines that appear to directly pertain to the arbitration process include:

LAWYER'S DUTIES TO OTHER COUNSEL

1. We will practice our profession with a continuing awareness that our role is to zealously advance the legitimate interests of our clients. In our dealings with others, we will not reflect the ill feelings of our clients. We will treat all other counsel, parties, and witnesses in a civil and courteous manner, not only in court, but also in all other written and oral communications. We will refrain from acting upon or manifesting bias or prejudice based upon race, sex, religion, national origin, disability, age, sexual orientation, or socioeconomic status toward any participant in the legal process.

2. We will not, even when called upon by a client to do so, abuse or indulge in offensive conduct directed to other counsel, parties, or witnesses. We will abstain from disparaging personal remarks or acrimony toward other counsel, parties, or witnesses. We will treat adverse witnesses and parties with fair consideration.

3. We will not encourage or knowingly authorize any person under our control to engage in conduct that would be improper if we engaged in such conduct.

---

17. The material contained in this section is adapted from Manuel San Juan, ABA Litigation Section's Civility Guidelines, February 2001 The Federal Lawyer 51.

4. We will not, absent good cause attribute bad motives or improper conduct to other counsel.

* * *

6. We will in good faith adhere to all express promises and to agreements with other counsel, whether oral or in writing, and to all agreements implied by the circumstances or local customs.

* * *

9. In civil actions, we will stipulate to relevant matters if they are undisputed and if no good faith advocacy basis exists for not stipulating.

* * *

10. We will not use any form of discovery or discovery scheduling as a means of harassment.

11. Whenever circumstances allow, we will make good faith efforts to resolve by agreement objections before presenting them to the [tribunal].

12. We will not time the filing or service of motions or pleadings in any way that unfairly limits another party's opportunity to respond.

13. We will not request an extension of time solely for the purpose of unjustified delay or to obtain unfair advantage.

14. We will consult other counsel regarding scheduling matters in a good faith effort to avoid scheduling conflicts.

15. We will endeavor to accommodate previously scheduled dates for hearings, depositions, meeting, conferences, vacations, seminars, or other functions that   produce good faith calendar conflicts on the part of other counsel.

16. We will promptly notify other counsel, and . . . other persons, when . . . meetings, or conferences are to be cancelled or postponed.

17. We will agree to reasonable requests for extensions of time and for waiver of procedural formalities, provided our clients' legitimate rights will not be materially or adversely affected.

18. We will not cause any default or dismissal to be entered without first notifying opposing counsel when we know his or her identity, unless the rules provide otherwise.

19. We will take depositions only when actually needed. We will not take depositions for the purposes of harassment or other improper purpose.

20. We will not engage in any conduct during a deposition that would not be appropriate in the presence of an [arbitrator].

21. We will not obstruct questioning during a deposition or object to deposition questions unless permitted under applicable law.

22. During depositions, we will ask only those questions we reasonably believe are necessary, and appropriate, for the prosecution or defense of an action.

23. We will carefully craft document production requests so they are limited to those documents we reasonably believe are necessary, and appropriate, for the prosecution or defense of an action. We will not design production requests to place an undue burden or expense on a party, or for any other improper purpose.

24. We will respond to document requests reasonably and not strain to interpret requests in an artificially restrictive manner to avoid disclosure of relevant and non-privileged documents. We will not produce documents in a manner designed to hide or obscure the existence of particular documents, or to accomplish any other improper purpose.

25. We will carefully craft interrogatories so they are limited to those matters we reasonably believe are necessary, and appropriate, for the prosecution or defense of an action, and we will not design them to place an undue burden or expense on a party, or for any other improper purpose.

26. We will respond to interrogatories reasonably and will not strain to interpret them in an artificially restrictive manner to avoid disclosure of relevant and non-privileged information, or for any other improper purpose.

27. We will base our discovery objections on a good faith belief in their merit and will not object solely for the purpose of withholding or delaying the disclosure of relevant information, or for any other improper purpose.

28. When a draft order is to be prepared by counsel to reflect an [arbitrator's] ruling, we will draft an order that accurately and completely reflects the [arbitrator's] ruling. We will promptly prepare and submit a proposed order to other counsel and attempt to reconcile any differences before the draft order is present to the [arbitrator].

29. We will not ascribe a position to another counsel that counsel has not taken.

30. Unless permitted or invited by the [arbitrator], we will not send copies of correspondence between counsel to the [arbitrator].

31. Nothing contained in these Guidelines is intended or shall be construed to inhibit vigorous advocacy, including vigorous cross-examination.

LAWYERS' DUTIES TO THE [ARBITRATOR(S)]

1. We will speak and write civilly and respectfully in all communications with the [arbitrator(s)].

2. We will be punctual and prepared for all . . . appearances so that all hearings, conferences, and trials may commence on time; if delayed, we will notify the [arbitrator(s)], if possible.

3. We will be considerate of the time constraints and pressures on the [arbitrator(s)] . . . inherent in their effort to administer justice.

4. We will not engage in any conduct that brings disorder or disruption to the [hearing]. We will advise our clients and witnesses appearing in [the hearing] of the proper conduct expected and required there and, to the best of our ability, prevent our clients and witnesses from creating disorder or disruption.

5. We will not knowingly misrepresent, mischaracterize, misquote, or miscite facts or authorities in any oral or written communication to the [arbitrator(s)].

6. We will not write letters to the [arbitrator(s)] in connection with a pending action, unless invited or permitted by the [arbitrator(s].

7. Before dates for hearings . . . are set, or if that is not feasible, immediately after such date has been set, we will attempt to verify the availability of necessary participants and witnesses so we can promptly notify the court of any likely problems.

◆ CHAPTER THREE ◆

Prehearing Advocacy

That's not writing. That's typing!
—Truman Capote

Similar to trial advocacy, the key to a successful arbitration is to prepare a persuasive trial story from the outset, and to prepare carefully both your client and your case for the arbitration hearing far in advance of its scheduled date.[1] If you are a claimant, prehearing advocacy will begin in earnest when you draft your arbitration demand and incorporated claims or when you draft your submission agreement. If you are a respondent, prehearing advocacy will commence when you draft your answer. These pleadings will provide sketches of the respective trial stories and, to a large extent, define the general limits of the stories as ultimately played out before the arbitration panel. These initial story designs will provide the basic templates against which the arbitrators will measure questions of relevance and materiality. They are important documents that should not just be drafted, but well crafted, or as Truman Capote might say, not just typed, but well-written. You should also take similar care in preparing motions, responses, position statements, discovery requests, and other pleadings during the arbitration's prehearing stage. In addition, you should view the preliminary hearing as a very useful, strategic tool to aid you in your prehearing preparation. Information you gather there will help you organize the document part of the case and advise your client and other witnesses on how to present their testimony at the hearing. In essence, it will aid you in performing your playwright and theatrical director functions, described in more detail in chapters 4 and 5, infra.

It is to all of these subjects that we now turn.[2]

3.1 Drafting the Arbitration Demand

You may initiate arbitration by demand or by submission agreement. If the arbitration is triggered by a contract's arbitration clause, you must draft the demand in accordance with that clause. The demand for arbitration is a written

---

1. *See generally*, Steven Lubet, *Modern Trial Advocacy* 7–13 (NITA, 1993). The reader is invited to consult the second edition of *Modern Trial Advocacy* (NITA, 1997), whenever the first edition is referenced throughout this Practical Guide Series book.
2. *See generally*, Thomas Oehmke, *Construction Arbitration*, chapter 11 (Lawyers Co-operative Publishing Co., 1988); Rodolphe J. A. De Seife, *Solving Disputes Through Commercial Arbitration*, chapter 6, (Callaghan, 1987); Roth, Wulff, and Cooper, *The Alternative Dispute Resolution Practice Guide*, chapters 8, 9, 10, and 11 (Lawyers Cooperative Publishing, 1993)

notice by one party to the other(s) of that party's intent to initiate the arbitration process. When arbitration is initiated by submission agreement, the disputants sign an agreement or, if the case is administered, a submission form agreeing to participate in the arbitration.

Pay close attention to any time limitations within which a claimant must present or file a demand. These time constraints may appear in the arbitration clause itself, in a court rule, or in a statute. If a demand is not timely filed with a dispute resolution organization or served on the other parties, the claimant may lose the right to have claims adjudicated in any forum, private or public. If you file a demand with a dispute resolution organization, you should be prepared to deposit a filing or administrative fee at that time.

To be arbitrable, the nature of the controversy must be within the parameter of the arbitration clause. Even though the parties have designated a particular dispute resolution organization to administer the arbitration, the clause's language will control over the language of the organization's published rules if there is an issue whether certain claims are arbitrable or whether certain procedures should be followed in relation to the demand.

You should draft the demand clearly and succinctly, while incorporating all of the case's pertinent facts. There is no set structure or format for a demand, although it is prudent to include, at a minimum, the following information: (1) the names of all parties involved in the dispute; (2) a succinct, straightforward statement of facts, in chronological order; (3) a quote containing the exact language of the arbitration clause, or an attachment with a copy of the clause; (4) a statement of the claim or claims, and how they relate to the contract and the arbitration clause; and (5) a statement of the relief sought. In complex cases, it is common for the claimant to attach to the demand a pleading in the form of a complaint that would be filed in court. Indeed, some dispute resolution organizations permit a court-filed complaint to serve as the demand and claims in arbitration when the parties opt to have their dispute resolved through arbitration rather than in the court system.

After drafting a demand, you must normally serve it on the other party or parties. This may usually be done in any manner of service that is acceptable for initiating a lawsuit in the court system. If you use the postal system, effect service by certified or registered mail. You should also be aware that under the rules of some dispute resolution organizations, the demand is first filed with the organization, which then serves it on the respondents. The organizations also have rules as to how many copies of the demand must be filed and served.

A checklist for drafting an arbitration demand appears in Appendix B.

3.2 Drafting the Response to the Demand

Once the claimant has filed the demand, the respondent can normally choose to answer or otherwise respond to the demand. Unlike the litigation setting, respondents are not usually required to file an answer. In fact, lack of an answer will not be construed as an admission of guilt but rather as a denial of the claim(s) presented in the demand. One important exception to these principles relates to securities cases. In recent years, dispute resolution organizations administering securities cases have promulgated rules requiring respondents to answer demands with specificity. Failure to be specific in your answer may prevent you from introducing evidence as to defenses not disclosed in the answer.

As a matter of common sense, in most situations where you have a choice as to filing an answer, it is in the respondent's best interest to respond to the demand in order to familiarize the arbitrator(s) with the case before the hearing. You certainly do not want to give the arbitrators the impression that your client is being disrespectful to them or is taking a cavalier attitude toward the arbitration proceeding. Also, you should be aware that, in addition to the exception for securities cases, some dispute resolution organizations routinely require that an answer be filed and still others require that an answer be filed if a claimant makes a demand for an answering statement. If a claimant makes such a demand, the respondent must file an answer or risk being barred from presenting any defense.

3.2.1 Drafting the answer

If the arbitration is taking place pursuant to the rules of a dispute resolution organization, the organization will notify the respondent of the proceedings. In such case, the respondent will usually have approximately seven to ten days to answer or acknowledge the claim. Again, a failure to answer will normally be considered a denial.

To put the respondent's position, defenses, and contentions on the record, your answer should contain at a minimum:

1. a general denial of all the claims, as appropriate;

2. a denial of each separate claim with a short explanation of your version of the facts, and if some of the claimant's allegations are true, an acknowledgment of the truth of the claims;

3. a protest of the relief being sought; and

4. if applicable, an unparticularized statement of the affirmative defenses. By not providing the particularized facts supporting your affirmative defenses, you can keep your defense options somewhat open during any discovery and through the course of the actual hearing. But be sure to

read any pertinent arbitration rules very carefully. Some may require you to include particularized affirmative defenses in your answer or waive them. Regardless of the existence of any such rules, you should be aware that an arbitrator, acting at his or her own discretion, may simply bar proof of an affirmative defense of which the claimant had no prehearing Typical affirmative defenses appear in the chart that follows.

TYPICAL AFFIRMATIVE DEFENSES	
Accord and Satisfaction	Duress
Assumption of Risk	Estoppel
Collateral Estoppel	Breach of Contract
Failure of Consideration	Failure to Exhaust Contractual Remedies
Failure to State a Claim	Fraud
Frustration of Purpose	Impossibility
Nonarbitrable Issue	Res Judicata
Statute of Frauds	Set-off
Statute of Limitations	Waiver
Comparative Negligence	Contributory Negligence
Condition Precedent	Failure to Mitigate Damages
Illegality	Privilege
Release	Unclean Hands

Although not required, an answer may also contain a request for a specific place for the hearing to be conducted, and it may reveal the name of the attorney or other party who will represent the respondent. An answer can also contain a request for a bill of particulars if the demand contains insufficient information for the respondent to be able to prepare a defense.

If the respondent chooses not to respond, the claimant can continue the arbitration process by selecting an arbitrator and scheduling the hearing. If the respondent fails to answer or appear, the claimant must proceed to prove the case based on proper evidence. The arbitrators will then determine an appropriate award based solely on the claimant's evidence.

3.2.2   Drafting counterclaims

In addition to answering the demand, the respondent may also file a counterclaim. A counterclaim is usually separate from the answer and any affirmative defenses. You should file this claim at the same time as the answer, and it should contain the same elements required in a demand. Also, the service and fee requirements are usually the same as filing a demand. Normally, if the respondent is simply filing an answer, no fee is required—only when filing a claim of some sort—even if that is a counterclaim.

Filing a counterclaim is the only opportunity for a respondent to present a new claim in the matter to be arbitrated. Under the Rules of the American Arbitration Association, for example, after the arbitrator has been appointed no new or different claims may be advanced without the arbitrator's consent. Therefore it is important to raise these claims in a counterclaim when filing the response. However, a counterclaim that arises out of a different and separate agreement that did not provide for arbitration cannot be alleged at this time.

3.2.3   Strategies for answering a demand

Here are a few general strategies for answering a demand in arbitration:

➢ Be general—not technical.

➢ Include only the facts pertinent to the explanation and understanding of your denials.

➢ State your responses in a logical, precise manner.

➢ If some of claimant's allegations are true, acknowledge the truth of the claims; if not, deny claimant's version and set forth your version of the facts.

➢ State affirmative defenses in general way, but touch on all of them.

3.3   Drafting Motions and Responses

Written motions are the exception, not the rule, in arbitration. They are generally used to dispose of law-based contested matters arising before the actual hearing. Because the arbitration process is not regulated by a universally applicable set of rules, arbitration motion practice may vary according to the needs and preferences of the arbitrators and practitioners in particular cases. Because the arbitration process is more informal than litigation, motions practice is informal as well. Generally, the best advice about written motions in arbitration is to strive to have none. If you must make written motions, limit them to situations where the relief you seek is fundamental to or dispositive of the case. Keep them short and simple (like this section); and responses likewise. Also, remember that in many arbitrations, motions are made orally by counsel and decided by the arbitrators in the preliminary hearing, as explained in more detail in section 3.5, infra. For a comprehensive listing of arguments to support rulings on various motions and objections during arbitration proceedings, see Appendix S

3.4   Drafting Position Statements

A position statement, also called a prehearing or opening brief, may be requested by the arbitrator in your case. Such statements are usually filed simultaneously by all parties by a designated date, although sometimes arbitrators request the claimant to submit first and the respondent to submit after reviewing the claimant's pleading. A statement or brief should be well organized; clearly written; and it should briefly apprise the arbitrators of the separate claims, the significant facts, the contentions, and the supporting case law. It should further inform the arbitrator or opposing counsel regarding your views on the remedies being sought, monetary and otherwise. It embodies the blueprint of your case, and the arbitrators may indeed refer to it from time to time during the course of the hearing.

When an arbitrator requests a position statement, the customary format is a short (five to ten-page) memorandum. There is no need to write an appellate court type of brief. You merely want to make an initial positive impression on the panel as to the merit of your positions. You will be able to round out this initial written impression at the actual hearing by means of your oral opening statement, testimonial and documentary evidence, cross examinations, and closing argument. The more "reader friendly" the statement or the brief, the more likely the arbitrator will begin the arbitration hearing with an accurate understanding of your case and position. With an effectively written position statement, you can get a "jump" on your opponent before the hearing even begins.

Because the opening statement is a persuasive document, you should state facts accurately and incorporate a few cases that strongly support your principal contentions. If the dispute involves interpretation of provisions of a contract or of a statute, quote those provisions in the fact portion of the position statement. Above all, be careful not to allege facts in the statement that you will not be able to prove during the hearing. If nonlawyers are on your panel, you must take special care to write in a straightforward way, without assuming they will understand legal terms. Explain Latin terms in plain English. Also, remember that if you cite cases or statutes, nonlawyers will not normally have easy access to law libraries. You should provide them with copies of pertinent cases and statutes. Though uncommon, when parties do not file position statements simultaneously, arbitrators occasionally permit a claimant to file a reply to respondent's position statement.

3.5 The Preliminary Hearing

A preliminary hearing, or prehearing conference, can be requested by the arbitrator or by any party. It can be conducted face-to-face or by telephone. In a large case with complex issues a preliminary hearing is indispensable. In other cases, if the arbitrator does not schedule a preliminary hearing, you will have to weigh the cost and benefits of having one. A one-hour preliminary hearing might obviate two hours of procedural arguments at the beginning of the actual hearing and may avoid the possibility that the actual hearing has to be postponed one or more times because of discovery and other prehearing squabbles. Cases which require little or no discovery and involve a few thousand dollars, of course, would probably not warrant scheduling a preliminary hearing.

A preliminary hearing provides many benefits to the parties. It is an opportunity to discuss the exchange of documents and witness lists; to stipulate to uncontested facts; estimate the hearing's length; and, outside the presence of the arbitrator(s), even to explore settlement possibilities. By accomplishing all of these goals during the preliminary hearing, your case is likely to proceed more smoothly at the hearing, and you will be able to concentrate more on the preparation and presentation of the case's substantive aspects and not have to worry so much about the procedural aspects.

The preliminary hearing is your first opportunity to make a favorable personal impression on the arbitrator. You should be as cooperative and collaborative as possible in working out the prehearing schedule and the rules which will be applicable to the hearing. It is very important that you do not present yourself as a nit-picker or an obstructionist, willing to argue with opposing counsel about any issue raised. If you take extreme positions not called for by the situation, you may find that later, the arbitrator may rule in a way that recognizes your unnecessary petulance or silliness. An arbitration in which Abe Lincoln was once involved provides a good example of what can happen when lawyers behave in a petty, unreasonable way. Actually, Lincoln served as an arbitrator in many disputes, both serious and frivolous. One day, two lawyers who had been arguing for hours about the correct proportion of the length of a man's legs to the size of his body called on Lincoln to settle the dispute. Lincoln listened gravely to the points on both sides, and then gave his summing up in full legal fashion. Recognizing that this was an issue of utmost significance that had caused much anguish in the past and would doubtless do so again in the future, and having applied the full extent of his mental prowess in agonizing over the appropriate decision, he nonetheless concluded, "It is my opinion, all side issues being swept aside, that a man's lower limbs, in order to preserve harmony of proportion, should be at least long enough to reach from his body to the ground." [3]

Customarily, the arbitrator will commence the preliminary hearing by explaining its purpose and then moving directly into a discussion of the necessary preparation of the case for hearing. The following topics, at a minimum, are normally discussed at a preliminary hearing.

3.5.1   Expectation of civility and professionalism

One of the first items on the arbitrator's agenda at the preliminary hearing will normally be his or her statement of expectation that the advocates and the parties will treat each other with the highest standards of civility and professionalism. Such statement communicates a theme of non-tolerance of petty squabbling and derisive behavior on the part of the participants and sets the tone for an efficient proceeding. (See section 2.14 for a discussion of the Standards of Civility).

3.5.2   Applicable rules and law governing the procedure in the particular arbitration and the parties' claims

Of course, it is important that the arbitrator knows what rules and what laws govern the interpretation of the arbitration clause, the arbitration procedures and the substantive law affecting the decision and the enforcement of the award in the case. Be prepared to confirm these matters with the arbitrator at the beginning of the preliminary hearing. If there is disagreement among counsel as to which rules or law apply to the case, the arbitrator will likely direct that the relevant issues be argued or briefed, if necessary. The arbitrator will want to decide these issues as soon as possible.

3.5.3   Arbitrability of all issues

The arbitrator will also want to know whether there is any dispute as to the arbitrability of all the issues raised in the demand, the cross-claims, and counterclaims, if any. The burden is usually on the party opposing arbitration to

---

3. Anecdote adapted from Fadiman, *supra* chapter 2, note 2, at 358.

establish that a particular claim, issue, or matter falls outside the scope of the arbitration agreement. Whether the arbitrator or a court must decide issues of arbitrability varies somewhat among jurisdictions, but as a general principle, if parties submit a matter to arbitration, a court will defer to the arbitrator's decision on the issue of arbitrability of a dispute if it appears that the parties intended for the arbitrator to decide the arbitrability issue(s). If a court must decide whether the parties agreed to arbitrate a certain issue—including the issue of arbitrability—courts normally apply state-law principles governing contract formation. However, it should be noted that courts generally do not assume that parties agreed to arbitrate the issue of arbitrability unless there is clear and unmistakable evidence that they did so. Thus, if an issue of arbitrability arises, before you decide the matter you should look to the arbitration clause or submission agreement to determine whether there is clear and unmistakable evidence that the parties intended for the arbitrator to decide issues of arbitrability.

Realize also, that questions of arbitrability are not always patent. Sometimes they are latent and intricate. Often, they can be raised with respect to various aspects of the validity of the underlying contracts containing arbitration clauses or of the clauses themselves, including aspects of fraud in the inducement, of lack of mutuality, or of contract termination. They can also involve issues of the power or authority of the arbitrator to grant certain kinds of relief or an appropriate remedy such as an injunction, specific performance, or the awarding of consequential or punitive damages. Thus, in some situations, a question may arise as to whether a party has waived the right to object to the arbitration on grounds of nonarbitrability if the objection was not made before or at the beginning of the hearing on the merits of the legal claims. Courts are split on how to properly decide waiver of arbitrability issues, and if such an issue arises in a case you are arbitrating, you would be well advised to review the applicable case law of the pertinent jurisdiction.

Federal cases vary as to the appropriate action courts should take when arbitrable and nonarbitrable claims arise out of the same transaction and are intertwined legally and factually. The decisions in these cases usually depend on the totality of the factual and procedural circumstances. Some cases hold that the court, in such circumstance, may hear and decide all of the claims; other cases hold that the court can stay the litigation of the nonarbitrable claims pending resolution of the arbitrable claims in arbitration; and still other cases hold that a court may sever a single claim and send part of the claim to arbitration. The best course for you to follow when an issue of arbitrability arises is to research the applicable law in your jurisdiction and be prepared to brief the issue.

3.5.4 Discovery

In smaller cases, any necessary informal discovery may have been completed prior to the preliminary hearing. When informal discovery has not occurred, sometimes counsel exchange documents during the preliminary hearing. In either situation, the arbitrator may hear counsel's arguments regarding relevancy, which may in fact have the advantage of clarifying the parties' claims and defenses in the arbitration.

In larger cases, you may have attempted more formal discovery prior to the preliminary hearing. If you and your opposing counsel have disagreed about the range of discovery requested by one side, the preliminary hearing is an opportunity to discuss the issue with the arbitrator. For example, if your opponent has intentionally withheld certain documents as part of an arbitration strategy, you can ask the arbitrator to direct your opponent to produce the withheld documents if they are not subject to a privilege. Such oral motions obviate the time-consuming, costly practice of drafting motions to compel the other side to produce this discovery. The parties can present their respective arguments to the arbitrator and receive an immediate ruling on the issue.

In complex cases where there are multiple parties, cabinets of relevant documents, and several witnesses to depose, arbitrators may require counsel to submit a discovery plan by a certain date. If that occurs, you will have to get together with the other counsel in the case and negotiate a schedule for the production of documents and the depositions of witnesses. Also, you should clarify at the preliminary hearing—with the arbitrator present—which discovery rules will apply. If there is a dispute about which discovery rules will apply or about the nature and scope of the discovery, the arbitrator can rule on these matters before you launch into discovery and waste time and money bickering over the rules of the game.

Normally, arbitrators permit the parties to take depositions of experts prior to the hearing on the merits. Cut-off dates for taking such depositions are normally set during the preliminary hearing. If these experts are not deposed before the hearing, counsel may waste much time at the hearing conducting exploratory questioning, commonly called a "fishing expedition." There is usually nothing "expedited" about it.

In the average case, it is generally not a good idea to deluge the arbitrator with motions or briefs prior to the preliminary hearing. You may be wasting your time and your client's money. Experienced arbitrators can hear and dispose of most procedural matters presented orally at the preliminary hearing. If briefing of a matter is required, the arbitrator can set a briefing schedule and a ruling date during the course of the preliminary hearing.

3.5.5 Amended pleadings

It may become apparent in discussing the state of the pleadings or the amount of needed discovery that a claim, answer, or counterclaim of your opponent is not sufficiently detailed. In such instance, you may wish to ask the arbitrator to direct that a pleading be amended to include more details.

3.5.6 Addition or joinder of parties

It may also become apparent during the preliminary hearing that other parties need to be notified of the arbitration and of their opportunity for voluntary addition as parties. Or they need to be joined as additional parties because of the existence of multiple arbitration clauses making them named parties to the dispute.

3.5.7 Witness lists

The arbitrator normally sets a date by which the parties must exchange a list of witnesses that they reasonably expect to call at the hearing on the merits. This list should contain the name of each witness and a short summary of anticipated testimony (when required). It should also have attached to it the curriculum vitae of any experts, and copies of any pertinent expert reports. If the arbitrator does not bring up the topic of witness lists at the preliminary hearing, you should do so. More arbitrations are stalled or interrupted because of complaints of "surprise witnesses" than for any other reason. You will need your opponent's list of witnesses at least two or three weeks before the hearing so you can prepare your cross examinations of those witnesses and so you can decide how to prepare your own witnesses. After receiving your opponent's list of witnesses, you may want to seek leave of the arbitrator to amend your list to add or delete witnesses. Counsel have a continuing obligation to update their witness lists as soon as such information becomes available. At the time you submit your witness list, you should double check the availability of your witnesses to appear at the hearing. Sometimes the arbitrator will require counsel to indicate on the witness list the order in which counsel intend to call witnesses at the hearing. Be aware that arbitrators may have to make ethics disclosures regarding the witnesses that counsel identify.

3.5.8 Observers and other attendees

In some cases, parties may wish to have persons present who are not actual parties or witnesses in the case. These observers or other attendees often have an interest in the proceeding and its outcome, or they simply want to be there to assist a party to present its case efficiently. Sometimes a spouse may desire to accompany a party to provide moral support; sometimes a corporate representative may want to be present to coordinate the timing of the appearance of witnesses as the hearing progresses. It is within the arbitrator's discretion to allow observers to be present and/or to limit their number. If an observer will predictably cause a disruption in the hearing, the arbitrator may decide to rule at the preliminary hearing that the person should not be permitted to be present

3.5.9   Hearing exhibits

Normally, the arbitrator will set a date by which counsel are to exchange exhibit lists or actual copies of premarked exhibits that will be introduced at the hearing on the merits. By that same date, counsel will be expected to provide the arbitrator or the administering organization with a list of the exhibits or, if the arbitrator directs, a hard copy of each of those exhibits. In more complex cases, counsel should place the exhibits in binders and tab them by exhibit number. The term "exhibits" also includes any schedules, diagrams, charts, audiotapes, videotapes, etc. which counsel intend to show the arbitrator for his review and consideration in making his or her decision on the merits. Arbitrators often require counsel to get together before the hearing and agree on a set of joint exhibits in order to avoid each side introducing duplicate exhibits.

3.5.10   Fact stipulations

Arbitrators will encourage counsel to submit a stipulation of uncontested facts, and will usually set a date by which the filing of the stipulation should occur. The stipulation may greatly reduce the amount of testimony and the number of exhibits that otherwise would have to be introduced at the hearing on the merits. If counsel submit such stipulation, it is a good practice for counsel—usually claimant's counsel—to read the stipulation aloud when the hearing on the merits commences. This procedure, of course, will vary depending on the preferences of individual arbitrators.

3.5.11   Order of evidence

In multiple party cases with counterclaims, crossclaims, etc., the arbitrator will discuss with the advocates the order in which the parties will be proceeding in the presentation of their evidence at the hearing on the merits. Often, the arbitrator will set time limits for the advocates' opening statements and even for case presentations if it is appropriate and the parties agree.

3.5.12   Sequestration of witnesses

The issue of whether witnesses will be permitted to be present in the hearing room when other witnesses testify should be discussed and decided at the preliminary hearing. Usually, the advocates will agree that the witnesses on both sides should be sequestered—that is, kept out of the hearing room at least until after they testify, and usually even after they testify. The purpose of sequestering witnesses, of course, is to guarantee to the extent possible that witnesses on one side of the case will not merely conform their testimony to each other rather than speaking from their separate memories of the events as they occurred. If there is a dispute on the sequestration issue, you can decide the matter at the preliminary hearing. Keep in mind that in corporate cases, it is customary that the corporation's counsel be permitted to have at least one corporate representative present during all the testimony, even if that person will be called to testify as a witness at some point in the case. If your witnesses will be sequestered, it is a good idea to suggest that they bring reading material with them on the hearing day to occupy themselves while they are waiting to testify.

3.5.13   Burden and standard of proof

Topics commonly omitted from the agenda of a preliminary hearing are the burden and standard of proof that will be applicable to the evidence adduced at the hearing on the merits. These are very important topics that deserve special attention, especially in multiparty cases or cases in which their are claims, counter-claims, cross-claims, and third-party claims. Which party has the burden of proof and the burden of going forward, and what standard of proof that each party must satisfy in order to prove their separate claims are matters that will have a very definite impact on how each advocate will prepare his or her case for the hearing. For example, if these matters are not discussed at the preliminary hearing, and an attorney comes to the hearing believing that the evidence supporting his affirmative claims will not have to be presented until the second or third day of the hearing, the attorney may be unprepared to go forward, not having pertinent documents with him and not having his witnesses available. Also, if an attorney comes to the hearing believing that the applicable standard of proof relating to his claims is preponderance of the evidence, when in fact the proper standard is clear and convincing evidence, which, if realized in advance of the hearing, could have been met, then the arbitrator will be deprived of the necessary evidence to fairly decide the case. These issues of burden and standard of proof can be discussed at the preliminary hearing in conjunction with the topic of order or sequence of proof to be presented at the hearing on the merits.

3.5.14   Position statements or prehearing briefs

In most cases, an arbitrator will direct the advocates to submit prehearing position statements or prehearing briefs a few days in advance of the hearing on the merits. Position statements, also called prehearing or opening briefs, are usually filed simultaneously by all parties by a designated date, though sometimes an arbitrator may direct that they be filed sequentially. A position statement or brief is a short memorandum, five to ten double-spaced pages in the average case, which succinctly apprizes the arbitrator of the significant facts,

the separate claims, the contentions, and supporting law. It should also contain
the advocates views on the remedies being sought, monetary and otherwise. It
should embody the blueprint of each party's case. If properly prepared, it will be
the type of document that the arbitrator will be referring to from time to time
during the course of the hearing to help put the parties' evidence in context.

3.5.15   Stenographer

If either party desires a stenographic record of the arbitration hearing, this
should be discussed and resolved at the preliminary hearing. Court reporters or
stenographers are not automatically provided at an arbitration hearing, nor are
they ordinarily required to be present. At some time before the preliminary hearing, you should check any statute governing the arbitration proceeding in your
jurisdiction to see if a stenographic record is required. At the preliminary hearing, the parties may decide on their own to secure the services of a court reporter
to make a record of the hearing. Rules of some dispute resolution organizations
require that a party desiring to arrange for a court reporter contact the court
reporting firm directly, and send notice to all other parties involved. If all parties so desire, the cost will be equally split among them. If only one party wishes
to have a reporter present, that party will bear the entire expense. Those rules
further provide that if the transcript will be the official record of the proceedings,
then both the arbitrator and the opposing parties are entitled to see a copy of the
transcript inspect for any errors. However, an opposing party who does not pay
an apportioned share of the expense is not entitled to a copy of the transcript.

Each party must decide on its own whether this extra expense should be
undertaken, depending on the particular circumstances. In large cases, with
several different issues, a stenographic record of the hearing will be beneficial,
particularly in the preparation of post-hearing briefs; if daily copy is available
during the course of the hearing, it may be helpful to the advocates in preparing
the cross-examination of their opponent's witnesses.

3.5.16   Interpreter

Any party desiring an interpreter at the hearing must arrange for one, and
unless otherwise agreed, must assume the service's costs. If applicable, it is wise
to discuss the need for an interpreter at the preliminary hearing. Lack of an interpreter on the hearing date may cause a hearing to be postponed. Normally, it
is not a good idea to have a family member or a fellow employee serve as an interpreter for a party or witness. Such persons may not have a good enough grasp of
one of the two languages and may not be familiar with all of the figures of speech.
When you need an interpreter, hire a person who is certified as an interpreter,
and ideally, one who provides interpreter services in court.

3.5.17 Special needs of sight, hearing, or otherwise physically impaired parties, witnesses, or counsel

At the preliminary hearing, the arbitrator will normally inquire whether any of the parties or witnesses, or even counsel, have special needs that will require special services relating to sight, hearing, or other physical impairments. If there are such special needs, you should discuss with the arbitrator and other advocates how these special needs can be satisfied and accommodated.

3.5.18 Setting a hearing date

The arbitrator will, of course, set a date for the hearing on the merits, taking the schedules of all counsel and, to the extent possible, the schedules of the parties and witnesses into account.

3.5.19 Designating the place of hearing; arrangement of hearing room

Another important task at the preliminary hearing is to designate the place where the hearing on the merits is to be conducted. If the arbitration is administered, the hearing normally will be held at the location of the administering organization. However, in a multi-party case or in a non-administered case, a larger hearing space may be required. The arbitrator may also desire a particular arrangement of the tables in the hearing room depending on the number of parties, counsel, and observers. These matters should be discussed and decided at the preliminary hearing.

3.5.20 Estimate of hearing length

The arbitrator will inquire as to the amount of time each side will need to present its case. Counsel have a tendency to underestimate their time needs. In fact, a standing joke among arbitrators is that, to arrive at an accurate estimate of the hearing time required by any case, they take the separate estimates of counsel for all parties, add them together, multiply by two, and then add an extra day. When you estimate the time required to present your case, be sure to take into account the time required for any preliminary matters, opening statements, direct examination of your witnesses, cross examination of your witnesses by your opponents, redirect examinations of your witnesses, recross examinations, arguments over evidence, extended lunch breaks to allow counsel to tend to their other clients, "dead time" waiting for witnesses to arrive, delays caused by taking witnesses out of order, delays caused by unanticipated evidence, rebuttal evidence, surrebuttal evidence, closing arguments, answering questions of the arbitrators, and site visits.

3.5.21   Subpoenas

In virtually all jurisdictions, arbitrators have the authority to issue subpoenas to require the parties and certain witnesses to attend the arbitration hearing and to require the production of documents. If the arbitrator in your case does not raise the matter of subpoenas, you should. It is important to subpoena every witness that you intend to call to testify in the arbitration proceeding. In many situations you will need to call the opposing party as an adverse witness and other witnesses who are employed by the opposing party or are under his or her control. Discuss these matters at the preliminary hearing so that opposing counsel is not surprised when the subpoenas issue. Also, let the arbitrator know you will be submitting the subpoenas far in advance of the hearing so that the witnesses will be able to adjust their schedules accordingly and so that you will have documents you need to prepare your case for the hearing. You will also want to ensure that the arbitrator will be available to sign the subpoenas when presented.

3.5.22   Prohibition against ex parte communications with arbitrators

Arbitrators invariably remind counsel that there should be no ex parte communication with them, with certain limited exceptions. In administered cases, counsel should normally send all pleadings to the administering organization which in turn sends the documents to the arbitrators. In emergency situations, counsel may have to send pleadings directly to the arbitrator with simultaneous service on opposing counsel. Obviously, where there is no administering organization, counsel must send their pleadings directly to the arbitrator, but those transmittals should not contain any communication that is not also provided to opposing counsel. Where arbitrators are party-appointed, they may have ex parte communication with their appointing parties and counsel to the extent permitted by applicable ethics rules or code.

3.5.23   Site inspections

In some arbitrations, the parties may perceive a need for the arbitrator to visit a particular site or accident scene. Site inspections are most common in construction and accident cases—particularly catastrophic accidents. The advocates will arrange the site visit and in most situations the arbitrator, the advocates, the parties, and some of the testifying witnesses will attend. Occasionally, advocates may request that they be permitted to take photographs of the site during the arbitrator's site visit for use later when the hearing resumes. These requests are usually granted. Photographs will not only preserve the scene as the arbitrator saw it, but they will also serve as a valuable visual aid for the advocates at the hearing when used in the context of other evidence to demonstrate a view of the site which either the arbitrator did not see, or saw but did not appreciate the relevance of what he or she was perceiving at the time.

3.5.24 Audio-visual aids

The use of demonstrative exhibits and audio-visual aids are important to the effective presentation of any case, but they are particularly important in cases where proof requires the demonstration of the condition of physical objects as they were at the time of or immediately before or after a particular event. At the preliminary hearing, the arbitrator will normally inquire of the advocates as to whether they will be using audio-visual aids so that there will be no surprises about these matters on the morning the hearing is to begin.

3.5.25 Experts

In arbitration, expert opinions are necessary where the matter in question is highly technical and only a person with specialized skills will be able to clarify the issue for the arbitrator(s). If one advocate intends to call an expert witness, the opposing advocate will most likely see a need to call an expert also. It is usually not prudent for an advocate to arrange for multiple experts to testify on the same technical issue. Rarely does cumulative expert evidence provide any tactical advantage to an advocate and its effect is only to prolong the hearing. Normally, at the preliminary hearing the arbitrator will inquire of the advocates as to whether they intend to introduce expert testimony at the hearing, and if they are the arbitrator will ask the parties and their counsel to agree to a deposition time frame—a date by which the depositions have to be taken. Another expert-related topic which often generates disagreement among advocates in arbitration is the timing of the exchange of the experts' curriculum vitae and their written expert opinions. These matters should also be discussed and decided at the preliminary hearing.

3.5.26 Need for final oral arguments; post-hearing proposed findings of fact; and conclusions of law

Although it may seem to be premature to raise at the preliminary hearing, it does no harm to discuss the issue of the need for final oral arguments or post-hearing findings or conclusions. This topic may have a direct impact on the advocates' thinking about how they intend to present their cases and whether they might need to arrange for the services of a court reporter. If the parties wish to defer these matters for discussion until near the end of the hearing on the merits, the arbitrator will move on to the next topic on the preliminary hearing agenda.

3.5.27   Nature and form of award

At the preliminary hearing, the arbitrator may want to confirm the nature and form of the award that the parties desire—the customary short award without a statement of reasons or an award incorporating a reasoned opinion. Realize that if you opt for an award with a reasoned opinion, there will be a basis to challenge the award by way of a motion for reconsideration. Such motion may be beneficial to you if you lose the case on the merits, but if your opponent is the losing party, such motion may extend the proceedings, cause additional costly briefing, and delay the enforcement of the award. In the rare case, the reasoned opinion may even provide the basis for a court challenge on the grounds that the arbitrators exceeded their authority or jurisdiction or that the award was manifestly unjust—whether or not there is actual merit to such challenges. Thus, before you opt for an award with a reasoned opinion, you should carefully weigh the advantages and disadvantages of having one in the particular circumstances of your case.

3.5.28   Appeal procedures

In recent years, certain dispute resolution organizations have added to their ADR rules, provisions allowing parties to pre-elect a second panel of arbitrators to hear any appeals from the first arbitration panel's decision. This appellate procedure is normally used in cases involving huge damage claims where the stakes are so high that the parties are unwilling to risk having a single arbitration panel issue an unchallengeable binding award. If you are representing a client in this type of arbitration, you may want to consider raising the matter of a possible appeal procedure at the preliminary hearing, or you may consider discussing this matter with a representative of the administering organization in a separate conference outside the presence of the arbitrator.

3.5.29   Pre-arbitration mediation

If the parties' arbitration clause or submission agreement does not provide for pre-arbitration mediation, the arbitrator may raise the possibility of the parties considering that option at the preliminary hearing. Alternatively, the arbitrator might ask the administering organization to raise this matter with the advocates in a separate conference. Normally, a neutral other than the arbitrator would conduct the mediation. Many cases which would require days or even weeks of arbitration can be resolved with the help of a skillful mediator in a matter of a few hours. Actually, in most situations, there is much benefit and very little risk of harm in trying mediation first. Even if the mediation process is not successful in resolving the dispute, it might result in the informal disclosure of information which may obviate the need to take any discovery in connection with the subsequent arbitration. Mediation might also be beneficial in draining anger and hostility from the dispute permitting the arbitration to proceed more efficiently, thereby guaranteeing a less-costly arbitration.

3.5.30 Additional preliminary hearings

If any issues are unresolved at the end of the preliminary hearing and require a later status report or briefing and oral argument by counsel, the arbitrator may schedule additional hearings.

3.6 Prehearing Discovery

Historically, there has been no right to formal discovery in arbitration proceedings. The opponents of arbitration discovery argue that the discovery process is incompatible with speedy, economical resolution of disputes—which is the goal of arbitration. Of course, the argument on the other side of the coin is that the preclusion of discovery leads to unjust results. Without discovery, parties cannot uncover key information relevant to the arbitrator's decision, and therefore injustice occurs. Also without discovery, there is a high risk that surprise evidence will be offered for introduction at the hearing and that the hearing will be interrupted to permit counsel to argue the admissibility of such evidence or to allow counsel time to arrange for and introduce controverting evidence. These interruptions and delays, argue the discovery proponents, may take up more time than limited prehearing discovery.

The upshot of all this is that in recent years there has been a trend toward permitting at least some limited discovery in arbitration proceedings. Most arbitrators, for example, will permit counsel to depose witnesses who will not be available for the hearing. Others will allow more extensive discovery, depending on the complexity of the case, and particularly where the parties can agree on the scope of discovery. When faced with a decision whether to ask for or resist discovery, you should ask yourself this question: "Without discovery, will the arbitration hearing simply be a series of glorified depositions, supervised by arbitrators whose time must be compensated, and consisting largely of a search for proof instead of a showing of truth?" If you answer yes to this question, it is probably in the best interests of your client to seek or accede to a reasonable amount of discovery.

Once you decide to participate in discovery, the next question is how to proceed to do it. Like litigation, discovery in an arbitration proceeding allows counsel to gather information they will use to support their various contentions at the arbitration hearing. However, unlike court litigation where a specific set of procedural rules governs the discovery process, absent a specific statutory provision or court rule, no uniform set of rules exists to govern arbitration discovery practice. Because of this lack of discovery rules, the manner of taking discovery in arbitration is left to the discretion and agreement of counsel. When counsel cannot agree, the arbitrator will specify the discovery procedures. The arbitrator may designate arbitration procedures of his or her own formulation or he or she may direct the parties to use all or a portion of the federal discovery rules or the discovery rules of the local jurisdiction. Discuss these matters at the preliminary hearing. Before you leave the preliminary hearing, you and your opposing counsel should have a clear understanding as to the specific limitations that the arbitrator has placed on various forms of discovery, including: (1) depositions, (2) interrogatories, (3) requests for production of documents, and (4) requests to admit.

3.7   Court Reporters

Court reporters or stenographers are not automatically provided at an arbitration hearing, nor are they ordinarily required to be present. At some time before the preliminary hearing, you should check any statute governing the arbitration proceeding in your area to see if a stenographic record is required. At the preliminary hearing, the parties may decide on their own to secure the services of a court reporter to make a record of the hearing. Rules of some dispute resolution organizations require that a party desiring to arrange for a court reporter contact the court reporting firm directly, and send notice to all other parties involved. If all parties so desire, the cost will be equally split among them. If only one party wishes to have a reporter present, that party will bear the entire expense. Those rules further provide that if the transcript will be the official record of the proceedings, then both the arbitrator and the opposing parties are entitled to see a copy of the transcript to inspect for any errors. However, an opposing party who does not pay an apportioned share of the expense is not entitled to a copy of the transcript.

Each party must decide on its own whether to undertake this extra expense, depending on the particular circumstances. In large cases with several different issues, a stenographic record of the hearing will be beneficial, particularly in the preparation of post-hearing briefs. If daily copy is available during the course of the hearing, it may be essential to your preparation of cross examination of your opponent's witnesses.

If you find that a court reporter is necessary in your particular arbitration situation, select one as you would in ordinary litigation. Be sure to choose one that you know and trust, or one who comes highly recommended.

Finally, you should be aware that some arbitrators tape record the arbitration proceedings and use the audiotape later when deciding the case. Even if you have a good objection to this procedure, it is usually not polite to object to the arbitrator's use of a tape recorder. If you or another counsel in the arbitration wants to tape record the proceedings, raise this matter prior to the hearing, either by way of motion or at the preliminary hearing. If you wait until the beginning of the hearing and one or more parties object and a heated argument ensues, you may be unnecessarily setting the stage for hostility and acrimony among counsel throughout the proceeding.

◆ CHAPTER FOUR ◆
Preparing for the Arbitration Hearing

*The artist sees the line of growth in a tree, the business man
an opportunity in a muddle, the lawyer a principle in a lot of
dramatic detail.*
                                    —*Oliver Wendell Holmes, Jr.*

Preparation for the hearing, although time consuming and tedious, is singularly important to a successful outcome in arbitration. Similar to preparing a case for a court trial, getting a case ready for an arbitration hearing includes preparing your client, your witnesses, and your exhibits. But of prime importance at this preparation stage of arbitration is the refinement of your initial trial story design—enhancing the drama of your story while making sure your principle is clearly perceptible through all the dramatic details. You must do this with the ultimate goal of achieving effective persuasion. Accomplishing this refinement task should precede everything else in your arbitration preparations.

If you approach all the hearing preparation tasks described in this chapter with an attitude of thoroughness and attention to detail, your ultimate hearing presentation will be able to weather any storm. Your experience will be much like that described in a story about a farmer's hired hand. It so happened that a farmer, when interviewing a potential helper, asked about his faults. "Well," the man answered with unabashed honesty, "the last fellow I worked for said I was awful hard to wake up during a bad wind storm at night." The farmer hired him, but a few weeks later had reason to remember the man's statement. A heavy wind storm hit the area and the farmer woke instantly and went to waken the hired hand so they could check on stock and equipment. But the man would not wake up. Finally the farmer went out alone. To his amazement, he found the barn doors securely fastened. The hay stack was tightly anchored with a heavy tarpaulin. The lumber pile had heavy stones on top. A great light dawned on the farmer. He now knew why his hired man slept soundly while the wind blew hard at night.[1]

---

1. Anecdote adapted from Jacob M. Braude, *New Treasury of Stories for Every Speaking and Writing Occasion* 306 (Prentice-Hall, Inc. 1959).

4.1   Designing the Persuasive Trial Story

If you are an effective advocate, by the time you get to the stage of the arbitration proceedings where you are preparing your client and your case for the hearing, you will already have given considerable thought to the design of a persuasive trial story to present to the arbitrators. It may be helpful at this point to review the techniques for designing such a story.[2]

A persuasive trial story has six basic characteristics:

1. It is told about people who have reasons for the way they act.
2. It accounts for or explains all the known or undeniable facts.
3. It is told by credible witnesses.
4. It is supported by factual details.
5. It accords with common sense and contains no implausible elements.
6. It is organized in a way that makes each succeeding fact increasingly more likely.

Your story must have two principal aspects: a theory and a theme. The theory is simply the adaptation of your story to the legal issues in the case. You should be able to communicate it in a short paragraph. A successful theory is simple, logical, credible, and it addresses the legal elements of your case. In developing your theory, you should ask yourself three questions:

1. What happened?
2. Why did it happen?
3. Why does that mean that my client should win?

Primarily, your theory should appeal to logic. Your theme, on the other hand, should be packageable in a single sentence and should appeal to moral force. It should justify the morality of your theory and appeal to a sense of justice.

A typical theme might be:

> The decedent lived the last three years of his life not knowing that the defendant was methodically draining all the assets from his estate.
>
> or,
>
> Defendant invested plaintiff's money in stocks which he, himself, thought were secure enough to risk a substantial part of his own wealth.

It may seem strange to you, but the best way to design a successful trial story is to plan your final argument. This technique will also lay the groundwork for

---

2. Lubet, *supra* chapter 3, note 1.

the structure of your opening statement. In your final arbitration preparations—before you prepare your client and witnesses and select your exhibits—think through that final argument. Ask yourself:

> What do I want to say in the final argument?

> What evidence must I introduce or elicit in order to be able to say it?

The answers to these questions will provide you with a broad outline of what your trial story should be. This will also provide an outline for how to prepare your case in chief for the hearing. When doing this you should:

> First list the legal elements of every claim or defense that you hope to establish through your story.

> List the evidence (potential testimony and documents) that you have available to support each element.

> Evaluate the strengths and weaknesses of each witness. Consider inconsistencies and gaps in each witness's testimony, the admissibility of the testimony, and the credibility of each witness.

> Select witnesses whose testimony is both necessary and sufficient to tell your story.

> Establish an order in which the witnesses will testify based on: (1) your need to have arbitrators remember the details of the testimony (usually testimony at the beginning and the end of a hearing is best remembered); (2) your need for logical progression of your story; (3) your need to maximize their dramatic impact.

Next, you should think about planning your cross examination of your opponent's witnesses. Your goal will be to diminish the persuasiveness of your opponent's trial story by defeating the logic of your opponent's theory and by undermining its theme or moral force. Planning for cross-examination has four steps:

1. List every potential witness that your opponent is likely to call to testify.

2. Consider all the grounds for precluding the testimony (e.g., competence, privilege, rank hearsay, etc.). Do the same thing for all documentary exhibits which your opponent might attempt to introduce through each witness.

3. Consider factual weaknesses related to the testimony of the witnesses (e.g., inconsistencies in testimony, witnesses' character, impeachable prior statements, etc.).

4. Consider how the witnesses can amplify your own theme and provide information favorable to your case.

When you have completed designing your persuasive trial story, go back and re-evaluate everything to ensure that your theory and theme are sufficiently developed and fully supported by credible, non-cumulative evidence, and that your planned cross examinations will defeat your opponent's trial story and not negatively impact your own. In designing your opening statement and final argument, you should plan each one to begin and end with your theme. You should also consider where you might invoke your theme to advantage in each while you are communicating a coherent theory of your case.

We now turn to a discussion of the details of preparing your client, your witnesses, and your exhibits for the arbitration hearing.

4.2   Preparing the Client

4.2.1   Explain the arbitration process

When preparing your client, first fully explain the arbitration process, how it works, how it is different from litigation, and, if the arbitration is binding, how the award becomes a final judgment when filed in court and is subject to extremely limited challenges on appeal. This last point is very important. If you should lose the arbitration, you do not want your client to complain that you never informed him that the arbitrator's award was, for all practical purposes, final and binding. In fact, during client preparation, it is a very good idea for you to have your client sign a statement to the effect that he understands the binding nature of the arbitrator's award. The key point here is to explain the process as clearly and as simply as possible.

4.2.2   Make your client feel at ease

You need to be especially attuned to anxious feelings your client may be experiencing. To counteract those feelings, you need to put him at ease and provide answers to any questions he might have about what he might expect to occur at the hearing. The more your client becomes comfortable while talking to you about the dispute, the more comfortable he will be in discussing it in front of the opposing counsel and the arbitrator. Share with him your strategy for winning the case. Identify the strong as well as the weak points of your case. Tell him how he is to help you implement your strategy through his testimony. Make sure he knows what part of his testimony is crucial to proving certain elements of your case.

4.2.3   Explain how to testify

He will of course want to know exactly what he should say at the hearing and how he should say it. Explain to him that the rules governing truthful testimony in arbitration are the same as in litigation, namely that untrue statements can constitute perjury. Advise him also that opposing counsel will have the opportunity to cross-examine him when he completes his direct examination. Tell him it is important that he does not say something that he knows is not fully true on direct examination, because he will most probably be forced to admit or imply its partial falsity on cross examination. This, you should advise, would be most damaging to his case and perhaps quite humiliating to him personally as well. Mark Twain learned this lesson once when he was returning from a trip to Europe. The world-acclaimed humorist, having just disembarked from a ship, became uncharacteristically annoyed when a customs official began rummaging through his baggage. "My good friend," he politely remarked to the official, "you don't have to mix up all my things. There are only clothes in there—nothing but clothes."

Continuing to root around in the baggage, the official struck something hard, and instantly pulled out and held high a full quart of the finest-quality bourbon. "You call this 'just clothes'?" the official exclaimed.

"Sure thing," Twain quickly retorted. "That's my nightcap!"[3]

4.2.4 Ask your client questions as you would on direct examination

Take your client through the direct examination as you will be doing it at the arbitration hearing.[4] Ask nonleading questions. Explain that narrative responses are fine with respect to certain questions, particularly relating to her educational background, work experiences, and the background events defining the dispute. But as to other questions, advise her to keep responses shorter. When she is answering your questions in this exercise, point out the answers where she has volunteered too much information so that she will know what not to do at the hearing. Take her through the whole case—touching on issues of both liability and damages—in this manner.

4.2.5 Subject your client to cross-examination

Cross-examine your client as your opposing counsel is most likely to do. Do not soft pedal. If possible, let your client experience the effects of impeachment in this exercise. Ask her a series of questions relating to her direct testimony. Then, if available, give her a copy of the transcript of her deposition taken some months before. Let her squirm in her chair while she searches for words to explain away seemingly contradictory statements appearing in the transcript. Allow her to recognize the limits of her memory, and instruct her that it is all right to say "I don't remember" in answer to a question of opposing counsel.

---

3. Anecdote adapted from Braude, *supra* note 1, at 24.
4. *See* section 5.4, *infra* in chapter 5.

4.2.6   Encourage your client to divulge to you both good and bad information relating to the case

Realize that even during preparations for the hearing, your client may avoid giving you all the pertinent information regarding her case for fear of damaging her claims or defenses. Let her know that it is very important that she tell you everything about the events in question—both good and bad—so that you will be prepared to adequately respond to the evidence adduced by opposing counsel at the hearing. Impress on your client that withholding "bad" evidence may seriously jeopardize your ability to adequately represent her at the hearing. Ask probing questions. Be thorough. Remember that your own professional reputation can be damaged if your client is impeached or is shown to be testifying falsely. If your preparatory questioning is incomplete, you may be placing yourself squarely in the jaws of an embarrassing defeat.

The importance of asking the right questions is ably illustrated by the story of the teenage country boy who was sitting one day on a log at the edge of a beautiful lake in a southern state. He was lazily watching his fishing line bobbing in the water. A car drove past, then stopped. Several male tourists looked over the fresh, inviting water of the lake, and one of them said to the boy, "Son, are there any snakes in this lake?"

"No, sir, no snakes in this lake," replied the boy. So the men peeled off their clothes and went in for a swim. For half an hour they swam and splashed in the cool water and had a good ol' time.

When they emerged from the lake, one of them had a thought, and he said to the boy, "Son, how come there are no snakes in this lake?"

With a half grin, the boy said, "Because the alligators done ate them all up." [5]

4.2.7   Avoid being judgmental or critical about your client's role in the events giving rise to the dispute

Do not give your client the impression that you are being judgmental in any way, or that you disapprove of any statements he made or actions he took with respect to the events which precipitated the dispute. If you do, you may cause him to skirt the important issues at the arbitration hearing and attempt to misrepresent what really happened. Keep a neutral tone during the preparatory session, and let your client know you are sympathetic to her situation. Most importantly, listen very carefully to everything your client says during the session. Make sure you fully understand all of the information she is trying to communicate to you. You may discover a new fact that is quite important to your case.

---

5. Anecdote adapted from Braude, *supra* note 1, at 386..

4.2.8 Warn your client to avoid inappropriate body language when not testifying

You should also counsel the client on the possible negative impact of the client's nonverbal communication during the arbitration hearing at the times he is not testifying. Your client's frowns, grimaces, sneers, scowls, mocking laughter, and the like during the presentations of either side will not advance his chances of a favorable award. You should counsel your client to appear interested, objective, and reasonable when the opposing side's witnesses are testifying. Even a silent face can speak a thousand words. A case in point is when Justice John Harlan played golf at the Chevy Chase Club outside Washington with his friend, the Episcopal Bishop of Washington. On the third tee, the Bishop missed the ball several times, but made no comment. However, he looked a picture of disgust. "Bishop," said Justice Harlan with a devilish grin, "that was the most profane silence I ever witnessed."[6]

4.3 Preparing the Witness

You may choose to call witnesses, in addition to your client, when you present your case. You should be selective in choosing your witnesses, and only call those with directly relevant testimony or information that is central to the case. A weak witness may hurt your case more than help it. The only way to anticipate how a witness will perform at the hearing is through preparation.[7]

The key to an effective witness preparation is to determine what information the witness will give in answer to your questions and those of opposing counsel. The best way to determine this is through a hearing simulation. Conducting a hearing simulation requires additional preparation, but will result in a great benefit during the hearing.

4.3.1 Conducting a hearing simulation

When conducting a hearing simulation, try to create an environment that will be similar to that of the actual hearing. Hold the simulation in a conference room or an empty office—somewhere away from familiar surroundings for your client or witnesses. Also, if you will be conducting the direct examination of the witnesses, be sure to prepare that witness yourself. You will lose much of the advantage of advance preparation if you rely on someone else to prepare your witnesses. The connection should be made between you and your witness; not between your associate and your witness.

---

6. Anecdote adapted from James C. Humes, *Speaker's Treasury of Anecdotes About the Famous*, 59 (Harper & Row Publishers, 1978).

7. *See* section 5.4, *infra* in chapter 5.

4.3.2   Both you and the witness should be fully aware of the witness's prior testimony

If the witness has made any written statements or has been deposed, go over this testimony in the hearing simulation. Make sure the witness does not change any facts previously stated or change the story in any way. If the witness has already made previous inconsistent statements, find out what the witness intends to say under oath during the hearing, and be prepared for your witness to be impeached by opposing counsel.

4.3.3   Put the witnesses through a direct examination

For your direct examination of the witness, prepare your questions ahead of time and use the hearing simulation to rehearse what will happen at the hearing. Try to proceed through this direct examination exercise without any critiques of the answers—as if the witness were actually giving testimony at the arbitration hearing. Do any critiquing at the end of the exercise. However, if you are completely surprised by an answer regarding a critical aspect of your case, stop and discuss it in detail so the witness can think through what she just said and clarify for you what the precise facts were or what she should have said. Re-ask the problem questions at the end of the exercise and evaluate the answers again. Remind the witness that you are only interested in her truthful testimony, but if answers are subject to misinterpretation by the arbitrator, you want the witness to use words which clearly and truthfully communicate what occurred.

4.3.4   Put the witnesses through a cross-examination

If your witness is not prepared for cross-examination, your opposing counsel may be able to neutralize any gains you made with the arbitrator during the direct examination. Prepare a list of questions you think the opposing counsel may ask (and even some difficult ones you don't think opposing counsel will ask) and see how the witness responds. If your witness seems unsure of the answers, even though you know she is giving true testimony, practice the routine until you both become comfortable with the procedure. Be sure to ask the questions in a tone and manner that the opposing counsel is likely to use. Get a feeling for how the witness may respond to a question asked in the accusatory tone of an adversary conducting a cross examination. Acting in the manner of the opposing attorney will prepare your witness for the hearing much more effectively than simply explaining the questions that the other side may ask.

4.3.5   Preparing expert witnesses

You must take special care in preparing your expert witnesses. Prepare each expert thoroughly including presenting the expert with a hypothetical question or questions regarding your case. Your expert must be prepared to convince the arbitrator that she is the person with the answers. Prepare your expert's testimony on qualifications, showing that his or her opinions on the precise topic at issue are highly valued by other experts in the same field. Stress to your expert that sound reasoning in her answers will determine whether or not she appears credible to the arbitrator. Warn the expert in advance that you will not stipulate to credentials at the hearing because you want the arbitrator to hear them firsthand. Also inform your expert that at the hearing you may offer to stipulate to the credentials of your opponent's expert to reduce any positive impact of his qualifications.

4.3.6 Remind witnesses of the danger of nonverbal communication

Just as you must advise your clients about the potential adverse effects of body language, you must similarly inform your witnesses. Body language—particularly facial expressions—may send signals that conflict with a witness's spoken words or that make it less credible. Watch for such facial expressions during the preparation of your witnesses and point them out to your witnesses, explaining to them the impact of the nonverbal communication in relation to their spoken words. Although there are exceptions, in most situations it is best if witnesses remain essentially expressionless when testifying. Though elementary in theory, this is not always simple in execution—even if your client is naturally expressionless. President Calvin Coolidge, for example, was widely known for being poker-faced and taciturn. Just before Will Rogers met President Coolidge for the first time, one of his friends said, "I'll bet you can't make Cal laugh in two minutes."

"I'll bet he laughs in 20 seconds," said Will. Then came the introduction: "Mr. President, this is Will Rogers; Mr. Rogers, President Coolidge."

Will held out his hand, looked confused, then said, "Excuse me, I didn't quite get the name." A grin spread across Coolidge's face.[8]

4.3.7 Advise witnesses as to proper attire

Instruct all of your witnesses to dress in attire appropriate for a courtroom trial. The informal setting should not induce your client or witnesses to dress inappropriately for a hearing of this nature. Ordinarily, your witnesses should dress in clean, neat, conservative clothes. There may be reasons for your witnesses to "dress down" depending on the location or setting of the arbitration or the impression you wish to convey to the arbitrators, and, obviously, you should give the witnesses specific instructions in such instances.

---

8. Anecdote adapted from P. Boller, *Presidential Anecdotes* 244 (Oxford University Press, 1981).

4.3.8   Inform witnesses of the order of testimony

Finally, if you will be calling more than one witness, make sure each witness knows when he or she is scheduled to testify. If witnesses are to be on call, make sure you know how to reach them to let them know when they should appear to testify.

4.3.9   Warn non-client witnesses regarding possible inquiry into witness preparation

Be sure to advise your non-client witnesses that they may be required to testify about the content of statements made in the course of their preparation for the arbitration hearing.

4.4   Preparing the Exhibits

After preparing your client and your witnesses, you will have a fairly clear idea of the exhibits you will need to present your case most effectively. Evidentiary exhibits—documentary evidence—should be premarked and placed in the sequence that you intend to introduce them into evidence. If there are group exhibits or summaries, mark them as such. In larger cases, place the exhibits in binders and tab them. You will need a set of exhibits for each arbitrator and, normally, a set for opposing counsel.

4.4.1   Preparing demonstrative exhibits

With respect to demonstrative exhibits to be used in an arbitration, as with a court hearing, you should prepare them so that they are both eye-catching and interesting. Demonstrative exhibits help tell your story to the arbitrator. They not only help the arbitrator understand your case, but to remember it as well. Large reproductions of original documents, in color as opposed to black and white, can be very persuasive in conveying your story, particularly if they are left exposed for reference by witnesses from time to time as the hearing proceeds.

4.4.2   Preparing photographs

As mentioned earlier, photographs of evidence should be taken by a professional photographer. This ensures the quality desired for an effective exhibit. Also, this allows the photographer, an outside party from the arbitration proceedings, to authenticate the location of the scene in the photograph. Always take several shots of the same scene, to offer a different view and perspective. When deciding on the particular photos to use as exhibits, look at the scene from the perspective of both parties and choose which photo best suits your case.

4.4.3 Securing physical objects

If you will be displaying an actual object (i.e., a piece of machinery) as an exhibit, locate and secure that object as soon as possible. This will prevent the object from becoming altered or disappearing. Also, be sure to label each object before the hearing.

4.4.4 Anticipating opponent's exhibits

Try to anticipate any exhibits your opponent will use, and be prepared to present your own form of that exhibit. For example, if you anticipate that your opponent will use a photograph of an accident scene as an exhibit, bring your own photo of the same scene so the arbitrator will be able to view it from both parties' perspectives. This prevents the other side from possibly obtaining an advantage by introducing one-sided evidence to the arbitrator.

4.4.5 Ensure witnesses have identical perceptions of exhibits

Make sure your client and your witnesses are familiar with all of the exhibits and that they can identify and explain any objects in the exhibits. Also, if the exhibits, for example, represent a particular area, make sure all of the witnesses are familiar enough with the area so they can identify what is in the picture as well as the surrounding area. Do not underestimate the risks of inconsistent testimony among witnesses caused by differing perceptions of exhibits. It is common knowledge that when looking at any object, some witnesses might observe something that is not there and other witnesses might not observe accurately what is there. Dr. Billroth, a famous Viennese surgeon, once told his medical students that a doctor needed two abilities: freedom from nausea and the power of observation. He then dipped his finger into a bitterly foul fluid and licked it off, requesting them to do the same. They did it quite mechanically and without flinching. Grinning broadly, Dr. Billroth said to his pride-filled class, "You have passed the first test well, but not the second, for none of you noticed that I dipped my first finger in the liquid but licked the second."[9]

---

9. Anecdote adapted from Humes, *supra* note 6, at 142.

◆ CHAPTER FIVE ◆

Advocacy During the Arbitration Hearing

My profession and that of an actor are somewhat akin, except that I have no scenes to help me, and no words are written for me to say. There is no black-cloth to increase the illusion. There is no curtain. But, out of the vivid, living dream of somebody else's life, I have to create an atmosphere—for that is advocacy.

—
Sir Edward Marshall Hall
British Lawyer (1858–1927)

In chapter two, dealing with initial choices in arbitration, we saw how the advocate's architect function helped the advocate do the spadework, pour the footings, and erect the skeletal structure of a successful arbitration. In chapters 3 and 4, we became familiar with the more aesthetic aspects of the advocate's architect function—which, in the advocate's medium of language, translated into the artistry of story designing and story telling. There we learned how that artistry assisted the advocate in the initial drafting, planning, and preparation stages of arbitration. In this chapter, we shall go one step further and examine the end product of the advocate-architect's artistic and scientific labors—the fully constructed arbitration hearing. As we shall learn, in this stage of arbitration, the advocate not only must draw on the story designing function discussed in the last chapter and the inner actor function as identified in this chapter's opening quote, but he or she must—perhaps even to a greater extent—draw upon his or her inner artistic functions as playwright and theatrical director.

As explained in more detail elsewhere,[1] the story designing/telling function is important to the arbitration advocate, but it is actually an incorporated part of a larger whole—the playwright function. It is the advocate-playwright who must mentally convert the story to a dialogue format and insert necessary actor cues and instructions. He must plot out the crossings and groupings of witnesses and the problems of set (audio-visual equipment, etc.). In his theatrical imagination, he must visualize each scene; hear the words of each witness. Playwrights use several devices in their scripts for heightening unity of effect, increasing dramatic impact, and economizing exposition. Examples of the last device include: the prologue in which the playwright tells the audience initially what it needs to know to understand the play as it unfolds, and the epilogue at the end of the play through which the audience is told what they should have observed. These

---

1. *See* John W. Cooley, *Appellate Advocacy Manual* (Vol. 1) §1:05C (Callaghan, 1989). *See generally*, David Ball, *Theater Tips and Strategies for Jury Trials* (NITA, 1993–94, 2003).

devices correspond quite neatly to the opening statement and the closing argument in arbitration.

After the advocate-playwright completes and delivers the converted mental script, the work really just begins. She must assume a role, more in the nature of theatrical director, by taking an active part in casting (choosing witnesses), rehearsing (pretrying witnesses), costuming (ensuring witnesses are properly dressed), staging (making hearing room arrangements), and nearly all aspects of pre-production.

In arbitration, the advocate-playwright cannot simply sit in the audience as the play is performed on stage; he or she must act in the play and direct it also. Thus, during an arbitration hearing, an advocate wears three artistic hats simultaneously—those of playwright, director, and actor. As playwright, the advocate is continuously refining the script while the "play" or hearing is in progress. In certain situations, the playwright may produce a final script called a "transcript." As director, the advocate adds depth to the playwright's script and coordinates all elements of the courtroom production to give the presentation unity and proportion and to assist each participant in making his or her maximum contribution to the hearing.

What makes the director role extremely difficult is that the activity on the hearing room stage is not controlled solely by the advocates. Also, unlike the ordinary play performance, the advocate-director actually performs as an actor in the play, while one or more other plays are being simultaneously scripted and directed by other advocates on the same hearing room stage. The "producers" of the whole theatrical production—the arbitrators—retain decisional authority as to all activity—even those aspects of the drama which the advocate-directors consider to be purely artistic. Nonetheless, the advocate-directors are ultimately responsible for communicating to the audience—the arbitrators-producers—their perception of the logical and emotional content of the playscripts ultimately created.

Yet, all of this artistry must be accomplished within the constraints of applicable procedural rules. To this topic, we now turn.

5.1   Procedural Rules

Do not expect that the procedural rules applicable to a trial will automatically apply in an arbitration hearing. Hearing rules may vary depending upon the content of the arbitration clause, the rules of any administering dispute resolution organization, the needs or desires of counsel, and the preferences of individual arbitrators.

Thus, before the scheduled hearing date and ideally even before the preliminary hearing, you should, at a minimum, carefully read the arbitration clause and the pertinent rules of the administering dispute resolution organization.

If you note any unusual and undesirable requirements, you should raise these matters for discussion at the preliminary hearing. Hearing rules drafted years before into an arbitration clause—and perhaps by counsel not currently involved in the arbitration—are sometimes inappropriate for application to the dispute as it actually evolved. You, along with opposing counsel and the arbitrator, can work out modifications of such rules during the preliminary hearing.

The same holds true for the rules of administering organizations. On many occasions, their rules need to be clarified in relation to your dispute's idiosyncrasies, or to the parties' identity and configuration. Here are a few illustrative examples:

5.1.1   Application of the Federal Rules of Civil Procedure

Your dispute resolution organization may require the arbitrators to apply the Federal Rules of Civil Procedure to any procedural question that arises in the hearing. If you believe the application of such rules will work a hardship on you or your client in arbitrating the dispute, you should bring specific matters to the arbitrator's attention prior to the hearing. If you have such problems with the application of the rules, because of expense or inconvenience, then your opposing counsel will likely be experiencing similar problems.

5.1.2   Testimony not required to be under oath

The rules of some organizations require witnesses to testify under oath only if it is required by law or requested by any party. Normally, you will want to make clear at the preliminary hearing that you want all witness statements made at the hearing on the merits to be under oath. Then, that will raise the question as to whether there will be someone at the hearing authorized to administer oaths. Ordinarily, by statute the arbitrator will have such authority, but in some cases he or she may not. If not, the court reporter, if one is scheduled to attend, may have such authority. The point is, if you want witnesses to make statements under oath, be sure there are means available at the hearing to ensure that it happens.

5.1.3   Evidence by affidavit

Also, some organizations' rules permit the arbitrators to consider affidavits of witnesses in lieu of their appearance and testimony at the hearing. If you object to affidavit evidence, and in most instances you will, you should notify your opposing counsel and the arbitrator of your objection before the hearing so you can either work out an agreement concerning it, or have the arbitrator rule on your objection.

5.1.4   Authorized representative

Ordinarily, organizations do not require parties to be represented by counsel during an arbitration hearing. Some rules permit a party to be represented by an "authorized representative" and to notify the opponent a few days before the hearing of such representation. If you receive notice of an authorized representative's identity, and it is a person whom you intend to subpoena and call as a witness at the hearing, immediately bring this matter to the attention of the opposing party and the arbitrator, so that the representative's "independence" problem can be resolved. Once the problem is brought to his attention, the opposing party may opt to enlist another authorized representative, who can serve better in the capacity of independent advisor.

5.1.5   Decision and award

Arbitration rules normally require arbitrators' decisions to be by a majority, unless a unanimous decision is required by the arbitration agreement or by law. If you and your opposing counsel for some reason desire that the liability determination be unanimous and that any damage award be by a majority, or some other such variation, then raise this matter with the arbitrators before the hearing. Also, rules rarely include a provision explaining what occurs if one of three arbitrators finds it necessary to withdraw during an arbitration hearing due to ill health or a discovered conflict of interest, etc., and the remaining two arbitrators disagree on the result. As arbitration becomes widely used, this problem may become more prevalent and the parties will have to deal with it by prehearing agreement. Some rules require the arbitrators to provide no reasons for the award, and others permit arbitrators to award prejudgment interest. If you would prefer something different than what such rules allow, you should raise these matters in the prehearing stage, and perhaps ideally in the preliminary hearing.

Above all, keep in mind that dispute resolution organizations' rules commonly have an automatic "waiver of rules" provision. Such provision usually states that any party who proceeds with an arbitration after knowledge that any provision or requirement of the rules has not been complied with, and who fails to state an objection in writing, is deemed to have waived the right to object. Thus, if you do not carefully review the arbitration rules pertinent to your case, you may find that you have wandered into a procedural quagmire from which you cannot gracefully escape. Some of these avoidable traps could affect your client's substantive, as well as procedural, rights. An ounce of prevention in these situations may, indeed, be worth a pound of cure.

5.2   Opening Statement

After the arbitrator calls the arbitration hearing to order, acknowledges his or her oath, and hears any preliminary matters, the arbitrator will request that counsel proceed with the opening statements. Both claimant and respondent—or if multiple parties, all parties—are entitled to an opportunity to present an opening statement. The claimant usually speaks first, followed by the respondent.

The opening statement's purpose is to help the arbitrator understand the evidence you are about to present. Its structure presents an oral synopsis, a prologue if you like, of the real life human drama which is to follow. The outline helps identify issues for the arbitrator while his or her mind is still fresh and uncluttered by volumes of evidence. It also alerts the arbitrator to questions of fact and law which the arbitrator will decide later.

The opening statement normally follows a simple format:

1. Introduction

2. Summary of facts, law, and theories

3. Presentation of facts

4. Brief statement of any applicable law, as appropriate

5. Comment on opposition's case

6. Restatement of summary of facts, law, and theories

7. Statement of any request for relief

We will explore each of these topics, but will devote the most attention to the presentation of facts. We will also touch on the rule against argument, delivery technique, and objections. But first, it is important that we review some fundamental differences between an opening statement in an arbitration and an opening statement in a trial.[2]

5.2.1   Basic differences between arbitration and trial opening statements

You might expect that the opening statement you present in arbitration is much the same as you would give in court before a jury or judge. However, be aware that not all arbitrators conduct arbitration proceedings in the same way. Lawyers with trial experience who serve as arbitrators are likely to expect trial-like opening statements. But nonlawyers who become professional arbitrators may have much different expectations about the opening statement's purpose and use and about the "rules of the game" related to it. You may encounter an

---

2. *See generally*, Thomas Oehmke, *Commercial Arbitration* 233–246 (The Lawyers Cooperative Publishing Co., 1987); Lubet, *supra* chapter 3, note 1 at 335–384.

arbitrator or a chair of an arbitration panel who is highly judgmental, a stickler for precision of words, and one who views the arbitration process through lenses of strict compliance and hypertechnicality. On the other hand, you may experience an arbitrator who fails to take control of the proceeding, allows counsel to dictate the direction process at whim, and permits counsel wide latitude in the opening statement's content and length. If you should have the misfortune to engage either of these types of arbitrators, be prepared for a trial by ordeal. Do not be surprised in such situations if you experience some of the following unusual opening statement procedures.

5.2.1.1   Written opening statements

Arbitrators who tend to comprehend information more easily by reading than by listening may require counsel to submit written opening statements prior to the hearing in lieu of presenting oral opening statements. Also, some arbitrators believe oral opening statements are a waste of time—time which parties can better use in presenting their evidence and making closing arguments. If you face such a situation and believe that an oral opening statement would be a better way to lay your trial story's groundwork, you will have to evaluate the pros and cons of requesting an opportunity to present an oral opening statement. Consider the personality of the arbitrator, his or her proclivity to resist change, and all the surrounding circumstances. You certainly would not want to antagonize an arbitrator by the very vehicle you intend to use to enlighten him.

5.2.1.2   Claimant may request to make opening
statement after respondent

As pointed out, supra, in arbitration as in a court trial, the claimant customarily makes an opening statement first, followed by the respondent. As is common knowledge, it is not unknown in a court trial for defense counsel to wait until the beginning of his or her case to present an opening statement. That also occurs routinely in arbitrations. But unlike a court trial, from time to time in arbitrations, a claimant might make a request to present an opening statement at the hearing's beginning, but after the respondent. Realize that in arbitration the parameters of the opening statement are entirely within the arbitrator's discretion. The arbitrator can set limitations on the opening statement's length and scope, its detail or brevity, and its general manner or character. He or she can also entertain requests for changing the sequence of the opening statements and may, in fact, permit the claimant to present an opening statement after the respondent. A claimant may have strategic or tactical reasons for presenting his or her opening statement second. First, such a request can throw the respondent off balance. A lawyer for a respondent who has not conscientiously prepared an opening statement waiting to hear claimant's opening statement first in order to respond, may find himself stumbling and at a loss for words if the arbitrator requires him to proceed first. In addition, claimant's counsel may find it advantageous to proceed second to have the last word. In the appropriate case, there might be a clear benefit to your client in addressing points covered by respondent's opening statement, outlining the claimant's position, and then quickly following that up with claimant's testimony while the pillars and framework of your trial story are still fresh in the arbitrator's mind. A nonlawyer arbitrator or an arbitrator who lets the lawyers control the hearing might permit a claimant to proceed second. As respondent's counsel, you can of course object to such request; as claimant's counsel, you may consider making the request in the appropriate situation.

5.2.1.3   Statements may be deemed to constitute admissions

Some arbitrators and hypertechnical opponents will listen carefully to your opening statement, hoping to catch you in some type of admission against your client's interest. Some arbitrators may hold you to these admissions of adverse facts—consciously or subconsciously—even though your evidence does not bear them out. Therefore, you may want to consider requesting that the arbitrator not hold against your client any inadvertent misstatement of fact that you might make in the opening statement.

5.2.1.4   Omissions may constitute waiver of claim or defense

Similar to admissions against interest, though to a much lesser extent, an arbitrator may view what you omit in your opening statement to be a waiver of a claim or defense. Thus, if the arbitrator is a stickler for details, make it clear in your opening statement that your remarks are intentionally abbreviated in the interest of efficiency and economy and that, even though you do not specifically address a matter in your opening statement, you are not waiving any claim in your written demand or any defense in your written answer, as the case may be.

5.2.1.5   Stipulations may be read aloud

Be prepared for the arbitrator who requires that stipulations be read aloud at the time of the opening statement. An arbitrator may require this to be done in more complex cases in which a stenographic record is taken and in which the award will contain a reasoned opinion. Some arbitrators like to have a clear understanding up front as to which facts are uncontested and which are not. Having the stipulations read at the beginning of the hearing will allow the arbitrator to truncate later testimony when he finds that it refers to already stipulated matters. Also, when preparing his reasoned opinion, all the stipulated facts will be consolidated conveniently in the beginning of the transcript for use in drafting a statement of facts, and for his occasional reference, as needed. If you do not anticipate the possibility of having to read fact stipulations at the hearing's beginning, you might be caught off guard, particularly if you have prepared a condensed trial story that integrates both stipulated and contested facts. In the appropriate case, you might want to clarify with the arbitrator at the preliminary hearing his or her preference regarding the handling of stipulations.

5.2.1.6   Arbitrator may permit a reply and surreply

Unlike a judge in a court proceeding, an arbitrator, on counsel's request, may permit a reply or a surreply to an opening statement. Although rare, this may occur in cases where there are counterclaims and/or where several arbitrations have been consolidated.

5.2.2   Rule against argument

Opening statements in court and in arbitration are aligned in the sense that, as a general proposition, argument is permitted in neither. However, argument is a relative concept, defined in the eye of the beholder. Thus, in arbitration, as in court proceedings, certain types of remarks by counsel in the opening statement would satisfy a "bright line" test for constituting argument; others would not. Examples of remarks falling in the "obviously prohibited argument" category might include: (1) urging the arbitrator to draw inferences from the facts and making certain conclusions; (2) explaining the importance of certain evidence; (3) suggesting how it should be weighed; (4) commenting directly on the credibility of witnesses; and (5) appealing overtly to a sense of mercy or justice.

As a general principle, impermissible argument occurs when an advocate seeks to tell the arbitrator how he or she should reach a decision. Because this broad principle is difficult to apply, other more narrow tests have been developed to help make distinctions. They are: the witness test, the verification test, and the "link" test. Under the witness test, one questions whether a witness will actually be called to testify to the information conveyed in the opening statement. If so, and if a witness would be permitted to testify because it was deemed to be factual information, then the opening statement would be proper. If the witness would be called to testify, and would not be permitted to testify as to the information because it was deemed a conclusion—not in the province of a witness—then the opening statement would be improper. Under the verification test, one questions whether the content of the opening statement can be verified, the point being that facts can be verified, argumentative conclusions cannot. Finally, under the "link" test, remarks descend to the level of impermissible argument when counsel must supply a non-evidence-based explanation—a rhetorical embellishment to link independent evidence with the point she is trying to make. An arbitrator may apply other tests, related to counsel's delivery style, to determine whether he or she has engaged in improper argument in the opening. Tone of voice can turn a simple factual statement into scornful argument. Rhetorical questions, even innocently formulated, can be piercingly argumentative and elicit anger. Finally, extreme repetition of facts can be deemed argumentative and even hostile during an opening statement.

The rule against argument does not mean that counsel can make no comments about the applicable law. In almost every opening statement, whether in court or in arbitration, there is a need to include some information about the law, if for no other reason than to let the trier of fact know what information is relevant to his or her determination. It is improper, however, for counsel in an opening statement to argue for a particular interpretation or construction of the law.

All of this discussion about trying to describe the essence of "argument" in the opening statement can perhaps best be summed up by the expression, "What is one person's expedient is another person's art."

There is a story told about Robert Henri, a well-known twentieth century artist and art teacher who was attending a private showing of paintings in a New York gallery. He was standing before a fine Sargent painting when his attention was attracted to a brawny individual admiring the same canvas and murmuring: "They have given me a good place at last."

"You in this sort of work?" Henri inquired.

"Been in it for years," replied the brawny man, "and this is the first time that I ever got on the line."

"Ah, indeed!" exclaimed Henri, "and where is your painting?" The man pointed to the Sargent.

"That?" asked Henri. "Why, Sargent painted that!"

"Painted it," sighed the man self-contentedly. "Yeah, I think Sargent was the bloke who painted the picture—but it was me who made the frame." [3]

5.2.3   Introduction and summary

Your introduction and summary should orient the arbitrator to the disputants and the dispute. After introducing yourself and your client, begin your summary of the more detailed story which is to follow immediately. The summary should contain a few sentences describing the dispute's factual contours, your theories of claims and defenses, and any necessary law to put the dispute in context. Often, counsel begins with a statement of theme—a single sentence that captures

---

3. Anecdote adapted from Braude, *supra* chapter 4, note 1, at 331.

the moral force of the case. After that, the introduction can focus on the overall theory of the case by answering the questions: What happened? Why did it happen? Why is my client's version correct? How can we be sure? Why does all this make sense? These questions are then answered in more detail during the next stage of the opening statement—the presentation of facts.

5.2.4   Presentation of facts

In your presentation of facts, state only facts which: (1) you will support with evidence; (2) you believe to be true; and (3) you believe to be admissible. Complying with these three constraints will protect you from discussing facts which you can only partially prove and from referring to facts which you have no evidence at all to support. They will also prevent you from straying into collateral matters or from referring to topics which are not admissible. Beyond this simple formula for selecting facts, you should always try to put the following principles into practice when planning and delivering your opening statement:[4]

5.2.4.1   Be brief and keep it interesting

Most arbitrators appreciate brevity in opening statements—particularly those arbitrators who prepare for the hearing by reading the demand, answer, pleadings, and position statements. Brevity, however, is a relative concept. If you represent a claimant in a case against several respondents and you have separate theories involving different facts concerning each one, a "brief" opening statement may take forty-five minutes or more. If you represent a respondent in such a case, your opening may extend only ten to fifteen minutes. Thus, you should frugally tailor the time to the task. In addition, you must keep your presentation interesting. You must convey to the arbitrator that listening to what you have to say will facilitate the performance of his or her decision making function in some important way.

5.2.4.2   Apply the principle of primacy

Keep in mind that the arbitrator is more apt to remember information that he or she hears first in an arbitration proceeding rather than information buried somewhere in its succeeding stages. Include information that will have the greatest impact on the arbitrator in decision making, and incorporate facts that have a key relationship with the most critical parts of your story.

5.2.4.3   Tie the evidence to legal issues

You must explain to the arbitrator why the facts you are presenting are important to the arbitrator's decision. You must clearly relate selected aspects of

---

4. *See* Lubet, *supra* chapter 3, note 1, at 348–75.

the evidence to the legal issues that the arbitrator must take into account when deciding the case.

5.2.4.4   Put the puzzle together

Tell your story in a narrative style and make it interesting. Use a chronological approach if it enhances the persuasive effect of your story. If combination or juxtaposition of facts yields more persuasion than chronology, jettison chronology. Do not use a witness-by-witness approach. The technique, such as, "Mr. Jones will testify that . . . " and "Ms. Smith will testify that . . . " is boring and noninte-grative. If there are a number of witnesses, the arbitrator is likely to get confused and start daydreaming. Once you lose the arbitrator's attention in your opening statement, you may also lose his sympathy for your client's plight—for good. Keep your story dynamic. To the extent possible, organize your story around a series of principal concepts supported by evidentiary details. Weave in references to witnesses while telling your story without making them the focal point of your narrative. Make all the factual connections for the arbitrator. Synthesize. Do not leave the arbitrator's understanding of your message to chance. You put the factual puzzle together; if you let the arbitrator do it, important pieces may be omitted and its communicative value lost.

5.2.4.5   Focus on operative facts

Arbitrations are won or lost most often on their facts—not on the applicable law. Thus it is important for you in the opening statement to have the arbitrator focus early in the proceeding on what you perceive to be the operative facts of your case. Operative facts include: action and key events; the physical scene; transactions and agreements, if any; relationship of the parties; business context, if any; and motives and motivations of the parties or key players.

5.2.4.6   Emphasize undisputed evidence

Your central evidence should occupy a special place in your story and you should communicate to the arbitrator the identity of your central evidence. It should consist of the facts most essential to your case and, at the same time, the facts least likely to be disputed.

5.2.4.7   Discard tangential facts

Eliminate "nice to know," nonessential information from your opening statement. The fact that your client, as a youth, won the national soapbox derby competition three years consecutively might be true, but it probably would not impress the average arbitrator. Furthermore, such tangential facts can distract the arbitrator from your true message and might even imply that your case is weak and that you are grasping at any straw to bolster your client's chances.

5.2.4.8   Deal minimally with bad facts

If you are absolutely certain that negative information will come out about your client or a witness during the course of an arbitration hearing, it is probably a good idea to let the arbitrator know about it in the opening statement. Use discretion, however, when disclosing such information. Wait until after you have disclosed all the favorable information about your client or witness before you reveal the negative, and then in only a passing sort of way, without dwelling on it.

5.2.5   Brief statement of law

In arbitration, as in a court trial, reserve the bulk of your legal arguments for the closing argument. But remember, an arbitration in which the arbitrator is a lawyer closely approximates a bench trial in court. When presenting an opening statement in a bench trial, advocates have much more latitude in discussing legal issues than they do in a jury trial. Thus, as mentioned supra, if you feel that an arbitrator must understand the law in order to comprehend your opening statement, then you may wish to refer sparingly to pertinent cases or statutes. In the appropriate case, you may also find that you need to refer to applicable administrative rules, regulations, or rulings. Refrain from arguing in the opening statement what you believe to be the proper interpretation or construction of the law or regulations.

5.2.6   Comments on opposition's case

In planning and presenting your opening statement, you will need to determine how much attention you wish to devote to the opposition's case. This is true whether you represent a claimant or a respondent. Here are some pointers you may wish to take into account.

5.2.6.1   Anticipating the respondent's opening

In most opening statements in arbitration, there will be no reply or surreply. This means, of course, that if you are representing a claimant and respondent's counsel will be discussing affirmative defenses or counterclaims in her opening statement, you will have no opportunity to reply. One way to handle this problem is simply to anticipate what the respondent is going to say about these topics and address them in your own opening statement. You should concentrate on your own case for the majority of the opening statement, and then address the affirmative defenses and counterclaims, if any, one by one. You should be firm, unapologetic, and straightforward.

5.2.6.2   Avoid being personally derisive

When you give your opening statement as claimant's counsel, you will not be absolutely certain that the respondent will actually be asserting the matters you anticipate. Acknowledge that you are addressing the matters because they were raised in the respondent's answer and related pleadings, and that you believe the arbitrator should be fully apprised of claimant's position with respect to them. Avoid being derisive of your opponent, because if you are, you can reasonably expect to receive the same back from the opponent in his or her opening statement.

George Bernard Shaw once sent Churchill a note inviting him to the first-night performance of Shaw's play, Saint Joan. He enclosed two tickets with a note which read, "One for yourself and one for a friend—if you have one."

In a return note expressing his regret at being unable to attend, Churchill asked if it would be possible to have tickets for the second night—"if there is one." [5]

5.2.6.3   Avoid addressing respondent's case in detail

Make references to respondent's case summarily; avoid going into factual details. In particular, do not make specific references to respondent's witnesses or to their expected testimony. Respondent's counsel may decide not to call certain witnesses or a witness may not actually testify to facts as you predict, and the arbitrator may feel misled. In the appropriate case, it can be quite crippling to an affirmative defense or a counterclaim by quoting directly from the respondent's own deposition, a letter he wrote at a critical time, or from a provision of the contract which she signed.

5.2.6.4   Commenting on the claimant's opening

If you are delivering your opening statement as respondent's counsel, you will have the distinct advantage of knowing precisely what your opponent's case will be. Listen carefully to your opponent's opening statement. Even though you may have sketched out your own opening comments, be flexible. Modify them as necessary to ensure that you make specific denials to each of claimant's specific assertions, accusations, or claims. A blanket denial will seem mechanical, and perhaps even pompous or insincere, to the arbitrator. Do not simply list all the claimant's unpleasant accusations, denying each one in sequence. Sanitize the accusation and then answer it by drawing on the positive aspects of your own case. If claimant has pointed to certain evidence as support for one of her important claims and you intend to introduce specific, controverting evidence, you should identify that evidence for the arbitrator.

---

5. Anecdote adapted from Fadiman, *supra* chapter 2, note 2, at 124.

When you listen to claimant's opening statement, also note what claimant has omitted telling the arbitrator. There may be several evidentiary gaps in his prima facie case that he will be unable to fill. You must exercise your discretion as to whether it is strategically sound to point out these omissions to the arbitrator in your opening statement. Despite what appears to be a chance to gain some points with the arbitrator, you may in fact succeed in educating the claimant on what evidence he needs in order to round out his case. You may want to save comments about those types of omissions until your closing argument. However, where claimant omits from his opening statement any comment on evidence which is harmful to his case and which cannot be explained away easily or be controverted by him, then you should bring these omissions to the arbitrator's attention. Do not gloat over these evidentiary defects. You just want to alert the arbitrator to these evidentiary gaps so the arbitrator will watch how the claimant deals with them in the hearing. There will be plenty of opportunity for you to argue these omissions vigorously in your closing argument.

Ordinarily, it is not a good idea to comment on the credibility of your opponent's witnesses in the opening statement. As pointed out, supra, the witnesses may not be called to testify. However, where claimant's counsel praises the superior credibility of his witnesses or attacks witnesses' credibility, then you must respond to such comments in your opening statement. You would not want to give the arbitrator the impression that you are acquiescing in your opponent's claims about witness credibility.

5.2.7   Summary and request for relief

The beginning of an opening statement is a preview of your positions and supporting evidence presented for the arbitrator's benefit. The concluding portion of an opening statement is a recapitulation of the preview to remind the arbitrator how you want him or her to perceive your story. Briefly summarize the facts you will present through your evidence. Restate any facts to which you have stipulated or admitted. Reiterate factual issues and your factual theories. Note the standard of proof and the required burden of proof. Explain how your evidence will disprove your opponent's theories. Finally, close by discussing what the arbitrator must find in order for you to prevail and conclude with a statement of the damages, remedies, or relief you seek, as appropriate.

5.2.8   Objections and responses

Generally speaking, arbitrators do not appreciate it when counsel object to their opponent's opening statement. Objections can be disruptive, distracting, rude, and antagonistic. They may give the arbitrator the impression that the speaker has struck a nerve and that the objector has something to hide. They can also draw attention to matters which the arbitrator may not have fully comprehended had the objection not been made. Thus, objections can be self-defeating in that they can accomplish the reverse of their intended purpose. However, there may be instances in which you feel compelled to object to your opponent's opening statement. Some of these instances follow.

5.2.8.1   Improper argument

If your opponent is essentially making a closing argument in the opening statement, it is appropriate to object. Arbitrators usually will not sustain an objection to a couple of sentences that seem to be argumentative. If you make an objection to such a peccadillo, you may irritate the arbitrator. But if your opponent is making extensive legal arguments—explaining the application of specific cases and attempting to draw legal conclusions based on evidence that has not yet been admitted—you should object. The arbitrator will most likely welcome it. He or she would also most probably sustain your objection to an opponent's misstatement or misquoting of the law and extended argument regarding the credibility of your witnesses who have not yet testified.

5.2.8.2   Personal knowledge of facts

Counsel is not a witness in the case. As a nonwitness, counsel should not give his or her personal opinion in the opening statement, tout his or her own credibility, or assert personal knowledge of the facts. This is irrelevant and improper. If such comments are extensive, you should object.

5.2.8.3   Raising issues or matters outside the pleadings

If your opponent begins discussing claims or defenses not framed by the pleadings, you may properly object. If you are representing a respondent, and your opponent's objectionable comments are very brief, you may decide to address them in your own opening statement.

5.2.8.4   Discussing excluded evidence

Your opponent's discussion of evidence ruled inadmissible by the arbitrator's prehearing ruling would clearly be a proper basis for an objection. Make such an objection immediately so as not to give the impression that you are waiving your prehearing objection. In the extreme situation, your opponent's flouting of the arbitrator's ruling might serve as a basis for requesting sanctions in the form of dismissal of a claim or defense or precluding introduction of certain documents or testimony.

5.2.8.5   Opponent's comments demeaning your client or witnesses

Your opponent may make disparaging remarks about your client's character or motives. Use your discretion in determining when your opponent has overstepped the bounds of fair play. If your client is present during your opponent's opening statement, you may feel compelled to object immediately to demonstrate you are intent on protecting your client's interests. If you are representing a respondent, you may decide that it makes more sense to respond to the demeaning comments in your own opening statement. These same considerations apply when your opponent makes demeaning comments about your witnesses.

Sometimes you can use humor to lighten the atmosphere when your opponent says something unpleasant about your client or witnesses in his or her opening statement, but you must carefully walk a diplomatic line here. Perhaps we can learn a lesson about this type of diplomacy from Mark Twain's response defending the reputation of a small-town Missouri newspaper he edited. His diplomacy substitutes artful deflection for hurtful retort. One day Twain got a letter from a residential subscriber complaining that he had found a spider inside his newspaper.

The sharp-witted editor penned this diplomatic response:

> ... The spider was merely looking over our paper to see which merchant was not advertising so that he could go to that store, spin his web across the door and lead a life of undisturbed peace ever afterward.[6]

5.2.8.6   Exceeding limits on the opening statement

If the arbitrator has set limits on the opening statement's scope or duration and your opponent exceeds them, you would be well within ambit of appropriate advocacy to object.

5.3   Evidentiary Rules

The procedural rules that govern an arbitration hearing are those to which the parties have agreed. The same is true of the rules of evidence. In arbitration, rarely do parties agree to observe formal evidentiary rules such as the Federal Rules of Evidence. It is believed that application of such rules spawn time-consuming evidence arguments which are antithetical to the goal of efficient dispute resolution. Also, most arbitrations are analogous to a bench trial in court. In most bench trials, the application of the rules of evidence are more relaxed than in a

---

6. Anecdote adapted from Edmund Fuller, *2500 Anecdotes for All Occasions* 370 (Avenel Books, 1978).

jury trial, the belief being that judges are better able than a jury to sort reliable evidence from the unreliable. Thus, in arbitration, the criteria for precluding evidence are quite narrow, usually limited to irrelevancy and immateriality. Only occasionally do arbitrators consult formal rules of evidence for guidance, and those are normally unique situations where a party asserts extreme prejudice to her case if the evidence is admitted. But, of course, even in those situations, the arbitrators will have to know what the evidence is in order to make a determination whether to exclude it. This fact renders a claim of prejudice questionable as a basis for objecting to evidence, because the objector may have to bring to the arbitrator's attention exactly the evidence she is trying to keep from his view.

Most arbitrators conduct arbitrations with a commonsense notion of what is important to resolve a case. They apply a low threshold for admitting evidence, and they weigh the reliability and importance of the evidence as the hearing continues and issues evolve. Some arbitrators view the arbitration process as an opportunity for the parties to vent pent-up anger and frustration as well as an arena to do legal combat. Also, many arbitrators liberally admit evidence in arbitration in order to obviate a later court challenge to their awards based on allegations of unfair preclusion of critical evidence.

From your point of view as an advocate, freedom from the rules of evidence creates an opportunity for you to use your ingenuity to convince an arbitrator of your case's merits. You will have expanded latitude in presenting your case without constantly worrying about the technical requirements concerning evidence foundations and hearsay. However, use discretion here. Arbitrators quickly become skeptical of the merit of a party's case where counsel consistently supports his or her position with unreliable evidence. The best rule of thumb is to take a conservative approach with evidence supporting critical elements of your claims or defenses, and a less conservative approach with evidence relating to background or peripheral matters. Thus, in relation to required elements of proof of claims or defenses, you should, when at all possible, lay proper foundations for your testimonial and documentary evidence and endeavor to comply with the rule against hearsay evidence. In relation to evidence less central to your legal claims, you can be less concerned with the technical requirements of foundations and of hearsay evidence.

On the flip side, be aware that if you seek to take at least some advantage of the relaxed evidence rules, your opponent will most assuredly be doing so to an equal or even greater degree. Thus, you must be on guard to detect your opponent's abuses of formal rules of evidence—not so much from the standpoint of objecting to the improper evidence at the time it is offered, but rather from the standpoints of: (1) ensuring that you respond to the objectionable evidence by later presentation of your own controverting or rehabilitating evidence; and/ or (2) reminding the arbitrator in your final argument that the objectionable evidence would not be admissible in a court of law, is unreliable, and therefore should be given little or no weight in the arbitration proceeding.

To ensure that your critical evidence conforms to the formal evidentiary requirements and to identify for the arbitrator portions of your opponent's critical evidence that do not comply with them and which are therefore unreliable, you must know and understand the generally accepted evidence requirements.[7] In this section, we will review some of the basic definitions, concepts and customs of evidence, applicable in arbitration hearings. In sections 5.4 through 5.9, infra, we shall review some of the approved techniques for introducing testimonial and documentary evidence, within the constraints of generally accepted evidence requirements. In section 5.9.6, we shall explore some of the grounds for making objections and motions related to evidence to assist you when confronted with a situation requiring you to make or respond to such objections and motions.

5.3.1   Direct and circumstantial evidence

There are two principal types of evidence, direct and circumstantial. Direct evidence takes several forms: oral testimony, written documents, and objects. Direct evidence directly proves the fact for which it is offered. Circumstantial evidence does not directly prove a fact but gives rise to an inference that a fact exists. For example, in a wrongful death case where a victim was killed by a hit-and-run driver, eyewitness testimony identifying the driver as the defendant would be direct evidence. Testimony identifying the make and model of the car that hit the victim, the color of the license plates, and that it was heading in the direction of defendant's home two blocks away, would be circumstantial evidence. While direct evidence is usually preferable over circumstantial evidence, the latter can be powerful if the inference which it raises is closely connected to the fact it is offered to prove. Often, circumstantial evidence may be the only type of evidence available for proof of a particular fact. Keep in mind, however, that an entire case built solely on circumstantial evidence may invite an arbitrator, in fairness to both parties, to draw inferences that may work against your theories.

Arbitrators will generally give more weight to direct than to circumstantial evidence. But as an advocate, you must be aware of the limitations of each type of evidence. For example, direct evidence may become less powerful when a witness's credibility is questionable. Circumstantial evidence loses potency when its relevancy is questionable. As an advocate, it is important to know the limitations of each type of evidence so that unreliable or irrelevant evidence is not admitted

---

7. *See generally*, Craig Peterson and Claire McCarthy, *Arbitration Strategy and Technique*, §7.2 (The Michie Company, 1986); Anthony J. Bocchino and David A. Sonenshein, *A Practical Guide to Federal Evidence* 37–38 (NITA, 1993, 2003).

during a hearing. If your opponent offers defective evidence, you should draw the arbitrator's attention to the problem of reliability or relevancy.

5.3.2   Relevance and materiality

Relevance is the relationship between a piece of evidence and the probability of the existence of a fact pertinent to a case. Relevance is a broader concept than materiality. Relevance pertains to the case generally and materiality pertains to specific propositions to be proved in a case. Although relevancy is one of the more common evidentiary objections in arbitration, arbitrators rarely sustain an evidence objection based solely on relevance, unless the proponent can make no plausible argument of its relatedness to a theory or fact in the case. Consequently, the only instance in which it may be sensible to object to evidence on grounds of relevancy is where the proponent of the evidence is attempting to raise a wholly collateral issue—for example a contract that has no connection whatsoever with the dispute in question. In certain situations it may be a good tactical move to wait for a short time to object on relevance grounds. This time will give the arbitrator an opportunity to realize that your opponent is trying to grind an ax not relevant to the proceeding and to waste everyone's time. The tolerated rambling may even result in the inadvertent disclosure of information helpful to you in relation to another dispute which might have otherwise remained hidden.

Evidence is material if it is offered to prove a proposition pertaining to an issue before an arbitrator for decision. Evidence can be factually relevant to a dispute—for example, with regard to background information—but may not be material to a particular area of inquiry. Thus, an arbitrator may sustain an objection to evidence on grounds of materiality where, although a line of questioning is tangentially relevant to a defense already presented and concluded, it is not material to the counterclaim issue with regard to which the witness was specifically called to testify. The line between relevance and materiality is fine indeed; do not expect every arbitrator to appreciate it.

5.3.3   Hearsay and exhibits

Hearsay evidence is normally admissible in arbitration, unless the parties agree otherwise. Like other forms of evidence, arbitrators will normally receive hearsay evidence and give it the weight they deem appropriate in the context of all the circumstances. Exhibits can be offered by either party and are admissible at the discretion of the arbitrator, regardless of foundation. All parties have an opportunity to examine exhibits.

5.3.4 Affidavits

Affidavits are admissible as evidence in an arbitration. An arbitrator will assign the affidavit the appropriate weight, taking into account that the affiant's testimony was not subject to cross-examination.

5.3.5 Admissions of fact

Written admissions of fact may be introduced in an arbitration hearing. However, you may be able to achieve more dramatic impact if the evidence is admitted orally through the opposing party on your cross-examination.

5.3.6 Stipulations of fact

As discussed supra with respect to the preliminary hearing, parties may submit stipulations of fact to the arbitrator before or during the hearing. Arbitrators generally encourage the parties to stipulate to facts to shorten the hearing's length. Sometimes you can orally stipulate to facts to undermine the dramatic effect of your opponent's proffer of evidence. For example, if your opposing counsel identifies documents she intends to introduce which will reveal your client's record of speeding convictions, you may take the wind out of her sails by simply telling the arbitrator that it is not necessary to receive the documents in evidence and that you will gladly stipulate to the three previous speeding convictions "because they have no direct relationship to what happened on the day in question."

5.3.7 Judicial notice

Similar to judges, arbitrators can take judicial notice of certain facts without the necessity of formal proof. Examples of facts appropriate for judicial notice include: laws, facts about government, geographical locations, history, language and abbreviations, dictionary definitions, natural phenomena, names of streets, and national holidays.

5.4 Direct Examination

Direct examination is your opportunity to present your case's substance. It is the time to offer the evidence available to establish the facts you need to prevail. Having planned your persuasive story, you must now prove the facts upon which it rests by eliciting the testimony of witnesses. In this section we will review the goals, basic rules, and planning considerations of direct examination. We shall also explore proper questioning technique, how to deal with adverse and hostile witnesses, and certain ethical issues related to direct examination.[8]

---

8. This section is a condensed and adapted version of Lubet, *supra* chapter 3, note 1, at 15–49. The reader is invited to consult that source for an in-depth threatment of the subject of direct examination, including detailed examples.

5.4.1   Goals of direct examination

Design your direct examinations to accomplish one or more of the following basic goals.

5.4.1.1   Introduce undisputed facts

In most arbitrations there will be many important facts that are not in dispute. Nonetheless, such facts cannot be considered by the arbitrator, and will not be part of the record for any later challenge, until and unless they have been placed in evidence through a stipulation or through a witness's testimony. Undisputed facts will often be necessary to establish an element of your case. Thus, failing to include them in direct examination could lead to an unfavorable award.

5.4.1.2   Enhance the likelihood of disputed facts

The most important facts in an arbitration will normally be those in dispute. Direct examination is your opportunity to put forward your client's version of the disputed facts. Furthermore, you must not only introduce evidence on disputed points, you must do so persuasively. The true art of direct examination consists in large part of establishing the certainty of facts that the other side claims are uncertain or untrue.

5.4.1.3   Lay foundations for the introduction of exhibits

In arbitration, on most occasions, the foundations for exhibits can be the subject of a stipulation. However, where particular exhibits, such as documents, photographs, writings, tangible objects, or other forms of real evidence, are critical to your case and your opposing counsel questions their reliability and will not stipulate to their foundation, you may have to call witnesses to lay appropriate foundations.

5.4.1.4   Reflect upon the credibility of witnesses.

You can expect the credibility of some witnesses to be attacked on cross-examination. In these situations you can blunt the assault by bolstering the witness's believability during direct examination. You can strengthen a witness by eliciting the basis of her knowledge, ability to observe, or lack of bias or interest in the outcome of the case. You may also call a witness to reflect adversely on the credibility of another witness's testimony, to provide direct evidence of bias or motive, to provide the background for an impeaching document, or simply to contradict other testimony.

5.4.1.5   Hold the attention of the arbitrator

No matter which of the above purposes predominates in any particular direct examination, conduct it in a manner that holds the arbitrator's attention. In addition to being the heart of your case, direct examination also has the highest potential for dissolving into boredom, inattention, and routine. Since it has none of the inherent drama or tension of cross-examination, you must take extreme care to prepare your direct examination so as to maximize its impact.

5.4.2   Basic rules governing direct examination

There are some very basic rules governing the manner and means by which testimony may be presented in an arbitration hearing. A discussion on some of these follows.

5.4.2.1   Competence of witnesses

Every witness called to testify on direct examination must be legally "competent" to do so. This generally means that the witness possesses personal knowledge of some matter at issue in the case, can perceive and relate information, recognizes the difference between truth and falsity, and understands the seriousness of testifying under oath or on affirmation.

5.4.2.2   Non-leading questions

Similar to the rule applying to court trials, in arbitration a principal rule of direct examination is that the attorney may not "lead" the witness. A leading question is one that contains or suggests its own answer. Since the party calling a witness to the stand is presumed to have conducted an interview and to know what the testimony will be, leading questions are disallowed in order to ensure that the testimony will come in the witness's own words.

There are, however, numerous exceptions to the rule against leading questions on direct examination. A lawyer is generally permitted to lead a witness on preliminary matters, on issues that are not in dispute, to direct the witness's attention to a specific topic, to expedite the testimony on non-essential points, and, in some jurisdictions, to refresh a witness's recollection. In addition, it is usually permissible to lead witnesses who are very young, very old, infirm, confused, or frightened. Finally, it is always within the arbitrator's discretion to permit leading questions in order to make the examination effective for the ascertainment of the truth, avoid needless consumption of time, protect the witness from undue embarrassment, or as is otherwise necessary to develop the testimony.

5.4.2.3 Narrative testimony

Another general rule is that witnesses other than experts may not testify on direct examination in "narrative" form. The term narrative has no precise definition but usually means an answer that goes beyond responding to a single specific question. Open ended questions that invite a lengthy or run-on reply are said to "call for a narrative answer." An example of a non-narrative question is, "What did you do next?" The objectionable, narrative version would be, "Tell us everything that you did that day."

5.4.2.4 The non-opinion rule

Witnesses are expected to testify as to their sensory observations. What did the witness see, hear, smell, touch, taste, or do? Witnesses other than experts generally are not allowed to offer opinions or to characterize events or testimony. A lay witness, however, is allowed to give opinions that are "rationally based upon the perception of the witness." Thus, witnesses will usually be permitted to draw conclusions on issues such as speed, distance, volume, time, weight, temperature, and weather conditions. Similarly, lay witnesses may characterize the behavior of others as angry, drunken, affectionate, busy, or even insane.

5.4.2.5 Refreshing recollection

Although witnesses are expected to testify in their own words, they are not expected to have perfect recall. It is permissible for the direct examiner to refresh the witness's recollection. It is most common to rekindle a witness's memory through the use of a document such as her prior deposition or report. It may also be permissible to use a photograph, an object, or even a leading question.

5.4.3 Planning the direct examination

Three fundamental aspects to every direct examination plan include:

- content
- organization
- technique

Content and organization are discussed in this subsection, and technique is addressed in the following subsection.

5.4.3.1 Content

"Content"—what the witness has to say—must be the driving force of every direct examination. Begin your planning by asking yourself the following questions:

> Why am I calling this witness?

> Which elements of my claims or defenses will the witness address?

> How can the witness be used to controvert an element of the other side's case?

> What exhibits can be introduced through the witness?

> How can the witness bolster or detract from the credibility of others who will testify?

> How can the witness add moral strength to the presentation of the case or appeal to the arbitrator's sense of justice?

After developing this information you must prioritize and discard. Here are some pointers on what you should include and exclude:

5.4.3.2 What to include

List the witness's facts that are necessary to establish your theory.

> What is the single most important thing the witness has to say?

> What are the witness's collateral facts that will make the central information more plausible?

> What is the next most important part of the potential testimony?

> What secondary facts make that testimony more believable?

Continue this process for every element of your case. Be sure to include those "thematic" facts that give your case moral appeal.

In addition to central facts and supporting details, your "content checklist" should include consideration of the following sorts of information:

> testimony regarding the reasons for the witness's own actions

> testimony providing more detailed explanation where the witness's words are not self-explanatory

> testimony bolstering the witness's own credibility

As to the last point, you should realize that in an arbitration hearing the witness's credibility is always in issue. Devote some part of every direct examination to establishing the witness's credibility. You can enhance credibility in numerous ways. Show that the witness is neutral and disinterested. Demonstrate that the witness had an adequate opportunity to observe. Allow the witness to deny any expected charges of bias or misconduct. Elicit the witness's personal background of probity and honesty.

5.4.3.3   What to exclude

Unless you have an extraordinarily compelling reason to include them, you will need to consider discarding facts that fall into the following categories:

Clutter. This may be the single greatest vice in direct examination. Details are essential to the corroboration of important evidence, and they are worse than useless virtually everywhere else. Aimless detail will detract from your true corroboration. To determine whether or not a certain fact is clutter, ask yourself the following questions:

> ➢ What does it contribute to your story's persuasiveness?

> ➢ Does it supply a reason for the way someone acted?

> ➢ Does it make an important fact more or less likely? Does it affect a witness's credibility?

> ➢ Does it enhance your story's moral value? If all of the answers are negative, you're looking at clutter.

Unprovables. "Unprovables" are facts that can successfully be disputed. While not "false," they may be subjected to such vigorous and effective dispute as to make them unusable.

> ➢ Is the witness the only person who claims to have observed a certain event, while many other credible witnesses swear to the precise contrary?

> ➢ Is the witness less than certain? Is the testimony contradicted by credible documentary evidence?

> ➢ It is usually better to pass up a line of inquiry than to pursue it and ultimately have it rejected.

Implausibles. Some facts need not be disputed in order to collapse under their own weight. They might be true, they might be useful, they might be free from possible contradiction, but they still just will not fly. Testimony that is simply too farfetched, if offered, will give the trier of fact something unnecessary to worry about. It will inject a reason to doubt the other testimony.

Impeachables .These are statements open to contradiction by the witness's own prior statements. By the time of the arbitration hearing, many witnesses will have given oral and/or written statements in the form of interviews, reports, and depositions. Many also will have signed or authored documents, correspondence, and other writings. With some limitations, the witnesses' previous words may be used to cast doubt upon their credibility; this is called impeachment by a prior inconsistent statement. The demonstration that a witness has previously made statements that contradict her hearing testimony is often one of the most dramatic, and damning, aspects of cross-examination in arbitration. Unless you can provide an extremely good explanation of why the witness has changed, or seems to have changed, her story, it is usually best to omit "impeachables" from direct testimony.

Door openers. Some direct testimony is said to open the door for inquiries on cross-examination that otherwise would not be allowed. The theory here is that fairness requires that the cross-examiner be allowed to explore any topic that was deliberately introduced on direct. Thus, before you open the door to any topic on direct, make sure you do not mind if a cross-examiner later follows you inside.

5.4.3.4   Organization

Organization is the tool through which you translate the witness's memory of events into a coherent and persuasive story. This requires idiom, art, and poetry. Artists do not paint everything they see. Rather, they organize shapes, colors, light, and impasto to present their own image of a landscape. In the same manner, an arbitration advocate does not simply ask a witness to "Tell everything you know," but instead uses the placement and sequence of the information to heighten and clarify its value.

Principles of organization. The key principles of this artistic process are primacy and recency, apposition, duration, and repetition. Primacy and recency refer to the widely accepted phenomenon that people tend to remember best those things that they hear first and last. Following this principle, the important parts of a direct examination should be brought out at its beginning, and again at its end. Less important information should be sandwiched in the middle. Apposition is the placement or juxtaposition of important facts in a manner that emphasizes their relationship. Duration refers to the relative amount of time that you spend on the various aspects of the direct examination. As a general rule you should dwell on the more important points, using the very length of coverage to emphasize the topic's significance. Less important matters should consume less of the direct examination. Repetition is a corollary of duration. Repeat important points, preferably throughout the direct examination, to increase the likelihood that the arbitrator will retain and rely on them.

Structural guidelines. When applying the previous principles, you should realize there is no set pattern for a direct examination's structure, just as there is no correct way to paint a landscape. The following structural guidelines, however, may be helpful.

Start strong and end strong. Both the overall direct examination and the sub-examinations should begin and end on strong points. Strong points possess these features:

> ➢ admissibility
> ➢ theory value
> ➢ thematic value

> ➢ dramatic impact
> ➢ undeniability

Use topical organization. Chronology is almost always the easiest form of organization. However, in many situations it is preferable to use a topical or thematic form of organization. In this way, you can arrange various components of the witness's testimony to reinforce each other, you can isolate weak points, and you can develop your theory in the most persuasive manner. The order in which events occurred is usually fortuitous. As an advocate, your challenge is to rearrange the telling so the story has maximum logical force.

Do not interrupt the action. A cardinal rule for the organization of direct examination is never to interrupt the action. Do not disrupt the dramatic flow of your story, the description of the crucial events, to fill in minor details.

Give separate attention to the details. Details add strength and veracity to a witness's testimony. Unfortunately, as pointed out immediately above, they can also detract from the flow of events. It is therefore usually best to give separate attention to the details, an approach that also allows you to explain their importance.

Avoid scattering circumstantial evidence. Circumstantial or inferential evidence is at its strongest when you can combine a series of circumstances to lead to the desired conclusion. It is therefore effective to present all of the related circumstantial evidence at a single point in the direct examination, rather than scatter it throughout. This will not always be possible. The logic of a witness's testimony may require that items of circumstantial evidence be elicited at different points in the testimony. Chronological organization will dictate introducing the circumstances in the order that they occurred or were discovered. Even topical organization may require assigning individual circumstances to separate topics. Nonetheless, it is always a good idea to attempt to cluster your circumstantial evidence.

Defensive direct examination. From time to time it will be necessary to bring out potentially harmful or embarrassing facts on direct in order to blunt their impact on cross-examination. The theory of such "defensive" direct examination is that the bad information will have less sting if the witness offers it, and conversely that it will be all the more damning if the witness is seen as having tried to hide the bad facts.

Affirmation before refutation. Witnesses are often called both to offer affirmative evidence of their own and to refute others' testimony. In such cases it is usually best to offer the affirmative evidence before proceeding to refutation. In this manner you will accentuate the positive aspects of your case and avoid making the witness appear to be scolding.

Get to the point. A direct examination is not a treasure hunt or murder mystery and there is seldom a reason to keep the arbitrator in suspense. The best form of organization is often to explain exactly where the testimony is headed, and then to go directly there.

End with a clincher. Every examination should end with a clincher, a single fact that capsulizes your theory or theme. To qualify as a clincher, a fact must be:

1. absolutely admissible

2. reasonably dramatic

3. simple and memorable

4. stated with certainty

5.4.4   Questioning technique

Since content is the moving force behind every direct examination, you must use questioning technique to focus attention on the witness and the credible testimony. Here are some suggested questioning techniques to help you achieve that goal.

5.4.4.1   Use short, open questions

Do not ask a witness, "Did you go to the bank?" The answer to that short question will probably be an even shorter "Yes." Instead, as much of your direct examination as possible should consist of questions that invite the witness to describe, explain, and illuminate the events of her testimony. Your witness will almost always be more memorable and believable if you can obtain information in her own words. Short, open questions will advance that goal.

5.4.4.2   Use directive and transitional questions

You cannot use open questions to begin an examination or to move from one area of the examination to another. To do so you would have to start with "When were you born," and proceed to ask "What happened next" in almost endless repetition. A better approach is to use directive and transitional questions. Directive questions, quite simply, direct the witness's attention to the topic that you want to cover.

5.4.4.3   Reinitiate primacy

As noted above, the principle of primacy tells us that the typical arbitrator will pay maximum attention to the witness at the very beginning of the testimony. You can make further use of this principle by continuously "re-beginning" the examination. That is, every time you seem to start anew, you will refocus the arbitrator's attention. You can reinitiate primacy by:

1.   using general headline questions

2.   explaining where you are going

3.   using body movement effectively

4.   using incremental questions

5.   drawing verbal images reflecting time, distance, and intensity

6.   repeating important points

7.   using visual aids

8.   avoiding the use of negative, lawyerly, and complex questions

5.4.5   Dealing with adverse and hostile witnesses

From time to time it may be necessary to call a witness, such as the opposing party, who will be hostile to your case. Because you cannot expect unfriendly witnesses to cooperate in preparation, most jurisdictions allow the use of leading questions for the direct examination of such witnesses. Unfriendly witnesses fall into two broad categories: adverse and hostile witnesses.

5.4.5.1   Adverse witnesses

Adverse witnesses include the opposing party and those identified with the opposing party. Examples of witnesses identified with the opposing party include employees, close relatives, business partners, and others who share a community of interest. There are limited situations in which it may be profitable to call an adverse witness. The first is where the adverse witness is the only person who can supply an essential element of your case. For the same reason, an adverse witness might also be called to authenticate a necessary document or to lay the foundation for some other critical exhibit. Finally, and most perilously, an adverse or hostile witness might be called solely for the purpose of making a bad impression on the arbitrator. Needless to say, this tactic has a strong potential to backfire. It is within the arbitrator's discretion to determine whether any particular witness is sufficiently identified with the opposition as to allow leading questions on direct examination. It is important to alert the arbitrator and opposing counsel to the fact that you are calling an adverse witness, in order to signal your intent to ask leading questions.

5.4.5.2   Hostile witnesses

A hostile witness is one who, while not technically adverse, displays actual hostility to the direct examiner or her client. The necessary characteristic may be manifested either through expressed antagonism or evident reluctance to testify. Additionally, a witness may be treated as hostile if his testimony legitimately surprises the lawyer who called him to the stand. Whatever the circumstances, it is generally necessary to have the arbitrator declare a witness to be hostile before proceeding with leading questions.

5.4.6   Redirect examination and rehabilitation

5.4.6.1   Purpose of redirect

Redirect allows counsel an opportunity to respond to the cross-examination. You can use redirect for a number of purposes. The witness may be asked to explain points explored during the cross, to untangle seeming inconsistencies, to correct errors or misstatements, or to rebut new charges or inferences. In other words, the purpose of redirect is to minimize or undo the damage, if any, that was effected during the cross-examination.

5.4.6.2   Basic rules of redirect

Scope. Because redirect is allowed for counteracting or responding to the cross-examination, the material you can cover on redirect is technically limited to the scope of the cross. The interpretation of this rule varies among arbitrators; some are quite strict and others are fairly lenient. Almost all arbitrators, however, insist that counsel is not free to introduce a wholly new matter on redirect. The redirect must always have some reasonable relationship to the cross-examination.

Some leading permitted. Many arbitrators will allow a certain amount of latitude during redirect, especially with regard to leading questions. Even without indulgence, leading questions are always permissible to direct the witness's attention or to introduce an area of questioning. A certain amount of leading may be necessary on redirect in order to focus the examination on the segment of the cross-examination you wish to explain or rebut.

Recross-examination and additional redirect. Redirect examination may be followed by recross which may be followed by additional redirect, and so on into the night. Each additional examination is limited to the scope of the one that immediately preceded it. Thus, recross is restricted to the scope of the redirect and a second redirect would be confined to the scope of the recross. There is no right to continue an infinite regression of successive "re-examinations." Rather, it is within the arbitrator's discretion to allow or deny a request for, say, re-recross. Most arbitrators routinely allow at least one redirect and one recross.

Reopening direct examination. Reopening direct examination is an alternative to redirect. Counsel can employ it to pursue a line of questioning that is beyond the scope of the cross-examination. It is strictly within the arbitrator's discretion to allow counsel to reopen a direct examination.

Conduct of redirect. Content is the most important aspect of redirect examination. The redirect should concentrate on a few significant points that definitely can be developed. These can typically include explanations or rehabilitation.

Explanations. Explanations are best obtained by asking for them. Focus the witness's attention on the pertinent area of the cross-examination and then simply ask her to give her explanation.

Rehabilitation. Redirect can be used specifically for rehabilitation of a witness who has been impeached with a prior inconsistent statement. Redirect can also be used to rehabilitate a witness with the witness's own prior consistent statements.

Rehabilitating after impeachment. The technique for rehabilitation is similar to that used for any other explanation. Direct the witness's attention to the supposed impeachment and request a clarification. It may be that the alleged inconsistency can be easily resolved, or that the earlier statement was the product of a misunderstanding or misinterpretation. Whatever the explanation, it is important to conclude the rehabilitation with the witness's affirmative statement of the witness's current testimony.

Rehabilitating through prior consistent statements. You can also rehabilitate a witness through the introduction of a prior consistent statement. Although a witness's own previous prior-to-arbitration account would ordinarily be hearsay, a Prior consistent statement is normally admissible to rebut an express or implied charge of recent fabrication or improper influence or motive. Accordingly, once the cross-examiner suggests the witness has changed his or her story, the direct examiner may show that the witness's testimony is consistent with an earlier report or other statement. Note that in some jurisdictions a prior consistent statement is admissible only if it predates the inconsistent statement used for impeachment.

5.4.7   Ethics of direct examination

Most of the ethical issues in direct examination involve the extent to which it is permissible to "assist" a witness to prepare or enhance her testimony and the lawyer's duty when he or she suspects that a client or witness may commit or has committed perjury.

5.4.7.1   Preparation of witnesses

A recurring question is the extent to which lawyers may coach witnesses in preparation for their testimony. In many countries it is considered unethical for a lawyer even to meet alone with a witness prior to the witness testifying because of the possibility for contamination of the testimony. In the United States, however, we take a far different view. Here it is generally considered incompetent for a lawyer to fail to meet with and prepare a witness before he or she testifies. Difficult issues arise, however, when counsel attempts to refresh a witness's recollection, to fill in gaps in her story, or to suggest alternative possibilities. Again, this practice is usually justified on the ground that it is necessary to ensure that the truth emerges fully. Witnesses can be forgetful, especially when they are unaware of the legal importance of certain facts. The guiding principle here is that counsel must, explicitly and implicitly, prepare the witness to give his or her own testimony and not the testimony the lawyer would favor or prefer. Most efforts to assist or empower the witness are ethical. Efforts at substitution or fabrication, no matter how well-cloaked, are not.

5.4.7.2   Offering inadmissible evidence

When evidence is admissible only for a limited purpose, it is unethical to attempt to put it to further use. The obligation of zealous advocacy does not require counsel to ignore or evade the arbitrator's rulings with regard to the restricted admissibility of evidence. By the same token, it is impermissible to prepare a witness to interject clearly inadmissible evidence. Where a motion in *limine* has been granted, for example, counsel cannot suggest or encourage a witness to use a narrative answer to volunteer the excluded information.

5.4.7.3   Perjury

The appropriate response to witness and client perjury has perplexed our profession endlessly. While no ethical lawyer would willingly be a party to perjury, questions arise as how best to prevent it without damaging the principles of confidentiality and zealous advocacy. There is no doubt that a lawyer may not call a non-client witness who is going to testify falsely, and must "take reasonable remedial measures, including, if necessary, disclosure to the tribunal."[9] The thorny problem, however, is the client. An attorney must certainly take all reasonable steps to dissuade a client from presenting untrue testimony. But what if the client insists on presenting a story that the lawyer firmly believes is false? Or what if the client's perjury on the stand takes the lawyer by surprise and becomes a fait accompli before the lawyer can stop it?

---

9. *See* Rules 3.3(a)(3) and 3.4(b), ABA Model Rules of Professional Conduct.

The ABA Model Rules of Professional Conduct provide that counsel, in both civil and criminal cases, must take reasonable steps to remedy client perjury, even at the cost of revealing a confidential communication.[10] Although there are not any easy solutions to these dilemmas, it is fair to say that the trend is toward diminished latitude for the client and increased disclosure by counsel.

5.5 Cross-Examination

If direct examination is your best opportunity to win your case, cross-examination may provide you with a chance to lose it. A poor direct can be aimless and boring, but the witnesses are generally helpful. Your worst fear on direct examination is usually that you have left something out. A poor cross-examination, on the other hand, can be truly disastrous. The witnesses can range from uncooperative to hostile, and you constantly run the risk of actually adding weight or sympathy to the other side's case. Moreover, the arbitrator inevitably perceives most cross-examinations as a contest between the lawyer and witness. You can seldom afford to appear to lose.

This section discusses the role of cross-examination, its basic rules, content, organization, and basic technique.[11] Several more advanced aspects of cross-examination—such as impeachment and the use of character evidence—are treated separately in section 5.6.

5.5.1 The role of cross-examination

Cross-examination is difficult. It is frequently dramatic, often exciting, and in many ways it defines the adversarial method of dispute resolution. It is the ultimate challenge for the arbitration advocate. It allows you to add to your case or detract from the opposition's case by extracting information from the other side's witnesses. Furthermore, cross-examination is inherently risky. The witness may argue with you. The witness may fill in gaps that were left in the direct testimony. The witness may make you look bad. You may make yourself look bad. Whatever good you accomplish may be subject to immediate cure on redirect examination. You cannot avoid these problems entirely, but you can minimize them. Although some cross-examination is usually expected of every witness, and the temptation is difficult to resist, as a general rule you should cross-examine carefully and briefly. You must always set realistic goals.

---

10. Rule 3.3(b), ABA Model Rules of Professional Conduct.
11. This section is a condensed and adapted version of Lubet, *supra* chapter 3, note 1, at 51–110. The reader is invited to consult that source for an in-depth treatment of the subject of cross-examination, including detailed examples.

5.5.2 Basic rules of cross-examination

Some rules of cross-examination vary depending on locality, but the following rules are nearly universal.

5.5.2.1 Leading questions permitted

The most obvious distinction between direct and cross-examination is the permissible use of leading questions. It is assumed that your adversary's witnesses will have little incentive to cooperate with you, and that you may not have been able to interview them in advance. Consequently, in arbitration, the cross-examiner is allowed to ask questions that contain their own answers. Moreover, the right to ask leading questions is usually understood to include the right to insist on a responsive answer.

5.5.2.2 Limitations on scope

Cross-examination is limited to the scope of the direct. Since cross-examination's purpose is to allow you to inquire of your adversary's witnesses, the inquiry's scope is restricted to those subjects that were raised during the direct examination. Note that the definition of scope may vary from arbitrator to arbitrator. A narrow application of this rule can limit the cross-examiner to the precise events and occurrences that the witness discussed on direct. A broader approach would allow questioning on related and similar events. For example, assume that the defendant in an auto collision case testified that his brakes had been inspected just a week before the accident. A strict approach to the "scope of direct" rule might limit the cross-examination to questioning on that particular inspection. A broader interpretation would allow inquiries into earlier brake inspections and other aspects of automobile maintenance. A more generous approach to the scope of cross-examination is definitely the modern trend.

There are two general exceptions to the "scope of direct" rule. First, the witness's credibility is always in issue. You may therefore always attempt to establish the bias, motive, interest, untruthfulness, or material prior inconsistency of a witness, without regard to the matters covered on direct examination. Second, you may cross-examine beyond the scope of the direct once the witness has "opened the door" to additional matters. In other words, a witness who voluntarily injects a subject into an answer on cross-examination may thereafter be questioned as though the subject had been included in the direct.

5.5.2.3 Other restrictions

A variety of other rules, most of which involve the manner or nature of questioning, also limit cross-examinations.

Argumentative questions. You may ask a witness questions. You may suggest answers. You may assert propositions. But you may not argue with the witness. As you may have guessed, the definition of an argumentative question is elusive. Much will depend on your demeanor; perhaps an argumentative question is one that is asked in an argumentative tone. The following is a reasonable working definition: an argumentative question insists that the witness agree with an opinion or characterization, as opposed to a statement of fact.

Intimidating behavior. You are entitled to elicit information on cross-examination by asking questions of the witness and insisting upon answers. You are not allowed to loom over the witness, to shout, to make threatening gestures, or otherwise to intimidate, bully, or (yes, here it comes) badger the witness.

Unfair characterizations. Your right to lead the witness does not include a right to mislead the witness. It is objectionable to attempt to mischaracterize a witness's testimony or to ask "trick" questions. If a witness has testified that it was dark outside, it would mischaracterize the testimony to begin a question, "So you admit that it was too dark to see anything?" Trick questions cannot be answered accurately. The most famous trick question is known as the "negative pregnant," as in Senator McCarthy's inquisitional, "Have you resigned from the Communist Party?"

Assuming facts. A frequently heard objection is that "Counsel has assumed facts not in evidence." Of course, a cross-examiner is frequently allowed to inquire as to facts that are not yet in evidence. This objection should only be sustained when the question uses the non-record fact as a premise rather than as a separate subject of inquiry, thus denying the witness the opportunity to deny its validity. An example of a question containing an unfair assumption would be: "Since you had been drinking, you were on foot instead of in your car that morning?" That the witness was drinking is an assumed fact. The problem with this sort of bootstrapping is that it does not allow the witness a fair opportunity to deny having been drinking in the first place.

Compound and other defective questions. Compound questions contain more than a single inquiry: "Are you related to the plaintiff, and were you wearing your glasses at the time of the accident?" The question is objectionable since any answer will necessarily be ambiguous. Cumulative or "asked and answered" questions are objectionable because they cover the same ground twice (or more). Vague questions are objectionable because they tend to elicit vague answers.

5.5.3 Content of Cross-Examination

The most frequent decision you will have to make regarding cross-examination is not whether to cross-examine, but how much. Make this evaluation at least twice: once in your prehearing preparation and again at the end of the direct examination. In preparation, you must consider the potential direct examination.

> What do you expect the witness to say and how, if at all, will you need to challenge or add to the direct?

At the arbitration hearing you must make a further determination.

> Did the actual direct examination proceed as you expected?

> Was it more or less damaging than you anticipated?

You must always reevaluate your cross-examination strategy in light of the direct testimony that was eventually produced. This process will often lead you to omit portions of your prepared cross, because they have become unnecessary. It is considerably more dangerous to elaborate on or add to your plan, although this is occasionally unavoidable. In either situation, always remember the risk inherent in cross-examination and ask yourself, "Is this cross-examination necessary?"

5.5.3.1   Consider the purposes of cross-examination

Though often an invigorating exercise, cross-examination should be undertaken only to serve some greater purpose within your theory of the case. A useful cross-examination should promise to fulfill at least one of the following objectives:

Repair or minimize damage

> Did the direct examination hurt your case?

> If so, can the harm be rectified or minimized?

> Can the witness be made to retract or back away from certain testimony?

> Can you elicit additional facts that will minimize the witness's impact?

Enhance your case

> Can you use the cross-examination to further one of your claims or defenses?

> Can you bring out positive facts that will support or contribute to your version of events?

Detract from their case

> Conversely, can the cross-examination be used to establish facts that are detrimental to your opponent's case?

> Can it be used to create inconsistencies among the other side's witnesses?

Establish foundation

> Is the witness necessary to the proper foundation for the introduction of a document or other exhibit, or for the offer of evidence by another witness?

Discredit direct testimony

➤ Is it possible to discredit the witness's direct testimony through means such as highlighting internal inconsistencies, demonstrating the witness's own lack of certainty or confidence, underscoring lack of opportunity to observe, illustrating the inherent implausibility of the testimony, or showing that it conflicts with the testimony of other, more credible witnesses?

Discredit the witness

➤ Can you show the witness to be biased or interested in the case's outcome?

➤ Does the witness have a reason to stretch, misrepresent, or fabricate the testimony?

➤ Has the witness been untruthful in the past?

➤ Can you show that the witness is otherwise unworthy of belief?

Reflect on the credibility of another. Can the cross-examination be used to reflect, favorably or unfavorably, on the credibility of a different witness? The length of your cross-examination will generally depend upon how many of the previous goals you expect to be able to fulfill. It is not necessary, and it may not be possible to attempt to achieve them all. You will often stand to lose more by over-reaching than you can possibly gain by seeking to cover all of the bases in cross-examination. Be selective.

5.5.3.2 Arrive at the "usable universe" of cross-examination

In preparing your cross-examination, you must first determine the entire universe of potential cross-examination and then you must determine your usable universe.

The entire universe. In preparing to cross-examine any witness you must first determine the broadest possible scope, or universe, for the potential cross-examination. From a review of all of the available materials and documents, construct a comprehensive list of the information available from the witness. In keeping with the purposes of cross-examination, place each potential fact in one of the following categories:

➤ Does it make my case more likely?

➤ Does it make their case less likely?

➤ Is it a predicate to the admissibility of other evidence?

➤ Does it make some witnesses more believable?

➤ Does it make some witnesses less believable?

This process will give you the full universe of theoretically desirable information from which you will structure your cross-examination.

The usable universe. To arrive at your "usable universe," ask yourself the following questions:

> ➢ Is a friendly witness available to present the same facts?
>
> ➢ Can the information be obtained only on cross-examination?
>
> ➢ Will the facts be uniquely persuasive on cross-examination?
>
> ➢ How certain is it that the witness will agree with you?

The construction of your usable universe depends almost entirely on your mastery of the case as a whole. To prepare for cross-examination you must know not only everything that the particular witness is liable to say, but also every other fact you might obtain from any other witness, document, or exhibit. You will want to choose those areas that will do you the most good, while risking the least harm.

5.5.3.3   Use a risk-averse approach to preparation

Risk-averse preparation for cross-examination begins with consideration of your anticipated final argument.

> ➢ What do you want to be able to say about this particular witness when you address the arbitrator at the end of the case?
>
> ➢ How much of that information do you expect to be included in the direct examination? The balance is what you will need to cover on cross.

Next, write out the portion of a final argument that you would devote to discussing the facts presented by this particular witness. This will at most serve as a draft for your actual closing, and you should limit this text to the facts contained in the witness's testimony. You need not include the characterizations, inferences, arguments, comments, and thematic references that will also be part of your real final argument. Depending upon the importance of the witness, the length of this argument segment can range from a short paragraph to a full page or more.

It is important that you write your text using short, single-thought, strictly factual sentences. You are not attempting to create literature. Do not worry about continuity, style, or transition. Simply arrange the declarative sentences one after another in the most persuasive order, referring to the witness in the third person.

The risk-averse approach is useful for developing the content of your cross-examination. The organization of the examination and the structure of your individual questions will depend upon additional analysis.

5.5.4   The organization of cross-examination

As with direct examination, the organization of a cross-examination can be based on the four principles of primacy and recency, apposition, repetition, and duration. Unlike direct examination, however, on cross-examination you will often have to deal with a recalcitrant witness. You may therefore have to recognize this reality and temper your plan, occasionally sacrificing maximum clarity and persuasion in order to avoid "telegraphing" your strategy to the uncooperative witness. Thus, we must include the additional organizing principles of indirection and misdirection when planning cross-examinations.

5.5.4.1   Additional organizing principles

Three further principles are basic to the organization, presentation, and technique of virtually every cross-examination. First, cross-examination is your opportunity to tell part of your client's story in the middle of the other side's case. Your object is to focus attention away from the witness's direct testimony and onto matters that you believe are helpful. On cross-examination, you want to tell the story. To do so, you must always be in control of the testimony and the witness. Second, cross-examination is never the time to attempt to gather new information. Never ask a witness a question simply because you want to find out the answer. Rather, you must use cross-examination to establish or enhance the facts you have already discovered. Finally, an effective cross-examination often succeeds through the use of indirection and misdirection. It is not necessary, and it is often harmful, to ask a witness the "ultimate question." By indirection, or indirect questioning, you first seek to establish small and uncontrovertible factual components of a theory, and only later address the theory itself. Final argument is your opportunity to point out the relationship between facts, make characterizations, and draw conclusions based upon the accumulation of details. Misdirection is an arch-relative of indirection, used when the witness is thought to be particularly deceptive or untruthful. Here the cross-examiner not only conceals the object of the examination but actually attempts to take advantage of the witness's own inclination to be uncooperative. Knowing that the witness will tend to fight the examination, the lawyer creates, and then exploits, a "misdirected" image.

5.5.4.2   Guidelines for organization

There are a variety of ways in which you can employ the previous principles.

Do not worry about starting strong. It would be desirable to begin every cross-examination with a strong, memorable point that absolutely drives home your theory and theme. Unfortunately, this will seldom be possible. Most cross-examinations will have to begin with a shake-down period, during which you acclimate yourself to the tenor of the witness's responses and when you also attempt to put the witness in a cooperative frame of mind. Unless you are able to start off with a true bombshell, it will usually be preferable to take the time necessary to establish predicate facts through indirection.

Use topical organization. Topical organization is essential in cross-examination. Your goal on cross-examination is not to retell the witness's story, but rather to establish a small number of additional or discrediting points. A topical format is the most effective in allowing you to move from area to area. Moreover, topical organization also allows you to take maximum advantage of apposition, indirection, and misdirection. You can use it to cluster facts in the same manner that you would on direct examination, or to separate facts in order to avoid showing your hand to the witness.

Give the details first. Within each segment of your cross-examination, it will usually be preferable to give the details first. No matter what your goal, the witness will be far more likely to agree with a series of small, incremental facts before the thrust of the examination has been made apparent. Once you have challenged, confronted, or closely questioned a witness, it will be extremely difficult to go back and fill in the details necessary to make the challenge stick.

Scatter inferential or circumstantial evidence. Inferential or circumstantial evidence is most persuasive when you can combine a series of facts or events in such a way as to create a logical path to the desired conclusion. Unfortunately, facts arranged in this manner on cross-examination will also be highly transparent to the witness. As you stack inference upon inference, your direction will become increasingly clear. A hostile or unfriendly witness will then become increasingly uncooperative, perhaps to the point of thwarting your examination. A far safer approach is to scatter the circumstantial evidence throughout the examination, drawing it together only during closing argument.

Save a zinger for the end. It is imperative that you plan carefully the very last point that you intend to make on cross-examination. It must be a guaranteed winner, the point on which you are willing to make your exit. Indeed, you should write this point down at the very bottom of your note pad, underlined and in bold letters. It should stand alone, with nothing to obscure it or distract you from it. Then if your entire examination seems to fail, if the witness denies every proposition, if the arbitrator sustains every objection, if the heavens fall and doom impends, you can always skip to the bottom of the page and finish with a flourish. Satisfied that you have made this single, telling, case-sealing point, you may proudly announce, "No further questions of this witness," and sit down. Your zinger should have all of the following characteristics. It should be:

1. absolutely admissible

2. central to your theory

3. crafted to evoke your theme

4. undeniable, and

5. stated with conviction

5.5.4.3   A classic format for cross-examination

The following classic format is designed to maximize witness cooperation. Of course, you may have a goal in mind for your cross-examination other than witness cooperation; in that case, feel free to ignore or alter this approach. As a rule of thumb, however, you can best employ principles such as indirection and "detail scattering" by seeking information in this order.

Friendly information. Be friendly first. Begin by asking all questions that the witness will regard as non-threatening. These will often be background questions. There is little doubt that a witness will be the most forthcoming when asked about aggrandizing information at the very outset of the cross-examination.

Affirmative information. After exhausting the friendly information, ask questions that build up your case's value, rather than tear down the opposition's. Much of this information will fill in gaps in the direct testimony. In fact, a good way to plan this portion of the cross is to list the information that you reasonably hope will be included in the direct. Although adverse witnesses may not be enthusiastic about supplying you with helpful information, they will be unlikely to fight you over answers that might logically have been included in their own direct.

Incontrovertible information. You can now proceed to inquire about facts that damage the opposition's case or detract from the witness's testimony, so long as they are well-settled or documentable. On these questions a witness may be inclined to hedge or quibble, but you can minimize this possibility by sticking to the sort of information that he ultimately must concede.

Challenging information. At some point, of course, you will have to ask questions that the witness will recognize as challenges: "Mr. Defendant, the fact is that the first thing you did after the collision was to telephone your office?" Such questions are necessary. When used in their proper place they will not prevent you from first exploiting the other, more cooperative testimony from the witness.

Hostile information. Hostile information involves directly confronting the witness. You may be able to extract the necessary answers to hostile questions, but certainly you can eliminate all hope of cooperation both then and thereafter.

Hostile questions involve assaults on the witness's honesty, probity, peacefulness, character, or background:

> Didn't you spend time in prison?

> You never intended to live up to the contract?

> That was a lie, wasn't it?

Zinger. Always end with one.

5.5.5　Questioning technique

You know what you want to cover on cross-examination, and you know the order in which you want to cover it. Next you need to know how to ask questions that will ensure your success.

The essential goal of cross-examination technique is witness control. Control can be either non-assertive or assertive. With a cooperative or tractable witness, control may mean nothing more than asking the right questions and getting the right answers. A hostile, evasive, or argumentative witness may require that you employ more assertive means. There are numerous questioning techniques, to be discussed below, that you can employ to ensure witness control. At a minimum, however, every question on cross-examination should have all of the following bedrock characteristics:

Short. Questions on cross-examination must be short in both execution and concept. If a question is more than ten words long, it is not short in execution. Try to shorten it. If a question contains more than a single fact or implication, it is not short in concept. Divide it.

Leading. Every question on cross-examination should be leading. Include the answers in the questions. Tell the witness exactly what to say. Cross-examination is no time to seek the witness's interpretation of the facts. It is the time for you to tell a story by obtaining the witness's assent. A non-leading question invites the witness to wander away from your story.

Propositional. The best questions on cross-examination are not questions at all. Rather, they are propositions of fact that you put to the witness in interrogative form. You already know the answer—you simply need to produce it from the witness's mouth. Every question on cross-examination should contain a proposition that falls into one of these three categories:

1. You already know the answer;

2. you can otherwise document or prove the answer; or

3. any answer will be helpful.

An example of the latter sort of question would be the classic inquiry to a witness who must admit having previously given a false statement: "Were you lying then, or are you lying now?"

5.5.5.1   Planning for control

Control of a witness on cross-examination begins with your plan and is achieved, in large measure, on your note pad. In other words, a cross-examination is only as good as your outline.

Avoid written questions. It can be useful to write out cross-examination questions in preparation for an arbitration hearing, but when it comes to the actual examination, it is usually a mistake to read from a prepared list of questions. The great majority of lawyers use notes, of course, but not in the form of written questions. Reading your questions will deprive your examination of the appearance of spontaneity. For all but the most accomplished thespians, reading from a script will sound just like reading from a script, or worse, a laundry list. It will be almost impossible to develop any rhythm with the witness. Reading from a set of questions will also deprive you of the control that comes from eye contact with the witness. The witness will be less likely to follow your lead, and you will be less able to observe the witness's demeanor of telltale signs of nervousness or retraction. Written questions are best used as a pre-examination device. Write them out, study them, hone them, rearrange them, and then discard them in favor of a topical outline.

Use an outline. You should make an outline of your cross-examination. Your outline should remind you of the points you intend to make on cross-examination and ensure that you do not inadvertently omit anything. Do not regard your notes as a script but rather as a set of cues or prompts, each of which introduces an area of questioning. Beneath each of the main prompts you will list the key details that you intend to elicit from the witness. Your outline can follow the same format that you have used since high school. Principal topics are represented by Roman numerals, subtopics are denoted by capital letters, and smaller points or component details are represented by Arabic numerals. Although the form for academic outlines goes on to involve lower case letters, small Roman numerals, and other levels ad infinitum, the outline for a cross-examination will become too complex if it extends beyond the third level.

Reference your outline. Once you have drafted the outline for your cross-examination, you should proceed to "reference" it. Referencing allows you to refresh the recollection of forgetful witnesses, and to impeach or contradict witnesses who give you evasive, unexpected, or false answers. Across from every important subtopic and crucial detail, record the source for the point you intend to make. You need not reference the major topic headings, but other than that it will often prove useful to reference your notes line by line. At a minimum, you must reference every point you consider essential to your case as well as those that you expect to be controverted or challenging to the witness. In addition to deposition transcripts, reference sources can come from letters, reports, memoranda, notes, and even photographs. The best sources, of course, are the witness's own prior words. Adequate secondary sources may include documents that the witness reviewed, acted upon, or affirmed by silence. In most circumstances, the testimony of a different person, though perhaps useful, will not be a reliable source for referencing a cross-examination.

Use questions that achieve control. Having reviewed the principles for organizing and outlining the cross-examination, we are now ready to consider the precise techniques that provide maximum control over a witness's testimony.

Use incremental questions. Cross-examination should proceed in a series of small, steady steps. This technique allows you to do two things. First, it blocks the escape route for a witness who is inclined to argue or prevaricate. The incremental questions provide small targets for a witness's inventiveness. More importantly, it lets you know early in the sequence whether the witness is likely to disagree with you. The use of incremental questions allows you to test the witness for cooperation, and to determine whether your own factual assumptions are correct, before you reach an embarrassing point of no return.

Use sequenced questions for impact. You can use sequencing on cross-examination for a variety of purposes. First, as on direct, you may use sequencing (or apposition) to clarify your story or enhance its impact upon the arbitrator. Eliciting two facts in close proximity can underscore relationships, contrasts, inconsistencies, connections, or motives. The apposition of otherwise disparate facts can help develop your theme.

Use sequenced questions for indirection. Unfortunately, what is clear to the arbitrator will also be clear to the witness. Alerted that you have decided to exploit a particular topic, the witness may decide not to concede so readily the topic's key details. In such situations you may use sequencing not for clarity and impact, but for indirection. You may therefore decide to simply abandon apposition, and instead scatter the information about the topic.

Use sequenced questions for commitment. Using sequenced questions in combination with incremental questions may occasionally allow you to compel an unwilling witness to make important concessions. Facts can often be arranged in a manner that gives their progression a logic of its own. When the initial facts in a sequence are sufficiently small and innocuous, a witness may be led to embark upon a course of concessions that will be impossible to stop.

Create a "conceptual corral." As we have seen, cross-examination's purpose is often to "box in" a witness so that crucial facts cannot be averted or denied. It is often useful to think of this process as building a "conceptual corral" around the witness. After building the first three sides of the corral, you may then close the gate with your final proposition. Each side of the conceptual corral is formed by a different sort of question. One side consists of the witness's own previous admissions or actions, another is formed by undeniable facts, and the third is based upon everyday plausibility. The length of any particular side, or the extent to which you will rely on any of the three sorts of information, will differ from case to case. With almost every witness, however, the three sides of the corral can be constructed to form an enclosure from which the witness cannot escape.

Avoid ultimate questions. It will often be tempting to confront an adverse witness with one last conclusory question: "So you just ignored the fire truck, didn't you?" Resist this temptation. If you have already established all of the incremental facts that lead to your conclusion, then you will have little to gain by making the question explicit. At best you will repeat what has become obvious, and at worst you will give the witness an opportunity to recant or amend the foundational testimony. Even worse, you may not have established the incremental facts as fully as you thought. Under these circumstances, you can expect the witness not only to disagree with your ultimate proposition, but to be prepared to explain exactly why you are wrong.

Listen to the witness and insist on an answer. There is more to controlling a witness on cross-examination than asking the right questions. You must also make sure that you have gotten the correct answers. This requires that you listen to the witness. Even the most painstakingly prepared question can elicit the wrong answer. The witness may not have understood you, or she may have detected an ambiguity in your inquiry. Some witnesses will argue with you for the sake of argument, some will try to deflect your examination, and some will simply answer a question different from the one you asked. In any event, you must always recall that it is the witness's answer that constitutes evidence, and you must listen carefully to ensure that the evidence is what you expected. You can often correct an incorrect answer by restating your question.

5.5.5.2   Avoid questions that lose control

The pitfalls of cross-examination are well known: refusals to answer; unexpected answers; and argumentative, evasive and slippery witnesses. Significantly, virtually all of these problems derive from the same basic error on the part of the cross-examiner—failure to control the testimony. You can avoid making this error by avoiding questions that make it likely that you will lose control of the witness. Here are a few examples of those sorts of questions.

Non-leading questions. The cardinal rule on cross-examination is to use leading questions. The cardinal sin is to abandon that tool. We have discussed at length the advantages of stating your questions in the form of leading propositions. For some reason, however, many lawyers seem impelled to drift into non-leading questions once an examination has begun. This is a mistake you should avoid like the plague.

"Why" or explanation questions. There is virtually never a need to ask a witness to explain something on cross-examination. If you already know the explanation, then use leading questions to tell it to the witness. If you do not already know the explanation, then cross-examination surely is not the time to learn it. No matter how assiduously you have prepared, no matter how well you think you understand the witness's motives and reasons, a witness can always surprise you by explaining the unexplainable. Asking a witness to explain is the equivalent of saying, "I've grown tired of controlling this cross-examination. Why don't you take over for a while?"

"Fishing" questions. Fishing questions are the ones that you ask in the hope that you might catch something. It has been said before and it is worth repeating here: Do not ask questions to which you do not know the answers. For every reason you have to think that the answer will be favorable, there are a dozen reasons you have not thought of, all of which suggest disaster.

Long questions. Long questions have an almost limitless capacity to deprive a cross-examiner of witness control. Long questions, by their very nature, multiply a witness's opportunity to find something with which to disagree. The more words you use, the more chance there is that a witness will refuse to adopt them all. A second problem with long questions is they are easily forgotten or misunderstood. The witness may insist on answering the question he or she thought you asked, rather than the one that you meant to ask.

"Gap" questions. "Gap" questions constitute an especially enticing subset of explanation questions. Gaps are found in direct testimony more often than one might expect. A witness may neglect to testify about one of a series of important events, or may omit testimony concerning a crucial document. Alternatively, a witness might leave out important evidence on damages, or may fail entirely to testify as to an element, such as proximate cause, of the opposition's case. How can you avoid the temptation to ask gap questions? The key is to remember that it is the opposition's burden to prove their case. Everything they leave out of their case works in your favor.

"You testified . . ." questions. Another common method of surrendering control to a witness is through the use of questions that seem to challenge the witness to recall the content of her earlier direct testimony. These can be referred to as "you testified" questions, because they inevitably contain some variant on those words. The problem with "you testified" questions is that they invite the witness

to quibble over the precise wording used on direct examination. The exact language of the witness's earlier answer is seldom essential, but the "you testified" format inflates its apparent importance, often almost to the point of seeming to pick a fight.

Characterizations and conclusions. Another way to risk losing control on cross-examination is to request that a witness agree with a characterization or conclusion. Assume that you are cross examining the plaintiff in a personal injury case. The plaintiff testified on direct that he was struck by a vehicle at midnight on a seldom-traveled country road. Your defense is misidentification of the driver. Wishing to take advantage of the time and place of the events, you ask this question: "It was too dark to see very well, wasn't it?" You have just asked the witness to agree with your characterization of the lighting conditions.

The plaintiff, being nobody's fool, answers: "I could see just fine." Instead, you should have asked the plaintiff about the facts that led you to the characterization: the sun had gone down, there was no moon that night, there were no street lamps, there were no house lights, there were no illuminated signs. The characterization could then be saved for final argument.

5.5.5.3   Reasserting control

Notwithstanding your best efforts and preparation, some witnesses will inevitably wander beyond your control. A witness typically falls out of control in one of three ways:

1.   she has refused to agree with you;

2.   she has been invited to explain an answer; or

3.   she is being impermissibly uncooperative.

In the first two instances the problem is your fault, and you can usually cure it with further questions. In the third case the witness is at fault, and you may need help from the arbitrator. To reassert control when the witness has failed to agree, you should: determine why the witness has refused to agree; break the question into constituent questions until the disagreement is eliminated. To reassert control when the witness explains, you should: determine why the witness has explained; avoid interrupting the witness (unless the witness is about to blurt out some devastating inadmissible fact or is violating the arbitrator's prior ruling prohibiting explanations); try a stern look, upraised hand, or sliding in a question during a pause in her testimony; or, if those techniques do not work, simply allow the witness to finish the answer and then proceed to another question that does not invite explanation. To reassert control when the witness is impermissibly uncooperative, you should: try the techniques just described; if unsuccessful, seek help from the arbitrator.

5.5.6   Ethics of cross-examination

While lawyers generally consider cross-examination to be an "engine" of truth-seeking, we are often criticized for using cross as a device for distortion and obfuscation. And in truth, like all powerful rhetorical tools, cross-examination can be used to mislead and deceive. Accordingly, certain ethical principles have developed that circumscribe a lawyer's use of cross-examination.

5.5.6.1   Factual and legal basis for questioning

To protect against the unscrupulous use of cross-examination, the general rule is that a lawyer may not, in trial, allude to any matter that the lawyer does not reasonably believe is relevant or that will not be supported by admissible evidence.[12] Ordinarily, in a court case subject to discovery, counsel is not free to make up assertions at trial, or even to fish for possibly incriminating material. Rather, as a predicate to any "propositional" question, counsel must ordinarily be aware of specific facts that support the allegation. In arbitration, where little or no discovery has been authorized, the good faith basis in fact requirement is somewhat relaxed because counsel may be examining a witness for the first time at the hearing itself.

Also, in a court trial, the "good faith" basis for a cross-examination question cannot be comprised solely of inadmissible evidence. Trial counsel cannot allude to any matter "that will not be supported by admissible evidence." Thus, in a court trial a good faith basis cannot be provided by rumors, uncorroborated hearsay, or pure speculation. In an arbitration, this rule is somewhat relaxed because hearsay is normally permitted. However, allegations based on evidence deemed inadmissible by the arbitrator may lead to a sustained objection, an admonition by the arbitrator, or even sanctions.

5.5.6.2   Assertions of personal knowledge

The general rule in a court trial is that it is unethical for counsel to "assert personal knowledge of facts in issue . . . or state a personal opinion as to the justness of a cause, the credibility of a witness, the culpability of a civil litigant or the guilt or innocence of an accused."[13] While this problem most frequently occurs during closing argument, it also arises during cross-examination. Cross-examination questions often take a "Do you know?" or "Didn't you tell me?" format. Both types of questions are improper, because they put the lawyer's own credibility in issue. "Do you know?" questions suggest the lawyer is aware of true facts which, while not appearing on the record, contradict the witness's testimony. "Didn't you tell me?" questions argue that the witness and the lawyer had a conversation, and that the lawyer's version is more believable. In either case, the

---

12. See Rule 3.4(e), ABA Model Rules of Professional Conduct.
13. *See* Rule 3.4(e), ABA Model Rules of Professional Conduct.

questions amount to an assertion of personal knowledge. In the informal setting of arbitration, some arbitrators may relax the enforcement of this rule, but other arbitrators may enforce it strictly.

5.5.6.3   Derogatory questions

It is unethical to ask questions that are intended solely to harass, degrade, or humiliate a witness, or to discourage him from testifying.

5.5.6.4   Discrediting a truthful witness

In arbitration, you cannot degrade or debase a witness simply to cast doubt on otherwise unchallenged testimony. On the other hand, true factual information may be used to undermine the credibility of a witness whose testimony is legitimately controverted.

5.5.6.5   Misusing evidence

The same rules apply on cross as on direct with regard to misusing evidence that has been admitted for a limited purpose.[14]

5.6   Impeachment

While much cross-examination consists of demonstrating inaccuracies or rebutting a witness's testimony, impeachment is intended actually to discredit the witness as a reliable source of information. Successful impeachment renders the witness less worthy of belief, as opposed to merely unobservant, mistaken, or otherwise subject to contradiction. There are three basic categories of witness impeachment, each of which provides a reason to place less credence in a witness's testimony.[15]

The most common method of impeachment is the use of a prior inconsistent statement, action, or omission. The elicitation of a prior inconsistency demonstrates that the witness's current testimony is at odds with her own previous statements or actions. In essence, this examination says, "Do not believe this witness because her story has changed."

A second method of impeachment is the use of character, or "characteristic" evidence. This form of impeachment is aimed at demonstrating that the witness possesses some inherent trait or characteristic, unrelated to the case at hand,

---

14. *See* section 5.4.7, *supra.*
15. This section is a condensed adaptation of Lubet, *supra* chapter 3, note 1 at 111–163, which contains an in-depth treatment of the subject of impeachment, with detailed examples

that renders the testimony less credible. Perhaps the witness is a convicted felon or suffers a memory defect. This examination says, "This witness is not trustworthy on any matter, because of who he is."

The third method, "case data" impeachment, involves the establishment of facts that make the witness less reliable, although only within the context of the case in arbitration. The witness might have a financial interest in the outcome of the case, or might be prejudiced against one of the parties. In other words, "Give less weight to the witness because of her relationship to the case."

Impeachment generally begins and ends during cross-examination. When a witness concedes the existence of the impeaching information, nothing further needs be done and the cross-examiner may go on to other matters. If, however, the witness denies the truth of the impeaching matter, the cross-examiner may be required to perfect or complete the impeachment by offering extrinsic evidence, or evidence that is adduced through the testimony of someone other than the subject of the impeachment. This can occur whether the original impeachment was based upon prior inconsistency, character, or case data.

5.6.1   Tactical considerations

Impeachment is a powerful tool. Unlike "standard" cross-examination, which may rely on unspoken premises and subtle misdirection, there can be no mistaking or hiding the intended impact of impeachment. All three kinds of impeachment are inherently confrontational. They challenge the witness's believability, perhaps even her veracity. For this reason, use the techniques of impeachment sparingly, both to preserve the method's potency and to avoid crying wolf over unimportant details.

5.6.1.1   Impeach the witness only on significant matters

It is important to avoid impeaching witnesses on irrelevant, trivial, or petty inconsistencies. The process of impeachment, particularly through the use of prior inconsistency, is generally so confrontational that there is a great risk of creating an annoying dissonance between expectation and reward. If the "punch line" fails to justify the build-up, the result can be embarrassing or damaging to your case.

5.6.1.2   Impeach the witness only on true inconsistencies

The purpose of impeachment through the use of a prior inconsistency is to show that the witness has made contradictory statements. The technique works only when the two statements cannot both be true. If the two statements can be harmonized, explained, or rationalized, the impeachment will fail.

5.6.1.3   Impeach a witness only when success is likely

Failed impeachment can be disastrous. A lawyer who begins an assault that cannot be completed will look ineffective at best and foolishly overbearing at worst.

5.6.1.4   Do not impeach favorable information

Impeachment is not like mountain climbing. It should not be undertaken simply because it is there. Impeachment's purpose is to cast doubt on the credibility of some or all of a witness's testimony. You gain nothing by casting doubt on testimony that was helpful to your own case. Thus, even if an opposing witness has given a prior inconsistent statement, do not be use it to impeach favorable hearing testimony.

5.6.1.5   Consider the "Rule of Completeness"

The Rule of Completeness provides that once a witness has been impeached from a prior inconsistent statement, opposing counsel may request the immediate reading of additional, explanatory portions of the same statement. Under the Federal Rules of Evidence, for example, the adverse party may introduce any other part of the statement "which ought in fairness to be considered contemporaneously with it." Thus, even a true gem of an impeaching statement may be immediately undercut if some other part of the impeaching document explains or negates the apparent contradiction.

5.6.1.6   Consider refreshing the witness's recollection

Not every gap or variation in a witness's testimony is the result of an intentional change. Witnesses often become confused or forgetful. A witness may have testified inconsistently with her prior statements quite innocently or inadvertently. In these circumstances it will often be possible to use the prior statement to refresh the witness's recollection, rather than to impeach her credibility. The technique for refreshing recollection is the same on cross-examination as it is on direct. Many arbitrators, however, will allow a cross-examiner to refresh a witness's recollection without first being required to establish that the witness's memory has been exhausted.

5.6.1.7   Evidentiary considerations

Prior inconsistent statements given under oath are admissible as substantive evidence; they can be used to prove the original statement's truth. Prior inconsistent statements that were not given under oath are generally admissible for the limited purpose of impeachment; they can be used only to reflect on the witness's credibility.

5.6.2   Prior Inconsistent Statements

Prior inconsistent statements damage a witness's credibility because they demonstrate the witness has changed his story. Depending upon the nature and seriousness of the change, you may show the witness to be evasive, opportunistic, error-prone, or even lying. To accomplish any of these goals, of course, it is necessary that the prior statement be clearly inconsistent with the current testimony, and that it be directed to a subject of true significance to the case. Semi-inconsistencies concerning tangential matters will have little or no impact.

There are three steps necessary to impeach a witness with a prior inconsistent statement: (1) recommit; (2) validate; and (3) confront. The following sub-sections treat each of the three steps in detail.

5.6.2.1   Recommit the witness

The first step in impeaching a witness with a prior inconsistent statement is to recommit the witness to his current testimony:

> Question: Mr. Kaye, you testified on direct examination that the light was green for the southbound traffic, correct?

This is an example of the traditional way to recommit the witness. The purpose of recommitting the witness is to underscore the gulf between the current testimony and the prior statement. There is no evidentiary requirement that the witness be allowed to repeat the direct testimony. On the other hand, it is difficult to imagine how the two statements could be effectively contrasted without restating the testimony that is about to be impeached.

There is an elegant alternative to the traditional approach to recommitting the witness by rephrasing the direct examination in language that is beneficial to the cross-examiner's own case. It is not necessary to repeat verbatim the witness's about-to-be-impeached testimony. Recommitment's purpose is only to focus attention on the inconsistency between the hearing testimony and the prior statement. It is therefore possible to recommit the witness to current testimony's content without repeating it word for word. The content, in turn, can be phrased in a virtually unlimited number of ways. Consider the simple traffic light example above. The witness testified on direct examination that the light was green for the southbound traffic, but his statement to the police was just the opposite. It is your theory that the light was red for the southbound traffic. Rather than repeat the direct testimony, the cross-examiner can recommit the witness as follows:

Question: Mr. Kaye, the light was red for the southbound traffic, correct?

Answer: No, that is not true.

Question: Mr. Kaye, I would like to show you the statement that you gave to Officer Berkeley.

You can now proceed to impeach the witness with his own prior statement. This format for recommittal avoids repetition of the direct testimony. It also allows you to describe your own case in affirmative language: "Wasn't the light red for the southbound traffic?" Since your case rests on the proposition that the light was red for the southbound traffic, you profit from stating that affirmative fact as often as possible.

5.6.2.2   Validate the prior statement

Once the witness has been recommitted, the next step in the impeachment is to validate the prior statement. Validation's initial purpose is to establish that the witness actually made the impeaching statement. Depending upon the case's circumstances, you can employ further validation to accredit or demonstrate the accuracy of the earlier statement, as opposed to the witness's direct testimony.

The fact that a witness has made a prior inconsistent statement is impeaching, but it does not necessarily demonstrate that the witness's current testimony is false or inaccurate. After all, the earlier statement may have been erroneous and the direct testimony correct. It is therefore frequently advantageous to show that the first statement was made under circumstances that make it the more accurate of the two. Since the two statements are by definition mutually exclusive, there is a natural syllogism: If the earlier statement is true, then the current testimony must be wrong. Thus, the "accreditation" of the prior inconsistent statement can further detract from the witness's credibility. Of course, no witness is likely to admit that her pre-arbitration statement was more accurate than her sworn testimony. It is therefore usually necessary to accredit the prior statement through the use of circumstantial evidence. Many indicia of accuracy can be attributed to the witness's earlier statement, including importance, duty, and proximity in time.

Accreditation through importance. You can accredit a witness's earlier statement by showing that the witness had an important reason to be accurate when giving it.

Accreditation through duty. You can also accredit prior statement by showing that the witness was under either a legal or business duty to be accurate. The most common example of a statement given under a legal duty is prior testimony, either at trial, arbitration, or deposition.

Accreditation through proximity in time. Because human memory inevitably fades, you can accredit an earlier statement because it was given closer in time to the events being described. You can employ this source of accreditation whether the impeaching material is a written statement, a deposition transcript, or a business document.

5.6.2.3   Confront the witness with the prior statement

The final stage of impeachment is to confront the witness with the prior statement. The purpose of this confrontation is to make the witness admit that he indeed made the earlier statement; recall that it is the fact of the prior inconsistency that is admissible as impeachment. This confrontation need not be "confrontational." It is frequently sufficient merely to require the witness to admit making the impeaching statement since most impeachment is based upon a witness's forgetfulness, confusion, or embellishment. You should reserve hostility or accusation for those rare situations when you can prove the witness to be lying or acting out of some other ill motive. To be effective, accomplish the confrontation in a clear and concise manner that leaves the witness no room for evasion or argument. The classic approach is simply to read the witness's own words.

You should follow two cardinal rules in confronting a witness with a prior inconsistent statement:

1.   Read the statement to the witness—do not ask the witness to read the statement aloud.

2.   Do not ask the witness to explain the inconsistency.

Both of these rules are applications of basic principles of cross-examination.

5.6.2.4   Ethical concerns

Two primary ethical issues arise in the context of impeaching a witness through the use of a prior inconsistent statement. The first issue, attempting to use the statement for a purpose other than that for which it was admitted.

It is unethical for a lawyer to "allude to any matter which the lawyer does not reasonably believe is . . . supported by admissible evidence."[16] Once an arbitrator has ruled that certain evidence is admissible only for a limited purpose, it is inadmissible on those issues for which it has been excluded. In light of a limiting instruction, no lawyer can reasonably believe otherwise. Thus, it is unethical to allude to a purely impeaching statement as though it had been admitted as substantive evidence.

The second ethical issue in impeachment involves the admonition not to allow a witness to explain the inconsistency. Assuming that there may be a perfectly reasonable explanation for the discrepancy between two statements, is it ethical to prevent the witness from explaining? The answer lies in the fact that it is not truly possible for a cross-examiner to prevent a witness from providing an explanation. It will always be possible for opposing counsel to ask the witness to elaborate during redirect examination. No admissible evidence can ultimately be excluded as the result of cross-examination tactics. Thus, the most the cross-examiner can accomplish will be to prevent the witness from explaining an inconsistency during cross-examination. As an advocate, it is the cross-examiner's task to present the evidence that is favorable to his or her client; the very purpose of redirect is to allow the other side to fill in gaps, remedy errors, and correct misperceptions. Thus, leaving potential explanations to redirect is perfectly permissible under the adversary system.

5.6.3   Other prior inconsistencies

In addition to prior inconsistent statements, witnesses may also be impeached through the use of prior omissions or silence, and on the basis of prior inconsistent actions.

5.6.3.1   Impeachment by omission or silence

Impeachment by omission generally follows the same theory as impeachment with a prior inconsistent statement. The witness's current testimony is rendered less credible because when she told the same story earlier it did not contain facts that she now claims are true. In essence, the impeachment is saying, "Do not believe this witness, because she is adding facts to her story." In other words, "If those things are true, why didn't you say them before?" To be impeaching, the witness's prior omission must be inconsistent with the current testimony. A prior omission is not impeaching, or even admissible, if it occurred in circumstances that do not render it incompatible with the witness's testimony at the hearing. Circumstances that create the necessary discontinuity between omission and testimony include opportunity, duty, and natural inclination.

---

16. Rule 3.4(e), ABA Model Rules of Professional Conduct.

5.6.3.2   Prior inconsistent actions

Finally, a witness may be impeached on the basis of prior inconsistent actions. The witness's current testimony is rendered less credible by pointing out that she did not act in conformity with her own story on some previous occasion: "If what you are saying now is true, why did you act inconsistently in the past?" Unlike impeachment through prior inconsistent statements or omissions, no elaborate set-up is necessary for the use of prior inconsistent actions. It is sufficient simply to put the questions to the witness.

5.6.4   Character and "characteristic" impeachment

"Character impeachment" refers to the use of some inherent trait or particular characteristic of the witness, essentially unrelated to the case at hand, to render the testimony less credible. The thrust of the impeachment is to show that the witness, for some demonstrable reason, is simply not trustworthy.

The most common forms of "characteristic impeachment" include:

➢ conviction of a crime,

➢ past untruthfulness and other bad acts, and

➢ impaired perception or recollection.

5.6.4.1   Conviction of a crime

A witness may be impeached on the basis of his or her past conviction of certain crimes. While the specifics vary from state to state, under the Federal Rules of Evidence a conviction is admissible for impeachment only if the crime:

1. was punishable by death or imprisonment in excess of one year under the law under which the witness was convicted, and the arbitrator determines that the probative value of admitting this evidence outweighs its prejudicial effect to the defendant, or

2. involved dishonesty or false statement, regardless of the punishment. In addition, Fed. R. Evid. 609(b),(d) provides that convictions generally may not be used if they are more than ten years old, and that juvenile adjudications are inadmissible under most circumstances.

5.6.4.2   Past untruthfulness and other bad acts

We have discussed the rules governing impeachment on the basis of a criminal conviction. What if a witness's untruthfulness or bad acts that were not the subject of a conviction? The Federal Rules of Evidence strike a balance by allowing the impeachment of witnesses on the basis of specific instances of past misconduct, apart from criminal convictions, only if they are probative of untruthfulness. Thus, a witness can be impeached with evidence that he has lied on a specific previous occasion but not on the basis of previous violence. Moreover, an arbitrator has discretion to exclude evidence even of past untruthfulness. Finally, incidents of prior untruthfulness may not be proven by extrinsic evidence. The cross-examiner is stuck with the witness's answer. Impeachment on the basis of past untruthfulness is therefore a very tricky matter. You must be certain that the witness will "own up" to the charge, since you will be unable to prove it otherwise.

5.6.4.3 Impaired perception or recollection

A witness can also be impeached on the basis of inability to perceive or recall events. Perception can be adversely affected by a wide variety of circumstances. The witness may have been distracted at the time of the events, or his vision may have been obscured. The witness may have been sleepy, frightened, or intoxicated. The witness may have poor eyesight or may suffer from some other sensory deficit. Any of these, or similar, facts can be used to impeach the credibility of a witness's testimony. As with so much else in cross-examination, this form of impeachment is usually most effective when counsel refrains from asking the ultimate question.

5.6.5 "Case data" impeachment

Some facts are impeaching only within the circumstances of a particular case. They would be innocuous, or perhaps even helpful, in any other context. The most common forms of case data impeachment are based on the witness's personal interest, motive, and bias or prejudice.

5.6.5.1 Personal interest

A witness who is personally interested in a case's outcome may be inclined to testify with less than absolute candor. Whether consciously or subconsciously, it is a well-recognized human tendency to shape one's recollection in the direction of the desired outcome. Impeachment on the basis of personal interest is therefore geared to take advantage of this phenomenon, by pointing out just how the witness stands to gain or lose as a consequence of the case's resolution. The technique may be applied to both party and non-party witnesses.

5.6.5.2 Motive

A witness's testimony may be affected by a motive other than financial interest. The witness may have a professional stake in the issues being litigated or may have some other reason to prefer one outcome to another.

5.6.5.3   Bias or prejudice

Bias and prejudice generally refer to a witness's relationship to one of the parties. A witness may be well-disposed, or ill-inclined, toward either the plaintiff or the defendant. Sadly, some witnesses harbor prejudices against entire groups of people. Bias in favor of a party is often the consequence of friendship or affinity.

5.7   Expert Testimony

Expert witnesses can be helpful in a wide variety of arbitration cases. They can be used in commercial cases to interpret complex financial data, in tort cases to explain the nature of injuries, and in legal or medical malpractice cases to establish the relevant standard of care. Given the extraordinarily broad scope of expert testimony, and its extreme potential for influencing the judgment of the trier of fact, certain rules have developed regarding the permissible use, extent, and nature of expert testimony.[17]

5.7.1 Standards for expert testimony

5.7.1.1   Areas of expertise

Fed. R. Evid. 702 provides that expert opinions are admissible where the expert's "scientific, technical, or other specialized knowledge will assist the arbitrator to understand the evidence or to determine a fact in issue."

Thus, there are two threshold questions:

➤ Does the witness possess sufficient scientific, technical, or other specialized knowledge?

➤ Will that knowledge be helpful to the trier of fact?

5.7.1.2   Scope of opinion

Fed. R. Evid. 704 provides that expert testimony, if otherwise admissible, "is not objectionable because it embraces an ultimate issue to be decided by the trier of fact." Arbitrators vary on their interpretations of the "ultimate issue" rule. Some arbitrators will allow experts to opine on virtually any issue, including such case-breakers as whether the claimant in a personal injury case was contributorily negligent or whether the respondent in a securities case violated exchange rules. Many arbitrators would also allow an expert in a medical malpractice case to testify that the failure to order the tests fell below the standard

---

17. This section is a condensed adaptation of Lubet, *supra,* chapter 3, note 1 at 171–213, which contains an in-depth treatment of expert testimony, including detailed examples.

of care generally exercised by practitioners in the relevant community. Most arbitrators, though not all, would balk at permitting the expert to testify that the defendant's conduct constituted malpractice, on the theory that malpractice is a legal conclusion that is not within a medical expert's specialized knowledge.

5.7.1.3   Basis for opinion

Under Fed R. Evid. 705, an expert can testify to her opinion with or without explaining the facts or data on which the opinion is based. In theory, then, an expert, once qualified, could simply state her opinion on direct examination, leaving the cross-examiner to search for its basis. In practice, of course, this approach is rarely followed, since the expert's opinion could hardly be persuasive until its foundation is explained. The rule's practical effect is to allow the witness to state her opinion at the   examination's beginning, followed by explication, rather than having to set forth all of the data at the outset.

5.7.2   The expert's overview

Just as a lawyer cannot succeed without developing a comprehensive case theory, neither will an expert be effective without a viable, articulated theory. An expert's theory is an overview or summary of the expert's entire position. The theory must not only state a conclusion, but must also explain, in commonsense terms, why the expert is correct.

➤ Why did she settle upon a certain methodology?

➤ Why did she review particular data?

➤ Why is her approach reliable?

➤ Why is the opposing expert wrong?

In other words, the expert witness must tell a coherent story that provides the arbitrator with reasons for accepting—and it is hoped—internalizing the expert's point of view.

The need for a theory is especially true in cases involving "dueling experts." It is common for each of the opposing parties in litigation to retain its own expert witnesses. The arbitrator is then faced with the task of sorting through the opinion testimony and choosing which witness to believe. It is likely that both experts will be amply qualified, and it is unlikely that either will make a glaring error in his analysis or commit an unpardonable faux pas in testimony. The arbitrator will therefore be inclined to credit the expert whose theory is most believable.

The importance of theory extends to all types of expert testimony. It is necessary, but not sufficient, for your expert to be thorough, exacting, highly regarded, incisive, honorable, and well prepared. Her testimony will suffer if she cannot support her opinion with commonsense reasons.

5.7.3   Offering expert testimony

There is a certain logic to most experts' direct examinations. While the particulars and details will vary, there are a limited number of possible patterns for organizing the testimony. It is absolutely necessary, for example, to qualify the expert before proceeding to her opinion. The following is a broad outline that can accommodate the specifics of most expert testimony.

5.7.3.1   Introduction and foreshadowing

The first step is to introduce the expert and explain her involvement in the case. Since expert testimony is qualitatively different from lay testimony, it is a good idea to clarify its purposes for the arbitrator so that he will understand what he is about to hear. Ask the witness how she came to be retained and why she is present at the arbitration. Be aware that the technical requirements of presenting expert testimony often result in a considerable time gap between the witness's introduction and the substantive high points of her testimony. Thus, it is generally desirable to foreshadow the expert's opinion at the very outset of the examination.

5.7.3.2   Qualification

To testify as an expert, a witness must be qualified by reason of knowledge, skill, experience, training or education.[18] This is a threshold question for the arbitrator, who must determine whether the witness is qualified before permitting her to give opinion testimony. The qualification of the witness, then, is a necessary predicate for all of the testimony to follow. Take care to qualify the expert in a manner that is both technically adequate and persuasive.

Technical requirements. The technical requirements for qualifying an expert witness are straightforward. It is usually adequate to show that the witness possesses some specialized skill or knowledge, acquired through appropriate experience or education, and that the witness is able to apply that skill or knowledge in a manner relevant to the case's issues.

There are of course, many other areas of basic qualification beyond education and experience. Examples include:

---

18. Rule 702, Federal Rules of Evidence.

- ➢ specialized training
- ➢ teaching and lecturing positions
- ➢ publications
- ➢ professional memberships
- ➢ continuing education courses
- ➢ licenses and certifications
- ➢ consulting experience
- ➢ awards and other professional honors

The establishment of basic qualifications, however, should not be counsel's entire objective. It is equally, if not more important to go on to qualify the witness as persuasively as possible.

Persuasive qualification. The technical qualification of an expert merely allows the witness to testify in the form of an opinion. Counsel's ultimate goal is to ensure that the arbitrator accepts the opinion. Persuasive qualification is particularly important in cases involving competing experts, since their relative qualifications may be one basis on which the arbitrator will decide which expert to believe. It is a mistake, however, to think that more qualifications are necessarily more persuasive. An endless repetition of degrees, publications, awards, and appointments may easily overload any arbitrator's ability, not to mention desire, to pay careful attention to the witness. It is often better to introduce the witness's detailed resumé or curriculum vitae and to use the qualification portion of the actual examination to focus in on several salient points. Experience is often more impressive than academic background. So, for example, a medical expert may be more impressive if she has actually practiced in the applicable specialty, as opposed to possessing knowledge that is strictly theoretical. When presenting such a witness, then, counsel should typically dwell on her experience, pointing out details such as the number of procedures she has performed, the hospitals where she is on staff, and the numbers of other physicians who have consulted her. Finally, it is frequently effective to emphasize areas of qualification where you know the opposing expert to be lacking. If your expert has a superior academic background, use the direct examination to point out why academic training is important. If your expert holds a certification that the opposing expert lacks, have her explain how difficult it is to become certified.

Tender the witness. It is customary with some arbitrators that, once qualifications have been concluded, the attorney must then tender the witness as an expert in a specified field. The purpose of the tender is to inform the arbitrator that qualification has been completed and to give opposing counsel an opportunity either to conduct a *voir dire* of the witness or to object to the tender. Opposing counsel may use voir dire examination to attempt to develop deficiencies in the witness's qualifications. This is done in the midst of the direct examination for two reasons. First, if it can be shown that the witness truly is not qualified, there will be no reason to continue the direct examination. Second, objections raised as a consequence of *voir dire* can often be cured through additional direct examination. Note that *voir dire* on qualifications, as with all *voir dire* examination, should be limited to the eventual admissibility of the expert testimony and should not be used as a substitute for cross-examination regarding weight or credibility.

5.7.3.3   Opinion and theory

Statement of opinion. Under Fed. R. Evid. 705, once the witness has been qualified and accepted as an expert, she may proceed to express her opinion without additional foundation. In other words, she may state her conclusions without first detailing the nature or extent of her background work or investigation. Many attorneys believe strongly in taking advantage of the "opinion first" provision. Expert testimony tends to be long, arcane, and boring. The intricate details of an expert's preparation are unlikely to be interesting or even particularly understandable. They will be even less captivating if they are offered in a void, without any advance notice of where the details are leading or why they are being explained. On the other hand, a clear statement of the expert's conclusion can provide the context for the balance of the explanatory testimony.

Statement of theory. Once the expert has stated her opinion, she should immediately provide the underlying theory. The theory should furnish the nexus between the expert's conclusion and the data used to support the conclusion. The examination should follow this pattern:

1. here is my opinion;

2. here are the principles that support my opinion; and

3. here is what I did to reach my final conclusion.

5.7.3.4   Explanation and support

Having stated and supported her theory choice, the expert can now go on to detail the nature of her investigation and calculations. The arbitrator cannot be expected to take the expert at her word, so she must establish the validity and accuracy of her data and assumptions.

Data. You should ask the expert how she chose and obtained her data. She should also explain why her information is reliable. The expert should also describe any tests or computations she performed. The treatment of underlying data is one of the trickiest aspects of expert testimony. Many experts will be in love with their data, and they will be anxious to lay them out in excruciating detail. Unfortunately, most arbitrators have little tolerance for lengthy descriptions of enigmatic scientific or technical processes. Counsel must therefore strike a balance, eliciting a sufficiently detailed treatment of the data to persuade the arbitrator of its reliability but stopping well short of the point where his or her attention span is exhausted. It is not sufficient for the expert simply to relate the data's nature. Rather, the expert should go on to explain how and why the data supports her conclusions.

Assumptions. Most experts rely upon assumptions. It is not necessary for your expert to explain or outline every hypothesis she used, but she should note and support the more important assumptions.

5.7.3.5 Theory differentiation

In cases involving dueling experts, there will also be competing theories. Properly prepared and presented, each expert will attempt to persuade the arbitrator to accept her theory. It can be particularly effective, therefore, to ask your expert to comment on the opposing expert's work. This technique can be called theory differentiation, because it is most convincing when your expert discusses the shortcomings of the opposition theory. The timing of theory differentiation can be important. As the claimant's counsel you will generally want to establish your expert's theory first, before proceeding to criticize the respondent's expert. Depending upon the case's circumstances, you might even want to forego theory differentiation entirely during your case in chief, and to recall your expert for that purpose on rebuttal. The respondent, on the other hand, should address the claimant's expert's theory at some point during the direct examination of the respondent's own expert. This can be done early in the examination (to rebut the claimant's expert immediately and forcefully), or it can be done toward the end of the testimony (to allow the respondent's expert to build up the positive aspects of her own theory before turning her attention to the opposition).

Conclusion. An expert's direct examination should conclude with a powerful restatement of her most important conclusions.

5.7.4 Persuasive expert examination techniques

You can use most of the direct examination methods discussed in section 5.4 with expert witnesses. In addition, you can apply the following techniques to expert testimony.

5.7.4.1 Humanize the expert witness

Many experts from scientific, technical, or financial backgrounds may appear aloof, intimidating, or even arrogant to those who do not share their special expertise. It is therefore important to humanize these witnesses as much as possible during the direct examination. If the arbitrator permits, bring out personal and family background information, and allow the witness to talk about more than strictly professional matters.

5.7.4.2   Use plain language

Virtually every field of expertise creates its own technical and shorthand terms, and expert witnesses will be inclined to use arcane and jargon-laden speech without even thinking about it. It is counsel's job to guide the witness away from the use of jargon and into the realm of everyday speech. There are three basic means to accomplish this task. First, thoroughly prepare the witness to avoid complex, professional terms. Spend sufficient time with the witness before the hearing so that she will understand the importance of plain, simple language. Second, ask for an explanation when your witness lapses into her native tongue, whether it is finance-talk, engineeringese, or accounting-speak. Do this gently and without reprimand or condescension. Finally, and possibly most importantly, avoid the temptation to adopt the expert's word choices. Too many lawyers, perhaps out of a desire to appear erudite or knowledgeable, tend to examine expert witnesses using the expert's own jargon. Such examinations can take on the characteristics of a private, and completely inaccessible, conversation between the lawyer and the witness. It is bad enough when lawyers use legalese; it is worse when they embrace the private speech of another profession.

Avoid narrative. Most arbitrators will allow expert witnesses considerable freedom to testify in narrative fashion. Many lawyers believe they should take advantage of this leeway, and they therefore encourage their experts to present their testimony in long, uninterrupted segments. This is a mistake. Long narratives are hard to follow and hard to digest. Anyone who ever sat through a long lecture or speech should understand how difficult it is to pay attention to a speaker for an extended period of time. This is particularly true of expert testimony, which often concentrates on complex or intricate details. Allowing an expert to testify in a long, unbroken stretch invites arbitrator inattention.

Use examples and analogies. Many complex ideas can be explained with examples, analogies, or metaphors. Encourage expert witnesses to clarify their testimony through the use of such imagery. You should not take the witness by surprise with a request for an example or metaphor. The time to consider using these explanatory tools is during preparation, not on the spur of the moment in the midst of direct examination.

Use visual aids. The use of visual aids can enhance the direct examination of almost every expert. Since expert testimony may be hard to follow, it can be particularly effective to portray the expert's concepts with charts, graphs, drawings, or models. A physician, for example, can bring testimony to life with an anatomical model or a series of colored overlays. Financial experts should illustrate their testimony with graphs or tables. An architectural or engineering expert should use diagrams or scale models. The possibilities for visual aids are practically infinite, limited only by counsel's (and the expert's) imagination.

Use internal summaries. Because of the potential length and complexity of expert testimony, it is important to use internal summaries to highlight significant points. Ask the expert to point out the relevance of the most critical steps in her analysis. Request that she summarize the implications of her findings. Think of the expert's testimony as containing a series of steps or elements. At the conclusion of each step the expert should explain how she got there, why it is important, and where she is going next.

Use the concept of consensus. Almost every field of expertise contains several contending schools of thought. Opposing experts often arrive at different opinions because they approach the issues from distinct perspectives. For example, a strict Freudian psychologist is likely to evaluate a patient's mental state quite differently from a Gestalt therapist. Your expert's testimony is more persuasive if you can show that she has presented the mainstream view, as opposed to a novel or untested theory. Do this by stressing such credentials as university affiliation, professional certification, or other indicia of widespread acceptance.

5.7.4.3   Use leading questions when called for

Two recurrent problems in expert testimony are boredom and pomposity. Many experts are inclined to drone on at length over unimportant details. Others present themselves with an air of excessive self-importance, especially in the course of presenting their credentials. You can resolve both of these difficulties through the judicious use of leading questions. You can often cut through a welter of details by using a leading question to direct the witness to the heart of the matter. You can also use leading questions to make the witness seem less haughty or pretentious.

5.7.4.4   Encourage powerful language

There is a tradition in many technical fields of hedging or qualifying the language in which conclusions are expressed. This makes great sense when discussing research, since one's results are always subject to further inquiry. Thus, professionals commonly use terms such as "to the best of my knowledge . . ." or "according to current indications . . ." or "as far as we can tell . . ." While this language is meant to convey open-mindedness as opposed to uncertainty, it can be fatal to a witness's testimony in an arbitration. To prevent inadvertent miscommunication, prepare your expert witnesses to testify in straightforward, unequivocal terms. Caution experts to avoid language that unintentionally qualifies or hedges their results, using instead wording that emphasizes accuracy and certainty.

5.7.4.5   Use enumeration

Audiences most often pay closer attention to information presented in numbered lists. Therefore, encourage expert witnesses to introduce concepts in terms of factors or considerations, rather than launching into extended explanations.

5.7.4.6   Consider inoculation

Expert witnesses may be open to several distinct lines of cross-examination. Counsel should therefore consider conducting a certain amount of explanatory or defensive direct examination to "inoculate" the witness against cross-examination on such matters as the payment of fees, the use of presumptions, reliance on secondary sources, and the like.

5.7.4.7   Do not stretch the witness's expertise

It may be tempting to try to stretch a witness's expertise, either as a cost-saving measure or in an effort to enlarge the scope of her testimony. Both of these undertakings are misguided. It is risky, bordering upon unethical, to seek to have an expert testify outside of her legitimate field.

5.7.5   Cross-examination of expert witnesses

You can adapt most of the basic approaches to cross-examination discussed in section 5.5 to expert testimony. In addition, there are certain tools you can use primarily or most effectively with expert witnesses.

Research, as much as technique, lies at the heart of expert witness cross-examination. You cannot conduct an adequate cross-examination without first thoroughly investigating all of the technical aspects of the expected testimony. It is often said that you cannot cross-examine an expert without first becoming an expert yourself. Moreover, your research should extend beyond the expert's subject matter area and into the witness's own professional background. Counsel should read everything the witness has ever published, and should also attempt to obtain transcripts of prior trial and/or deposition testimony. There is nothing so effective as impeaching an expert with his or her own prior assertions. Other fruitful areas of investigation may include the expert's professional affiliations, past clients, governmental positions, and the like. Don't view such research as an effort to dig up dirt (although once in a lifetime you might stumble across something juicy), but rather as an attempt to obtain a rounded picture of the expert's professional status. Many experts have become closely associated with certain positions over the course of their careers, and this knowledge can be very helpful in shaping a cross-examination.

The research necessary to cross-examine an expert witness will necessarily vary considerably from case to case. The balance of this section is therefore limited to techniques that can be applied to expert witnesses in general.

5.7.5.1   Challenge the witness's credentials

An expert witness's credentials are subject to challenge either on *voir dire* or during cross-examination. You can use *voir dire* to object to the legal sufficiency of the expert's qualifications, while cross-examination is the time to attack their weight.

Voir dire on credentials. Once the proponent of an expert has concluded the qualification segment of the direct examination, opposing counsel is entitled to conduct a *voir dire* of the witness. A *voir dire* examination temporarily suspends the direct so that the opponent of the proffered evidence can inquire as to its evidentiary sufficiency. With regard to the qualification of experts, this means that opposing counsel can interrupt the direct examination to conduct a mini-cross limited to the witness's credentials. It is frequently an uphill battle to persuade an arbitrator that a proffered witness should not be allowed to testify as an expert. Arbitrators often respond to such objections by ruling that they go only to the weight, and not the admissibility, of the expert testimony. Nonetheless, it is possible to disqualify an expert through the use of *voir dire*. You can disqualify purported experts by establishing the remoteness of their credentials, the inapplicability of their specialties, the lack of general acceptance of their purported expertise, or the unreliability of their data.

5.7.5.2   Cross-examination on credentials

The arbitrator's ruling that a witness may testify as an expert means only that the witness possesses sufficient credentials to pass the evidentiary threshold. It still may be possible to diminish the weight of the witness's qualifications during cross-examination. There are three basic methods for discrediting the value of a witness's credentials.

Limit the scope of the witness's expertise. Although a witness may be well-qualified in a certain area or sub-specialty, it may be possible to recast the case's issues in such a way as to place them beyond the witness's competence.

Stress missing credentials. An expert witness may be minimally qualified to testify, but still lack certain important certifications, degrees, or licenses.

Contrast your expert's credentials. It is most effective to contrast an adverse witness's missing credentials with your own expert's superior qualifications. You can contrast experts' credentials on the basis of certification and other matters. It is fair game, for example, to point out your own witness's greater or more specific experience, your witness's teaching or publication record, or any other disparity that will enhance your expert and diminish the opposition. Note, however, that all of the rules of basic cross-examination apply here as well. You must be satisfied to elicit the fact of the contrasting qualifications. It will do you little good to argue with the opposing witness, or to try to extract a concession that her credentials are inadequate.

5.7.5.3   Obtain favorable information

You can often obtain favorable concessions from the opposing party's expert witness. As with all cross-examination, it is usually wisest to attempt to extract such information near the examination's beginning. Needless to say, one must be positive of the answers before launching into this sort of cross-examination. In general, the helpful material available from opposing experts will fall into the following categories.

Affirm your own expert. Even experts who ultimately disagree may have many shared understandings. You may therefore contribute to your own expert's accreditation by asking the opposing expert to acknowledge the reliability of your expert's data, the validity of her assumptions, or the caliber or her credentials.

Elicit areas of agreement. In addition, it may be possible to elicit concessions from the opposing expert that go to the case's merits. The adverse expert may, for example, be willing to agree with several of your major premises, even while disagreeing with your ultimate conclusion.

Criticize the opposing party's conduct. Finally, it may be possible to draw from an opposing expert significant criticism of his or her own party's conduct. Though the expert reached a final conclusion favorable to the party, she may be unwilling to approve of all of their underlying actions.

5.7.5.4   Use of learned treatises

One form of cross-examination unique to expert witnesses is impeachment through the use of a learned treatise. Under Fed. R. Evid. 803(18), you can confront an expert witness with statements contained in *"published treatises, periodicals, or pamphlets on a subject of history, medicine, or other science or art,"* so long as they are established as reliable authority. Contrary to the belief of many lawyers, judges, and arbitrators, it is not necessary to establish that the witness has relied on the particular treatise, or even that the witness acknowledge it as authoritative. Under the Federal Rules, the reliability of a learned treatise may be established either by admission of the witness, or by other expert testimony, or by judicial notice. Once the reliability of the treatise is confirmed, the impeachment may proceed in one of two ways. You may read a passage from the treatise into evidence without asking the expert any questions about it; the Federal Rules require only that the passage be called to the witness's attention. The more traditional approach is to ask the witness whether she agrees with the particular quotation. At that point the witness must either accede or disagree. If she accepts the statement, your job is done. If she disagrees, you may argue later that she is out of step with recognized authority. Finally, note that this rule allows an excerpt from a learned treatise to be read into evidence, but that the treatise itself may not be received as an exhibit.

5.7.5.5   Challenge the witness's impartiality

Expert witnesses are supposed to be independent analysts, not advocates. The worst thing you can say about an expert witness is that he or she has altered her opinion to fit a party's needs. Accordingly, it can be very effective to cross-examine an expert on the issue of bias, if the material is there to be exploited. Cross-examination on bias falls into three basic categories.

Fees. In arbitration, it is generally productive to cross-examine an expert concerning her fee only in fairly limited circumstances. For example, it may demonstrate bias if the fee is extraordinarily large. Similarly, it may be evidence of something less than objectivity if the witness has a large unpaid fee outstanding at the time that she testifies.

Relationship with party or counsel. An expert's relationship with a party or with counsel may also indicate a lack of impartiality. Some witnesses seem to work hand in glove with certain law firms, testifying to similar conclusions in case after case. While such an ongoing relationship is not proof of bias, it does suggest that the association may have been sustained for a reason. It can become questionable when a firm has engaged the same expert on a dozen or more occasions. While there may be a perfectly innocent explanation for this constancy, it is certainly reasonable to bring it out on cross-examination. The same analysis pertains to witnesses who have testified repeatedly for the same party, although retained by different law firms. Finally, some cases may involve testimony by in-house experts, perhaps a company's own accountant or engineer. In most cases, such experts are susceptible to no more suggestion of bias than would be any other employee. In some situations, however, the in-house expert's own judgment will be at issue in the case. An accountant, for example, may have failed to see that a debt was under collateralized; an engineer may not have not have foreseen the need for more exacting tolerances. In these circumstances the cross-examination must bring out the witness's personal stake in the litigation's outcome.

Positional bias. With or without regard to past retention, some experts seem wedded to certain professional, scientific, or intellectual positions. Experts frequently come to testify only for plaintiffs or only for defendants. Others reach only one of a range of conclusions. Some psychiatrists, for example, have been known never to find a single criminal defendant to be sane or competent. Where they exist, these rigidly held positional biases can be exploited effectively on cross-examination.

Preparation for cross-examination on bias. You should prepare diligently before cross examining an expert witness on bias. Partiality is a serious accusation to make against an expert witness, and you should not level it without a good faith basis for the claim. Cross-examination is not the time to make random inquiries, much less baseless charges, as to lack of objectivity or independence.

5.7.5.6   Point out omissions

An expert may be vulnerable on cross-examination if he or she has failed to conduct essential tests or procedures, or neglected to consider all significant factors. The question of neglected tests or experiments will depend upon each case's unique factors. Other sorts of omissions are more commonplace. Witnesses are frequently asked to evaluate the validity or accuracy of other experts' work. A consulting pathologist, for example, might be asked to re-evaluate the protocol of an autopsy conducted by the local medical examiner. No matter how prominent, a "second-opinion" witness can almost always be undermined by the fact that he or she did not conduct the primary investigation:

5.7.5.7   Substitute information

Change assumptions. As we have seen, almost all experts must use assumptions of one sort or another in the course of formulating their opinions. An expert's assumptions, however, might be unrealistic, unreliable, or unreasonably favorable to the retaining party. It can be extremely effective, therefore, to ask the witness to alter an assumption, substituting one that you believe to be more in keeping with the case's evidence.

Vary the facts. A related technique is to vary the facts upon which the expert has relied, or to suggest additional facts.

Degree of certainty. It is also possible to challenge an expert's degree of certainty by suggesting alternative scenarios or explanations.

Dependence on other testimony. An expert witness's opinion often depends upon facts to be established by other witnesses. Thus, the expert's testimony may be undermined, not by anything you ask the expert directly, but rather by challenging its factual underpinnings during the cross-examination of the fact witnesses. It is necessary only to obtain the expert's concession that the other witness's facts are essential to her opinion.

5.7.5.8   Challenge technique or theory

The most difficult, though frequently the most tempting, form of expert cross-examination is to challenge the witness's method, theory, or logic. It is possible, but extremely unlikely, that an expert will agree that she made a mistake or that her reasoning is faulty. In most cases you have little to gain by confronting an expert with any but the most glaring flaws, since that will only afford her an opportunity to explain. It is usually far more effective to use your own expert to point out the opposition's errors, and then to draw your own conclusions during closing argument.

5.7.6   Ethics of expert examination

Fees. Unlike other witnesses who can be reimbursed only for expenses, an expert may be paid a fee for preparing and testifying in an arbitration.[19] There is authority that an expert's fee must be "reasonable," but that limit has never been well-defined. In any event, an unreasonably large fee would render the witness extremely vulnerable on cross-examination. A more salient restriction is the rule against paying contingent fees to expert witnesses, which is found in virtually every jurisdiction. Contingent fees are prohibited because they provide the expert with an unacceptable incentive to tailor her opinion to the interests of the party retaining her.

Influencing testimony. Lawyers typically retain experts for one reason only: to help win the case. Given the expense involved, there may be a temptation to view the expert as simply another team member you can enlist to provide whatever advocacy is necessary. Thus, it is not unknown for attorneys to attempt to persuade experts to alter the content of their opinions. This is wrong. It is no more acceptable to attempt to persuade an expert to change her opinion than it would be to try to convince a percipient witness to change his account of the facts. The entire system of expert testimony rests upon the assumption that experts are independent of the retaining attorneys. Counsel must take care not to attempt or appear to use the fee relationship to corrupt the expert's autonomy.[20] As with other witnesses, it is not unethical to assist an expert to prepare for trial. You may inform the witness of the questions you will ask on direct examination, and may alert the witness to potential cross-examination. You can advise an expert to use powerful language, to avoid jargon, to use analogies, to refrain from long narratives, or to use other means that will help her convey her opinion accurately.

Disclosure and discovery. In arbitration, where discovery is usually the exception and not the rule, testifying experts are generally subject to discovery. Purely consulting experts, other than in extreme circumstances, are usually exempt from discovery. The question that arises is whether it is ethical to attempt to interview

---

19. Rule 3.4(b) comment 3, ABA Model Rules of Professional Conduct.
20. Rule 3.4(b), ABA Model Rules of Professional Conduct.

an opposing party's consulting witness, from whom formal discovery is not available. Needless to say, you must take care to determine the relevant jurisdiction's law on this issue—or better yet, obtain the arbitrator's permission—before attempting to interview the opposition's non-testifying expert.

5.8   Foundations for Evidence

Before any evidence can be considered in a court trial, there must be some basis for believing it to be relevant and admissible. This basis is called the foundation for the evidence. In an arbitration hearing in which the parties have agreed that rules of evidence do not apply, the requirement for foundations is relaxed. But even in some of those hearings, where a piece of evidence is critical to the case, the arbitrator will require counsel to lay a proper foundation. Where the arbitration agreement or the rules of a court mandatory arbitration program require the application of the rules of evidence, you of course will be required to comply with them and lay appropriate foundations for the evidence you wish to introduce. Moreover, many foundations, whether or not required by the arbitrator, will enhance the reliability or credibility of your evidence. This section will prepare you for those situations where foundations are necessary or well-advised.[21]

5.8.1   Evidentiary foundations—general

5.8.1.1   Components of foundation

There are three aspects to virtually all evidentiary foundations. To be received, evidence must be shown to be: (1) relevant, (2) authentic, and (3) admissible under the applicable laws of evidence. While the discrete elements of foundation will differ according to the evidence's nature and purpose for which it is offered, these three considerations must always apply.

Relevance. Relevance defines the relationship between the proffered evidence and some fact that is at issue in the case. Evidence will not be admitted simply because it is interesting or imaginative. Rather, it must be shown to be probative in the sense that it makes some disputed fact either more or less likely. The relevance of most evidence is generally made apparent from the case's context, but occasionally it must be demonstrated by the establishment of foundational facts.

Authenticity. The concept of authenticity refers to the requirement of proof that the evidence actually is what the proponent claims it to be. In other words,

---

21. This section is a condensed adaptation of Lubet, *supra* chapter 3, note 1 at 261–333, which contains and in-depth treatment of the subject of evidentiary foundations, including detailed examples.

Cross-examination. Foundation requirements apply equally during cross and direct examinations. You must lay testimonial foundations on cross-examination for personal knowledge, voice identification, hearsay exceptions, and in every other circumstance where a foundation would be necessary on direct examination. In addition, there are special foundations for certain cross-examination techniques such as impeachment by past omission or prior inconsistent statement. It is also often necessary to use cross-examination to lay the foundation for the admission of exhibits. Defense counsel in particular can avoid the need to call adverse witnesses by attempting to establish foundations for her own exhibits while cross-examining a plaintiff's witness.

5.8.2   Foundations for testimonial evidence

5.8.2.1   Personal knowledge

Witnesses are expected to testify from personal knowledge. The most common sort of personal knowledge is direct sensory perception: information gained through sight, hearing, touch, taste, and smell. Witnesses may also have personal knowledge of more subjective information, such as their own intentions or emotions, or the reputation of another person.

5.8.2.2   Special foundations for certain testimonial evidence

While most testimony requires a showing of personal knowledge, certain testimony calls for the establishment of additional foundational facts.

Conversations. Witnesses are often called upon to testify to conversations between two or more parties. To authenticate the conversation, and thereby allow opposing counsel to conduct a meaningful cross-examination, testimony concerning a conversation generally must be supported by a foundation establishing the date, time, and place of the conversation, as well as the persons present at the time.

Telephone conversations and voice identification. The foundation for a telephone conversation includes the additional element of voice identification, or of a reasonable circumstantial substitute. In the absence of a basis for voice identification, you can use circumstantial evidence as the foundation for a telephone conversation. You can authenticate a telephone call placed by the witness by showing that the call was made to a listed number. You can use numerous other circumstances to authenticate telephone conversations. Subsequent verifying events can form the foundation for telephone calls either placed or received by the witness.

Prior identification. Under Fed. R. Evid. 801 (d)(1)(C), a witness may testify to his or her previous, out-of-court identification of an individual. This rule evidence is not to be admitted until there has been a threshold showing that it is "the real thing." The arbitrator decides whether an item of evidence has been sufficiently authenticated, and the criteria vary according to the nature of the evidence involved. The requirement of authenticity is not limited to tangible objects. It also applies to certain testimonial evidence. For example, a witness generally may not testify to a telephone conversation without first establishing her basis for recognizing the voice of the person on the other end of the line. That is, the identity of the other speaker must be authenticated.

Specific admissibility. While evidence will generally be received if it is relevant and authentic, the law of evidence contains a host of specific provisions that govern the admissibility of various sorts of proof. In many cases you can admit evidence only following the establishment of foundational facts. Most exceptions to the hearsay rule, for example, require such a preliminary showing. Similarly, you must lay a foundation for the admission of evidence of habit or routine practice, or for the admission of evidence of subsequent remedial measures.

5.8.2.3   Establishing foundations

Single or multiple witnesses. The most common approach to the establishment of a foundation is simply to call a witness who can provide the necessary facts, and then to offer the evidence after that testimony has been elicited. Some foundations cannot be laid by a single witness. In such cases counsel must establish separate parts of the foundation from each of several witnesses before offering the evidence.

Conditional admissibility. It is not always possible to complete a foundation during the testimony of a single witness. However, a witness who is responsible for part of the foundation will in many cases have other important information concerning the exhibit. Fed. R. Evid. 104(b) embodies the doctrine of conditional admissibility, which allows the temporary or conditional admission of the evidence based upon counsel's representation that the foundation will be completed through the testimony of a subsequent witness.

Using adverse witnesses. You can often simplify potentially complex foundations through the use of adverse examination. In a case where executed contracts have been exchanged through the mail, for example, it may be extremely difficult for one party to authenticate the other party's signature. You can completely alleviate this problem, however, simply by calling the opposing party as an adverse witness.

applies to both criminal and civil matters. The foundation for this testimony is that the witness made the out-of-court identification after perceiving the person identified.

Habit and routine. To lay the foundation for evidence of habit or routine practice, you must call a witness with personal knowledge of the regular conduct of the person or organization involved. Furthermore, counsel must establish that the asserted conduct was, in fact, of a consistently repeated nature. You can accomplish this through proof of either extended observation or of the existence of a formal policy or procedure.

Individual habit. The most common foundation for an individual's habit is through evidence of a pattern of conduct repeated over a substantial period of time. The alleged habit must be clearly differentiated from independent or distinct activities.

Business practice. You can establish the routine practice of a business or organization either through direct observation or through evidence of an existing policy or practice.

5.8.2.4   Foundations for hearsay statements

The rule against hearsay excludes evidence of out-of-court statements if offered to prove the truth of the matter asserted.[22] Numerous exceptions to the hearsay rule allow for the admissibility of out-of-court statements, provided you establish the necessary foundation. The foundations for those exceptions that apply primarily to testimonial evidence are discussed below. A later section discusses foundations for hearsay exceptions that typically apply to documentary evidence. The following sub-sections are an abbreviated outline of the foundations for the various hearsay exceptions for those arbitrations in which the hearsay rule applies.

Party admissions. Out-of-court statements made by the opposing party are generally admissible to prove the truth of the matter asserted. In brief, the opposing party's previous statements are admissible if:

1. the witness can authenticate the statement,

2. the statement was made by the party against whom it is offered, and

3   the statement is adverse to the opposing party's claim or defense.

The party admission exception also applies to statements made by the agent or employee of a party.[23] In such situations there are two additional elements to the foundation:

---

22. Fed. R. Evid. 801.
23. Fed. R. Evid. 801(d)(2)(D).

1. the declarant was an agent or employee of the opposing party at the time that the statement was made, and

2. the statement concerned a matter that was within the scope of the agency or employment.

Present sense impression. The present sense impression exception allows the admission of out-of-court statements "describing or explaining an event or condition made while the declarant was perceiving the event or condition, or immediately thereafter." [24] The foundation for the exception is that:

1. the declarant perceived an event,

2. the declarant described the event, and

3. the description was given while the event occurred or immediately afterwards.

A witness may testify as to her own present-sense impression statement or that of another. It is generally necessary for the statement to have been made in the witness's presence, in order to satisfy the foundational requirement of personal knowledge.

Excited utterance. The excited utterance exception is quite similar to the present sense impression rule. It allows for the admission of hearsay when the statement relates "to a startling event or condition made while the declarant was under the stress of excitement caused by the event or condition." [25] The foundation for an excited utterance is that:

1. the declarant perceived a startling event or experienced a stressful condition,

2. the declarant made a statement concerning the event or condition, and

3. the statement was made while the declarant was under the stress of the event or condition.

As with present sense impressions, a witness may testify to her own excited utterance or to that of another.

State of mind. "State of mind" provides one of the broadest exceptions to the hearsay rule. It allows the admission of statements concerning the declarant's "then existing state of mind emotion, sensation, or physical condition (such as intent, plan, motive, design, mental feeling, pain, and bodily health)."[26] The foundation for this exception is that the statement actually be probative of the declarant's mental, emotional, or physical condition. You can best demonstrate this by the statement's content. Apart from the statement's content, there is no

---

24. Fed. R. Evid. 803(1).
25. Fed. R. Evid. 803(2).
26. Fed. R. Evid Rule 803(3).

special foundation for the state of mind exception. However, the witness still must establish the statement's authenticity by testifying as to:

1. when the statement was made,

2. where it was made,

3. who was present, and

4. what was said.

Note also that the statement must have been made during the existence of the mental, emotional, or physical condition that it describes.

Statement made for medical treatment. The foundation for this exception is that the declarant made a statement for the purpose of obtaining medical care or diagnosis. The statement may be made to a physician, medical worker, or other person, so long as its purpose was to obtain or facilitate treatment. The statement may include medical history or past symptoms, but it must relate to a present bodily condition.[27]

Dying declaration. The hearsay exception for dying declarations requires the following foundation: (1) The declarant made a statement while believing that his or her death was imminent, (2) concerning what he or she believed to be the cause of death.[28]

5.8.3   Foundations for documents

In addition to the usual issues of relevance and authenticity, the foundation for a document usually includes two other elements. Because documents invariably contain out-of-court statements, they must be brought within an exception or exclusion to the hearsay rule. Additionally, the proffer must comply with the "best evidence" or "original writing" rule.

5.8.3.1   Authentication

The authentication of documents typically requires proof of authorship or origin and, depending on the issues in the case, may also call for proof of transmission or receipt.

Handwriting and signature. You can authenticate the signature or other handwriting on a document through a variety of means. A witness may recognize a signature based on past observation or may authenticate it on the basis of circumstantial evidence. Other possibilities include expert testimony and in-arbitration comparison by the arbitrator. A witness may always authenticate her own handwriting or signature. A witness may also authenticate the handwriting of another if sufficient familiarity can be shown.

---

27. Fed. R. Evid. 803(4).
28. Fed. R. Evid. 804(b)(2).

Circumstantial evidence of authorship or origin. Many documents are printed or typewritten and do not contain signatures or other handwriting. Unless such a document is somehow uniquely marked, you will need to authenticate it via circumstantial evidence. Such evidence can be in the form of a letterhead, seal, or stamp, or it can be provided by the context of the case.

Mailing or transmission. A document's admissibility will often depend upon its receipt by, or at least transmission to, another party. This is an authenticity issue since the document is made admissible only by its status as one that was actually or constructively received. In other words, proof of mailing authenticates the document as truly having been sent to the other party. Mailing can be proven either directly or through evidence of a routine business practice. Direct proof of mailing can be given in a single sentence: "I placed the document in an envelope, with the correct address, and I deposited it in the United States mail with sufficient postage."

The original writing (best evidence) rule. The so-called "best evidence" rule was once a formidable obstacle to the admission of documentary evidence. In its harshest form, the rule excluded all but the original copy of any writing, unless certain conditions could be met. Today, the rule has been softened considerably, and now allows for the easy admissibility of most copies.[29] The rule constitutes an authenticity requirement, but its terms are sufficiently unique so as to call for separate treatment. The essence of the "original writing" rule is that a document's content can be proved only by producing the original, or an acceptable duplicate, unless the original is lost, destroyed, or unavailable. Because under most circumstances a duplicate is admissible on the same terms as the original, the rule now operates primarily to exclude testimonial summaries or paraphrases of a document. Note also that the original writing rule applies only to proof of a document's content, not its signing, acknowledgment, or delivery.

5.8.3.2   Foundations for hearsay exceptions

The offer of a document inevitably sets the hearsay bell ringing in opposing counsel's mind. While writings may be admissible for non-hearsay purposes, such as proof of notice or acceptance, they are frequently submitted precisely to prove that their contents are true. Various exceptions allow the use of such documents, each requiring its own foundation. The following section discusses the more common exceptions.

Business records. Business records can include ledgers, accounts, calendar entries, memoranda, notices, reports, statements, and similar writings. All of these documents constitute hearsay if they are offered to prove that their contents are

---

29. Fed. R. Evid. 1002.

true. Under the Federal Rules, the records of any regularly conducted activity are admissible if they:

1. were made at or near the time of a transaction or event;

2. were made by, or based on information transmitted from, a person with knowledge;

3. were kept in the course of a regularly conducted business activity; and

4. were made as a part of the regular practice of that business activity.[30]

Computer print-outs. Computer-generated print-outs have become a common form of business record. In the early days of computing it was considered necessary to prove that computer data entry and retrieval systems were reliable means for storing information, but this is no longer the case. The Federal Rules specifically recognize "data compilations" as an acceptable form of business record. Thus, the foundation for a computer print-out is basically the same as that for any other business record.

Summaries. Many business records or other sets of data are so lengthy and ponderous that they cannot be conveniently produced in an arbitration hearing. Even if you could produce them, they may be so extensive and technical as to be impenetrable. In these circumstances it is permissible to substitute a "chart, summary, or calculation" that fairly presents the relevant information in a usable or understandable form.[31] The foundation for such a summary includes these elements:

1. the original documents are so voluminous that they cannot be conveniently examined in the arbitration hearing;

2. the witness has examined the original data;

3. the witness is qualified to produce a summary of the information; and

4. the exhibit is a fair and accurate summary of the underlying information.

Recorded recollection. A witness's written notes, or other recorded recollection, may be admitted into evidence only if the witness, at the time of trial, "has insufficient recollection to enable him to testify fully and accurately." [32] The foundation for this exception to the hearsay rule comprises these elements:

1. the witness once had personal knowledge of the relevant facts or events;

2. the witness cannot currently recall the events fully and accurately;

3. the witness previously made an accurate memorandum or record of the facts; and

---

30. Fed. R. Evid. 803(6).
31. Fed. R. Evid. 1006.
32. Fed. R. Evid. 803(5).

4.   at a time when the events were fresh in the witness's memory.

Public records. There are a number of hearsay exceptions that allow for the admissibility of public records, statistics, and reports. Such records are generally admissible if they were made by a public office or agency and they set forth:

1.   the activities of the office or agency; or

2.   matters observed pursuant to a duty imposed by law; or

3.   in limited circumstances, certain investigative findings; or

4.   officially required records of vital statistics.[33]

Because most government records are "self-authenticating," it is not usually necessary to call a witness to testify to their authenticity.[34]

Absence of public record. You can also use public records to show the non-occurrence of events. The foundation for this evidence is:

1.   that such events, occurrences or matters were regularly recorded in some form;

2.   by a public office or agency; and

3.   that a diligent search has failed to disclose a record of a particular fact or event.

This evidence may be offered by certification from the appropriate official, in which case no witness needs to be called. The evidence may also be offered via testimony.

Previous testimony. The transcript of a person's previous testimony may be admitted into evidence if:

1.   the declarant is currently "unavailable" to testify;

2.   the testimony was given under oath in court or at a deposition;

3.   the party against whom the testimony is being offered had a fair opportunity to examine the witness when the testimony was originally given.[35]

Note that this exception allows the admission of the earlier statement as a substitute for current testimony. Unlike the use of prior testimony for impeachment, there is no requirement that the previous testimony be inconsistent with the declarant's current position. Under the Federal Rule, a witness can be deemed "unavailable" for a variety of reasons, including:

1.   the valid assertion of a privilege;

2.   persistent refusal to testify;

---

33. Fed. R. Evid. 803(8) and 803(9).
34. Fed. R. Evid. 902.
35. Fed. R. Evid. 804(b)(1)·

3. inability to attend the hearing due to illness;

4. death;

5. failure of memory; or

6. absence from the hearing notwithstanding the efforts of the proponent of the testimony to procure attendance.

Party admissions. The party admission exception applies to documents as well as to oral statements. A party admission can be contained in a letter, report, memorandum, journal, progress chart, or virtually any other form of writing. Once the exhibit has been authenticated, the only remaining foundation is that it was made or adopted by a party against whom it is being offered, or by an agent, servant, or employee of such a party.

5.8.4 Foundations for real and demonstrative evidence

5.8.4.1   Real evidence/tangible objects

You must show real evidence to be relevant and authentic. The relevance of real evidence is typically established by the case's context, and often requires no additional attention when it comes to laying the foundation. Authenticity, on the other hand, must always be carefully established as it is the fact of authenticity that qualifies the exhibit as real evidence. In many cases you can show the authenticity of real evidence by a witness's recognition of the exhibit. Other cases require a more detailed and complex foundation, usually referred to as chain of custody.

Recognition of the exhibit. You can establish the authenticity of real evidence through the testimony of a witness who is able to recognize the item in question. Many objects can be identified by virtue of their unique features. Others may have been given some identifying mark in anticipation of litigation. In either case, the witness must testify (1) that she was familiar with the object at the time of the underlying events, and (2) that she is able to recognize the exhibit in the arbitration hearing as that very same object.

Chain of custody. A chain of custody establishes the location, handling, and care of an object between the time of its recovery and the time of trial. A chain of custody must be shown whenever (1) the exhibit is not uniquely recognizable and has not been marked, or (2) when the exhibit's physical properties are in issue.

5.8.4.2   Photography and other recording devices

Photographs and other recordings bridge the gap between real and demonstrative evidence. While a visual or audio recording of any sort is, strictly speaking, an illustration of a past event, its capacity to portray a scene with accuracy is so great that many arbitrators treat photographs and other recordings as tantamount to real evidence.

Still photographs. The basic foundation for the admission of a still photograph is that it "fairly and accurately" portrays the scene shown. In all but a few situations it is not necessary to call the photographer to testify. It is generally possible to introduce a photograph through the testimony of any witness who is familiar with the scene as it appeared at a relevant time.

Motion pictures and videotapes. As with photographs, a motion picture or videotape may be authenticated by any witness who is familiar with the scene or scenes portrayed. It is necessary to call the operator of the camera only if special features were employed, or if the date of the filming is in issue. A more difficult problem arises in the case of remote taping, when no person actually observed the events as they were recorded. In these circumstances the foundation must include additional information on operating procedures as well as the equipment's condition.

Audiotapes. The foundation for an audiotape recording depends upon the purpose for which it is offered. A tape recording that is submitted merely as a voice exemplar, for example, may be authenticated by any witness who is able to recognize the voices of the various speakers. The same holds true for recorded music, as might be offered in a copyright dispute. Any witness who is familiar with the material recorded can lay the foundation.

X-rays and similar images. X-rays and other images produced by means such as computerized axial tomography (CAT scans) and magnetic resonance imaging (MRIs), are essentially photographs of the body's internal composition. To lay a foundation a physician or other qualified person must testify that an X-ray, CAT scan, or MRI is a fair representation of the internal structure of a given patient's body. The identifying marks on the film (which allow the physician to recognize which X-ray belongs to which patient) are usually considered to be business records of the hospital or clinic.

5.8.4.3   Demonstrative evidence

Demonstrative evidence is used to illustrate, clarify, or explain other testimony or real evidence. When such an exhibit is sufficiently accurate or probative, it may be admitted into evidence.

Admissible demonstrative evidence. The foundation for a map, chart, blueprint, or other diagram is essentially the same as that for a photograph. The witness must be familiar with the scene, location, or structure as it appeared at a relevant time, and must testify that the exhibit constitutes a fair representation. Additional foundation is necessary if the exhibit is drawn to scale.

Models and reproductions. The foundation for a model or reproduction is similar to that for a photograph. The witness must be familiar with the real location or object and must testify to the model's accuracy. Issues regarding scale are identical to those concerning maps and diagrams.

Illustrative aids. Exhibits that are insufficiently accurate to be allowed into evidence may often still be used for illustrative purposes. The foundation includes a witness's testimony that the exhibit will assist in explaining her testimony, as well as a general explanation or description of the inaccuracy.

5.9   Shaping the Process Toward a Favorable Decision

In a trial held in court, you should constantly be concerned with preserving the record for appeal. You must ensure that the record is complete, accurate, and that all appeal issues have been preserved in the record by rulings on appropriate motions or objections. In an arbitration, you are not usually concerned with preserving the record for appeal. Rather, much like a sculptor, you are actively engaged in shaping the process toward a favorable decision by the arbitrator. In the words of Michelangelo, "The more the marble wastes, the more the statue grows." This process-shaping consists of several activities including:

1. introducing all pertinent evidence;

2. proper handling and use of exhibits;

3. using exhibits persuasively;

4. ensuring complete and accurate transcripts;

5. making and responding to offers of proof; and

6. making and responding to objections.

5.9.1   Introducing all pertinent evidence

One would hardly think of maintaining a checking account at a bank without keeping a record or log of deposits and withdrawals. Such a record allows one to know the account's balance (i.e., usable or available cash), what was deposited and when, what was withdrawn and when, what checks and deposits eventually cleared (i.e., actually admitted or acknowledged by the bank), and which were rejected for insufficient funds or other reasons. So too, one would hardly consider arbitrating a case, particularly one involving multiple documentary and other physical exhibits, without keeping a log or record of which exhibits were admitted (i.e., cleared), or rejected (for insufficient foundation, irrelevancy, etc.), or offered and withdrawn. During the course of an arbitration hearing, keep an exhibit log for the exhibits that you seek to introduce into evidence and also, separately, for the exhibits that the other party or parties seek to introduce. An example of an exhibit log format appears in the figure below:

Date	Ex. No.	Des-script.	ID	Offer'd	Offer of Proof	Admit	Ruling Reserve	Reason	Party Admit. Angst.

Several advantages flow from using an exhibit log during an arbitration. In arbitrations involving many exhibits and/or having several parties and lasting several days, it is essential that you or an assistant keep an exhibit log, if for no other reason than to assist you in determining what evidence you may properly refer to in your closing argument to the arbitrator. Evidence not admitted cannot be the basis of any assertion in closing argument. Thus, a quick reference to the exhibit log can give you an instant picture of the parameters governing the scope of your argument. A log of your opponent's exhibits can assist you in making valid objections that the evidence being argued to the arbitrator (or later in connection with post-hearing motions) was not admitted into evidence (or was withdrawn, as the case may be). Clearly, the exhibit log can also be a helpful reference source when you begin to refamiliarize yourself with the evidence to draft any required post-hearing briefs. In performing such task, it may serve as your overview document indicating which piece of evidence was rejected, when it was rejected during the course of the hearing (pointing you to the appropriate date of transcript), and the reason the arbitrator rejected the evidence. It may also help you sift out what may appear, at least initially, to be a significant evidentiary issue to raise in a motion for reconsideration of an arbitration award. Also, exhibit logs of your and your opponents' exhibits will quickly refresh your memory as to which items of your evidence were received despite your opponent's objections and why. It will also serve as a handy exhibit index when you are reviewing the hearing record when preparing a response to a motion for reconsideration of an arbitration award.

In addition to these post close-of-evidence uses, the exhibit log also benefits its users during the course of an arbitration hearing. One horrible nightmare seems to be recurrent among arbitration advocates. That is the one where a trial lawyer inadvertently omits introducing into evidence one otherwise *de minimis* or insignificant document which, however, is critical to the proof of an essential element of his or her claim or defense. In such an instance, even small things may turn the scale. Not only can this be terribly embarrassing if it actually occurs, but it can provide the basis for a potential legal malpractice action by the client. An exhibit log can help prevent this from happening. You can review the log prior to the case's close and prior to the close of all the evidence so you can satisfy yourself that you have offered and admitted all critical pieces of evidence (or that there is a record of rejection). Also, you can review the exhibit log to ensure that all your objections to your opponent's exhibits have been clearly and comprehensively stated to the arbitrator. Sometimes additional reasons for your objecting to certain evidence will become apparent to you during the hearing's course and you may wish to have the arbitrator reconsider his previous ruling in light of your additional basis for objections. If you do not overdo it, most arbitrators will accommodate you in this regard, particularly with respect to a critical piece of evidence whose admissibility is in dispute.

Occasionally, an arbitrator will reserve ruling on the admissibility of certain exhibits, pending counsel's providing additional evidence "connecting them up" and establishing their relevance or materiality. The exhibit log assists by reminding you which exhibits require a ruling by the arbitrator. Also, arbitrators often reject evidence, but, on request, permit counsel to make an offer of proof immediately or later during the course of proceedings. The exhibit log can remind you which exhibits need to be supported by an offer of proof prior to the close of the evidence.

In summary, keeping an exhibit log can ensure that an accurate record of the hearing evidence is properly preserved for later use, either in connection with briefing on post-hearing briefs, a motion for reconsideration of the award, or a court challenge to the award.

5.9.2   Proper handling and use of exhibits

5.9.2.1   The role of exhibits

Exhibits are the tangible objects, documents, photographs, video and audio tapes, and other items offered for the arbitrator's consideration. Exhibits are the only form, apart from the testimony of witnesses, in which evidence can be received. In an arbitration hearing, exhibits enhance or supplement the testimony of the witnesses. Exhibits can make information clearer, more concrete, more understandable, and more reliable. The sub-sections immediately following will discuss the general procedures for handling, introducing, and using exhibits.[36]

5.9.2.2   Types of exhibits

While the categories tend to overlap and the lines cannot be drawn with precision, it is often helpful to think of exhibits as falling into these three categories:

1. real evidence,

2. demonstrative evidence, and

3. documentary evidence.

Real evidence. The term "real evidence" generally refers to tangible objects that played an actual role in the events at issue in the hearing. Photographs, while obviously different from tangible objects, are so close to reality that they are also often treated as real evidence. Documents such as contracts, memoranda, letters, and other primary writings can also be considered real evidence, although the special rules that apply to out-of-court writings generally make it more convenient to treat "documentary evidence" as a separate category.

Demonstrative evidence. The term "demonstrative evidence" refers to exhibits that did not play an actual role in the events underlying the case, but that are used to illustrate or clarify a witness's testimony. As compared with real evidence—which exists by virtue of the activities of the parties and witnesses in the case—demonstrative evidence is lawyer-generated. Demonstrative evidence can take the form of models, graphs, diagrams, charts, drawings, or any other objects that can explain or illustrate issues in the case.

Documentary evidence. "Documentary evidence" is the term used to refer to virtually all writings, including letters, contracts, leases, memoranda, reports, and business records. Written documents, almost by definition, contain out-of-court statements, and they are typically offered because their contents are relevant to the case. Thus, most documents face hearsay hurdles in a way that real and demonstrative exhibits do not. Tangible objects are admitted into evidence because of what they are; documentary exhibits are admitted because of what they say. The value of documentary evidence cannot be overstated. Intrinsic writings can provide proof of past events in a way that mere testimony cannot.

---

36. This subsection is a condensed adaptation of Lubet, *supra* chapter 3, note 1 at 287–299.

5.9.2.3 Prehearing procedures for the admission of exhibits

In arbitration, the arbitrator can deal with and rule on contested exhibits in a preliminary hearing. You can file motions "in limine" (Latin for "at the threshold") prior to the hearing and to obtain the exclusion of evidence or to seek a ruling declaring certain evidence admissible. The arbitrator can rule on such motions in a preliminary hearing. Stipulations and requests to admit can also be worked out in such hearing.

5.9.2.4 Offering exhibits during the hearing

Whether they consist of real, demonstrative, or documentary evidence, there is one basic protocol for offering exhibits at an arbitration hearing. Although the details vary somewhat from one arbitration setting to another, the following steps form a nearly universal procedure.

Mark the exhibit for identification. Mark every exhibit for identification before you offer it into evidence, or even refer to it in the course of a hearing. Marking the exhibit identifies it for the record so it will be uniquely recognizable to anyone who later reads a transcript of the proceedings. References to "this letter" or "the first broken fastener" may be understood in the hearing room, but they will be meaningless to a reader of the transcript. "Respondent's exhibit three," on the other hand, can mean only one thing, assuming that the exhibit was appropriately marked and identified.

Exhibits are generally marked sequentially and further identified according to the designation of the party who has first offered them. Thus, the exhibits in a two-party arbitration will be called claimant's exhibit one, claimant's exhibit two, respondent's exhibit one, respondent's exhibit two, and so forth. In multiple-party hearings it is necessary to identify an exhibit by the name, and not merely the designation, of the party who offers it. Accordingly, you will see references to claimant Bennett exhibit one, or Weber exhibit two. In some arbitrations, claimants may be expected to use sequential numbers for their exhibits, while respondents are requested to use letters. Hence, claimant's exhibit one and respondent's exhibit A. The details of the particular marking system are unimportant, so long as it clearly indicates which exhibit is which.

The "mark" itself usually takes the form of a sticker placed directly on the object or document. Stickers are available in a variety of forms. Many attorneys use color-coded sets that already contain the words plaintiff or defendant, with a space left blank for the number assigned to each exhibit. The procedure of requiring the court reporter to mark exhibits has been widely replaced by the attorneys' premarking of exhibits, either at a prehearing conference or in the attorney's office. The term "marked for identification" means the exhibit has been marked, and can be referred to in arbitration, but has not yet been admitted into evidence. Exhibits that have been marked for identification may be shown to witnesses and may be the subject of limited examinations for the purpose of establishing a foundation. Many arbitrators shun "for identification" notation as redundant. All exhibits need to be marked, and the record will show which have been allowed into evidence even in the absence of a special inscription.

Identify the exhibit for opposing counsel. Exhibits should be identified for opposing counsel before they are shown to the witness. This may be done by referring to the exhibit number or by indicating its designation in the prehearing order if one has been prepared. Most arbitrators will expect you to hand or display the exhibit to opposing counsel before proceeding.

Examine the witness on the exhibit's foundation. Having identified the exhibit, you may now proceed to lay the foundation for its admission.

Show the exhibit to the witness. The first step is to show the exhibit to the witness. This is typically done by handing it to the witness. If the exhibit is something as large as a life-sized model or an enlarged photograph, you may point to it and direct the witness's attention. In either case you should announce for the record what you are doing, using a shorthand description of the exhibit and its identification number:

> Counsel: Ms. Bowman, I am handing you respondent's exhibit eleven, which is a letter dated July 26.

The description ensures clarity and must be scrupulously neutral. While you are allowed to ask a leading question on preliminary matters, you are not allowed to begin arguing your case under the pretext of laying a foundation. Thus, you cannot say:

> Counsel: Ms. Bowman, I am handing you respondent's exhibit eleven, which is the letter in which the claimant agreed to provide repair service at no additional cost.

Identify the exhibit. Next, have the witness identify the exhibit. The witness should state the basis for her familiarity with the exhibit, and then describe it in some detail:

> Question: Have you ever seen claimant's exhibit seven before?
>
> Answer: Yes, I have seen it many times.
>
> Question: What is claimant's exhibit seven?
>
> Answer: It is a piece of the stationery that I received when my order was delivered from Quickset Printing.
>
> Question: How is it that you recognize it?
>
> Answer: I remember how it looked when I took it out of the box.

Complete the foundation. In some situations, particularly those involving real evidence, the identification of the exhibit will provide a sufficient foundation for admission. In other circumstances the foundation will be much more elaborate, perhaps calling for chain of custody or the establishment of a hearsay exception. These and other foundations for the introduction of real, demonstrative, and documentary evidence are discussed in sections 5.8.3 and 5.8.4.

Offer the exhibit into evidence. Once you have completed the foundation, you can offer the exhibit into evidence. Jurisdictions vary as to the formality with which this must be done. In the simplest version:

Counsel: Mr. Arbitrator, we offer claimant's exhibit three.

In any case, the exhibit must be shown to the arbitrator, who will then ask opposing counsel if there are any objections to its admission. If there are no objections, the arbitrator will receive the exhibit into evidence.

Use of the exhibit. Once an exhibit has been admitted into evidence, a witness can testify about its contents and you can use it to illustrate or amplify a witness's testimony. Tangible objects can be used in demonstrations.

5.9.3   Persuasive use of exhibits

For suggestions on ways to use exhibits persuasively in arbitration *see* section 5.11.2.

5.9.4   Ensure completeness and accuracy of transcripts

First, being courteous to your court reporter will be a small investment that will reap huge returns. The court reporter is part of the team—consisting of yourself, your opposing counsel, and the arbitrator—whose goal is to produce a complete and accurate record of events as they occur in the hearing. As a team, you as members must help the court reporter achieve that end.

5.9.4.1   Ensure completeness of transcripts

To help the court reporter make a complete record you should:

Avoid speaking when the court reporter is changing paper, or marking exhibits, etc. Important statements may be unintentionally excluded.

Avoid speaking simultaneously with other lawyers or the arbitrator—or worse yet—speaking before the witness is finished answering your questions. Even the most competent court reporters are sometimes unable to completely unscramble simultaneous oral statements and may omit important information from the subsequently prepared transcript.

When appropriate, describe off-the-record trial events on the record, and invite other counsel and the arbitrator to clarify your characterization as they perceived the events or discussion.

Orally (and accurately) describe witnesses' gestures if it is in your client's interest to do so. For example, if a witness for the opposing party uses body language or gestures indicating an evasive, untruthful, disrespectful attitude, you might want to describe this particular conduct, diplomatically, for the record.

Be aware that witnesses are not usually experienced at telling their stories in anything other than everyday language. Sometimes witnesses omit details because they assume they are communicating only with people in the hearing room. Thus, you must carefully fill in the omitted details through additional questioning. For example, a witness who describes the distance between herself and the point of impact of two automobiles as the distance between the witness and the rear wall of the hearing room would have little meaning to a reader of the transcript who was not present in the hearing room.

Clearly indicate when you wish to go off the record and when you wish to resume on the record.

5.9.4.2   Ensure accuracy of transcripts

Aside from ensuring there will be no unintentional omissions in the testimony, colloquies, or oral descriptions on the record, you must ensure that the printed words ultimately appearing in the transcript will be accurate. Ways in which you can help the court reporter produce an accurate transcript are:

Take reasonable measures to acquaint the court reporter with the nature of the case. Provide the court reporter with a pleading or order which contains an accurate case caption and the names of counsel. If the pleading briefly encapsulates the nature of the case and stage of the proceedings, all the better. Physically identify the counsel and other persons (parties, interpreters, paralegals, etc.) present at the hearing.

If the proceedings will involve complicated terminology and spellings (medical malpractice case, environmental case, etc.), provide the court reporter with a glossary of terms in advance of the proceeding. Also, it is helpful to provide the court reporter with passages from text of complicated material or list of case citations you will be referring to in an oral argument before the arbitrator.

Avoid blocking the court reporter's view of the witness when questioning the witness in the hearing room.

If a witness uses a figure of speech or metaphor ("the claimant appeared to be 'knee high to a grasshopper' next to the towering respondent"), *make sure through questioning that the record is clarified regarding the height of the claimant in relation to the respondent.*

Make sure the spellings of persons' names, street names, etc., are accurate. Ask the witness to spell them if they are the least bit unusual. However, be certain the witness knows how to spell them. It can be embarrassing for the witness and you, if he or she boggles the spelling. If you know the witness may be unprepared or unable to spell the word, ask for a stipulation of the correct spelling of the word.

Ensure that dates and times are accurately stated and that there is no ambiguity about which date or time the witness is testifying.

Be careful how a witness uses pronouns (he, she, they, etc.). Sometimes, when testifying about several individuals, it is necessary that the witness minimize the use of pronouns, and attribute conduct to named persons.

Refer to documents by exhibit number (and page) at all times.

Markings made by witnesses on a photograph or large demonstrative exhibit should be designated by the witness's initials or designated number or letter.

5.9.5   Making and responding to offers of proof

An offer of proof consists of actual evidence (testimonial or documentary) or of a statement of counsel (oral or written) demonstrating what evidence counsel would be seeking to introduce into evidence if the arbitrator had not sustained opposing counsel's objection. You should make an offer of proof only after the arbitrator has sustained an objection to a question propounded to a witness or to a proffered exhibit. Its primary purpose is to preserve the record so that if judicial review becomes necessary, the reviewing court will have a basis for determining whether or not the arbitrator properly excluded the evidence. A secondary purpose of an offer of proof is to serve as a basis for having the arbitrator reconsider the ruling excluding the evidence.

You may make an offer of proof in one of two forms: formally, through tendering the actual evidence (testimony or exhibits); or informally, through statement of counsel on the record. A formal offer of proof is generally preferred. Usually, testimonial offers of proof occur during your direct examination of a witness. You should make clear on the record which portion of the offer of proof is being submitted.

In responding to an offer of proof, you should state your objections clearly and succinctly on the record. This will generally be effective in dissuading the arbitrator from reversing the original ruling sustaining your objection to the area of questioning or exhibit(s), as the case may be. You should also seek to cross-examine the witness who is the vehicle for a testimonial offer of proof to further buttress your position that the arbitrator has properly excluded the evidence. Opposing counsel should state all grounds for his/her opposition to the proposed evidence when the offer of proof is made, or the grounds not stated may be deemed waived on later court review.

5.9.6   Making and responding to objections.

Objections are the means by which evidentiary disputes are raised and resolved.[37] You may make objections to an attorney's questions, to a witness's testimony, to the introduction or use of exhibits, to a lawyer's demeanor or behavior, and even to the arbitrator's conduct. In many arbitrations, particularly those that are not recorded by a court reporter, very few objections are made. However, in some arbitrations which involve high stakes and a court reporter is present, and/or where the parties have agreed that rules of evidence will apply, objections are made as if proceeding in court. Because objections are really the exception and not the rule in most arbitrations, this subsection is intentionally abbreviated, consisting of only a short list of common objections and some ethical considerations related to objections.

5.9.6.1   Form-of-question objections

The following list and descriptions of some common objections (and responses) is intended only as a reference or guide, not as a substitute for a thorough knowledge of evidence and procedure.

Leading question. A leading question suggests or contains its own answer. Leading questions are objectionable on direct examination. They are permitted on cross-examination. See Fed. R. Evid. 611.

> *Responses.* The question is preliminary, foundational, directing the witness's attention, or refreshing the witness's recollection. The witness is very old, very young, infirm, adverse, or hostile. Leading questions can most often be rephrased in non-leading form.

Compound question. A compound question contains two separate inquiries that are not necessarily susceptible of a single answer. For example, "Wasn't the fire engine driving in the left lane and flashing its lights?"

> *Responses.* Dual inquiries are permissible if the question seeks to establish a relationship between two facts or events. For example, "Didn't he move forward and then reach into his pocket?" Other than to establish

---

37. This subsection is a condensed and adapted version of Lubet, *supra* chapter 3, note 1, at 215–259 which contains and in-depth treatment of objections, including detailed examples.

a relationship, compound questions are objectionable and should be rephrased.

Vague question. A question is vague if it is incomprehensible, or incomplete, or if any answer will necessarily be ambiguous. For example, the question "When do you leave your house in the morning?" is vague, since it does not specify the day of the week to which it refers.

> *Responses.* A question is not vague if the arbitrator understands it. Many arbitrators will ask the witness whether he or she understands the question. Unless the precise wording is important, it is often easiest to rephrase a vague question.

Argumentative question. An argumentative question asks the witness to accept the examiner's summary, inference or conclusion, rather than to agree with the existence (or non-existence) of a fact. Questions can be made more or less argumentative depending upon the examiner's tone of voice.

> *Responses.* Treat the objection as a relevance issue, and explain its probative value to the arbitrator: "Mr. Arbitrator, it goes to prove . . ." It will not be persuasive to say, "Mr. Arbitrator, I am not arguing." It might be persuasive to explain the non-argumentative point that you are trying to make. Alternatively, make no response, but wait to see if the arbitrator thinks that the question is argumentative. If so, rephrase the question.

Narratives. Witnesses are required to testify in the form of question and answer. This requirement ensures that opposing counsel will have the opportunity to frame objections to questions before the answer is given. A narrative answer is one which proceeds at some length in the absence of questions. An answer that is more than a few sentences long can usually be classified as a narrative. A narrative question is one that calls for a narrative answer, such as, "Tell us everything that you did on July 14." Objections can be made both to narrative questions and narrative answers.

> *Responses.* The best response is usually to ask another question that will break up the narrative. Note that expert witnesses are often allowed to testify in narrative fashion, since technical explanations cannot be given easily in question-and-answer format. Even then, however, it is usually more persuasive to interject questions to break up big answers.

Asked and answered. An attorney is not entitled to repeat questions and answers. Once an inquiry has been "asked and answered," further repetition is objectionable.

> *Responses.* If the question has not been asked and answered, counsel can point out to the arbitrator the manner in which it differs from the earlier testimony. Otherwise, it is best to rephrase the question so as to vary the exact information sought.

Assuming facts not in evidence. A question, usually on cross-examination, is objectionable if it includes as a predicate a statement of fact that has not been proven. The reason for this objection is that the question is unfair; it cannot be answered without conceding the unproven assumption.

> *Responses.* A question assumes facts not in evidence only when it uses an introductory predicate as the basis for another inquiry. Simple, one-part cross-examination questions do not need to be based upon facts that are already in evidence. For example, it would be proper to ask a witness "Didn't you leave home late that morning?" whether or not there had already been evidence as to the time of the witness's departure. As a consequence of misunderstanding this distinction, "facts not in evidence" objections are often erroneously made to perfectly good cross-examination questions. If the objection is well taken, most questions can easily be divided in two.

Non-responsive answers. It was once hornbook law that only the attorney who asked the question could object to a non-responsive answer. The theory for this limitation was that opposing counsel had no valid objection so long as the content of the answer complied with the rules of evidence. The more modern view is that opposing counsel can object if all, or some part, of an answer is unresponsive to the question, since counsel is entitled to insist that the examination proceed in question-and-answer format.

> *Responses.* Ask another question.

5.9.6.2   Substantive objections

Hearsay objections. Depending upon the agreed procedures, hearsay may or may not be admissible in arbitrations. The Federal Rules of Evidence define hearsay as "[A] statement, other than one made by the declarant while testifying at the trial or hearing, offered in evidence to prove the truth of the matter asserted." Fed. R. Evid. 801(c). Thus, any out-of-arbitration statement, including the witness's own previous statement, is potentially hearsay. Whenever a witness testifies, or is asked to testify, about what she or someone else said in the past, the statement should be subjected to hearsay analysis. Statements are not hearsay if they are offered for a purpose other than to "prove the truth of the matter asserted." For example, consider the statement, "I warned him that his brakes needed work." This statement would be hearsay if offered to prove that the brakes were indeed defective. On the other hand, it would not be hearsay if offered to prove that the driver had notice of the condition of the brakes and was therefore negligent in not having them repaired. There are also numerous exceptions to the hearsay rule.

> *Responses.* Out-of-arbitration statements are admissible if they are not hearsay, or if they fall within one of the exceptions to the hearsay rule. In addition to statements that are not offered for their truth, the Federal Rules of Evidence define two other types of statements as non-hearsay. The witness's own previous statement is not hearsay if (A) it was given under oath and it is inconsistent with the current testimony; or (B) it is consistent with the current testimony and it is offered to rebut a charge of recent fabrication; or (C) it is a statement of past identification. *See* Fed. R. Evid. 801(d)(1). In addition, an admission of a party opponent is defined as non-hearsay, if offered against that party. Fed. R. Evid. 801(D)(2). Some of the more frequently encountered exceptions to the hearsay rule are as follows:

Present sense impression. A statement describing an event made while the declarant is observing it. For example, "Look, there goes the President." Fed. R. Evid. 803(1).

Excited utterance. A statement relating to a startling event made while under the stress of excitement caused by the event. For example, "A piece of plaster fell from the roof, and it just missed me." Fed. R. Evid. 803(2).

State of mind. A statement of the declarant's mental state or condition. For example, "He said that he was so mad he couldn't see straight." Fed. R. Evid. 803(3).

Past recollection recorded. A memorandum or record of a matter about which the witness once had knowledge, but which she has since forgotten. The record must have been made by the witness when the events were fresh in the witness's mind and must be shown to have been accurate when made. Fed. R. Evid. 803(5).

Business records. The business records exception applies to the records of any regularly conducted activity. To qualify as an exception to the hearsay rule, the record must have been made at or near the time of the transaction, by a person with knowledge or transmitted from a person with knowledge. It must have been made and kept in the ordinary course of business. The foundation for a business record must be laid by the custodian of the record, or by some other qualified witness. Fed. R. Evid. 803(6).

Reputation as to character. Evidence of a person's reputation for truth and veracity is an exception to the hearsay rule. Note that there are restrictions other than hearsay on the admissibility of character evidence. Fed. R. Evid. 803(21). See also Fed. R. Evid. 404–405.

Prior testimony. Testimony given at a different proceeding, or in deposition, qualifies for this exception if (1) the testimony was given under oath; (2) the adverse party had an opportunity to cross-examine; and (3) the witness is currently unavailable. Fed. R. Evid. 804(b)(1).

Dying declaration. A statement by a dying person as to the cause or circumstances of what he or she believed to be impending death. Admissible only in homicide prosecutions or civil cases. Fed. R. Evid. 804(b)(2).

Statement against interest. A statement so contrary to the declarant's pecuniary, proprietary, or penal interest, that no reasonable person would have made it unless it were true. The declarant must be unavailable, and certain other limitations apply in criminal cases. Fed. R. Evid. 804(b)(3).

Catch-all exception. Other hearsay statements may be admitted if they contain sufficient circumstantial guarantees of trustworthiness. The declarant must be unavailable, and advance notice must be given to the adverse party. Fed. R. Evid. 807.

Irrelevant. Evidence is irrelevant if it does not make any fact of consequence to the case more or less probable. Evidence can be irrelevant if it proves nothing, or if it tends to prove something that does not matter. Fed. R. Evid. 401, 402.

> *Response.* Explain the relevance of the testimony.

Unfair prejudice. Relevant evidence may also be excluded if its probative value is substantially outweighed by confusion of issues, or by misleading the fact-finder, or by considerations of undue delay, waste of time, or needless presentaion of cumulative evidence. Fed. R. Evid. 403.

> *Responses.* Most arbitrators are hesitant to exclude evidence on this basis. A measured explanation of the probative value of the testimony is the best response.

Improper character evidence, generally. Character evidence is generally not admissible to prove that a person acted in conformity with his or her character. For example, a driver's past accidents cannot be offered as proof of current negligence. Fed. R. Evid. 404(a).

Responses. Past crimes and bad acts may be offered to prove motive, opportunity, intent, preparation, plan, knowledge, identity, or absence of mistake. Fed. R. Evid. 404(b).

Improper character evidence, conviction of crime. As noted above, the commission, and even the conviction, of past crimes is not admissible to prove current guilt. The credibility of a witness who takes the stand and testifies, however, may be impeached on the basis of a prior criminal conviction, but only if the following requirements are satisfied: the crime must have been either (1) a felony, or (2) one which involved dishonesty or false statement, regardless of punishment. With certain exceptions, the evidence is not admissible unless it occurred within the last ten years. Juvenile adjudications are generally not admissible. Fed. R. Evid. 609.

Responses. If the crime was not a felony, the conviction may still be admissible if it involved dishonesty. If the conviction is more than ten years old, it may still be admissible if the arbitrator determines that its probative value, supported by specific facts and circumstances, substantially outweighs its prejudicial effect. Fed. R. Evid. 609.

Improper character evidence. As noted above, the past bad acts of a person may not be offered as proof that he or she committed similar acts. Specific instances of conduct are admissible for the limited purpose of attacking or supporting credibility. A witness may therefore be cross-examined concerning past bad acts only if they reflect upon truthfulness or untruthfulness. Note, however, that such bad acts (other than conviction of a crime) may not be proved by extrinsic evidence. The cross-examiner is stuck with the witness's answer. Fed. R. Evid. 608(b).

Responses. Explain the manner in which the witness's past bad acts are probative of untruthfulness.

Improper character evidence, reputation. Reputation evidence is admissible only with regard to an individual's character for truthfulness or untruthfulness. Moreover, evidence of a truthful character is admissible only after the witness's character has been attacked. Fed. R. Evid. 608(a).

Responses. Explain the manner in which the reputation evidence is probative of truthfulness or untruthfulness.

Lack of personal knowledge. Witnesses (other than experts) must testify from personal knowledge, which is more or less defined as sensory perception. A witness's lack of personal knowledge may be obvious from the questioning, may be inherent in the testimony, or may be developed by questioning on *voir dire*. Fed. R. Evid. 602.

> *Responses.* Ask further questions that establish the witness's personal knowledge.

Improper lay opinion. Lay witnesses (non-experts) are generally precluded from testifying as to opinions, conclusions, or inferences. Fed. R. Evid. 701.

> *Responses.* Lay witnesses may testify to opinions or inferences if they are rationally based upon the perception of the witness. Common lay opinions include estimates of speed, distance, value, height, time, duration, and temperature. Lay witnesses are also commonly allowed to testify as to the mood, sanity, demeanor, sobriety, or tone of voice of another person.

Speculation or conjecture. Witnesses may not be asked to speculate or guess. Such questions are often phrased as hypotheticals, such as, "What would have happened if . . . ?"

> *Responses.* Witnesses are permitted to make reasonable estimates rationally based upon perception.

Authenticity. You must authenticate exhibits before they may be admitted. Authenticity refers to adequate proof that the exhibit actually is what it seems or purports to be. Virtually all documents and tangible objects must be authenticated. Since exhibits are authenticated by laying a foundation, objections may be raised on the ground of either authenticity or foundation.

> *Responses.* Ask additional questions that establish authenticity.

Lack of foundation. Nearly all evidence, other than a witness's direct observation of events, requires some sort of predicate foundation for admissibility. An objection to lack of foundation requires the arbitrator to make a preliminary ruling as to the admissibility of the evidence. Fed. R. Evid. 104. The evidentiary foundations vary widely.[38]

Best evidence. The "best evidence" or "original document" rule refers to the common law requirement that copies or secondary evidence of writings could not be admitted into evidence unless the absence of the original could be explained. Under modern practice, most jurisdictions have significantly expanded upon the circumstances in which duplicates and other secondary evidence may be admitted. Fed. R. Evid. 1001–1003.

---

38. *See* section 5.8, *supra*.

Responses. Ask additional questions demonstrating either that the item offered is a duplicate, or that the original is unavailable.

Privilege. Numerous privileges may operate to exclude otherwise admissible evidence. Among the most common are attorney-client, physician-patient, marital, clergy, mediator, psychotherapist-patient, and a number of others that exist either by statute or at common law. Each privilege has its own foundation and its own set of exceptions. Fed. R. Evid. 501 did not change the common law privileges, but note that state statutory privileges may not pertain in arbitrations governed by federal rules.

Responses. Virtually all privileges are subject to some exceptions, which vary from jurisdiction to jurisdiction.

Subsequent remedial measures. Evidence of subsequent repair or other remedial measures is not admissible to prove negligence or other culpable conduct. Fed. R. Evid. 407. The primary rationale for this rule is that parties should not be discouraged from remedying dangerous conditions, and should not have to choose between undertaking repairs and creating proof of their own liability.

Responses. Subsequent remedial measures may be offered to prove ownership, control, or feasibility of precautionary measures, if controverted. Fed. R. Evid. 407. Evidence of subsequent repair may also be admissible in strict liability cases, as opposed to negligence cases.

Settlement offers. Offers of compromise or settlement are not admissible to prove or disprove liability. Statements made during settlement negotiations are also inadmissible. Fed. R. Evid. 408.

Responses. Statements made during settlement discussions may be admissible to prove bias or prejudice of a witness, or to negate a contention of undue delay. Fed. R. Evid. 408.

5.9.6.3   Ethics and objections

Ethical issues frequently arise in the context of making and meeting objections. Because the objecting process is one of the most confrontational aspects of the trial, it often tests counsel's reserves of good will, civility, restraint, and sense of fair play. The three most common problems are discussed below.

Asking objectionable questions. It is unethical to attempt to use the information contained in questions as a substitute for testimony that cannot be obtained. Some lawyers apparently believe that the idea of zealous advocacy allows them to slip information before an arbitrator by asserting it in a question, knowing full well that the witness will not be allowed to answer. The usual scenario is something as follows:

Lawyer: Isn't it true that you were once fired from a job for being drunk?

Objection: Objection, relevance.

Lawyer: I withdraw the question. (Sotto voce: Who cares about the ruling? I never expected to get it in, but now the arbitrator knows that the witness is a drunk.)

This conduct, even if the information is true, is absolutely unethical. Testimony is to come from witnesses, with admissibility ruled upon by the arbitrator. It subverts the very purpose of an adversary hearing when lawyers abuse their right to question witnesses in order to slip inadmissible evidence before the arbitrator.

Making questionable objections.. The same general analysis applies to the use of objections as it does to the offer of evidence. Counsel need not be positive that an objection will be sustained but must only believe that there is a reasonable basis for making it. Again, in arbitration it is up to the arbitrator to decide whether to admit the evidence.

Making "tactical" objections. Many lawyers, and more than a few trial advocacy texts, tout the use of so-called "tactical" objections. Since an objection is the only means by which one lawyer can interrupt the examination of another, it is suggested that objections should occasionally be made to "break up" the flow of a successful examination. An objection can throw the opposing lawyer off stride, or give the witness a rest, or distract the arbitrator from the testimony's content. This advice is usually tempered with the admonition that there must always be some evidentiary basis for the objection, but the real message is that you can use an objection for any purpose whatsoever, so long as you can make it with a straight face. This view is unfortunate. It amounts to nothing more than the sneaky use of objections for a wholly improper purpose. No arbitrator would allow a lawyer to object on the ground that the opposition's examination is going too well. The fact that disruption can be accomplished *sub silentio* does not justify it. The same is true of other "tactical" uses of objections such as suggesting testimony to a witness.

5.10 Final Argument

5.10.1 The role and function of the final argument.

5.10.1.1 The whole story

Final argument in arbitration is the advocate's only opportunity to tell the case's story in its entirety, without interruption, free from most constraining formalities.[39] Unlike witness examinations, counsel delivers the final argument in her own words, and without the need intermittently to cede the stage to the opposition. Unlike the opening statement, it is not bound by strict rules governing proper and improper content. In other words, final argument is the moment for pure advocacy when all of the lawyer's organizational, analytic, interpretive, and forensic skills are brought to bear on the task of persuading the arbitrator. The final argument cannot be fully successful unless the preceding stages of the arbitration hearing were also successful. The opening statement's mental image will not stay with the arbitrator unless it is sustained by evidence from the witness stand. More to the point, the final argument cannot paint a picture that is contrary to, or unsupported by, the evidence. While final argument can and should be the capstone of a well-tried case, it is unlikely to be the saving grace of a poor one.

5.10.1.2 Use of theory and theme

Theory. If nothing else, the final argument must communicate the advocate's theory of the case. Some witnesses can be disregarded, some details can be omitted, some legal issues can be overlooked, but the theory of the case is absolutely essential. You must use the final argument, therefore, to illuminate your theory. This means that you must tell the arbitrator why your client is entitled to an award. A simple recitation of facts is not sufficient. Rather, the argument should bring together information from the various witnesses and exhibits in a way that creates only one result. To be successful, the theory you present in a final argument must be logical, believable, and legally sufficient.

Logical. A case theory, and consequently a final argument, must be logical in the sense that the component facts lead to the desired conclusions. It is often helpful, therefore, to reason backward, starting with the end result and then providing supportive facts.

Believable. The most logical theory in the world will not win a case if the arbitrator doesn't believe it. For a theory to be sound it must be based on facts that are likely to be accepted. The most believable information is often that which is

---

39. This section on final argument is a condensed adaptation of Lubet, *supra* chapter 3, note 1, at 385–440 which contains an in-depth treatment of the subject, including detailed examples.

produced by the other side—admissions. Although not quite so powerful as admissions, undisputed facts can provide a sturdy cornerstone for case theory and final argument and can be marshaled to cast light on disputed evidence. When key events or occurrences are in dispute, you can make your perception of events believable by arguing from commonsense and experience. Finally, an advocate can establish believability by relying upon the witnesses' credibility.

Legally sufficient. The final component of a solid theory is legal sufficiency. The logic and believability of a final argument must lead to the desired legal result. In other words, a final argument must address the law as well as the facts.

Theme. Your theme should be a constant presence throughout the final argument. Unlike opening statement and witness examinations, where you can only use a theme intermittently, you can organize the entire final argument so as to emphasize your theme. You can begin with a statement of the theme and constantly return to it in each segment of the argument.

5.10.1.3   What makes it argument

Recall the cardinal rule of opening statements that you may not argue. In final argument, on the other hand, you may, should, and must argue if you are serious about winning your case. The gloves are off and the limitations are removed, but what precisely distinguishes argument from mere presentation of the facts? The following are some of the most useful elements of "argument."

Conclusions. The attorney in final argument is free to draw and urge conclusions based upon the evidence. A conclusion is a result, consequence, or repercussion that follows from the evidence in the case. It is not sufficient for a final argument to draw, or even urge, conclusions. The argument must go on to explain why the desired conclusions are the correct ones.

Inferences. While a final argument can and should include broad conclusions, it may also include the sort of narrow conclusions commonly known as inferences. An inference is a deduction drawn from the existence of a known fact. In other words, you need not prove the inferred fact so long as it is a commonsense consequence of some established fact. An inference will be accepted only if it is well-grounded in common understanding. For that reason, it is often necessary or desirable to explain the basis of all but the most obvious inferences. For example, everyone will be willing to infer a child's age from knowledge of her grade in school. There is no need to explain that third graders are typically eight or nine years old. Other inferences, however, may be more complicated.

Details and circumstantial evidence. Final argument is counsel's only opportunity to explain the relevance and consequences of circumstantial evidence. Much of the art of direct and cross-examination consists of the accumulation of details that lead to a certain conclusion or result. The knowledge of the individual witnesses, not to mention trial strategy and luck, may result in the scattering of such details throughout the trial. It is during final argument that the attorney can reassemble the details so they lead to the desired result.

5.10.1.4   Analogies, allusions, and stories.

Analogies. An analogy can explain human conduct through reference to everyday human behavior. You can strengthen or diminish a witness's testimony by comparing her version of events to some widely understood experience or activity. While analogies can be very powerful, there is always the danger that the other side can invert and exploit them. Thus, so long as the opposing counsel has yet to argue, take care to ensure that any analogies are "airtight." For the same reason, claimant's counsel often reserves the use of analogies until rebuttal when the respondent will no longer be able to reply.

Allusions. An allusion is a literary or similar reference that adds persuasive force to an argument. In earlier days, before the advent of mass culture, trial lawyers' allusions were most commonly drawn from Shakespeare or the Bible. Today references are just as likely to be taken from motion pictures, television, popular songs, fairy tales, or (alas) even advertisements.

Stories. Stories, in the form of either hypotheticals or anecdotes, can be used effectively in final argument. It is permissible to illustrate an argument with a hypothetical story, so long as the story is based on facts that are in evidence.

Credibility and motive. Counsel may also use the final argument to comment on, and compare, witnesses's motive and credibility. Many, perhaps most, arbitrations involve competing renditions of past events which the arbitrator must resolve in order to reach a decision. Final argument is the only time when the attorney may directly confront witness character and explain why some witnesses should be believed and others discounted. Witness examinations can bring out impeaching facts, and the opening statement can use apposition to contrast the credibility of different witnesses. But only in final argument can counsel make direct comparisons. Finally, you can argue motive on the basis either of proven facts or logical inferences. You may tell the arbitrator why a witness would exaggerate, waffle, conceal information, quibble, or lie. The suggested reasons need not be based on outright admissions, so long as they follow rationally from the testimony in the case.

Weight of the evidence. While the opening statement is limited to a recitation of the expected evidence, you can use the final argument to assert the weight of the evidence.

> ➢ Why is one version preferable to another?

> ➢ Why should some facts be accepted and others rejected?

➢   Why is one case stronger than the other?

Demeanor. It is fair game in final argument to comment on a witness's demeanor. Demeanor arguments are usually negative in nature, since it is easier to characterize untrustworthy conduct. An argument that counsel's own witness "looked like he was telling the truth" will tend to seem insincere or over-protective. Negative comments, on the other hand, can be effective so long as they are adequately based on observable fact. One caveat: demeanor argument is based strictly on perception, and there is little way to ensure that counsel's perception of the witness will be the same as the arbitrator's. Conduct that the attorney sees as evidence of deception might be regarded by an arbitrator as a reasonable response to unfair questioning. Be careful. Use demeanor argument only when the witness's behavior has been blatant and unambiguous.

Refutation. Another distinguishing feature of argument is refutation of opposing positions. Opening statements and witness examinations may recite and elicit facts that are contrary to the opposition case, but final argument can refute it directly by pointing out errors, inconsistencies, implausibilities, and contradictions.

Application of law. Final argument provides the attorney an occasion to apply the law to the case's facts. Discussion of law is extremely limited during the opening statement and all but forbidden during witness examinations, but it is a staple of the final argument.

Moral appeal. Final argument allows counsel to elaborate on the case's moral theme. Recall that a theme states, usually in a single sentence, a compelling moral basis for a verdict in your client's favor. Your theme invokes shared values, civic virtues, or common motivations. You can state the theme during the opening statement and allude to it in witness examinations, but you can hammer it home in the final argument.

5.10.2   Format

In most arbitrations, the parties' final arguments are divided into three distinct segments, which are presented in the following order: the claimant's argument in chief, the respondent's argument in chief, and claimant's rebuttal. In some arbitrations, the claimant will be allowed to opt to argue second; thus, there are only two components: the respondent's argument and the claimant's rebuttal.

5.10.2.1   Claimant's argument in chief

The claimant must use argument in chief to define the issues and lay out the case's entire theory. The claimant's argument in chief will not be successful unless it provides the arbitrator with compelling reasons to find for the claimant on every necessary issue. Claimant's initial argument in arbitration must be comprehensive. The claimant must usually prevail by a preponderance of the evidence and must establish all of the elements of her cause of action. Failing to address an element can be fatal. In contrast, the respondent may often be considerably more selective during final argument. The respondent can frequently prevail simply by disproving a single element of the claimant case and therefore need not address issues as comprehensively as the claimant. To counterbalance this advantage, a claimant's attorney will often use the final argument to issue a series of challenges to the respondent, thus drawing the respondent into a discussion of issues that respondent's counsel might prefer to leave alone.

5.10.2.2   Respondent's argument in chief

The respondent generally has substantially more latitude than the claimant in determining the content of the argument in chief. While the claimant must address every element, the respondent is usually free to "cherry pick," selecting only those elements or issues in which counsel has the most confidence. The defense theory, of course, must be comprehensive in the sense that it explains all of the relevant evidence, but its legal thrust may be significantly more pointed than the claimant's. The defining characteristic of the defendant's argument in chief is that it is sandwiched between the claimant's two arguments. Respondent's counsel must respond to the claimant's argument in chief but will not be able to respond to rebuttal.

Responding to the claimant's argument in chief. It is essential that respondent reply directly to the claimant's argument in chief. After listening to the claimant's prolonged excoriation of the respondent, the arbitrator will immediately want to know what the respondent has to say in return. This does not mean that respondent's counsel should adopt the claimant's organization or respond point by point, but the respondent's argument cannot be entirely divorced from the structure that the claimant creates. At a minimum, the respondent should deny the specific charges leveled in the claimant's argument. It is a natural human response to deny unfair or untrue accusations. The arbitrator will expect as much from a wrongly blamed respondent. Unless there is a good reason for doing otherwise, the denial should come early in the respondent's argument. Finally, the watchword for the respondent's argument in chief is flexibility. While the claimant may have the luxury of composing her entire final argument, the respondent must always be alert to new issues and nuances raised once the arguments have begun. It simply will not do for respondent's counsel to deliver a set piece, because the respondent's argument is most effective to the extent that it rebuts the claimant's case as presented at the end of the hearing.

Anticipating rebuttal. The greatest difficulty for respondent's counsel is knowing that, ordinarily, she cannot speak again following the claimant's rebuttal. The claimant may comment on, criticize, or even ridicule respondent's argument, but the respondent may not reply. Respondent's counsel may have perfectly good answers for everything that the claimant says on rebuttal, but no matter. The rule is that the defense may argue only once. Respondent can request permission to give a surrebuttal argument, but arbitrators do not always grant such requests. Thus, it is extremely important that counsel do whatever is possible to blunt the rebuttal in advance. One approach is to anticipate and reply specifically to the claimant's possible rebuttal arguments.

5.10.2.3   Claimant's rebuttal

Effective use of rebuttal can be elusive. While the claimant's argument in chief can be completely planned in advance and the respondent's argument in chief can be mostly planned, rebuttal must generally be delivered extemporaneously. Preparation for rebuttal typically takes place while claimant's counsel listens to the respondent's argument in chief. Nonetheless, you can apply certain principles to make rebuttal more forceful and compelling. The most important principle of rebuttal is to organize it according to the claimant's own theory of the case.

Structure response around claimant's issues. A common approach to rebuttal is simply to make notes of the respondent's arguments and then to reply to the most important of them in the order in which they were delivered. This technique is easy to use, and it has the virtue of minimizing the potential for overlooking arguments. Its vice, however, is that it organizes the rebuttal according to the respondent's agenda, rather than the claimant's. It also tends to promote a boring delivery, since a rebuttal that follows this approach is likely to fall into a repetitive cadence of short paragraphs, each one beginning, "The respondent also argued . . . "

A more effective technique involves matching the respondent's arguments to the major propositions in the claimant's own case. To do this, claimant's counsel needs only to prepare a truncated outline of the three or four most important, or hotly contested, issues in the case, leaving a blank half-page or so under each heading. In this manner, you can spread four major arguments over two sheets of paper, and arrange them in the order most advantageous to the claimant. Then, as respondent's counsel argues, claimant's attorney can write her notes under the appropriate heading. When it comes time to deliver rebuttal, claimant's counsel will have automatically organized her notes of the respondent's remarks according to the claimant's own structure. You can then deliver the rebuttal topically, without regard to the order of argument used by the respondent.

Present claimant's case affirmatively. A second principle of rebuttal is to present the claimant's case in an affirmative light. Even when it is well organized, rebuttal is weakened if it becomes nothing more than a series of retorts. As with all argument, it is more effective to present the positive side of your own case, and this is particularly important when you represent the burdened party. Consequently, even in rebuttal, you should frame every position as a constructive statement of the claimant's own theory, and refute the defense being used to explain further or elaborate on the claimant's case.

Avoid sandbagging an argument. It is inherently risky for the claimant to sandbag by completely omitting a subject from the argument in chief and then trying to argue it in rebuttal. If the respondent does not touch on the same or related topic in his argument, then the arbitrator may not permit claimant to raise the topic for the first time in rebuttal. It usually is not risky, however, to withhold the use of an analogy or story until rebuttal, thereby preventing the respondent from reversing it.

5.10.2.4   Variations

It is always within the arbitrator's discretion to alter the usual order of argument to reflect the actual burden of proof in the particular case. In cases involving counterclaims or affirmative defenses, the respondent may be allowed to present the first and last arguments, or may be given a surrebuttal to follow the claimant's rebuttal. In multi-party cases the arbitrator will determine the order in which the various claimants and respondents will proceed. It is also the arbitrator's prerogative to apportion the time for argument, although the court may not effectively deny a party the opportunity to argue its case. Finally, some arbitrators do not provide automatically for rebuttal but rather require the claimant affirmatively to reserve time from the argument in chief.

5.10.3   Structure

You must develop the final argument's structure for maximum persuasive weight. The central thrust of the final argument must always be to provide reasons—logical, moral, legal, emotional—for the issuance of an award in your client's favor. Every aspect of the final argument should contribute in some way to the completion of the sentence "We win because . . . " In the broadest sense, of course, the desired conclusion should simply follow from the case's facts and law. Few cases, however, will go to arbitration unless the facts are capable of multiple interpretations. Effective argument therefore places a premium on arrangement and explanation. Topical organization is the guiding principle in the structure of final arguments. The following section will discuss the various methods of employing topical organization and the drawbacks and advantages of alternative structures.

5.10.3.1   Topical organization

The importance of topical organization in final argument cannot be over emphasized. Seemingly natural methods of organization, such as chronology and witness listing, will not present the evidence in its most persuasive form. Topical organization, on the other hand, allows counsel to determine the best way to address the case's issues. Topical organization can use, or combine, any of the following strategies.

Issues. One of the simplest and most effective forms of organization is to divide the case into a series of discrete factual or legal issues. Large issues, such as liability and damages, are obvious, but they are also so broad as to provide relatively little help in ordering an argument. It is more useful to think of issues as narrower propositions of fact or law.

Elements. A second form of topical organization revolves around elements and claims. Every legal cause or defense is composed of various discrete elements. A claim of negligence, for instance, must be supported by proof of duty, breach of duty, cause in fact, proximate cause, and damages. A claimant can therefore develop her final argument by discussing the evidence as it supports each of the distinct elements of her cause of action. A respondent, who needs to challenge only a single element in order to win, can use the same form of organization, but can truncate it by focusing only on those elements that are truly likely to be negated.

Turning points. Modern cognitive theory tells us that fact-finders are likely to regard the information in a case as a series of turning points or problems. Rather than resolving the truth or falsity of every distinct fact, they are far more likely to focus on a limited number of contested issues. Once an arbitrator decides those issues, she will be inclined to fit the individual facts into a picture that fits that view of reality. Thus, an attorney can persuade an arbitrator by identifying the key turning points in the hearing and explaining them in a way that comports with the arbitrator's life experience and sense of reality.

5.10.3.2   Alternative structures

Chronological organization. Chronology is the most obvious alternative structure for a final argument. Since the case's events manifestly occurred in a chronological order, it seems obvious to replay them in the same progression during final argument. While chronology certainly plays an important role in final argument, it is usually not the best approach to overall structure. The difficulty with chronology is that events are unlikely to have occurred in the most persuasive possible sequence. Early events can frequently be illuminated by their subsequent consequences.

Witness listing. Some lawyers persist in presenting final argument as a series of witness descriptions and accounts, essentially recapitulating each witness's testimony. This approach is unlikely to succeed, as it diminishes the argument's logical coherence and force. Where topical organization focuses on the importance of issues and chronological organization focuses on the real-life sequence of events, witness listing depends on nothing more than the serendipity of which witness said what. It is a lazy, and usually ineffective, method of organization. While it will often be necessary to compare witness accounts in the course of a final argument, this should not be the primary focus of the argument.

5.10.3.3   Other organizing tools

Start strong and end strong. The principles of primacy and recency apply with full force to the final argument. In presenting a final argument, counsel has a limited window in which to attempt to shape the arbitrator's imagination of the acts, events, and circumstances at issue in the case. Eliminate anything that bores the arbitrator, or that distracts her from the task at hand, from the final argument. And devote prime time—the very beginning and the very end of the argument—to the case's most important considerations.

Claimant should advance affirmative case first. Most final arguments will consist of two distinct components: developing the affirmative case and debunking the opposing party's claims and/or defenses. As a general rule, it is preferable to build up your own case first and then proceed to debunk the opposition. Claimants in particular should resist the temptation to begin by criticizing the defense case. No matter how weak or ridiculous the defenses, it is usually best to begin with the strong points of your own case. The claimant, after all, bears the burden of proof, and cannot win without establishing all of the elements of an affirmative case. Thus, you gain little by refuting the defense if you cannot prove your own case first. Moreover, a claimant who launches immediately into an assault on the respondent's case may be seen as confessing a lack of confidence in her own position. And if the arbitrator does not jump immediately to that conclusion, you can be sure that respondent's counsel will argue that precise inference: "If claimant's case is so strong, why did counsel begin by attacking the defense; they must be worried." The respondent has more latitude. Having just heard the claimant's argument, an arbitrator is unlikely to draw any adverse inference should respondent's counsel begin by refuting the claimant's case. Indeed, most arbitrators will be waiting to hear the respondent's denial. Therefore, the respondent should almost always begin with a denial.

Cluster circumstantial evidence and accumulate details. We have seen that details can give texture and support to a case's theory, and that circumstantial evidence can establish major propositions. These small, constituent facts are often presented at different times during the trial's testimonial phase. One witness may testify to several details, the importance of which will become apparent only in light of other evidence supplied by other witnesses. Moreover, on cross-examination counsel may deliberately separate details, so as not to alert the witness to the examination's intended thrust. Final argument is the time to gather all of these details and harmonize them to create a symphony of persuasive thought.

Bury your concessions. In the course of almost every argument it will be necessary to concede certain of the opposition's claims or facts, if only to minimize or discount them. As a corollary to the "start and end strong" rule, you should usually "bury" such concessions in the middle of your argument.

Weave in witness credibility. We noted above that witness listing is an ineffective format for final argument. Witness credibility, on the other hand, is often a subject you must address. The solution is to weave discussion of the witnesses, and their relative credibility, into the story's fabric.

Carefully consider how to approach damages. In arbitration, when issues of both liability and damages are present, claimant's counsel should argue liability first and then damages. If you are respondent's counsel, you may want to address damages first briefly, but spend most of your argument picking apart the claimant's case on liability.

5.10.4   Content

The specific content of any final argument will obviously be determined by the case's facts and issues. However, you should consider certain sorts of information for inclusion in every final argument.

5.10.4.1   Tell a persuasive story

Virtually every final argument should contain all of the elements of a persuasive story. The argument should detail the evidentiary support for counsel's case theory and should consistently invoke the trial theme. A persuasive story has four basic elements, each of which answers an important question:

What happened? A persuasive story accounts for all of the known facts. It is not premised on incomplete information, and it does not glide over or ignore inconvenient occurrences. This is not to say that a final argument must mention every minor detail in the case, but rather that it should, in some fashion, accommodate all of the established facts. The final argument must, of course, cover the central facts of counsel's case, taking care to provide support for all of the legally necessary elements. It must also consider the evidence produced by the opposing party.

Why did it happen? Explain the reasons for the actions of the parties and other witnesses. It is not enough to state that an individual did something. Rather, counsel should go on to reveal why those activities were consistent with that individual's self-interest, announced intentions, past behavior, life style, or other understandable motivations. The articulation of reasons gives logical weight to the argument, and can transform it from an attorney's assertion into an acceptable statement of fact.

How can we be sure? As we have seen throughout, persuasion often rests on the accumulation of supportive details. An essential aspect of final argument is the marshaling of details that give weight to counsel's argument. The inclusion or exclusion of details is a tricky problem. While the right details at the right time can add an airtight quality to your case, the use of too many details (or their use in support of unimportant propositions) can drag a final argument into the depths of boredom and despair. There is no single key to making judgments in this area, but it is safe to look to the following guidelines:

Use details when important facts are in dispute. Whenever there is a disagreement as to an occurrence or incident, you can use details effectively to support your client's version of events.

Use details when motivations are in issue. The presence (or absence) of motive can frequently be established through recourse to constituent facts. Explain why a party would want to act in a certain way. Look at the details that show the benefits of the actions' consequences.

Use details to support an interpretation of the evidence. The meaning of certain evidence is often contested even when the underlying facts are not in dispute. Use an interpretation of the details which best supports your theory.

Do not use details for unimportant reasons. The arbitrator will have a limited tolerance for details. Every time you use one detail, you diminish the effectiveness of those you will use later. It is therefore necessary to reserve your use of details for truly important situations. For example, you will not want to use details, even if they are available, to attack the credibility of a witness whose testimony was not damaging to your case.

Is it plausible? Perhaps the ultimate test of every final argument is plausibility. Even if an argument accounts for the known facts, gives reasons for every action, is supported by credible witnesses, and might be replete with convincing details, it still will not be accepted if it does not make sense to the arbitrator. Almost every other failing can be overcome or forgiven. You cannot, however, win with an implausible argument. It is essential, therefore, that every final argument address the subject of commonsense. Explain why your theory is realistic, using

examples and analogies from everyday life. You can also use "commonsense" arguments to belittle or even ridicule the opposition's case. It is
every lawyer's dream that the arbitrator will adjourn the hearing and
immediately conclude that the opposition's case just doesn't stack up.

5.10.4.2   Tie up cross-examinations

Final argument is the time to tie up the issues that you intentionally left un-
addressed during cross-examination. Recall the questions that are forbidden to
the prudent cross-examiner: Never ask a witness to explain; never ask a witness
to fill in a gap; never ask a witness to agree with a characterization or conclusion.
These questions, and others like them, all risk losing control of the witness. All
authorities agree that it is better to refrain from asking the ultimate question,
and to make the point instead during the final argument. Thus, if your cross-examinations were artful and effective, you should be able to spend some portion
of the final argument drawing the previously unspoken conclusions. You can use
the same approach with regard to explanations and characterizations. You did
not ask a witness why something happened; be sure to use the final argument
to tell the arbitrator why it happened. You did not ask a witness to agree with
a conclusion or characterization; be sure to use the final argument to draw the
conclusion yourself.

5.10.4.3   Comment on promises

Attorneys on both sides of a case will inevitably make various promises and
commitments to the arbitrator during the hearing's course. These promises may
be overt, as is often the case during opening statements: "We will produce a series of documents and work records that prove that the respondent was nowhere
near the scene of the accident." Or the commitments may be implicit in the case's
theory. When a claimant seeks damages for personal injury, there is obviously an
implied promise of certain proof. Whatever the case, final argument is the time
for counsel to comment on promises made, kept, or broken. Point out the ways in
which you fulfilled your commitments. Perhaps more importantly, and certainly
more dramatically, underscore the ways in which the opposition failed to live up
to their own promises.

5.10.4.4   Resolve problems and weaknesses.

You can also use final argument to solve problems and confront weaknesses.
No matter how well the evidentiary phase of the hearing proceeded, you are sure
to be left with a number of difficult or troublesome issues. Once identified, you
can address and resolve these issues in the course of final argument. There are
several schools of thought as to the best timing for addressing weaknesses or
problems. Some authorities believe that weaknesses should never be addressed

unless the opposing side raises them first. Others believe you should deal with at least certain weaknesses "defensively," on the theory that you can preempt the sting by discussing the issue first. The decision is not always simple. Claimants' attorneys have the choice of dealing with weaknesses during either argument in chief or rebuttal. Thus, they can either initiate the discussion, or they can wait to see whether the defense brings up the issue during its argument in chief. Respondents, on the other hand, must be more wary. Even if the claimant omits a problem area from the argument in chief, counsel can still exploit it mercilessly on rebuttal.

5.10.4.5   Discuss damages

An arbitration can often be divided into the conceptual areas of liability and damages. Although liability is the threshold issue, it is a mistake to underestimate the importance of damages.

Claimant. Unless the hearing has been bifurcated, claimants in particular should devote a significant portion of the final argument to the development of damages. It may be helpful to think of damages as comprising a "second persuasive story" in the case. Once liability has been established, you can address damages using all of the persuasive story elements that we have discussed earlier. Counsel should account for the known facts that bear on damages, give the reasons for the actions of the people involved, address the credibility of the specific witnesses, delineate the crucial details, and explain why the requested damage award accords with commonsense. There are two significant aspects involved in most arguments for damages: method and amount. It is important to explain to the arbitrator precisely how damages have been (or should be) calculated. It is also usually important to request a specific amount, rather than leaving the award to the arbitrator's guesswork.

Respondent. Some defense attorneys prefer to avoid or minimize the issue of damages, reasoning that any discussion may be seen as an implicit admission of liability. Many lawyers, however, choose not to "roll the dice" on liability, concluding that a reduced damage award is the next best thing to winning the case outright. When discussing damages, as a respondent's lawyer, you have a choice. You may simply rebut the claimant's damage claim, or you may present a competing estimate of your own. The decision will rest upon the particular case's circumstances. Note, however, that the presentation of a competing damage estimate does run a greater risk of seeming to concede liability.

5.10.4.6   Thanks

It is only common courtesy to thank the arbitrator for serving as the decision maker in the case. Do not overdo it or you will sound phony. A simple statement of thanks, on behalf of yourself and your client, is usually sufficient.

5.10.5   Persuasive delivery techniques for final argument

For some suggestions on persuasive delivery techniques for final argument see section 5.11.1, *infra*.

5.10.6   Ethics and objections

The rules of ethics, evidence, and procedure combine to place a number of very real, though definitely manageable, limits on what you can say during final argument.

5.10.6.1   Impermissible argument

Statements of personal belief. It is improper and unethical for an attorney to "assert personal knowledge of facts in issue . . . or state a personal opinion as to the justness of a cause, the credibility of a witness, the culpability of a civil litigant . . . ." [40] This rule's purpose is twofold. First, it prevents lawyers from putting their own credibility at issue in a case. The decision maker is required to decide a case on the basis of the law and evidence, not on their affinity for or faith in a particular lawyer. While every advocate strives to be trusted and believed, it subverts the adversary system to make an overt, personal pitch. Moreover, a statement of personal belief inevitably suggests that the lawyer has access to off-the-record information, and therefore invites the decision maker to decide the case on the basis of non-record evidence.

Appeals to prejudice or bigotry. It is unethical to attempt to persuade a decision maker through appeals to racial, religious, ethnic, gender, or other forms of prejudice. People—including arbitrators—can be swayed by their own biases, but lawyers cannot and should not seek to take advantage of this unfortunate phenomenon. An appeal to prejudice asks the decision maker to disregard the evidence and to substitute an unreasonable stereotype or preconception. Thus, such arguments violate the rule against alluding to "any matter the lawyer does not reasonably believe is relevant or that will not be supported by admissible evidence." [41] The mention of race, gender, or ethnicity is not always improper. It may, for example, be permissible to refer to a party's race if it is relevant to identification by an eyewitness. On the other hand, it is definitely unethical to make racial or similar

---

40. Rule 3.4(e) ABA Model Rules of Professional Conduct.
41. Id.

appeals implicitly or through the use of code words. An argument based on bigotry cannot be saved through subtle language.

Misstating the evidence. While it is permissible to draw inferences and conclusions, it is improper intentionally to misstate or mischaracterize evidence in the course of final argument. Arbitrators are usually reluctant to resolve questions raised by the rule, but even so, two lessons accompany the "misstatement" rule. First, do not take the arbitrators' general reluctance to resolve questions raised by the rule as license to ignore the rule. Second, do not use the "misstatement" rule as an excuse to make spurious objections, to interrupt opposing counsel's argument, or to quibble over the meaning of the evidence. Make objections only when opposing counsel has seriously and prejudicially departed from the record.

Misstating the law. In most jurisdictions attorneys may use final argument to explain the relevant law and to apply the law to the facts of the case. Counsel may not, however, misstate the law, or argue for legal interpretations that are contrary to the court's decisions.

Misusing evidence. When evidence has been admitted only for a limited or restricted use, it is improper to attempt to use it for any other purpose.

Exceeding the scope of rebuttal. It is objectionable to attempt to argue new matters on rebuttal.

5.10.6.2   The protocol of objections

Making objections. Objections during final argument follow the same general pattern as objections during witness examinations. Counsel should state succinctly the ground for the objection. There is usually no need to present argument unless requested by the arbitrator. Most attorneys attempt to avoid objecting during opposing counsel's final argument. It is considered a common courtesy to allow opposing counsel to speak uninterrupted. Moreover, the overuse of objections may result in the interruption of one's own final argument. This does not mean, of course, that you should tolerate seriously improper arguments. It is unethical to make spurious objections simply for the purpose of interfering with opposing counsel's argument.

Responding to objections. The best response to an objection is often no response. An objection disrupts the flow of final argument, and an extended colloquy with the arbitrator will only prolong the interruption. A dignified silence will usually be sufficient to allow the arbitrator to rule. Once the arbitrator rules, whether favorably, unfavorably, or inscrutably, counsel should simply proceed by adapting the argument to the arbitrator's ruling.

5.11 Persuasive Techniques

In this section we shall review some of the persuasive delivery and examination techniques you can use to advantage in arbitration when making your opening statements and final arguments and when using exhibits.[42]

5.11.1   Opening statement and final argument

5.11.1.1   Do not read

Do not read your opening statement or final argument from a prepared text. Only the most skilled professional actors can deliver a scripted speech and still appear to be spontaneous and sincere. Everyone else will seem to be stilted or labored. Your goal during your presentation should be to communicate directly to the arbitrators, not to lecture to them from a manuscript. You will want to make eye contact, you will want to pick up on the arbitrator's reactions, and you will want to respond to objections and rulings by the arbitrator. Respondent's counsel, moreover, will want to reply to challenges, weaknesses, and omissions in the claimant's presentation. A written presentation will prevent you from doing any of these things effectively.

Much the same can be said of attempting to memorize your presentation. While exceptional memorization is better than reading, you will still run the risk of forgetting a line (or more), of losing your place, or of being thrown off track by an objection. Very experienced lawyers may be able to deliver their presentations from memory. Novices should be wary of trying. The best approach is often to make your presentation from an outline. It should be possible to list all of your major points, as well as the most important supporting details, on one or two sheets of paper. An outline will allow you to organize the material and ensure that you don't leave anything out, while avoiding all of the perils of reading or memorization. The key, of course, is for your notes to be unobtrusive. Hence, the outline as opposed to the text.

5.11.1.2   Use simple, straightforward language

Your presentation should be reasonably straightforward and direct. In your opening statement allow your facts to speak for themselves; it is not a time for emotional pleas or impassioned argument. In any event, in the opening statement you will not be allowed to make elaborate use of metaphors, literary allusions, biblical quotations, or any of the other rhetorical devices that can be so helpful during final argument. You should never talk down to an arbitrator.

---

42. This section is a condensed adaptation of Lubet, *supra* chapter 3, note 1 at 375–378; 428–432; 324–333, which includes an in-depth treatment of delivery and persuasion techniques, including detailed examples.

Simple language is generally the best. In final arguments, apply simple, active language in argumentative form. There may be a strong temptation during final argument to use judgmental or conclusory terms such as heinous, brutal, deceptive, unfair, virtuous, naive, and the like. Although usually not permitted during opening statements, such language is allowed on final argument. Nonetheless, counsel would do well to remember that conclusory adjectives and adverbs are almost always less persuasive than are active nouns and verbs. It is one thing to assert that a crime was heinous, and quite another to describe its awful, vivid details.

5.11.1.3   Verbal pacing

The speed, tone, inflection and volume of your speech can be important persuasive tools. You can use changes in speed, tone, inflection and volume to signal transitions and to maintain the arbitrator's attention. It is important, of course, to avoid speaking too quickly or too loudly. You can pace your speech to convey perceptions of time, distance, and intensity. If you describe an event rapidly, it will seem to have taken place very quickly. If you describe it at a more leisurely pace, the time frame will expand. In similar fashion, rapid speech will tend to magnify intensity and reduce distance. Slower delivery will reduce intensity and increase distance.

5.11.1.4   Movement for emphasis and transition

In some arbitrations, the hearing room's size will dictate how much movement you may engage in during your presentations. In many arbitrations, counsel present their opening statements and final arguments while seated. However, if space allows, and you can make your presentations while standing, the following suggestions may be beneficial. A certain amount of body and hand movement will enliven your final argument and increase the arbitrator's attentiveness. You can use gestures to emphasize important points or to accent differences between your case and the opposition's. You can also use body movement for emphasis or transition. Pausing and taking a step or two will alert the arbitrator that you are about to change subjects. Moving toward the arbitrator will underscore the importance of what you are about to say. Moving away from the arbitrator will signal the conclusion of a line of argument. Note that body movement can only be used effectively if you avoid aimless pacing. Constant movement not only distracts the arbitrator, but it also deprives you of the ability to use movements purposefully. Use a lectern if you need it.

5.11.1.5   Visuals and exhibits

You need not confine your opening statement and final argument to your words alone. The use of visual aids and exhibits can enormously enhance the value of your presentations.

Exhibits. Since your presentation's purpose is to explain what the evidence will show or has shown, you are entitled to read from or display documents and other exhibits that you expect to be admitted into evidence or which are already in evidence. If the case involves a contract, quote from the central clause. If there is a key letter in evidence, have it enlarged and show it to the arbitrator during your opening statement, and use the same exhibit in your final argument. Use a pointer so that the arbitrator can read along with you as you recite the opposing party's damning admission. During your presentations you can show the arbitrator photographs, models, maps, and charts, as well as other tangible exhibits such as weapons, machinery, or even prosthetics.

Visual aids. In addition to displaying actual exhibits, you may also use visual aids during your presentations. The general rule is that any visual aid must be likely to help the arbitrator understand the hearing evidence. Thus, lawyers routinely use visual aids in arbitration to show "time lines," or to draw free-hand diagrams that are not offered or received into evidence. There are limitations, of course. The visual aids must fairly summarize the evidence, and in the opening statement, they cannot be misleading, and they cannot be argumentative. You could not, for example, produce in opening statement a chart captioned "Three Reasons Not To Believe The Claimant." Use of such a chart, however, would be quite permissible in final argument. You should show visual aids to opposing counsel before your presentation begins. It is advisable also to show visuals to the arbitrator and to obtain advance permission for their use.

Other evidence. Not all exhibits are visual. It is permissible to play tape recordings during presentations—such as legally taped telephone conversations or 911 emergency calls—if they will later be offered or have been accepted in evidence.

Use of emotion in final argument. There are different schools of thought regarding the use of emotion in final argument. Many lawyers believe emotion has little place at any point during an arbitration, while others believe emotion can communicate as effectively as logic or reason. There is a strong consensus, however, that false emotion will backfire. Insincerity has a way of showing through, and there is little that is less persuasive than an overtly insincere attorney. The best approach to emotion is to save it for the times when you are discussing your case's moral dimension. There is no reason to wax passionate over the date on which a contract was signed. It is understandable, however, to show outrage or resentment toward a party who intentionally breached a contract, knowing that it would cause great harm to another. The absence of emotion may be taken as a lack of belief in your case's righteousness. What reasonable person would be unmoved when discussing crippling injuries to a child or perjury by the opposing party? There will be points in many arbitrations that virtually call out for an outward display of feeling, and a flat presentation may be regarded as an absence of conviction.

5.11.2   Persuasive use of exhibits

It is important to present and use exhibits as persuasively as possible in arbitration.

5.11.2.1   Persuasive foundations

You can use two approaches to enhance the persuasiveness of foundations. Your choice will depend on the circumstances.

Minimalism. Whenever possible, use stipulations and pretrial rulings to avoid the need for developing foundations in arbitration. If you must present foundational testimony, keep it as short as possible. You can use leading questions, permissible on preliminary matters, to move the testimony along.

Maximalism. Foundations are not always rote technicalities. Particularly where the exhibit's authenticity is in issue, the thoroughness of the foundation can play an important role in persuasion. In such circumstances it is important to develop the foundation fully.

5.11.2.2   Creative exhibits

The most valuable exhibits in any case seldom step forward and present themselves. Rather, you must seek, search out, and discover them. Often they must be developed and created. Even those exhibits that are simply handed to counsel by the client can be presented in an enhanced form. The following sections discuss creative means of finding, developing, and presenting exhibits.

Looking for exhibits. It is essential to ensure your complete access to all real and documentary exhibits. While you will rarely want to introduce everything that you find, you cannot adequately represent your client until you have examined every potential item of evidence. No competent attorney would go to an arbitration hearing without having learned the identity of every witness, and exhibits are essentially silent witnesses. You must find them all—both documentary exhibits and real evidence.

Developing exhibits. All exhibits fall essentially into two categories: those that predate the arbitration and those attorneys create. You must take the pre-arbitration, or integral, exhibits as they are found, but you have wide latitude in shaping and developing other exhibits for use at the hearing. Some of the more common sorts of lawyer-generated exhibits are:

1. enlargement of a key section of the deposition transcript of an adverse witness's testimony;

2. photographs and videotapes;

3. models;

4. diagrams and maps;

5. explanatory graphs and charts.

The creation of these, and similar, exhibits should be considered in virtually every case.

Presenting exhibits. The presentation of an exhibit can be as important as its composition or foundation. No matter how well thought out, no matter how solidly admissible, an exhibit will not accomplish its purpose if it is not understood and accepted by the trier of fact. In addition to selecting key integral documents for enhanced presentation, effective arbitration preparation also involves the design of lawyer-generated exhibits. Particularly when it comes to diagrams and graphs, an ounce of professional preparation is usually worth several pounds of hearing room drawing. You must decide whether a chart, graph, or diagram can improve a witness's testimony. If so, develop the desired exhibit in advance of the hearing. While witnesses can draw on blackboards or poster boards while testifying, you should usually avoid this approach. Freehand drawing is unreliable under the best circumstances, and witnesses are notoriously prone to make embarrassing mistakes when called upon to draw before the arbitrator. Use of a blackboard, in particular, seldom leads to a satisfying result.

Size. Exhibits must be seen to be appreciated. When creating an exhibit, create a big one. When using integral exhibits, such as pre-existing documents, make enlargements.

There is no reason for a lawyer-produced exhibit to be visually inaccessible. Charts, graphs, and diagrams should be made on oversize pieces of stiff poster board. Thin tagboard is unacceptable, since even a masterpiece will be useless if it cannot be made to stand up. Ensure that a display easel will be available in the hearing room. You can also use an overhead projector to display documents. Unfortunately, the visual quality of overhead projection is often poor. The exhibit may be distorted or the image may be faint. Although overhead transparencies are inexpensive and easy to obtain, photographic enlargements are preferred. Photographs, whether pre-existing or taken at counsel's direction, should also be enlarged.

Computer generated graphics may have the greatest visual and persuasive impact, but they are prone to frustrating technical glitches. If you intend to use computer displays or models, be certain to have a contingency plan.

Copies. You should enter the hearing room with enough copies of every exhibit. At a minimum, this should include an original, additional copies for the witness and the arbitrator, and copies for each opposing attorney if they have not already been produced. Distributing copies at the appropriate time in the examination will prevent delays and can forestall objections. There is nothing more awkward and distracting than a lawyer leaning over a witness's shoulder while they attempt to share an exhibit. When enlargements are impractical or unavailable, make enough copies of the exhibits, whether documents or photographs, to distribute to the arbitrators. You can also assemble documents into a bound or loose-leaf "exhibit book," and provide copies to the arbitrators and to witnesses as necessary.

5.12 Summary of the Elements of Classical Persuasion

We know from the classical Greek philosopher Aristotle that there are five objectives of persuasive messages and three artistic means of persuasion.

5.12.1 The five objectives of persuasive messages.

Persuasion in its broadest sense may be described as the art of moving human beings to action. Persuasion starts by creating a relationship between oneself and others. The primary purpose of creating such relationship is not merely to connect people who were previously unconnected; rather, its primary purpose is to make them aware of the connections which they already have. An artful arbitration advocate accomplishes this task by mastering the five objectives of persuasive messages. Persuasive messages must: (1) command the attention of the receiver; (2) be understood by the receiver as intended by the sender; (3) warrant the receiver's belief that the information presented is credible or accurate; (4) present information which conforms to the receiver's values of what is right and wrong; and (5) motivate the receiver to act. Persuasive messages influence how receivers choose or decide which information to process. This implies the utility of strategy and theory and the criticality of audience analysis. Thus, as an advocate in arbitration, you must analyze your audiences and apply those analyses when determining how best to effectuate the five objectives of the persuasive message.

5.12.2   The three artistic means of persuasion

Aristotle's teachings about persuasion are as relevant today as they were when he first conceived them. As early as the fourth century B.C., Aristotle identified and labeled three "artistic means of persuasion": *ethos* (character of speaker); *pathos* (emotions aroused in audience); and *logos* (logical— true or probable argument). These three means of persuasion bear a striking resemblance to the three dimensions of attitude in modern-day psychology: behavioral (*ethos*), affective (*pathos*), and cognitive (*logos*).

Of major importance to you as an arbitration advocate is the behavioral component of persuasion, *ethos*. It concerns the analysis of a speaker's character and credibility. *Ethos* encompasses the personal characteristics of the speaker and how perceptions of wisdom, decency, and personal goodness influence a listener's motivation to act or think as the in consonance with the speaker's urging. According to Aristotle, the speaker's trustworthy character was the test of the *truth* of what was being said. *Ethos* was the "controlling factor" in persuasion. He identified two aspects of *ethos*: (1) personal qualities of the speaker; (2) the stereotypes by which the audience may judge the character of the speaker. Thus, in an arbitration, you must be continually conscious of your own personal qualities which project trustworthiness and those qualities of stereotypes which detract from your trust worthiness and which you should therefore avoid and those which enhance your trustworthiness and which you should therefore exhibit.

As an arbitration advocate, you also need to have an intimate understanding of the affective component of persuasion, *pathos*. Simply defined, pathos is the art of putting the audience in a desired frame of mind by appealing to their emotions, personal involvement, or needs reduction or satisfaction. At its foundation, *pathos* is an appeal to how one feels about concepts, values, conduct, and situations generally.

Finally, you additionally need to know, understand, and apply *logos* in the arbitration setting. *Logos*, the cognitive component of persuasion, refers to how the listener thinks, and is probably best described as an appeal to an audience's sense of reason through structured argument and evidentiary proof which favors logical consistency. The interrelationship between Aristotle's three means of persuasion and the three psychological components of persuasion is demonstrated in the diagram appearing on the following page:[43]

---

43. This chart appears in Raymond Ross, *Understanding Persuasion* 7 (Prentice Hall, Inc., 1990) (3rd ed.) reprinted by permission of Allyn and Bacon.

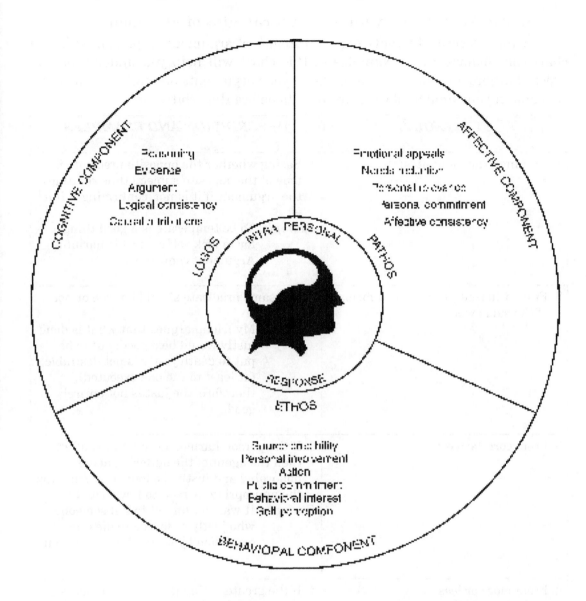

By knowing your audiences in arbitration, you will be able to adjust the amount of each ingredient, *ethos*, *pathos*, and *logos*, in conveying a persuasive message to accomplish your goal in a particular interchange. If there is no opportunity to analyze your audience, or if you are unable accurately classify it, you will probably want to use a balanced approach, and incorporate all three means, realizing at all times that *ethos* will be the controlling factor in the persuasiveness of your message.

5.12.3 Aristotle's twenty-eight strategies of argument

Aristotle described twenty-eight strategies of argument as presented in the chart that follows.[44] The examples in this chart will help you understand the types of arguments that you can make in your arguments on motions in arbitration and in your final or closing arguments before the arbitrator.

STRATEGIES	DESCRIPTION AND EXAMPLES
1. Arguing: from opposites;	1. Seeing whether the opposite predicate is true of the opposite subject; thus refuting the argument if it is not, confirming it if it is; *Example:* To be temperate is a good thing; for to lack self control is harmful. Argument confirmed.
2. From different grammatical forms of the same word;	2. The same predicate should be true or not true; *Example:* My friend argues that what is done justly would be a good; but to be put to death justly is not desirable (at least to the one executed); therefore, the just is not entirely good.
3. From correlatives;	3. If the person harmed deserved to suffer, then the agent of the suffering acted honorably and justly (so long as he/she was the appropriate person to have acted); *Example:* It was not unjust to kill someone who justly deserved to die (i.e. execution by state after a fair trial).
4. From more or less	4. If the greater thing is true, the lesser is also true (and vice versa); or if something is not the fact in the case where it would be more expected, it clearly is not the case where it would be less expected; *Example:* If not even the judges know everything, attorneys can hardly do so.

---

44. This chart is developed from information contained in George A. Kennedy, *Aristotle on Rhetoric: A Theory of Civic Discourse* 190-203 (1991); *see also* John W. Cooley, *A Classical Approach to Mediation— Part I: Classical Rhetoric and the Art of Persuasion in Mediation*, 19 U. of Dayton L. Rev. 83 (1993).

5. From a view of time;	5. Arguing from what was true in the past to what is more true in the present; (a fortiori—from the stronger); *Example:* Yesterday, you agreed to consent to the entry of an injunction because, as you admitted, "my client's conduct is predatory"; today you refuse to consent to the injunction, even though your client, in the meantime, has expanded his unlawful conduct into other sales territories?
6. From turning what has been said against oneself upon the one who said it;	6. Discrediting the accuser; *Example:* Even the prosecutor has had speeding tickets.
7. From definition;	7. Making arguments from the essence of meanings of words; *Example:* What is divine? Is it not either a god or the work of a god? If it is the work of a god, does not a god exist?
8. From varied meanings of a word;	8. *Example:* The word "sharp" has several meanings: capable of cutting, intelligent, and a notation in music.
9. From division;	9. Limiting the available alternatives, and excluding most, if not all, of them; *Example:* All people do wrong for one of three reasons: either this, or this, or this; now two of these are impossible in this case, but even the plaintiff's counsel herself does not assert the third.
10. From induction;	10. To prove on the basis of many similar instances; *Example:* Three times in the past the respondent has been found guilty of sabotaging parts shipments delivered by strike-breakers, yet he asks management to believe that he was home watching television by himself when the latest sabotage occurred.

11. From a previous judgment about the same or a similar or opposite matter;	11. Argument based on precedent; *Example:* The agreement we reached previously in Jones v. Acme is ideally suitable to resolve the issues now before the arbitrator.
12. From the parts;	12. Arguing by shifting focus to a species within a defined genus; *Example:* Defense counsel has argued that plaintiff could not prove his case if this dispute went to trial, but which element of the plaintiff's prima facie case could not be proved?
13. On the basis of the consequences;	13. Exhorting or dissuading, accusing or defending, praising or blaming on the basis of the good or bad which will result from some conduct; *Example:* Ms. Arbitrator, if the employee is not suspended for a substantial period of time, other employees will be tempted to engage in the same kind of misconduct.
14. From equally undesirable alternatives;	14. Argument by posing a dilemma in which the same or opposite act performed in each of two (ore more) situations presented yields an undesirable consequence; arguing a "Catch-22 situation"; *Example:* Since my client did not report the alleged child abuse to the authorities as required by law, she is subject to a fine and incarceration; but if she had reported the child abuse she would have suffered physical abuse personally from her spouse, and possibly death.
15. From exposition of opponent's true position or motivation;	15. *Example:* Plaintiff does not want her deposition postponed because of a previously scheduled appointment here at Bel-Nor Hospital for minor surgery. I have evidence that she made preparations to go on a 10 day trip to the Bahamas after she received the notice of deposition.

16. From consequences by analogy;	16. Argument by showing the irrationality of the reverse proposition; *Example:* If underage boys can be drafted into military service because they are tall, tall boys must be men; if so, short men must be boys.
17. From same results to same causes;	17. Arguing that "you can't have it both ways" or "either way"; *Example:* Mr. Arbitrator, the government contends that even though there was a technical defect in the way this law was enacted, it became effective before my client allegedly violated it. I respectfully suggest that this law could not have been defective and effective at the same time.
18. From contraries;	18. Arguing that it is not always appropriate to choose the same thing before and after an event, but rather the reverse; *Example:* Was it not shameful that this young mother, while staying with her parents, fought to come home to see her children, and having come home, was forced by her husband to go back to her parents in order not to fight?
19. From purpose to cause;	19. Arguing that the purpose for which something might exist or might happen is the cause for which it does exist or has happened;
20. From reasons why people act and why they avoid action;	20. Arguing as to what turns the mind in favor or against something; *Example:* Would not a man, such as Mr. Smith, who had a serious gambling habit and who was about to experience a foreclosure of his home mortgage, be tempted, if not inclined, to "borrow" money from his employer without his employer knowing it?

21. From things which have happened previously, though implausible;	21. Arguing that truth is often stranger than fiction; *Example:* Who, in 1985, would have predicted that the Berlin Wall would be rubble by 1992? Why then is it not possible for Ms. Murphy, against all odds, to have made $3,000,000 investing in the stock market on one day without access to any inside information?
22. From the refutative;	22. Argument by looking at contradictions in three separate ways: (1) as applying to the opponent; (2) as applying to the speaker; and (3) as applying to the speaker and the opponent; *Example 1:* He says he loves his company; yet he gives his company's secrets to his company's enemies. *Example 2:* She says that I am litigious, yet she cannot state the name of a single case which I allegedly have filed. *Example 3:* Her employer has never lent her any money, but I have rescued her from foreclosure.
23. From the possibility of false impression;	23. Arguing by analogy from the possibility of false impression; *Example:* For centuries, many people believed the world to be flat. When the facts became known, the people discovered that they were initially wrong. So, too, of my Mr. Walton's alleged misconduct.
24. From cause and effect;	24. Arguing that if the cause exists, the effect does; if it does not, there is no effect; *Example:* It is clear that the Ms. Carlton's preoccupation with tuning her car radio resulted in her driving through the red light and crashing into Mr. Fenster's car, broadside.
25. From the possibility of an untried, better plan;	25. Arguing that there is possibly a better way of doing something than the present way; *Example:* Perhaps this case is more suitable for mediation than arbitration.

26. From a comparison to things done in the past?	26. Argument by focusing on the comparison between what is being proposed to be done, and what has been done in the past; *Example:* Ms. Arbitrator, I respectfully point out that you have given us ten days in the past to submit our post-hearing briefs, rather than the five days which you have just proposed.
27. On the basis of mistake;	27. Accusing or defending on the basis that mistakes have been made; *Example:* Because all the other identically phrased clauses in the contract were scratched through with initials of the contracting parties, it must have been a mistake that this single identical clause remained.
28. From the meaning of a proper name;	28. Argument by association with a proper name of a person, place, or thing, known generally to the audience; *Example:* Management's decision on this matter has created a Loch Ness in the workplace.

5.12.4   Aristotle's nine fallacious arguments

Aristotle identified nine fallacious arguments. As an advocate in arbitration, you should be aware of them in order to avoid using them and to be able to detect when a speaker is employing them. Some of the examples appearing in the chart below are those of Aristotle, some are those of this author, and some are combinations of both.[45]

---

45. This chart is developed from information contained in George A. Kennedy, *Aristotle on Rhetoric: A Theory of Civic Discourse* 204–210 (1991); *see also* John W. Cooley, *A Classical Approach to Mediation—Part I: Classical Rhetoric and the Art of Persuasion in Mediation*, 19 U. of Dayton L. Rev. 83, 115–16 (1993).

ARISTOTLE'S NINE FALLACIOUS ARGUMENTS	
FALLACIES	*DESCRIPTIONS AND EXAMPLES*
1. Fallacy Resulting: From the shape of the expression;	1. Using words that sound the same but have different meanings; *Example:* Plaintiff's counsel: "After the injury to my client, the barber admitted his 'sheer' misfunction." Opposing counsel: "That's not true. What my client said was 'my shears malfunctioned.'"
2. From combining what is divided and dividing what is combined;	2. Connecting facts or arguments, and then drawing an inference without basis in fact; dividing facts or arguments to make things seem what they are not; *Example:* Defendant was not at work and not at home, so he must have sabotaged his employer's power station.
3. From exaggeration;	3. The absence of argument or enthymeme; opponent attempts to persuade by bombast; amplification of alleged action without proof; *Example:* What defendant did here has sent a clear signal to every last teenager in the country that they can engage in computer piracy and become rich doing it.
4. From an unnecessary sign;	4. A nonsyllogistic statement; *Example:* Every wicked man is a thief.
5. From an accidental result;	5. Drawing a conclusion based on seeming circumstances and not on the facts or reason; *Example:* The Chief Executive Officer was angry because he felt the Union leaders intentionally dishonored him by not inviting him to the retirement luncheon, when, in fact, his name was overlooked completely by mistake.
6. From a fallacious assumption;	6. *Example:* Because the beggars sing and dance in the subway station, they are happy.

7. From treating a non-cause as a cause;	7. Treating what happens later as though it happened because of what preceded; *Example:* Three hours after the train blew its whistle, the shop owner found his front window cracked from top to bottom. There is no question that the railroad is responsible for the damage.
8. By omission of consideration of when and how;	8. *Example:* A person may always kill another in self-defense. [In the pertinent jurisdiction, the proposition is valid only if the person does not use excessive force and does not initially provoke hostility].
9. By confusing what is general and what is not general with the particular;	9. Arguing that the improbable will be probable because some things happen contrary to probability; arguing a qualified (rather than a general) probability without clearly saying so; *Example:* If a strong man is charged with assault, he should be acquitted because it is not likely that he would start the fight for the very reason that it would seem probable that he would be accused of starting it.

◆ CHAPTER SIX ◆

Post-Hearing Advocacy

The meaning of a sentence may be more than that of separate words, as a melody is more than the notes, and no degree of particularity can ever obviate recourse to the setting in which all appear, and which all collectively create.

—Learned Hand

This chapter traces the possible activities of the arbitration advocate from the completion of the arbitration hearing through an appeal. You will perceive an overriding theme as you read this chapter: The law and courts discourage all post-hearing activity beyond enforcement of the arbitrator's award. This is because arbitration's primary purpose is to avoid the cost and time required for traditional in-court dispute resolution. Courts, both state and federal, generally frown upon the judicial challenge of any arbitration award whether at the trial or appeal level. The bases upon which a losing party may challenge the arbitrator's award provisions are, by federal and state statutes, extremely limited. That clear legislatively established policy coupled with a strong judicial preference toward enforcement, allows very few opportunities to a losing party to complain about an arbitrator's award. For all practical purposes, if the parties have agreed to binding arbitration, the award is final and the parties must live with it.

There are, however, a few exceptions to the rigid no-court-challenge rule, and these are discussed in sections 6.5 and 6.6, infra. Because these exceptions will rarely apply to an arbitration in which you are involved, you are probably better advised to expend your effort convincing the arbitrator of your position's merit before issuance of the award—in your post-hearing briefs, if they are requested; or, if it is necessary, after the issuance of the award—in a motion for reconsideration of the award or for rehearing. In these post-hearing and post-award briefing situations you will put your story-telling skills to the ultimate test. It is in these situations that, as the opening quote suggests, something as simple as a sentence's meaning can be our most helpful ally or our most ruthless enemy. To these post-hearing advocate activities—most of which rely on the power of the pen—we now turn.

6.1   Drafting Post-Hearing Briefs

Occasionally, an arbitrator will request counsel to file post-hearing briefs in lieu of closing arguments or in addition to them. If the arbitrator requests such briefs, you should take the request very seriously and ask the arbitrator what format and content he or she prefers. Usually, arbitrators request such briefs in complex factual cases where it is not completely clear, even from the counsel's oral arguments, whether there is sufficient evidence to sustain particular elements of claims or defenses. However, there may be other reasons for requesting briefs. For example, there might be very difficult legal questions which the arbitrator must decide and which require citations to the particular cases supporting the parties' respective positions. In other situations, arbitrators may need the parties' respective views on how scientific or highly technical testimony of expert witnesses supports their legal positions. Thus, it is very important, before leaving the hearing room for the last time, that you ask the arbitrator whether he or she wants you to focus on any particular topics covered by the evidence submitted and the arguments heard.

If the arbitrator does not request that post-hearing briefs be filed, you should consider requesting permission to file a brief. Occasionally, there are evidence situations that are so delicate, so intricate, or so fraught with the potential for misunderstanding, that the only way to handle them effectively is through a meticulous review and marshaling of the evidence. There may be other reasons why you might conclude that post-hearing briefs are necessary. In a high-stakes case, where defeat would mean substantial monetary loss to your client, you should request permission to file briefs. If you do not, and your client loses big, you may always wonder whether a brief might have made the difference. Briefing will, of course, cost your client further expense and will most likely delay the award's issuance. You should advise your client of these facts when you discuss your reasons for seeking to file a brief.

If you are directed or are permitted to file a post-hearing brief, you should draft it with the same care you would take in drafting a good appellate brief. You should place particular emphasis on qualities of brevity, clarity and succinctness, bearing in mind that the more there is to read, the more time it will take the arbitrator to read it. Follow all rules and requests of the arbitrator. By no means should you exceed any page limitation. Where possible, make thorough referencing and citation to the hearing transcript, if there is one, and to any pertinent exhibits introduced during the hearing. Avoid superfluous arguments and minimize alternative arguments. If an arbitrator has asked the parties to address a specific point for the sake of clarity, address only that point. Additional ramblings about what you think is important will not endear you or your client to the arbitrator.

When you draft a post-hearing brief, think like the arbitrator. That is, put yourself in the arbitrator's shoes and think what you want to know about the case in order to render a fair and just decision. Craft the facts so as to capitalize on the persuasive trial story you have created through your hearing evidence. Concentrate on the important factual and legal issues—the ones that the arbitrator may have asked questions about at the hearing. Realize that the arbitrator might be swayed as much by the situation's equities as by the legal technicalities. This is a particularly important consideration if your arbitrator is a non-lawyer. Sometimes the mechanical application of law can yield results that defy common sense. As you write the brief, continuously ask yourself "What seems fair?" and "What would be the common sense approach to this situation?" If you harp on hypertechnicalities in your brief, completely disregarding the human element, do not be surprised if you receive an unfavorable decision from the arbitrator.

Make your brief reader-friendly, well-organized, and divided by headings and subheadings where appropriate. Your writing style should be simple and direct. Use of unnecessary words and legalese, archaic, or intellectual language is always inappropriate, and more so when the arbitrator is a non-lawyer. Choose words carefully, and heed appropriate conventions of style, grammar, construction, and punctuation. Do not repeat yourself. Avoid bluster and a self-important style with a passion. Keep your writing simple and unpretentious and its greatness will shine through.

There is a story told that when Eleanor Roosevelt visited California's Monterey Peninsula, a local mother took her youngsters to the airport to see her arrive. Before the plane landed, the mother gave them a thorough briefing on just who Mrs. Roosevelt was, and concluded, "She's a very great lady."

As the First Lady disembarked, one of the children, a little girl, slipped away from her mother and trotted alongside Mrs. Roosevelt to the terminal, looking interestedly up at her face. Returning to her mother, she remarked thoughtfully, "You know, I don't think she knows she's a great lady."[1]

In sum, arbitrators rarely require the parties to submit post-hearing briefs. If briefs are required, consider the request's gravity, and seize the opportunity to make a good showing for your client. Above all, view your task through the arbitrator's eyes—what you are inclined to write in your adversarial role may not be what the arbitrator wants to see.

Keep in mind that a post-hearing brief which successfully builds rapport with the arbitrator's sense of justice and fairness will, more often than not, precipitate a decision in your favor.

---

1. Jacob M. Braude, *Lifetime Speaker's Encyclopedia* (Vol 2) 754 (Prentice Hall, Inc. 1962).

6.2   Requisites of an Award

An arbitrator fashions an award based upon her evaluation of the case's facts and the applicable law. The arbitrator may grant any just and equitable relief within the scope of her authority. The parties may, however, limit the scope of the allowable remedies or relief available to the arbitrator, and by agreement may exclude specific remedies. This can be done either in the submission agreement or in the arbitration clause included in the original contract.

The arbitrator's award should always be in writing, signed by the arbitrator, and, if required by rules or the parties' agreement, notarized and witnessed. It should be clear and concise. Normally, the award does not include a written opinion explaining the arbitrator's reasoning, but it must contain a ruling on all claims (principal claims, counter-claims, third-party claims, etc.) and damage requests (compensatory, consequential, punitive, etc.) in issue. It must name the winning party on each claim, and the party against whom the award is rendered. The precise dollar amount of the award on each claim must also be specified. The award is the arbitrator's last act in the discharge of her duties. As such, in addition to making liability and damage determinations, it also apportions all administrative fees and expenses for the hearing and assesses the arbitrator's fees and attorney's fees, if appropriate.

A written opinion is usually not required in arbitration because it slows down the process and encourages appeals by losing parties who wish to challenge the arbitrator's reasoning. Court challenges to reasoning in an arbitrator's opinion are usually unsuccessful, even if the arbitrator completely misconstrues the applicable law.

An award may be either binding or non-binding, depending on the parties' pre-arbitration agreement. Binding awards are enforceable under applicable breach of contract laws. In most jurisdictions, a binding arbitration award, if properly filed and confirmed in court, has the same effect as a court judgment, except that it is not usually subject to appeal. A non-binding award has no legal effect, but, of course, the parties can still agree to accept it. Even if the parties do not accept the non-binding award, they can still use it to facilitate settlement. In some jurisdictions, a party who rejects the result of a court-annexed arbitration may in certain circumstances be liable for the opponent's costs and attorney's fees.

Normally, the parties will set the time period in which the arbitrator must render the award. They may do this through the pre-arbitration agreement or in the arbitration clause in the original contract. This time period may also be fixed by dispute resolution organization rules, local court rules, judge's guidelines, or statute. Dispute resolution organizations commonly have rules allowing thirty days for an arbitrator to issue an award. An experienced arbitrator with knowledge of the subject matter should, however, be able to render an award almost immediately after an arbitration hearing.

6.3   Motion to Reopen Hearing or to Modify or Correct Award

After closing the hearing, the arbitrator may reopen it on his own motion or on the motion of any party.[2] Reasons for an arbitrator's reopening of a hearing might include: apparent insufficient evidence on an aspect of the case; doubt as to applicable law; or additional briefing is needed. Customarily, if the hearing's reopening would delay issuance of the award beyond the time limitation specified in the arbitration agreement, the arbitrator may not reopen the hearing without the parties' consent. Usually, a hearing may not be reopened after the award is issued.

If a party moves to reopen the hearing, the party must demonstrate good cause. Satisfactory "good cause" would normally include newly discovered evidence that could not have been known or presented at the time of the hearing. The moving party must show that the evidence was unavailable at the time of the hearing or that there is a reasonable explanation for its nonproduction. The movant must also demonstrate that the reopening will not seriously affect a substantial right of the other party.

More common than the motion to reopen proceedings is the motion to modify or correct the award. The latter is in the nature of a motion for reconsideration, but normally the reconsideration does not permit any material modification of the award. A motion to modify or correct an award is made where:[3]

> There is an evident material mistake in the figures referred to in the award.

> There is an evident material mistake in the description of any person, thing, or property referred to in the award.

> The arbitrators have issued an award concerning a matter not submitted to them.

> The form of the award is incorrect.

> Information needs to be added or deleted to effect the intent of the award.

> Clarification is needed to promote justice between the parties.

---

2. *See generally* Oehmke, *Commercial Arbitration* (Revised Edition), chapter 125 (Clark Boardman Callaghan, 1995).
3. Id. at §128:04.

A motion for modification or clarification must demonstrate indefiniteness or confusion in the interpretation of the award. A sufficient basis for such motion would be a movant's assertion of no reasonable certainty as to how to comply with the award.

6.4   Enforcing the Award

The procedure for enforcing arbitration awards is summary in nature. The filing in court of a petition to confirm an award and to enter judgment (with a proposed order and judgment) is the usual method of enforcement provided by most state statutes. Typically, the state court statutory period for filing the petition is one year from the date of the award. The Uniform Arbitration Act permits objections or a counterclaim to vacate the award within ninety days of filing the petition to confirm.[4]

The procedure is similar in the federal court system under the Federal Arbitration Act (9 U.S.C.§9). One party petitions to confirm an award; and a disagreeing opponent may cross-move to vacate it. Where there are no genuine issues of material fact, the confirmation order is granted and summary judgment is entered. To enter summary judgment, the court normally requires the following documents to be on file:[5]

> ➢ the arbitration agreement;

> ➢ papers dealing with the selection or appointment, if any, of an additional umpire;

> ➢ any written extension of time within which to make the award;

> ➢ the award; and

> ➢ each notice, affidavit, or other paper used upon an application to confirm the award, and a copy of each court order upon such application.

A judgment confirming an arbitration award is docketed as in any other action and has the same force and effect as any other judgment.

6.5   Challenging the Award

There are only a few grounds for challenging arbitration awards in court, and even those are very narrowly construed. Usually only statutory exceptions apply. These exceptions do not include mistakes of fact, errors of law, poor reasoning on the part of the arbitrator, or arbitrary and unjustified determinations. In fact, to secure judicial inquiry, a challenging party must demonstrate extraordinary circumstances which indicate an arbitrator's abuse of power or use of power

---

4. Oehmke *supra* chapter 5, note 2, at chapter 21.
5. Oehmke, *supra* note 2, at §137:05.

beyond his or her jurisdiction. The challenging party also carries the burden of proof.

In almost every instance, when a court is considering statutory exceptions to enforcement, it does so with a very strong pro-enforcement bias. There are, however, several grounds upon which an arbitration award might be vacated.[6] These include:

Contract

> no written agreement to arbitrate

> party breached part of agreement to arbitrate

> arbitration agreement is invalid

> arbitration was demanded after contract or statutory limitation

Hearing

> arbitrator conducted hearing contrary to the arbitration statute or rules

> party committed fraud in the arbitration

> arbitrator refused to consider material facts

> parties agreed to reopen the hearing because of the discovery of new evidence, but the arbitrator refused

Arbitrator

> arbitrator displayed bias and partiality

> arbitrator failed to disclose a serious conflict of interest

> arbitrator was corrupt

> arbitrator refused to postpone hearing when good cause was shown

> arbitrator exceeded authority

Award

> arbitrator decided non-arbitrable matters

> arbitrators failed to make a mutual, final, and definite award

> award was procured by corruption, fraud, or undue means

> award was not timely rendered, despite party's protest

> evident material miscalculation of figures in the award

---

6. *See* Oehmke, *supra* note 2, at §142:04.

> ➢ evident material mistake in the description of a person, thing, or property referred to in the award

> ➢ award is contrary to public policy

Non-arbitrability of a dispute is a threshold matter of enforceability which can generally be resolved at the outset of the arbitration hearing and, if necessary, ruled upon by a court at that time. Some courts will hold that this issue is waived if it is not brought up at the appropriate time. Arbitrability may also be challenged on the ground that the arbitration clause is invalid under the laws governing the original contract entered into by the parties. This type of challenge is rare because the mere existence of an arbitration clause in a valid contract is difficult to rebut.

If an arbitrator makes a decision regarding a matter not included within the arbitration's scope, a party may challenge the award. This challenge is construed as narrowly as any other challenge, however, and the burden of proof is just as high. Courts are normally unwilling to second-guess an arbitrator's interpretation of the parties' agreement. Courts often uphold provisions outside the scope of the arbitration agreement on the ground that the arbitrator had simply interpreted the clause as ineffective to deny his own jurisdiction.

Evident partiality or corruption are also grounds upon which you may challenge an award. However, standards of conduct for arbitrators differ depending on who appointed them. An arbitrator appointed by a party, as opposed to one appointed as a neutral, often will not be held to the same requirement of impartiality. Courts have ruled that an arbitrator will not be held to the same standards of impartiality as a judge. There are also circumstances under which parties may not have the defense of bias available to them. These include prior knowledge of facts suggesting the arbitrator's partiality and waiver based on lack of objections to partiality at the time that knowledge was gained.

Improperly refusing a postponement or refusing to hear evidence may constitute a procedural due process ground upon which an award may be challenged. However, as in all other cases of award challenges, the threshold of proof is very high. The challenger must demonstrate not only disregard of due process, but actual harm as a result of such disregard. Inability to fully cross examine a witness and inability to reschedule a hearing because of a witness's prior speaking engagement have both been found to not violate a party's procedural due process rights.

Rulings contrary to law are also difficult to establish as a basis for challenging an arbitrator's award. The challenging party must demonstrate that an arbitrator appreciated the existence of a clearly governing standard, but decided to ignore it. In some jurisdictions, in order to be judicially vacated, the arbitrator's finding must be completely irrational. Courts will find a foundation for any award so long as in some logical way the award is derivable from the original contract's wording.

Challenges based on awards being contrary to public policy have rarely been successful. This is generally because courts view the pubic policy favoring arbitration to override any dissatisfaction with an award based on its violation of some lesser public policy consideration.

The standard of proof required to establish corruption, fraud, or undue means is clear and convincing evidence. A party must demonstrate that it could not have discovered the fraud with the exercise of due diligence prior to the arbitration. The challenger must also demonstrate that the fraud was materially related to an issue in contest in the arbitration. Proof of perjury can be a successful challenge if it meets the clear and convincing standard. So might a failure to disclose fees paid by one party to the arbitrator. In any case, in order for a challenge based on fraud, corruption, or undue means to be successful, that fraud, corruption, or undue means must stem from the arbitrator's behavior.

Because the grounds for challenging an arbitration award are very narrow, agreed-to challenges may be a subject that parties might wish to explore, negotiate, and specify in an arbitration agreement. As an alternative, in appropriate situations counsel may wish to design the arbitration process initially to provide for a pre-designated appellate tribunal, should the losing party in the arbitration wish to appeal.

6.6   Appeal

If an arbitration award is challenged in court and a final judgment is entered, the judgment, as in any other case, is appealable to the appellate court. On appeal, the appellate court can confirm, vacate, recommit, modify, clarify, or correct an award. Rarely, if ever, would an appellate court reverse an award on the merits, even if there were a transcript of the arbitration proceedings. Instead, the appellate court might vacate an award, requiring the arbitration process to begin anew.[7]

Most appellate courts in reviewing appeals from judgments entered on arbitration awards abide by these presumptions:[8]

➢   the award is presumed to be valid

➢   there is no review for errors or misinterpretations of fact or law

---

7. *See* Oehmke, *supra* chapter 5, note 2 at §22:4.
8. *See* Oehmke, *supra* note 2, at §141:09.

> ➤ the arbitration proceedings will not be invalidated for failure to meet rules of evidence or other procedural requirements applicable to trials.

> ➤ the arbitrator does not have to give reasons for the award.

The Federal Arbitration Act (9 U.S.C. §16 et seq.) specifies district court orders related to arbitration proceedings that are appealable and those that are not appealable.[9]

The appealable orders and decisions are as follows:

> ➤ order refusing to stay litigation

> ➤ order refusing to compel arbitration

> ➤ order confirming an arbitrator's award or partial award

> ➤ order denying confirmation of an arbitrator's award or partial award

> ➤ order modifying an arbitrator's award

> ➤ order correcting an arbitrator's award

> ➤ order vacating an arbitrator's award

> ➤ interlocutory order granting, continuing, or modifying an injunction against an arbitration

> ➤ a final decision with respect to an arbitration

The non-appealable orders and decisions are:

> ➤ order staying litigation which allows arbitration to proceed

> ➤ order compelling or directing arbitration to proceed

> ➤ order refusing to modify or correct an award

> ➤ order refusing to grant, continue, or modify an injunction against an arbitration subject to the Act.

> ➤ order which is interim and nonfinal

From the above listings, it is evident that the Federal Arbitration Act contains an intended legislative bias in favor of honoring parties' agreements to arbitrate their disputes to conclusion without judicial interference. Note especially that where a district court rejects a party's request to modify or correct an award, the decision is non-appealable.

---

9. *See* Oehmke, *supra* note 2 at §§ 156:07 and 156:08.

◆ CHAPTER SEVEN ◆

Description of the Hybrid Processes

No trumpets sound when the important decisions . . . are made.
—Agnes DeMille

Pure mediation or pure arbitration may not be the most appropriate alternative means for resolving a particular dispute. In these situations you need to exercise creativity in selecting or designing an appropriate hybrid process to satisfy your client's specific needs. Med-arb, discussed in section 1.1, is just one of many available hybrids. In binding mediation—which on its face seems to be an oxymoron—if mediation is unsuccessful, the mediator makes a binding decision at a figure within the mediated bracket.

New hybrids seem to be emerging all the time. For example, if you are dissatisfied with the neutral-biasing potential of med-arb and binding mediation, you may be attracted to the clearer role distinctions for the neutral in arb-med. In that process, the parties first proceed to arbitration before an arbitrator who renders a binding decision. The arbitrator does not show the decision to the parties; rather the arbitrator places the decision in a sealed envelope. The parties can then negotiate a resolution on their own, or they can involve the arbitrator as a mediator to help mediate a resolution. The arbitrator's decision, having already been made, is not influenced by any confidential information of the parties. If the mediation or negotiations are unsuccessful, the parties open the sealed envelope and are bound by the award. Parties negotiating in the shadow of the sealed award tend to reach a joint decision for themselves rather than to entrust their fate to an imposed solution of unknown value.

As the opening quote suggests, trumpets won't sound to let you know that you have decided on the best ADR process for resolving your client's dispute. You must simply examine the alternatives and use your best judgment to select or design the appropriate process. To do this effectively, you must have a clear understanding of the principal hybrid processes already in standard use. Some of the principal hybrid ADR processes are described below.[1]

---

1. *See generally* Branton and Lovett, *supra* chapter 7, note 7, at 3–4 to 3–6.

7.1   High-Low Arbitration

A form of arbitration increasingly used in personal injury and other types of disputes is high-low arbitration, also called bracketed arbitration. It is commonly used where liability is not an issue, though that condition is not a prerequisite. In this process, the parties negotiate to impasse, and then proceed to arbitration. Plaintiff's last settlement demand and defendant's last offer establish a bracket defining the limits of the arbitrator's award in the case. The arbitrator conducts the arbitration without knowledge of the endpoints of the bracket. The parties are free to make any evidence-based arguments they wish regarding damages, and if the arbitrator determines the defendant is liable, he or she makes a decision on damages as if it were ordinary arbitration. When the arbitrator renders an award, neither party will be liable for a figure outside the agreed-to bracket.

For example, assume that in a particular case the plaintiff's last demand was $100,000 and the defendant's last offer was $50,000. The parties then proceed to an arbitration hearing at which the plaintiff argues entitlement to damages in the amount of $150,000 and the defendant argues that plaintiff is entitled to $25,000, at most. If the arbitrator renders an award of $125,000, the defendant will pay no more than $100,000. If the arbitrator renders an award of $35,000, the plaintiff will receive $50,000. If the arbitrator renders an award of $75,000, the plaintiff will receive $75,000 because that figure falls within the pre-agreed bracket.

There are several advantages to high-low arbitration. First, it reduces the risk of allowing a third party to decide your fate. Going to the arbitration, both parties know the lower and upper limits on the award. Second, it encourages vigorous bargaining because the plaintiff wants to establish the highest minimum award possible and the defendant seeks to fix the lowest maximum award possible. This situation usually forces the parties to find a reasonable settlement range, and at the same time, a reasonably narrow bracket. If the bracket is too large, say, $25,000 and $1,000,000, when the parties proceed to arbitration, there is very little advantage of high-low arbitration over ordinary arbitration—unless, of course, one side or the other has thoroughly misjudged the case's value. Finally, high-low arbitration is more economical than going to trial after an unsuccessful mediation. Typically, a skillful mediator helps the parties arrive at a reasonable settlement range, which can serve as the bracket in a subsequent high-low arbitration conducted by another neutral.

7.2   Baseball Arbitration

Baseball arbitration is a type of final-offer arbitration in which the disputing parties agree in writing to negotiate to only one position—their last and best offer—and then submit the dispute to arbitration. In baseball arbitration, the arbitrator must choose the final offer of one of the parties and may not find a different result in any circumstance.

This type of final-offer arbitration had its origin in player salary negotiations in major league baseball but now is an ADR method adaptable to practically any type of dispute involving a monetary solution. A quick decision is a valuable feature of the classic version of baseball arbitration. The arbitrator must pick one figure or the other and is encouraged to render his or her decision within twenty-four hours. The decision is binding, and there can be no compromise. Also, the arbitrator may give no explanation for the decision.

The rigidity of final-offer arbitration is its main selling point. It is also its own deterrent. Labor experts believe that the risk involved in having your offer rejected and the other side's offer selected promotes good faith bargaining, encourages a narrow negotiated settlement bracket, and in practice provides an incentive for parties to resolve differences without an arbitration hearing.

7.3   Fact-Finding

Fact-finding is a dispute resolution process that provides a more efficient, speedy, and sensitive resolution of claims. It is particularly helpful in resolving claims for which the traditional adversarial resolution process cannot meet all participants' needs, for example, sexual harassment claims.

In a fact-finding intervention, the court normally appoints a fact-finder or team of fact-finders to investigate the complaint and issue a written report of findings. Because fact-finders are generally used in cases involving sensitive issues, confidentiality is a paramount requirement. A fact-finder must be someone who is sensitive to others' concerns, a good judge of credibility using little information, able to keep absolute strict confidentiality, and a skillful interviewer. Whenever possible, fact-finders should have expertise in the field that they are investigating.

A fact-finder must also have unlimited access to relevant information, witnesses, and documentation. Parties who agree to the fact-finding process will gain little by not cooperating. The fact-finder must conduct interviews with the pertinent parties and any other persons who have relevant information. Where at all possible, this is done outside the presence of the parties' lawyers with the knowledge and permission of the parties and their lawyers.

The fact-finder's report states what the fact-finder believes happened and identifies any issues about which the fact-finder is unable to draw conclusions. Since the fact-finder is neutral and uninvolved, this report serves as a basis for resolving the conflict. The report does not reach any legal conclusions. For example, in a sexual harassment case, the report does not say whether sexual harassment has occurred. Unless the parties have previously agreed otherwise, the report does not recommend remedies. It does, however, assess the credibility of all those interviewed.

The fact-finder's report is submitted to the court and to each party. The court usually gives the parties a reasonable time period to resolve the dispute on their own before it takes its next step—which may be to commence the litigation process or to move on to a mediation or arbitration process. Generally, it is not a good idea to have the fact-finder go on to serve as either a mediator or arbitrator following the investigation. Depending on the specific circumstances and the agreements of the parties, the court may provide the fact-finder's report to the mediator or arbitrator. At this stage, the parties are usually represented by counsel.

In some sexual harassment claim situations, the court appoints two fact-finders, one man and one woman. This team approach allows the process to avoid the insensitivity of the usual adversary process to both the accuser and the accused in a sexual harassment claim. The more sensitive, specialized environment provided by fact-finding greatly increases the likelihood that the parties will reach mutually acceptable results on their own and avoid litigation that would be costly, both financially and emotionally, to all involved.

7.4   Co-Med-Arb

The ADR process called co-med-arb has emerged in recent years as an antidote to many of the ills which plague the process of med-arb, described in section 1.1. As you recall, med-arb is a combination of the mediation and arbitration processes in which a neutral serves in the role of mediator initially and attempts to settle the dispute. If mediation is unsuccessful, the same neutral serves in the role of arbitrator, hears evidence presented by the parties, and then renders an arbitral award. Med-arb "has been praised for its efficiency gains and condemned for resulting in a 'confusion of roles' that jeopardizes both the effectiveness of mediation and the integrity of arbitral decision making."[2]

The basic concept of co-med-arb is to use two neutrals, one in the role of mediator and one as arbitrator, but to have them work as closely as possible together to maximize their efficiency while avoiding confusion of roles. Even though co-med-arb employs two neutrals, the design of the process seeks to avoid duplicative expenses by saving time needed to bring the arbitrator "up to speed" should the mediation prove unsuccessful.

---

2. Christian Buehring-Uhle, *Co-Med-Arb Technique Holds Promise for Getting Best of Both Worlds*, 3 World Arbitration and Mediation Report 21 (1992). *See also*, Roth, Wulff, & Cooper, *supra*, chapter 3, note 2, at §37:12.

The parties select both the mediator and the arbitrator prior to the dispute or after the dispute arises. The two neutrals jointly tend to procedural matters such as conducting a pre-hearing conference, setting dates for meetings, and scheduling the filing of briefs. The mediator and arbitrator review all submitted documents prior to the hearing. At the initial session of the hearing, they sit as a panel to hear the parties' opening statements in what is called the open phase. During this open phase, the arbitrator presides and both the arbitrator and mediator may ask clarifying questions of counsel, but the mediator withholds asking "sensitive" questions regarding the parties' needs and interests until the second, or confidential, phase of the process. After the open phase closes, the rules preclude the mediator from discussing the substance of the dispute with the arbitrator, though the two neutrals may usually confer on procedural matters.

In the confidential phase, the mediator attempts to mediate the dispute to resolution. If the parties reach an impasse, they proceed to the third phase of the process and present their evidence to the arbitrator. When this occurs, the mediator is usually "on call" in the event that the parties desire to resume mediation at one or more points during the arbitration. If the parties resume mediation, the mediator sets strict time limits on the mediation conference.

Although mediation efforts may not be successful initially in resolving the entire dispute, they can lead to a variety of possible beneficial results including streamlining the arbitration, achieving a stipulation of facts or agreed limitation of issues, and resolving several of the contested issues. The mediator may also be helpful after the arbitration hearing concludes. If the parties desire, the arbitrator may withhold the award until after the parties have a limited-duration final session with the mediator to attempt to work out a mutually satisfactory settlement. If the mediation is successful, the parties agree that the award should not issue, and they enter into a settlement agreement. If the mediation is unsuccessful, the arbitrator issues the award, and if the parties desire, they can request that the mediator conduct a post-award settlement conference.

Although the co-med-arb process is generally more expensive than pure mediation or pure arbitration, use of the process can prove to be a very wise investment. In complex, high-stakes disputes, the value of co-med-arb's collateral benefits may far outweigh its cost in dollars. Because of the continuous availability of mediation, there is opportunity for a settlement early in the co-med-arb process, or at any number of points during the process. Moreover, the process may avoid damaging continuing relationships that your client needs to maintain with one or more of the parties. In short, choosing the two-neutral co-med-arb tandem process may allow you to extract the best of both the mediation and the arbitration processes while minimizing the disadvantages associated with using one or the other or with using their sequenced amalgam, med-arb.

7.5   Summary Jury Trial

In 1980, Federal District Judge Thomas D. Lambros created the summary jury trial method of alternative dispute resolution as a case management option, because he found himself with a massive docket of toxic tort cases, primarily asbestos cases. Each of these cases had reached a point where the parties considered them unsettlable. In conceiving the summary jury trial, Judge Lambros had three objectives. First, he wished to facilitate settlements by allowing parties who have failed to settle in traditional pretrial settlement conferencing the opportunity, at very low cost, to see the reactions of actual jurors to their case, within the courtroom environment. Second, he wished to give parties the opportunity to define their issues and learn how the presiding judge would rule on their arguments. Third, he sought to give parties the opportunity to debrief jurors following a proceeding in order to give the lawyers and parties an idea of how a jury would react to and understand their arguments.

A summary jury trial is an actual nonbinding trial that can usually be completed in less than one day. It is designed to facilitate a settlement. A party may entirely disregard the findings of the summary trial jury, but when cases that have been argued in summary proceedings go to full trial, it is quite likely that the full-trial jury will find in the same way.

To ensure that a trial with the potential to last for weeks can be completed in one day, the lawyers and the judge must work together to strip from the summary trial all unnecessary tasks. To accomplish this, the lawyers present all the evidence in a narrative fashion, based on affidavits and depositions gathered throughout discovery which usually has already been completed. Evidentiary objections are not made at the summary trial, rather they are resolved at a comprehensive pre-summary trial conference.

At the final pre-summary trial conference, the judge rules on all pending motions and sets a date for the summary trial. Since no witnesses will be called, lengthy notice periods can be avoided, allowing a summary trial to commence within a week of the decision to have one. The judge normally directs each party, a few days prior to the summary trial, to submit a short trial brief, arguing only the issues pertinent to the summary trial. These briefs also contain proposed jury instructions. The judge normally requires the parties to accompany their attorneys to the summary trial so they are able to see firsthand how a jury will react to their arguments. The judge also sets time limitations on counsels' presentations. Usually, each side is given roughly fifteen minutes for an opening statement, one hour for its case-in-chief, one-half hour to rebut, and the opportunity to carve out time in reserve for a closing statement, at the party's option.

This final pre-summary trial conference serves more than just the purpose of laying the hearing's ground rules. It is an opportunity to provide momentum for the case to settle. Roughly one third of all summary jury cases settle between the final pre-summary trial conference and the summary trial. This happens for several reasons. Parties have had their first opportunity to see how the judge is likely to rule on motions in limine and evidentiary objections, and they begin to realize how the judge will probably rule on those motions in a full trial. For this reason, it is necessary for the judge to use all of the same evidentiary standards at the summary trial that he or she would at a full trial and to try to rule in a similar way. Also, attorneys are made more aware of the risk of having their claims defeated, which makes settlement all the more attractive. And, certainly it is true that a party who has lost a summary jury trial, whether he intended to go to full trial or not, has had his bargaining power diminished greatly.

It is vitally important that the summary jury trial mirror an actual trial. A jury is empaneled through a voir dire process, just as in a full trial. The major differences are that the jury in summary jury proceedings is usually six persons rather than ten or twelve, and that the judge conducts the voir dire. The judge may ask jurors to fill out profiles before the date of the summary trial. Furthermore, the judge must be careful to empanel a jury that would be just like a jury at a full trial in order for the litigants to gain the full effect of the summary trial jury's input. For this reason, the judge may allow each party's attorney two peremptory challenges.

Once the jury is empaneled and sworn, the trial proceeds in much the same order as a full trial would, with the attorneys presenting evidence in narrative form. Some judges permit videotapes of expert witnesses and critical occurrence witnesses to be played. The attorneys may use any physical evidence, exhibits, or other devices that they would be permitted to use in a full trial. If the summary jury trial does not proceed in the same way a full trial would proceed, litigants will not have as much confidence in the jury's findings as they normally would and will have less incentive to settle.

Following the verdict, the jurors are debriefed by the judge and the lawyers, and sometimes by the litigants themselves. The debriefing is quite instructive, making the parties aware of the specific reasons supporting the jury's evaluation of the case.

Immediately following the debriefing, post-summary trial settlement conferencing begins. This conferencing may last for several weeks, as needed. If a reasonable period of time elapses without a settlement being reached, the court may set the case for full trial. A very large majority of cases that go through the summary jury trial process settle. But even in those that do not, the summary trial allows a streamlined full trial, usually shorter and usually with stronger arguments from both sides.

7.6   Mini-Trial

The mini-trial, as apparent from its name, is an abbreviated trial or hearing. This method of dispute resolution is a relatively new approach with two major advantages: first, mini-trials curtail much of the discovery process; and second, mini-trials involve high-level business persons early in the dispute resolution process. Because discovery is limited, and because the hearing itself is in fact a miniature hearing, this method of dispute resolution can be dramatically less expensive than traditional litigation. However, compared to other methods of dispute resolution, the mini-trial is relatively more expensive.

The mini-trial method is best suited to large disputes and complex litigation, such as cases involving breaches of complex contracts, particularly if there are intricate technical issues; patent cases; antitrust cases; major construction cases; and product liability cases. This is because the panel asked to decide the case will include business experts in the field—a high-level management executive of each party. The parties initiate a mini-trial by negotiating a mini-trial agreement.

Mini-trials are most successful when each party makes a genuine effort to limit discovery to only those documents and depositions that will be absolutely necessary to resolve the particular issue or issues at hand. The mini-trial agreement usually prohibits mass exchange of documents and limits the number and length of depositions. In some instances, depending on how much discovery has already taken place when the decision for a mini-trial is made, discovery may not be necessary at all. If the decision for a mini-trial is made early in the litigation process and discovery is necessary, the mini-trial agreement should always establish a discovery time limit. Sixty days seems to be standard. When possible, the mini-trial agreement lists the deponents and fixes a time limit, perhaps two hours, for each deposition. If the mini-trial agreement does not appropriately limit discovery, the cost-saving purpose of the mini-trial may be defeated.

When discovery is complete, the parties to the mini-trial exchange brief position summaries, which include document and witness lists to be used at the hearing. The summaries help avoid surprises and advise the panel members of each party's position before the hearing. The number of witnesses and trial exhibits designated in the summaries is kept to a minimum. The parties make a concerted effort to use a simplified process for the dispute's resolution. Without such an effort, the mini-trial is ineffective.

The mini-trial agreement also specifies who will make up the panel for the mini-trial. This panel normally consists of three people: a business executive from each side and a third-party neutral. The third-party neutral is instrumental in keeping the resolution process on course. For example, a party may be over inclusive when designating documents and witnesses in its summary. The third-party neutral ensures that only relevant witnesses and documents are listed and used. The neutral is usually an attorney with expertise in the dispute's subject matter.

The business executives appointed to the panel by the parties must have the full authority to negotiate a settlement. Without that power, the hearing may be for naught. Also, it is advisable that an executive deeply involved with the case not be designated as a panel member. No panel member should be asked to pass judgment on a superior or a person who reports directly to her, in the ordinary course of the party's business. The panel members selected should also be provided with a technical advisor from their respective companies if complex issues demand it. This will, of course, increase the hearing's cost, but will provide the panel members with necessary assistance regarding difficult technical issues.

At the hearing's close, negotiation commences. The success of the entire process rests on this period of negotiation. To ensure its success, the mini-trial agreement sets up its parameters in a way most conducive to achieving settlement. The negotiation normally extends into several sessions. Ideally, the two business executives should be the only people present. The third-party neutral may be consulted for advice or clarification but should not be an active participant. This is a time for the parties to resolve their dispute. Normally the lawyers for the parties do not participate. In the event that negotiations break down completely, the mini-trial agreement normally provides for a mandatory period of time to elapse before the decision is made to resume the original litigation. A "cool-down" period often allows the parties an opportunity to rethink their reasons for entering mini-trial negotiations in the first place and often generates new settlement ideas.

Mini-trials result in settlements a high percentage of the time. They can quickly turn complex business disputes into mutual-gain settlements. As a result, the mini-trial stands as a highly effective tool for cost cutting, and it has substantial future potential for reducing the amount of complex business litigation burdening our court systems.

7.7   Simulated Juries

Any party may employ a simulated or mock jury to evaluate a case for trial or settlement. Use of a simulated jury is very much like a "dress rehearsal." In most situations, it is a one-party endeavor. Its singular advantage as an ADR method is that the party employing it has complete control over the process. You may decide to use a mock jury simply to rehearse your case. Or you may use it to choose one of two or more case theory options.

The simulated jury experience allows you to observe how a panel of people, assembled purposefully to "mirror" potential jury makeup, will evaluate each aspect of a case. It is a useful tool in pointing out the case's weaknesses and the strengths. You may also use it to demonstrate for a client a reaction to certain trial strategies about which you and the client disagree. Watching the jury deliberate after hearing your presentation of the case, or of both sides of the case, can provide valuable insight into the hearts and minds of an average jury panel. The experience may convince you and your client to settle the case.

For these reasons, you must take great care to ensure that a simulated jury resembles, as closely as possible, an actual potential jury. If your client can afford it, you may hire a consulting firm to research and assemble a simulated jury. This is helpful, but expensive, and by no means a necessity. As an alternative, you or a paralegal can assemble a jury at minimal cost through telephone solicitation or posting with local employment agencies or college campuses.

Many attorneys assume this process is too expensive. However, if used as a tool to facilitate settlement, the expense can be a cost saver when considering the time and energy you avoid expending by settling prior to trial. If used as a tool to fine-tune a case during trial preparation, it may also provide a more favorable trial result.

7.8   Special Masters

Fed. R. Civ. P. 53 creates the special master. Special masters are judicial adjuncts who provide judges specialized assistance in managing their dockets and facilitating settlement. In the past, special masters were viewed primarily as fact-finders with respect to discrete issues in complex cases. However, in recent years courts have begun to expand the special master's role to include case management in preparation for trial. This can include overseeing certain aspects of the discovery process or overseeing the entire pretrial stage of the litigation. Special masters also have become more active as settlement facilitators, mediating the resolution of specified issues and conducting settlement conferences, particularly in complex cases.

Generally the intervention of a special master occurs pursuant to the parties' agreement. However, the court may appoint a special master without such agreement. The goal in either case is usually cost reduction. Special masters may even choose to incorporate other forms of mediation or arbitration, such as early neutral evaluation or mini-trial. These forms of dispute resolution are particularly useful since they, as well as special master intervention, are well suited for cases involving technical subject matter with complex issues that could benefit from the experience of a seasoned intervenor. Usually the special master is an attorney with many years of experience in litigation and settlement negotiation. Magistrates or retired judges are also commonly appointed to serve as special masters.

The new applications of the special master, those of case manager and mediator, are most intriguing. A judge may appoint a special master solely to develop a case management plan expressly for settlement. Typically a judge selects a special master, directs the parties to attend a status hearing, and defines the special master's objectives in the presence of both parties and their counsel. The judge may set a deadline by which the special master must submit a plan that will include schedules of limited discovery and a deposition schedule, both pared to include only what is needed for the purposes of settlement. The special master works with the parties to help them eliminate issues on which there is essential agreement. The schedules help streamline the process and keep the case moving toward settlement.

Once the special master has submitted the case management plan for settlement, depending on the parties' desires or the court's orders, the special master's duties may end. Alternatively, he or she may continue in the capacity of mediator. Some judges and special masters believe it is not appropriate to have the same person who developed the case management plan act as the settlement mediator. Some judges and masters prefer that the settlement special master ("settlement master") not have the authority to rule on discovery disputes. Each of these determinations must be made at the initial status conference with the parties, their counsel, and the special master present. Other details may also need to be discussed there, such as whether or not ex parte communication will be allowed and how much the special master will communicate, and for what purpose, with the judge.

The settlement master hosts and conducts settlement conferences, mediating actual disputes between parties, or at least identifying them, and eliminating areas of essential agreement. Often the parties prefer to have ex parte meetings with the settlement master, although this is not generally done without each party's consent. Through such caucuses, the settlement master very often can shepherd the case to a successful settlement.

7.9   Early Neutral Evaluation

In 1985, the United States District Court for the Northern District of California began a judicial experiment in alternative dispute resolution now known as early neutral evaluation. A committee had been set up to consider how the court could reduce the cost of litigation for the client. The committee determined that the greatest wasted expense was in the pretrial stage of litigation. Pretrial posturing by attorneys, vague pleading that did not allow the opposition to understand the claims against it, and poor pretrial communication all contributed to inflated expense.

The committee came up with the early neutral evaluation system as a response to these problems. In this type of ADR process, a neutral evaluator conducts a short, usually two-hour, case evaluation conference early on in the litigation process. The evaluator is normally a highly respected private attorney chosen by the court. The evaluators have essentially no judicial power. They enter no binding orders.

The court usually requires the parties themselves to attend the evaluation conference with their counsel. At the evaluation conference each party presents its position within a fifteen to thirty-minute time period. The evaluator then identifies areas of agreement or near agreement to allow trial counsel to limit the dispute's scope. Stipulations are encouraged. The evaluator also makes an effort to discourage alternative arguments, arguments with multiple themes, or boilerplate arguments. This phase of the conference helps limit discovery to actual, rather than perceived, disputes. The evaluator has in mind at this stage of the conference that he or she will recommend a discovery plan which will help keep the case moving toward settlement. This may save the court and both parties considerable time, energy, and money.

In the next phase of the evaluation conference, the evaluator assesses for each party the relative strengths and weaknesses of their case, and, if possible, their opponent's case. The evaluator also attempts to predict, within a certain range, each party's chance for liability and the amount of damages. In doing this, the evaluator draws upon considerable trial and settlement experience and, of course, to do this effectively, the evaluator must be credible and respected. The evaluator also comments on the likely cost of full discovery without settlement.

At this point the evaluator may offer to explore settlement possibilities with the parties, or if the parties wish, the process may end here. If the parties choose to explore further settlement talks, the evaluator relies on her experience to help the parties develop a plan to approach settlement. If the parties choose to explore settlement, the evaluator develops a discovery plan and shares it with the parties. The discovery plan is geared to preparing the case to put it in the best possible posture for settlement. The evaluator may also suggest a motion plan or a deposition schedule. The evaluator must be consistent in her effort to separate information that would be necessary for settlement negotiations and that which may be necessary at full trial. Preparation for settlement, not trial, is the goal.

When early neutral evaluation works as intended, it helps parties lower their litigation costs, improve pretrial communication with their opponents, and analyze their cases realistically while considering the input of a highly respected attorney in the field. Parties also avoid unnecessary discovery and normally increase their chances for early settlement.

7.10 Expert Panels

A court may appoint a panel of experts to help it in any number of ways, but the most typical use of an expert panel is to instruct and educate a court on complex scientific evidence in order for the court to determine the admissibility of such evidence. More and more, however, parties are using expert panels to facilitate settlements. Generally, a court issues an order that functions much like a pre-arbitration agreement which defines each aspect that the panel of experts will be expected to cover. As an alternative, the parties may accomplish this by agreement.

Included in the order or agreement are the panel's composition, or the selection method; the subject matter of the area of inquiry; any specific duties of the panel, such as conducting physical examination of evidence; time limits for accomplishing these duties; whether a report will be filed, and what is to be included in that report; how the panel members will function throughout the rest of the discovery process and trial; and how much the panel is to be compensated and by whom.

Courts can employ expert panels to manage and control discovery in cases where a judge may be wholly unqualified to do so. Scientific expert panels, therefore, can be most helpful in large-scale cases involving difficult scientific issues. These cases include asbestos litigation, pharmaceutical products liability cases, and tobacco industry litigation. Experts in these cases can help parties strip their cases of superfluous arguments, identify important issues of actual and significant disagreement, and guide parties in meaningful settlement negotiation. A judge may ask experts to serve as a conduit for either the parties or the judge to convey scientific issues to the court, or legal issues to the parties, respectively. A judge may accomplish this by scheduling frequent status meetings with the parties and the experts.

When serving in a settlement mode, a court-appointed expert normally confers with both parties together and each party individually. This approach promotes candor and enables the expert or experts to freely discuss settlement in light of the party's overall case. The court-appointed experts also can consult with the judge outside the parties' presence regarding the panel's investigation and findings. This process works most effectively when the judge appointing the experts for settlement purposes is not the judge who will serve as the trial judge in the case. The experts typically have access to all relevant documents, deposition transcripts, and witnesses, including the parties' experts. Fully informed about the litigation's subject matter, expert panels can conduct their own investigation, draw their own conclusions, and draft a report that will be used to facilitate settlement.

For this reason, the parties must agree on an expert or experts. The parties must be confident in these individuals' abilities and must respect their ability to draw intelligent conclusions from the information they gather. The court must take great care to ensure the experts have no ties to any party. Impartiality is vital. A court selects credible, impartial experts by submitting a reasonably short list of ten or twenty experts to the parties. Each party has unlimited peremptory challenges to any potential panelist. The list then is pared down to only those experts who the parties believe are impartial and credible. Experts must remove themselves from consideration for conflict of interest reasons.

The process of information gathering by the experts may take a few months to complete, but when considered in the light of litigation that has the potential to last five or ten years, the investment of a few months of earnest effort toward a mutually agreeable settlement may well be worth it. The expert panel provides its findings to the court and to all parties. On the basis of this report, the parties begin settlement conferencing facilitated by the experts. By the time the settlement conferencing begins, the panel of experts may have already ascertained what each party would require in a mutually satisfactory settlement. The court, without conducting a settlement conference, may use the panel's information and conclusions to fashion a settlement proposal on its own. It has knowledge of the parties' requirements for a settlement and may forego further negotiations if it thinks a settlement can be accomplished solely on the basis of the work of the expert panel.

7.11 Co-Mediation

An ADR hybrid that has gained increased use over the past few years is co-mediation. Simply defined, co-mediation is a process in which more than one person serves as a mediator. It involves the concepts of team mediation and interdisciplinary problem solving, and it can be tailored to the needs of a particular dispute. Depending on the ethnic, cultural, gender, or age characteristics of the disputants, two or more mediators having characteristics matching those of the adverse parties may be able to facilitate rapport-building and communication more easily than a single mediator with whom the disputants have difficulty identifying. Multiple mediators are commonly used in complex disputes where there are multiple parties, sometimes on each side of the case, and an intricate configuration of claims, cross-claims, and counterclaims. Such complex cases routinely exist in the fields of construction, tort, and environmental law. In such situations, the mediators may be assigned specific functions, or they may be assigned to specific disputants or specific aspects of the dispute. One mediator is designated as the lead mediator. That person is the chief strategist, coordinating the mediation activities of the other mediators and serving as an advisor and clearinghouse of information for them.

The most widespread application of co-mediation is in the field of family law, particularly in divorce mediation. Divorce cases especially lend themselves to resolution by interdisciplinary problem solving. Usually the co-mediators in a divorce case are a lawyer and a nonlawyer, though in some situations two non-lawyers may share the mediator role. The nonlawyers are usually from disciplines other than law, for example, counseling, psychotherapy, financial or estate planning, or accounting. In a combined-neutral arrangement the lawyer usually serves as the process expert and the nonlawyer as the technical expert to provide independent opinions on particular issues (value of a business enterprise, or an investment portfolio, etc.) or to help develop alternative solutions that could be part of a negotiated settlement.

7.12 Arb-Med

In arb-med, a process free of the impediments of med-arb (*see* section 1.1) and binding mediation (*see* section 7.13 below), the parties first proceed to arbitration before an arbitrator who will render a binding decision. When the arbitrator reaches a decision and drafts the award, it is not shown to the parties. Rather the arbitrator places the award in a sealed envelope. Thereafter, the parties can negotiate a resolution on their own, or they can involve the arbitrator as a mediator to help mediate a resolution. The arbitrator's decision, having already been made, will not be influenced by any confidential information of the parties. If the negotiations or mediation are unsuccessful, the parties open the sealed envelope, read the award, and, by preagreement, are bound by it. Parties negotiating in the shadow of the sealed award tend to reach a joint decision for themselves rather than to entrust their fate to an imposed solution of unknown value.

7.13 Binding Mediation

Med-arb is often confused with a relative newcomer to the ADR process spectrum—"binding mediation." Insurance companies and plaintiffs' lawyers in search of finality in smaller-damage personal injury cases are turning to binding mediation routinely to avoid the disadvantages of arbitral or court adjudication —namely, the substantial delay and costs associated with discovery, trial preparation, trial, and possibly appeal. The concept of binding mediation is simple: if the parties and their counsel spend two hours in a mediation with an experienced mediator or former judge, why should the parties not have that neutral determine what the fair settlement value of the case is and preagree to be bound by that determination? Med-arb and binding mediation have distinctive and significant differences in their respective results. The result of a med-arb is an award—a decision on the merits of the parties' claims and defenses, based on evidence—which can be filed and enforced in a court of law. The result of a binding mediation is a neutral evaluation of the fair settlement value of a case—which may in fact have little relation to the ultimate merits of the case. Rather, fair settlement value is based on the risks of going forward to proof and the probabilities of success measured at the present stage of the litigation, sometimes without the benefit of expert evidence. This is definitely a process of speculation and "best guess" evaluation by a mediator, and the parties and counsel using it should be so informed. Binding mediation, which has no separate evidentiary phase, has been criticized for this "best guess" feature and for its susceptibility to being abused by unscrupulous counsel who exaggerate the strength of their potential evidence in caucuses. Neutrals who conduct binding mediations must be careful to detect such exaggerations and evaluate them accordingly. Counsel who participate in binding mediations must be careful to limit their risk of an unfair outcome by requiring the other side to preagree to a reasonable high-low bracket of which the mediator is unaware. This bracket safeguards each party to the binding mediation against the possibility of a "runaway" or biased evaluation. Alternatively, counsel may consider using other mediation hybrids, including arb-med and co-med-arb.

7.14 Hybrid ADR Process Selection

This section presents a tool to assist neutrals, parties, and their counsel in designing the appropriate hybrid ADR process for a particular dispute. The chart takes into account the hybrid mediation processes and also the other hybrid processes discussed above in this chapter. The chart identifies special needs of a client or situation and simultaneously describes the hybrid process having features satisfying those special needs. An assumption underlying the use of this chart is that the general needs of the client are: (1) to accelerate resolution of the dispute as compared to the time required for resolution by traditional court adjudication; and (2) to lessen or minimize the costs of resolution.

HYBRID ADR SELECTION CHART		
HYBRID PROCESS	*SPECIAL NEED(S) OF CLIENT OR SITUATION*	*PROCESS FEATURE SATISFYING SPECIAL NEED(S) OF CLIENT OR SITUATION*
High-Low Arbitration	Desires binding result Wants to minimize risk of aberrant adverse binding award Does not want arbitrator(s) to be influenced by final negotiated offers and demands	Binding award Parties preagree to maximum/minimum award bracket Parties preagree not to disclose bracket to arbitrator(s)
Baseball Arbitration	Wants to limit potential losses to a known tolerable level and to maximize potential gain Desires to maximize effectiveness of the negotiation process.	Parties preagree to limit the arbitrator's function to choosing either the high or the low end of the parties' negotiated bracket Arbitrator's limited function influences parties to negotiate to a narrow bracket and cases often settle without need of arbitration
Med-Arb and Co-Med-Arb	Wants to go through evidentiary hearing only if absolutely necessary. Wants to preserve relationship with other side, if at all possible Desires to first attempt to find a creative solution Desires to use threat of arbitration to enhance opportunity for mediated result	Evidentiary arbitration hearing conducted only if mediation unsuccessful Mediation can help heal and preserve relationships Mediation can result in creative solutions Expense or inconvenience of arbitration can influence parties to work hard to settle case in mediation

(cont'd.) Med-Arb and Co-Med-Arb	Desires finality Situation appropriate for use of two neutrals Wants to preserve option for mediated result throughout arbitration process	Arbitration yields a final, enforceable award if mediation is unsuccessful One neutral serves as mediator, the other, as arbitrator Dual neutrals preserves opportunity for settlement
Arb-Med	Does not want mediation process to taint evidentiary hearing in arbitration. Wants an arbitrated result only as absolutely final alternative	Arbitration award withheld pending post-hearing mediation Arbitration award revealed only in instance where mediated result is not possible
Binding Mediation	Does not want an evidentiary hearing (e.g., case not fully discovered; unfavorable evidence, etc.) Wants to settle case without neutral's evaluation, if possible Desires neutral to evaluate case based on information disclosed in mediation Desires finality	Mediator attempts to settle dispute by facilitative caucusing; if unsuccessful, makes binding evaluation Mediator attempts to settle dispute, first Mediator gives opinion of case value if mediation is unsuccessful Binding case evaluation
Co-mediation	Wants input of expert or person with special expertise or having ethnic, cultural, or gender characteristics matching those of parties. Wants to facilitate rapport building and communication	Mediator teams up with psychologist, technical expert, accountant, etc. Mediation team relates to needs and interests of parties

Mini-Trial	Capitalize on executives' expertise in making effective business decisions	Corporate executives are on panel that hears the abbreviated case presentations
		A disinterested neutral facilitates negotiation between executives after case presentations
	Enhance opportunities for collaboration by executives	
		Presentations made to panel by the attorneys on both (or all) sides
	Executives need to see evidence on both or all sides	
		Objectivity is achieved by putting executives in a temporary "neutral" role
	Executives need to separate themselves from dispute to get objective view of case	
		Process is non-binding
	Parties need to limit risk of adverse result	
Simulated Juries	Party needs private rehearsal to learn strengths and weaknesses of its strategies/tactics	Case is presented in an abbreviated manner to pre-selected jury
		Jurors deliberate and reach a verdict
	Need for impartial evaluation by people closely mirroring potential jury	Party and counsel debrief jurors
		Jurors' verdict(s) and comments often lead to decision to settle
	Party needs opportunity for feedback from one or more juries	
	Party needs to determine whether case should be settled	

Special Master	Need for individualized case management Need for overseeing certain aspects of discovery process Need for issue-framing, issue-shaping, issue reduction Need for specialized settlement skills or experience Need for neutral to help parties and counsel design a case-appropriate dispute resolution process or case-management plan Court needs neutral to read pleadings, hear evidence and oral argument and report and recommend an appropriate disposition	Court-appointed attorney or former judge can provide individualized case management and serve the other needs described in the adjacent column
Early Neutral Evaluation	Need to minimize retrial posturing by attorneys early in the life of the case Need to clarify vague pleadings Need to improve pretrial communication among counsel Need for early evaluation of strengths and weaknesses of claims and defenses Need to limit case to actual rather than merely perceived disputes	Highly respected, court-appointed panel attorney conducts evaluation conference early in case, minimizes pretrial posturing, and serves the other needs described in the adjacent column

Fact-finding	Facts needed before decision made on approach to resolution High degree of confidentiality required Sensitivity to parties' feelings/reputation is paramount	Fact-finder or team appointed to investigate and issue report Fact-finder/team maintains strict confidentiality Fact-finder is sensitive to others' concerns and is skillful interviewer
Expert Panels	Judge or private neutral needs to be educated on one or more areas of complex scientific evidence Scientific specialist needed to manage or control discovery Parties need to explore settlement options in technically complex case	Experts can examine complex information and translate it into simple-to-understand concepts Technical experts are able to communicate on counsel's and parties' level Experts' report can be used as a tool by parties to settle case
Summary Jury Trial	Need to see jury reaction to facts in an accelerated judicial proceeding in a courtroom environment Need to define critical legal issues and to learn how judge would rule on them Need to know why jury ruled a certain way	Six jurors selected by profiles; brief videotapes of expert and critical witness testimony Comprehensive pretrial conference; evidentiary objections and jury instructions ruled on by judge Through jury debriefing, parties learn specific reasons for jury's evaluation of case

◆ CHAPTER EIGHT ◆

Effective Advocacy in Cyberarbitration

The same way that e-commerce is the road ahead for conventional trade, e-arbitration and e-mediation are the beacons for solving disputes in the twenty-first century.

—*Dr. Petronio R. G. Muniz*
President, Instituto Arbiter
Recife, Brazil

Not since the invention of the printing press has there been such great progress in the technology of communication as the development of the Internet.[1] In less than a decade, the Internet rapidly developed from a simple network of government, military, and research computer networks to a global medium for the instantaneous exchange of ideas and information. Today, the Internet renders anyone with a computer and a connecting device the ability communicate with and transfer documents to anyone else globally who is similarly equipped. It has been said that this electronic revolution, or "E-Revolution," may have an even greater impact on the world of commerce than the Industrial Revolution.[2]

It most definitely has had a faster impact. The time it took for other new technologies to be used by at least fifty million people in the twentieth century much exceeded the time the public has needed to adapt to the Internet. For example, radio required a thirty-eight-year user acclimation period; television, thirteen years; and cable television, ten years. In contrast, it has been estimated that in the first five years of commercial Internet use, 200 million connected to the Internet in more than a hundred countries worldwide. The United States Commerce Department has estimated by the year 2005, there will be more than one billion commercial users worldwide, generating more than $3.2 trillion in revenue. Indeed, the growth of Internet use is unparalleled by the usage of any other communication technology or commercial innovation in recorded history.

What does all of this mean for the twenty-first century advocate who wants to represent clients effectively not only in traditional business and personal transactions and dispute settings but also in new Internet-created cyberspace settings? It means, quite simply, that advocates have to quickly learn and adapt to new methods of communication and related technology so that they can best

---

1.   Frank A. Cona, *Focus on Cyberlaw: Application of Online Systems in Alternative Dispute Resolution*, 45 Buffalo L. Rev. 975 (1997).
2.   John W. Cooley, *New Challenges for Consumers and Businesses in the Cyber Frontier: E-Contracts, E-Torts, and E-Dispute Resolution*, 13 Loyola Consumer L. Rev. 102 (2001); *see generally* Robert Hemmesfaur (Ed.), *@ Risk: Internet and E-Commerce Insurance and Reinsurance Legal Issues* (Reactions Publishing Group, Ltd., London, 2000).

represent their clients in a dynamic and ever-expanding world of high-velocity information exchange, resulting in both durable deals and derisive disputes. The enormous quantity of personal interactions and commercial transactions occurring on the Internet is bound, unquestionably, to generate millions of disagreements over time and much thinking, on lawyers' parts, about how to resolve the resulting disagreements efficiently. Advocates may have to discard some traditional legal concepts and old ways of doing things in favor of more cyber-apropos methods. Newer and faster ways of conducting commerce via the Internet will continue to present a wide variety of risks and exposures for companies and consumers alike. Advocates and their clients will need to focus on some of the new legal issues that are certain to arise in electronic contract (e-contract) and electronic tort (e-tort) disputes. They will also need to consider new ways of incorporating the use of the Internet in resolving disputes which arise both in "real world" traditional ways and in cyberspace itself.[3] It is predictable that advocates, more and more, will be representing clients involved in disputes, commercial and otherwise, of an international character.[4] In doing so, advocates will need to become proficient in Electronic Dispute Resolution, which includes cyberarbitration (e-arbitration) and cybermediation (e-mediation). It is the purpose of this chapter to prepare you to represent clients effectively, as the opening quote suggests, in one of these twenty-first century "beacons for solving disputes"—the process of cyberarbitration.

8.1   Basic Definitions

Vocabulary is a basic ingredient to effective communication and learning. As advocates representing someone else's positions and interests in a new forum for dispute resolution—cyberspace—you cannot afford to misuse vocabulary. You must know the commonly accepted meaning of new terms and how to use the terms appropriately. Once you know and understand the vocabulary of cyberarbitration, you will feel much more comfortable engaging in this new dispute resolution process. Appropriate word selection and word usage are especially important first steps in your development of new cyberadvocacy skills. The purposes of including definitions of internet terms here are to shorten your learning curve and to decrease your anxiety about representing clients in cyberarbitration.[5] The

---

3. *See generally*, Ethan Katsh and Janet Rifkin, *Online Dispute Resolution* (Jossey-Bass, 2001); Ethan Katsh, *Online Dispute Resolution: Some Lessons from the E-Commerce Revolution*, 28 N. Ky. L. Rev. 810 (2001).

4. *See generally*, Robert C. Bordone, *Electronic Dispute Resolution: A Systems Approach —Potential, Problems, and a Proposal*, 3 Harv. Negotiation L. Rev. 175 (1998); Alan Wiener, *Regulations and Standards for Online Dispute Resolution: A Primer for Policymakers and Stakeholders* (Part 1) (Feb. 15, 2001), (http://www.mediate.com/articles/awiener2.cfm).

5. The definitions contained in this section are, in part, adapted from Bryan Pfaffenberger, *Webster's New World Computer Dictionary* (9th Ed.)(Hungry Minds, Inc. 2001) and Philip E. Margolis, Random House *Webster's Computer & Internet Dictionary* (3d Ed.) (Random House, 2000).

definitions presented here are not in alphabetical order, but rather are listed in an order that promotes and facilitates understanding of terms, beginning, where possible, with the broadest definitions and continuing with related or included definitions of terms.

8.1.1 Cyberspace

Cyberspace is a metaphor used to describe the non-physical, virtual terrain created by computer systems. (The prefix "cyber" means anything related to computers or to the Internet.) Like physical space, cyberspace contains objects (files, mail messages, graphics, etc.) and different modes of transportation and delivery.

Unlike real space, exploring cyberspace does not require any physical movement other than pressing keys on a keyboard or moving a computer mouse. The following definitions are general terms related to cyberspace.

Internet. An enormous and rapidly growing system of linked computer networks, connecting millions of computers worldwide, that facilitates data communication services such as remote login, file transfer, electronic mail (e-mail), the World Wide Web, and newsgroups. Using TCP/IP, also called the Internet protocol suite, the Internet assigns every online computer a unique Internet address, also called an IP address, so that any two connected computers can locate each other on the network and exchange data. "Online" means connected to a network or more commonly, the Internet. "Protocol" is a standard in data communications and networking that specifies the format of data as well as the rules to be followed.

World Wide Web. A global hypertext system or "Web" that uses the Internet as its transport mechanism. Communication between Web clients (browsers) and Web servers is defined by the Hypertext Transport Protocol (HTTP). In a hypertext system, users navigate by clicking a hyperlink embedded in the current document; this action displays a second document in the same or a separate browser window. Web documents are created using HTML, a declarative markup language. Incorporating hypermedia (graphics, sounds, animations, and video), the Web has become the ideal medium for publishing information on the Internet and serves as a platform for the emerging electronic economy.

Domain. In a computer network, a group of computers that are administered as a unit. On the Internet, this term refers to all the computers that are collectively addressable within one of the four parts of an *Internet Protocol (IP) address*. For example, the first part of an IP address specifies the number of a computer network. All the computers within this network are part of the same domain.

Domain name. In the system of domain names used to identify individual Internet computers, a single word or abbreviation that makes up part of a computer's unique name. Consider this unique, fictitious name: (cool.law.nwu.edu). "Cool" is a specific computer in the "law" school at Northwestern University (nwu). At the end of the series of domain names is the top-level domain (here, edu), which includes hundreds of colleges and universities throughout the United States.

Domain name system (DNS). In the Internet, the conceptual system, standards, and names that make up the hierarchical organization of the Internet into named domains.

IP. Abbreviation for Internet Protocol. It is the standard that describes how an Internet-connected computer should break data down into packets for transmission across the network, and how those packets should be addressed so that they arrive at their destination. IP is the connectionless part of the TCP/IP protocols. The Transmission Control Protocol (TCP) specifies how two Internet computers can establish a reliable data link.

URI. Abbreviation for uniform resource identifier. In the hypertext Transfer Protocol (HTTP), a string of characters that identifies and Internet resource, including the type of resource and its location. There are two types of URIs: uniform resource locators (URLs) and relative URLs (RELURLs).

URL. An acronym for uniform resource locator. On the World Wide Web, it is one of two basic kinds of URIs. It is the string of characters that precisely identifies an Internet resource's type and location. For example, consider the following fictitious URL:

http://www.wildcats.northwestern.edu/toros/refs/parking.html

This URL identifies a World Wide Web document (http://), indicates the domain name of the computer on which it is stored www.wildcats.northwestern.edu), fully describes the document's location within the directory structure (toros/refs), and includes the document's name and extension (parking.html).

RELURL. One of two basic kinds of uniform resource identifiers (URIs). It is a string of characters that gives a resource's file name (such as parking.html) but does not specify its type or exact location.

Hot link. A method of copying information from one document (the source document) to another (the destination document) so that the destination document's information is updated automatically when the source document's information changes.

Cold link. A method of copying information from one document (the source document) to another (the target document) so that a link is created. Cold links are distinguished from hot links in that cold links are not automatically updated; one must update them manually with a command that opens the source document, reads the information, and recopies the information if it has changed.

Hyperlink. In a hypertext system, an underlined or otherwise emphasized word or phrase that displays another document when clicked with the mouse.

Hypertext. A method of preparing and publishing text, ideally suited to the computer, in which readers can choose their own paths through the material. In preparing hypertext, information is first "chunked" into small, manageable units, such as single pages of text. These units are called nodes. Then the hyperlinks (also called anchors) are embedded in the text. When a reader clicks on a hyperlink, the hypertext software displays a different node. The process of navigating among the nodes linked in this way is called browsing. A collection of nodes that are interconnected by hyperlinks is called a web.

HTML. Acronym for Hypertext Markup Language. It is a markup language for identifying the portions of a document (called elements) so that, when accessed by a program called a Web browser, each portion appears with a distinctive format. The agency responsible for standardizing HTML is the World Wide Web Consortium (W3C).

HTTP. The Internet standard that supports the exchange of information on the World Wide Web. HTTP enables Web authors to embed hyperlinks in Web documents. HTTP defines the process by which a Web client, called a browser, originates a request for information and sends it to a Web server, a program designed to respond to HTTP requests and provide the desired information.

Web site. Web site (location) on the World Wide Web. Each Web site contains a home page, which is the first document users see when they enter the site. The site might also contain additional documents and files. Each site is owned and managed by an individual, company, or organization.

Web browser. A software application used to locate and display Web pages. Most modern browsers can present multimedia information, including sound and video.

Web server. A computer that delivers (serves up) Web pages. Every Web server has an IP address and possibly a domain name. For example, if you enter the URL http://www.advocacy.com/index.html this sends a request to the server whose domain name is advocacy.com. The server then fetches the page named index.html and sends it to your browser. Any computer can be turned into a Web server by installing server software and connecting the machine to the Internet.

Web master. An individual who manages a Web site. Depending on the size of the site, the Webmaster might be responsible for any of the following:

1. making sure that the Web server hardware and software are running properly;

2. designing the Web site;

3. creating and updating Web pages;

4. replying to user feedback;

5. creating CGI scripts;

6. monitoring traffic through the site.

8.1.2 Electronic Dispute Resolution (EDR)

Electronic Dispute Resolution (EDR) is an umbrella term encompassing all forms of electronic-based methods of dispute resolution (e.g. cyberarbitration, cybermediation) and their related electronic support and information-delivery technology, such as telephone conferencing and voicemail, the Internet, videoconferencing technology, fax machines, and fax software.

EDR should not be confused with E-dispute Resolution. An "e-dispute" means a dispute arising out of online business transactions or online usage. Typical e-disputes stem from electronic contracts (e-contracts) in electronic commerce (e-commerce), or they are based on electronic torts (e-torts) which result in harm to a person or property in connection with Internet use.[6]

8.1.3   Videoconferencing

Videoconferencing means conducting a conference between two or more participants at different sites by using computer networks to transmit audio and video data. For example, a point-to-point (two person) video conferencing system works much like a video telephone. Each participant has a video camera, microphone, and speakers mounted on his or her computer. As the two participants speak to each other, their voices are carried over the network and delivered to the other's speakers, and whatever images appear in front of the video camera appear in a window on the other participant's monitor. Multipoint videoconferencing allows three or more participants to sit in a virtual conference room and communicate as if they were sitting right next to one another.

8.1.4   Telephonic Dispute Resolution (TDR)

"Telephone Dispute Resolution" (TDR) is a term that encompasses telephone-based methods of dispute resolution, including telephone negotiation, telephone mediation, telephone arbitration, or telephone depositions. TDR can be used in conjunction with face-to-face and online dispute resolution processes.

8.1.5   EDR information acquisition and delivery technology

The definitions in this subsection provide meanings for Electronic Dispute Resolution information acquisition and delivery technology. These are also called EDR "tools."

> *Fax machine.* Abbreviation of facs(imile) machine, a fax machine is an electronic device that can send or receive text and pictures over a telephone line. It consists of an optical scanner for digitizing (dividing into a grid of dots) images on paper, a printer for printing incoming fax messages, and a telephone for making the connection.
>
> *A related device is the fax modem.* That device you can attach to a personal computer in order for you to transmit and receive electronic documents as faxes. Documents sent through a fax modem must already be in an

---

6. John W. Cooley, *New Challenges for Consumers and Businesses in the Cyber-Frontier: E-Contracts, E-Torts, and E-Dispute Resolution,* 13 Loyola Consumer Law Review 102 (2001).

electronic form (that is, in a disk file). Documents you receive are stored in files on your disk or received as hard copy on a fax machine. To create fax documents from images on paper, you need an optical scanner.

Voice mail. A communications system in which telephone voice messages are transformed into digital form and are stored in a network. When the person to whom the message is directed logs on to the system and discovers that a message is waiting, the system plays the message. Voice mail also refers to e-mail systems that support audio. Users can leave spoken messages for one another and listen to the messages by executing the appropriate command in the e-mail system.

E-mail. Short for e(lectronic) mail, it refers to the transmission of messages over communications networks. The messages can be notes entered from the keyboard or electronic files stored on disk. Most e-mail systems include a rudimentary text editor for composing messages, but many allow you to edit your messages using any editor you want. You then send the message to the recipient by specifying the recipient's e-mail address. You can also send the same message to several users at once. This is called broadcasting. Sent messages are stored in electronic mailboxes until the recipient accesses and displays them. Many systems visually and audibly alert the recipient when mail is received. After reading your mail, you can store it in a text file, forward it to others, or delete it. Copies of memos and attachments can be printed out on a printer if you want a hard copy. Emerging standards are making it possible for users of all types of different e-mail systems to exchange messages.

WebTV. A general term for a whole category of products and technologies that enable one to surf the Web on your TV. Most WebTV products today consist of a small box that connects to a telephone line and a television. It makes a connection to the Internet via one's telephone service and then converts the downloaded Web pages to a format that can be displayed on the TV. These products also come with a remote control device so that one can navigate through the Web. In the future, WebTV products will not require telephone connections, but will instead access the Internet directly through the cable TV lines.

Chat Room. Chat is real-time online communication between two or more computer users. Once an online chat has been initiated, either user can enter text in the conversation by typing on the keyboard and the entered text will appear on the other user's monitor. A chat room is a virtual space where a chat session takes place. Technically, a chat room is really a channel, but the term "room" is used to promote the chat metaphor. Web sites can be equipped with a chat room feature.

Threaded Discussions. In online discussions, a thread is a series of messages that have been posted as replies to one another. A single forum or conference may contain a single topic or it may consist of many threads covering different subjects. Replies to messages are normally nested directly under the related message instead of messages being arranged in some other order, such as chronological or alphabetical order. Web sites can be equipped with a threaded discussion feature.

Instant Messaging. A type of online service that enables you to create a private chat room with another individual. Typically, the instant messaging system alerts you whenever somebody on your private list is online. You can then initiate a chat session with that individual.

8.1.6 Online Dispute Resolution (ODR)

Online Dispute Resolution (ODR), also referred to as Cyber/Dispute Resolution and electronic Alternative Dispute Resolution, and by their more aesthetic acronyms (C/DR) and eADR respectively,[7] encompasses processes for resolving disputes predominantly by online means. The term includes both disputes that arise off-line—in the real world—but are handled online and those disputes that arise in cyberspace (e.g. in electronic commerce).[8] It includes recognized forms of ADR, such as arbitration, mediation, and negotiation, which, in a cyberspace context are called cyberarbitration, cybermediation, and cybernegotiation. These cyberprocesses are also referred to respectively as e-arbitration, e-mediation, and e-negotiation. Cybernegotiation consists of two types: automated negotiation and assisted negotiation. Offline dispute resolution refers to traditional face-to-face negotiation, mediation, and arbitration.

8.1.7 Cyberarbitration

Arbitration that is conducted predominantly in cyberspace is referred to as cyberarbitration.

---

7. *See* T. Schultz, G. Kaufmann-Kohler, D. Langer, V. Bonnet, *Online Dispute Resolution: The State of the Art and the Issues, E-Com Research Project of the University of Geneva*, Geneva, 2001, http://www.online-adr.org,

8. *See generally* Louise Ellen Teitz, *Symposium: Providing Legal Services for the Middle Class in Cyberspace: The Promise and Challenge of On-line Dispute Resolution*, 70 Fordham L. Rev. 985, 991 (2001).

Cyberarbitrator. A cyberarbitrator who is experienced and/or trained in conducting cyberarbitration.

Cyberparty. A disputant in an ODR process, including cyberarbitration.

Cyberadvocate. A lawyer who represents a cyberparty in an ODR process, including cyberarbitration.

8.1.8   Cybermediation

Mediation that is conducted predominantly in cyberspace is referred to as cybermediation.

Cybermediator. A mediator who is experienced and/or trained in conducting cybermediation.

Cyberparty. A disputant in a an ODR process, including cybermediation.

Cyberadvocate. A lawyer who represents a cyberparty in an ODR process, including cybermediation.

8.1.9   Cybernegotiation

Negotiation that is conducted predominantly in cyberspace is referred to as cybernegotiation. There are two types of cybernegotiation: automated negotiation and assisted negotiation.

Cybernegotiator. A person who negotiates in cyberspace.

Cyberparty. A disputant in an ODR process, including cybernegotiation.

Cyberadvocate. A lawyer who represents a cyberparty in an ODR process, including cybernegotiation.

Automated negotiation. Negotiation (bidding) by means of high automation programs. These are programs that basically consist of software that match demand/settlement responses without human intervention.[9]

---

9. T. Schultz, G. Kaufmann-Kohler, D. Langer, V. Bonnet, *Online Dispute Resolution: The State of the Art and the Issues*, E-Com Research Project of the University of Geneva, Geneva, 2001, http://www.online-adr.org, 4–5.

Assisted negotiation. This process should not be confused with cybermediation. Assisted negotiation is a C/DR process in which the ODR organization provides only a secure site and possibly a storage means and other features, such as a threaded message board. No actual negotiation service (neutral third-party assistance) is provided. In this process, the parties have to reach an agreement without any external entity having the capacity to decide for them, not even a computer, as in automated negotiation.[10]

8.1.10   Internet regulatory organizations and related terms[11]

ICANN. Abbreviation for Internet Corporation for Assigned Names and Numbers. It is a private, California-based, non-profit corporation managing Internet domain names and Internet Protocol (IP) addresses. It administers as dispute resolution system for resolving domain name disputes.

UDRP. Abbreviation for Uniform Dispute Resolution Policy. This policy establishes a procedure for the online resolution of disputes that concern domain names. This policy has been established by ICANN. The UDRP is a non-national authority for the resolution of domain name disputes. Its purpose is to avoid the competition and conflicts that arise from a variety of national courts and rules. The UDRP is intended to be applied only to very flagrant types of cybersquatting. The four institutions designated by ICANN to resolve domain name disputes are: WIPO, eResolution, the National Arbitration Forum, and the CPR Institute for Dispute Resolution.

ICC. Abbreviation for the International Chamber of Commerce. This organization advocates for minimal government regulation of e-commerce and asserts that self-regulation by the industry is the most effective way to build confidence in e-commerce.

GBDe. Abbreviation for Global Business Dialogue on Electronic Commerce. This initiative involves seventy-two companies around the world. Its objective is to endeavor to make e-commerce reach its full economic

---

10. T. Schultz, G. Kaufmann-Kohler, D. Langer, V. Bonnet, *Online Dispute Resolution: The State of the Art and the Issues*, E-Com Research Project of the University of Geneva, Geneva, 2001, http://www.online-adr.org, 5–6.

11. Adapted in part from T. Schultz, G. Kaufmann-Kohler, D. Langer, V. Bonnet, *Online Dispute Resolution: The State of the Art and the Issues*, E-Com Research Project of the University of Geneva, Geneva, 2001, http://www.online-adr.org, 84–86.

and social potential. It makes recommendations on ADR to Internet merchants, to ADR service providers, and to governments.

E-Commerce Group. Abbreviation for Electronic Commerce and Consumer Protection Group. It is a coalition of large companies that are involved in business-to-consumer e-commerce. The group seeks to foster consumer confidence and consumer protection by creating industry best practices and a predictable legal framework. It further promotes fair, timely, and affordable means to settle disputes and obtain redress concerning online transactions, and it encourages merchants to provide in-house procedures to resolve complaints and to provide third party dispute resolution programs, including online dispute resolution processes.

EuroCommerce. This is a lobby group that acts as the trade representation to the European Union institutions. It has published a European Code of Conduct for online commercial relations. It encourages online merchants to provide an in-house procedure for handling complaints. FEDMA. Abbreviation for Federation of European Direct Marketing. It has twelve partners in national Direct Marketing Associations in the European Union and all those of Switzerland, Hungary, Poland, and the Czech and Slovak Republics. It has published a code on e-commerce and interactive marketing.

DSA. Abbreviation for the Direct Selling Association. This is a national trade association in the United States which represents companies that market products through personal explanation and demonstration. It has established Guidelines for Internet Use and a Code of Ethics for its members. Through its educational arm, the Direct Selling Education Foundation (DSEF), it conducts international seminars and other training on online transactions and dispute resolution.

8.2   Types of Alternative ODR Services—General

Dispute resolution organizations are increasingly providing mediation, arbitration, and other innovative dispute resolution services over the Internet.[12] The purpose of this section is to make you aware of the variety of types of ODR services available, generally. A more detailed description of ODR service providers and their respective service offerings appears in section 8.6. A listing of online dispute resolution service providers and their Web site addresses appears in Appendix L.

---

12. *See generally*, Alan Wiener, *Opportunities and Initiatives in Online Dispute Resolution*, SPIDR News, Vol. 24, No.3, page 17 (Summer 2000).

8.2.1   Examples of primary ODR services

8.2.1.1   Cyberarbitration

Several dispute resolution organizations (e.g. WEBdispute.com) currently offer online arbitration services, also called cyberarbitration. Some service providers limit their services to particular types of disputes (e.g. e-Resolution—Internet domain name disputes).[13] Typically, parties complete and submit online an agreement to cyberarbitration. The service provider then issues a schedule for stating and answering positions on various disputed issues. When that part of the process is completed, the provider schedules a five-day e-mail hearing. The parties select the arbitrator and he or she opens the Hearing. Each party presents his or her case online. The cyberarbitrator may pose questions online to the parties as the hearing progresses. On the last day of the hearing, the parties submit final arguments to the cyberarbitrator by e-mail. The cyberarbitrator then closes the hearing, reviews and considers the evidence, and renders a decision by United States mail within twenty days.

8.2.1.2   Cybermediation

Both online and traditional dispute resolution service providers (e.g. onlineresolution.com) are increasingly offering online mediation services, also called cybermediation. This form of ODR and others described in this section have come to fruition, in significant part, through the combined supportive efforts of ODR pioneers John Helie, Jim Melamed, and Colin Rule. In the pure form of cybermediation, one party initiates the process by completing a confidential form on the service provider's Internet site. The form requires a party to identify the disputants, the nature of the dispute, and the desired outcome. The service provider then contacts the other named parties, advises them of the submission, explains the online mediation process, and invites their participation. If the parties desire to participate, they typically sign an agreement to abide by the online mediation ground rules, protocols, and procedures. The parties then mutually agree to use a cybermediator from a list provided by the service provider. The selected cybermediator then conducts e-mail communication with the parties, jointly or in caucuses as appropriate, and attempts to facilitate a mutually agreeable solution. If an agreement is reached, it is commonly reduced to writing.

Another type of cybermediation (e.g. the Online Ombuds Office) has a conference room where, using technology like Internet Relay Chat (IRC) and chat rooms, the cyberneutral can meet with all the parties simultaneously or can put each party in a separate room and shuttle back and forth.[14]

---

13. *See generally*, Joseph W. Goodman, *The Pros and Cons of Online Dispute Resolution: An Assessment of Cyber-Mediation Websites*, 2003 Duke L. & Tech. Rev. 4 (2003).

14. *See generally* M. Ethan Katsh, *Dispute Resolution in Cyberspace*, 28 Conn. L. Rev. 953, 966–72 (1996).

8.2.1.3   Cybernegotiation: blind bidding

Also called "automated negotiation" and "blind negotiation," this widely offered service has proven, for some users, to be a popular online method of resolving monetary disputes. At least one company (SettleSmart) permits blind negotiation of non-monetary settlement terms also. In this process, parties confidentially submit, normally by e-mail, monetary offers and demands in "rounds" to the service provider. If the offer and demand of negotiating parties match, or fall within a defined range, or overlap, the parties, by pre-agreement, settle the case for the matching amount, the average of the offer or demand if within a defined range, or for the demand in the event of an overlap. In most systems, parties can keep the negotiation open and confidentially e-mail their respective offers and demands at will. This allows parties to continue to engage in blind negotiation over a period of time, even as discovery ensues. If there is a settlement, the service provider immediately notifies the parties by e-mail.

8.2.1.4   Cybernegotiation: private online forum

Some dispute resolution service providers (e.g. SquareTrade) offer an online forum permitting buyers and sellers to resolve disagreements involving online purchases. Claimants can initiate a case by completing a form online describing what occurred and what relief they want. The service provider then e-mails notice of the complaint to the other party and provides an opportunity to respond. When there is a response, the service provider posts the complaint and response on a secure Web page and the parties are permitted, for as long as they desire, to exchange information about the disputed matter. If the matter is not resolved through this Web page discussion, the complainant may request the service provider to assign a mediator to help resolve the parties' differences.

8.2.1.5   Cybernegotiation: online forum with public assessment option

At least one organization (e.g., iLevel) permits its members to submit complaints against vendors and their requested relief online. The organization sends the member's complaint to the vendor and permits the disputing parties a period of time to resolve the matter privately. If the dispute does not resolve, the member can request the organization to post the gathered information online for public comment. Online public may then review the information and state their views in favor of the member or vendor. The theory is that public will provide impartial feedback and the public pressure will ultimately assist the disputing parties in finding a fair or equitable solution.

8.2.1.6   Cybernegotiation: technology-assisted optimized negotiation

At least one online dispute resolution service provider (e.g. One Accord) offers disputing parties technology-assisted negotiation services at a patented neutral site.[15] The goal of this type of service provider is to integrate interest-based negotiation principles with technology that is designed to optimize settlements. As one commentator describes this service:

> A facilitator helps parties jointly model their negotiation problem and then assists each party individually input their confidential preferences from their private computer terminal. The system "elicits complex preferences by allowing parties to associate confidence in relative importance of issues and package ratings" and "accurately models negotiation cases and party satisfaction functions allowing parties to experiment with *'what if'* scenarios." Finally, the system "generates fair compromises, equivalents and optimal solutions apportioning benefits according to an equity reference established by negotiating parties."[16]

8.2.1.7   Online simulated juries

Another forum for online dispute resolution (e.g.,iCourthouse), offers simulated jury services called "Peer Jury" and "Panel Jury." In Peer Jury cases, the disputants preagree whether the jurors' verdict will be binding or advisory. The volunteer jurors then select the cases they desire to decide, review the parties' "trial books," ask any questions of the disputants, and then render their verdicts. The service provider informs the parties of the verdict, the number of votes cast, the median award, and a summary of the jurors' comments. In a variation of this process, the parties first review potential jurors' answers to *voir dire* questionnaires. They then choose specific jurors comprising what is called a "Panel Jury." A unique feature of the Panel Jury process permits the parties to monitor the jurors online written deliberations in real time. Besides rendering verdicts, the Panel Jury can also answer questionnaires from parties about the effectiveness of the evidence and arguments presented.

---

15. *See generally*, Ernest M. Thiessen, P. Eng, and Joseph P. McMahon, *Beyond Win-Win in Cyberspace*, 15 Ohio St. J. on Disp. Resol. 643 (2000); Stephen J. Ware and Sarah Rudolph Cole, *Introduction: ADR in Cyberspace*, 15 Ohio St. J. on Disp. Resol. 589, 592–93 (2000).

16. Alan Wiener, *Opportunities and Initiatives in Online Dispute Resolution*, SPIDR News, Vol. 24, No.3, pages 18–19 (Summer 2000).

8.2.2   Examples of secondary ODR services[17]

Aside from their primary ADR services, some ODR organizations provide secondary or supplemental ODR services. Some of these services are described below.

8.2.2.1   Dispute prevention

Some ODR services provide background checks of potential corporate employees, advice in the use of standard business contracts and forms, and training for employees and employers.

8.2.2.2   Assistance in drafting dispute resolution clauses

Some ODR organizations, provide assistance in drafting dispute resolution clauses for negotiation (e.g. NewCourtCity), mediation (e.g. Internet Neutral), and arbitration (e.g. NovaForum.com).

8.2.2.3   Training and information

Some ODR organizations simply provide general consumer information in the nature of training and dispute resolution information (e.g. WebAssured.com and Resolution Forum), or links to specific legal publications (e.g. NewCourtCity).

8.2.2.4   Complaint assistance

This is a form of technologically assisted negotiation often provided in seal or trustmark cases (*see* below). Some trustmark organizations serve as intermediaries, forwarding complaints to the certified merchant sites (e.g. BBBOnline and WebAssured) or requesting them to take action (e.g. iLevel). Some trustmark organizations also recommend appropriate ways for customers to deal with the allegedly offending merchant sites (Online Ombuds Office).

8.2.2.5   Portal to other ODR providers

Some ODR organizations provide links to other ODR organizations (e.g. ICANN).

8.2.2.6   Legal assistance

Some ODR organizations post a list of attorneys on a Web site or have the personnel communicate with potential users regard legal assistance (e.g. Online Resolution, e-Mediator, NewCourtCity, IRIS, and ClaimChoice.com). Mediation

---

17. Adapted from T. Schultz, G. Kaufmann-Kohler, D. Langer, V. Bonnet, *Online Dispute Resolution: The State of the Art and the Issues*, E-Com Research Project of the University of Geneva, Geneva, 2001, http://www.online-adr.org, 30–33.

advocates with ODR advocacy experience may wish to contact such organizations to register on their lawyer referral lists.

8.2.2.7   Evaluation

This service can take the form of expert evaluation or of a procedure to test the merits of the case. It does not require the participation or cooperation of the opponent. Essentially, the first form involves a neutral expert examining the legal and technical issues and assessing the merit and value of the claim. If all parties participate in the expert evaluation, they can agree that the results will be fact-binding (e.g. Online Resolution) or entirely binding. The second form can be non-binding or binding and consists of a mock trial by a retired judge or a jury (e.g. 1-2-3 Settle.Com and clickNsettle.com).

8.2.2.8   Trustmarks or seals

These are tools whereby companies can be obligated to establish internal procedures for the handling of conflicts (e.g. Web Trader and MARS), companies' agreement to be bound by the outcome of the ODR system (e.g. WebAssured.com), or declarations by companies of their good intentions (e.g. Web Trader). These kinds of tools are often incorporated into a code of conduct governing the conduct of licensee companies and licensees are permitted to display the seal or trustmark. One ODR organization provides for a limited amount of free dispute resolution services to licensees (e.g. NovaForum.com). Trustmarks and seals may be the principal mechanism for the promotion of self-regulation and consumer confidence in e-commerce.

8.2.2.9   Publication of complaints

This is a procedure used in seal or trustmark programs. It is usually in the form of either an agreement by Internet merchants to invite their consumers to post comments on special forums about their transactional experience with the merchants (e.g. Web Trader) or the publication by the ODR organization of the results of a negotiation between a consumer and Internet merchant or of the lack of response by a merchant (e.g. iLevel and iCourthouse).

8.3   Comparison of Face-To-Face, Telephone, and Written Communication in Arbitration

The twenty-first century advocate who represents a client in arbitration is constantly confronted with the question of what mode of communication he or she should be using at various stages of the arbitration process. The reason for this is that the advocate in arbitration has many modes of communication from which to choose including face-to-face, videoconferencing, telephone, letter, e-mail, fax, or combinations of these modes. In this section we will review the relative advantages and disadvantages of the three primary modes of communication: face-to-face, telephonic, and written. It is hoped that the information here will assist you in choosing the appropriate mode of communication as the arbitration progresses.[18]

8.3.1   Face-to-face communication in arbitration

When people communicate with one another, ninety-three percent of the meaning of their messages is contained in their facial and vocal cues, rather than in the content of the messages. Thus, generally speaking, the most communicatively efficient mode of arbitration is face to face. However, there may be situations where the disputing parties are so emotionally hostile toward one another that a face-to-face arbitration would do more harm than good. In such situations, a face-to-face meeting might also be counter-indicated because there is no continuing relationship to be preserved. In some situations, face-to-face arbitration may be simply impossible because of geographical distance between or among the parties and their counsel. In some such situations videotelephones or videoconferencing may serve as a near-equivalent substitute for a face-to-face meeting. In other arbitration situations, while a face-to-face meeting may be helpful during a portion of the process, an advocate might conclude for strategic, tactical, or other reasons, that another mode of communication might be more appropriately used in other phases of the process.

8.3.2.   Telephonic communication in arbitration

For some people, the telephone offers a more effective and efficient way to arbitrate than arbitrating in person. Some advocates, for example, are better skilled at sensing audible cues suggesting true meaning of a participant's telephone statement than they are at discerning nonverbal aspects of messages in a face-to-face meeting. These audible cues consist of, among others, pitch, pace, tone, volume, inflection, sighs, and pauses. Actually, nonverbal, visual cues to meaning can be distracting and overwhelming to some people in an in-person situation.

There are some major disadvantages to arbitrating over the telephone. For example, it is often difficult to discern the identity of the speakers if a number of participants, including the arbitrator and several disputing parties, are engaged

---

18. *See generally*, Charles B. Craver, Effective *Legal Negotiation and Settlement* (4th Ed.) 310–16 (LEXIS Publishing, 2001); Edward Brunet and Charles B. Craver, *Alternative Dispute Resolution: The Advocate's Perspective* (2d Ed.) 159–62 (LexisNexis, 2001); Ethan Katsh, Janet Rifkin, and Alan Gaitenby, *E-Commerce, E-Disputes, and E-Dispute Resolution: In the Shadow of Ebay Law,* 15 Ohio St. J. on Disp. Resol. 705 (2000); Janice Nadler, *Electronically-Mediated Dispute Resolution and E-Commerce* 17 Negotiation Journal No. 4 (2001); Michael Morris, Janice Nadler, Terri Kurtzberg, and Leigh Thompson, *Schmooze or Lose: Social Friction and Lubrication in E-mail Negotiations Group Dynamics: Theory Research and Practice* Vol. 6, No. 1 (March 2002).

in the teleconference. Furthermore, in a document-rich case, discussing documents over the telephone can often be a cumbersome task if the documents are not quickly identifiable by volume and page number. Also, teleconferences can also become rambling, directionless conversations without strong supervision by the arbitrator. Teleconferences are usually less personal than face-to-face conversations. Such faceless verbal exchanges sometimes facilitate competitive or even deliberately deceptive tactics.

8.3.3 Written communication in arbitration

8.3.3.1 Letter and fax communication

Written communication in arbitration permits the transmission of detailed information to the arbitrator and/or the other parties. The writer has the luxury of not being interrupted during the course of his or her written communication. Written communication also serves as a permanent record of an opposing counsel's offers and concessions.

Furthermore, as an advocate, you can avoid misunderstandings by taking the time to be careful and accurate in your written communications to the arbitrator, opposing parties, and co-counsel. Letters or faxes received by you in an arbitration normally allow you as much time as necessary to review proposals and obtain input from you client, your partners, or co-counsel.

8.3.3.2 E-mail communication

There are many advantages to e-mail communication in arbitration. First, you can instantaneously communicate your pleadings to the arbitrator and opposing counsel simultaneously. Amending and correcting pleadings is also facilitated by use of e-mail. Advocates can prepare and transmit their pleadings from any place in the world; likewise, arbitrators can issue their rulings from any location. Another advantage of e-mail arbitration is that split second tactical decisions do not have to be made. Advocates and their clients can take time to consider and respond to positions or pleadings. Also, studies have shown that the absence of social status cues can influence people to respond openly and less hesitatingly than in a face-to-face setting.

E-mail communication in arbitration, however, is not without its shortcomings. The informality of e-mail communication is its strength as well as its weakness. People using e-mail can easily lapse into a mode where they are totally unconcerned about making a good appearance. In such state, they can be inappropriately informal and even offensive. One study showed that people are eight times more likely to "flame" in electronic discussion than in face-to-face discussion. Recipients of participants' messages can easily misunderstand or misinterpret them. The reason for this is that the recipient cannot always discern the emotive aspect accompanying the content of the message. Consider the e-mail statement, "You consistently have all the right answers." It is not clear whether the writer is exhibiting deference or sarcasm. Emoticons (typographical symbols indicating emotional cues) can help solve this problem, if used tastefully. Also, and more problematically, insults take on permanence. Hostile exchanges can escalate rapidly. Even intended innocuous language can be perceived as deliberately inflammatory and reinforce prior preliminary impressions of recipients, causing misinterpretations to be compounded to a crisis point. In addition, behavioral research has demonstrated that it can take four times as long for a three-person group to make a decision in a real-time (chat room-type) computer conference as in a face-to-face conference. It can take ten times as long for a four-person group, having no time restrictions, to come to a joint decision. These research results have implications for arbitrators in decision making as well as for advocates who try to jointly decide how to plan a discovery schedule. Unless you exercise special care, you can also easily compromise the confidentiality of the arbitration process. The split-second sending of an e-mail to an unintended addressee can be disastrous. Finally, research has shown that people are more intolerant about changing their decision on an issue when they commit their decision to writing, and especially when they publish that written decision to other persons. Written positions or hard-line proposals in e-mail can be more intractable than when they are expressed in person or over the telephone.

Using letters and faxes in arbitration may have its downside. It may cause an unwanted slowdown of the arbitration process. If you use regular mail, the arbitrator and opposing counsel may do likewise and thereby retard the progress of the arbitration. With regard to faxes, if time is of the essence, realize that there is a chance that faxes might get backlogged for transmission in your own mail room, and even if sent, they may get lost in opposing counsel's mail room or they may be misrouted.

These and other advantages and disadvantages of using letter, fax, and e-mail communication in arbitration are outlined in the following charts.

8.3.3.3 Arbitrating using traditional means of writing— letter and fax

ARBITRATING USING TRADITIONAL MEANS OF WRITING (LETTER AND FAX)	
ADVANTAGES	*DISADVANTAGES*
Transmit detailed information	May cause unwanted slowdown of arbitration
No interruptions	Inflexible; you may have to take a position too early in the arbitration process
Permanent record of opponent's positions, pleadings, and correspondence	Lawyer time involved may be more extensive
Misunderstandings more easily avoided	May spawn antagonistic responses
You have time to review proposals and get input	Faxes may be backlogged for transmission
	Faxes may get lost in opponent's mail room

8.3.3.4 Arbitrating using non-traditional means of writing—E-mail

ARBITRATING USING NON-TRADITIONAL MEANS OF WRITING (E-MAIL)	
ADVANTAGES	*DISADVANTAGES*
Messages instantaneously communicated	Messages can be misunderstood and/or misinterpreted
Advocates can prepare and transmit pleadings and arbitrators can issue rulings from anywhere in the world	Insults take on permanence; hostile exchanges can escalate rapidly
Amendments or corrections to pleadings can be distributed immediately and simultaneously	Frustrating delays; takes up to four times longer for a group to reach consensus or a joint decision
Messages can be broadcasted to any number of people simultaneously	Unless care is exercised, confidentiality can be easily compromised
Absence of social status cues can influence people to respond openly and less hesitatingly than in a face-to-face setting	Positions or hard-line proposals can be more intractable than when they are expressed in person or over the telephone
Split second tactical decisions do not normally have to be made	

8.4   Benefits and Limitations of Cyberarbitration

There are both benefits and limitations associated with the use of cyberarbitration.[19] These are discussed generally in section 8.4.1. Two topics that deserve special analysis under this heading are confidentiality and cost of service. These topics are discussed in sections 8.4.3 and 8.4.4, respectively.

8.4.1 Benefits

8.4.1.1   Cost

Some of the benefits of cyberarbitration are as follows. One of the obvious advantages of cyberarbitration over face to face arbitration is reduced cost. Expense of travel and accommodations is often prohibitive in small-dispute situations. Also sending multiple faxes to several parties or telephoning many parties is also time consuming and expensive. In contrast, sending documents via e-mail or posting them on a web site is virtually effortless. Other cost considerations are discussed, *infra*, section 8.4.4.

8.4.1.2   Speed

Instantaneous transmission of information by electronic means in most cases accelerates the resolution process. Often, after the arbitrators reach consensus, using their generated written discussions and the digital findings and conclusions submitted by the advocates, they can quickly formalize, draft, and issue their award and supporting opinion, as appropriate.

8.4.1.3   Availability

Participants can be located anywhere in the world Participants may communicate asynchronously—they choose when they want to respond, day or night.

8.4.1.4   Arbitrator expertise

A worldwide pool of arbitrators with special expertise can enhance the quality of the arbitration process.

---

19. *See generally*, Paul Schiff Berman, *The Globalization of Jurisdiction*, 151 U. Pa. L. Rev. 311 (2002); Karen Stewart and Joseph Matthews, *Online Arbitration of Cross-Border, Business to Consumer Disputes*, 56 U. Miami L. Rev. 1111 (2002); Lucille M. Ponte, *Throwing Bad Money after Bad: Can Online Resolution (ODR) Really Deliver the Goods for the Unhappy Internet Shopper?* 3 Tul. J. Tech. & Intell. Prop. 55 (2001); William Krause, *Do You Want to Step Outside? An Overview of Online Alternative Dispute Resolution* 19 J. Marshall J. Computer & Info. L. 457 (2001); Richard Michael Victorio, *Internet Dispute Resolution (IDR): Bringing ADR into the 21st Century*, 1 Pepp. Disp. Resol. L. J. 279 (2001); Elizabeth G. Thornburg, *Going Private: Technology, Due Process, and Internet Dispute Resolution*, 34 U.C. Davis L. Rev. 151 (2000); Paul D. Carrington, *Virtual Arbitration*, 15 Ohio St. J. on Disp. Resol. 669 (2000); Tiffany J. Lanier, *Where on Earth Does Cyber-Arbitration Occur? International Review of Arbitral Awards Rendered Online*, 7 ILSA J Int'l & Comp L 1 (2000); Frank A. Cona, *Application of Online Systems in Alternative Dispute Resolution*, 45 Buffalo L. Rev. 975 (1997).

8.4.1.5   Less confrontational

The parties are able to choose when they want to respond or participate in the process as it proceeds through its various stages. This allows time for parties to reflect on the materials they receive from opposing parties and co-parties, get initial legal advice, strategize with counsel or co-parties, carefully craft what they want to say, and even get final input from counsel or co-parties before they finally commit to a response or argument that their counsel will communicate to the arbitrator and to the other side. The online nature of the process eliminates the pressure to respond immediately to a received communication. Moreover, advocates can quickly consult legal and expert sources online and help their clients realistically assess the predictable outcome of a phase of the cyberarbitration proceedings. Cyberarbitration minimizes the effects of confrontational dynamics.

8.4.1.6   Cyberspace ensures a neutral forum

Cyberspace itself provides a neutral forum in the nature of an arbitrator's office or conference room. A dominant party is not able to exploit "home court advantage."

8.4.2   Limitations

8.4.2.1   Enforcement of arbitral awards

Determining what law governs the initial commercial contract and the terms of any award may be challenging. The parties can circumvent these problem areas by carefully crafting an arbitration agreement to include terms defining jurisdiction, applicable laws, and enforcement and review procedures. Self-executing award mechanisms, trustmark withdrawal, and escrow accounts are a few of the measures that can be used to ensure the enforcement of arbitral awards.

8.4.2.2   Uncertainty regarding confidentiality, privacy, anonymity, and authenticity

As discussed more thoroughly in section 8.4.3, *infra*, maintaining confidentiality of communications in cyberspace can be a difficult task. The parties' fear of information leaks and invasion of privacy can create barriers to unfettered communication. Also, because of the faceless interaction in cyberspace, the identity of communicators and the authenticity of communications can sometimes be difficult to guarantee.

8.4.2.3   Absence of human factors

Online communication often lacks the spontaneity and vigor of face-to-face interaction and oral discussion. Also studies have shown that parties proceeding online are more likely to distrust and suspect lying or deceit on the part of other participants and they are more likely to "flame" and reach impasse in negotiation of fact stipulations or resolution of discovery matters.

8.4.2.4   Computer accessibility and literacy

Varying degrees of computer accessibility and literacy may affect the quality of online communication between counsel and client. Occasionally, use of online technology can create a power imbalance among the parties or counsel. This imbalance may result from varying quality of computer equipment or software, the relative competence of the cyberarbitration participants to use the Internet or online information resources, or the unequal experience with using the services of a cyberarbitrator.

8.4.2.5   Unsuitability of disputes for cyberarbitration

Some disputes are comfortably amenable to resolution by cyberarbitration. These includes disputes originating in cyberspace—intellectual property disputes and e-commerce disputes; disputes that are fundamentally economic (insurance claims and construction defects; and disputes that concern undeveloped areas of the law—for example, a body of cyberspace customary law. Certain types of disputes may not be as appropriate for cyberarbitration. For example, a situation where the credibility of the parties is a crucial issue in a dispute might be more appropriate for a face-to-face (or a videoconference) arbitration so that the arbitrator could assess the parties' relative truthfulness. Moreover, personal injury cases where plaintiffs need to demonstrate the nature of their injuries, scars, etc. may be more appropriate for traditional arbitration or video-conferenced arbitration. Similarly, a patent or product liability case, where it is helpful to a resolution for the arbitration participants to see the configuration or operation of a particular piece of equipment, may be a candidate for a traditional arbitration.

The above-described benefits and limitations of cyberarbitration and others are outlined in the following chart.

8.4.2.6   Benefits and limitations of cyberarbitration

BENEFITS AND LIMITATIONS OF CYBERARBITRATION	
BENEFITS	**LIMITATIONS**
Reduced cost in comparison with face-to-face arbitration	Enforcement of arbitral awards may be a problem
Accelerated proceedings	Determining what law governs the initial commercial contract and the terms of any award may be challenging
Participants can be located anywhere in the world	
Participants may communicate asynchronously—they choose when they want to respond, day or night	Varying degrees of computer accessibility and literacy may exist among counsel and their clients
Arbitrators with special expertise may be hired worldwide	Power imbalance may be created by unequal online expertise/experience/equipment of parties or counsel.
Cyberarbitration minimizes the effects of confrontational dynamics	Online communication lacks the spontaneity and vigor of face-to-face interaction and oral discussion
Cyberspace itself provides a neutral forum in the nature of an arbitrator's office or conference room	Parties are more likely to distrust and suspect lying or deceit on the part of other participants
Parties can craft communications in an emotion-free setting	Parties are more likely to "flame" and reach impasse
Advocates have easy access to legal and expert sources to help them give realistic advice to clients at particular points in the arbitration proceedings	Parties may have uncertainty regarding confidentiality, privacy, anonymity, and authenticity.
Often, after the arbitrators reach consensus, using their generated written discussions, they can quickly formalize, draft, and issue their award and supporting opinion, as appropriate	Some disputes may not be suitable for resolution by means of cyberarbitration.
	When the parties' credibility is in issue, traditional arbitration may be more effective than cyberarbitration

8.4.3   Confidentiality

Confidentiality has always been an important aspect of the arbitration process. The participants' agreement to maintain the confidentiality of the arbitration proceedings is usually sufficient in face-to-face arbitrations to guarantee nondisclosure of sensitive information. It is the responsibility of each participant in offline (or online) arbitrations not to mistakenly disclose information by e-mail or other means. ODR, however, has created a new threat to arbitration confidentiality.[20] Regardless of the participants' agreement to maintain confidentiality of online arbitration proceedings, breaches of security can originate externally from nonparticipants who intentionally invade, acquire, and perhaps even alter information the participants want to preserve as confidential and unchanged. It is generally accepted among the ODR provider community that electronic messages need to be protected by electronic means and that electronic arbitration communications and access to the data must be secured, before, during, and after the cyberarbitration. Thus, protection is needed with respect to both the transmission and the storage of confidential arbitration information. These two aspects require different means of protection. The risks to be protected against are: the risk that unauthorized third parties will gain access to the information (i.e. risk of compromising the confidentiality of the message); and the risk that such third parties will alter it (i.e. the risk of compromising the integrity of the message). A current serious limitation of cyberarbitration is that ODR providers cannot always guarantee that arbitration communications and documentation will not be disclosed.

8.4.3.1   Transmission of information

Unencrypted e-mail is considered to be about as secure as postcards. E-mail is capable, however, of being secured by several means. One means is through a software called Secure Multipurpose Internet Mail Exchange Protocol (S/MIME). If correctly used, the software provides the recipient with strong evidence of the origin of the contents of the message. It also has a feature that confirms to the sender that his or her message was delivered to a specific recipient. Another product that is free of charge but difficult to employ by non-specialists is Pretty Good Privacy (PGP). It is a message protection software with the same quality of service as S/MIME and is available from the Massachusetts Institute of Technology.

Alteration of a transmitted message can be reduced by digital signatures. These are cryptographic instruments trusted to third parties called signature or

---

20. *See generally*, T. Schultz, G. Kaufmann-Kohler, D. Langer, V. Bonnet, Online Dispute Resolution: *The State of the Art and the Issues, E-Com Research Project of the University of Geneva*, Geneva, 2001, http://www.online-adr.org, 44–50.

key-holders. If a sender uses such private key to electronically sign a message, the receiver can verify both the origin and the integrity of the message.

Other means of protection must be used to secure information that is posted on a Web site, as opposed to being sent by e-mail.

The Hypertext Transfer Protocol (HTTP) is the generally accepted protocol for online transactions. In addition to this Web-based security feature, Secure Sockets Layer (SSL) provides protection of the confidentiality and integrity of Web-based communications.

Web site storage of confidential information is also a risk area. Site storage systems consist of a database and Web server. ODR providers must protect these against such risks as intrusions, viruses, and disk crashes. These storage systems can be protected by firewalls, but it is more effective to implement protection for each document instead of the system as a whole.

Because security systems are not yet widely available to satisfy high expectations of security in the ODR provider field, advocates may do well to carefully weigh the risks of using ODR for disputes in which the financial stakes are very high.

8.4.4   Cost or financing of service

Fees for use of ODR services are generally of three types: bilateral (or multilateral), unilateral, or external source.[21] In the bilateral (or multilateral) model, each party pays its proportional share of the user fee. This seems fair on its face, but one problem with this model is that the cost for the consumer may be disproportionate compared to the amount at stake. A very large majority of ODR providers charge users under this model.

In the unilateral user fee model, the business (merchant or insurance company) pays the entire fee for the ODR service. The payment can be in the form of an annual membership fee (e.g. a trustmark fee) or a fee per case. The problem with this model is the inevitable appearance of bias. It might appear to the non-business user, for example, that the business payor of the user fee is being favored in the process. The appearance of bias can be lessened by the ODR provider's implementation of strict procedural rules, ensuring the availability of an adequate selection of independent neutrals, publishing clear policies of neutrality and impartiality, and establishing an independent supervisory or auditing body. Approximately 12 percent of the ODR service providers in existence as of December, 2001 have implemented the unilateral fee model.

---

21. *See generally*, T. Schultz, G. Kaufmann-Kohler, D. Langer, V. Bonnet, *Online Dispute Resolution: The State of the Art and the Issues*, E-Com Research Project of the University of Geneva, Geneva, 2001, http://www.online-adr.org, 74–77.

Approximately 10 percent of ODR service providers operate under the external source fee model. In this model, a third party—university or a governmental or non-governmental organization (e.g. a consumer association) pays the entire fee for the ODR service. In general, this model provides the highest guarantee of independence and impartiality. As of December, 2001, ODR service providers employing this fee model were: ECODIR, ODR.NL, IRIS, Virtual Magistrate, and Online Ombuds Office.

On the question of independence, advocates selecting ODR provider organizations may want to take into account the provider's organizational structure and outside financial support. As of December, 2001, a large majority of the ODR providers were for-profit organizations; approximately 20 percent operated on a not-for-profit basis.

8.5   Ethics of Cyberadvocacy

The State codes of professional conduct for lawyers, most of which incorporate the American Bar Association's Model Rules of Professional Conduct, guide an advocate's conduct in representing clients in cyberarbitration.[22] (*See* section 2.7 and Appendix J). The ABA maintains a Web site (http://www.elawyering.org) that provides guidance for lawyers that practice online. The site also provides ethical guidance at http://www.elawyering.org/ethics/advice.asp. The Elawyering Task Force, ABA, Legal Web sites Best Practice Guidelines (2001) can be accessed at http://www.elawyering.org/tools/practices/asp.

Arbitrators' conduct is generally governed by the Code of Ethics for Arbitrators in Commercial Disputes—Revised 2004, which have been developed in conjunction with the American Bar Association. (*See* section 2.12 and Appendix I). Currently, some large associations of dispute resolution providers have proposed, or are considering, common policies or codes of conduct for ODR. Guidelines published by the American Arbitration Association, entitled eCommerce Dispute Management Protocol, Principles for Managing B2B [business to business] Relationships, acknowledges the important of fairness, clear policies, a range of options, and resources of technology. In May of 2001, the American Bar Association Task Force on E-Commerce and ADR, after investigating core features of effective ODR, produced a Draft Preliminary Report & Concept Paper. Among other topics covered, it addressed issues of impartiality, confidentiality, security, and qualifications and responsibilities of neutrals. The task force released its final

---

22. *See generally*, Louise Ellen Teitz, P*roviding Legal Services for the Middle Class in Cyberspace: The Promise and Challenge of On-Line Dispute Resolution*, 70 Fordham L. Rev. 985, 987–91 (2001).

report and concept paper on April 5, 2002, and it was posted on the internet at < http://www.law.washington.edu/ABA-eADR/home.html>.[23]

One critical ethical duty of advocates in cyberarbitration is maintaining client confidences. Online communication presents a minefield of opportunities for inadvertent and harmful disclosures of client information by incautious and unwary advocates.[24] Following the guidance presented below will help you avoid making those instant, and unintentional harmful disclosures.

8.5.1   Carefully manage the power of the "cc"

Anyone who is or who has been a subscriber to a Listserv knows how useful some of the received information is and how annoying some of it can be. Thus when communicating by e-mail or by e-mail list, make a quick check to see if all the addressees actually need to receive or would even want to receive the information you are sending. There are times when, on behalf of your client, you will want to communicate with all participants in the arbitration, but there will be other times when the information sent will be merely ministerial and applicable to only one or two participants or co-parties. Do not bother participants with a message that has no relevance to them only because it is convenient for you to click only once without thinking, sorting, and deciding. Also, while the "cc" option is a powerful e-mail tool, it is a horrible "accident waiting to happen." Critical, highly confidential information can be disclosed in a split, unthinking, second and can compromise an arbitration and perhaps put a lawyer's career in jeopardy. Before commencing an online arbitration, arbitrators normally take great pains to advise parties and counsel about the dangers of unintentional disclosures of client confidences and to discuss procedures for preventing it from happening. This advice should be explicitly heeded.

8.5.2   Use caucuses judiciously

Realize that when you engage in cybermediation, you may be caucusing privately with several participants simultaneously. By that I mean you may send a confidential communication to counsel for a co-party, and while that lawyer is considering it, you may receive a communication from opposing counsel requiring your immediate response—before you respond to counsel for the co-party. You may also receive responses out of order—which could be confusing. Consider, for example that you send one confidential e-mail message to the first participant now, and another confidential message to a second participant two hours from now. The second participant responds immediately and the first participant

---

23. *See* Benjamin Davis, *A Status Report on the American Bar Association Task Force on E-Commerce and Alternative Dispute Resolution*, 8 Tex. Wesleyan L. Rev. 29 (2002).
24. M. Ethan Katsh, *Dispute Resolution in Cyberspace*, 28 Conn. L. Rev. 953, 971–74 (1996).

responds a couple hours later. If you are not careful to note which participant is e-mailing you, it is possible that your expectations about receiving a response from the first party more quickly might cause you to err by directing your confidential response to the wrong party. Thus, you must take great care not to disclose confidential information accidentally when communicating online. And, of course, when you are dealing online with four or five co-parties and opposing parties and the arbitrator(s), the pressure to guard against unintentional disclosures of confidential information is extremely intense and your ethical obligation to maintain confidentiality becomes magnified proportionately.

8.5.3   Take security precautions vis-a-vis other Web users

If you are engaged in the arbitration of a high-profile case online, do not be too surprised if you have interlopers—related to the dispute or not—trying to acquire information on the arbitration's progress. If you use chat rooms, make sure they are secure and keep an eye out for new entrants whose identity you do not know.

8.5.4   Maintain appropriate confidentiality within your groups

It was pointed out above that the "cc" feature of e-mail is a powerful and useful tool, but that it can cause disastrous disclosures of information. Before you send any e-mail messages, you should ensure that the principal addressees and the "cc" addressees are appropriate. You may be involved in several online mediations and arbitrations at once. If you are simultaneously involved in several cyber-adr processes, it is important for you to keep the e-mail addresses of participants in the various cases segregated from each other so that you don't inadvertently dispatch an e-mail to a participant in a separate cyber-adr process.

8.6   Considerations in Selecting a Cyberarbitration Service and Cyberarbitrator

8.6.1   The cyberarbitration process

Before you select an ODR service provider and a cyberarbitrator or a panel of cyberarbitrators, you should decide what kind of cyberarbitration process you, your client, and the opposing side desire. One of the first questions you want to ask yourself is whether you want to be limited in your choice of arbitrators by an ODR provider's "mandatory" list of neutrals. If you and your opposing counsel have in mind a particular arbitrator want to hire, you may want to consider eliminating from consideration those providers that limit your choice of arbitrators to their list or panel.

Also, as described more fully in section 8.6.2, all ODR providers do not provide the same type of arbitration process. The nature of the arbitration process provided by each ODR provider depends on the type of technology available on the Web site. For example, some provider Web sites only allow for e-mail communication and do not provide a chat room feature. Thus, if you and opposing counsel desire a traditional arbitration conference format of all the mediation participants, you might want to consider eliminating from consideration all those providers that do not offer the real-time chat feature. Similarly, if there are several parties on your side of the dispute you may want a Web site real-time chat feature that allows private caucusing for one or more parties and their counsel. This desired feature may further result in narrowing your search for providers. In some situations, you may need instant messaging, threaded discussion, and videoconferencing availability. You may also want a provider that offers mediation as a tandem process option as you proceed through the arbitration. In still other situations, you may desire a provider that provides only a technology platform for arbitration, which the parties can use together with their independently selected arbitrator(s). Thus, in many respects, choosing the appropriate provider of online arbitration is often much more challenging than selecting an offline arbitration service provider.

8.6.2 Selecting a cyberarbitration service

In addition to reasons stated in section 8.6.1, choosing a cyberarbitration service is much more challenging than choosing a provider of face-to-face (or offline) arbitration services because there are no geographic limitations. In offline arbitration, counsel normally select an arbitration service that is conveniently located geographically. If several parties are located in one city and two parties are from out of state, for example, usually parties will agree to hold the arbitration in the city where the most parties are located. That is not true in the case of online dispute resolution. The location of the parties is not a factor. Parties located anywhere in the United States can choose a provider of ODR services located in any state or in any foreign country. This fact greatly increases the spectrum of choice. Not limited by geography, parties can choose any ODR service provider worldwide based on, among other criteria, reputation for high-quality service, reputation for high-quality justice, Web site confidentiality features, specialty in processing specific types of disputes, competence and impartiality of neutrals, availability of binding and nonbinding process alternatives, speed of resolution process, satisfaction of foreign language needs, and effective enforcement mechanisms.

When you and your client discuss the need to select a cyberarbitration service, one of the first questions you should address is whether binding cyberarbitration is the only process that is appropriate to resolve your dispute. On reflection, you might conclude that non-binding cyberarbitration would be a better choice or that a cybernegotiation service (such as blind bidding) or a cybermediation service might adequately satisfy your needs and be less costly than proceeding to the more formal and time-consuming binding cyberarbitration process.[25] Alternatively, you might conclude that you really need cyberarbitration, but that you want to have available the option to proceed to a consensual dispute resolution process. Thus, in such situation, you need to know the criteria both for selecting a service provider that offers adjudication (cyberarbitration) and consensual dispute resolution (cybermediation or online facilitated negotiation).[26]

8.6.2.1   Selection criteria for cyberarbitration service

With regard to an adjudicative hearing, in general, experts identify eleven procedural requirements that must be present to ensure due process.[27] They are as follows:

1. Unbiased neutral(s)

2. The parties' right to be represented by counsel

3. Notice and a statement of reasons giving rise to the dispute

4. Statement in response to the reasons giving rise to the dispute

5. The parties' opportunity to present evidence including witnesses, in support of their positions

6. The parties' right to know opposing evidence

7. The right to cross-examine opposing witnesses

8. The decision maker's duty to keep a record of the evidence presented

9. The decision maker's duty to render a decision based on and limited to the evidence in the record and the applicable law

10. The decision maker's duty to give reasons to the parties supporting the decision

11. The availability of appellate review of the decision

---

25. *See* Thomas Schultz, *Online Arbitration: Binding or Non-binding*, U. Mass. ADR online Monthly, <http://ombuds.org/center/adr2002-11-schultz.html>.

26. *See generally*, Louise Ellen Teitz, *Providing Legal Services for the Middle Class in Cyberspace: The Promise and Challenge of On-line Dispute Resolution*, 70 Fordham L. Rev. 985, 1007–09 (2001); Lucille M. Ponte, *Throwing Bad Money After Bad: Can Online Dispute Resolution (ODR) Really Deliver the Goods for the Unhappy Internet Shopper?* 3 Tul. & Intell. Prop. 55 (2001).

27. Henry H. Perritt, Jr., *Dispute Resolution in Cyberspace: Demand for New Forms of ADR*, 15 Ohio St. J. on Disp. Resol. 675, 677–84 (2000).

While most of these requirements would equally serve as due process criteria for cyberarbitration, some of them have not been due process requirements even in traditional arbitration. As to criteria 10 and 11 in the list above—the arbitrator's issuance of a reasoned decision and the parties being provided the opportunity for appellate review, while they may be "nice-to-have" court-type due process criteria, they are not absolutely necessary requirements for adequate due process in a cyberarbitration. An important criteria for cyberarbitration not included in the list above is cost of the process. Criteria 10 and 11 could significantly and unreasonably increase the cost of any arbitration, and would certainly do so in cyberarbitration. These cost issues, however, are really for the parties to agree upon. Even in some traditional arbitrations parties frequently opt for the arbitrator issuing reasoned findings and conclusions supporting and in a few arbitrations, and in some rare cases, parties preagree to an appellate arbitration panel to be used in the event that one or more parties desires review of the arbitration hearing panel's decision. In summary, then, an arbitration service provider whose arbitration system satisfies criteria 1 through 9, above, will normally satisfy at least the minimum due process interests of your clients. If a client seeks more that minimal due process and is not opposed to paying additionally for it, you may want to explore the possibility of choosing an arbitration process that incorporates criteria 10 and 11 as well.

8.6.2.2 Selection criteria for an ODR service generally

When selecting an ODR provider that can offer an optional cybermediation service, one commentator suggests that the advocate consider only the first three criteria set forth in the above eleven-point list, since the remaining eight criteria are not relevant to a consensual settlement process, such as mediation.[28] Thus, you would want to ensure that a cybermediation service provider offers the parties, at a minimum: (1) a means by which they can select a neutral third party to mediate their dispute; (2) the right for the parties to be represented by counsel; (3) and opportunity to have notice and a statement of reasons giving rise to the dispute.

Other commentators have identified what they believe to be three fundamental building blocks for a proper ODR system of any kind: convenience, trust, and expertise.[29] They believe that some measure of each factor must be present in any selected system. They also assert that the relative presence of each factor

---

28. Henry H. Perritt, Jr., *Dispute Resolution in Cyberspace: Demand for New Forms of ADR*, 15 Ohio St. J. on Disp. Resol. 675, 683–84 (2000).
29. Ethan Katsh and Janet Rifkin, *Online Dispute Resolution: Resolving Conflicts in Cyberspace* 71–92 (Jossey-Bass, 2001).

determines whether, in any particular instance, one ODR system should be used over another or whether ODR should be used (as opposed offline ADR systems) at all. Included in the convenience factor, are "any logistical and financial factors that positively or negatively affect access to and participation in the process."

The basic question is whether an online ODR option is more convenient for a particular dispute application than, for instance, writing a letter, using the phone, a combination of these two, or even a face-to-face meeting. Would it be more convenient to drive to a nearby suburb on a sunny day for the initial joint session of a mediation conference rather than engaging in an online joint session? If so, probably the parties would opt for a face-to-face conference. If in this same scenario, the mediation was in the agreement-drafting stage, it might make more sense to hold the mediation session online so that drafts of agreement provisions could be immediately exchanged and modified in writing online and to everyone's satisfaction. Another fundamental factor required of any ODR system is trust. The parties and their counsel must be absolutely assured that when using a particular ODR system, their confidential information will not be revealed to the other side—or in fact to anyone who has no right to see or hear it. Some ODR systems have a seal or trustmark provided by an independent third party which vouches for the trustworthiness of the ODR service provider. Finally, expertise is a necessary requirement for any ODR company. Expertise involves an interactive informational process—one that satisfies the specific interactive needs of its users. Some ODR systems, such as blind bidding, can provide online dispute resolution services that cannot be done as well or efficiently offline. ODR by its very online nature has a worldwide Web of online information available to its users. It is the twenty-first century challenge of the ODR providers to capitalize on its available expertise and informational resources to make the ODR experience as effective and rewarding online as it has proven over the years to be offline.

Several research studies have demonstrated that in most conflict situations, disputants are more concerned with issues of exoneration, with obtaining an adequate hearing, and with being treated respectfully than they are with the actual outcome of the dispute resolution process in which they engage.[30] In effect, disputants are more concerned about the adequacy and fairness of the procedure ("procedural justice") by which the dispute is resolved than the outcome or settlement result itself.

Studies show that there three key components of procedural justice:

1.   perceived trust (did the neutral fully consider my views and needs?);

---

30. *See generally*, Janice Nadler, *Electronically-Mediated Dispute Resolution and E-Commerce*, 17 Negotiation Journal No.4 (2001).

2.   standing (did the neutral treat me with politeness, dignity and respect?); and

3.   neutrality (did the neutral treat me in an evenhanded, nondiscriminatory way and behave in an open, fact-based fashion?).

As to perceived trust, it has been shown that the extent to which disputants are willing settle a dispute and to abide by the terms of the settlement in the future can be strongly influenced by the feeling that they have been given the opportunity to tell their side of the story. This "voice" effect stems from whether the neutral is perceived as giving adequate consideration to the disputant's views. Above all, disputants seem to be concerned with telling their story because the perception of being heard is a signal that the authority (e.g. an arbitrator) can be trusted to view them and treat them in a way that is benevolent and fair. In addition, the process must be dignified in itself, and confer standing on the disputants to be entitled to dignity and respect. Finally, the process must be neutral in the sense that the third party (e.g. an arbitrator) conducts himself or herself in an unbiased way and with a concern for achieving and accurate understanding of the facts and other relevant information.

Finally, it should be noted that in a 2001 study of forty-nine ODR organizations reported by the Private International Law Department of the Geneva University Law School, the core principles of fundamental due process in online dispute resolution of consumer disputes were identified to be:

1.   reasonable cost to the consumer;

2.   independence and impartiality of the ODR organization and process;

3.   transparency of the ODR organization (clear policies and full disclosure of statistics and corporate and/or financial support and links);

4.   speed of ODR process;

5.   accessibility to consumers.[31]

From this discussion, we can distill the following criteria for selecting an ODR service. The ODR service provider should, at a minimum:

1.   provide an adequate means for parties and their counsel to select a neutral third party;

2.   allow parties to be represented by counsel;

3.   provide parties an opportunity to receive notice and a statement of reasons giving rise to the dispute, and an opportunity to respond;

---

31. T. Schultz, G. Kaufmann-Kohler, D. Langer, V. Bonnet, *Online Dispute Resolution: The State of the Art and the Issues*, E-Com Research Project of the University of Geneva, Geneva, 2001, http://www.online-adr.org, 89–90.

4.   make the ADR process as accessible and convenient as possible for the parties, at a reasonable cost;

5.   ensure that ODR communications are confidentially maintained;

6.   provide adequate expertise or instruction to assist the parties, technologically, in the use of the online dispute resolution services;

7.   ensure that cyberneutrals permit the parties and counsel to voice their views and needs fully;

8.   ensure that cyberneutrals accord standing to the parties and counsel by treating them with politeness, dignity, and respect.

9.   ensure that cyberneutrals act in an unbiased and impartial manner and with a concern for achieving and accurate understanding of the facts and other relevant information.

10.   ensure that the ODR process is reasonably speedy and that the ODR organization has clear operational policies and provides full disclosure of statistics and financial support and links.

If the ODR process is cyberarbitration, these six additional criteria apply:

11.   the parties have the opportunity to present evidence including witnesses, in support of their positions

12.   the parties' right to know opposing evidence

13.   the right to cross-examine opposing witnesses

14.   the decisionmaker has a duty to keep a record of the evidence presented

15.   the decisionmaker has a duty to render a decision based on and limited to the evidence in the record and the applicable law

16.   the decisionmaker has a duty to give reasons to the parties supporting the decision

8.6.2.3   ODR service providers and principal services offered

The chart below identifies organizations that provided (or have planned offerings of) ODR services as of June, 2003.[32] It also states the principal type or types of dispute serviced, the principal type of ODR service or services offered, and other descriptive information. Web site addresses for each of the organizations are contained in Appendix L. The letter key for each principal type of dispute serviced by the ODR organization is as follows:

---

32.   Much of the initial information compiled in this table was derived from T. Schultz, G. Kaufmann-Kohler, D. Langer, V. Bonnet, *Online Dispute Resolution: The State of the Art and the Issues*, E-Com Research Project of the University of Geneva, Geneva, 2001, <http://www.online-adr.org>. The Web sites of the ODR service providers shown in the table were last visited in June, 2003. The Web sites are listed in Appendix L.

A. all disputes or unspecified disputes

B. consumer disputes

C. insurance disputes

D. commercial disputes

E. domain-name disputes

F. race discrimination and violence

G. individual and public liberties

H. employment

I. online auction disputes

J. online marketplaces

The numerical key for each principal ODR service offered by a listed ODR organization is as follows:

1. automated negotiation

2. assisted negotiation

3. cybermediation

4. cyberarbitration

5. case evaluation

6. trustmark or seal programs

7. complaint filing for offline ADR

8. a decision-type process, with written decisions, but neither arbitration nor mediation, technically;

9. linking cite to ADR providers

10. cybernegotiation

11. mock trial; jury verdicts

12. technology-assisted optimized negotiation with neutral facilitator

13. communication platform for cybermediation

14. court of law using simultaneous videoconferencing, online windows showing exhibits and instant-messenger programs with real-time written discussions of legal issues.

15. non-binding cyberarbitration

16. automated complaint assistance

8.6.2.4   ODR Organizations services chart

ODR ORGANIZATIONS	PRINCIPAL TYPE OF DISPUTE(S)	PRINCIPAL TYPE OF ODR SERVICE(S)	COMMENTS
Better Business Bureau Online	B	6 (Reliability, privacy, and Children's Privacy); 7; planned: 1, 3, 4	United States (U.S.)-based non-profit industry association to promote relationship between businesses and consumers worldwide
ClickNSettle.com	A	1	U.S.-based private business venture
CPR Institute for Dispute Resolution	E	8	U.S.-based alliance of 500 counsel of corporations and lawyers seeking to promoted ADR
Cyberarbitration	A	Planned: 4	Indian-based private venture
Cybercourt	A	Planned: 3, 4	Germany-based program operated by Price Waterhouse Coopers
Cybersettle	A	1	North American private business venture; exclusive online settlement tool of the Association of Trial Lawyers of America
The Domain Magistrate	E	9	Assistance center to link to three of the four ODR providers approved by ICANN
ECODIR	A	3, 5, 10	European Comsumer Dispute Resolution; a free online dispute resolution program promoted by the European Commission
E-Mediation (also ODR.NL)	B, D	Planned: 3, 4	Netherlands-based venture created by the Dutch Electronic Commerce Platform

e-Mediator	B, D	3	Pilot project of an offline mediation institution called Consensus
eResolution (under development)	D, E	3, 4, 8	Canadian-based private business venture
FordJourney	B	4	Service provided by the Chartered Institute of Arbitrators, in Ireland for online sales of Ford cars
FSM	F	6	German ODR Company based in Bonn; companies agree to abide by code of conduct
iCourthouse	A	4, 5, 11	U.S.-based business venture; free for parties; subscription basis to attorneys
iLevel	B	2	U.S.-based consumer service
Internet Neutral	A	3	U.S.-based private business venture
Intersettle	A	1	Scotland-based private business venture
IRIS	G	3	French based organization
Judicial Dispute Resolution, Inc.	A	3, 4, 5	Chicago-based private business venture of former judges providing offline ADR for domestic and international commercial disputes
Mediation Arbitration Resolution Services (MARS)	A	1, 3, 4	U.S.-based private business ventures
National Arbitration Forum	A	4	U.S.-based arbitration institution providing DR services under UDRP; accredited by ICANN

NovaForum.com	D, H	3, 4	Canadian-based private business venture, providing ADR services after exhaustion of internal corporate procedures
One Accord	A	12	ODR provider with goal of integrating interest-based negotiation principles with technology that is designed to optimize settlements
Online Ombuds Office	I	3	US-based non-profit research project created by University of Massachusetts
Online Resolution	A	2, 3, 4	U.S.-based organization created by the Mediation Information and Research Center (MIRC)
Resolution Forum	A	2, 3, 4	U.S.-based non-profit program to make ODR more accessible and affordable to the general public
SettlementOnline	A	1, 13	Private business venture
SettleOnline	A	1	U.S.-based private business venture created by Resolution Systems, Inc., a provider of offline ADR
SettleTheCase	A	3, 4	Private business venture
SquareTrade	J	2, 3, 4	U.S.-based private business venture
State of Michigan	D	Planned:14	Michigan court of law for claims greater than $25,000
The Claim Room	A	1, 2, 13	U.K.-based private business venture
TRUSTe	D	2	Non-profit initiative operated by a private business venture

Virtual Magistrate	A	15	U.S.-based academic and non-profit institution, operated by the Chicago-Kent College of Law
WebAssured.com	A	3, 4, 16	U.S.-based private business venture
WEBDispute.com	A	4, Planned: 3	U.S.-based private business venture
WebMediate	A	1, 3, 4	U.S.-based private business venture
WeCanSettle	A	1	U.K.-based private business venture
World Intellectual Property Organization (WIPO)	E	3, 4	DR provider approved by ICANN, applying the UDRP and its own supplemental rules
Word&Bond	A	6, 4	U.K.-based private business venture

8.6.3 Selecting a cyberarbitrator

If you are selecting a cyberarbitrator, apart from all the criteria discussed in section 2.6.3, two obvious attributes you would be looking for are a candidate's degree of computer literacy and his or her training or experience in resolving disputes online. Until cyberarbitration is used more widely, you may have to be content with finding a candidate that is simply computer literate. Do not be afraid to interview a cyberarbitrator candidate and ask him or her direct questions about his or her online resolution experience. Also talk to other counsel that you know who have participated in one or more cyberarbitrations and obtain their suggestions as to effective cyberarbitrators. Dispute resolution organizations that provide online dispute resolution services exclusively would be a good source for identifying and locating experienced cyberarbitrators. (*See* Appendix L). The American Bar Association operates a Web site (http://www.elawyering.org) that provides guidance for lawyers who practice online. That Web site eventually may be a resource for lawyers to network in order to facilitate selection of cyberneutrals.

8.6.4 Cyberarbitration "walk through"

In order to have a realistic "feel" for what it is like to prepare and plan for a cyberarbitration, we will "walk through" the next few sections with the aid of a four-party dispute scenario.[33] To take full advantage of the "walk-through" experience, you are encouraged to put yourself in the role of counsel for each of these parties immediately before and during the preliminary hearing as you think through the design and planning of the appropriate cyberarbitration process and communication format procedures. As in traditional arbitration, the preliminary hearing in cyberarbitration is a critical stage of the arbitration process where critical decisions are reached by the parties or imposed by the arbitrator concerning the conduct of the evidentiary part of the proceeding. In actuality, the results of the preliminary hearing—particularly in cyberarbitration—can make or break a party's chances of prevailing on the merits in a cyberarbitration hearing. The advocate's ability to negotiate the appropriate evidentiary and communication procedures or to prevail in his or her arguments with respect to them can have a significant impact on the ultimate results in the cyberarbitration proceeding.

8.6.4.1 Cyberarbitration "walk through" scenario

The dispute concerns the construction of a new medical office building in the Chicago, Illinois area that tenant doctors complain has a faulty air conditioning system. The building was completed in the last week of August, and the doctors moved in during the first week of September. The owner of the building is withholding a final $100,000 payment to the General Contractor until the problem is corrected. The four parties to the dispute are the General Contractor, Best Contracting Co., ("BEST")(a national company headquartered in New York, with local office in Chicago), the Heating and Cooling subcontractor, Perfectemp Co.,("PERFECTEMP")(Milwaukee, Wisconsin), with outside counsel in Milwaukee, the Project Engineer, Imagineering, Inc. ("IMAGINEERING") (national engineering firm headquartered in San Diego, California), and Aircon Fabricators Ltd., ("AIRCON"), the manufacturer of the cooling system, a company in Frankfurt, Germany with International counsel in London, England. Perfectemp had purchased the cooling system from AIRCON through a business-to-business Internet transaction. Because of the importance of solving the problem within a few months time, the relatively modest dollar amount of the corrective measures that might need to be taken, the geographic distances separating the parties and

---

33. This scenario is a time-frame modified version of the one that appears in *Mediation Advocacy 2d Ed.* 275–82 (NITA 2002). It is used here in order to demonstrate the differences in preparation and planning strategies employed in cyberarbitration vis-a-vis cybermediation.

even counsel to parties, the prohibitive costs of a face-to-face meeting, the parties and their lawyers have agreed to engage in cyberarbitration to avoid extremely costly and time consuming face to face arbitration or litigation. AIRCON would not consent to cybermediation because it felt it needed an arbitrator's decision to defend against claims in the future that it manufactures faulty products. Counsel for the parties have secured the services of a cyberarbitrator on the panel of CYBERSOLUTIONS, a full service ODR provider located in Sydney Australia. The chart below identifies the participants in the cyberarbitration and their geographic locations. The parties have chosen as their neutral, the world famous construction dispute mediator and arbitrator, Michael Fairman ("FAIRMAN") who is located in Melbourne, Australia.

8.6.4.2   Cyberarbitration participants and their locations

PARTY	PARTY'S REP.	LOCATION OF PARTY'S REP.	PARTY'S COUNSEL	LOCATION OF PARTY'S COUNSEL
BEST	Dist. Mgr. of General Contractor	Chicago, Illinois	BEST's in-house general counsel	New York, New York
PERFEC-TEMP	CEO of Heating and Cooling Installation Subcontractor	Milwaukee, Wisconsin	Outside Litigation Counsel	Milwaukee, Wisconsin
IMAGINEER-ING	President of Engineering Firm	San Diego, California	Retained Local Litigation Counsel	Chicago, Illinois
AIRCON	Technical Supr. and Sales Mgr. of Air conditioner Mfr.; bi-lingual	Frankfurt, Germany	International bi-lingual counsel; mega law firm	London, England

8.6.4.3   General information concerning construction dispute

BEST completed construction of a two-story (98,000 square feet) medical office building in the Chicago, Illinois area during the last week of August. The tenants—who are all doctors practicing in various medical specialties—moved in during the first week in September. The first two weeks in September were unusually hot in Chicago. The doctors complained to the building's OWNER that the building's air conditioning system was not operating properly. Four doctors reported having to send their office staffs home early on four occasions because their office temperatures approached 90 degrees. These four doctors wrote letters to the OWNER documenting their complaints. The temperature fortunately cooled down during the third week of September and so did the tempers of the doctors. During the next few months the air conditioning will not be an issue. But the air conditioning matter must be resolved prior to April of next year when cooling of the building will be necessary.

After faxing the four letters of complaint to BEST's District Manager in Chicago in the third week of September, the OWNER called the District Manager and told him to get the air conditioning corrected. The OWNER told BEST that the medical building's Director of Maintenance had carefully followed the procedures detailed in AIRCON's air conditioner manual in an effort to correct the problem, but to no avail. The Director of Maintenance e-mailed AIRCON's Technical Supervisor and Sales Manager in Frankfurt, Germany who informed the Director of Maintenance that the procedures he followed were correct and that the problem was "definitely not with the air conditioning equipment." AIRCON suggested that the problem was with the ductwork, and that if anyone was at fault, it was either the Heating and Cooling Subcontractor (PERFECTEMP), or the Project Engineer (IMAGINEERING). The Director of Maintenance e-mailed each of these companies, and they both denied responsibility, claiming the problem was caused by the other or by the air conditioner manufacturer, AIRCON.

BEST's District Manager e-mailed his company's in-house General Counsel in New York, who contacted the lawyers for the other three parties to discuss the possibility of cybermediation. Because of AIRCON's objection to that process, the parties finally agreed to use the cyberarbitration process After e-mail back and forth for a few days in the first week of October, they all agreed to use CYBERSOLUTIONS in Australia as the ODR provider, and specifically, FAIRMAN, a broadly experienced and highly skilled construction cyberarbitrator and cybermediator.

8.6.4.4   Confidential information for BEST, the general contractor

You are BEST's in house General Counsel in New York. You have interviewed your BEST's Chicago District Manager by telephone and he has told you the general information appearing immediately above and the following information.

He said that when the OWNER called him, the OWNER was irate. Many doctors had called the OWNER "raising Cain" about the air conditioning problem. The OWNER said he wanted the situation corrected immediately. The doctors were demanding 50 percent discounts on their monthly rent payments and the OWNER told your District Manager that he would have to recoup the value of such discounts from BEST. The OWNER further told your District Manager that he was withholding paying BEST the final $100,000 owed on the project "until the doctors are happy as larks" with the temperatures of their offices. The OWNER said he wanted to stay out of it—he didn't want any more expense, like hiring a lawyer or paying for a mediation or arbitration. He said it was BEST's responsibility to "straighten out this mess."

BEST's Chicago District Manager further told you that, after he talked to the OWNER, he immediately telephoned PERFECTEMP's CEO and advised him of the situation. The Chicago District Manger also reminded PERFECTEMP's CEO that, under his contract with BEST, he was subject to liquidated damages in the amount of $1,000 a day if it was determined that his installation of the cooling system was faulty. PERFECTEMP's CEO got angry. He vigorously asserted that his crews installed the equipment and ductwork according to IMAGINEERING's and AIRCON's specifications. He further said that any problems with the air conditioning were not his fault. He said either IMAGINEERING or AIRCON or both were to blame.

Also, BEST's Chicago District Manager told you that he had no idea whether the equipment, the installation, or the engineering was to blame, but he was convinced that this problem had to be solved quickly so as to minimize any costs to BEST.

Finally BEST tells you that it still owes AIRCON $48,500 for the medical building cooling system and that it has initiated the purchase of ten other cooling systems for buildings it is constructing around the United States. Also, BEST still owes PERFECTEMP $20,000 for the installation work on the medical building complex. The cash flow of the Chicago District Office is currently in dire straits pending receipt of final payment from the OWNER of the Chicago medical building and due to other substantial unpaid receivables.

8.6.4.5   Confidential information for PERFECTEMP, the installer

You are PERFECTEMP'S outside litigation counsel in Milwaukee, Wisconsin. You have interviewed President of PERFECTEMP in person. Since the President's office is in Milwaukee, you see him quite often and know him well. In the interview, he told you the general information appearing above and the following information.

He said that BEST's District Manager told him in a phone call that, under PERFECTEMP's contract with BEST, PERFECTEMP is subject to liquidated damages in the amount of $1000 per day if PERFECTEMP is found to be responsible for the faulty cooling condition of the building. PERFECTEMP's President further told you that he vigorously asserted in the phone conversation that PERFECTEMP was not at fault here, but that either IMAGINEERING or AIRCON were to blame.

PERFECTEMP's President also admitted to you that despite what he told BEST's District Manager on the phone, he in fact did not know whether PERFECTEMP may be responsible or partially responsible here. He said that when the building was completed, he himself tested and balanced the air conditioning system. It was a relatively cool day—about 70 degrees. He said that he noted in his internal report that even under those mild temperatures, the building took an inordinate amount of time to cool down and that the temperatures fluctuated from floor to floor. In examining some of the exposed ductwork, he noticed that several sections had much smaller dimensions than IMAGINEERING's specifications in the engineering drawings. At the time, he believed this to be inconsequential, and so he did nothing about it. He, however, took pictures of the undersized ductwork.

Finally, PERFECTEMP's President told you that BEST still owes PERFECTEMP $20,000 for the installation work on the medical building complex.

8.6.4.6 Confidential information for IMAGINEERING, project engineer

You are IMAGINEERING'S locally retained litigation counsel in Chicago, Illinois. IMAGINEERING is headquartered in San Diego, California. You have done some minor litigation work for IMAGINEERING in Chicago in the past, but you have never worked with the President of the company directly. You have interviewed IMAGINEERING'S President by telephone recently. In the interview, he told you the general information appearing above and the following information.

IMAGINEERING's President told you that he is taking this complaint very seriously because his company is in the process of doing engineering drawings for approximately ten similar medical buildings around the United States. He also has several engineering contracts in process and about to be executed. He did not want any bad publicity over this Chicago medical building because it might adversely affect his relationships with his present clients and the development of relationships with new clients. He was very happy that this dispute was being kept out of court through cyberarbitration conducted by someone in Australia. He preferred to use cybermediation, but he will accede to using cyberarbitration to minimize any adverse publicity.

IMAGINEERING's President further told you that the IMAGINEERING engineer that worked on the project originally had since left the company. He said that when he first got word about the air conditioning problem in the Chicago medical building, he pulled the file on the project and reviewed it.

He said that he noticed something startling. He said that because of a typographical error in an early analysis of the project, an error was made in specifying the appropriate tonnage of the cooling system for the project. This error was carried through to all documents and specifications related to the project. The final specifications called for a 250-ton cooling system, whereas the tonnage specification based on the building size and floor area should have been 280 tons. Luckily, the error was smaller than it could have been, but it certainly does carry with it some professional malpractice implications.

Finally, he told you that luckily, all the other specifications, including the size of the ductwork, were appropriate for the higher tonnage (280-ton) cooling system.

Now we are ready to analyze how this dispute might be processed in a cyberarbitration. Apart from the advocacy suggestions presented below in the next four Sections, you are encouraged to imagine other ways you might handle each situation as counsel for one of the four parties. By agreement of the participants, the manager of CYBERSOLUTIONS has e-mailed the contact information to all participants, including e-mail addresses, regular addresses, telephone numbers, fax numbers, and company Web site addresses.

8.7 Designing the Cyberarbitration Procedures Through the Vehicle of the Preliminary Hearing

As pointed out in section 8.6.4, supra, the preliminary hearing is a most critical stage of the arbitration process, including the cyberarbitration process. While some of the issues covered in a normal preliminary hearing can be addressed in the arbitration agreement itself (either pre-dispute or post-dispute) the relevant procedural issues typically do not fully crystallize until the parties and their counsel have attempted to negotiate an early resolution of the dispute and have failed in their efforts. Before that occurs, parties usually do not want to incur substantial legal expense to plan for an arbitration that may become moot through a negotiated settlement.

Thus, the period of time immediately before a preliminary hearing and during the preliminary hearing itself present excellent opportunities for counsel and their respective clients to design an arbitration process that is as efficient, economical, and just as is possible. The following matrix shows the configuration of claims that exist as the parties in the "walk-through" scenario proceed to a preliminary hearing.

8.7.1   Claims Matrix

COMPLAINANT	RESPONDENT	NATURE OF CLAIMS	REMEDIES SOUGHT
BEST	AIRCON	Breach of Contract Breach of Warranty	Damages; Substitution of Equipment
BEST	IMAGINEERING	Professional Negligence Breach of Contract	Damages
BEST	PERFECTEMP	Breach of Contract	Compensatory Damages; Liquidated Damages
AIRCON	BEST	Breach of Contract	Payment of Amounts Owed $48,500; Consequential Damages
PERFECTEMP	BEST	Breach of Contract	Payment of Amounts Owed; $20,000 Consequential Damages

In the analysis that follows in this Section, you should assume that, by agreement of the parties, you are an approved observer witnessing a preliminary hearing in progress, conducted in a teleconference set up by CYBERSOLUTIONS in late October. CYBERSOLUTIONS has technology that converts the voice discussion to a digital format, from which hard copies can be made. Thus, the teleconference discussion will be preserved as part of the record in the case in both digital and hard copy form. Some of the parties are also listening to the telephonic discussions of counsel and the arbitrator. Other parties opted not to be on the conference call because they could review the full text of the discussions later, either online, or by printing out hard copies of them.

You should also know that for a couple weeks prior to the preliminary hearing, the parties have already communicated by e-mail, chat rooms, and instant messaging in an effort to agree on the procedures to be employed in the cyberarbitration proceedings. There was no pre-dispute arbitration agreement. They have entered into a bare bones post-dispute agreement to arbitrate and have signed a strict confidentiality agreement. In their recent e-mail discussions, counsel have agreed on some procedural issues and not others. Further negotiations regarding procedures will occur during the preliminary hearing itself, with input from the cyberarbitrator. Counsel for BEST volunteered to consolidate from counsel's prior online discussions, a summary of the points of agreement and contested points and respective arguments relating to preliminary hearing topics. He e-mailed a copy of this summary to each of the other counsel for approval. After receiving approval from counsel, he e-mailed a copy of the summary to the arbitrator (with copies to counsel) to be used by the arbitrator and counsel in the telephonic preliminary hearing. The summary was prepared in order to minimize the time that might otherwise have to be spent in the preliminary hearing sorting the agreed points from the contested ones and arguing respective positions.

It is understood by counsel and their clients that if counsel reach impasse as to certain procedures, the arbitrator will have to decide the pertinent procedural issues. As you witness the unfolding of this design process, put yourself in the role of each counsel for the parties and of the arbitrator. Consider how you would handle these procedural issues if you were in the shoes of each counsel, and how you would decide these issues—or foster agreement—on them, if you were the arbitrator. Be creative. You may think of much better solutions to the procedural issues than all the counsel and the arbitrator in the case! Good luck.

8.7.2   Stages of the arbitration process and communication formats and technology

8.7.2.1   All counsel

CYBERSOLUTIONS, the ODR provider jointly selected by counsel, has an extremely limited number of procedural rules, most of which are protocols relating to confidentiality, privacy, and security of information. This is because CYBERSOLUTIONS' business philosophy is that the parties, working with counsel, can tailor-make the procedures to fit the dispute. Thus, during their online discussions prior to the preliminary hearing, counsel considered using aspects of the American Arbitration Association's Supplementary Procedures for Online Arbitration ("AAA Supplementary Procedures")(*see* Appendix P) and the Supplementary Rules of the E-Arbitration-Tribunal ("EAT Supplementary Rules)(*see* Appendix Q) in their efforts to design a mutually acceptable arbitration process. They will continue to refer to them for guidance throughout the preliminary hearing. In those online discussions, counsel also discussed the various technologies and communication formats available to them in constructing the appropriate process. Ironically, the variety of communication tools available through CYBERSOLUTIONS made their task more difficult. The list of communication tools and formats include: regular mail, e-mail, telephone (voice and fax), chat rooms, threaded discussions, instant messaging, web cams, net cams, and videoconferencing. CYBERSOLUTIONS also has hybrid forms of these tools, depending on the parties' needs. It is this availability of numerous communication options that makes the cyberarbitration preliminary hearing more challenging that one held in a traditional face-to-face arbitration. Finally, counsel agreed that a copy of all pleadings and documents (digital or hardcopy, as the arbitrator might direct, would as a matter of course be provided to CYBERSOLUTIONS' administrator she has agreed to assume the responsibility to maintain the official record in the case. The following chart shows, in order of increasing expense, the available communication modes, the best situation(s) for use, and some of their respective advantages and disadvantages. The face to face communication mode, which is normally the optimal, but most expensive mode, does not appear in the chart.

8.7.2.2   Communication Modes

COMMUNICATION MODES			
COMMUN. MODE	**BEST USE**	**ADVANTAGES**	**DISADVANTAGES**
E-mail	For sequential, leisurely written communication where quick reply is not normally needed or expected.	Messages can be broadcast to any number of people simultaneously. *See also* the chart in section 8.3.3.6	Confidentiality can be easily compromised. *See also* the chart in section 8.3.3.6
Threaded Discussions	For sequential, leisurely communication in which all the written dialogue of a number of participants remains on the screen.	By scrolling up, participants can view all dialogue occurring previously on a particular topic. It produces a "record" of the conversation.	A couple participants may dominate dialogue on minor points while other participants are trying to get them involved in discussing topics more important to the group as a whole.
Instant Messaging	Provides a private space for real-time written conversation with another individual.	System can alert the two users that they are simultaneously online so they can engage in conversation.	Normally, the two participants must have the same internet provider.

Chat Rooms	Provide a private space where several persons may engage in real-time written conversation.	Persons can schedule a chat room meeting at mutually convenient times, accommodating time zones and locations of participants.	Conversations can become sarcastic and hostile, depending on the topic being discussed.
Regular Mail or Traceable Carrier	Provides an alternative to digitally sent written materials, where addressees do not have the necessary or adequate equipment to send or receive the material by internet means.	Addressees are more likely to receive accurate duplicates of original hard copy pages. Objects may be sent by mail, which is not possible using the internet.	Mail sent internationally may be delayed in arriving at its destination, or it may get lost. There may be customs problems, also. Cost of mailing may be prohibitive.
Voice Mail	For use when called person is unavailable, but can return the call later; also useful to record a message containing information that needs no response by called person.	Minimizes or eliminates "phone tag" and can facilitate the transfer of extensive information to the called person.	Voice mail messages in which caller does not leave a telephone number or e-mail address where he/she can be reached can be annoying.
FAX	For use when transmitting a reasonably small number of pages of information.	Faxing is a very useful alternative to internet transmission of information where time is of the essence and digital copy of document is unavailable.	Sometimes faxed copies are illegible or incomplete; sometimes it is impossible to tell who the sender is.

Teleconference	For use when it is more efficient for people to talk orally with one another.	It allows full exploration of topics by a limited number of participants in a relatively short period of time when they are prepared by reading pre-conference material. It facilitates and accelerates decision making.	It is often difficult to know who the speaker is during the course of the conversation. The number of participants in a teleconference is limited by practical considerations of complexity of interactions, time, and expense.
Webcam	For use by two persons when seeing images of each other is important while communicating.	Webcam imitates face to face communication between two people.	Special cameras and software need to be purchased by each participant
Netcam	For use when it is important that several known recipients on a network see images of each other while communicating.	Netcam imitates face-to-face communication between several persons in a network.	Special equipment needs to be purchased by the participants in netcam communication.
Videoconference	For use when it is important that several participants at different sites interact electronically with each other visually and auditorially; useful for meetings and for depositions where seeing and hearing the testifying witness is important.	The videoconference most closely imitates face to face communication between any number of participants.	Cost of extensive use of this medium of communication can be prohibitive.

8.7.3   Civility and professionalism

8.7.3.1   All counsel

In their e-mail discussions prior to the preliminary hearing, BEST'S counsel wrote first and suggested that all counsel and parties deal with one another with civility and professionalism. He cautioned against allowing e-mail conversations or chat room or telephone discussions to career out of control into fields of hostility and personal attack. He said that he had been involved in several other CYBERARBITRATIONS in which this occurred and it led to continuing animosity, distrust, and an unnecessarily extended process. He suggested that counsel, up front in the preliminary hearing, jointly tell the cyberarbitrator that they intended to proceed through the process with an attitude of mutual professional respect and consideration. He thought that would get them off to a good start before the arbitrator. The other counsel agreed to communicate similar intentions to ARBITRATOR FAIRMAN at the beginning of the preliminary hearing, which they did.

8.7.4   Applicable rules and law governing the procedure in the arbitration; law applicable to claims

Counsel could not come to an agreement on this topic, except to agree that their respective positions would be argued to the cyberarbitrator in the preliminary hearing and that the rules of any jurisdiction would not apply strictly. Hearsay would be admissible in the cyberarbitration proceedings, subject to counsel's arguments of non-relevance, substantial unreliability, and/or substantial prejudice. Since there was no pre-dispute arbitration agreement, the issues of the applicable procedural and evidentiary rules (for guidance) and the law governing the procedure and the award are wide open.

8.7.4.1   As counsel for BEST

In the teleconference at the preliminary hearing, BEST argues that Illinois' rules and laws relating to arbitration procedure, evidence (for guidance), the parties' claims, and the award should govern the cyberarbitration proceedings. He premises his argument on the facts that the building and the allegedly defective product is located in that state, practically all the significant events are clustered there, and if BEST filed a law suit against these parties, it would naturally file it in the Circuit Court of Cook County, in Illinois.

8.7.4.2   As counsel for AIRCON

AIRCON sees the applicable rules and law issues quite differently. AIRCON argues at the preliminary hearing that this is not a simple inter-state dispute. It is an international dispute and, accordingly, international rules and law should apply. He points out that he could easily file an action for declaratory judgment in the court in Frankfurt Germany where AIRCON is headquartered. He asserts that the rules of an international arbitration firm, such as the Chartered Institute of Arbitrators or the American Arbitration Association, should govern the procedural rules and that the laws of Germany should govern issues related to the claims between BEST and AIRCON and the award. If he were allowed to prevail on these issues, he would agree to having the Federal Rules of Evidence be used for guidance, if necessary, on evidentiary questions.

8.7.4.3   As counsel for IMAGINEERING

A primary concern of IMAGINEERING is the integrity and security of the arbitration process. It wants to avoid any possibility of information leaks that could damage its professional reputation in the business world. Counsel for IMAGINEERING has heard that California, where the company is located, has very strict rules relating to confidentiality of the arbitration process and competence of arbitrators. Thus, IMAGINEERING argues in favor of having California arbitration rules apply. It would concede that Illinois law could apply to issues relating to the claims and the award. It would not object to having the Federal Rules of Evidence be used for guidance if significant evidentiary questions arise.

8.7.4.4   As counsel for PERFECTEMP

In the view of PERFECTEMP, the position of BEST seems to make the most sense. Besides, PERFECTEMP wants more business from BEST in the future, so he doesn't want to aggravate BEST over an issue that is inconsequential. He has compared Illinois and Wisconsin law and those states' respective arbitration rules and has not detected any material differences.

8.7.4.5   Arbitrator FAIRMAN

After reading their prefiled summary and hearing counsel's arguments during the preliminary hearing, FAIRMAN rules as follows:

> The AAA International Arbitration Rules and the AAA Supplementary Procedures for Online Arbitration shall apply, as modified by the agreement of the parties or the rulings of the arbitrator where no clear guidance is contained in those rules. Furthermore, the Federal Rules of Evidence shall be used as guidance, when necessary, on evidentiary questions, and the law of the State of Illinois shall govern all issues related to the related to the parties' claims and to the entry and/or enforcement award. For purposes of the award, the State of Illinois is the site of the arbitration.

8.7.5   Ability to arbitrate all issues

8.7.5.1   All counsel

Counsel agreed in their e-mail discussions that all issues related to the present factual circumstances involving all four parties would be arbitrable. Counsel for PERFECTEMP wanted to arbitrate, in the present arbitration, an outstanding bill that BEST had refused to pay from another building project. BEST agreed in e-mail correspondence to mediate that matter separately after the present arbitration is completed and after the time for objecting to or appealing the award had expired. PERFECTEMP acquiesced in BEST's suggestion for a later mediation of the other dispute.

8.7.6   Discovery

8.7.6.1   All counsel

In their e-mail discussions, counsel had very different ideas about the quantity and the type of discovery that should be undertaken, and the communication mode(s) that should be used. The only item that they could agree to was that the question of experts and expert testimony would be discussed separately from document and fact witness depositions.

8.7.6.2   As counsel for BEST

At the preliminary hearing, BEST takes the position that document requests should be exchanged by November 7 and that documents should be produced or e-mail objections sent to CYBERSOLUTIONS by November 21. BEST thinks that documents could be sent by traceable carrier in hard copy form with two-day delivery directions. BEST wants to depose PERFECTEMP's president (who inspected the ductwork), IMAGINEERING'S president (who reviewed and approved the cooling system specifications), and AIRCON'S chief design engineer (who was very familiar with all aspects of the cooling system in question). BEST thinks that these depositions could be in the form of written interrogatories, with the deponents providing written responses under oath. BEST further thinks that this should be accomplished in a hard copy format by overnight mail sent through a traceable carrier. BEST suggests that the questions be served on the deponents and counsel by November 14 and the responses should be received by BEST by November 28.

8.7.6.3   As counsel for AIRCON

Counsel for AIRCON points out that arbitration "discovery" does not exist in Germany, where AIRCON is headquartered. In Germany, applications can be made to a court before or during a pending arbitration for the court to undertake a judicial inspection, question witnesses, or take expert evidence. AIRCON'S counsel acknowledges that such procedure would not be appropriate here. Instead, he argues that relevant documents should be produced by all counsel immediately in digital form. Documents not in digital form should be scanned and produced in digital form. Confidentially, AIRCON believes it has nothing to hide. The complaints from the Brazilian and Italian purchases have not been fully resolved, but they should be resolved within the next couple of weeks. Besides, AIRCON has letters from purchasers of the cooling system from all over the world praising the functioning of the system. AIRCON strongly believes that its cooling system is not defective and it wants to prove that fact as soon as possible. It has numerous purchase orders for the cooling system pending worldwide (ten have been ordered by BEST alone). AIRCON further argues that no depositions of fact witnesses are necessary. It strongly opposes any request by a party to depose AIRCON's chief design engineer. He speaks German only and securing his testimony (indeed his cooperation) would be very difficult. These people are very proud of their products and a deposition would be viewed as an insult.

8.7.6.4 As counsel for IMAGINEERING

The President of IMAGINEERING wants to get this arbitration over quickly. IMAGINEERING believes that no formal discovery requests need to be made, and it says so at the preliminary hearing. Counsel for the parties, it argues, should cooperate and turn over to each other, the relevant documents. IMAGINEERING privately believes that the documents containing the typographical error, buried in the mound of plans and drawings, might be overlooked by the other counsel, or "lost in the shuffle." At the preliminary hearing, IMAGINEERING takes the position that no depositions should be taken. It does this in part to shield its President from being deposed and having to admit to errors in tonnage specifications.

8.7.6.5 As counsel for PERFECTEMP

It is PERFECTEMP'S position that discovery should be limited to document exchange in hard copy form, through a traceable carrier guaranteeing two-day delivery. PERFECTEMP could live with BEST'S proposed document production schedule. PERFECTEMP believed that no depositions need to be taken. In its view, they are a waste of time and money, since the parties would have to live through the testimony a second time when they went before the cyberarbitrator at the "hearing." PERFECTEMP wants to keep the costs of the cyberarbitration as low as possible. In comparison to the other parties, PERFECTEMP is a very small company with limited cash flow. It could not justify spending much money on this case, considering that it only had a $20,000 claim. Also, PERFECTEMP has a low level of computer literacy and does not have fancy hardware and software supporting video technology. PERFECTEMP's President never learned how to type. However, PERFECTEMP knows that it was behind the curve technologically and that it has to bite the bullet soon and update its communication systems to stay competitive in the construction field. Its President is thinking about hiring someone to design a Web site for the company.

8.7.6.6   Arbitrator FAIRMAN

After reviewing counsel's arguments in the summary and hearing the points they made in the teleconference, arbitrator FAIRMAN states that it is his goal to rule as fairly as possible on these discovery issues, while taking into account the economical, technological, and efficiency concerns of the parties. He says that he has to balance the parties' desire to obtain a speedy resolution of this dispute with realistic predictions of time and work required for them to accomplish the quantity and quality of discovery to enable them to adequately present their cases. He then rules as follows:

1.   Counsel will e-mail (with copies to all) their document requests by November 7.

2.   Counsel will respond to the document requests, by either producing responsive documents or submitting objections to the requests (with reasons) by November 21. Any responses to the objections will be e-mailed to all by December 1. Documents will be produced in hard copy form, through a traceable carrier guaranteeing two-day delivery. Every document produced will have an identifying number stamped on each page.

3.   The arbitrator will rule on all document objections by December 8.

4.   A maximum of four fact witness depositions will be taken in this case. Each of the four parties in this dispute has the option to depose one fact witness. By December 8, counsel shall advise each other of their desire to take a deposition, and the identity of the person to be deposed. If one or more counsel decide not to take a deposition, their deposition opportunity will then pass to the remaining counsel who have opted to take a deposition. Thus, if three counsel opt to take a deposition and one does not, the three counsel shall determine whether any of them want to take an additional deposition. If two or three of them do want to take another deposition, they will determine by lot, who will have the right to choose the fact witness deponent. If two counsel opt to take a deposition, and two counsel do not, each of the two counsel opting to take depositions will have the option to take an additional deposition. If one those two deposing counsel do not want to take an additional deposition, the other deposing counsel has an option to take a third deposition.

5.   All depositions will be taken by videoconference set up by CYBERSO-LUTIONS. Each deposition will be limited to two hours. The counsel who seeks to depose the fact witness will be limited to one hour of questioning. Counsel may reserve part of his one-hour limit to question the witness after the other three counsel have their opportunity to examine the witness. Each of the other three counsel will be entitled to question the witness for twenty minutes.

6.   CYBERSOLUTIONS will arrange to record the videoconferences and provide the arbitrator with a copy of the videorecording as soon as possible after each deposition. Deponents will testify under oath during the videoconferences and their testimony there will serve as their testimony at the hearing on the merits of this matter.

7.   All depositions will be noticed and taken by January 15 of next year. Any counsel who, without good cause, fails to notice and take a deposition or depositions by that date will forfeit the right to take the deposition(s).

8.   If necessary, the arbitrator may schedule a chat room session or a teleconference with counsel and a fact witness or witnesses so that the arbitrator can ask them additional questions.

8.7.7   Prehearing motions, pleading amendments, and briefing schedules

8.7.7.1   All counsel

In their e-mail discussions prior to the preliminary hearing, counsel agreed that there would be no formal prehearing written motions, related briefing, or amendments to pleadings. All prehearing requests would be made in the preliminary hearing teleconference.

8.7.8   Addition or joinder of parties

8.7.8.1   All counsel

In their prehearing discussion, the parties agreed that all the necessary parties were participating in the cyberarbitration.

8.7.9   Witness lists; experts; expert reports; subpoenas

8.7.9.1   All counsel

In their e-mail discussions, counsel agreed that, except for AIRCON'S chief design engineer, all fact witnesses would be willing to cooperate and make themselves available to testify. Thus, subpoenas would be unnecessary. If the chief design engineer was noticed for deposition and he objected, the noticing counsel would, if he deemed necessary, move for a ruling of the arbitrator and the issuance of a subpoena. They also agreed that their combined witness list would be composed of the person(s) who were deposed in prehearing discovery. They disagreed, however, on several matters relating to experts.

8.7.9.2   As counsel for BEST

Counsel for BEST wants to call two experts of his choice—experts that he had used in other construction-related cases. One is an expert in the technical aspects of manufacturing cooling systems; the other is an expert in the installation of cooling systems. Both reside and work in Chicago. He would be willing to produce their reports a week before their depositions. He prefers that the depositions be taken in a chat room session.

8.7.9.3   As counsel for AIRCON

Counsel for AIRCON wants to call one expert of his choice—an English-speaking German professor of engineering reputed to be the foremost expert in the world in the technical aspects of cooling systems. He had used this expert in several cases around the world in the last two years. AIRCON thinks that the deposition of this expert should be taken by videoconference. Counsel for AIRCON would produce the expert's report three days before this deposition.

8.7.9.4   As counsel for PERFECTEMP

Focusing on the additional costs of having experts testify and noting that counsel would have to be present for several depositions of experts, PERFECTEMP takes the position that no expert testimony is necessary in the case. PERFECTEMP believes that this case can be decided on the basis of the documents and any fact witness testimony presented by counsel for the parties.

8.7.9.5   As counsel for IMAGINEERING

Counsel for IMAGINEERING also takes the position that no expert is needed in this case. Confidentially, it is paranoid that an expert going through the documents may notice the typographical errors in the tonnage requirements.

8.7.9.6 Arbitrator FAIRMAN

Making it clear that he is trying to minimize the costs of the arbitration and referring to Article 22 of the AAA International Arbitration Rules, FAIRMAN rules that he will appoint an independent expert to report in writing to the arbitrator. The written report will in turn be distributed to counsel by e-mail attachment. CYBERSOLUTIONS will provide counsel with a list of five experts (together with their curriculum vitae), located geographically near Chicago, each of whom are combined experts in cooling system technology, specifications, and installation. Counsel will have seven days to strike any expert or experts from the list. If no expert on the list survives this process of elimination, CYBERSOLUTIONS will provide counsel with another list, until counsel can agree on one expert. Counsel will provide the expert so selected with pertinent documentation. The expert also will be instructed by CYBERSOLUTIONS to visit the site prior to his deposition. CYBERSOLUTIONS will schedule a videoconference deposition of the expert at a time convenient to all counsel during the period January 15 to January 30 of next year. The deposition will be limited to two hours and counsel will each have thirty minutes to ask the expert questions. CYBERSOLUTIONS will have the videoconference video recorded and provided to the arbitrator as soon as possible after the deposition. If necessary, the arbitrator may schedule a chat room session or teleconference with counsel and the expert so that the arbitrator can ask additional questions of the expert.

8.7.10 Observers and other attendees

8.7.10.1 All counsel

In their e-mail sessions, Counsel for BEST said that the OWNER of the building expressed an interest in being present for some of the chat room, teleconference, or videoconference sessions. Counsel agreed that they would e-mail each other with the names and relationship to the dispute subject of any persons they are requesting to be present at such sessions. They stipulated that approved observers would have to sign a confidentiality agreement and the counsel who is sponsoring the observer to the participants in a session that the approved person is present at the session.

8.7.11 Hearing exhibits and fact stipulations

8.7.11.1 All counsel

In their e-mail session, counsel agreed that the hearing exhibits would consist of all the documents produced in discovery, with their pages appropriately stamped with identifying numbers. They also agreed that they could come up with an agreed statement of the background facts before any formal hearing or arguments before the arbitrator.

8.7.12   Order of presenting evidence

8.7.12.1   All counsel

In their e-mail session, counsel agreed to the following order of the presentation of evidence or of their final arguments to the arbitrator, as the case may be. BEST would make its presentation first, with AIRCON, PERFECTEMP, and IMAGINEERING following in sequence. BEST would have an opportunity to reply to all three presentations in a combined presentation. They agreed that an e-mail closing argument with a subsequent teleconference session with the arbitrator might be the best format. If documents are referenced in the e-mail closing argument, they would be identified by stamped page numbers. This would give counsel to emphasize certain aspects of their closing and allow the arbitrator to ask questions of counsel.

8.7.13   Sequestration of witnesses

8.7.13.1   All counsel

In their e-mail session, counsel agreed that all non-party witnesses would not participate in any chat room sessions, teleconferences, or videoconference, except those in which they were actually testifying. Party witnesses, of course, could be present in the cyberspace sessions at any time.

8.7.14   Burden and standard of proof

8.7.14.1   All counsel

In their e-mail discussions, counsel agreed that the complainant (or the couter-claimant) would have the burden of proof, and the applicable standard of proof would be "preponderance of the evidence." IMAGINEERING had requested the more stringent "clear and convincing" standard of proof for the professional negligence claim, but had no legal support for requesting it. Eventually, IMAGINEERING acquiesced in "preponderance of evidence" standard for all claims.

8.7.15   Position statements or prehearing briefs

8.7.15.1   All counsel

In their e-mail discussions and subject to the arbitrator's approval, counsel would present only closing arguments in writing by e-mail attachments.

Those closing arguments would contain references to documents and pages of documents by stamped page number. The testimony of witnesses would be referenced by identifying the page or pages of the digital recording made from the videoconference. As a practical matter, the arbitrator would review the closing arguments and related evidence prior to their final teleconference when counsel would be available to answer the arbitrator's questions.

8.7.16 Stenographer and interpreter

8.7.16.1 All counsel

In their e-mail discussions, counsel agreed that no stenographer or interpreter was necessary. The only exception concerning an interpreter would be if AIRCON's chief design engineer were to be deposed.

8.7.17 Special needs of the physically impaired

8.7.17.1 All counsel

In their e-mail discussions, counsel for BEST pointed out that his client was deaf in one ear. That, he said, should be taken into account if he were to be deposed orally in the cyberarbitration proceedings. No other counsel had special needs issues.

8.7.18 Scheduling of hearing; length of proceedings

8.7.18.1 All counsel

In their e-mail and chat room discussions, counsel agreed that the final hearing in the matter (the closing arguments) should occur in the last week of February of next year. This would allow time for all the depositions—fact witnesses and the expert—to be viewed by the arbitrator, and also, it would allow counsel enough time to prepare their e-mail closing arguments.

8.7.19 Final oral arguments; post-hearing proposed findings and conclusions

8.7.19.1 All counsel

In their e-mail and chat room discussions, counsel agreed that their final oral arguments would be preceded by e-mail attachments, properly citing the record, sent to the arbitrator and to each other. There would be no post-hearing proposed findings and conclusions. They also agreed that their final oral argument would be by teleconference, and each counsel would be allotted twenty minutes, with the arbitrator being allotted whatever time necessary to ask questions of counsel.

8.7.20   Nature and form of award

8.7.20.1   As counsel for BEST

Counsel for BEST wants an award with a reasoned opinion so that there will be no question as to which party or parties are liable and why.

8.7.20.2   As counsel for AIRCON

Counsel for AIRCON wants an award and a reasoned opinion because he wants an opportunity, if necessary, to ask the arbitrator to reconsider his conclusions.

8.7.20.3   As counsel for IMAGINEERING

Counsel for IMAGINEERING wants no reasoned opinion. The less the better, if the company is found to be negligent.

8.7.20.4   As counsel for PERFECTEMP

PERFECTEMP wants no reasoned opinion because that would mean that PERFECTEMP would have more expenses—the arbitrator's additional fees.

8.7.20.5   Arbitrator FAIRMAN

The arbitrator rules that a brief supporting opinion will accompany the award.

8.7.21   Appeal procedures and enforcement of the award

8.7.21.1   All counsel

In their e-mail and chat room discussions, counsel agreed that the arbitrator's decision would be final, and that their would be no pre-planned appeal process.

Of course, if a party had a claim of manifest injustice during the course of the arbitration, it could challenge the award as the law allowed in the jurisdiction which the arbitrator designated to be the site of the arbitration for purposes of the award. They also agreed in writing to abide by the arbitrator's award and to subject themselves to the laws of the State of Illinois regarding the enforcement of judgments entered on arbitration awards.

8.7.22 Pre-arbitration mediation

8.7.22.1 All counsel

Because one of the parties objected to pre-arbitration mediation, counsel agreed that none would take place.

8.7.23 Additional preliminary hearings

8.7.23.1 All counsel

In their e-mail and chat room discussions, counsel agreed that there would be no additional preliminary hearings, except on motion by counsel.

8.7.24 Prohibition against ex parte communication with arbitrator

8.7.24.1 All counsel

In their e-mail and chat room discussions, counsel agreed not to engage in ex parte communication with the arbitrator.

At the conclusion of the telephonic preliminary hearing, counsel for BEST volunteered to draft a ruling incorporating counsel's agreements and the arbitrator's rulings on the preliminary hearing topics. He agreed to e-mail the draft ruling to counsel for their suggestions and approval prior to e-mailing it to the arbitrator for signing and issuance.

8.8 Cyberarbitration Protocols

Several ODR service providers publish protocols on their Web sites. These protocols establish the ground rules governing the participants' conduct in the particular ODR process selected. Online Resolution (www.onlineresolution.com) has one of the most sophisticated, elegant, and complete set of ground rules among the ODR service providers. Some of its protocols are reproduced here, with permission. The American Arbitration Association's "eCommerce Dispute Management Protocol" is also reproduced below, with permission. These are examples of ground rules that you might expect to see on a professionally operated Web site.

8.8.1 Example of Online Resolution's Protocol

8.8.1.1 Arbitration

Online arbitration is similar to traditional arbitration, except that all communications take place online. The online arbitrator appointed for your case will be an experienced professional, who knows the subject area of your dispute. The

Arbitrator "convenes" the arbitration, manages the process efficiently, maintains confidentiality, and issues a decision based on the evidence presented. The Online Arbitrator coordinates and schedules the presentation of data, makes rulings on admissibility of evidence, keeps the process moving forward, and renders a decision promptly after the conclusion of the hearing. Of course, in the online setting, all communications, including the presentation of evidence, is supplied in electronic form-text, image, audio, or video. Participants in Online Arbitration agree in advance to abide by the Arbitrator's decision, and that the award may be filed in any appropriate court.

Following completion of the Online Arbitration, each participant completes a brief evaluation of the Arbitrator and the process.

8.8.1.2   Protocol

Confidentiality and Security. Online Resolution requires our neutrals to operate within the boundaries of the Model Standards of Practice of the ABA, SPIDR, and AAA.

Under these standards, confidentiality is taken very seriously.

Neutrals will not share information designated as confidential with the other party/parties unless there is an explicit agreement to do so. Unless waived, no negotiation, mediation, arbitration, or evaluation communications may be utilized in any contested action between participants. Participant Settlement Agreement will be presumed not confidential, but may be made confidential by agreement of participants.

Communications are between the neutral and participants. Online Resolution does not review nor retain these communications. Online Resolution does maintain case files indicating the fact that parties entered into a dispute resolution process, who the neutral was, who the parties were and whether the session is reported to have resulted in agreement or not. Online Resolution also retains, analyzes and displays information regarding participant satisfaction With the Online Neutral and with the Online Resolution program as a whole.

Online Resolution's disagreement information forms will be viewed only by the individual participant, the case manager who assigns the neutral, and the neutral. Unless required by law, this information will not be released to any party not explicitly authorized to see it.

Under no circumstances will the Online Resolution Neutral be asked to testify in any contested hearing nor provide materials from the Online Resolution.

Our Web site utilizes secure Web technologies and a firewall to protect all of the date we collect. Our full-time network coordinator is constantly monitoring our system and protecting it from outside threats.

That being said, the Internet is not a perfectly secure environment. We commit to work to the best of our abilities to keep the Online Resolution site secure and to keep information visible only to those authorized to view it, but we cannot give any absolute assurance, nor can any Internet site, that our system will remain secure at all times.

8.8.2 Example of American Arbitration Association's protocols

The American Arbitration Association has a more generic protocol for eCommerce dispute management and resolution as follows:

8.8.2.1 eCommerce Dispute Management Protocol

PRINCIPLES FOR MANAGING BUSINESS-TO-BUSINESS RELATIONSHIPS

Global commerce is entering a rare time in history—a time in which business is conducted at unprecedented speed and traditional business practices are being reevaluated. Today, businesses have an extraordinary opportunity to shape the way they conduct themselves in this new world of eCommerce, and they are doing it with foresight and deliberation.

Recognizing the importance of maintaining valued business relationships, forward-thinking companies are incorporating sound dispute management principles in all aspects of their relationships to avoid traditional costly and time-consuming methods of resolving disputes. In the global marketplace, businesses acknowledge the value of fostering an environment in which controversies are anticipated, minimized and resolve in a fair, timely and final manner. By adopting the principles set forth in the eCommerce Dispute Management Protocol, companies can resolve disputes and get back to business.

Fairness

We believe that all businesses are entitled to a fundamentally fair dispute management process that includes access to Neutral dispute resolution providers.

Continuity of Business

We believe it is important to isolate disputes and resolve them with minimal disruption to other transactions.

Clear Dispute Management Policies

We believe it is important to clearly identify and support the mechanisms for the prevention and resolution of disputes.

Range of Options

We encourage the use of a variety of cost-effective methods to resolve disputes at the earliest possible stage.

Commitment to Technology

We support the use of appropriate technology to aid the swift and economical management of disputes.

8.9   Cyberspace Netiquette

Communication on the Internet involves different dynamics and rules than does communication through other media.[34] Thus, when you are communicating messages or conducting an arbitration online, you will have to take into account the benefits and limitations of this medium in order to capitalize on the experience. One principal difference between online communication and ordinary verbal communication is that in e-mail or threaded discussions you have the opportunity to compose, read, reflect, and modify the content of your message before you send or convey it. Thus, you can catch errors or unintentional misstatements of facts before you actually communicate them. In a chat-room mode, this advantage is not present and you must take care to carefully and tactfully craft your message as your fingers fly.

---

34. *See generally*, Jeffrey G. Kichaven, *Virtual Mediation* 7–8 (Business Law Today, ABA, May/June 1996).

When you are arbitrating online, you may find this set of communication guidelines—or "netiquette"—helpful.[35] In the discussion that follows, it should be understood that no communications are ex parte; that is, no counsel or party is communicating with the arbitrator without simultaneously copying the opposing party and that the arbitrator is sending e-mails to the parties simultaneously.

8.9.1 Communicate only with permission

You must take special precautions to ensure that you know who is "in the loop" for communicating online. You should clarify with other counsel whether they prefer to have all of your e-mail sent solely to them, or whether they want copies sent to their clients also. You should also, of course, specify whether or not you want your client to be a recipient of participants' e-mail. In some situations you may want your client to receive the arbitrator's e-mail, but not the e-mail of other lawyers. There may be other people outside of the circle of actual participants in the cyberarbitration who need to be kept abreast of various happenings during the course of the arbitration. Make sure you know whom you are authorized to contact and whom you are not to contact. Sending an e-mail message to a person not authorized to receive it could doom an arbitration in some situations.

8.9.2 Don't take time for granted

When you are communicating sequentially in cyberspace, you may find that people behave as though there are no time constraints—as if they have "all the time in the world." Because this phenomenon is widespread, accomplishing simple tasks, such as receiving a ruling from the arbitrator or receiving co-parties' views on certain issues by e-mail, may seem to take forever. To minimize this problem, at the outset of the arbitration, you may want to suggest that the arbitrator establish a protocol covering time periods within which counsel are expected to respond by e-mail.

8.9.3 Be conscious of time zones

While you may need to set time limits for replies, be conscious that the arbitrator's or a party's ability to reply may be hampered by the timing of your request. On the Web, you may be communicating with people who live and work in various parts of the United States and even in various countries in the world

---

35. *See generally*, Jeffrey Krivis, *Mediating in Cyberspace* 128–31 (CPR Institute for Dispute Resolution, *Alternatives to the High Cost of Litigation*, Vol. 14, No. 10, November 1996); John R. Helie and James C. Melamed, *Email Management and Etiquette*, (http://www.mediate.com/articles/email.cfm).

who are in different time zones. Some of these people may even be traveling through various time zones during the course of an extended cyberarbitration. Thus, if you send an e-mail to someone in the early morning from New York to San Francisco, don't expect even the earliest response to be before about mid-afternoon. You must factor in not only the time-zone differential, but also the time it will take the party to communicate with others—perhaps even by e-mail—before the party will be able to respond to you. Also, if an attorney, for example, had to be in court early in the morning, he or she may not even have a chance to check e-mail until later in the day, which will additionally delay the response. Thus, be mindful of these delaying factors and take care to avoid setting unrealistic reply deadlines for your cyberarbitration participants.

8.9.4   Respect people's space

Avoid overwhelming the arbitrator, the parties, and their counsel with e-mail messages. It is disconcerting for someone to open his or her mailbox to find a whole list of e-mails from the same person. People have lives; and counsel not only have personal lives, but they also have other clients to represent. Neutrals may have several separate cases they are cyberarbitrating or cybermediating simultaneously. While the cyberarbitration you are engaged in may be the only one you are currently working on, do not convey that impression to the participants, and do not let the arbitration overtake your life. Sometimes people arbitrate online because they like the often leisurely pace and opportunity for considered attorney-client decision making. Be cognizant of that possibility and avoid being obsessive. Also, realize that your unrelenting e-mail involvement may unnecessarily increase the costs for all parties in the case, including your own client. Realize that every e-mail you send not only documents time you've spent on the case, but also the takes up time of the arbitrator and of other counsel who must communicate with their clients and get back to you and the arbitrator. High aggregate fees can mount quickly.

8.9.5   Request and provide confirmations

Breakdown in communication may occur simply because the arbitrator and other counsel never received your e-mail communication. This may occur because of an address error, misdirection, or even an inadvertent failure to "send" the prepared message. Thus, if you are dispatching an important e-mail message, it is a good idea to request the addressees to acknowledge receipt of the message even before they review and consider its content. If you do not receive confirmation from each addressee, then you will be able to investigate right away to determine whether you will need to resend the message or relay it to him or her via another mode of communication. Similarly, if the arbitrator or other counsel request that you acknowledge receipt of an e-mail, you should confirm receipt immediately and respond to the substance of the message later.

8.9.6   Check and answer e-mail regularly

As an advocate in a cyberarbitration, you will need to develop the discipline of checking and answering e-mail periodically during each day. Because e-mail is not as intrusive as telephone contact, you will find that some counsel, or parties, or the arbitrator, as the case may be, may send you e-mail on the weekend. The policy you adopt for handling e-mail communication on the weekends will conform to your individual preferences or lifestyle. Some cyberarbitration participants prefer not to respond to such communications until the next business day; others prefer to respond in order to sustain the momentum of dialogue or to keep their mailboxes cleared out.

8.9.7   Give notice of extended absences

If you are involved in a cyberarbitration, it is important that you let your participants know when you are going to be unavailable for e-mail communication for a day or more. They will appreciate your courtesy, and by mutual agreement you and they might be able to arrange some alternate mode of communication to substitute for e-mail, in case of an emergency for example.

8.9.8   Forward e-mails with an explanation

You have probably received forwarded e-mails from senders who provide no accompanying explanation. This can be disconcerting and annoying. Often, when you receive such an unadorned forwarded message, you are not sure why you have received it and what you are expected to do with it now that you have it. Thus, when you are forwarding messages, you should get into the habit of inserting a short explanatory note prior to any message you forward so that the receiving party will understand why you are sending it and whether he or she needs to respond to you in some way.

8.9.9   Attach only necessary documents

Be respectful of people's time. If you attach a document to an e-mail, make sure that each addressee needs to review it. Before you attach a document, review your list of addressees and segregate those out who do not need to receive it. Then send a separate e-mail to those people without the document attached.

8.9.10   Police hostile or hurtful language

E-mail is a type of communication that can quickly degenerate into an abusive exchange. It can create a faceless "bunker" mentality among opposing counsel that is regrettably conducive to sniping and taking "pot shots" at others in an insulting way. Insults can be exchanged privately—one on one—or in the open for all to see. Such exchanges can quickly escalate into situations that are difficult to bring back into balance. As a professional matter, you must be vigilant to halt even the slightest signs of hostile or hurtful language. Left unattended, such offensive remarks can disrupt the cyberarbitration at the very least, and at worst they can cause the process to disintegrate.

8.9.11   Be polite and diplomatic in your own language

As a cyberadvocate, you can provide a model for the type of written communication that you expect the others to use in an online mediation. You will find, generally speaking, that if you make an effort to use polite, respectful, and diplomatic language, the other participants will do likewise.

8.9.12   Keep communications crisp, pithy, and relevant

Most of us have experienced online communication where a participant goes well outside the relevant topic and writes interminably about matters that fail to move the discussion to a common goal. In an online arbitration, counsel may engage in this type of communication to divert the process from an issue where his position is weak to issues where he can speak from a position of strength. This kind of communication may also indicate a desire on counsel's part to control the agenda. Normally the arbitrator will nip this kind of communication in the bud and encourage the participants to keep communications crisp, pithy, and relevant. But if the arbitrator does not control this behavior, you may want to e-mail the arbitrator (with a copy sent to other counsel) and suggesting that the arbitrator set length limits on the e-mail communications.

8.9.13   Mind your grammar, spelling, and punctuation

Your e-mail communications need not be perfect, but you should pay respect to common rules of grammar, spelling, and punctuation. Consider this sentence from a hypothetical e-mail message between co-counsel in a cyberarbitration:

> i think your principle goal here, mary, is far out. don't go there.
> you'll be disappointed and hack-off the our oponents.

This sentence communicates much about its writer. Failure to use capital letters and to spell properly says that the writer is in a hurry and may be invested only superficially in the communication process. Use of slang and failure to capitalize names can be degrading to receivers of e-mail. A good rule of thumb is to take the type of drafting care with your e-mail communications that you expect others to take when they are sending e-mails to you.

8.9.14 Use emoticons and abbreviations minimally

Emoticons are groups of punctuation and other symbols used to convey emotions. Do not assume that everyone knows what emoticons mean. You may do harm in an e-mail communication if you intend one meaning by your use of an emoticon and your addressee infers another meaning. Here is a list of common emoticons so that you will be able to understand them if you receive them in online communication:

|-)	*happy, humorous*
|-(	*unhappy*
|-0	*shocked*
|-}	*wry, ironic*
<g>	*grin*
<s>	*sigh*
<VBG>	*very big grin*

Abbreviations can save time and space, but if your addressees do not understand what they mean, they can be aggravating to them. It is a wise practice to use abbreviations minimally or not at all, or when you first use them, to put their meanings in parentheses. Here are a few common abbreviations that you may receive or even use in your online communications:

BTW	*by the way*
F2F	*face to face*
FYI	*for your information*
imo	*in my opinion*

imho	*in my humble opinion*
LOL	*laughing out loud*
TIA	*thanks in advance*
BR	*best regards*
BPR	*best personal regards*

8.9.15   Use telephone backup

When arbitrating online, sometimes there is no equal substitute for picking up the telephone and talking directly to someone, such as your opposing counsel. Some people communicate better verbally than in writing. Also, people can often relay communications more effectively and meaningfully by voice. For example, in a speaking context, you can give support, provide detailed explanations, and answer questions more quickly and sensitively. Thus, while written online communication can be very effective in arbitration, telephone backup will also be quite useful from time to time.

8.9.16   Save your e-mail correspondence

It is a wise practice to save (and digitally back up) all your e-mail correspondence relating to a particular arbitration, at least until the arbitration has concluded, and sometimes well beyond the conclusion. You will find it helpful to refer back to certain e-mail communications from time to time—especially near the end of the arbitration when you are drafting your final briefs or preparing your closing argument. You may also find it useful during the course of the arbitration to print out hard copies of critical communications for your reference in your final arguments. The e-mail correspondence may also be helpful to you long after the arbitration if an issue arises as to whether a party is in compliance with the arbitrator's award. Exactly how long you retain your e-mail correspondence after the conclusion of the arbitration will be dictated by your firm's own retention policies or, perhaps, the rules of your particular jurisdiction.

8.10 Gathering Relevant Internet Information

8.10.1   General

In your preparation for a cyberarbitration, apart from selecting documents relevant to your case, you should realize that you have at your fingertips a virtual wealth of Internet information useful to your arbitration presentation.

Remember that, in cyberarbitration, oftentimes you can ask the arbitrator to take judicial notice of certain facts. Through web research in advance of the cyberarbitration, advocates can also gather information highly relevant to the matters at issue in the arbitration, other than the information disclosed to you by opposing counsel. This information could be used as part of your direct case or on cross-examination. Of course, if you intended to use information discovered by use of the Internet, you would have to disclose to opposing counsel the nature of this information and your intent to use it at the cyberarbitration hearing. Such research might yield these types of information, to name only a few:

1. applicable cases decided by relevant courts in the last few days (or hours)(LEXIS, WestLaw, etc.);

2. newspaper articles concerning statements made by various arbitration parties publicly (NEXIS);

3. background information on the parties and their counsel contained in Web professional directories or on corporate Web sites (this might be appropriate research in the medical building scenario);

4. prospecti or annual reports of corporate parties;

5. information showing structures of corporations, identifying subsidiaries, interlocking directorates, or other linkages;

6. articles or book synopses written by various parties, and/or their counsel or other experts, taking positions opposite those being taken in the cyberarbitration;

7. items of information in the judicial notice category: day of week on a particular date, weather conditions on a particular date in a particular city, date and time of day that a particular historical or catastrophic event occurred, etc.;

8. state government information; and (9) federal government information.[36]

To gather this information, you must be able to use not only computer-aided legal research techniques (in which lawyers are by now reasonably skilled) but also general web research techniques. Some tips on using the latter techniques follow.

---

36. For a comprehensive collection of Internet reference tools covering topics of: arbitration institutions and rules, link collections and bookmarks, foreign laws, arbitration journals and newsletters, national arbitration laws, international treaties and model laws, currency converters, public company information, online newspapers, and travel and weather information, *see* Bernhard F. Meyer-Hauser, *Online Aid for Arbitrators and Arbitration Counsel*, 8 Croat.Arbit. Yearb. 9 (2001)

8.10.2   Search engines

A search engine is a program that searches one or more documents for specified key words and returns a list of locations where those keywords were found. Some search engines are capable of doing Boolean searches; others are not. A Boolean search involves using Boolean operators (i.e. AND, OR, and NOT) that are used to refine or broaden a search. (*See* below in this subsection). You may find the following legal search engines useful in preparing for cyberarbitration: (type first http://www.)

> abanet.org
> American Law Sources Online
> Catalaw (meta search engine)
> CyberAttorney
> Findlaw
> GSU Law (meta search engine)
> Hieros Gamos
> InternetLegalResourceGuide
> Law.com
> LawCrawler
> LawGuru

8.10.2.1   Search engines chart

The chart below identifies the leading general search engines and describes relevant attributes.

SEARCH ENGINES	RELEVANT ATTRIBUTES
Alta Vista	Searches in any language using Boolean operators and date limitation
Excite	Uses Boolean operators and offers extensive retrieval options
Fast/All the Web	Allows Boolean queries and content limitors
GO	Good coverage of Web, Newsgroup information, and news and company sites

Google.com Google/Uncle Sam	No Boolean operators; very accurate searching; specialized search engine for searching for government information
Hot Bot	"Super Search" feature offers the user word filters, page, location, and media type limitation; drop down menus give user straight-forward limiting options
Lycos	Full Boolean search available; indexing of fifty million Web pages
Northern Light	Great degree of precision searching; limits include dates, subjects, sources, and document types
Yahoo!	Considered more of a search directory than a traditional search engine

Other search engines and meta search engines include: (type first http://www.

About.com	SavvySearch	Metacrawler
Ask Jeeves	ProFusion	Inference
Search.com	Looksmart	Cyber 411

8.10.3 Other Internet reference tools chart

Other reference tools that you can use to find information to aid problem solving are listed in the following chart, with comments as appropriate: (type first http://www.)

REFERENCE TOOL	COMMENTS
clearinghouse.net	Argus Clearinghouse Reviews and rates top Web sites
ipl.org	Internet Public Library
lli.org	Librarian's Index to the Internet
vlib.stanford.edu/overview.html	The WWW Virtual Library

anywho.com	Phone and address lookup site from AT&T locates people when you have only partial information; includes a reverse telephone number lookup feature
switchboard.com	Phone and address lookup site
whowhere.com	Phone and address lookup site
infospace.com	Email, business, and residential address lookup site
zip2.com	Business address and phone number lookup site
companysleuth.com	Background on businesses, including information on litigation and patent applications
mapquest.com	Detailed street maps for any place in the U.S.
nyp.org/branch/eresources.html	New York Public Library. A library card is required; library barcode number is used as a password; has several excellent electronic databases available to the public, including Proquest, which provides full-text articles from many newspapers and periodicals
iTools.com/research-it	All-in-one reference desk: dictionary, quotes, translators, and more
onelook.com	Four hundred dictionaries; specialized and general
britannica.com	Encyclopedia Brittanica; free of charge
thesaurus.com	Roget's Internet Thesaurus
infoplease.com/	Information Please Almanac; dictionary and full Columbia Encyclopedia

biography.com/find/find.html	Cambridge Biographical Encyclopedia; brief cross-referenced biographies of more that 15,000 notable people
dictionaries.travlang.com/	Provides word translation from English into many other languages
nolo.com/dictionary/wordindex.cfm	Nolo's legal dictionary
odci.gov/cia/publications/pubs.html	C.I.A. World Factbook; brief profiles of countries around the world
usps.gov	U.S. Postal Service's Zip Code finder and express mail tracker
ups.com	Track UPS packages
fedex.com	Tack Fedex packages

8.10.4 Tips for using search engines

When conducting a search, break down the topic into key concepts. For example, to find out what the Federal Aviation Administration (FAA) has said about making handicapped seating available on commercial airliners, the keywords might be:

FAA handicapped seating

> **Boolean AND** If you connect search terms with AND, you tell the search engine to retrieve Web pages containing all the keywords. Consider the following search command:

FAA and handicapped and seating

In this example, the search engine will not return pages with just the word FAA; nor will it return pages with the word FAA and the word handicapped.

Rather the search engine will only return pages where the words FAA, handicapped, and seating all appear somewhere on the page. Thus, the word AND helps to narrow your search results to pages where all keywords appear.

➤ **Boolean OR** If you connect search terms with OR, you tell the search engine to return pages with a single keyword, several keywords, and all keywords. Thus, OR expands your search results. Use OR when you have synonyms for a keyword. It is best to surround OR statements with parentheses. Combine OR statements with AND statements if you wish to narrow your results as much as possible. For example, the following search statement locates information on buying an insolvent company:

(company or corporation or business) and (buy or purchase) and insolvent

➤ **Boolean AND NOT** If you connect search terms with AND NOT, you tell the search engine to retrieve Web pages containing one keyword but not the other. Consider this example:

insurance and not life

This search statement tells the search engine to return web pages about insurance, but not web pages concerning life insurance. Essentially, you should use AND NOT when you have a keyword that has multiple meanings.

➤ **Implied Boolean: Plus and Minus** In some search engines, plus and minus symbols can be used as alternatives to full Boolean AND and AND NOT. The plus sign is the equivalent of AND, and the minus sign is the equivalent of AND NOT. No space is placed between the plus or minus sign and the keyword.

➤ **Phrase searching** Placing a group of words in double quotes tells the search engine to only retrieve documents in which those words appear side by side. Phrase searching is a powerful tool for narrowing searches. Examples are: "arbitration advocacy training"; "evaluative mediator"; "online dispute resolution service."

➤ **Combining phrase searching with implied Boolean or full Boolean.** Consider the following examples:

+"deep vein thrombosis" +cause

"deep vein thrombosis" and cause

These search statements tell the search engine to retrieve pages where the words "deep vein thrombosis" appear side-by-side and the word cause appears somewhere on the page.

> **Plural forms, capital letters, and alternate spellings.** Most search engines interpret singular keywords as singular or plural. If you desire plural forms only, type your keywords that way. If you want both upper and lower case occurrences returned, type your keywords in all lower case letters. On the other hand, if you want to limit your results to initial capital letters (e.g. Abraham Lincoln) or all upper case letters (TOP SECRET), you should type your keywords accordingly. A few search engines allow variations in spelling or word forms by use of the asterisk (*) symbol. For example, capital* returns web pages with capital, capitals, capitalize, and capitalization.

> **Title Search.** A web page is composed of a number of fields, such as title, domain, host, URL, and link. If you combine field searches with phrase searches and Boolean logic, you increase your search effectiveness. Consider these examples:

+title: "Abraham Lincoln" +President +"Mary Todd"

title: "Abraham Lincoln" and President and "Mary Todd"

The above title search tells the search engine to return web pages where the phrase Abraham Lincoln appears in the title and the words President and Mary Todd appear somewhere on the page. Like plus and minus, there is no space between the colon after title and the keyword.

> **Domain search.** The domain search allows you to limit your results to certain domains such as websites from educational institutions, other countries, or the government. The current United States domains include the following:

.com = commercial business

.edu = educational institution

.gov = governmental institution

.org = a non-profit organization

.mil = a military site

.net = a network site

Consider these examples:

domain:edu and "cloning" and animal*

domain:uk and title: "Winston Churchill"

domain:gov and "freedom of information" and bribe*

➢ **Host search.** This type of search allows to search all the pages at a Web site for keywords or phrases of interest. An example is shown below.

+host:www.abanet.org +cyber*

host:www.abanet.org and cyber*

➢ **URL search.** If you do a URL search, you tell the search engine to return the web pages where the keyword appears in the URL or Web site address. A URL search narrows results to web pages devoted to the keyword topic. Consider these examples:

+url:arbitration +title:articles

url:arbitration and title:articles

➢ **Link search.** If you want to know what Web sites are linked to a particular site of interest, use a link search. For example, you would use this type of search if you have a home page and you want to know if anyone has put a link to your page on their Web site. Typically, researchers use link searches for conducting backward citations. Consider these examples:

link:www.nita.org

link:www.arbitrate.com

link:www.onlineresolution.com

Epilogue

We have made our journey through arbitration advocacy with the aid of many anecdotes from the lives of some well-known people, including lawyers, judges, political leaders, humorists, novelists, painters, musicians, and other artists. It seems only fitting that we end with an anecdote from the life of the poet, essayist, novelist, and physician, Oliver Wendell Holmes, Sr., the father of one of history's most revered U. S. Supreme Court justices. A man of letters, the senior Holmes achieved sufficient distinction in medicine to be appointed professor of anatomy and physiology at Harvard, a post he held for thirty-five years. This is known to many, but what may not be as widely recognized as the natural ability he reputedly had as an arbitrator. The story is told that the Massachusetts Historical Society wanted to pay tribute to the discoverer of anesthesia, and so it commissioned the creation of a monument. A bitter dispute arose over whose bust should adorn it, for both William Morton and Charles Jackson claimed the discovery. When asked to informally arbitrate this matter, the senior Holmes quickly announced his decision: the busts of both men would be used, with the inscription "To Ether."[1]

We sincerely hope this book will enhance your effectiveness as an arbitration advocate, and we wish you luck in always having an arbitrator as wise, fair, and creative as the senior Holmes to decide your cases.

---

1. Anecdote adapted from Fadiman, *supra* chapter 2, note 2, at 285.

◆ CONTENTS OF APPENDICES ◆

◆APPENDIX A◆

Arbitration Forum and Panel Selection Checklist

1.   Choosing the appropriate arbitration forum

—Court-annexed arbitration programs

—State or local government arbitration programs

—Bar Association arbitration programs

—Nonprofit ADR organizations

—Private for-profit ADR organizations

2.   Deciding on the number of arbitrators

—Single arbitrator

    —Three arbitrators

    —Other

3.   Choosing individuals to serve as arbitrators

—What is the nature of the dispute?

    —Area of law requiring special arbitrator knowledge or experience

    —Technical or scientific subject requiring special arbitrator knowledge or experience

    —Mostly factual issues

    —Mostly legal issues

    —Mixed factual and legal issues

—Considering the type of dispute and the nature of the parties, what status of arbitrator would be ppropriate?

    —Former judge

    —Attorney

    —Non-attorney

    —Academic

    —Business expert

    —Technical expert

    —Financial expert

—Scientific expert

—Other

—Does the arbitrator you are considering possess the most important basic qualities of a good arbitrator?

—Honesty, integrity, ethical standards

—Impartiality,neutrality,confidentiality

—Patience

—Flexibility

—Open-mindedness

—Ability to control proceedings

—Good listening and communication skills

—Appropriate sense of humor

—Respect for lawyers and clients

—Good judgment

—Does the arbitrator possess the necessary training and experience to decide this dispute?

—Training in arbitration

—Certified as an arbitrator by a court system or dispute resolution organization

—Conducts training in arbitration

—Substantial arbitration experience appropriate to the present dispute

—Candidate has been appointed by the court as an arbitrator or special master in the past

—Sufficient litigation experience, if required

—Candidate will provide lawyer references from prior arbitrations he or she has conducted

—Is listed on the panels of one or more dispute resolution organizations

—Has a reputation for professional excellence among dispute resolution practitioners

—Member or officer in local or national professional associations

—Can the arbitrator satisfy the practical needs of the parties?

—Affordable fees: hourly, daily, by sessions

—Policy on fees if hearing is canceled or postponed

—Willing to conduct preliminary hearings if parties believe it necessary

—Willing to travel to provide arbitration services

—Fees charged for travel time

—Types of expenses

—Provide, schedule, or suggest facilities where the arbitration can be held

—Available to serve as arbitrator for the number of sessions and at the times the parties and their counsel are available

◆APPENDIX B◆

Pleading, Drafting, and Preliminary Hearing Checklist

1. Drafting Arbitration Demands

    —Timing

    —Specific time period specified in the arbitration clause?

    —Statute of limitations apply to any claims?

    —Court rule time limit?

    —Requirements of arbitration clause

    —Does the nature of the dispute fall within the arbitration clause?

    —Does the arbitration clause provide for a specific arbitrator or arbitration association?

    —Claims

    —Names of all parties involved?

    —Chronological statement of the facts?

    —Arbitration clause quoted directly or a copy of the clause attached?

    —Specific statement of the dispute?

    —Detailed synopsis of the relief sought?

    —Signed by claimant or counsel?

    —Filing

    —What do the dispute resolution organization's rules require?

    —Service by certified or registered mail?

    —Filing fee or administrative fee included?

2. Drafting the Response to the Demand

    —Drafting the answer

    —Include a general denial of the claim.

    —Include a protest of the relief sought.

    —Describe the facts of your side of the matter, and support any legal conclusions with proper authority.

    —If desired, include general, unspecific affirmative defenses.

    —If desired, request a specific place for the hearing.

    —Sign the answer.

—Drafting counterclaims

   —File at the same time as the response.

   —Include the same elements required in a demand.

   —Pay the appropriate fee requirements (same as a demand).

   —Serve the counterclaim in the same manner as you would a demand.

—Drafting motions and responses

   —Always present a dispositive motion or a motion seeking fundamental relief in writing.

   —Give the factual background of the request for relief.

   —Specify the relief requested in simple terms.

   —Give the legal basis for the relief requested (rules, statutes, case law).

   —State why your client needs the specific relief.

   —Evaluate your strategy before filing any motion or response to make sure it won't do more harm than good.

   —Send a copy of your motion to your opposing counsel.

3.   Drafting Position Statements

Claimant:

   —A caption containing the names of the claimant(s), respondent(s), and the case number, if applicable

   —The date of the cause of action

   —A brief summary of the facts of the case

   —A statement of the issues presented for arbitration

   —An argument stating your position supported by a few important citations to case law and any applicable statutes

   —Your name, address and telephone number

Respondent:

   —A caption containing the names of the claimant(s), respondent(s), and the case number, if applicable

   —A restatement of the facts if your knowledge of the facts is different from claimant's

   —If responding to claimant's position statement, a direct reply to each of claimant's arguments, supported by case law and applicable statutes. This part of your brief should distinguish claimant's cases and cite cases favorable to your position.

   —Your name, address, and telephone number

4.   Preliminary Hearing

__Cover all pertinent topics with parties and counsel

   __Expectation of civility and professionalism

   __Applicable rules and governing law

   __Arbitrability of all issues

   __Discovery

   __Prehearing motions and briefing schedules

   __Amended pleadings

   __Addition or joinder of parties

   __Witness lists

   __Observers and other attendees

   __Hearing exhibits

   __Fact stipulations

   __Order of evidence

   __Sequestration of witnesses

   __Burden and standard of proof

   __Position statements or prehearing briefs

   __Stenographer

   __Interpreter

   __Special needs for physically impaired attendees

   __Hearing date

   __Place of hearing; arrangement of hearing room

   __Length of hearing

   __Subpoenas

   __Prohibition against ex parte communications

   __Site inspections

   __Audio-visual aids

   __Experts

   __Need for final oral arguments; post-hearing briefs

   __Nature and form of award

   __Any appeal procedures

   __Pre-arbitration mediation

      __Additional preliminary hearings

__Considering procedural alternatives

      __Videotaped or telephone testimony

      __ Bifurcation

      __ Consolidation of claims

      __ Phasing the arbitration

      __ Class action procedure

◆APPENDIX C◆

Client, Witness, and Exhibit Preparation Checklist

1. Client Preparation Checklist

   —Explain the arbitration process.

   —Make your client feel at ease.

   —Explain how to testify.

   —Take client through a direct examination.

   —Subject client to realistic cross-examination.

   —Encourage client to divulge both good and bad information.

   —Avoid being critical about client's role in the events giving rise to dispute.

   —Ensure client(s) (and witnesses) have identical perceptions of exhibits.

   —Warn client to avoid inappropriate body language.

   —Advise client as to proper attire for hearing.

   —Advise client of the date, time, and place of hearing.

2. Witness Preparation Checklist

   —Cover same points with witness as with client. In addition:

   > —Ensure you are aware of any prior relevant testimony or written statements of witness.

   > —Warn non-client witnesses regarding possible inquiry into witness preparation.

3. The Do's and Don'ts of Testifying

   —The do's of testifying

   > —Do tell the truth.

   > —Do listen carefully to each question.

   > —Do ask for clarification if you don't understand a question.

   > —Do take your time when answering questions.

   > —Do allow the questioner to finish the question before answering.

   > —Do testify politely—refrain from being hostile, defensive, or humorous.

—Do speak clearly, distinctly, and confidently when answering questions.

—Do look the questioner squarely in the eye when responding.

—Do be cautious of friendly cross examiners.

—Do keep your answers brief.

—The don'ts of testifying

—Don't answer a question on cross-examination until the arbitrator rules on your counsel's objection to it.

—Don't let the other side "bully" you into giving answers that you don't believe are true.

—Don't give memorized answers or read answers from notes—this will look rehearsed and will not have as much credibility as natural, spontaneous answers.

—Don't be afraid to clarify any statements you make, or correct any mistakes in your testimony.

—Don't volunteer any information on cross-examination—don't elaborate.

—Don't be afraid to answer "I don't know" or "I don't remember" if you don't know the answer to a question.

—Don't try to impress the arbitrator or opposing counsel with a large vocabulary.

—Don't limit your later memory of events. Don't say "That's all that happened" or "No one said anything more."

—Don't be inconsistent. During cross-examination, don't try to improve on the story you told on direct examination.

—Don't testify about what you heard from someone else or about information which you cannot personally verify.

4.   Exhibit Preparation Checklist

—Demonstrative exhibits

—Photographs

—Physical exhibits

—Anticipate opponent's exhibits

◆APPENDIX D◆
Arbitration Hearing Checklist

1. Procedural Rules

   —Rules to apply to proceeding

   —Are statements to be taken under oath?

   —Is evidence by affidavit admissible?

   —Rules regarding decision and award

2. Opening Statement

   —Oral/written

   —Introduction and summary

   —Presentation of facts

        —Be brief.

        —Apply principles of primacy and recency.

        —Tie evidence to legal issues.

        —Put puzzle together.

        —Focus on operative facts.

        —Emphasize undisputed evidence.

        —Discard tangential facts.

        —Deal with bad facts minimally.

   —Brief statement of law

   —Comments on opposition's case

        —Anticipate the respondent's opening.

        —Avoid being personally derisive.

        —Avoid addressing respondent's case in detail.

        —Commenting on claimant's opening.

   —Summary and request for relief

   —Objections and responses during the opening statement

        —Improper argument

        —Personal knowledge of facts

        —Raising issues or matters outside the pleadings

   —Discussing excluded evidence

—Comments demeaning client or witnesses

3.   Direct Examination

—Goals

—Introduce undisputed facts.

—Enhance likelihood of disputed facts.

—Lay foundations for introduction of exhibits.

—Reflect upon the credibility of witnesses.

—Hold attention of the arbitrator.

—Basic rules governing direct examination

—Witnesses must be legally competent.

—Use non-leading questions.

—Avoid questions eliciting narrative testimony.

—Avoid opinion testimony from lay witnesses, with narrow exceptions.

—Recollection may be refreshed by document or a leading question.

—Questioning technique

—Use short, open questions.

—Use directive and transitional questions.

—Reinitiate primacy.

4.   Cross-Examination

—Basic rules governing cross-examination

—Leading questions permitted.

—Limit to scope of direct examination.

—Avoid argumentative questions.

—Avoid intimidating behavior.

—Avoid unfair characterizations.

—Do not assume facts not in evidence.

—Avoid asking compound or other defective questions.

—Purposes of cross-examination

—Repair or minimize damage.

—Enhance your case.

—Detract from their case.

—Establish foundation.

—Discredit direct testimony.

—Discredit witness.

—Reflect on credibility of another.

—Organization of cross-examination

—No need to start strong.

—Use topical organization.

—Give details first.

—Scatter inferential or circumstantial evidence.

—Save a zinger for the end.

—A classic format for cross-examination

—Friendly information

—Affirmative information

—Uncontrovertible information

—Challenging information

—Hostile information

—Zinger

—Questioning Technique

—Use short, leading, propositional questions.

—Use questions that achieve control.

—Use incremental questions.

—Use sequenced questions for impact.

—Use sequenced questions for indirection.

—Use sequenced questions for commitment.

—Create a "conceptual corral."

—Avoid ultimate questions.

—Listen to the witness and insist on an answer.

—Avoid questions that lose control.

—Avoid non-leading questions.

—Avoid "why" questions.

—Avoid "fishing" questions.

—Avoid long questions.

—Avoid "gap" questions.

—Avoid "you testified" questions.

—Avoid characterization questions.

5.   Impeachment

—Tactical considerations

—Impeach witness only on significant matters.

—Impeach only on true inconsistencies.

—Impeach only when success is likely.

—Do not impeach favorable information.

—Consider "rule of completeness."

—Consider refreshing witness's recollection.

—Procedure for impeaching a witness with a prior inconsistent statement

—Recommit witness.

—Validate prior statement.

—Confront witness with prior statement.

—Impeachment with other prior inconsistencies

—By omission or silence

—By prior inconsistent actions

—Character impeachment

—Conviction of crime

—Past untruthfulness and other bad acts

—Impaired perception or recollection

—"Case data" impeachment

—Personal interest

—Motive

—Bias or prejudice

6.   Expert Testimony

—Direct examination of expert witness

—Humanize the expert witness.

—Use plain language.

       —Avoid narrative.

       —Use examples and analogies.

       —Use visual aids.

       —Use internal summaries.

       —Use concept of consensus.

       —Use leading questions as necessary.

       —Encourage powerful language.

       —Use enumeration.

       —Consider inoculation.

       —Don't stretch witness's expertise.

—Cross-examination of expert witness

       —Challenge the witness's credentials.

       —Voir dire on credentials.

       —Cross-examine on credentials.

              —Limit scope of witness's expertise.

               —Stress missing credentials.

               —Contrast your expert's credentials.

—Obtain favorable information.

       —Affirm your own expert.

       —Elicit areas of agreement.

       —Criticize opposing party's conduct.

       —Use learned treatises.

       —Challenge witness's impartiality.

               —Fees

               —Relationship with party or counsel

               —Positional bias

—Point out omissions.

—Substitute information.

       —Change assumptions.

       —Vary the facts.

       —Challenge expert's degree of certainty.

       —Challenge factual underpinnings of opinion.

—Challenge technique or theory.

7.   Foundations for Evidence

—General requirements

—Relevance

—Authenticity

—Specific requirements depending on nature of evidence

—Foundations for testimonial evidence

—Conversations

—Date, time, and place of conversation

—Persons present

—Telephone conversations and voice identification

—Same as for conversations, plus

—Voice identification

—Prior identification

—Witness made prior identification

—After perceiving the person identified

—Habit and routine

—Witness with personal knowledge of the regular conduct of the person or organization involved

—Asserted conduct was, in fact, of a consistently repeated nature

—Foundations for oral hearsay statement exceptions

—Foundation for oral party admissions (and also for written party admissions)

—Witness can authenticate the statement.

—Statement was made by the party against whom it is offered.

—Statement is adverse to the opposing party's claim or defense.

—Foundation for oral (or written) admissions of an agent or employee of party.

—Same as for party above, plus

—Declarant was an agent or employee of the opposing party at the time that the statement was made.

—Statement concerned a matter that was within the scope of the agency or employment.

—Foundation for present sense impression

—Declarant perceived an event.

—Declarant described the event.

—Description was given while the event occurred or immediately afterwards.

—Foundation for excited utterance

—Declarant perceived a startling event or experienced a stressful condition.

—Declarant made a statement concerning the event or condition.

—Statement was made while the declarant was under the stress of the event or condition.

—Foundation for state of mind

—Statement actually probative of declarant's mental, emotional, or physical condition.

—Statement made during the existence of such condition.

—Date and time statement was made.

—Where it was made.

—Who was present.

—What was said.

—Foundation for medical treatment

—Declarant made a statement for purpose of obtaining medical care or diagnosis.

—Declarant made statement to physician or medical person.

Statement may include medical history or past symptoms, but it must relate to a then present bodily condition.

—Foundation for dying declaration

—Declarant made a statement while believing that his or her death was imminent.

—Statement concerned what he or she believed to be the cause of death.

—Foundations for documents

—General foundation requirements

   —Authentication

     —Handwriting and signature

     —Circumstantial evidence of authorship and origin

     —Mailing or transmission

    —Original writing (or "best evidence") rule

—Foundations for documentary hearsay exceptions

 —Foundation for business records and computer print-outs:

   —Documents are records kept in the course of a regularly conducted business activity:

     —made at or near the time of a transaction or event.

     —made by, or based on information transmitted from, a person with knowledge.

     —made as a part of the regular practice of that business activity.

 —Foundation for summaries

   —Original documents are so voluminous that they cannot be conveniently examined in the arbitration hearing.

   —Witness has examined the original data.

   —Witness is qualified to produce a summary of the information.

   —Exhibit is a fair and accurate summary of the underlying information.

 —Foundation for recorded recollection:

   —Witness once had personal knowledge of the relevant acts or events.

   —Witness cannot currently recall the events fully and accurately.

   —Witness previously made an accurate memorandum or record of the facts at a time when the events were fresh in his or her memory.

 —Foundation for public records

Note: most government records are self-authenticating, not requiring a government witness to testify.

   —Document must be made by a public office or agency.

—Set forth the activities of the office or agency, or

—Set forth matters observed pursuant to a duty imposed by law, or

—Set forth, in limited circumstances, certain investigative findings, or

—Set forth officially required records of vital statistics

—Foundation for absence of public record:

Note: this evidence may be offered by certification from the appropriate official, in which case no witness needs to be called. The evidence may also be offered via testimony.

—Certain events, occurrences or matters were regularly recorded in some form by a public office or agency.

—A diligent search has failed to disclose a record of a particular fact or event.

—Foundation for previous testimony

—Declarant is currently "unavailable" to testify.

—Testimony was given under oath in court or at a deposition.

—Party against whom the testimony is being offered had a fair opportunity to examine the witness when the testimony was originally given.

—Foundation for written admissions of a party

—Same as for oral admissions, above.

—Proof that writing was made or adopted by the party against whom it is being offered, or by an agent, servant, or employee of such party.

—Foundations for real and demonstrative evidence

—Foundation for real evidence/tangible objects

—Recognition of exhibit

—Witness was familiar with the object at the time of the underlying events.

—Witness is able to recognize the exhibit as that very same object.

—Chain of custody

—Location, handling, and care of an object between the time of its recovery and the time of trial.

—Needed where

—Object is not uniquely recognizable and has not been marked, or

—Object's physical properties are in issue.

—Foundations for photography and other recording devices

—Foundation for still photographs

—Photograph "fairly and accurately" portrays the scene shown.

—Witness may be photographer or any person who is familiar with the scene as it appeared at a relevant time.

—Foundation for motion pictures and videotapes

—Similar to requirements for photographs.

—Operator of the camera needs to be called only if special features were employed, or if the date of the filming is in issue.

—Foundation for audiotapes

—Depends upon the purpose for which it is offered.

—Voice exemplar: witness who is able to recognize the voices of the various speakers.

—Recorded music: witness who is familiar with the material recorded.

—Foundation for X-rays and similar images

—Qualified witness testifies that X-ray, CAT scan, or MRI image is a fair representation of internal structure of the patient's body.

—Witness testifies to identifying marks on film to demonstrate it is a business record of the hospital or clinic.

—Foundations for demonstrative evidence

—Foundation for map, charts, or other diagrams

—Similar to photograph.

—Witness must be familiar with the scene, location, or structure as it appeared at a relevant time, and

—Witness must testify that exhibit constitutes a fair representation.

—Foundation for models and reproductions

—Similar to photograph.

—Witness must be familiar with the real location or object, and must testify to the model's accuracy.

—Foundation for illustrative aids

—Exhibit is accurate.

—Exhibit will assist witness in explaining his or her testimony.

8.   Common Objections

—Form of question objections

—Leading question

—Compound question

—Vague question

—Argumentative question

—Narrative question

—Asked and answered

—Assuming facts not in evidence

—Non-responsive answer to question

—Substantive objections

—Hearsay objection

—Irrelevant

—Unfair prejudice

—Improper character evidence

—Lack of personal knowledge

—Improper lay opinion

—Speculation or conjecture

—Authenticity

—Lack of foundation

—Best evidence

—Privilege

—Subsequent remedial measures

—Settlement offers

9.   Final Argument

—Structure

    —Topical organization

    —Chronological organization

    —Other organizing tools

        —Start and end strong.

        —Claimant should advance affirmative case first.

        —Cluster circumstantial evidence and accumulate details.

        —Bury your concessions.

        —Weave in witness credibility.

        —Carefully consider how to approach damages.

—Content

    —Tell a persuasive story

    —What happened?

    —Why did it happen?

    —How can we be sure?

        —Is it plausible?

    —Tie up cross-examinations.

    —Comment on promises.

    —Resolve problems and weaknesses.

    —Discuss damages.

    —Thank arbitrator(s).

◆ APPENDIX E ◆
Post-Hearing Advocacy Checklist

1.   Drafting Post-hearing Briefs

—Think like an arbitrator.

—Format and language

   —Reader friendly

   —Well organized

   —Divided by headings and subheadings

   —Avoid using unnecessary words and legalese

   —Avoid bluster and self-important style

   —Avoid harping on technicalities

   —Use simple and direct writing style

2.   Challenging Awards in Court

—Rarely successful

—Bases for challenge

   —Contract

      —No written agreement to arbitrate.

      —Party breached part of agreement to arbitrate.

      —Arbitration agreement is invalid.

      —Arbitration was demanded after contract or statutory limitation.

   —Hearing

      —Arbitrator conducted hearing contrary to the arbitration statute or rules.

      —Party committed fraud in the arbitration.

      —Arbitrator refused to consider material facts.

      —Parties agreed to reopen the hearing because of the discovery of new evidence, but the arbitrator refused.

   —Arbitrator

      —Arbitrator displayed bias and partiality.

—Arbitrator failed to disclose a serious conflict of interest.

—Arbitrator was corrupt.

—Arbitrator refused to postpone hearing when good cause was shown.

—Arbitrator exceeded authority.

—Award

—Arbitrator decided non-arbitrable matters.

—Arbitrators failed to make a mutual, final, and definite award.

—Award was procured by corruption, fraud, or undue means.

—Award was not timely rendered, despite party's protest.

—Evident material miscalculation of figures in the award.

—Evident material mistake in the description of a person, thing, or property referred to in the award.

—Award is contrary to public policy.

◆APPENDIX F◆

Sample Arbitration Clauses for a Commercial Contract

Reproduced with permission of the American
Arbitration Association and JAMS

STANDARD ARBITRATION AGREEMENTS

It is not enough to state that disputes arising under the agreement shall be settled by arbitration. While this language indicates the parties' intent to arbitrate and may authorize a court to enforce the clause, it leaves many issues unresolved. Issues such as to when, where, how, and before whom a dispute will be arbitrated are subject to disagreement, with no way to resolve them except to go to court.

The standard arbitration clause suggested by the American Arbitration Association addresses those questions. It has proven highly effective in over a million disputes. The parties can provide for the arbitration of future disputes by inserting the following in their contract:

- *Any controversy or claim arising out of or relating to this contract, or the breach thereof, shall be settled by arbitration administered by the American Arbitration Association in accordance with its [applicable] rules and judgment upon the award rendered by the arbitrator may be entered in any court having jurisdiction thereof.*

The arbitration of existing disputes may be accomplished by use of the following:

- *We, the undersigned parties, hereby agree to submit to arbitration administered by the American Arbitration Association under its [applicable] rules the following controversy [cite briefly]. We further agree that we will faithfully observe this agreement and the rules, and that we will abide by and perform any award rendered by the arbitrator(s), and that a judgment of the court having jurisdiction may be entered upon the award.*

The above clauses, which refer to the time-tested rules of the AAA, have consistently received judicial support. The standard clause is often the best to include in a contract. By invoking the AAA's rules, these clauses meet the requirements of an effective arbitration clause.

1. It makes clear that all disputes are arbitrable. Thus, it minimizes dilatory court actions to avoid the arbitration process.

2. It is self-enforcing. Arbitration can continue despite an objection from a party, unless the proceedings are stayed by court order or by agreement of the parties.

3. It provides for a complete set of rules and regulations. This feature eliminates the need to spell out rules and regulations in the parties' agreement.

4. It provides for the appointment of an impartial neutral. Arbitrators are selected by the parties from a large pool of available experts. Under the AAA rules, a procedure is available to disqualify an arbitrator for bias.

5. It settles disputes over the locale of the proceeding. When the parties disagree, locale determinations are made by the AAA as administrator, alleviating the need for direction from the courts.

6. It can provide for administrative conferences. If the clause provides for the AAA's Commercial Arbitration Rules, Construction Industry Arbitration Rules, or related rules for resolving business disputes, there is a provision for an administrative conference with the parties' representatives and an AAA staff member to expedite the arbitration proceedings.

7. It can provide for preliminary hearings. If the clause provides for the AAA's various commercial arbitration rules, a preliminary hearing can be arranged in large and complex cases to specify the issues to be resolved, clarify claims and counter-claims, provide for an exchange of information, and consider other matters that will expedite the arbitration proceedings.

8. Mediation is available. If the clause provides for the AAA's various commercial arbitration rules, mediation conferences can be arranged to facilitate a mutual settlement, without additional administrative cost to the parties.

9. It establishes time limits to assure prompt disposition of disputes. An additional feature of the AAA's various commercial arbitration rules are the Expedited Procedures which are used to resolve smaller claims.

10. It insulates the arbitrator from the parties. Under the vast majority of rules which provide for the resolution of business disputes, the AAA channels communications between the parties and the arbitrator, which serves to protect the continued neutrality of the arbitrator and the process.

11. It establishes a procedure for the serving of notices. Depending on the rules used and the type of the case, notices can be served by regular mail, addressed to the party or its representative at the last known address. Under most of the rules, the AAA and the parties may use facsimile transmission, telex, telegram, or other written forms of electronic communication to give the notices required by the rules.

12. It gives the arbitrator the power to decide matters equitably and to fashion any appropriate relief, including specific performance. The AAA rules allow the arbitrator to grant any remedy or relief that the arbitrator deems just and equitable and within the scope of the agreement of the parties, including, but not limited to, specific performance of a contract.

14. It provides for enforcement of the award. The award can be enforced in any court having jurisdiction, with only limited grounds for resisting the award.

JAMS

B-2. Mediation Followed By Arbitration

This clause should be used if you want to first attempt to resolve your disputes through non-binding mediation, with an agreement to proceed to final and binding arbitration if necessary. This clause should be used with either Clause C-1 or Clause C-2, depending on whether you want Streamlined or Comprehensive Arbitration procedures. If you want to require that the parties first attempt to resolve the dispute by negotiation, then this clause should be used in conjunction with Clause A-2.

The parties agree that any and all disputes, claims or controversies arising out of or relating to this Agreement shall be submitted to JAMS, or its successor, for mediation, and if the matter is not resolved through mediation, then it shall be submitted to JAMS, or its successor, for final and binding arbitration. Either party may commence mediation by providing to JAMS and the other party a written request for mediation, setting forth the subject of the dispute and the relief requested. The parties will cooperate with JAMS and with one another in selecting a mediator from JAMS' panel of neutrals, and in scheduling the mediation proceedings. The parties covenant that they will participate in the mediation in good faith, and that they will share equally in its costs. All offers, promises, conduct and statements, whether oral or written, made in the course of the mediation by any of the parties, their agents, employees, experts and attorneys, and by the mediator or any JAMS employees, are confidential, privileged and inadmissible for any purpose, including impeachment, in any arbitration or other proceeding involving the parties, provided that evidence that is otherwise admissible or discoverable shall not be rendered inadmissible or non-discoverable as a result of its use in the mediation. Either party may initiate arbitration with respect to the matters submitted to mediation by filing a written demand for arbitration at any time following the initial mediation session or 45 days after the date of filing the written request for mediation, whichever occurs first. The mediation may continue after the commencement of arbitration if the parties so desire. Unless otherwise agreed by the parties, the mediator shall be disqualified from serving as arbitrator in the case. The provisions of this Clause may be enforced by any Court of competent jurisdiction, and the party seeking enforcement shall be entitled to an award of all costs, fees and expenses, including attorneys fees, to be paid by the party against whom enforcement is ordered.

Clause B-2 can be adapted to an existing dispute by replacing the first sentence with the following:

The parties hereto presently are parties to a dispute (describe briefly) that they wish to submit to mediation and, if necessary, to arbitration, at JAMS.

C. ARBITRATION

C-1. Streamlined Arbitration

If you want to attempt to resolve your dispute through mediation prior to arbitration, then this clause should be used with Clause B-2. If you want to require that the parties first attempt to resolve the dispute by negotiation, you should also use Clause A-2. If you want to attempt negotiation of your dispute prior to arbitration, but do not wish to use mediation as an intermediate step, please refer to the instructions preceding Clause A-2.

Any dispute, claim or controversy arising out of or relating to this Agreement or breach, termination, enforcement, interpretation or validity thereof, including the determination of the scope or applicability of this Agreement to arbitrate, shall be determined by arbitration in (location of arbitration), before a sole arbitrator, in accordance with the laws of the State of _____ for agreements made in and to be performed in that State. The arbitration shall be administered by JAMS pursuant to its Streamlined Arbitration Rules and Procedures. Judgment on the Award may be entered in any court having jurisdiction. Allocation of Fees and Costs. The arbitrator shall, in the Award, allocate all of the costs of the arbitration (and the mediation, if applicable), including the fees of the arbitrator and the reasonable attorneys' fees of the prevailing party, against the party who did not prevail.

C-2. Comprehensive Arbitration

This clause should be selected if you want to use arbitration governed by JAMS' Comprehensive Arbitration Rules to resolve your dispute. If you want to attempt to resolve your dispute through mediation prior to arbitration, then this clause should be used with Clause B-2. If you want to require that the parties first attempt to resolve the dispute by negotiation, you should also use Clause A-2. If you want to provide for negotiation of your dispute prior to arbitration, but do not wish to use mediation as an intermediate step, please refer to the instructions preceding Clause A-2.

Any dispute, claim or controversy arising out of or relating to this Agreement or the breach, termination, enforcement, interpretation or validity thereof, including the determination of the scope or applicability of this Agreement to arbitrate, shall be determined by arbitration in (location of arbitration), before a sole arbitrator, in accordance with the laws of the State of _____ for agreements made in and to be performed in that State. The arbitration shall be administered by JAMS pursuant to its Comprehensive Arbitration Rules and Procedures. Judgment on the Award may be entered in any court having jurisdiction.

Allocation of Fees and Costs. The arbitrator shall, in the Award, allocate all of the costs of the arbitration (and the mediation, if applicable), including the fees of the arbitrator and the reasonable attorneys' fees of the prevailing party, against the party who did not prevail.

C-3. Submission to Arbitration

The parties hereto presently are parties to a dispute (describe briefly) that they wish to submit to mediation and thereafter to arbitration at JAMS. Such dispute shall be determined by arbitration in (location of arbitration), before a sole arbitrator, in accordance with the laws of the State of _____ for agreements made in and to be performed in that State. The arbitrator shall have the power to determine the scope or applicability of this Agreement to arbitrate. The arbitration shall be administered by JAMS pursuant to its Comprehensive Rules. Judgment on the Award may be entered in any court having jurisdiction.

Allocation of Fees and Costs. The arbitrator shall, in the Award, allocate all of the costs of the arbitration (and the mediation, if applicable), including the fees of the arbitrator and the reasonable attorneys' fees of the prevailing party, against the party who did not prevail.

C-4. Waiver of Right to Litigate in Court

Whenever you agree to final and binding arbitration, you likewise agree to forego your right to resolve your disputes through litigation in court. Some states require that for enforcement of arbitration agreements in certain, specified types of contracts in which the parties may be viewed as possessing unequal bargaining power (e.g. consumer contracts, etc.), there must be evidence of a knowing and intelligent waiver of the right to litigate in court. You should familiarize yourself with, and follow precisely any requirements of, relevant state law when incorporating a mandatory arbitration clause in this type of contract, including provisions regarding the placement and prominence of the notice of waiver. Subject to the specific requirements of state law, the legal requirements for enforcement of a mandatory arbitration clause in this type of contract may usually be satisfied by use of a disclosure clause similar to the following one.

NOTICE: By initialing in the space below you are agreeing to have all disputes, claims or controversies arising out of or relating to this Agreement decided by neutral binding arbitration, and you are giving up any rights you might possess to have those matters litigated in a court or jury trial. By initialing in the space below you are giving up your judicial rights to discovery and appeal except to the extent that they are specifically provided for under this Agreement. If you refuse to submit to arbitration after agreeing to this provision you may be compelled to arbitrate under federal or state law. Your agreement to this arbitration provision is voluntary.

◆ APPENDIX G ◆

AAA Commercial Arbitration Rules
Effective July 1, 2003

Reproduced with permission from the American Arbitration Association

1.   R-1. Agreement of Parties*+

(a) The parties shall be deemed to have made these rules a part of their arbitration agreement whenever they have provided for arbitration by the American Arbitration Association (hereinafter AAA) under its Commercial Arbitration Rules or for arbitration by the AAA of a domestic commercial dispute without specifying particular rules. These rules and any amendment of them shall apply in the form in effect at the time the administrative requirements are met for a demand for arbitration or submission agreement received by the AAA. The parties, by written agreement, may vary the procedures set forth in these rules. After appointment of the arbitrator, such modifications may be made only with the consent of the arbitrator.

(b) Unless the parties or the AAA determines otherwise, the Expedited Procedures shall apply in any case in which no disclosed claim or counterclaim exceeds $75,000, exclusive of interest and arbitration fees and costs. Parties may also agree to use these procedures in larger cases. Unless the parties agree otherwise, these procedures will not apply in cases involving more than two parties. The Expedited Procedures shall be applied as described in Sections E-1 through E-10 of these rules, in addition to any other portion of these rules that is not in conflict with the Expedited Procedures.

(c) Unless the parties agree otherwise, the Procedures for Large, Complex Commercial Disputes shall apply to all cases in which the disclosed claim or counterclaim of any party is at least $500,000, exclusive of claimed interest, arbitration fees and costs. Parties may also agree to use the Procedures in cases involving claims or counterclaims under $500,000, or in nonmonetary cases. The Procedures for Large, Complex Commercial Disputes shall be applied as described in Sections L-1 through L-4 of these rules, in addition to any other portion of these rules that is not in conflict with the Procedures for Large, Complex Commercial Disputes.

(d) All other cases shall be administered in accordance with Sections R-1 through R-54 of these rules.

* The AAA applies the *Supplementary Procedures for Consumer-Related Disputes* to arbitration clauses in agreements between individual consumers and businesses where the business has a standardized, systematic application of arbitration clauses with customers and where the terms and conditions of the purchase of standardized, consumable goods or services are nonnegotiable or

primarily non-negotiable in most or all of its terms, conditions, features, or choices. The product or service must be for personal or household use. The AAA will have the discretion to apply or not to apply the Supplementary Procedures and the parties will be able to bring any disputes concerning the application or non-application to the attention of the arbitrator. Consumers are not prohibited from seeking relief in a small claims court for disputes or claims within the scope of its jurisdiction, even in consumer arbitration cases filed by the business.

+A dispute arising out of an employer promulgated plan will be administered under the AAA's National Rules for the Resolution of Employment Disputes.

R-2. AAA and Delegation of Duties

When parties agree to arbitrate under these rules, or when they provide for arbitration by the AAA and an arbitration is initiated under these rules, they thereby authorize the AAA to administer the arbitration. The authority and duties of the AAA are prescribed in the agreement of the parties and in these rules, and may be carried out through such of the AAA's representatives as it may direct. The AAA may, in its discretion, assign the administration of an arbitration to any of its offices.

R-3. National Roster of Arbitrators

The AAA shall establish and maintain a National Roster of Commercial Arbitrators ("National Roster") and shall appoint arbitrators as provided in these rules. The term "arbitrator" in these rules refers to the arbitration panel, constituted for a particular case, whether composed of one or more arbitrators, or to an individual arbitrator, as the context requires.

R-4. Initiation under an Arbitration Provision in a Contract

(a) Arbitration under an arbitration provision in a contract shall be initiated in the following manner:

(i) The initiating party (the "claimant") shall, within the time period, if any, specified in the contract(s), give to the other party (the "respondent") written notice of its intention to arbitrate (the "demand"), which demand shall contain a statement setting forth the nature of the dispute, the names and addresses of all other parties, the amount involved, if any, the remedy sought, and the hearing locale requested.

(ii) The claimant shall file at any office of the AAA two copies of the demand and two copies of the arbitration provisions of the contract, together with the appropriate filing fee as provided in the schedule included with these rules.

(iii) The AAA shall confirm notice of such filing to the parties.

(b) A respondent may file an answering statement in duplicate with the AAA within 15 days after confirmation of notice of filing of the demand is sent by the AAA. The respondent shall, at the time of any such filing, send a copy of the answering statement to the claimant. If a counterclaim is asserted, it shall contain a statement setting forth the nature of the counterclaim, the amount involved, if any, and the remedy sought. If a counterclaim is made, the party making the counterclaim shall forward to the AAA with the answering statement the appropriate fee provided in the schedule included with these rules.

(c) If no answering statement is filed within the stated time, respondent will be deemed to deny the claim. Failure to file an answering statement shall not operate to delay the arbitration.

(d) When filing any statement pursuant to this section, the parties are encouraged to provide descriptions of their claims in sufficient detail to make the circumstances of the dispute clear to the arbitrator.

R-5. Initiation under a Submission

Parties to any existing dispute may commence an arbitration under these rules by filing at any office of the AAA two copies of a written submission to arbitrate under these rules, signed by the parties. It shall contain a statement of the nature of the dispute, the names and addresses of all parties, any claims and counterclaims, the amount involved, if any, the remedy sought, and the hearing locale requested, together with the appropriate filing fee as provided in the schedule included with these rules. Unless the parties state otherwise in the submission, all claims and counterclaims will be deemed to be denied by the other party.

R-6. Changes of Claim

After filing of a claim, if either party desires to make any new or different claim or counterclaim, it shall be made in writing and filed with the AAA. The party asserting such a claim or counterclaim shall provide a copy to the other party, who shall have 15 days from the date of such transmission within which to file an answering statement with the AAA. After the arbitrator is appointed, however, no new or different claim may be submitted except with the arbitrator's consent.

R-7. Jurisdiction

(a) The arbitrator shall have the power to rule on his or her own jurisdiction, including any objections with respect to the existence, scope or validity of the arbitration agreement.

(b) The arbitrator shall have the power to determine the existence or validity of a contract of which an arbitration clause forms a part. Such an arbitration clause shall be treated as an agreement independent of the other terms of the contract. A decision by the arbitrator that the contract is null and void shall not for that reason alone render invalid the arbitration clause.

(c) A party must object to the jurisdiction of the arbitrator or to the arbitrability of a claim or counterclaim no later than the filing of the answering statement to the claim or counterclaim that gives rise to the objection. The arbitrator may rule on such objections as a preliminary matter or as part of the final award.

R-8. Mediation

At any stage of the proceedings, the parties may agree to conduct a mediation conference under the Commercial Mediation Procedures in order to facilitate settlement. The mediator shall not be an arbitrator appointed to the case. Where the parties to a pending arbitration agree to mediate under the AAA's rules, no additional administrative fee is required to initiate the mediation.

R-9. Administrative Conference

At the request of any party or upon the AAA's own initiative, the AAA may conduct an administrative conference, in person or by telephone, with the parties and/or their representatives. The conference may address such issues as arbitrator selection, potential mediation of the dispute, potential exchange of information, a timetable for hearings and any other administrative matters.

R-10. Fixing of Locale

The parties may mutually agree on the locale where the arbitration is to be held. If any party requests that the hearing be held in a specific locale and the other party files no objection thereto within 15 days after notice of the request has been sent to it by the AAA, the locale shall be the one requested. If a party objects to the locale requested by the other party, the AAA shall have the power to determine the locale, and its decision shall be final and binding.

R-11. Appointment from National Roster

If the parties have not appointed an arbitrator and have not provided any other method of appointment, the arbitrator shall be appointed in the following manner:

(a) Immediately after the filing of the submission or the answering statement or the expiration of the time within which the answering statement is to be filed, the AAA shall send simultaneously to each party to the dispute an identical list of 10 (unless the AAA decides that a different number is appropriate) names of persons chosen from the National Roster. The parties are encouraged to agree to an arbitrator from the submitted list and to advise the AAA of their agreement.

(b) If the parties are unable to agree upon an arbitrator, each party to the dispute shall have 15 days from the transmittal date in which to strike names objected to, number the remaining names in order of preference, and return the list to the AAA. If a party does not return the list within the time specified, all persons named therein shall be deemed acceptable. From among the persons who have been approved on both lists, and in accordance with the designated order of mutual preference, the AAA shall invite the acceptance of an arbitrator to serve. If the parties fail to agree on any of the persons named, or if acceptable arbitrators are unable to act, or if for any other reason the appointment cannot be made from the submitted lists, the AAA shall have the power to make the appointment from among other members of the National Roster without the submission of additional lists.

(c) Unless the parties agree otherwise when there are two or more claimants or two or more respondents, the AAA may appoint all the arbitrators.

R-12. Direct Appointment by a Party

(a) If the agreement of the parties names an arbitrator or specifies a method of appointing an arbitrator, that designation or method shall be followed. The notice of appointment, with the name and address of the arbitrator, shall be filed with the AAA by the appointing party. Upon the request of any appointing party, the AAA shall submit a list of members of the National Roster from which the party may, if it so desires, make the appointment.

(b) Where the parties have agreed that each party is to name one arbitrator, the arbitrators so named must meet the standards of Section R-17 with respect to impartiality and independence unless the parties have specifically agreed pursuant to Section R-17(a) that the party-appointed arbitrators are to be non-neutral and need not meet those standards.

(c) If the agreement specifies a period of time within which an arbitrator shall be appointed and any party fails to make the appointment within that period, the AAA shall make the appointment.

(d) If no period of time is specified in the agreement, the AAA shall notify the party to make the appointment. If within 15 days after such notice has been sent, an arbitrator has not been appointed by a party, the AAA shall make the appointment.

R-13. Appointment of Chairperson by Party-Appointed Arbitrators or Parties

(a) If, pursuant to Section R-12, either the parties have directly appointed arbitrators, or the arbitrators have been appointed by the AAA, and the parties have authorized them to appoint a chairperson within a specified time and no appointment is made within that time or any agreed extension, the AAA may appoint the chairperson.

(b) If no period of time is specified for appointment of the chairperson and the party-appointed arbitrators or the parties do not make the appointment within 15 days from the date of the appointment of the last party-appointed arbitrator, the AAA may appoint the chairperson.

(c) If the parties have agreed that their party-appointed arbitrators shall appoint the chairperson from the National Roster, the AAA shall furnish to the party-appointed arbitrators, in the manner provided in Section R-11, a list selected from the National Roster, and the appointment of the chairperson shall be made as provided in that Section.

R-14. Nationality of Arbitrator

Where the parties are nationals of different countries, the AAA, at the request of any party or on its own initiative, may appoint as arbitrator a national of a country other than that of any of the parties. The request must be made before the time set for the appointment of the arbitrator as agreed by the parties or set by these rules.

R-15. Number of Arbitrators

If the arbitration agreement does not specify the number of arbitrators, the dispute shall be heard and determined by one arbitrator, unless the AAA, in its discretion, directs that three arbitrators be appointed. A party may request three arbitrators in the demand or answer, which request the AAA will consider in exercising its discretion regarding the number of arbitrators appointed to the dispute.

R-16. Disclosure

(a) Any person appointed or to be appointed as an arbitrator shall disclose to the AAA any circumstance likely to give rise to justifiable doubt as to the arbitrator's impartiality or independence, including any bias or any financial or personal interest in the result of the arbitration or any past or present relationship with the parties or their representatives. Such obligation shall remain in effect throughout the arbitration.

(b) Upon receipt of such information from the arbitrator or another source, the AAA shall communicate the information to the parties and, if it deems it appropriate to do so, to the arbitrator and others.

(c) In order to encourage disclosure by arbitrators, disclosure of information pursuant to this Section R-16 is not to be construed as an indication that the arbitrator considers that the disclosed circumstance is likely to affect impartiality or independence.

R-17. Disqualification of Arbitrator

(a) Any arbitrator shall be impartial and independent and shall perform his or her duties with diligence and in good faith, and shall be subject to disqualification for

(i) partiality or lack of independence,

(ii) inability or refusal to perform his or her duties with diligence and in good faith, and

(iii) any grounds for disqualification provided by applicable law. The parties may agree in writing, however, that arbitrators directly appointed by a party pursuant to Section R-12 shall be nonneutral, in which case such arbitrators need not be impartial or independent and shall not be subject to disqualification for partiality or lack of independence.

(b) Upon objection of a party to the continued service of an arbitrator, or on its own initiative, the AAA shall determine whether the arbitrator should be disqualified under the grounds set out above, and shall inform the parties of its decision, which decision shall be conclusive.

R-18. Communication with Arbitrator

(a) No party and no one acting on behalf of any party shall communicate ex parte with an arbitrator or a candidate for arbitrator concerning the arbitration, except that a party, or someone acting on behalf of a party, may communicate ex parte with a candidate for direct appointment pursuant to Section R-12 in order to advise the candidate of the general nature of the controversy and of the anticipated proceedings and to discuss the candidate's qualifications, availability, or independence in relation to the parties or to discuss the suitability of candidates for selection as a third arbitrator where the parties or party-designated arbitrators are to participate in that selection.

(b) Section R-18(a) does not apply to arbitrators directly appointed by the parties who, pursuant to Section R-17(a), the parties have agreed in writing are non-neutral. Where the parties have so agreed under Section R-17(a), the AAA shall as an administrative practice suggest to the parties that they agree further that Section R-18(a) should nonetheless apply prospectively.

R-19. Vacancies

(a) If for any reason an arbitrator is unable to perform the duties of the office, the AAA may, on proof satisfactory to it, declare the office vacant. Vacancies shall be filled in accordance with the applicable provisions of these rules.

(b) In the event of a vacancy in a panel of neutral arbitrators after the hearings have commenced, the remaining arbitrator or arbitrators may continue with the hearing and determination of the controversy, unless the parties agree otherwise.

(c) In the event of the appointment of a substitute arbitrator, the panel of arbitrators shall determine in its sole discretion whether it is necessary to repeat all or part of any prior hearings.

R-20. Preliminary Hearing

(a) At the request of any party or at the discretion of the arbitrator or the AAA, the arbitrator may schedule as soon as practicable a preliminary hearing with the parties and/or their representatives. The preliminary hearing may be conducted by telephone at the arbitrator's discretion.

(b) During the preliminary hearing, the parties and the arbitrator should discuss the future conduct of the case, including clarification of the issues and claims, a schedule for the hearings and any other preliminary matters.

R-21. Exchange of Information

(a) At the request of any party or at the discretion of the arbitrator, consistent with the expedited nature of arbitration, the arbitrator may direct

(i) the production of documents and other information, and

(ii) the identification of any witnesses to be called.

(b) At least five business days prior to the hearing, the parties shall exchange copies of all exhibits they intend to submit at the hearing.

(c) The arbitrator is authorized to resolve any disputes concerning the exchange of information.

R-22. Date, Time, and Place of Hearing

The arbitrator shall set the date, time, and place for each hearing. The parties shall respond to requests for hearing dates in a timely manner, be cooperative in scheduling the earliest practicable date, and adhere to the established hearing schedule. The AAA shall send a notice of hearing to the parties at least 10 days in advance of the hearing date, unless otherwise agreed by the parties.

R-23. Attendance at Hearings

The arbitrator and the AAA shall maintain the privacy of the hearings unless the law provides to the contrary. Any person having a direct interest in the arbitration is entitled to attend hearings. The arbitrator shall otherwise have the power to require the exclusion of any witness, other than a party or other essential person, during the testimony of any other witness. It shall be discretionary with the arbitrator to determine the propriety of the attendance of any other person other than a party and its representatives.

R-24. Representation

Any party may be represented by counsel or other authorized representative. A party intending to be so represented shall notify the other party and the AAA of the name and address of the representative at least three days prior to the date set for the hearing at which that person is first to appear. When such a representative initiates an arbitration or responds for a party, notice is deemed to have been given.

R-25. Oaths

Before proceeding with the first hearing, each arbitrator may take an oath of office and, if required by law, shall do so. The arbitrator may require witnesses to testify under oath administered by any duly qualified person and, if it is required by law or requested by any party, shall do so.

R-26. Stenographic Record

Any party desiring a stenographic record shall make arrangements directly with a stenographer and shall notify the other parties of these arrangements at least three days in advance of the hearing. The requesting party or parties shall pay the cost of the record. If the transcript is agreed by the parties, or determined by the arbitrator to be the official record of the proceeding, it must be provided to the arbitrator and made available to the other parties for inspection, at a date, time, and place determined by the arbitrator.

R-27. Interpreters

Any party wishing an interpreter shall make all arrangements directly with the interpreter and shall assume the costs of the service.

R-28. Postponements

The arbitrator may postpone any hearing upon agreement of the parties, upon request of a party for good cause shown, or upon the arbitrator's own initiative.

R-29. Arbitration in the Absence of a Party or Representative

Unless the law provides to the contrary, the arbitration may proceed in the absence of any party or representative who, after due notice, fails to be present or fails to obtain a postponement. An award shall not be made solely on the default of a party. The arbitrator shall require the party who is present to submit such evidence as the arbitrator may require for the making of an award.

R-30. Conduct of Proceedings

(a) The claimant shall present evidence to support its claim. The respondent shall then present evidence to support its defense. Witnesses for each party shall also submit to questions from the arbitrator and the adverse party. The arbitrator has the discretion to vary this procedure, provided that the parties are treated with equality and that each party has the right to be heard and is given a fair opportunity to present its case.

(b) The arbitrator, exercising his or her discretion, shall conduct the proceedings with a view to expediting the resolution of the dispute and may direct the order of proof, bifurcate proceedings and direct the parties to focus their presentations on issues the decision of which could dispose of all or part of the case.

(c) The parties may agree to waive oral hearings in any case.

R-31. Evidence

(a) The parties may offer such evidence as is relevant and material to the dispute and shall produce such evidence as the arbitrator may deem necessary to an understanding and determination of the dispute. Conformity to legal rules of evidence shall not be necessary. All evidence shall be taken in the presence of all of the arbitrators and all of the parties, except where any of the parties is absent, in default or has waived the right to be present.

(b) The arbitrator shall determine the admissibility, relevance, and materiality of the evidence offered and may exclude evidence deemed by the arbitrator to be cumulative or irrelevant.

(c) The arbitrator shall take into account applicable principles of legal privilege, such as those involving the confidentiality of communications between a lawyer and client.

(d) An arbitrator or other person authorized by law to subpoena witnesses or documents may do so upon the request of any party or independently.

R-32. Evidence by Affidavit and Post-hearing Filing of Documents or Other Evidence

(a) The arbitrator may receive and consider the evidence of witnesses by declaration or affidavit, but shall give it only such weight as the arbitrator deems it entitled to after consideration of any objection made to its admission.

(b) If the parties agree or the arbitrator directs that documents or other evidence be submitted to the arbitrator after the hearing, the documents or other evidence shall be filed with the AAA for transmission to the arbitrator. All parties shall be afforded an opportunity to examine and respond to such documents or other evidence.

R-33. Inspection or Investigation

An arbitrator finding it necessary to make an inspection or investigation in connection with the arbitration shall direct the AAA to so advise the parties. The arbitrator shall set the date and time and the AAA shall notify the parties. Any party who so desires may be present at such an inspection or investigation. In the event that one or all parties are not present at the inspection or investigation, the arbitrator shall make an oral or written report to the parties and afford them an opportunity to comment.

R-34. Interim Measures**

(a) The arbitrator may take whatever interim measures he or she deems necessary, including injunctive relief and measures for the protection or conservation of property and disposition of perishable goods.

(b) Such interim measures may take the form of an interim award, and the arbitrator may require security for the costs of such measures.

(c) A request for interim measures addressed by a party to a judicial authority shall not be deemed incompatible with the agreement to arbitrate or a waiver of the right to arbitrate.

** The Optional Rules may be found below.

R-35. Closing of Hearing

The arbitrator shall specifically inquire of all parties whether they have any further proofs to offer or witnesses to be heard. Upon receiving negative replies or if satisfied that the record is complete, the arbitrator shall declare the hearing closed. If briefs are to be filed, the hearing shall b e declared closed as of the final date set by the arbitrator for the receipt of briefs. If documents are to be filed as provided in Section R-32 and the date set for their receipt is later than that set for the receipt of briefs, the later date shall be the closing date of the hearing. The time limit within which the arbitrator is required to make the award shall commence, in the absence of other agreements by the parties, upon the closing of the hearing.

R-36. Reopening of Hearing

The hearing may be reopened on the arbitrator's initiative, or upon application of a party, at any time before the award is made. If reopening the hearing would prevent the making of the award within the specific time agreed on by the parties in the contract(s) out of which the controversy has arisen, the matter may not be reopened unless the parties agree on an extension of time. When no specific date is fixed in the contract, the arbitrator may reopen the hearing and shall have 30 days from the closing of the reopened hearing within which to make an award.

R-37. Waiver of Rules

Any party who proceeds with the arbitration after knowledge that any provision or requirement of these rules has not been complied with and who fails to state an objection in writing shall be deemed to have waived the right to object.

R-38. Extensions of Time

The parties may modify any period of time by mutual agreement. The AAA or the arbitrator may for good cause extend any period of time established by these rules, except the time for making the award. The AAA shall notify the parties of any extension.

R-39. Serving of Notice

(a) Any papers, notices, or process necessary or proper for the initiation or continuation of an arbitration under these rules, for any court action in connection therewith, or for the entry of judgment on any award made under these rules may be served on a party by mail addressed to the party, or its representative at the last known address or by personal service, in or outside the state where the arbitration is to be held, provided that reasonable opportunity to be heard with regard to the dispute is or has been granted to the party.

(b) The AAA, the arbitrator and the parties may also use overnight delivery or electronic facsimile transmission (fax), to give the notices required by these rules. Where all parties and the arbitrator agree, notices may be transmitted by electronic mail (E-mail), or other methods of communication.

(c) Unless otherwise instructed by the AAA or by the arbitrator, any documents submitted by any party to the AAA or to the arbitrator shall simultaneously be provided to the other party or parties to the arbitration.

R-40. Majority Decision

When the panel consists of more than one arbitrator, unless required by law or by the arbitration agreement, a majority of the arbitrators must make all decisions.

R-41. Time of Award

The award shall be made promptly by the arbitrator and, unless otherwise agreed by the parties or specified by law, no later than 30 days from the date of closing the hearing, or, if oral hearings have been waived, from the date of the AAA's transmittal of the final statements and proofs to the arbitrator.

R-42. Form of Award

(a) Any award shall be in writing and signed by a majority of the arbitrators. It shall be executed in the manner required by law.

(b) The arbitrator need not render a reasoned award unless the parties request such an award in writing prior to appointment of the arbitrator or unless the arbitrator determines that a reasoned award is appropriate.

R-43. Scope of Award

(a) The arbitrator may grant any remedy or relief that the arbitrator deems just and equitable and within the scope of the agreement of the parties, including, but not limited to, specific performance of a contract.

(b) In addition to a final award, the arbitrator may make other decisions, including interim, interlocutory, or partial rulings, orders, and awards. In any interim, interlocutory, or partial award, the arbitrator may assess and apportion the fees, expenses, and compensation related to such award as the arbitrator determines is appropriate.

(c) In the final award, the arbitrator shall assess the fees, expenses, and compensation provided in Sections R-49, R-50, and R-51. The arbitrator may apportion such fees, expenses, and compensation among the parties in such amounts as the arbitrator determines is appropriate.

(d) The award of the arbitrator(s) may include:

(i) interest at such rate and from such date as the arbitrator(s) may deem appropriate; and

(ii) an award of attorneys' fees if all parties have requested such an award or it is authorized by law or their arbitration agreement.

R-44. Award upon Settlement

If the parties settle their dispute during the course of the arbitration and if the parties so request, the arbitrator may set forth the terms of the settlement in a "consent award." A consent award must include an allocation of arbitration costs, including administrative fees and expenses as well as arbitrator fees and expenses.

R-45. Delivery of Award to Parties

Parties shall accept as notice and delivery of the award the placing of the award or a true copy thereof in the mail addressed to the parties or their representatives at the last known addresses, personal or electronic service of the award, or the filing of the award in any other manner that is permitted by law.

R-46. Modification of Award

Within 20 days after the transmittal of an award, any party, upon notice to the other parties, may request the arbitrator, through the AAA, to correct any clerical, typographical, or computational errors in the award. The arbitrator is not empowered to redetermine the merits of any claim already decided. The other parties shall be given 10 days to respond to the request. The arbitrator shall dispose of the request within 20 days after transmittal by the AAA to the arbitrator of the request and any response thereto.

R-47. Release of Documents for Judicial Proceedings

The AAA shall, upon the written request of a party, furnish to the party, at the party's expense, certified copies of any papers in the AAA's possession that may be required in judicial proceedings relating to the arbitration.

R-48. Applications to Court and Exclusion of Liability

(a) No judicial proceeding by a party relating to the subject matter of the arbitration shall be deemed a waiver of the party's right to arbitrate.

(b) Neither the AAA nor any arbitrator in a proceeding under these rules is a necessary or proper party in judicial proceedings relating to the arbitration.

(c) Parties to an arbitration under these rules shall be deemed to have consented that judgment upon the arbitration award may be entered in any federal or state court having jurisdiction thereof.

(d) Parties to an arbitration under these rules shall be deemed to have consented that neither the AAA nor any arbitrator shall be liable to any party in any action for damages or injunctive relief for any act or omission in connection with any arbitration under these rules.

R-49. Administrative Fees

As a not-for-profit organization, the AAA shall prescribe an initial filing fee and a case service fee to compensate it for the cost of providing administrative services. The fees in effect when the fee or charge is incurred shall be applicable. The filing fee shall be advanced by the party or parties making a claim or counterclaim, subject to final apportionment by the arbitrator in the award. The AAA may, in the event of extreme hardship on the part of any party, defer or reduce the administrative fees.

R-50. Expenses

The expenses of witnesses for either side shall be paid by the party producing such witnesses. All other expenses of the arbitration, including required travel and other expenses of the arbitrator, AAA representatives, and any witness and the cost of any proof produced at the direct request of the arbitrator, shall be borne equally by the parties, unless they agree otherwise or unless the arbitrator in the award assesses such expenses or any part thereof against any specified party or parties.

R-51. Neutral Arbitrator's Compensation

(a) Arbitrators shall be compensated at a rate consistent with the arbitrator's stated rate of compensation.

(b) If there is disagreement concerning the terms of compensation, an appropriate rate shall be established with the arbitrator by the AAA and confirmed to the parties.

(c) Any arrangement for the compensation of a neutral arbitrator shall be made through the AAA and not directly between the parties and the arbitrator.

R-52. Deposits

The AAA may require the parties to deposit in advance of any hearings such sums of money as it deems necessary to cover the expense of the arbitration, including the arbitrator's fee, if any, and shall render an accounting to the parties and return any unexpended balance at the conclusion of the case.

R-53. Interpretation and Application of Rules

The arbitrator shall interpret and apply these rules insofar as they relate to the arbitrator's powers and duties. When there is more than one arbitrator and a difference arises among them concerning the meaning or application of these rules, it shall be decided by a majority vote. If that is not possible, either an arbitrator or a party may refer the question to the AAA for final decision. All other rules shall be interpreted and applied by the AAA.

R-54. Suspension for Nonpayment

If arbitrator compensation or administrative charges have not been paid in full, the AAA may so inform the parties in order that one of them may advance the required payment. If such payments are not made, the arbitrator may order the suspension or termination of the proceedings. If no arbitrator has yet been appointed, the AAA may suspend the proceedings.

EXPEDITED PROCEDURES

E-1. Limitation on Extensions

Except in extraordinary circumstances, the AAA or the arbitrator may grant a party no more than one seven-day extension of time to respond to the demand for arbitration or counterclaim as provided in Section R-4.

E-2. Changes of Claim or Counterclaim

A claim or counterclaim may be increased in amount, or a new or different claim or counterclaim added, upon the agreement of the other party, or the consent of the arbitrator. After the arbitrator is appointed, however, no new or different claim or counterclaim may be submitted except with the arbitrator's consent. If an increased claim or counterclaim exceeds $75,000, the case will be administered under the regular procedures unless all parties and the arbitrator agree that the case may continue to be processed under the Expedited Procedures.

E-3. Serving of Notices

In addition to notice provided by Section R-39(b), the parties shall also accept notice by telephone. Telephonic notices by the AAA shall subsequently be confirmed in writing to the parties. Should there be a failure to confirm in writing any such oral notice, the proceeding shall nevertheless be valid if notice has, in fact, been given by telephone.

E-4. Appointment and Qualifications of Arbitrator

(a) The AAA shall simultaneously submit to each party an identical list of five proposed arbitrators drawn from its National Roster from which one arbitrator shall be appointed.

(b) The parties are encouraged to agree to an arbitrator from this list and to advise the AAA of their agreement. If the parties are unable to agree upon an arbitrator, each party may strike two names from the list and return it to the AAA within seven days from the date of the AAA's mailing to the parties. If for any reason the appointment of an arbitrator cannot be made from the list, the AAA may make the appointment from other members of the panel without the submission of additional lists.

(c) The parties will be given notice by the AAA of the appointment of the arbitrator, who shall be subject to disqualification for the reasons specified in Section R-17.

The parties shall notify the AAA within seven days of any objection to the arbitrator appointed. Any such objection shall be for cause and shall be confirmed in writing to the AAA with a copy to the other party or parties.

E-5. Exchange of Exhibits

At least two business days prior to the hearing, the parties shall exchange copies of all exhibits they intend to submit at the hearing. The arbitrator shall resolve disputes concerning the exchange of exhibits.

E-6. Proceedings on Documents

Where no party's claim exceeds $10,000, exclusive of interest and arbitration costs, and other cases in which the parties agree, the dispute shall be resolved by submission of documents, unless any party requests an oral hearing, or the arbitrator determines that an oral hearing is necessary. The arbitrator shall establish a fair and equitable procedure for the submission of documents.

E-7. Date, Time, and Place of Hearing

In cases in which a hearing is to be held, the arbitrator shall set the date, time, and place of the hearing, to be scheduled to take place within 30 days of confirmation of the arbitrator's appointment. The AAA will notify the parties in advance of the hearing date.

E-8. The Hearing

(a) Generally, the hearing shall not exceed one day. Each party shall have equal opportunity to submit its proofs and complete its case. The arbitrator shall determine the order of the hearing, and may require further submission of documents within two days after the hearing. For good cause shown, the arbitrator may schedule additional hearings within seven business days after the initial day of hearings.

(b) Generally, there will be no stenographic record. Any party desiring a stenographic record may arrange for one pursuant to the provisions of Section R-26.

E-9. Time of Award

Unless otherwise agreed by the parties, the award shall be rendered not later than 14 days from the date of the closing of the hearing or, if oral hearings have been waived, from the date of the AAA's transmittal of the final statements and proofs to the arbitrator.

E-10. Arbitrator's Compensation

Arbitrators will receive compensation at a rate to be suggested by the AAA regional office.

PROCEDURES FOR LARGE, COMPLEX COMMERCIAL DISPUTES

L-1. Administrative Conference

Prior to the dissemination of a list of potential arbitrators, the AAA shall, unless the parties agree otherwise, conduct an administrative conference with the parties and/or their attorneys or other representatives by conference call. The conference will take place within 14 days after the commencement of the arbitration. In the event the parties are unable to agree on a mutually acceptable time for the conference, the AAA may contact the parties individually to discuss the issues contemplated herein. Such administrative conference shall be conducted for the following purposes and for such additional purposes as the parties or the AAA may deem appropriate:

(a) to obtain additional information about the nature and magnitude of the dispute and the anticipated length of hearing and scheduling;

(b) to discuss the views of the parties about the technical and other qualifications of the arbitrators;

(c) to obtain conflicts statements from the parties; and

(d) to consider, with the parties, whether mediation or other non-adjudicative methods of dispute resolution might be appropriate.

L-2. Arbitrators

(a) Large, Complex Commercial Cases shall be heard and determined by either one or three arbitrators, as may be agreed upon by the parties. If the parties are unable to agree upon the number of arbitrators and a claim or counterclaim involves at least $1,000,000, then three arbitrator(s) shall hear and determine the case. If the parties are unable to agree on the number of arbitrators and each claim and counterclaim is less than $1,000,000, then one arbitrator shall hear and determine the case.

(b) The AAA shall appoint arbitrator(s) as agreed by the parties. If they are unable to agree on a method of appointment, the AAA shall appoint arbitrators from the Large, Complex Commercial Case Panel, in the manner provided in the Regular Commercial Arbitration Rules. Absent agreement of the parties, the arbitrator(s) shall not have served as the mediator in the mediation phase of the instant proceeding.

L-3. Preliminary Hearing

As promptly as practicable after the selection of the arbitrator(s), a preliminary hearing shall be held among the parties and/or their attorneys or other representatives and the arbitrator(s). Unless the parties agree otherwise, the preliminary hearing will be conducted by telephone conference call rather than in person. At the preliminary hearing the matters to be considered shall include, without limitation:

(a) service of a detailed statement of claims, damages and defenses, a statement of the issues asserted by each party and positions with respect thereto, and any legal authorities the parties may wish to bring to the attention of the arbitrator(s);

(b) stipulations to uncontested facts;

(c) the extent to which discovery shall be conducted;

(d) exchange and premarking of those documents which each party believes may be offered at the hearing;

(e) the identification and availability of witnesses, including experts, and such matters with respect to witnesses including their biographies and expected testimony as may be appropriate;

(f) whether, and the extent to which, any sworn statements and/or depositions may be introduced;

(g) the extent to which hearings will proceed on consecutive days;

(h) whether a stenographic or other official record of the proceedings shall be maintained;

(i) the possibility of utilizing mediation or other non-adjudicative methods of dispute resolution; and

(j) the procedure for the issuance of subpoenas.

By agreement of the parties and/or order of the arbitrator(s), the pre-hearing activities and the hearing procedures that will govern the arbitration will be memorialized in a Scheduling and Procedure Order.

L-4. Management of Proceedings

(a) Arbitrator(s) shall take such steps as they may deem necessary or desirable to avoid delay and to achieve a just, speedy and cost-effective resolution of Large, Complex Commercial Cases.

(b) Parties shall cooperate in the exchange of documents, exhibits and information within such party's control if the arbitrator(s) consider such production to be consistent with the goal of achieving a just, speedy and cost-effective resolution of a Large, Complex Commercial Case.

(c) The parties may conduct such discovery as may be agreed to by all the parties provided, however, that the arbitrator(s) may place such limitations on the conduct of such discovery as the arbitrator(s) shall deem appropriate. If the parties cannot agree on production of documents and other information, the arbitrator(s), consistent with the expedited nature of arbitration, may establish the extent of the discovery.

(d) At the discretion of the arbitrator(s), upon good cause shown and consistent with the expedited nature of arbitration, the arbitrator(s) may order depositions of, or the propounding of interrogatories to, such persons who may possess information determined by the arbitrator(s) to be necessary to determination of the matter.

(e) The parties shall exchange copies of all exhibits they intend to submit at the hearing 10 business days prior to the hearing unless the arbitrator(s) determine otherwise.

(f) The exchange of information pursuant to this rule, as agreed by the parties and/or directed by the arbitrator(s), shall be included within the Scheduling and Procedure Order.

(g) The arbitrator is authorized to resolve any disputes concerning the exchange of information.

(h) Generally hearings will be scheduled on consecutive days or in blocks of consecutive days in order to maximize efficiency and minimize costs.

OPTIONAL RULES FOR EMERGENCY MEASURES OF PROTECTION

O-1. Applicability

Where parties by special agreement or in their arbitration clause have adopted these rules for emergency measures of protection, a party in need of emergency relief prior to the constitution of the panel shall notify the AAA and all other parties in writing of the nature of the relief sought and the reasons why such relief is required on an emergency basis. The application shall also set forth the reasons why the party is entitled to such relief. Such notice may be given by facsimile transmission, or other reliable means, but must include a statement certifying that all other parties have been notified or an explanation of the steps taken in good faith to notify other parties.

O-2. Appointment of Emergency Arbitrator

Within one business day of receipt of notice as provided in Section O-1, the AAA shall appoint a single emergency arbitrator from a special AAA panel of emergency arbitrators designated to rule on emergency applications. The emergency arbitrator shall immediately disclose any circumstance likely, on the basis of the facts disclosed in the application, to affect such arbitrator's impartiality or independence. Any challenge to the appointment of the emergency arbitrator must be made within one business day of the communication by the AAA to the parties of the appointment of the emergency arbitrator and the circumstances disclosed.

O-3. Schedule

The emergency arbitrator shall as soon as possible, but in any event within two business days of appointment, establish a schedule for consideration of the application for emergency relief. Such schedule shall provide a reasonable opportunity to all parties to be heard, but may provide for proceeding by telephone conference or on written submissions as alternatives to a formal hearing.

O-4. Interim Award

If after consideration the emergency arbitrator is satisfied that the party seeking the emergency relief has shown that immediate and irreparable loss or damage will result in the absence of emergency relief, and that such party is entitled to such relief, the emergency arbitrator may enter an interim award granting the relief and stating the reasons therefore.

O-5. Constitution of the Panel

Any application to modify an interim award of emergency relief must be based on changed circumstances and may be made to the emergency arbitrator until the panel is constituted; thereafter such a request shall be addressed to the panel. The emergency arbitrator shall have no further power to act after the panel is constituted unless the parties agree that the emergency arbitrator is named as a member of the panel.

O-6. Security

Any interim award of emergency relief may be conditioned on provision by the party seeking such relief of appropriate security.

O-7. Special Master

A request for interim measures addressed by a party to a judicial authority shall not be deemed incompatible with the agreement to arbitrate or a waiver of the right to arbitrate. If the AAA is directed by a judicial authority to nominate a special master to consider and report on an application for emergency relief, the AAA shall proceed as provided in Section O-1 of this article and the references to the emergency arbitrator shall be read to mean the special master, except that the special master shall issue a report rather than an interim award.

O-8. Costs

The costs associated with applications for emergency relief shall initially be apportioned by the emergency arbitrator or special master, subject to the power of the panel to determine finally the apportionment of such costs.

◆ APPENDIX H ◆
JAMS COMPREHENSIVE ARBITRATION
RULES AND PROCEDURES (effective April, 2003)
Reproduced with permission from JAMS

Table of Contents

Rule 1.   Scope of Rules

(a)   The JAMS Comprehensive Arbitration Rules and Procedures ("Rules") govern binding Arbitrations of disputes or claims that are administered by JAMS and in which the Parties agree to use these Rules or, in the absence of such agreement, any disputed claim or counterclaim that exceeds $250,000, not including interest or attorneys' fees, unless other Rules are prescribed.

(b)   The Parties shall be deemed to have made these Rules a part of their Arbitration agreement whenever they have provided for Arbitration by JAMS under its Comprehensive Rules or for Arbitration by JAMS without specifying any particular JAMS Rules and the disputes or claims meet the criteria of the first paragraph of this Rule.

(c)   The term "Party" as used in these Rules includes Parties to the Arbitration and their counsel or representative.

Rule 2.   Party-Agreed Procedures

The Parties may agree on any procedures not specified herein or in lieu of these Rules that are consistent with the applicable law and JAMS policies (including, without limitation, Rules 15(i), 30 and 31). The Parties shall promptly notify the JAMS Case Manager of any such Party-agreed procedures and shall confirm such procedures in writing. The Party-agreed procedures shall be enforceable as if contained in these Rules.

Rule 3.   Amendment of Rules

JAMS may amend these Rules without notice. The Rules in effect on the date of the commencement of an Arbitration (as defined in Rule 5) shall apply to that Arbitration, unless the Parties have specified another version of the Rules.

Rule 4.   Conflict with Law

If any of these Rules, or a modification of these Rules agreed on by the Parties, is determined to be in conflict with a provision of applicable law, the provision of law will govern, and no other Rule will be affected.

Rule 5.   Commencing an Arbitration

(a)   The Arbitration is deemed commenced when JAMS confirms in a Commencement Letter one of the following:

(i)   The submission to JAMS of a post-dispute Arbitration agreement fully executed by all Parties and that specifies JAMS administration or use of any JAMS Rules; or

(ii)   The submission to JAMS of a pre-dispute written contractual provision requiring the Parties to arbitrate the dispute or claim and which specifies JAMS administration or use of any JAMS Rules or which the Parties agree shall be administered by JAMS; or

(iii)   The oral agreement of all Parties to participate in an Arbitration administered by JAMS or conducted pursuant to any JAMS Rules, confirmed in writing by the Parties; or

(iv)   A court order compelling Arbitration at JAMS.

(b)   The Commencement Letter shall confirm that one of the above requirements for commencement has been met and that JAMS has received any payment required under the applicable fee schedule. The date of commencement of the Arbitration is the date of the Commencement Letter.

(c)   If a Party who has signed a pre-dispute written contractual provision specifying these Rules or JAMS administration fails to agree to participate in the Arbitration process, JAMS shall confirm in writing that Party's failure to respond or participate and, pursuant to Rule 22, the Arbitrator shall schedule, and provide appropriate notice of a Hearing or other opportunity for the Party demanding the Arbitration to demonstrate its entitlement to relief.

(d)   The definition of "commencement" in these Rules is not intended to be applicable to any legal requirement, such as the statute of limitations or a contractual limitations period, unless actually so specified by that requirement.

Rule 6.   Administrative Conference

(a)   The Case Manager may conduct an Administrative Conference with the Parties by telephone. The Administrative Conference may occur within seven (7) calendar days after the date of commencement of the Arbitration. Unless the Parties agree otherwise, if the Administrative Conference does not take place within the time specified above, the Case Manager shall proceed with the Arbitrator selection process pursuant to Rule 15 as if the Administrative Conference had, in fact, been held.

(b)   The Case Manager shall answer any questions regarding these Rules and may discuss procedural matters such as the pleading or notice of claim sequence, Arbitrator selection, the Preliminary Conference process and the expectations of the Parties as to the length of the Arbitration Hearing. The Parties may agree to a date for the Hearing subject to Arbitrator availability. In the absence of agreement, the Hearing date shall be set by the Arbitrator pursuant to Rule 19(a).

(c)   At the request of a Party and in the absence of Party agreement, JAMS may make a determination regarding the location of the Hearing, subject to Arbitrator review. In determining the location of the Hearing such factors as the subject matter of the dispute, the convenience of the Parties and witnesses and the relative resources of the Parties shall be considered.

(d)   The Case Manager may convene, or the Parties may request, additional Administrative Conferences.

Rule 7.   Number of Arbitrators and Appointment of Chairperson

(a)   The Arbitration shall be conducted by one neutral Arbitrator unless all Parties agree otherwise. In these Rules, the term "Arbitrator" shall mean, as the context requires, the Arbitrator or the panel of Arbitrators in a tripartite Arbitration.

(b)   In cases involving more than one Arbitrator the Parties shall agree on, or in the absence of agreement the Case Manager shall designate, the Chairperson of the Arbitration Panel. If the Parties and the Arbitrator agree, the Chairperson may, acting alone, decide discovery and procedural matters.

Rule 8.   Service

(a)   Service under these Rules is effected by providing one copy of the document with original signatures to each Party and two copies in the case of a sole Arbitrator and four copies in the case of a tripartite panel to the Case Manager. Service may be made by hand-delivery, overnight delivery service or U.S. mail. Service by any of these means is considered effective upon the date of deposit of the document. Service by facsimile transmission is considered effective upon transmission, but only if followed within one week of delivery by service of an appropriate number of copies and originals by one of the other service methods.

(b)   In computing any period of time prescribed or allowed by these Rules for a Party to do some act within a prescribed period after the service of a notice or other paper on the Party and the notice or paper is served on the Party only by U.S. Mail, three (3) calendar days shall be added to the prescribed period.

Rule 9.   Notice of Claims

(a)   If a matter has been submitted for Arbitration after litigation has been commenced in court regarding the same claim or dispute, the pleadings in the court case, including the complaint and answer (with affirmative defenses and counterclaims), may be filed with JAMS within fourteen (14) calendar days of the date of commencement, and if so filed, will be considered part of the record of the Arbitration. It will be assumed that the existence of such pleadings constitutes appropriate notice to the Parties of such claims, remedies sought, counterclaims and affirmative defenses. If necessary, such notice may be supplemented pursuant to Rule 9(b).

(b)   If a matter has been submitted to JAMS prior to or in lieu of the filing of a case in court or prior to the filing of an answer, the Parties shall give each other notice of their respective claims, remedies sought, counterclaims and affirmative defenses (including jurisdictional challenges). Such notice may be served upon the other Parties and filed with JAMS, in the form of a demand for Arbitration, response or answer to demand for Arbitration, counterclaim or answer or response to counterclaim. Any pleading shall include a short statement of its factual basis.

(c)   Notice of claims, remedies sought, counterclaims and affirmative defenses may be served simultaneously, in which case they should be filed with JAMS within fourteen (14) calendar days of the date of commencement of the Arbitration, or by such other date as the Parties may agree. The responding Parties may, however, in their sole discretion, wait to receive the notice of claim before serving any response, including counterclaims or affirmative defenses. In this case, the response, including counterclaims and affirmative defenses, should be served on the other Parties and filed with JAMS within fourteen (14) calendar days of service of the notice of claim. If the notice of claim has been served on the responding Parties prior to the date of commencement, the response, including counterclaims and affirmative defenses, shall be served within fourteen (14) calendar days from the date of commencement.

(d)   Any Party that is a recipient of a counterclaim may reply to such counterclaim, including asserting jurisdictional challenges. In such case, the reply must be served on the other Parties and filed with JAMS within fourteen (14) calendar days of having received the notice of counterclaim. No claim, remedy, counterclaim or affirmative defense will be considered by the Arbitrator in the absence of prior notice to the other Parties, unless all Parties agree that such consideration is appropriate notwithstanding the lack of prior notice.

Rule 10.   Changes of Claims

After the filing of a claim and before the Arbitrator is appointed, any Party may make a new or different claim. Such claim shall be made in writing, filed with JAMS and served on the other Parties. Any response to the new claim shall be made within fourteen (14) calendar days after service of such claim. After the Arbitrator is appointed, no new or different claim may be submitted except with the Arbitrator's approval. A Party may request a Hearing on this issue. Each Party has the right to respond to any new claim in accordance with Rule 9(c).

Rule 11.   Interpretation of Rules and Jurisdictional Challenges

(a)   Once appointed, the Arbitrator shall resolve disputes about the interpretation and applicability of these Rules and conduct of the Arbitration Hearing. The resolution of the issue by the Arbitrator shall be final.

(b)   Whenever in these Rules a matter is to be determined by "JAMS" (such as in Rules 6(c), 11(d), 15(d), (f) or (g), 24(i) or 31(e)), such determination shall be made in accordance with JAMS' administrative procedures.

(c)   Jurisdictional and arbitrability disputes, including disputes over the existence, validity, interpretation or scope of the agreement under which Arbitration is sought, and who are proper

Parties to the Arbitration, shall be submitted to and ruled on by the Arbitrator. The Arbitrator has the authority to determine jurisdiction and arbitrability issues as a preliminary matter.

(d)   Disputes concerning the appointment of the Arbitrator and the venue of the Arbitration, if that determination is relevant to the selection of the Arbitrator, shall be resolved by JAMS.

(e)   The Arbitrator may upon a showing of good cause or sua sponte, when necessary to facilitate the Arbitration, extend any deadlines established in these Rules, provided that the time for rendering the Award may only be altered in accordance with Rules 22(i) or 24.

Rule 12.   Representation

The Parties may be represented by counsel or any other person of the Party's choice. Each Party shall give prompt written notice to the Case Manager and the other Parties of the name, address and telephone and fax numbers of its representative. The representative of a Party may act on the Party's behalf in complying with these Rules.

Rule 13.   Withdrawal from Arbitration

(a)   No Party may terminate or withdraw from an Arbitration after the issuance of the Commencement Letter (see Rule 5) except by written agreement of all Parties to the Arbitration.

(b)   A Party that asserts a claim or counterclaim may unilaterally withdraw that claim or counterclaim without prejudice by serving written notice on the other Parties and on the Arbitrator. However, the opposing Parties may, within fourteen (14) calendar days of service of notice of the withdrawal of the claim or counterclaim, request that the Arbitrator order that the withdrawal be with prejudice.

Rule 14.   *Ex Parte* Communications

No Party may have any *ex parte* communication with a neutral Arbitrator regarding any issue related to the Arbitration. Any necessary *ex parte* communication with JAMS, whether before, during or after the Arbitration Hearing, shall be conducted through the Case Manager. The Parties may agree to permit *ex parte* communication between a Party and a non-neutral Arbitrator.

Rule 15.   Arbitrator Selection and Replacement

(a)   Unless the Arbitrator has been previously selected by agreement of the Parties, the Case Manager at the Administrative Conference may attempt to facilitate agreement among the Parties regarding selection of the Arbitrator.

(b)   If the Parties do not agree on an Arbitrator, the Case Manager shall send the Parties a list of at least five (5) Arbitrator candidates in the case of a sole Arbitrator and ten (10) Arbitrator candidates in the case of a tripartite panel. The Case Manager shall also provide each Party with a brief description of the background and experience of each Arbitrator candidate.

(c)   Within seven (7) calendar days of service upon the Parties of the list of names, each Party may strike two (2) names in the case of a sole Arbitrator and three (3) names in the case of a tripartite panel, and shall rank the remaining Arbitrator candidates in order of preference. The remaining Arbitrator candidate with the highest composite ranking shall be appointed the Arbitrator.

(d)   If this process does not yield an Arbitrator or a complete panel, JAMS shall designate the sole Arbitrator or as many members of the tripartite panel as are necessary to complete the panel.

(e)   If a Party fails to respond to the list of Arbitrator candidates within seven (7) calendar days of service by the Parties of the list, the Case Manager shall deem that Party to have accepted all of the Arbitrator candidates.

(f)   Entities whose interests are not adverse with respect to the issues in dispute shall be treated as a single Party for purposes of the Arbitrator selection process. JAMS shall determine whether the interests between entities are adverse for purposes of Arbitrator selection, considering such factors as whether the entities are represented by the same attorney and whether the entities are presenting joint or separate positions at the Arbitration.

(g)   If, for any reason, the Arbitrator who is selected is unable to fulfill the Arbitrator's duties, a successor Arbitrator shall be chosen in accordance with this Rule. If a member of a panel of Arbitrators becomes unable to fulfill his or her duties after the beginning of a Hearing but before the issuance of an Award, a new Arbitrator will be chosen in accordance with this Rule unless, in the case of a tripartite panel, the Parties agree to proceed with the remaining two Arbitrators. JAMS will make the final determination as to whether an Arbitrator is unable to fulfill his or her duties, and that decision shall be final.

(h)   Any disclosures regarding the selected Arbitrator shall be made as required by law or within ten (10) calendar days from the date of appointment. The obligation of the Arbitrator to make all required disclosures continues throughout the Arbitration process.

(i)   At any time during the Arbitration process, a Party may challenge the continued service of an Arbitrator for cause. The challenge must be based upon information that was not available to the Parties at the time the Arbitrator was selected. A challenge for cause must be in writing and exchanged with opposing Parties who may respond within seven (7) days of service of the challenge. JAMS shall make the final determination on such challenge. Such determination shall take into account the materiality of the facts and any prejudice to the parties. That decision will be final.

Rule 16.   Preliminary Conference

At the request of any Party or at the direction of the Arbitrator, a Preliminary Conference shall be conducted with the Parties or their counsel or representatives. The Preliminary Conference may address any or all of the following subjects:

(a)   The exchange of information in accordance with Rule 17 or otherwise;

(b)   The schedule for discovery as permitted by the Rules, as agreed by the Parties or as required or authorized by applicable law;

(c)   The pleadings of the Parties and any agreement to clarify or narrow the issues or structure the Arbitration Hearing;

(d)   The scheduling of the Hearing and any prehearing exchanges of information, exhibits, motions or briefs;

(e)   The attendance of witnesses as contemplated by Rule 21;

(f)   The scheduling of any dispositive motion pursuant to Rule 18;

(g)   The premarking of exhibits; preparation of joint exhibit lists and the resolution of the admissibility of exhibits;

(h)   The form of the Award; and

(i)   Such other matters as may be suggested by the Parties or the Arbitrator.

The Preliminary Conference may be conducted telephonically and may be resumed from time to time as warranted.

Rule 17.   Exchange of Information

(a)   The Parties shall cooperate in good faith in the voluntary, prompt and informal exchange of all non-privileged documents and other information relevant to the dispute or claim immediately after commencement of the Arbitration.

(b)   The Parties shall complete an initial exchange of all relevant, non-privileged documents, including, without limitation, copies of all documents in their possession or control on which they rely in support of their positions, names of individuals whom they may call as witnesses at the Arbitration Hearing, and names of all experts who may be called to testify at the Arbitration Hearing, together with each expert's report that may be introduced at the Arbitration Hearing, within twenty-one (21) calendar days after all pleadings or notice of claims have been received. The Arbitrator may modify these obligations at the Preliminary Conference.

(c)   Each Party may take one deposition of an opposing Party or of one individual under the control of the opposing Party. The Parties shall attempt to agree on the time, location and duration of the deposition, and if the Parties do not agree these issues shall be determined by the Arbitrator. The necessity of additional depositions shall be determined by the Arbitrator based upon the reasonable need for the requested information, the availability of other discovery options and the burdensomeness of the request on the opposing Parties and the witness.

(d)   As they become aware of new documents or information, including experts who may be called upon to testify, all Parties continue to be obligated to provide relevant, non-privileged documents, to supplement their identification of witnesses and experts and to honor any informal agreements or understandings between the Parties regarding documents or information to be exchanged. Documents that have not been previously exchanged, or witnesses and experts not previously identified, may not be considered by the Arbitrator at the Hearing, unless agreed by the Parties or upon a showing of good cause.

(e)   The Parties shall promptly notify the Case Manager when an unresolved dispute exists regarding discovery issues. The Case Manager shall arrange a conference with the Arbitrator, either by telephone or in person, and the Arbitrator shall decide the dispute. With the written consent of all Parties, and in accordance with an agreed written procedure, the Arbitrator may appoint a special master to assist in resolving a discovery dispute.

Rule 18.   Summary Disposition of a Claim or Issue

(a)   The Arbitrator shall decide a Motion for Summary Disposition of a particular claim or issue, either by agreement of all interested Parties or at the request of one Party, provided other interested Parties have reasonable notice to respond to the request.

(b)   The Case Manager shall facilitate the Parties' agreement on a briefing schedule and record for the Motion. If no agreement is reached, the Arbitrator shall set the briefing and Hearing schedule and contents of the record.

Rule 19.   Scheduling of Hearing

(a)   The Arbitrator, after consulting with the Parties that have appeared, shall determine the date and time of the Hearing. The Arbitrator and the Parties shall attempt to schedule consecutive Hearing days if more than one day is necessary.

(b)   If a Party has failed to answer a claim and the Arbitrator reasonably believes that the Party will not participate in the Hearing, the Arbitrator may set the Hearing without consulting with that Party. The non-participating Party shall be served with a Notice of Hearing at least thirty (30) calendar days prior to the scheduled date unless the law of the relevant jurisdiction allows for shorter notice.

Rule 20.   Pre-Hearing Submissions

(a)   Subject to any schedule adopted in the Preliminary Conference (Rule 16), at least fourteen (14) calendar days before the Arbitration Hearing, the Parties shall exchange a list of the witnesses they intend to call, including any experts, a short description of the anticipated testimony of each such witness, an estimate of the length of the witness's direct testimony, and a list of exhibits. In addition, at least fourteen (14) calendar days before the Arbitration Hearing, the Parties shall identify all exhibits intended to be used at the Hearing and exchange copies of such exhibits to the extent that any such exhibit has not been previously exchanged. The Parties should pre-mark exhibits and shall attempt themselves to resolve any disputes regarding the admissibility of exhibits prior to the Hearing. The list of witnesses, with the description and estimate of the length of their testimony and the copies of all exhibits that the Parties intend to use at the Hearing, in pre-marked form, should also be provided to JAMS for transmission to the Arbitrator, whether or not the Parties have stipulated to the admissibility of all such exhibits.

(b)   The Arbitrator may require that each Party submit concise written statements of position, including summaries of the facts and evidence a Party intends to present, discussion of the applicable law and the basis for the requested Award or denial of relief sought. The statements, which may be in the form of a letter, shall be filed with JAMS and served upon the other Parties, at least seven (7) calendar days before the Hearing date. Rebuttal statements or other pre-Hearing written submissions may be permitted or required at the discretion of the Arbitrator.

Rule 21.   Securing Witnesses and Documents for the Arbitration Hearing

At the written request of another Party, all other Parties shall produce for the Arbitration Hearing all specified witnesses in their employ or under their control without need of subpoena. The Arbitrator may issue subpoenas for the attendance of witnesses or the production of documents. Pre-issued subpoenas may be used in jurisdictions which permit them. In the event a Party or a subpoenaed person objects to the production of a witness or other evidence, the Party may file an objection with the Arbitrator, who will promptly rule on the objection, weighing both the burden on the producing Party and the need of the proponent for the witness or other evidence.

Rule 22.   The Arbitration Hearing

(a)   The Arbitrator will ordinarily conduct the Arbitration Hearing in the manner set forth in these Rules. The Arbitrator may vary these procedures if it is determined reasonable and appropriate to do so.

(b)   The Arbitrator shall determine the order of proof, which will generally be similar to that of a court trial.

(c)   The Arbitrator shall require witnesses to testify under oath if requested by any Party, or otherwise in the discretion of the Arbitrator.

(d)   Strict conformity to the rules of evidence is not required, except that the Arbitrator shall apply applicable law relating to privileges and work product. The Arbitrator shall consider evidence that he or she finds relevant and material to the dispute, giving the evidence such weight as is appropriate. The Arbitrator may be guided in that determination by principles contained in the Federal Rules of Evidence or any other applicable rules of evidence. The Arbitrator may limit testimony to exclude evidence that would be immaterial or unduly repetitive, provided that all Parties are afforded the opportunity to present material and relevant evidence.

(e)   The Arbitrator shall receive and consider relevant deposition testimony recorded by transcript or videotape, provided that the other Parties have had the opportunity to attend and cross-examine. The Arbitrator may in his or her discretion consider witness affidavits or other recorded testimony even if the other Parties have not had the opportunity to cross-examine, but will give that evidence only such weight as the Arbitrator deems appropriate.

(f)   The Parties will not offer as evidence, and the Arbitrator shall neither admit into the record nor consider, prior settlement offers by the Parties or statements or recommendations made by a mediator or other person in connection with efforts to resolve the dispute being arbitrated, except to the extent that applicable law permits the admission of such evidence.

(g)   The Hearing or any portion thereof may be conducted telephonically with the agreement of the Parties or in the discretion of the Arbitrator.

(h)   When the Arbitrator determines that all relevant and material evidence and arguments have been presented, the Arbitrator shall declare the Hearing closed. The Arbitrator may defer the closing of the Hearing until a date agreed upon by the Arbitrator and the Parties, to permit the Parties to submit post-Hearing briefs, which may be in the form of a letter, and/or to make closing arguments. If post-Hearing briefs are to be submitted, or closing arguments are to be made, the Hearing shall be deemed closed upon receipt by the Arbitrator of such briefs or at the conclusion of such closing arguments.

(i)   At any time before the Award is rendered, the Arbitrator may, on his or her own initiative or on application of a Party for good cause shown, re-open the Hearing. If the Hearing is re-opened and the re-opening prevents the rendering of the Award within the time limits specified by these Rules, the time limits will be extended for an appropriate period of time.

(j)   The Arbitrator may proceed with the Hearing in the absence of a Party who executed an Arbitration agreement, or who is otherwise bound to arbitrate, and who after receiving notice of the Hearing pursuant to Rule 19, fails to attend. The Arbitrator may not render an Award solely on the basis of the default or absence of the Party, but shall require any Party seeking relief to submit such evidence as the Arbitrator may require for the rendering of an Award. If the Arbitrator reasonably believes that a Party will not attend the Hearing, the Arbitrator may schedule the Hearing as a telephonic Hearing and may receive the evidence necessary to render an Award by affidavit. The notice of Hearing shall specify if it will be in person or telephonic.

(k)   (i) Any Party may arrange for a stenographic or other record be made of the Hearing and shall inform the other Parties in advance of the Hearing. The requesting Party shall bear the cost of such stenographic record. If all other Parties agree to share the cost of the stenographic record, it shall be made available to the Arbitrator and may be used in the proceeding.

(ii) If there is no agreement to share the cost of the stenographic record, it may not be provided to the Arbitrator and may not be used in the proceeding unless the Party arranging for the stenographic record either agrees to provide access to the stenographic record at no charge or on terms that are acceptable to the Parties and the reporting service.

(iii) If the Parties agree to an Optional Arbitration Appeal Procedure (see Rule 34), they shall ensure that a stenographic or other record is made of the Hearing and shall share the cost of that record

(iv) The Parties may agree that the cost of the stenographic record shall or shall not be allocated by the arbitrator in the award.

Rule 23.   Waiver of Hearing

The Parties may agree to waive the oral Hearing and submit the dispute to the Arbitrator for an Award based on written submissions and other evidence as the Parties may agree.

Rule 24.   The Award

(a)   Absent good cause for an extension, and except as provided in Rule 22(i) or 31(d), the Arbitrator shall render the Award within thirty (30) calendar days after the date of the closing of the Hearing (as defined in Rule 22(h)) or, if a Hearing has been waived, within thirty (30) calendar days after the receipt by the Arbitrator of all materials specified by the Parties. The Arbitrator shall provide the Award to the Case Manager for issuance in accordance with this rule.

(b)   Where a panel of Arbitrators has heard the dispute, the decision and Award of a majority of the panel shall constitute the Arbitration Award and shall be binding on the Parties.

(c)   Unless the Parties specify a different standard, in determining the Award the Arbitrator shall be guided by principles of law and equity as applied to the facts found at the Arbitration Hearing. The Arbitrator may grant any remedy or relief that is just and equitable and within the scope of the Parties' agreement, including but not limited to specific performance of a contract.

(d)   In addition to the final Award, the Arbitrator may make other decisions, including interim or partial rulings, orders and Awards.

(e)   Interim Measures. The Arbitrator may take whatever interim measures are deemed necessary, including injunctive relief and measures for the protection or conservation of property and disposition of disposable goods. Such interim measures may take the form of an interim Award, and the Arbitrator may require security for the costs of such measures. Any recourse by a Party to a court for interim or provisional relief shall not be deemed incompatible with the agreement to arbitrate or a waiver of the right to arbitrate.

(f)   In any Award, order or ruling, the Arbitrator may also assess Arbitration fees, Arbitrator compensation and expenses if provided by agreement of the Parties, allowed by applicable law or pursuant to Rule 31(c), in favor of any Party.

(g)   The Award will consist of a written statement signed by the Arbitrator regarding the disposition of each claim and the relief, if any, as to each claim. Unless all Parties agree otherwise, the Award shall also contain a concise written statement of the reasons for the Award.

(h)   After the Award has been rendered, and provided the Parties have complied with Rule 31, the Award shall be issued by serving copies on the Parties. Service may be made by U.S. Mail. It need not be sent certified or registered.

(i)   Within seven (7) calendar days after issuance of the Award, any Party may serve upon the other Parties and on JAMS a request that the Arbitrator correct any computational, typographical or other error in an Award (including the reallocation of fees pursuant to Rule 31(c)), or the Arbitrator may *sua sponte* propose to correct such errors in an Award. A Party opposing such correction shall have seven (7) calendar days in which to file any objection. The Arbitrator may make any necessary and appropriate correction to the Award within fourteen (14) calendar days of receiving a request or seven (7) calendar days after the Arbitrator's proposal to do so. The corrected Award shall be served upon the Parties in the same manner as the Award.

(j)   The Award is considered final, for purposes of either an Optional Arbitration Appeal Procedure pursuant to Rule 34 or a judicial proceeding to enforce, modify or vacate the Award pursuant to Rule 25, fourteen (14) calendar days after service is deemed effective if no request for a correction is made, or as of the effective date of service of a corrected Award.

Rule 25.   Enforcement of the Award

Proceedings to enforce, confirm, modify or vacate an Award will be controlled by and conducted in conformity with the Federal Arbitration Act, 9 U.S.C. Sec 1 *et seq.* or applicable state law.

Rule 26.   Confidentiality and Privacy

(a)   The Case Manager and the Arbitrator shall maintain the confidential nature of the Arbitration proceeding and the Award, including the Hearing, except as necessary in connection with a judicial challenge to or enforcement of an Award, or unless otherwise required by law or judicial decision.

(b)   The Arbitrator may issue orders to protect the confidentiality of proprietary information, trade secrets or other sensitive information.

(c)   Subject to the discretion of the Arbitrator or agreement of the Parties, any person having a direct interest in the Arbitration may attend the Arbitration Hearing. The Arbitrator may exclude any non-Party from any part of a Hearing.

Rule 27.   Waiver

(a)   If a Party becomes aware of a violation of or failure to comply with these Rules and fails promptly to object in writing, the objection will be deemed waived, unless the Arbitrator determines that waiver will cause substantial injustice or hardship.

(b)   If any Party becomes aware of information that could be the basis of a challenge for cause to the continued service of the Arbitrator, such challenge must be made promptly, in writing, to the Arbitrator or JAMS. Failure to do so shall constitute a waiver of any objection to continued service by the Arbitrator.

Rule 28.   Settlement and Consent Award

(a)   The Parties may agree, at any stage of the Arbitration process, to submit the case to JAMS for mediation. The JAMS mediator assigned to the case may not be the Arbitrator or a member of the Appeal Panel, unless the Parties so agree pursuant to Rule 28(b).

(b)   The Parties may agree to seek the assistance of the Arbitrator in reaching settlement. By their written agreement to submit the matter to the Arbitrator for settlement assistance, the Parties will be deemed to have agreed that the assistance of the Arbitrator in such settlement efforts will not disqualify the Arbitrator from continuing to serve as Arbitrator if settlement is not reached; nor shall such assistance be argued to a reviewing court as the basis for vacating or modifying an Award.

(c)   If, at any stage of the Arbitration process, all Parties agree upon a settlement of the issues in dispute and request the Arbitrator to embody the agreement in a Consent Award, the Arbitrator shall comply with such request unless the Arbitrator believes the terms of the agreement are illegal or undermine the integrity of the Arbitration process. If the Arbitrator is concerned about the possible consequences of the proposed Consent Award, he or she shall inform the Parties of that concern and may request additional specific information from the Parties regarding the proposed Consent Award. The Arbitrator may refuse to enter the proposed Consent Award and may withdraw from the case.

Rule 29.   Sanctions

The Arbitrator may order appropriate sanctions for failure of a Party to comply with its obligations under any of these Rules. These sanctions may include, but are not limited to, assessment of costs, exclusion of certain evidence, or in extreme cases ruling on an issue submitted to Arbitration adversely to the Party who has failed to comply.

Rule 30.   Disqualification of the Arbitrator as a Witness or Party and Exclusion of Liability

(a)   The Parties may not call the Arbitrator, the Case Manager or any other JAMS employee or agent as a witness or as an expert in any pending or subsequent litigation or other proceeding involving the Parties and relating to the dispute that is the subject of the Arbitration. The Arbitrator, Case Manager and other JAMS employees and agents are also incompetent to testify as witnesses or experts in any such proceeding.

(b)   The Parties shall defend and/or pay the cost (including any attorneys' fees) of defending the Arbitrator, Case Manager and/or JAMS from any subpoenas from outside Parties arising from the Arbitration.

(c)   The Parties agree that neither the Arbitrator, Case Manager nor JAMS is a necessary Party in any litigation or other proceeding relating to the Arbitration or the subject matter of the Arbitration, and neither the Arbitrator, Case Manager nor JAMS, including its employees or agents, shall be liable to any Party for any act or omission in connection with any Arbitration conducted under these Rules, including but not limited to a recusal by the Arbitrator.

Rule 31.   Fees

(a)   Each Party shall pay its pro-rata share of JAMS fees and expenses as set forth in the JAMS fee schedule in effect at the time of the commencement of the Arbitration, unless the Parties agree on a different allocation of fees and expenses. JAMS agreement to render services is jointly with the Party and the attorney or other representative of the Party in the Arbitration.

(b)   JAMS requires that the Parties deposit the fees and expenses for the Arbitration prior to the Hearing and may preclude a Party that has failed to deposit its pro-rata or agreed-upon share of the fees and expenses from offering evidence of any affirmative claim at the Hearing. JAMS may waive the deposit requirement upon a showing of good cause.

(c)   The Parties are jointly and severally liable for the payment of the fees and expenses of JAMS. In the event that one Party has paid more than its share of the fees, the Arbitrator may award against any other Party any costs or fees that such Party owes with respect to the Arbitration.

(d)   JAMS may defer issuance of an Arbitration Award rendered by the Arbitrator if any and/or all outstanding invoices are not paid. If JAMS declines to issue an Arbitration Award in accordance with this Rule, it shall not be issued to any Party.

(e)   Entities whose interests are not adverse with respect to the issues in dispute shall be treated as a single Party for purposes of JAMS' assessment of fees. JAMS shall determine whether the interests between entities are adverse for purpose of fees, considering such factors as whether the entities are represented by the same attorney and whether the entities are presenting joint or separate positions at the Arbitration.

Rule 32.   Bracketed (or High-Low) Arbitration Option

(a)   At any time before the issuance of the Arbitration Award, the Parties may agree, in writing, on minimum and maximum amounts of damages that may be awarded on each claim or on all claims in the aggregate. The Parties shall promptly notify the Case Manager, and provide to the Case Manager a copy of their written agreement setting forth the agreed-upon maximum and minimum amounts.

(b)   The Case Manager shall not inform the Arbitrator of the agreement to proceed with this option or of the agreed-upon minimum and maximum levels without the consent of the Parties.

(c)   The Arbitrator shall render the Award in accordance with Rule 24.

(d)   In the event that the Award of the Arbitrator is in between the agreed-upon minimum and maximum amounts, the Award shall become final as is. In the event that the Award is below the agreed-upon minimum amount, the final Award issued shall be corrected to reflect the agreed-upon minimum amount. In the event that the Award is above the agreed-upon maximum amount, the final Award issued shall be corrected to reflect the agreed-upon maximum amount.

Rule 33.   Final Offer (or Baseball) Arbitration Option

(a)   Upon agreement of the Parties to use the option set forth in this Rule, at least seven (7) calendar days before the Arbitration Hearing, the Parties shall exchange and provide to the Case Manager written proposals for the amount of money damages they would offer or demand, as applicable, and that they believe to be appropriate based on the standard set forth in Rule 24 (c). The Case Manager shall promptly provide a copy of the Parties' proposals to the Arbitrator, unless the Parties agree that they should not be provided to the Arbitrator. At any time prior to the close of the Arbitration Hearing, the Parties may exchange revised written proposals or demands, which shall supersede all prior proposals. The revised written proposals shall be provided to the Case Manager who shall promptly provide them to the Arbitrator, unless the Parties agree otherwise.

(b)   If the Arbitrator has been informed of the written proposals, in rendering the Award the Arbitrator shall choose between the Parties' last proposals, selecting the proposal that the Arbitrator finds most reasonable and appropriate in light of the standard set forth in Rule 24(c). This provision modifies Rule 24(g) in that no written statement of reasons shall accompany the Award.

(c)   If the Arbitrator has not been informed of the written proposals, the Arbitrator shall render the Award as if pursuant to Rule 24, except that the Award shall thereafter be corrected to conform to the closest of the last proposals, and the closest of the last proposals will become the Award.

(d)   Other than as provided herein, the provisions of Rule 24 shall be applicable.

Rule 34.   Optional Arbitration Appeal Procedure

At any time before the Award becomes final pursuant to Rule 24, the Parties may agree to the JAMS Optional Arbitration Appeal Procedure. All Parties must agree in writing for such procedure to be effective. Once a Party has agreed to the Optional Arbitration Appeal Procedure, it cannot unilaterally withdraw from it, unless it withdraws, pursuant to Rule 13, from the Arbitration.

◆ APPENDIX I ◆

The text of The Code of Ethics For Arbitrators in Commercial Disputes—2004 Revision can be found here:

https://www.americanbar.org/content/dam/aba/migrated/dispute/commercial_disputes.pdf

✦ APPENDIX J ✦

Selected ABA Model Rules of Professional Conduct*

PREAMBLE AND SCOPE:
A LAWYER'S RESPONSIBILITIES

[1] A lawyer, as a member of the legal profession, is a representative of clients, an officer of the legal system and a public citizen having special responsibility for the quality of justice.

[2] As a representative of clients, a lawyer performs various functions. As advisor, a lawyer provides a client with an informed understanding of the client's legal rights and obligations and explains their practical implications. As advocate, a lawyer zealously asserts the client's position under the rules of the adversary system. As negotiator, a lawyer seeks a result advantageous to the client but consistent with requirements of honest dealings with others. As an evaluator, a lawyer acts by examining a client's legal affairs and reporting about them to the client or to others.

[3] In addition to these representational functions, a lawyer may serve as a third-party neutral, a nonrepresentational role helping the parties to resolve a dispute or other matter. Some of these Rules apply directly to lawyers who are or have served as third-party neutrals. See, e.g., Rules 1.12 and 2.4. In addition, there are Rules that apply to lawyers who are not active in the practice of law or to practicing lawyers even when they are acting in a nonprofessional capacity. For example, a lawyer who commits fraud in the conduct of a business is subject to discipline for engaging in conduct involving dishonesty, fraud, deceit or misrepresentation. See Rule 8.4.

[4] In all professional functions a lawyer should be competent, prompt and diligent. A lawyer should maintain communication with a client concerning the representation. A lawyer should keep in confidence information relating to representation of a client except so far as disclosure is required or permitted by the Rules of Professional Conduct or other law.

[5] A lawyer's conduct should conform to the requirements of the law, both in professional service to clients and in the lawyer's business and personal affairs. A lawyer should use the law's procedures only for legitimate purposes and not to harass or intimidate others. A lawyer should demonstrate respect for the legal system and for those who serve it, including judges, other lawyers and public officials. While it is a lawyer's duty, when necessary, to challenge the rectitude of official action, it is also a lawyer's duty to uphold legal process.

[6] As a public citizen, a lawyer should seek improvement of the law, access to the legal system, the administration of justice and the quality of service rendered by the legal profession. As a member of a learned profession, a lawyer should cultivate knowledge of the law beyond its use for clients, employ that knowledge in reform of the law and work to strengthen legal education. In addition, a lawyer should further the public's understanding of and confidence in the rule of law and the justice system because legal institutions in a constitutional democracy depend on popular participation and support to maintain their authority. A lawyer should be mindful of deficiencies in the administration of justice and of the fact that the poor, and sometimes persons who are not poor, cannot afford adequate legal assistance. Therefore, all lawyers should devote professional time and resources and use civic influence to ensure equal access to our system of justice for all those who because of economic or social barriers cannot afford

---

* Reprinted with the permission of the American Bar Association.

or secure adequate legal counsel. A lawyer should aid the legal profession in pursuing these objectives and should help the bar regulate itself in the public interest.

[7] Many of a lawyer's professional responsibilities are prescribed in the Rules of Professional Conduct, as well as substantive and procedural law. However, a lawyer is also guided by personal conscience and the approbation of professional peers. A lawyer should strive to attain the highest level of skill, to improve the law and the legal profession and to exemplify the legal profession's ideals of public service.

[8] A lawyer's responsibilities as a representative of clients, an officer of the legal system and a public citizen are usually harmonious. Thus, when an opposing party is well represented, a lawyer can be a zealous advocate on behalf of a client and at the same time assume that justice is being done. So also, a lawyer can be sure that preserving client confidences ordinarily serves the public interest because people are more likely to seek legal advice, and thereby heed their legal obligations, when they know their communications will be private.

[9] In the nature of law practice, however, conflicting responsibilities are encountered. Virtually all difficult ethical problems arise from conflict between a lawyer's responsibilities to clients, to the legal system and to the lawyer's own interest in remaining an ethical person while earning a satisfactory living. The Rules of Professional Conduct often prescribe terms for resolving such conflicts. Within the framework of these Rules, however, many difficult issues of professional discretion can arise. Such issues must be resolved through the exercise of sensitive professional and moral judgment guided by the basic principles underlying the Rules. These principles include the lawyer's obligation zealously to protect and pursue a client's legitimate interests, within the bounds of the law, while maintaining a professional, courteous and civil attitude toward all persons involved in the legal system.

[10] The legal profession is largely self-governing. Although other professions also have been granted powers of self-government, the legal profession is unique in this respect because of the close relationship between the profession and the processes of government and law enforcement. This connection is manifested in the fact that ultimate authority over the legal profession is vested largely in the courts.

[11] To the extent that lawyers meet the obligations of their professional calling, the occasion for government regulation is obviated. Self-regulation also helps maintain the legal profession's independence from government domination. An independent legal profession is an important force in preserving government under law, for abuse of legal authority is more readily challenged by a profession whose members are not dependent on government for the right to practice.

[12] The legal profession's relative autonomy carries with it special responsibilities of self-government. The profession has a responsibility to assure that its regulations are conceived in the public interest and not in furtherance of parochial or self-interested concerns of the bar. Every lawyer is responsible for observance of the Rules of Professional Conduct. A

lawyer should also aid in securing their observance by other lawyers. Neglect of these responsibilities compromises the independence of the profession and the public interest which it serves.

[13] Lawyers play a vital role in the preservation of society. The fulfillment of this role requires an understanding by lawyers of their relationship to our legal system. The Rules of Professional Conduct, when properly applied, serve to define that relationship.

SCOPE

[14] The Rules of Professional Conduct are rules of reason. They should be interpreted with reference to the purposes of legal representation and of the law itself. Some of the Rules are imperatives, cast in the terms "shall" or "shall not." These define proper conduct for purposes of professional discipline. Others, generally cast in the term "may," are permissive and define areas under the Rules in which the lawyer has discretion to exercise professional judgment. No disciplinary action should be taken when the lawyer chooses not to act or acts within the bounds of such discretion. Other Rules define the nature of relationships between the lawyer and others. The Rules are thus partly obligatory and disciplinary and partly constitutive and descriptive in that they define a lawyer's professional role. Many of the Comments use the term "should." Comments do not add obligations to the Rules but provide guidance for practicing in compliance with the Rules.

[15] The Rules presuppose a larger legal context shaping the lawyer's role. That context includes court rules and statutes relating to matters of licensure, laws defining specific obligations of lawyers and substantive and procedural law in general. The Comments are sometimes used to alert lawyers to their responsibilities under such other law.

[16] Compliance with the Rules, as with all law in an open society, depends primarily upon understanding and voluntary compliance, secondarily upon reinforcement by peer and public opinion and finally, when necessary, upon enforcement through disciplinary proceedings. The Rules do not, however, exhaust the moral and ethical considerations that should inform a lawyer, for no worthwhile human activity can be completely defined by legal rules. The Rules simply provide a framework for the ethical practice of law.

[17] Furthermore, for purposes of determining the lawyer's authority and responsibility, principles of substantive law external to these Rules determine whether a client-lawyer relationship exists. Most of the duties flowing from the client-lawyer relationship attach only after the client has requested the lawyer to render legal services and the lawyer has agreed to do so. But there are some duties, such as that of confidentiality under Rule 1.6, that attach when the lawyer agrees to consider whether a client-lawyer relationship shall be established. See Rule 1.18. Whether a client-lawyer relationship exists for any specific purpose can depend on the circumstances and may be a question of fact.

[18] Under various legal provisions, including constitutional, statutory and common law, the responsibilities of government lawyers may include authority concerning legal matters that ordinarily reposes in the client in private client-lawyer relationships. For example, a lawyer for a government agency may have authority on behalf of the government to decide upon settlement or whether to appeal from an adverse judgment. Such authority in

various respects is generally vested in the attorney general and the state's attorney in state government, and their federal counterparts, and the same may be true of other government law officers. Also, lawyers under the supervision of these officers may be authorized to represent several government agencies in intragovernmental legal controversies in circumstances where a private lawyer could not represent multiple private clients. These Rules do not abrogate any such authority.

[19] Failure to comply with an obligation or prohibition imposed by a Rule is a basis for invoking the disciplinary process. The Rules presuppose that disciplinary assessment of a lawyer's conduct will be made on the basis of the facts and circumstances as they existed at the time of the conduct in question and in recognition of the fact that a lawyer often has to act upon uncertain or incomplete evidence of the situation. Moreover, the Rules presuppose that whether or not discipline should be imposed for a violation, and the severity of a sanction, depend on all the circumstances, such as the willfulness and seriousness of the violation, extenuating factors and whether there have been previous violations.

[20] Violation of a Rule should not itself give rise to a cause of action against a lawyer nor should it create any presumption in such a case that a legal duty has been breached. In addition, violation of a Rule does not necessarily warrant any other nondisciplinary remedy, such as disqualification of a lawyer in pending litigation. The Rules are designed to provide guidance to lawyers and to provide a structure for regulating conduct through disciplinary agencies. They are not designed to be a basis for civil liability. Furthermore, the purpose of the Rules can be subverted when they are invoked by opposing parties as procedural weapons. The fact that a Rule is a just basis for a lawyer's self-assessment, or for sanctioning a lawyer under the administration of a disciplinary authority, does not imply that an antagonist in a collateral proceeding or transaction has standing to seek enforcement of the Rule. Nevertheless, since the Rules do establish standards of conduct by lawyers, a lawyer's violation of a Rule may be evidence of breach of the applicable standard of conduct.

[21] The Comment accompanying each Rule explains and illustrates the meaning and purpose of the Rule. The Preamble and this note on Scope provide general orientation. The Comments are intended as guides to interpretation, but the text of each Rule is authoritative.

RULE 1.1 COMPETENCE

A lawyer shall provide competent representation to a client. Competent representation requires the legal knowledge, skill, thoroughness and preparation reasonably necessary for the representation.

RULE 1.2 SCOPE OF REPRESENTATION AND ALLOCATION OF AUTHORITY BETWEEN CLIENT AND LAWYER

(a) Subject to paragraphs (c) and (d), a lawyer shall abide by a client's decisions concerning the objectives of representation and, as required by Rule 1.4, shall consult with the client as to the means by which they are to be pursued. A lawyer may take such action on behalf of the client as is impliedly authorized to carry out the representation. A lawyer shall abide by a client's decision whether to settle a matter. In a criminal case, the lawyer shall abide by the client's decision, after consultation with the lawyer, as to a plea to be entered, whether to waive jury trial and whether the client will testify.

(b) A lawyer's representation of a client, including representation by appointment, does not constitute an endorsement of the client's political, economic, social or moral views or activities.

(c) A lawyer may limit the scope of the representation if the limitation is reasonable under the circumstances and the client gives informed consent.

(d) A lawyer shall not counsel a client to engage, or assist a client, in conduct that the lawyer knows is criminal or fraudulent, but a lawyer may discuss the legal consequences of any proposed course of conduct with a client and may counsel or assist a client to make a good faith effort to determine the validity, scope, meaning or application of the law.

RULE 1.3 DILIGENCE

A lawyer shall act with reasonable diligence and promptness in representing a client.

RULE 1.4 COMMUNICATION

(a) A lawyer shall:

(1) promptly inform the client of any decision or circumstance with respect to which the client's informed consent, as defined in Rule 1.0(e), is required by these Rules;

(2) reasonably consult with the client about the means by which the client's objectives are to be accomplished;

(3) keep the client reasonably informed about the status of the matter;

(4) promptly comply with reasonable requests for information; and

(5) consult with the client about any relevant limitation on the lawyer's conduct when the lawyer knows that the client expects assistance not permitted by the Rules of Professional Conduct or other law.

(b) A lawyer shall explain a matter to the extent reasonably necessary to permit the client to make informed decisions regarding the representation.

RULE 1.6: CONFIDENTIALITY OF INFORMATION

(a) A lawyer shall not reveal information relating to the representation of a client unless the client gives informed consent, the disclosure is impliedly authorized in order to carry out the representation or the disclosure is permitted by paragraph (b).

(b) A lawyer may reveal information relating to the representation of a client to the extent the lawyer reasonably believes necessary:

(1) to prevent reasonably certain death or substantial bodily harm;

(2) to prevent the client from committing a crime or fraud that is reasonably certain to result in substantial injury to the financial interests or property of another and in furtherance of which the client has used or is using the lawyer's services;

(3) to prevent, mitigate or rectify substantial injury to the financial interests or property of another that is reasonably certain to result or has resulted from the client's commission of a crime or fraud in furtherance of which the client has used the lawyer's services;

(4) to secure legal advice about the lawyer's compliance with these Rules;

(5) to establish a claim or defense on behalf of the lawyer in a controversy between the lawyer and the client, to establish a defense to a criminal charge or civil claim against the lawyer based upon conduct in which the client was involved, or to respond to allegations in any proceeding concerning the lawyer's representation of the client; or

(6) to comply with other law or a court order.

RULE 1.7 CONFLICT OF INTEREST: CURRENT CLIENTS

(a) Except as provided in paragraph (b), a lawyer shall not represent a client if the representation involves a concurrent conflict of interest. A concurrent conflict of interest exists if:

(1) the representation of one client will be directly adverse to another client; or

(2) there is a significant risk that the representation of one or more clients will be materially limited by the lawyer's responsibilities to another client, a former client or a third person or by a personal interest of the lawyer.

(b) Notwithstanding the existence of a concurrent conflict of interest under paragraph (a), a lawyer may represent a client if:

(1) the lawyer reasonably believes that the lawyer will be able to provide competent and diligent representation to each affected client;

(2) the representation is not prohibited by law;

(3) the representation does not involve the assertion of a claim by one client against another client represented by the lawyer in the same litigation or other proceeding before a tribunal; and

(4) each affected client gives informed consent, confirmed in writing.

RULE 1.9 DUTIES TO FORMER CLIENTS

(a) A lawyer who has formerly represented a client in a matter shall not thereafter represent another person in the same or a substantially related matter in which that person's interests are materially adverse to the interests of the former client unless the former client gives informed consent, confirmed in writing.

(b) A lawyer shall not knowingly represent a person in the same or a substantially related matter in which a firm with which the lawyer formerly was associated had previously represented a client

(1) whose interests are materially adverse to that person; and

(2) about whom the lawyer had acquired information protected by Rules 1.6 and 1.9(c) that is material to the matter; unless the former client gives informed consent, confirmed in writing.

(c) A lawyer who has formerly represented a client in a matter or whose present or former firm has formerly represented a client in a matter shall not thereafter:

(1) use information relating to the representation to the disadvantage of the former client except as these Rules would permit or require with respect to a client, or when the information has become generally known; or

(2) reveal information relating to the representation except as these Rules would permit or require with respect to a client.

RULE 1.12 FORMER JUDGE, ARBITRATOR, MEDIATOR
OR OTHER THIRD-PARTY NEUTRAL

(a) Except as stated in paragraph (d), a lawyer shall not represent anyone in connection with a matter in which the lawyer participated personally and substantially as a judge or other adjudicative officer or law clerk to such a person or as an arbitrator, mediator or other third-party neutral, unless all parties to the proceeding give informed consent, confirmed in writing.

(b) A lawyer shall not negotiate for employment with any person who is involved as a party or as lawyer for a party in a matter in which the lawyer is participating personally and substantially as a judge or other adjudicative officer or as an arbitrator, mediator or other third-party neutral. A lawyer serving as a law clerk to a judge or other adjudicative officer may negotiate for employment with a party or lawyer involved in a matter in which the clerk is participating personally and substantially, but only after the lawyer has notified the judge or other adjudicative officer.

(c) If a lawyer is disqualified by paragraph (a), no lawyer in a firm with which that lawyer is associated may knowingly undertake or continue representation in the matter unless:

(1) the disqualified lawyer is timely screened from any participation in the matter and is apportioned no part of the fee therefrom; and

(2) written notice is promptly given to the parties and any appropriate tribunal to enable them to ascertain compliance with the provisions of this rule.

(d) An arbitrator selected as a partisan of a party in a multimember arbitration panel is not prohibited from subsequently representing that party.

RULE 1.13: ORGANIZATION AS CLIENT

(a) A lawyer employed or retained by an organization represents the organization acting through its duly authorized constituents.

(b) If a lawyer for an organization knows that an officer, employee or other person associated with the organization is engaged in action, intends to act or refuses to act in a matter related to the representation that is a violation of a legal obligation to the organization, or a violation of law that reasonably might be imputed to the organization, and that is likely to result in substantial injury to the organization, then the lawyer shall proceed as is reasonably necessary in the best interest of the organization. Unless the lawyer reasonably believes that it is not necessary in the best interest of the organization to do so, the lawyer shall refer the matter to higher authority in the organization, including, if warranted by the circumstances to the highest authority that can act on behalf of the organization as determined by applicable law.

(c) Except as provided in paragraph (d), if

(1) despite the lawyer's efforts in accordance with paragraph (b) the highest authority that can act on behalf of the organization insists upon or fails to address in a timely and appropriate manner an action, or a refusal to act, that is clearly a violation of law, and
(2) the lawyer reasonably believes that the violation is reasonably certain to result in substantial injury to the organization, then the lawyer may reveal information relating to the representation whether or not Rule 1.6 permits such disclosure, but only if and to the extent the lawyer reasonably believes necessary to prevent substantial injury to the organization.

(d) Paragraph (c) shall not apply with respect to information relating to a lawyer's representation of an organization to investigate an alleged violation of law, or to defend the organization or an officer, employee or other constituent associated with the organization against a claim arising out of an alleged violation of law.

(e) A lawyer who reasonably believes that he or she has been discharged because of the lawyer's actions taken pursuant to paragraphs (b) or (c), or who withdraws under circumstances that require or permit the lawyer to take action under either of those paragraphs, shall proceed as the lawyer reasonably believes necessary to assure that the organization's highest authority is informed of the lawyer's discharge or withdrawal.

RULE 2.4 LAWYER SERVING AS THIRD-PARTY NEUTRAL

(a) A lawyer serves as a third-party neutral when the lawyer assists two or more persons who are not clients of the lawyer to reach a resolution of a dispute or other matter that has arisen between them. Service as a third-party neutral may include service as an arbitrator, a mediator or in such other capacity as will enable the lawyer to assist the parties to resolve the matter.

(b) A lawyer serving as a third-party neutral shall inform unrepresented parties that the lawyer is not representing them. When the lawyer knows or reasonably should know that a party does not understand the lawyer's role in the matter, the lawyer shall explain the difference between the lawyer's role as a third-party neutral and a lawyer's role as one who represents a client.

RULE 3.3 CANDOR TOWARD THE TRIBUNAL

(a) A lawyer shall not knowingly:

(1) make a false statement of fact or law to a tribunal or fail to correct a false statement of material fact or law previously made to the tribunal by the lawyer;

(2) fail to disclose to the tribunal legal authority in the controlling jurisdiction known to the lawyer to be directly adverse to the position of the client and not disclosed by opposing counsel; or

(3) offer evidence that the lawyer knows to be false. If a lawyer, the lawyer's client, or a witness called by the lawyer, has offered material evidence and the lawyer comes to know of its falsity, the lawyer shall take reasonable remedial measures, including, if necessary, disclosure to the tribunal. A lawyer may refuse to offer evidence, other than the testimony of a defendant in a criminal matter, that the lawyer reasonably believes is false.

(b) A lawyer who represents a client in an adjudicative proceeding and who knows that a person intends to engage, is engaging or has engaged in criminal or fraudulent conduct related to the proceeding shall take reasonable remedial measures, including, if necessary, disclosure to the tribunal.

(c) The duties stated in paragraphs (a) and (b) continue to the conclusion of the proceeding, and apply even if compliance requires disclosure of information otherwise protected by Rule 1.6.

(d) In an ex parte proceeding, a lawyer shall inform the tribunal of all material facts known to the lawyer that will enable the tribunal to make an informed decision, whether or not the facts are adverse.

RULE 3.4 FAIRNESS TO OPPOSING PARTY AND COUNSEL

A lawyer shall not:

(a) unlawfully obstruct another party' s access to evidence or unlawfully alter, destroy or conceal a document or other material having potential evidentiary value. A lawyer shall not counsel or assist another person to do any such act;

(b) falsify evidence, counsel or assist a witness to testify falsely, or offer an inducement to a witness that is prohibited by law;

(c) knowingly disobey an obligation under the rules of a tribunal except for an open refusal based on an assertion that no valid obligation exists;

(d) in pretrial procedure, make a frivolous discovery request or fail to make reasonably diligent effort to comply with a legally proper discovery request by an opposing party;

(e) in trial, allude to any matter that the lawyer does not reasonably believe is relevant or that will not be supported by admissible evidence, assert personal knowledge of facts in issue except when testifying as a witness, or state a personal opinion as to the justness of a cause, the credibility of a witness, the culpability of a civil litigant or the guilt or innocence of an accused; or

(f) request a person other than a client to refrain from voluntarily giving relevant information to another party unless:

(1) the person is a relative or an employee or other agent of a client; and
(2) the lawyer reasonably believes that the person's interests will not be adversely affected by refraining from giving such information.

RULE 3.5 IMPARTIALITY AND DECORUM OF THE TRIBUNAL

A lawyer shall not:

(a) seek to influence a judge, juror, prospective juror or other official by means prohibited by law;

(b) communicate ex parte with such a person during the proceeding unless authorized to do so by law or court order;

(c) communicate with a juror or prospective juror after discharge of the jury if:

(1) the communication is prohibited by law or court order;
(2) the juror has made known to the lawyer a desire not to communicate; or
(3) the communication involves misrepresentation, coercion, duress or harassment; or

(d) engage in conduct intended to disrupt a tribunal.

RULE 4.1 TRUTHFULNESS IN STATEMENTS TO OTHERS

In the course of representing a client a lawyer shall not knowingly:

(a) make a false statement of material fact or law to a third person; or

(b) fail to disclose a material fact to a third person when disclosure is necessary to avoid assisting a criminal or fraudulent act by a client, unless disclosure is prohibited by Rule 1.6.

RULE 4.3 DEALING WITH UNREPRESENTED PERSON

In dealing on behalf of a client with a person who is not represented by counsel, a lawyer shall not state or imply that the lawyer is disinterested. When the lawyer knows or reasonably should know that the unrepresented person misunderstands the lawyer's role in the matter, the lawyer shall make reasonable efforts to correct the misunderstanding. The lawyer shall not give legal advice to an unrepresented person, other than the advice to secure counsel, if the lawyer knows or reasonably should know that the interests of such a person are or have a reasonable possibility of being in conflict with the interests of the client.

RULE 4.4 RESPECT FOR RIGHTS OF THIRD PERSONS

(a) In representing a client, a lawyer shall not use means that have no substantial purpose other than to embarrass, delay, or burden a third person, or use methods of obtaining evidence that violate the legal rights of such a person.

(b) A lawyer who receives a document relating to the representation of the lawyer's client and knows or reasonably should know that the document was inadvertently sent shall promptly notify the sender.

◆APPENDIX K◆

Organizaions Offering ADR Services

ORGANIZATION	LOCATION AND CONTACT INFORMATION	TYPES OF DISPUTES
EASTERN UNITED STATES		
American Arbitration Association	www.adr.org New York, N.Y (212) 484-4000 Boston, Mass. (617) 451-6600 Atlanta, Ga. (404) 325-0101 Miami, Fla. (305) 358-7777	General civil
Arbitration Forums Inc.	www.arb.file.org Tampa, Fla. (813) 931-4004	Insurance claims
Clean Sites	Alexandria, Va. (703) 683-8522	Environmental
JAMS, Inc.	www.jamsadr.com Boston, Mass. (617) 228-0200 New York, N.Y. (212) 751-2700 Washington, D.C. (202) 942-9180 Atlanta, Ga. (213) 620-1133	General civil
International Centre for Settlement of investment Disputes (Public International Organization)	www.worldbank.org Washington, D.C. (202) 477-1234	International Investment
Resolution Resources Inc.	www.clrp.com Atlanta, Ga. (404) 215-9800	General civil
World Wildlife Fund	www.worldwildlife.org Washington, D.C. (202) 293-4800	Environmental, natural resources

ORGANIZATION	LOCATION AND CONTACT INFORMATION	TYPES OF DISPUTES
CENTRAL UNITED STATES		
ADR Systems of America, LLC	www.adrsystems.com e-mail: adrsystems@aol.com Chicago, Illinois (312) 960-2260	General civil
American Arbitration	www.adr.org Chicago, Ill (312) 616-6560 Denver, Colorado(303) 831-0823 Cincinnati, Ohio (513) 241-8434 Minneapolis, Minnesota (612) 332-6545 St. Louis, Missouri (314) 621-7175	General civil
Center for Resolution of Disputes	ww.cfrdemediation.com Cincinnati, Ohio (513) 721-4466	Private and public disputes
Chicago International Dispute Resolution Association (CIDRA)	www.cidra.org Chicago, Illinois (312) 409-1373	International
Global solutions	e-mail: globalbohn.msn.com Inverness, Illinois (847) 358-8856	Commerical and International

JAMS, Inc.	Chicago, Illinois (312) 739-0200 www.jams.com	General civil
	Indianapolis, Indiana (317) 231-6320 www.vbradr.com	
	Denver, Colorado (303) 534-1254 www.jamsadr.com	
	Dallas, Texas (214) 744-5267 www.jamsadr.com	
	Houston, Texas (713) 651-1400 www.jamsadr.com	
Judicial Dispute Resolution, Inc.	e-mail: jdrinc@jdrinc.com Chicago, Illinois (312) 917-2888	General civil
Mediation Research and Education Project, Inc.	www.mrep.org Chicago, Ill (810) 356-0870	Coal industry, manufacturing, communications, education

ORGANIZATION	LOCATION AND CONTACT INFORMATION	TYPES OF DISPUTES
WESTERN UNITED STATES		
American Arbitration Association	www.adr.org San Francisco, California (415) 981-3901 Los Angeles, California (213) 383-6516 Seattle, Washington (206) 622-6435	General civil
CDR Associates	www.mediate.org Boulder, Colo. (303) 442-7367	Commercial, government
JAMS, Inc.	www.jamsadr.org San Francisco, California (415) 982-5267 Los Angeles, California (213) 620-1133 Portland, Oregon (800) 626-5267 Tacoma, Washington (206) 627-3059 Seattle, Washington (206) 622-5267	General civil
Judicial Arbiter Group, Inc.	www.jaginc.com Colorado Springs, Colorado (719) 473-8282 Denver, Colorado (303) 572-1919	General civil
United States Arbitration and Mediation, Inc.;	www.usamwa.com Seattle, Washington (206) 467-0794	Commercial, tort

ORGANIZATION	CONTACT INFORMATION	PRINCIPLE SERVICES
NONPROFIT ORGANIZATIONS THAT STUDY AND PROMOTE ADR		
ABA Section of Dispute Resolution 740 15th Street, N.W. Washington, DC 20005	www.abanet.org/dispute e-mail: dispute@abanet.org (202) 662-1680	ADR services to ABA members and general public
Association for Conflict Resolution 1015 18th St. N.W. Washington, DC 20036	www.acresolution.org info@acresolution.org (202) 464-9700	
CPR Institute for Dispute Resolution 366 Madison Avenue New York, NY 10017	www.cpradr.org (212) 949-6490	Promotes ADR through corporate policy statements
American Arbitration Association 1633 Broadway New York, NY 10020	www.adr.org e-mail: usadrpub@arb.com (212) 484-4000	ADR publications, training, meetings, and seminars.
Center for Analysis of Alternative dispute Resolution Systems 11 E. Adams St. Suite 500 Chicago, IL 60603	www.caadrs.org e-mail: caadrs@caadrs.org (312) 922-6475, ext. 924	Conducts studies of the effectiveness of court-sponsored ADR programs
Center for Conflict Resolution 11 E. Adams St. Suite 500 Chicago, IL 60603	www.caads.org (312) 922-6464	ADR training and mediation center

◆APPENDIX L ◆
Online Dispute Resolution Organizations

Unless otherwise indicated below, the listed websites of ODR service providers were active as of June, 2003.

Better Business Bureau Online (http://www.bbbonline.org)

ClickNSettle.com (http://www.clicknsettle.com)

CPR Institute for Dispute Resolution (http://www.cpradr.org)

Cyberarbitration (planned) (http://www.cyberarbitration.com)

Cybercourt (planned) (http://www.cybercourt.com)

Cybersettle (http://www.cybersettle.com)

The Domain Magistrate (http://www.domainmagistrate.com)

ECODIR (http://www.ecodir.org)

E-Mediation (also ODR.NL)(planned)

(http://www.e-mediation.nl)

e-Mediator (http//www.consensus.uk.com/e-mediator.html)

eResolution (htp://www.eresolution.com)

FordJourney (http://www.arbitrators.org/fordjourney/INDEX.HTM)

FSM (http://www.fsm.de)

iCourthouse (http://www.icourthouse.com)

iLevel (http://www.ilevel.com/)

Internet Neutral (http://www.internetneutral.com)

Intersettle (http://www.intersettle.co.uk)

IRIS (http://www.iris.sgdg.org/mediation)

Judicial Dispute Resolution, Inc. (http://www.jdrinc.com)

Mediation Arbitration Resolution Services (MARS) (http://www.resolvemydispute.com)

National Arbitration Forum (http://www.arb-forum.com/domains)

NovaForum.com (http://www.novaforum.com)

One Accord (http://www.oneaccordinc.com/)

Online Ombuds Office (http://www.ombuds.org)

Online Resolution (http://www.onlineresolution.com)

Resolution Forum (http://www.resolutionforum.org)

SettlementOnline (http://www.settlementonline.com/Index.html)

SettleOnline (http://www.settleonline.com)

SettleTheCase (http://www.settlethecase.com/main.html)

SquareTrade (http://www.squaretrade.com)

State of Michigan (planned) (http://www.michigancybercourt.net)

The Claim Room (http://www.theclaimroom.com)

TRUSTe (http://www.truste.org)

Virtual Magistrate (http://www.vmag.org)

WebAssured.com (http://www.webassured.com)

WEBDispute.com (mediation planned) (http://www.webdispute.com)

WebMediate (http://www.webmediate.com)

WeCanSettle (http://www.wecansettle.com)

World Intellectual Property Organization (WIPO)
(http://www.arbiter.wipo.int/domains)

Word&Bond (http://www.wordandbond.com)

✦APPENDIX M ✦

UNIFORM ARBITRATION ACT
(Last Revisions Completed Year 2000)
Drafted by the

NATIONAL CONFERENCE OF COMMISSIONERS ON UNIFORM STATE LAWS

and by it

APPROVED AND RECOMMENDED FOR ENACTMENT IN ALL THE STATES
at its
ANNUAL CONFERENCE

ANNUAL CONFERENCE
MEETING IN ITS ONE-HUNDRED-AND-NINTH YEAR
ST. AUGUSTINE, FLORIDA

JULY 28–AUGUST 4, 2000
WITHOUT COMMENTS

UNIFORM ARBITRATION ACT

The Committee that acted for the National Conference of Commissioners on Uniform State Laws in preparing the Revised Uniform Arbitration Act is as follows:

FRANCIS J. PAVETTI, 83 Huntington Street, New London, CT 06320, *Chair*

FRANCISCO L. ACEVEDO, P.O. Box 190998, 16th Floor, Banco Popular Center, Hato Rey, PR 00919

RICHARD T. CASSIDY, 100 Main Street, P.O. Box 1124, Burlington, VT 05402

M. MICHAEL CRAMER, 216 N. Adams Street, Rockville, MD 20850

BARRY C. HAWKINS, One Landmark Square, 17th Floor, Stamford, CT 06901

TIMOTHY J. HEINSZ, University of Missouri-Columbia, School of Law, 203 Hulston Hall, Columbia, MO 65211, *National Conference Reporter*

ROGER C. HENDERSON, University of Arizona, James E. Rogers College of Law, Mountain and Speedway Streets, Tucson, AZ 85721, *Committee on Style Liaison*

JEREMIAH MARSH, Suite 4300, Three First National Plaza, Chicago, IL 60602

RODNEY W. SATTERWHITE, P.O. Box 1540, Midland, TX 79702

JAMES A. WYNN, JR., Court of Appeals, One W. Morgan Street, P.O. Box 888, Raleigh, NC 27602

JOAN ZELDON, Superior Court, 500 Indiana Avenue, N.W., Room 1640, Washington, DC 20001

EX OFFICIO

JOHN L. McCLAUGHERTY, P.O. Box 553, Charleston, WV 25322, *President*

STANLEY M. FISHER, 1100 Huntington Building, 925 Euclid Avenue, Cleveland, OH 44115-1475, *Division Chair*

AMERICAN BAR ASSOCIATION ADVISORS

RICHARD CHERNICK, 3055 Wilshire Boulevard, 7th Floor, Los Angeles, CA 90010-1108, *Co-Advisor*

JAMES L. KNOLL, 1500 S.W. Taylor Street, Portland, OR 97205, *Tort and Insurance Practice Section Advisor*

JOHN K. NOTZ, JR., 3300 Quaker Tower, 321 N. Clark Street, Chicago, IL 60610-4795, *Senior Lawyers Division Advisor*

YARKO SOCHYNSKY, 350 The Embarcadero, 6th Floor, San Francisco, CA 94105-1250, *Real Property, Probate and Trust Law Section Advisor*

RONALD M. STURTZ, 27 Badger Drive, Livingston, NJ 07039, *Co-Advisor*

MAX ZIMNY, Floor 3, 1710 Broadway, New York, NY 10019-5254, *Labor and Employment Law Section Advisor*

EXECUTIVE DIRECTOR

FRED H. MILLER, University of Oklahoma, College of Law, 300 Timberdell Road, Norman, OK 73019, *Executive Director*

WILLIAM J. PIERCE, 1505 Roxbury Road, Ann Arbor, MI 48104, *Executive Director Emeritus*

Copies of this Act may be obtained from:

NATIONAL CONFERENCE OF COMMISSIONERS
ON UNIFORM STATE LAWS
211 E. Ontario Street, Suite 1300
Chicago, Illinois 60611
312/915-0195   www.nccusl.org

UNIFORM ARBITRATION ACT
TABLE OF CONTENTS [summary]

UNIFORM ARBITRATION ACT

Prefatory Note

The Uniform Arbitration Act (UAA), promulgated in 1955, has been one of the most successful Acts of the National Conference of Commissioners on Uniform State Laws. Forty-nine jurisdictions have arbitration statutes; 35 of these have adopted the UAA and 14 have adopted substantially similar legislation. A primary purpose of the 1955 Act was to insure the enforceability of agreements to arbitrate in the face of oftentimes hostile state law. That goal has been accomplished. Today arbitration is a primary mechanism favored by courts and parties to resolve disputes in many areas of the law. This growth in arbitration caused the Conference to appoint a Drafting Committee to consider revising the Act in light of the increasing use of arbitration, the greater complexity of many disputes resolved by arbitration, and the developments of the law in this area.

The UAA did not address many issues which arise in modern arbitration cases. The statute provided no guidance as to (1) who decides the arbitrability of a dispute and by what criteria; (2) whether a court or arbitrators may issue provisional remedies; (3) how a party can initiate an arbitration proceeding; (4) whether arbitration proceedings may be consolidated; (5) whether arbitrators are required to disclose facts reasonably likely to affect impartiality; (6) what extent arbitrators or an arbitration organization are immune from civil actions; (7) whether arbitrators or representatives of arbitration organizations may be required to testify in another proceeding; (8) whether arbitrators have the discretion to order discovery, issue protective orders, decide motions for summary dispositions, hold prehearing conferences and otherwise manage the arbitration process; (9) when a court may enforce a preaward ruling by an arbitrator; (10) what remedies an arbitrator may award, especially in regard to attorney's fees, punitive damages or other exemplary relief; (11) when a court can award attorney's fees and costs to arbitrators and arbitration organizations; (12) when a court can award attorney's fees and costs to a prevailing party in an appeal of an arbitrator's award; and (13) which sections of the UAA would not be waivable, an important matter to insure fundamental fairness to the parties will be preserved, particularly in those instances where one party may have significantly less bargaining power than another; and (14) the use of electronic information and other modern means of technology in the arbitration process. The Revised Uniform Arbitration Act (RUAA) examines all of these issues and provides state legislatures with a more up-to-date statute to resolve disputes through arbitration.

There are a number of principles that the Drafting Committee agreed upon at the outset of its consideration of a revision to the UAA. First, arbitration is a consensual process in which autonomy of the parties who enter into arbitration agreements should be given primary consideration, so long as their agreements conform to notions of fundamental fairness. This approach provides parties with the opportunity in most instances to shape the arbitration process to their own particular needs. In most instances the RUAA provides a default mechanism if the parties do not have a specific agreement on a particular issue. Second, the underlying reason many parties choose arbitration is the relative speed, lower cost, and greater efficiency of the process. The law should take these factors, where applicable, into account. For example, section 10 allows consolidation of issues involving multiple parties. Such a provision can be of special importance in adhesion situations where there are numerous persons with essentially the same claims against a party to the arbitration agreement. Finally, in most cases parties intend the decisions of arbitrators to be final with minimal court involvement unless there is clear unfairness or a denial of justice. This contractual nature of arbitration means that the provision to vacate awards in section 23 is limited. This is so even where an arbitrator may award attorney's fees, punitive damages or other exemplary relief under section 21. Section 14 insulates arbitrators from unwarranted litigation to insure their independence by providing them with immunity.

Other new provisions are intended to reflect developments in arbitration law and to insure that the process is a fair one. Section 12 requires arbitrators to make important disclosures to the parties. Section 8 allows courts to grant provisional remedies in certain circumstances to protect the integrity of the arbitration process. Section 17 includes limited rights to discovery while recognizing the importance of expeditious arbitration proceedings.

In light of a number of decisions by the United States Supreme Court concerning the Federal Arbitration Act (FAA), any revision of the UAA must take into account the doctrine of preemption. The rule of preemption, whereby FAA standards and the emphatically pro-arbitration perspective of the FAA control, applies in both the federal courts and the state courts. To date, the preemption-related opinions of the Supreme Court have centered in large part on the two key issues that arise at the front end of the arbitration process—enforcement of the agreement to arbitrate and issues of substantive arbitrability. *Prima Paint Corp. v. Flood & Conklin Mfg. Co.*, 388 U.S. 35 (1967); *Moses H. Cone Mem'l Hosp. v. Mercury Constr. Corp.*, 460 U.S. 1 (1983); *Southland Corp. v. Keating*, 465 U.S. 2 (1984); *Perry v. Thomas*, 482 U.S. 483 (1987); *Allied-Bruce Terminix Cos. v. Dobson*, 513 U.S. 265 (1995); *Doctor's Assocs. v. Cassarotto*, 517 U.S. 681 (1996). That body of case law establishes that state law of any ilk, including adaptations of the RUAA, mooting or limiting contractual agreements to arbitrate must yield to the pro-arbitration public policy voiced in sections 2, 3, and 4 of the FAA.

The other issues to which the FAA speaks definitively lie at the back end of the arbitration process. The standards and procedure for vacatur, confirmation and modification of arbitration awards are the subject of sections 9, 10, 11, and 12 of the FAA. In contrast to the "front end" issues of enforceability and substantive arbitrability, there is no definitive Supreme Court case law speaking to the preemptive effect, if any, of the FAA with regard to these "back end" issues. This dimension of FAA preemption of state arbitration law is further complicated by the strong majority view among the United States Circuit Courts of Appeals that the section 10(a) standards are not the exclusive grounds for vacatur.

Nevertheless, the Supreme Court's unequivocal stand to date as to the preemptive effect of the FAA provides strong reason to believe that a similar result will obtain with regard to section 10(a) grounds for vacatur. If it does, and if the Supreme Court eventually determines that the section 10(a) standards are the sole grounds for vacatur of commercial arbitration awards, FAA preemption of conflicting state law with regard to the "back end" issues of vacatur (and confirmation and modification) would be certain. If the Court takes the opposite tack and holds that the section 10(a) grounds are not the exclusive criteria for vacatur, the preemptive effect of section 10(a) would most likely be limited to the rule that state arbitration acts cannot eliminate, limit or modify any of the four grounds of party and arbitrator misconduct set out in section 10(a). Any definitive federal "common law," pertaining to the nonstatutory grounds for vacatur other than those set out in section 10(a), articulated by the Supreme Court or established as a clear majority rule by the United States Courts of Appeals, likely would preempt contrary state law. A holding by the Supreme Court that the Section 10(a) grounds are not exclusive would also free the States to codify other grounds for vacatur beyond those set out in section 10(a). These various, currently nonstatutory grounds for vacatur are discussed at length in the section C to the Comment to section 23.

An important caveat to the general rule of FAA preemption is found in *Volt Information Sciences, Inc. v. Stanford Univiversity*, 489 U.S. 468 (1989) and *Mastrobuono v. Shearson Lehman Hutton, Inc.*, 514 U.S. 52 (1995). The focus in these cases is on the effect of FAA preemption on choice-of-law provisions routinely included in commercial contracts. *Volt* and *Mastrobuono* establish that a clearly expressed contractual agreement by the parties to an arbitration contract to conduct their arbitration under state law rules effectively trumps the preemptive effect of the FAA. If the parties elect to govern their contractual arbitration mechanism by the law of a particular State and thereby limit the issues that they will arbitrate or the procedures under which the arbitration will be conducted, their bargain will be honored—as long as the state law principles invoked by the choice-of-law provision do not conflict with the FAA's prime directive that agreements to arbitrate be enforced. *See, e.g., ASW Allstate Painting & Constr. Co. v. Lexington Ins. Co.*, 188 F.3d 307 (5th Cir. 1999); *Russ Berrie & Co. v. Gantt*, 988 S.W.2d 713 (Tex. Ct. App. 1999). It is in these situations that the RUAA will have most impact. Section 4(a) of the RUAA also explicitly provides that the parties to an arbitration agreement may waive or vary the terms of the Act to the extent otherwise permitted by law. Thus, when parties choose to contractually specify the procedures to be followed under their arbitration agreement, the RUAA contemplates that the contractually-established procedures will control over contrary state law, except with regard to issues designated as "nonwaivable" in section 4(b) and (c) of the RUAA.

The contractual election to proceed under state law instead of the FAA will be honored presuming that the state law is not antithetical to the pro-arbitration public policy of the FAA. *Southland* and *Terminix* leave no doubt that anti-arbitration state law provisions will be struck down because preempted by the federal arbitration statute.

Besides arbitration contracts where the parties choose to be governed by state law, there are other areas of arbitration law where the FAA does not preempt state law, in the absence of definitive federal law set out in the FAA or determined by the federal courts. First, the Supreme Court has made clear its belief that ascertaining when a particular contractual agreement to arbitrate is enforceable is a matter to be decided under the general contract law principles of each State. The sole limitation on state law in that regard is the Court's assertion that the enforceability of arbitration agreements must be determined by the same standards as are used for all other contracts. *Terminix*, 513 U.S. at 281 (1995) (quoting *Volt*, 489 U.S. at 474 (1989)) and quoted in *Cassarotto*, 517 U.S. 681, 685 (1996); and *Cassarotto*, 517 U.S. at 688 (quoting *Scherk v. Alberto-Culver Co.*, 417 U.S. 506, 511 (1974)). Arbitration agreements may not be invalidated under state laws applicable only to arbitration provisions. *Id.* The FAA will preempt state law that does not place arbitration agreements on an "equal footing" with other contracts.

During the course of its deliberations the Drafting Committee considered at length another issue with strong preemption undertones—the question of whether the RUAA should explicitly sanction contractual provisions for "opt-in" review of challenged arbitration awards beyond that presently contemplated by the FAA and current state arbitration acts. "Opt-in" provisions of two types are in limited use today. The first variant permits a party who is dissatisfied with the arbitral result to petition directly to a designated state court and stipulates that the court may vacate challenged awards, typically for errors of law or fact. The second type of "opt-in" contractual provision establishes an appellate arbitral mechanism to which challenged arbitration awards can be submitted for review, again most typically for errors of law or fact.

As explained in detail in section B of the Comment to section 23, there were a number of reasons that resulted in the decision not to include statutory sanction of the "opt-in" device for expanded judicial review in the RUAA: (1) the current uncertainty as to the legality of a state statutory sanction of the "opt-in" device,

(2) the "disconnect" between the Act's purpose of fostering the use of arbitration as a final and binding alternative to traditional litigation in a court of law, and (3) the inclusion of a statutory provision that would permit the parties to contractually render arbitration decidedly non-final and non-binding. Simply stated, the potential gain to be realized by codifying a right to opt-into expanded judicial review that has not yet been definitively confirmed to exist does not outweigh the potential threat that adoption of an opt-in statutory provision would create for the integrity and viability of the RUAA as a template for state arbitration acts.

Unlike the "opt-in" judicial review mechanism, there are few, if any, legal concerns raised by statutory sanction of "opt-in" provisions for appellate arbitral review. Nevertheless, as explained in the Section B of the Comments to section 23, because the current, contract-based view of arbitration establishes that the parties are free to design the inner workings of their arbitration procedures in any manner they see fit, the Drafting Committee determined that codification of that right in the RUAA would add nothing of substance to the existing law of arbitration.

The decision not to statutorily sanction either form of the "opt-in" device in the RUAA leaves the issue of the legal propriety of this means for securing review of awards to the developing case law under the FAA and state arbitration statutes. Parties remain free, within the constraints imposed by the existing and developing law, to agree to contractual provisions for arbitral or judicial review of challenged awards.

It is likely that matters not addressed in the FAA are also open to regulation by the States. State law provisions regulating purely procedural dimensions of the arbitration process (*e.g.*, discovery [RUAA Section 17], consolidation of claims [RUAA Section 10], and arbitrator immunity [RUAA Section 14]) likely will not be subject to preemption. Less certain is the effect of FAA preemption with regard to substantive issues like the authority of arbitrators to award punitive damages (RUAA Section 21) and the standards for arbitrator disclosure of potential conflicts of interest (RUAA Section 12) that have a significant impact on the integrity and/or the adequacy of the arbitration process. These "borderline" issues are not purely procedural in nature but unlike the "front end" and "back end" issues they do not go to the essence of the agreement to arbitrate or effectuation of the arbitral result. Although there is no concrete guidance in the case law, preemption of state law dealing with such matters seems unlikely as long as it cannot be characterized as anti-arbitration or as intended to limit the enforceability or viability of agreements to arbitrate.

The subject of international arbitration is not specifically addressed in the RUAA. Twelve States have passed arbitration statutes directed to international arbitration. Seven States have based their statutes on the Model Arbitration Law proposed in 1985 by the United Nations Commission on International Trade Law (UNCITRAL). Other States have approached international arbitration in a variety of ways, such as adopting parts of the UNCITRAL Model Law together with provisions taken directly from the 1958 United Nations Convention on Recognition and Enforcement of Foreign Arbitral Awards (commonly referred to as the New York Convention) or by devising their own international arbitration provisions.

Any provisions of these state international arbitration statutes that are inconsistent with the New York Convention, to which the United States adhered in 1970 (terms of the New York Convention can be found at 9 U.S.C. § 201), or with the federal legislation in chapter 2 of Title 9 of the United States Code are preempted. Chapter 2 creates federal-question jurisdiction in the federal district courts for any case "falling under the [New York] Convention" and permits removal of any such case from a state court to the federal court "at any time prior to trial." 9 U.S.C. §§ 203, 205. The statute covers any commercial agreement to arbitrate and the resultant arbitration award unless the matter involves only American citizens and has no reasonable relationship to any foreign country and the courts have broadly applied the statute. Therefore, it is unlikely that state arbitration law will have major application to an international case. There are two instances where state arbitration law might apply in the international context: (1) where the parties designate a specific state arbitration law to govern the international arbitration and (2) where all parties to an arbitration proceeding involving an international transaction decide to proceed on a matter in state court and do not exercise their rights of removal under chapter 2 of Title 9 and the relevant provision of state arbitration law is not preempted by federal arbitration law or the New York Convention. In these relatively rare cases, the state courts will refer to the RUAA unless the State has enacted a special international arbitration law.

Because few international cases are likely to be dealt with in state courts and because of the diversity of state law already enacted for international cases, the Drafting Committee decided not to address international arbitration as a specific subject in the revision of the UAA; however, the Committee utilized provisions of the UNCITRAL Model Law, the New York Convention, and the 1996 English Arbitration Act as sources of statutory language for the RUAA.

The members of the Drafting Committee to revise the Uniform Arbitration Act wish to acknowledge our deep indebtedness and appreciation to Professor Stephen Hayford and Professor Thomas Stipanowich who devoted extensive amounts of time by providing invaluable advice throughout the entire drafting process.

UNIFORM ARBITRATION ACT

SECTION 1. DEFINITIONS. In this [Act]:

(1) "Arbitration organization" means an association, agency, board, commission, or other entity that is neutral and initiates, sponsors, or administers an arbitration proceeding or is involved in the appointment of an arbitrator.

(2) "Arbitrator" means an individual appointed to render an award, alone or with others, in a controversy that is subject to an agreement to arbitrate.

(3) "Court" means [a court of competent jurisdiction in this State].

(4) "Knowledge" means actual knowledge.

(5) "Person" means an individual, corporation, business trust, estate, trust, partnership, limited liability company, association, joint venture, government; governmental subdivision, agency, or instrumentality; public corporation; or any other legal or commercial entity.

(6) "Record" means information that is inscribed on a tangible medium or that is stored in an electronic or other medium and is retrievable in perceivable

SECTION 2. NOTICE.

(a) Except as otherwise provided in this [Act], a person gives notice to another person by taking action that is reasonably necessary to inform the other person in ordinary course, whether or not the other person acquires knowledge of the notice.

(b) A person has notice if the person has knowledge of the notice or has received notice.

(c) A person receives notice when it comes to the person's attention or the notice is delivered at the person's place of residence or place of business, or at another location held out by the person as a place of delivery of such communications.

SECTION 3. WHEN [ACT] APPLIES.

(a) This [Act] governs an agreement to arbitrate made on or after [the effective date of this [Act]].

(b) This [Act] governs an agreement to arbitrate made before [the effective date of this [Act]] if all the parties to the agreement or to the arbitration proceeding so agree in a record.

(c) On or after [a delayed date], this [Act] governs an agreement to arbitrate whenever made.

SECTION 4. EFFECT OF AGREEMENT TO ARBITRATE NON WAIVABLE PROVISIONS.

(a) Except as otherwise provided in subsections (b) and (c), a party to an agreement to arbitrate or to an arbitration proceeding may waive or, the parties may vary the effect of, the requirements of this [Act] to the extent permitted by law.

(b) Before a controversy arises that is subject to an agreement to arbitrate, a party to the agreement may not:

(1) waive or agree to vary the effect of the requirements of Section 5(a), 6(a), 8, 17(a), 17(b), 26, or 28;

(2) agree to unreasonably restrict the right under Section 9 to notice of the initiation of an arbitration proceeding;

(3) agree to unreasonably restrict the right under Section 12 to disclosure of any facts by a neutral arbitrator; or

(4) waive the right under Section 16 of a party to an agreement to arbitrate to be represented by a lawyer at any proceeding or hearing under this [Act], but an employer and a labor organization may waive the right to representation by a lawyer in a labor arbitration.

(c) A party to an agreement to arbitrate or arbitration proceeding may not waive, or the parties may not vary the effect of, the requirements of this section or

SECTION 5. [APPLICATION] FOR JUDICIAL RELIEF.

(a) Except as otherwise provided in Section 28, an [application] for judicial relief under this [Act] must be made by [motion] to the court and heard in the manner provided by law or rule of court for making and hearing [motions].

(b) Unless a civil action involving the agreement to arbitrate is pending, notice of an initial [motion] to the court under this [Act] must be served in the manner provided by law for the service of a summons in a civil action. Otherwise, notice of the motion must be given in the manner provided by law or rule of court for serving [motions] in pending cases.

SECTION 6. VALIDITY OF AGREEMENT TO ARBITRATE.

(a) An agreement contained in a record to submit to arbitration any existing or subsequent controversy arising between the parties to the agreement is valid, enforceable, and irrevocable except upon a ground that exists at law or in equity for the revocation of a contract.

(b) The court shall decide whether an agreement to arbitrate exists or a controversy is subject to an agreement to arbitrate.

(c) An arbitrator shall decide whether a condition precedent to arbitrability has been fulfilled and whether a contract containing a valid agreement to arbitrate is enforceable.

(d) If a party to a judicial proceeding challenges the existence of, or claims that a controversy is not subject to, an agreement to arbitrate, the arbitration proceeding may continue pending final resolution of the issue by the court, unless

SECTION 7. [MOTION] TO COMPEL OR STAY ARBITRATION.

(a) On [motion] of a person showing an agreement to arbitrate and alleging another person's refusal to arbitrate pursuant to the agreement:

(1) if the refusing party does not appear or does not oppose the [motion], the court shall order the parties to arbitrate; and

(2) if the refusing party opposes the [motion], the court shall proceed summarily to decide the issue and order the parties to arbitrate unless it finds that there is no enforceable agreement to arbitrate.

(b) On [motion] of a person alleging that an arbitration proceeding has been initiated or threatened but that there is no agreement to arbitrate, the court shall proceed summarily to decide the issue. If the court finds that there is an enforceable agreement to arbitrate, it shall order the parties to arbitrate.

(c) If the court finds that there is no enforceable agreement, it may not pursuant to subsection (a) or (b) order the parties to arbitrate.

(d) The court may not refuse to order arbitration because the claim subject to arbitration lacks merit or grounds for the claim have not been established.

(e) If a proceeding involving a claim referable to arbitration under an alleged agreement to arbitrate is pending in court, a [motion] under this section must be made in that court. Otherwise a [motion] under this section may be made in any court as provided in Section 27.

(f) If a party makes a [motion] to the court to order arbitration, the court on just terms shall stay any judicial proceeding that involves a claim alleged to be subject to the arbitration until the court renders a final decision under this section.

(g) If the court orders arbitration, the court on just terms shall stay any judicial proceeding that involves a claim subject to the arbitration. If a claim subject to the arbitration is severable, the court may limit the stay to that claim.

SECTION 8. PROVISIONAL REMEDIES.

(a) Before an arbitrator is appointed and is authorized and able to act, the court, upon [motion] of a party to an arbitration proceeding and for good cause shown, may enter an order for provisional remedies to protect the effectiveness of the arbitration proceeding to the same extent and under the same conditions as if the controversy were the subject of a civil action.

(b) After an arbitrator is appointed and is authorized and able to act:

(1) the arbitrator may issue such orders for provisional remedies, including interim awards, as the arbitrator finds necessary to protect the effectiveness of the arbitration proceeding and to promote the fair and expeditious resolution of the controversy, to the same extent and under the same conditions as if the controversy were the subject of a civil action and

(2) a party to an arbitration proceeding may move the court for a provisional remedy only if the matter is urgent and the arbitrator is not able to act timely or the arbitrator cannot provide an adequate remedy.

(c) A party does not waive a right of arbitration by making a [motion] under subsection (a) or (b).

SECTION 9. INITIATION OF ARBITRATION.

(a) A person initiates an arbitration proceeding by giving notice in a record to the other parties to the agreement to arbitrate in the agreed manner between the parties or, in the absence of agreement, by certified or registered mail, return receipt requested and obtained, or by service as authorized for the commencement of a civil action. The notice must describe the nature of the controversy and the remedy sought.

(b) Unless a person objects for lack or insufficiency of notice under Section 15(c) not later than the beginning of the arbitration hearing, the person by appearing at the hearing waives any objection to lack of or insufficiency of notice.

SECTION 10. CONSOLIDATION OF SEPARATE ARBITRATION PROCEEDINGS.

(a) Except as otherwise provided in subsection (c), upon [motion] of a party to an agreement to arbitrate or to an arbitration proceeding, the court may order consolidation of separate arbitration proceedings as to all or some of the claims if:

(1) there are separate agreements to arbitrate or separate arbitration proceedings between the same persons or one of them is a party to a separate agreement to arbitrate or a separate arbitration proceeding with a third person;

(2) the claims subject to the agreements to arbitrate arise in substantial part from the same transaction or series of related transactions;

(3) the existence of a common issue of law or fact creates the possibility of conflicting decisions in the separate arbitration proceedings; and

(4) prejudice resulting from a failure to consolidate is not outweighed by the risk of undue delay or prejudice to the rights of or hardship to parties opposing consolidation.

(b) The court may order consolidation of separate arbitration proceedings as to some claims and allow other claims to be resolved in separate arbitration proceedings.

(c) The court may not order consolidation of the claims of a party to an agreement to arbitrate if the agreement prohibits consolidation.

SECTION 11. APPOINTMENT OF ARBITRATOR; SERVICE AS A NEUTRAL ARBITRATOR.

(a) If the parties to an agreement to arbitrate agree on a method for appointing an arbitrator, that method must be followed, unless the method fails. If the parties have not agreed on a method, the agreed method fails, or an arbitrator appointed fails or is unable to act and a successor has not been appointed, the court, on [motion] of a party to the arbitration proceeding, shall appoint the arbitrator. An arbitrator so appointed has all the powers of an arbitrator designated in the agreement to arbitrate or appointed pursuant to the agreed method.

(b) An individual who has a known, direct, and material interest in the outcome of the arbitration proceeding or a known, existing, and substantial relationship with a party may not serve as an arbitrator required by an agreement to be

SECTION 12. DISCLOSURE BY ARBITRATOR.

(a) Before accepting appointment, an individual who is requested to serve as an arbitrator, after making a reasonable inquiry, shall disclose to all parties to the agreement to arbitrate and arbitration proceeding and to any other arbitrators any known facts that a reasonable person would consider likely to affect the impartiality of the arbitrator in the arbitration proceeding, including:

(1) a financial or personal interest in the outcome of the arbitration proceeding; and

(2) an existing or past relationship with any of the parties to the agreement to arbitrate or the arbitration proceeding, their counsel or representatives, a witness, or another arbitrators.

(b) An arbitrator has a continuing obligation to disclose to all parties to the agreement to arbitrate and arbitration proceeding and to any other arbitrators any facts that the arbitrator learns after accepting appointment which a reasonable person would consider likely to affect the impartiality of the arbitrator.

(c) If an arbitrator discloses a fact required by subsection (a) or (b) to be disclosed and a party timely objects to the appointment or continued service of the arbitrator based upon the fact disclosed, the objection may be a ground under Section 23(a)(2) for vacating an award made by the arbitrator.

(d) If the arbitrator did not disclose a fact as required by subsection (a) or (b), upon timely objection by a party, the court under Section 23(a)(2) may vacate an award.

(e) An arbitrator appointed as a neutral arbitrator who does not disclose a known, direct, and material interest in the outcome of the arbitration proceeding or a known, existing, and substantial relationship with a party is presumed to act with evident partiality under Section 23(a)(2).

(f) If the parties to an arbitration proceeding agree to the procedures of an arbitration organization or any other procedures for challenges to arbitrators before an award is made, substantial compliance with those procedures is a condition precedent to a [motion] to vacate an award on that ground under Section 23(a)(2).

SECTION 13. ACTION BY MAJORITY. If there is more than one arbitrator, the powers of an arbitrator must be exercised by a majority of the arbitrators, but all of them shall conduct the hearing under Section 15(c).

SECTION 14. IMMUNITY OF ARBITRATOR; COMPETENCY TO TESTIFY; ATTORNEY'S FEES AND COSTS.

(a) An arbitrator or an arbitration organization acting in that capacity is immune from civil liability to the same extent as a judge of a court of this State acting in a judicial capacity.

(b) The immunity afforded by this section supplements any immunity under other law.

(c) The failure of an arbitrator to make a disclosure required by Section 12 does not cause any loss of immunity under this section.

(d) In a judicial, administrative, or similar proceeding, an arbitrator or representative of an arbitration organization is not competent to testify, and may not be required to produce records as to any statement, conduct, decision, or ruling occurring during the arbitration proceeding, to the same extent as a judge of a court of this State acting in a judicial capacity. This subsection does not apply:

(1) to the extent necessary to determine the claim of an arbitrator, arbitration organization, or representative of the arbitration organization against a party to the arbitration proceeding; or

(2) to a hearing on a [motion] to vacate an award under Section 23(a)(1) or (2) if the [movant] establishes prima facie that a ground for vacating the award exists.

(e) If a person commences a civil action against an arbitrator, arbitration organization, or representative of an arbitration organization arising from the services of the arbitrator, organization, or representative or if a person seeks to compel an arbitrator or a representative of an arbitration organization to testify or produce records in violation of subsection (d), and the court decides that the arbitrator, arbitration organization, or representative of an arbitration organization is immune from civil liability or that the arbitrator or representative of the organization is not competent to testify, the court shall award to the arbitrator, organization, or representative reasonable attorney's fees and other reasonable

SECTION 15. ARBITRATION PROCESS.

(a) An arbitrator may conduct an arbitration in such manner as the arbitrator considers appropriate for a fair and expeditious disposition of the proceeding. The authority conferred upon the arbitrator includes the power to hold conferences with the parties to the arbitration proceeding before the hearing and, among other matters, determine the admissibility, relevance, materiality and weight of any evidence.

(b) An arbitrator may decide a request for summary disposition of a claim or particular issue:

(1) if all interested parties agree; or

(2) upon request of one party to the arbitration proceeding if that party gives notice to all other parties to the proceeding, and the other parties have a reasonable opportunity to respond.

(c) If an arbitrator orders a hearing, the arbitrator shall set a time and place and give notice of the hearing not less than five days before the hearing begins. Unless a party to the arbitration proceeding makes an objection to lack or insufficiency of notice not later than the beginning of the hearing, the party's appearance at the hearing waives the objection. Upon request of a party to the arbitration proceeding and for good cause shown, or upon the arbitrator's own initiative, the arbitrator may adjourn the hearing from time to time as necessary but may not postpone the hearing to a time later than that fixed by the agreement to arbitrate for making the award unless the parties to the arbitration proceeding consent to a later date. The arbitrator may hear and decide the controversy upon the evidence produced although a party who was duly notified of the arbitration proceeding did not appear. The court, on request, may direct the arbitrator to conduct the hearing promptly and render a timely decision.

(d) At a hearing under subsection (c), a party to the arbitration proceeding has a right to be heard, to present evidence material to the controversy, and to cross-examine witnesses appearing at the hearing.

(e) If an arbitrator ceases or is unable to act during the arbitration proceeding, a replacement arbitrator must be appointed in accordance with Section 11 to continue the proceeding and to resolve the controversy.

SECTION 16. REPRESENTATION BY LAWYER. A party to an arbitration proceeding may be represented by a lawyer.

SECTION 17. WITNESSES; SUBPOENAS; DEPOSITIONS; DISCOVERY.

(a) An arbitrator may issue a subpoena for the attendance of a witness and for the production of records and other evidence at any hearing and may administer oaths. A subpoena must be served in the manner for service of subpoenas in a civil action and, upon [motion] to the court by a party to the arbitration proceeding or the arbitrator, enforced in the manner for enforcement of subpoenas in a civil action.

(b) In order to make the proceedings fair, expeditious, and cost effective, upon request of a party to or a witness in an arbitration proceeding, an arbitrator may permit a deposition of any witness to be taken for use as evidence at the hearing, including a witness who cannot be subpoenaed for or is unable to attend a hearing. The arbitrator shall determine the conditions under which the deposition is taken.

(c) An arbitrator may permit such discovery as the arbitrator decides is appropriate in the circumstances, taking into account the needs of the parties to the arbitration proceeding and other affected persons and the desirability of making the proceeding fair, expeditious, and cost effective.

(d) If an arbitrator permits discovery under subsection (c), the arbitrator may order a party to the arbitration proceeding to comply with the arbitrator's discovery-related orders, issue subpoenas for the attendance of a witness and for the production of records and other evidence at a discovery proceeding, and take action against a noncomplying party to the extent a court could if the controversy were the subject of a civil action in this State.

(e) An arbitrator may issue a protective order to prevent the disclosure of privileged information, confidential information, trade secrets, and other information protected from disclosure to the extent a court could if the controversy were the subject of a civil action in this State.

(f) All laws compelling a person under subpoena to testify and all fees for attending a judicial proceeding, a deposition, or a discovery proceeding as a witness apply to an arbitration proceeding as if the controversy were the subject of a civil action in this State.

(g) The court may enforce a subpoena or discovery-related order for the attendance of a witness within this State and for the production of records and other evidence issued by an arbitrator in connection with an arbitration proceeding in another State upon conditions determined by the court so as to make the arbitration proceeding fair, expeditious, and cost effective. A subpoena or discovery-related order issued by an arbitrator in another State must be served in the manner provided by law for service of subpoenas in a civil action in this State and, upon [motion] to the court by a party to the arbitration proceeding or the arbitrator, enforced in the manner provided by law for enforcement of subpoenas in a civil action in this State.

SECTION 18. JUDICIAL ENFORCEMENT OF PREAWARD RULING BY ARBITRATOR. If an arbitrator makes a preaward ruling in favor of a party to the arbitration proceeding, the party may request the arbitrator to incorporate the ruling into an award under Section 19. A prevailing party may make a [motion] to the court for an expedited order to confirm the award under Section 22, in which case the court shall summarily decide the [motion]. The court shall issue an order to confirm the award unless the court vacates, modifies, or corrects the award under Section 23 or 24.

SECTION 19. AWARD.

(a) An arbitrator shall make a record of an award. The record must be signed or otherwise authenticated by any arbitrator who concurs with the award. The arbitrator or the arbitration organization shall give notice of the award, including a copy of the award, to each party to the arbitration proceeding.

(b) An award must be made within the time specified by the agreement to arbitrate or, if not specified therein, within the time ordered by the court. The court may extend or the parties to the arbitration proceeding may agree in a record to extend the time. The court or the parties may do so within or after the time specified or ordered. A party waives any objection that an award was not timely made unless the party gives notice of the objection to the arbitrator before receiving notice of the award.

SECTION 20. CHANGE OF AWARD BY ARBITRATOR.

(a) On [motion] to an arbitrator by a party to an arbitration proceeding, the arbitrator may modify or correct an award:

(1) upon a ground stated in Section 24(a)(1) or (3);

(2) because the arbitrator has not made a final and definite award upon a claim submitted by the parties to the arbitration proceeding; or

(3) to clarify the award.

(b) A [motion] under subsection (a) must be made and notice given to all parties within 20 days after the movant receives notice of the award.

(c) A party to the arbitration proceeding must give notice of any objection to the [motion] within 10 days after receipt of the notice.

(d) If a [motion] to the court is pending under Section 22, 23, or 24, the court may submit the claim to the arbitrator to consider whether to modify or correct the award:

(1) upon a ground stated in Section 24(a)(1) or (3);

(2) because the arbitrator has not made a final and definite award upon a claim submitted by the parties to the arbitration proceeding; or

(3) to clarify the award.

(e) An award modified or corrected pursuant to this section is subject to Sections 19(a), 22, 23, and 24.

SECTION 21. REMEDIES; FEES AND EXPENSES OF ARBITRATION PROCEEDING.

(a) An arbitrator may award punitive damages or other exemplary relief if such an award is authorized by law in a civil action involving the same claim and the evidence produced at the hearing justifies the award under the legal standards otherwise applicable to the claim.

(b) An arbitrator may award reasonable attorney's fees and other reasonable expenses of arbitration if such an award is authorized by law in a civil action involving the same claim or by the agreement of the parties to the arbitration proceeding.

(c) As to all remedies other than those authorized by subsections (a) and (b), an arbitrator may order such remedies as the arbitrator considers just and appropriate under the circumstances of the arbitration proceeding. The fact that such a remedy could not or would not be granted by the court is not a ground for refusing to confirm an award under Section 22 or for vacating an award under Section 23.

(d) An arbitrator's expenses and fees, together with other expenses, must be paid as provided in the award.

(e) If an arbitrator awards punitive damages or other exemplary relief under subsection (a), the arbitrator shall specify in the award the basis in fact justifying and the basis in law authorizing the award and state separately the amount of the punitive damages or other exemplary relief.

SECTION 22. CONFIRMATION OF AWARD. After a party to an arbitration proceeding receives notice of an award, the party may make a [motion] to the court for an order confirming the award at which time the court shall issue a confirming order unless the award is modified or corrected pursuant to Section 20 or 24 or is vacated pursuant to Section 23.

SECTION 23. VACATING AWARD.

(a) Upon [motion] to the court by a party to an arbitration proceeding, the court shall vacate an award made in the arbitration proceeding if:

(1) the award was procured by corruption, fraud, or other undue means;

(2) there was:

(A) evident partiality by an arbitrator appointed as a neutral arbitrator;

(B) corruption by an arbitrator; or

(C) misconduct by an arbitrator prejudicing the rights of a party to the arbitration proceeding;

(3) an arbitrator refused to postpone the hearing upon showing of sufficient cause for postponement, refused to consider evidence material to the

controversy, or otherwise conducted the hearing contrary to Section 15, so as to prejudice substantially the rights of a party to the arbitration proceeding;

(4) an arbitrator exceeded the arbitrator's powers;

(5) there was no agreement to arbitrate, unless the person participated in the arbitration proceeding without raising the objection under Section 15(c) not later than the beginning of the arbitration hearing; or

(6) the arbitration was conducted without proper notice of the initiation of an arbitration as required in Section 9 so as to prejudice substantially the rights of a party to the arbitration proceeding.

(b) A [motion] under this section must be filed within 90 days after the [movant] receives notice of the award pursuant to Section 19 or within 90 days after the [movant] receives notice of a modified or corrected award pursuant to Section 20, unless the [movant] alleges that the award was procured by corruption, fraud, or other undue means, in which case the [motion] must be made within 90 days after the ground is known or by the exercise of reasonable care would have been known by the [movant].

(c) If the court vacates an award on a ground other than that set forth in subsection (a)(5), it may order a rehearing. If the award is vacated on a ground stated in subsection (a)(1) or (2), the rehearing must be before a new arbitrator. If the award is vacated on a ground stated in subsection (a)(3), (4), or (6), the rehearing may be before the arbitrator who made the award or the arbitrator's successor. The arbitrator must render the decision in the rehearing within the same time as that provided in Section 19(b) for an award.

(d) If the court denies a [motion] to vacate an award, it shall confirm the award unless a [motion] to modify or correct the award is pending.

Comment

A. Comment on Section 23(a)(2), (5), (6), and (c)

SECTION 24. MODIFICATION OR CORRECTION OF AWARD.

(a) Upon [motion] made within 90 days after the [movant] receives notice of the award pursuant to Section 19 or within 90 days after the [movant] receives notice of a modified or corrected award pursuant to Section 20, the court shall modify or correct the award if:

(1) there was an evident mathematical miscalculation or an evident mistake in the description of a person, thing, or property referred to in the award;

(2) the arbitrator has made an award on a claim not submitted to the arbitrator and the award may be corrected without affecting the merits of the decision upon the claims submitted; or

(3) the award is imperfect in a matter of form not affecting the merits of the decision on the claims submitted.

(b) If a [motion] made under subsection (a) is granted, the court shall modify or correct and confirm the award as modified or corrected. Otherwise, unless a motion to vacate is pending, the court shall confirm the award.

(c) A [motion] to modify or correct an award pursuant to this section may be joined with a [motion] to vacate the award.

SECTION 25. JUDGMENT ON AWARD; ATTORNEY'S FEES AND LITIGATION EXPENSES.

(a) Upon granting an order confirming, vacating without directing a rehearing, modifying, or correcting an award, the court shall enter a judgment in conformity therewith. The judgment may be recorded, docketed, and enforced as any other judgment in a civil action.

(b) A court may allow reasonable costs of the [motion] and subsequent judicial proceedings.

(c) On [application] of a prevailing party to a contested judicial proceeding under Section 22, 23, or 24, the court may add reasonable attorney's fees and other reasonable expenses of litigation incurred in a judicial proceeding after the award is made to a judgment confirming, vacating without directing a rehearing, modifying, or correcting an award.

SECTION 26. JURISDICTION.

(a) A court of this State having jurisdiction over the controversy and the parties may enforce an agreement to arbitrate.

(b) An agreement to arbitrate providing for arbitration in this State confers exclusive jurisdiction on the court to enter judgment on an award under this [Act].

SECTION 27. VENUE. A [motion] pursuant to Section 5 must be made in the court of the [county] in which the agreement to arbitrate specifies the arbitration hearing is to be held or, if the hearing has been held, in the court of the [county] in which it was held. Otherwise, the [motion] may be made in the court of any [county] in which an adverse party resides or has a place of business or, if no adverse party has a residence or place of business in this State, in the court of any [county] in this State. All subsequent [motions] must be made in the court hearing the initial [motion] unless the court otherwise directs.

SECTION 28. APPEALS.

(a) An appeal may be taken from:

(1) an order denying a [motion] to compel arbitration;

(2) an order granting a [motion] to stay arbitration;

(3) an order confirming or denying confirmation of an award;

(4) an order modifying or correcting an award;

(5) an order vacating an award without directing a rehearing; or

(6) a final judgment entered pursuant to this [Act].

(b) An appeal under this section must be taken as from an order or a judgment in a civil action.

SECTION 29. UNIFORMITY OF APPLICATION AND CONSTRUCTION.
In applying and construing this uniform act, consideration must be given to the need to promote uniformity of the law with respect to its subject matter among States that enact it.

SECTION 30. RELATIONSHIP TO ELECTRONIC SIGNATURES IN GLOBAL AND NATIONAL COMMERCE ACT. The provisions of this Act governing the legal effect, validity, and enforceability of electronic records or electronic signatures, and of contracts performed with the use of such records or signatures conform to the requirements of Section 102 of the Electronic Signatures in Global and National Commerce Act.

SECTION 31. EFFECTIVE DATE. This [Act] takes effect on [effective date].

SECTION 32. REPEAL. Effective on [delayed date should be the same as that in Section 3(c)], the [Uniform Arbitration Act] is repealed.

2. This repeal section is based on Section 1205 of the Revised Uniform Partnership Act and Section 1209 of the 1996 Amendments constituting the Uniform Limited Liability Partnership Act. Both of these statutes have transition provisions similar to Section 3 of the RUAA.

SECTION 33. SAVINGS CLAUSE. This [Act] does not affect an action or proceeding commenced or right accrued before this [Act] takes effect. Subject to Section 3 of this [Act], an arbitration agreement made before the effective date of this [Act] is governed by the [Uniform Arbitration Act].

◆APPENDIX N ◆

The Federal Arbitration Act

1. Title 9, US Code, Section 1-14, was first enacted February 12, 1925 (43 Stat. 883), codified July 30, 1947 (61 Stat. 669), and amended September 3, 1954 (68 Stat. 1233). Chapter 2 was added July 31, 1970 (84 Stat. 692), two new Sections were passed by the Congress in October of 1988 and renumbered on December 1, 1990 (PLs669 and 702); chapter 3 was added on August 15, 1990 (PL 101-369); and Section 10 was amended on November 15.

ARBITRATION

THE FEDERAL ARBITRATION ACT

CHAPTER 1. GENERAL PROVISIONS

Section 1. "Maritime transactions" and "commerce" defined; exceptions to operation of title

"Maritime transaction", as herein defined, means charter parties, bills of lading of water carriers, agreements relating to wharfage, supplies furnished vessels or repairs to vessels, collisions, or any other matters in foreign commerce which, if the subject of controversy, would be embraced within admiralty jurisdiction; "commerce", as herein defined, means commerce among the several States or with foreign nations, or in any Territory of the United States or in the District of Columbia, or between any such Territory and another, or between any such Territory and any State or foreign nation, or between the District of Columbia and any State or Territory or foreign nation, but nothing herein contained shall apply to contracts of employment of seamen, railroad employees, or any other class of workers engaged in foreign or interstate commerce.

Section 2. Validity, irrevocability, and enforcement of agreements to arbitrate

A written provision in any maritime transaction or a contract evidencing a transaction involving commerce to settle by arbitration a controversy thereafter arising out of such contract or transaction, or the refusal to perform the whole or any part thereof, or an agreement in writing to submit to arbitration an existing controversy arising out of such a contract, transaction, or refusal, shall be valid, irrevocable, and enforceable, save upon such grounds as exist at law or in equity for the revocation of any contract.

Section 3. Stay of proceedings where issue therein referable to arbitration

If any suit or proceeding be brought in any of the courts of the United States upon any issue referable to arbitration under an agreement in writing for such arbitration, the court in which such suit is pending, upon being satisfied that the issue involved in such suit or proceeding is referable to arbitration under such an agreement, shall on application of one of the parties stay the trial of the action until such arbitration has been had in accordance with the terms of the agreement, providing the applicant for the stay is not in default in proceeding with such arbitration.

Section 4. Failure to arbitrate under agreement; petition to United States court having jurisdiction for order to compel arbitration; notice and service thereof; hearing and determination.

A party aggrieved by the alleged failure, neglect, or refusal of another to arbitrate under a written agreement for arbitration may petition any United States district court which, save for such agreement, would have jurisdiction under Title 28, in a civil action or in admiralty of the subject matter of a suit arising out of the controversy between the parties, for an order directing that such arbitration proceed in the manner provided for in such agreement. Five days' notice in writing of such application shall be served upon the party in default. Service thereof shall be made in the manner provided by the Federal Rules of Civil Procedure. The court shall hear the parties, and upon being satisfied that the making of the agreement for arbitration or the failure to comply therewith is not in issue, the court shall make an order directing the parties to proceed to arbitration in accordance with the terms of the agreement. The hearing and proceedings, under such agreement, shall be within the district in which the petition for an order directing such arbitration is filed. If the making of the arbitration agreement or the failure, neglect, or refusal to perform the same be in issue, the court shall proceed summarily to the trial thereof. If no jury trial be demanded by the party alleged to be in default, or if the matter in dispute is within admiralty jurisdiction, the court shall hear and determine such issue. Where such an issue is raised, the party alleged to be in default may, except in cases of admiralty, on or before the return day of the notice of application, demand a jury trial of such issue, and upon such demand the court shall make an order referring the issue or issues to a jury in the manner provided by the Federal Rules of Civil Procedure, or may specially call a jury for that purpose. If the jury find that no agreement in writing for arbitration was made or that there is no default in proceeding thereunder, the proceeding shall be dismissed. If the jury find that an agreement for arbitration was made in writing and that there is a default in proceeding thereunder, the court shall make an order summarily directing the parties to proceed with the arbitration in accordance with the terms thereof.

Section 5. Appointment of arbitrators or umpire

If in the agreement provision be made for a method of naming or appointing an arbitrator or arbitrators or an umpire, such method shall be followed; but if no method be provided therein, or if a method be provided and any party thereto shall fail to avail himself of such method, or if for any other reason there shall be a lapse in the naming of an arbitrator or arbitrators or umpire, or in filling a vacancy, then upon the application of either party to the controversy the court shall designate and appoint an arbitrator or arbitrators or umpire, as the case may require, who shall act under the said agreement with the same force and effect as if he or they had been specifically named therein; and unless otherwise provided in the agreement the arbitration shall be by a single arbitrator.

Section 6. Application heard as motion

Any application to the court hereunder shall be made and heard in the manner provided by law for the making and hearing of motions, except as otherwise herein expressly provided.

Section 7. Witnesses before arbitrators; fees; compelling attendance

The arbitrators selected either as prescribed in this title or otherwise, or a majority of them, may summon in writing any person to attend before them or any of them as a witness and in a proper case to bring with him or them any book, record, document, or paper which may be deemed material as evidence in the case. The fees for such attendance shall be the same as the fees of witnesses before masters of the United States courts. Said summons shall issue in the name of the arbitrator or arbitrators, or a majority of them, and shall be signed by the arbitrators, or a majority of them, and shall be directed to the said person and shall be served in the same manner as subpoenas to appear and testify before the court; if any person or persons so summoned to testify shall refuse or neglect to obey said summons, upon petition the United States district court for the district in which such arbitrators, or a majority of them, are sitting may compel the attendance of such person or persons before said arbitrator or arbitrators, or punish said person or persons for contempt in the same manner provided by law for securing the attendance of witnesses or their punishment for neglect or refusal to attend in the courts of the United States.

Section 8. Proceedings begun by libel in admiralty and seizure of vessel or property

If the basis of jurisdiction be a cause of action otherwise justiciable in admiralty, then, notwithstanding anything herein to the contrary, the party claiming to be aggrieved may begin his proceeding hereunder by seizure of the vessel or other property of the other party according to the usual course of admiralty proceedings, and the court shall then have jurisdiction to direct the parties to proceed with the arbitration and shall retain jurisdiction to enter its decree upon the award.

Section 9. Award of arbitrators; confirmation; jurisdiction; procedure

If the parties in their agreement have agreed that a judgment of the court shall be entered upon the award made pursuant to the arbitration, and shall specify the court, then at any time within one year after the award is made any party to the arbitration may apply to the court so specified for an order confirming the award, and thereupon the court must grant such an order unless the award is vacated, modified, or corrected as prescribed in sections 10 and 11 of this title. If no court is specified in the agreement of the parties, then such application may be made to the United States court in and for the district within which such award was made. Notice of the application shall be served upon the adverse party, and thereupon the court shall have jurisdiction of such party as though he had appeared generally in the proceeding. If the adverse party is a resident of the district within which the award was made, such service shall be made upon the adverse party or his attorney as prescribed by law for service of notice of motion in an action in the same court. If the adverse party shall be a nonresident, then the notice of the application shall be served by the marshal of any district within which the adverse party may be found in like manner as other process of the court.

Section 10. Same; vacation; grounds; rehearing

(a) In any of the following cases the United States court in and for the district wherein the award was made may make an order vacating the award upon the application of any party to the arbitration

(1) Where the award was procured by corruption, fraud, or undue means.

(2) Where there was evident partiality or corruption in the arbitrators, or either of them.

(3) Where the arbitrators were guilty of misconduct in refusing to postpone the hearing, upon sufficient cause shown, or in refusing to hear evidence pertinent and material to the controversy; or of any other misbehavior by which the rights of any party have been prejudiced.

(4) Where the arbitrators exceeded their powers, or so imperfectly executed them that a mutual, final, and definite award upon the subject matter submitted was not made.

(5) Where an award is vacated and the time within which the agreement required the award to be made has not expired the court may, in its discretion, direct a rehearing b the arbitrators.

(b) The United States district court for the district wherein an award was made that was issued pursuant to section 590 of title 5 may make an order vacating the award upon the application of a person, other than a party to the arbitration, who is adversely affected or aggrieved by the award, if the use of arbitration or the award is clearly inconsistent with the factors set forth in section 582 of Title 5.

Section 11. Same; modification or correction; grounds; order

In either of the following cases the United States court in and for the district wherein the award was made may make an order modifying or correcting the award upon the application of any party to the arbitration

(a) Where there was an evident material miscalculation of figures or an evident material mistake in the description of any person, thing, or property referred to in the award.

(b) Where the arbitrators have awarded upon a matter not submitted to them, unless it is a matter not affecting the merits of the decision upon the matter submitted.

(c) Where the award is imperfect in matter of form not affecting the merits of the controversy.

The order may modify and correct the award, so as to effect the intent thereof and promote justice between the parties.

Section 12. Notice of motions to vacate or modify; service; stay of proceedings

Notice of a motion to vacate, modify, or correct an award must be served upon the adverse party or his attorney within three months after the award is filed or delivered. If the adverse party is a resident of the district within which the award was made, such service shall be made upon the adverse party or his attorney as prescribed by law for service of notice of motion in an action in the same court. If the adverse party shall be a nonresident then the notice of the application shall be served by the marshal of any district within which the adverse party may be found in like manner as other process of the court. For the purposes of the motion any judge who might make an order to stay the proceedings in an action brought in the same court may make an order, to be served with the notice of motion, staying the proceedings of the adverse party to enforce the award.

Section 13. Papers filed with order on motions; judgment; docketing; force and effect; enforcement

The party moving for an order confirming, modifying, or correcting an award shall, at the time such order is filed with the clerk for the entry of judgment thereon, also file the following papers with the clerk:

(a) The agreement; the selection or appointment, if any, of an additional arbitrator or umpire; and each written extension of the time, if any, within which to make the award.

(b) The award.

(c) Each notice, affidavit, or other paper used upon an application to confirm, modify, or correct the award, and a copy of each order of the court upon such an application.

The judgment shall be docketed as if it was rendered in an action.

The judgment so entered shall have the same force and effect, in all respects, as, and be subject to all the provisions of law relating to, a judgment in an action; and it may be enforced as if it had been rendered in an action in the court in which it is entered.

Section 14. Contracts not affected

This title shall not apply to contracts made prior to January 1, 1926.

Section 15. Inapplicability of the Act of State doctrine

Enforcement of arbitral agreements, confirmation of arbitral awards, and execution upon judgments based on orders confirming such awards shall not be refused on the basis of the Act of State doctrine.

Section 16. Appeals

(a) An appeal may be taken from

(1) an order

(A) refusing a stay of any action under section 3 of this title,

(B) denying a petition under section 4 of this title to order arbitration to proceed,

(C) denying an application under section 206 of this title to compel arbitration,

(D) confirming or denying confirmation of an award or partial award, or

(E) modifying, correcting, or vacating an award;

(2) an interlocutory order granting, continuing, or modifying an injunction against an arbitration that is subject to this title; or

(3) a final decision with respect to an arbitration that is subject to this title.

(b) Except as otherwise provided in section 1292 (b) of title 28, an appeal may not be taken from an interlocutory order

(1) granting a stay of any action under section 3 of this title;

(2) directing arbitration to proceed under section 4 of this title;

(3) compelling arbitration under section 206 of this title; or

(4) refusing to enjoin an arbitration that is subject to this title.

THE FEDERAL ARBITRATION ACT

CHAPTER 2. CONVENTION ON THE RECOGNITION AND ENFORCEMENT OF FOREIGN ARBITRAL AWARDS

Section 201. Enforcement of Convention

The Convention on the Recognition and Enforcement of Foreign Arbitral Awards of June 10, 1958, shall be enforced in United States courts in accordance with this chapter.

Section 202. Agreement or award falling under the Convention

An arbitration agreement or arbitral award arising out of a legal relationship, whether contractual or not, which is considered as commercial, including a transaction, contract, or agreement described in section 2 of this title, falls under the Convention. An agreement or award arising out of such a relationship which is entirely between citizens of the United States shall be deemed not to fall under the Convention unless that relationship involves property located abroad, envisages performance or enforcement abroad, or has some other reasonable relation with one or more foreign states. For the purpose of this section a corporation is a citizen of the United States if it is incorporated or has its principal place of business in the United States.

Section 203. Jurisdiction; amount in controversy

An action or proceeding falling under the Convention shall be deemed to arise under the laws and treaties of the United States. The district courts of the United States (including the courts enumerated in section 460 of Title 28) shall have original jurisdiction over such an action or proceeding, regardless of the amount in controversy.

Section 204. Venue

An action or proceeding over which the district courts have jurisdiction pursuant to section 203 of this title may be brought in any such court in which save for the arbitration agreement an action or proceeding with respect to the controversy between the parties could be brought, or in such court for the district and division which embraces the place designated in the agreement as the place of arbitration if such place is within the United States.

Section 205. Removal of cases from State courts

Where the subject matter of an action or proceeding pending in a State court relates to an arbitration agreement or award falling under the Convention, the defendant or the defendants may, at any time before the trial thereof, remove such action or proceeding to the district court of the United States for the district and division embracing the place where the action or proceeding is pending. The procedure for removal of causes otherwise provided by law shall apply, except that the ground for removal provided in this section need not appear on the face of the complaint but may be shown in the petition for removal. For the purposes of Chapter 1 of this title any action or proceeding removed under this section shall be deemed to have been brought in the district court to which it is removed.

Section 206. Order to compel arbitration; appointment of arbitrators

A court having jurisdiction under this chapter may direct that arbitration be held in accordance with the agreement at any place therein provided for, whether that place is within or without the United States. Such court may also appoint arbitrators in accordance with the provisions of the agreement.

Section 207. Award of arbitrators; confirmation; jurisdiction; proceeding

Chapter 1 applies to actions and proceedings brought under this chapter to the extent that chapter is not in conflict with this chapter or the Convention as ratified by the United States.

Section 208. Chapter 1; residual application

Chapter 1 applies to actions and proceedings brought under this chapter to the extent that chapter is not in conflict with this chapter or the Convention as ratified by the United States.

CHAPTER 3. INTER-AMERICAN CONVENTION ON INTERNATIONAL COMMERCIAL ARBITRATION

Section 301. Enforcement of Convention

The Inter-American Convention on International Commercial Arbitration of January 30, 1975, shall be enforced in United States courts in accordance with this chapter.

Section 302. Incorporation by reference

Sections 202, 203, 204, 205, and 207 of this title shall apply to this chapter as if specifically set forth herein, except that for the purposes of this chapter "the Convention" shall mean the Inter-American Convention.

Section 303. Order to compel arbitration; appointment of arbitrators; locale

(a) A court having jurisdiction under this chapter may direct that arbitration be held in accordance with the agreement at any place therein provided for, whether that place is within or without the United States. The court may also appoint arbitrators in accordance with the provisions of the agreement.

(b) In the event the agreement does not make provision for the place of arbitration or the appointment of arbitrators, the court shall direct that the arbitration shall be held and the arbitrators be appointed in accordance with Article 3 of the Inter-American Convention.

Section 304. Recognition and enforcement of foreign arbitral decisions and awards; reciprocity

Arbitral decisions or awards made in the territory of a foreign State shall, on the basis of reciprocity, be recognized and enforced under this chapter only if that State has ratified or acceded to the Inter-American Convention.

Section 305. Relationship between the Inter-American Convention and the Convention on the Recognition and Enforcement of Foreign Arbitral Awards of June 10, 1958

When the requirements for application of both the Inter-American Convention and the Convention on the Recognition and Enforcement of Foreign Arbitral Awards of June 10, 1958, are met, determination as to which Convention applies shall, unless otherwise expressly agreed, be made as follows:

(1) If a majority of the parties to the arbitration agreement are citizens of a State or States that have ratified or acceded to the Inter-American Convention

and are member States of the Organization of American States, the Inter-American Convention shall apply.

(2) In all other cases the Convention on the Recognition and Enforcement of Foreign Arbitral Awards of June 10, 1958, shall apply.

Section 306. Applicable rules of Inter-American Commercial Arbitration Commission

(a)For the purposes of this chapter the rules of procedure of the Inter-American Commercial Arbitration Commission referred to in Article 3 of the Inter-American Convention shall, subject to subsection (b) of this section, be those rules as promulgated by the Commission on July 1, 1988.

(b) In the event the rules of procedure of the Inter-American Commercial Arbitration Commission are modified or amended in accordance with the procedures for amendment of the rules of that Commission, the Secretary of State, by regulation in accordance with section 553 of Title 5, consistent with the aims and purposes of this Convention, may prescribe that such modifications or amendments shall be effective for purposes of this chapter.

Section 307. Chapter 1; residual application

Chapter 1 applies to actions and proceedings brought under this chapter to the extent chapter 1 is not in conflict with this chapter or the Inter-American Convention as ratified by the United States.

◆APPENDIX O ◆

AMERICAN ARBITRATION ASSOCIATION INTERNATIONAL ARBITRATION RULES

As Amended and Effective November 1, 2001

Table of Contents [summary]

Introduction

The world business community uses arbitration to resolve commercial disputes arising in the global marketplace. Supportive laws are in place. The New York Convention of 1958 has been widely adopted, providing a favorable legislative climate. Arbitration clauses are enforced. International commercial arbitration awards are recognized by national courts in most parts of the world, even more than foreign court judgments.

Arbitration institutions have been established in many countries to administer international cases. Many have entered into cooperative arrangements with the American Arbitration Association.

These International Arbitration Rules have been developed to encourage greater use of such services. By providing for arbitration under these rules, parties can avoid the uncertainty of having to petition a local court to resolve procedural impasses. These rules are intended to provide effective arbitration services to world business through the use of administered arbitration.

As the International Centre for Dispute Resolution (ICDR) is a division of the American Arbitration Association (AAA), parties can arbitrate future disputes under these rules by inserting either of the following clauses into their contracts:

"Any controversy or claim arising out of or relating to this contract shall be determined by arbitration in accordance with the International Arbitration Rules of the International Centre for Dispute Resolution."

or

"Any controversy or claim arising out of or relating to this contract shall be determined by arbitration in accordance with the International Arbitration Rules of the American Arbitration Association."

The parties may wish to consider adding:

(a)   "The number of arbitrators shall be (one or three)";

(b)   "The place of arbitration shall be (city and/or country)"; or

(c)   "The language(s) of the arbitration shall be _____."

Parties are encouraged, when writing their contracts or when a dispute arises, to request a conference, in person or by telephone, with the ICDR, to discuss an appropriate method for selection of arbitrators or any other matter that might facilitate efficient arbitration of the dispute.

Under these rules, the parties are free to adopt any mutually agreeable procedure for appointing arbitrators, or may designate arbitrators upon whom they agree. Parties can reach agreements concerning appointing arbitrators either when writing their contracts or after a dispute has arisen. This flexible procedure permits parties to utilize whatever method they consider best suits their needs. For example, parties may choose to have a sole arbitrator or a tribunal of three or more. They may agree that arbitrators shall be appointed by the ICDR, or that each side shall designate one arbitrator and those two shall name a third, with the ICDR making appointments if the tribunal is not promptly formed by that procedure. Parties may mutually request the ICDR to submit to them a list of arbitrators from which each can delete names not acceptable to it, or the parties may instruct the ICDR to appoint arbitrators without the submission of lists, or may leave that matter to the sole discretion of the ICDR. Parties also may agree on a variety of other methods for establishing the tribunal. In any event, if parties are unable to agree on a procedure for appointing arbitrators or on the designation of arbitrators, the ICDR, after inviting consultation by the parties, will appoint the arbitrators. The rules thus provide for the fullest exercise of party autonomy, while assuring that the ICDR is available to act if the parties cannot reach mutual agreement.

Whenever a singular term is used in the rules, such as "party," "claimant" or "arbitrator," that term shall include the plural if there is more than one such entity.

Parties may choose to use the ICDR's mediation services. The ICDR can schedule the mediation for anywhere in the world and will propose a list of specialized international mediators.

Parties filing an international case with the American Arbitration Association's International Centre for Dispute Resolution may do so by contacting any one of the AAA's regional offices or by contacting the International Centre for Dispute Resolution's New York, N.Y. office which is supervised by multilingual attorneys and case managers who have the requisite expertise in international matters.

Further information about these rules can be secured by contacting the International Centre for Dispute Resolution at 888-855-9575.

INTERNATIONAL CENTRE FOR DISPUTE RESOLUTION
International Arbitration Rules

Article 1

1.   Where parties have agreed in writing to arbitrate disputes under these International Arbitration Rules or have provided for arbitration of an international dispute by the International Centre for Dispute Resolution or the American Arbitration Association without designating particular rules, the arbitration shall take place in accordance with these rules, as in effect at the date of commencement of the arbitration, subject to whatever modifications the parties may adopt in writing.

2.   These rules govern the arbitration, except that, where any such rule is in conflict with any provision of the law applicable to the arbitration from which the parties cannot derogate, that provision shall prevail.

3.   These rules specify the duties and responsibilities of the administrator, the International Centre for Dispute Resolution, a division of the American Arbitration Association. The administrator may provide services through its Centre, located in New York City, or through the facilities of arbitral institutions with which it has agreements of cooperation.

I.   Commencing the Arbitration

Notice of Arbitration and Statement of Claim

Article 2

1.   The party initiating arbitration ("claimant") shall give written notice of arbitration to the administrator and at the same time to the party against whom a claim is being made ("respondent").

2.   Arbitral proceedings shall be deemed to commence on the date on which the administrator receives the notice of arbitration.

3.   The notice of arbitration shall contain a statement of claim including the following:

(a)   a demand that the dispute be referred to arbitration;

(b)   the names and addresses of the parties;

(c)   a reference to the arbitration clause or agreement that is invoked;

(d)   a reference to any contract out of or in relation to which the dispute arises;

(e)   a description of the claim and an indication of the facts supporting it;

(f)   the relief or remedy sought and the amount claimed; and

(g)   may include proposals as to the means of designating and the number of arbitrators, the place of arbitration and the language(s) of the arbitration.

4. Upon receipt of the notice of arbitration, the administrator shall communicate with all parties with respect to the arbitration and shall acknowledge the commencement of the arbitration.

Statement of Defense and Counterclaim

Article 3

1. Within 30 days after the commencement of the arbitration, a respondent shall submit a written statement of defense, responding to the issues raised in the notice of arbitration, to the claimant and any other parties, and to the administrator.

2. At the time a respondent submits its statement of defense, a respondent may make counterclaims or assert setoffs as to any claim covered by the agreement to arbitrate, as to which the claimant shall within 30 days submit a written statement of defense to the respondent and any other parties and to the administrator.

3. A respondent shall respond to the administrator, the claimant and other parties within 30 days after the commencement of the arbitration as to any proposals the claimant may have made as to the number of arbitrators, the place of the arbitration or the language(s) of the arbitration, except to the extent that the parties have previously agreed as to these matters.

4. The arbitral tribunal, or the administrator if the arbitral tribunal has not yet been formed, may extend any of the time limits established in this article if it considers such an extension justified.

Amendments to Claims

Article 4

During the arbitral proceedings, any party may amend or supplement its claim, counterclaim or defense, unless the tribunal considers it inappropriate to allow such amendment or supplement because of the party's delay in making it, prejudice to the other parties or any other circumstances. A party may not amend or supplement a claim or counterclaim if the amendment or supplement would fall outside the scope of the agreement to arbitrate.

II. The Tribunal

Number of Arbitrators

Article 5

If the parties have not agreed on the number of arbitrators, one arbitrator shall be appointed unless the administrator determines in its discretion that three arbitrators are appropriate because of the large size, complexity or other circumstances of the case.

Appointment of Arbitrators

Article 6

1. The parties may mutually agree upon any procedure for appointing arbitrators and shall inform the administrator as to such procedure.

2. The parties may mutually designate arbitrators, with or without the assistance of the administrator. When such designations are made, the parties shall notify the administrator so that notice of the appointment can be communicated to the arbitrators, together with a copy of these rules.

3. If within 45 days after the commencement of the arbitration, all of the parties have not mutually agreed on a procedure for appointing the arbitrator(s) or have not mutually agreed on the designation of the arbitrator(s), the administrator shall, at the written request of any party, appoint the arbitrator(s) and designate the presiding arbitrator. If all of the parties have mutually agreed upon a procedure for appointing the arbitrator(s), but all appointments have not been made within the time limits provided in that procedure, the administrator shall, at the written request of any party, perform all functions provided for in that procedure that remain to be performed.

4. In making such appointments, the administrator, after inviting consultation with the parties, shall endeavor to select suitable arbitrators. At the request of any party or on its own initiative, the administrator may appoint nationals of a country other than that of any of the parties.

5. Unless the parties have agreed otherwise no later than 45 days after the commencement of the arbitration, if the notice of arbitration names two or more claimants or two or more respondents, the administrator shall appoint all the arbitrators.

Impartiality and Independence of Arbitrators

Article 7

1. Arbitrators acting under these rules shall be impartial and independent. Prior to accepting appointment, a prospective arbitrator shall disclose to the administrator any circumstance likely to give rise to justifiable doubts as to the arbitrator's impartiality or independence. If, at any stage during the arbitration, new circumstances arise that may give rise to such doubts, an arbitrator shall promptly disclose such circumstances to the parties and to the administrator. Upon receipt of such information from an arbitrator or a party, the administrator shall communicate it to the other parties and to the tribunal.

2.   No party or anyone acting on its behalf shall have any ex parte communication relating to the case with any arbitrator, or with any candidate for appointment as party-appointed arbitrator except to advise the candidate of the general nature of the controversy and of the anticipated proceedings and to discuss the candidate's qualifications, availability or independence in relation to the parties, or to discuss the suitability of candidates for selection as a third arbitrator where the parties or party-designated arbitrators are to participate in that selection. No party or anyone acting on its behalf shall have any ex parte communication relating to the case with any candidate for presiding arbitrator.

Challenge of Arbitrators

Article 8

1.   A party may challenge any arbitrator whenever circumstances exist that give rise to justifiable doubts as to the arbitrator's impartiality or independence. A party wishing to challenge an arbitrator shall send notice of the challenge to the administrator within 15 days after being notified of the appointment of the arbitrator or within 15 days after the circumstances giving rise to the challenge become known to that party.

2.   The challenge shall state in writing the reasons for the challenge.

3.   Upon receipt of such a challenge, the administrator shall notify the other parties of the challenge. When an arbitrator has been challenged by one party, the other party or parties may agree to the acceptance of the challenge and, if there is agreement, the arbitrator shall withdraw. The challenged arbitrator may also withdraw from office in the absence of such agreement. In neither case does withdrawal imply acceptance of the validity of the grounds for the challenge.

Article 9

If the other party or parties do not agree to the challenge or the challenged arbitrator does not withdraw, the administrator in its sole discretion shall make the decision on the challenge.

Replacement of an Arbitrator

Article 10

If an arbitrator withdraws after a challenge, or the administrator sustains the challenge, or the administrator determines that there are sufficient reasons to accept the resignation of an arbitrator, or an arbitrator dies, a substitute arbitrator shall be appointed pursuant to the provisions of Article 6, unless the parties otherwise agree.

Article 11

1.   If an arbitrator on a three-person tribunal fails to participate in the arbitration for reasons other than those identified in Article 10, the two other

arbitrators shall have the power in their sole discretion to continue the arbitration and to make any decision, ruling or award, notwithstanding the failure of the third arbitrator to participate. In determining whether to continue the arbitration or to render any decision, ruling or award without the participation of an arbitrator, the two other arbitrators shall take into account the stage of the arbitration, the reason, if any, expressed by the third arbitrator for such nonparticipation, and such other matters as they consider appropriate in the circumstances of the case. In the event that the two other arbitrators determine not to continue the arbitration without the participation of the third arbitrator, the administrator on proof satisfactory to it shall declare the office vacant, and a substitute arbitrator shall be appointed pursuant to the provisions of Article 6, unless the parties otherwise agree.

2. If a substitute arbitrator is appointed under either Article 10 or Article 11, the tribunal shall determine at its sole discretion whether all or part of any prior hearings shall be repeated.

III. General Conditions

Representation

Article 12

Any party may be represented in the arbitration. The names, addresses and telephone numbers of representatives shall be communicated in writing to the other parties and to the administrator. Once the tribunal has been established, the parties or their representatives may communicate in writing directly with the tribunal.

Place of Arbitration

Article 13

1. If the parties disagree as to the place of arbitration, the administrator may initially determine the place of arbitration, subject to the power of the tribunal to determine finally the place of arbitration within 60 days after its constitution. All such determinations shall be made having regard for the contentions of the parties and the circumstances of the arbitration.

2. The tribunal may hold conferences or hear witnesses or inspect property or documents at any place it deems appropriate. The parties shall be given sufficient written notice to enable them to be present at any such proceedings

Language

Article 14

If the parties have not agreed otherwise, the language(s) of the arbitration shall be that of the documents containing the arbitration agreement, subject to the power of the tribunal to determine otherwise based upon the contentions of the parties and the circumstances of the arbitration. The tribunal may order that any documents delivered in another language shall be accompanied by a translation into the language(s) of the arbitration.

Pleas as to Jurisdiction

Article 15

1. The tribunal shall have the power to rule on its own jurisdiction, including any objections with respect to the existence, scope or validity of the arbitration agreement.

2. The tribunal shall have the power to determine the existence or validity of a contract of which an arbitration clause forms a part. Such an arbitration clause shall be treated as an agreement independent of the other terms of the contract. A decision by the tribunal that the contract is null and void shall not for that reason alone render invalid the arbitration clause.

3. A party must object to the jurisdiction of the tribunal or to the arbitrability of a claim or counterclaim no later than the filing of the statement of defense, as provided in Article 3, to the claim or counterclaim that gives rise to the objection. The tribunal may rule on such objections as a preliminary matter or as part of the final award.

Conduct of the Arbitration

Article 16

1. Subject to these rules, the tribunal may conduct the arbitration in whatever manner it considers appropriate, provided that the parties are treated with equality and that each party has the right to be heard and is given a fair opportunity to present its case.

2. The tribunal, exercising its discretion, shall conduct the proceedings with a view to expediting the resolution of the dispute. It may conduct a preparatory conference with the parties for the purpose of organizing, scheduling and agreeing to procedures to expedite the subsequent proceedings.

3. The tribunal may in its discretion direct the order of proof, bifurcate proceedings, exclude cumulative or irrelevant testimony or other evidence, and direct the parties to focus their presentations on issues the decision of which could dispose of all or part of the case.

4. Documents or information supplied to the tribunal by one party shall at the same time be communicated by that party to the other party or parties.

Further Written Statements

Article 17

1. The tribunal may decide whether the parties shall present any written statements in addition to statements of claims and counterclaims and statements

of defense, and it shall fix the periods of time for submitting any such statements.

2. The periods of time fixed by the tribunal for the communication of such written statements should not exceed 45 days. However, the tribunal may extend such time limits if it considers such an extension justified.

Notices

Article 18

1. Unless otherwise agreed by the parties or ordered by the tribunal, all notices, statements and written communications may be served on a party by air mail, air courier, facsimile transmission, telex, telegram, or other written forms of electronic communication addressed to the party or its representative at its last known address or by personal service.

2. For the purpose of calculating a period of time under these rules, such period shall begin to run on the day following the day when a notice, statement or written communication is received. If the last day of such period is an official holiday at the place received, the period is extended until the first business day which follows. Official holidays occurring during the running of the period of time are included in calculating the period.

Evidence

Article 19

1. Each party shall have the burden of proving the facts relied on to support its claim or defense.

2. The tribunal may order a party to deliver to the tribunal and to the other parties a summary of the documents and other evidence which that party intends to present in support of its claim, counterclaim or defense.

3   At any time during the proceedings, the tribunal may order parties to produce other documents, exhibits or other evidence it deems necessary or appropriate.

Hearings

Article 20

1. The tribunal shall give the parties at least 30 days' advance notice of the date, time and place of the initial oral hearing. The tribunal shall give reasonable notice of subsequent hearings.

2. At least 15 days before the hearings, each party shall give the tribunal and the other parties the names and addresses of any witnesses it intends to present, the subject of their testimony and the languages in which such witnesses will give their testimony.

3. At the request of the tribunal or pursuant to mutual agreement of the parties, the administrator shall make arrangements for the interpretation of oral testimony or for a record of the hearing.

4. Hearings are private unless the parties agree otherwise or the law provides to the contrary. The tribunal may require any witness or witnesses to retire during the testimony of other witnesses. The tribunal may determine the manner in which witnesses are examined.

5. Evidence of witnesses may also be presented in the form of written statements signed by them.

6. The tribunal shall determine the admissibility, relevance, materiality and weight of the evidence offered by any party. The tribunal shall take into account applicable principles of legal privilege, such as those involving the confidentiality of communications between a lawyer and client.

Interim Measures of Protection

Article 21

1. At the request of any party, the tribunal may take whatever interim measures it deems necessary, including injunctive relief and measures for the protection or conservation of property.

2. Such interim measures may take the form of an interim award, and the tribunal may require security for the costs of such measures.

3. A request for interim measures addressed by a party to a judicial authority shall not be deemed incompatible with the agreement to arbitrate or a waiver of the right to arbitrate.

4. The tribunal may in its discretion apportion costs associated with applications for interim relief in any interim award or in the final award.

Experts

Article 22

1. The tribunal may appoint one or more independent experts to report to it, in writing, on specific issues designated by the tribunal and communicated to the parties.

2. The parties shall provide such an expert with any relevant information or produce for inspection any relevant documents or goods that the expert may require. Any dispute between a party and the expert as to the relevance of the requested information or goods shall be referred to the tribunal for decision.

3. Upon receipt of an expert's report, the tribunal shall send a copy of the report to all parties and shall give the parties an opportunity to express, in writing, their opinion on the report. A party may examine any document on which the expert has relied in such a report.

4. At the request of any party, the tribunal shall give the parties an opportunity to question the expert at a hearing. At this hearing, parties may present expert witnesses to testify on the points at issue.

Default
Article 23

1. If a party fails to file a statement of defense within the time established by the tribunal without showing sufficient cause for such failure, as determined by the tribunal, the tribunal may proceed with the arbitration.

2. If a party, duly notified under these rules, fails to appear at a hearing without showing sufficient cause for such failure, as determined by the tribunal, the tribunal may proceed with the arbitration.

3. If a party, duly invited to produce evidence or take any other steps in the proceedings, fails to do so within the time established by the tribunal without showing sufficient cause for such failure, as determined by the tribunal, the tribunal may make the award on the evidence before it.

Closure of Hearing
Article 24

1. After asking the parties if they have any further testimony or evidentiary submissions and upon receiving negative replies or if satisfied that the record is complete, the tribunal may declare the hearings closed.

2. The tribunal in its discretion, on its own motion or upon application of a party, may reopen the hearings at any time before the award is made.

Waiver of Rules
Article 25

A party who knows that any provision of the rules or requirement under the rules has not been complied with, but proceeds with the arbitration without promptly stating an objection in writing thereto, shall be deemed to have waived the right to object.

Awards, Decisions and Rulings
Article 26

1. When there is more than one arbitrator, any award, decision or ruling of the arbitral tribunal shall be made by a majority of the arbitrators. If any arbitrator fails to sign the award, it shall be accompanied by a statement of the reason for the absence of such signature.

2. When the parties or the tribunal so authorize, the presiding arbitrator may make decisions or rulings on questions of procedure, subject to revision by the tribunal.

Form and Effect of the Award
Article 27

1.   Awards shall be made in writing, promptly by the tribunal, and shall be final and binding on the parties. The parties undertake to carry out any such award without delay.

2.   The tribunal shall state the reasons upon which the award is based, unless the parties have agreed that no reasons need be given.

3.   The award shall contain the date and the place where the award was made, which shall be the place designated pursuant to Article 13.

4.   An award may be made public only with the consent of all parties or as required by law.

5.   Copies of the award shall be communicated to the parties by the administrator.

6.   If the arbitration law of the country where the award is made requires the award to be filed or registered, the tribunal shall comply with such requirement.

7.   In addition to making a final award, the tribunal may make interim, interlocutory, or partial orders and awards.

Applicable Laws and Remedies
Article 28

1.   The tribunal shall apply the substantive law(s) or rules of law designated by the parties as applicable to the dispute. Failing such a designation by the parties, the tribunal shall apply such law(s) or rules of law as it determines to be appropriate.

2.   In arbitrations involving the application of contracts, the tribunal shall decide in accordance with the terms of the contract and shall take into account usages of the trade applicable to the contract.

3.   The tribunal shall not decide as amiable compositeur or ex aequo et bono unless the parties have expressly authorized it to do so.

4.   A monetary award shall be in the currency or currencies of the contract unless the tribunal considers another currency more appropriate, and the tribunal may award such pre-award and post-award interest, simple or compound, as it considers appropriate, taking into consideration the contract and applicable law.

5.   Unless the parties agree otherwise, the parties expressly waive and forego any right to punitive, exemplary or similar damages unless a statute requires that compensatory damages be increased in a specified manner. This provision

shall not apply to any award of arbitration costs to a party to compensate for dilatory or bad faith conduct in the arbitration.

Settlement or Other Reasons for Termination

Article 29

1. If the parties settle the dispute before an award is made, the tribunal shall terminate the arbitration and, if requested by all parties, may record the settlement in the form of an award on agreed terms. The tribunal is not obliged to give reasons for such an award.

2. If the continuation of the proceedings becomes unnecessary or impossible for any other reason, the tribunal shall inform the parties of its intention to terminate the proceedings. The tribunal shall thereafter issue an order terminating the arbitration, unless a party raises justifiable grounds for objection.

Interpretation or Correction of the Award

Article 30

1. Within 30 days after the receipt of an award, any party, with notice to the other parties, may request the tribunal to interpret the award or correct any clerical, typographical or computation errors or make an additional award as to claims presented but omitted from the award.

2. If the tribunal considers such a request justified, after considering the contentions of the parties, it shall comply with such a request within 30 days after the request.

Costs

Article 31

The tribunal shall fix the costs of arbitration in its award. The tribunal may apportion such costs among the parties if it determines that such apportionment is reasonable, taking into account the circumstances of the case.

Such costs may include:

(a) the fees and expenses of the arbitrators;

(b) the costs of assistance required by the tribunal, including its experts;

(c) the fees and expenses of the administrator;

(d) the reasonable costs for legal representation of a successful party; and

(e) any such costs incurred in connection with an application for interim or emergency relief pursuant to Article 21.

Compensation of Arbitrators

Article 32

Arbitrators shall be compensated based upon their amount of service, taking into account their stated rate of compensation and the size and complexity of the case. The administrator shall arrange an appropriate daily or hourly rate, based on such considerations, with the parties and with each of the arbitrators as soon as practicable after the commencement of the arbitration. If the parties fail to agree on the terms of compensation, the administrator shall establish an appropriate rate and communicate it in writing to the parties.

Deposit of Costs

Article 33

1.   When a party files claims, the administrator may request the filing party to deposit appropriate amounts as an advance for the costs referred to in Article 31, paragraphs (a), (b) and (c).

2.   During the course of the arbitral proceedings, the tribunal may request supplementary deposits from the parties.

3.   If the deposits requested are not paid in full within 30 days after the receipt of the request, the administrator shall so inform the parties, in order that one or the other of them may make the required payment. If such payments are not made, the tribunal may order the suspension or termination of the proceedings.

4.   After the award has been made, the administrator shall render an accounting to the parties of the deposits received and return any unexpended balance to the parties.

Confidentiality

Article 34

Confidential information disclosed during the proceedings by the parties or by witnesses shall not be divulged by an arbitrator or by the administrator. Unless otherwise agreed by the parties, or required by applicable law, the members of the tribunal and the administrator shall keep confidential all matters relating to the arbitration or the award.

Exclusion of Liability

Article 35

The members of the tribunal and the administrator shall not be liable to any party for any act or omission in connection with any arbitration conducted under these rules, except that they may be liable for the consequences of conscious and deliberate wrongdoing.

Interpretation of Rules

Article 36

The tribunal shall interpret and apply these rules insofar as they relate to its powers and duties. The administrator shall interpret and apply all other rules.

◆ APPENDIX P ◆

AMERICAN ARBITRATION ASSOCIATION
SUPPLEMENTARY PROCEDURES FOR ONLINE ARBITRATION
(Effective July 1, 2001)

1.   Introduction

The purpose of the Supplementary Procedures for Online Arbitration is to permit, where the parties have agreed to arbitration under these Supplementary Procedures, arbitral proceedings to be conducted and resolved exclusively via the Internet. The Supplementary Procedures provide for all party submissions to be made online, and for the arbitrator, upon review of such submissions, to render an award and to communicate it to the parties via the Internet. These Supplementary Procedures further authorize the parties and the arbitrator in certain circumstances to use methods of communication other than the Internet.

Definitions

a. **Administrative Site** refers to the Internet site www.adr.org. At the Administrative Site, parties may initiate arbitration under the Supplementary Procedures and pay filing fees and other administrative costs. The Administrative Site also provides schedules of applicable fees and costs, technical guidelines regarding the format of submissions, as well as other important information and resources.

b. **Arbitrator** refers to a sole arbitrator or a three person panel appointed according to the Supplementary Procedures.

c. **Case Site** refers to the Internet site established to maintain the case files and submissions. All of the parties' written submissions shall be posted on the Case Site, and no one other than the AAA, the parties, and the Arbitrator shall have access to the Case Site.

d. **Hearing**, whether used in the singular or plural, refers to any meeting or meetings of the parties before the Arbitrator, whether conducted in-person or by telephone, video-conference, or other means.

e. **Internet** and **online** are used interchangeably to refer to the world-wide electronic online medium.

f. **Portal Terms** shall refer to the terms and conditions of use of the Case Site and Administrative Site, as may be amended from time to time by the AAA.

g. **Submit** refers to (i) the electronic transmittal of pleadings, exhibits, communications, or other documents to the Case Site, or (ii) such other method of transmitting pleadings, exhibits, communications, or other documents as may be authorized by the Arbitrator under Section 12(a). **Submissions** refers to all such pleadings, exhibits, communications, or other documents, however transmitted.

h. **Writing** refers not only to the customary definition of "writing" but also to an "electronic record" as the term is defined the Uniform Electronic Transactions Act (U.L.A.), § 2.

Procedures

1.   Agreement to Arbitrate under these Supplementary Procedures

a. The parties shall be deemed to have made these Supplementary Procedures a part of their arbitration agreement whenever they have provided for arbitration by the American Arbitration Association (the "AAA") under its Supplementary Procedures for online Arbitration. These Supplementary Procedures may also be used, by agreement of the parties and Arbitrator, in arbitrations initiated under other sets of rules. The Supplementary Procedures and any amendment to them shall apply in the form in effect at the time of commencement of the arbitration. The parties, by agreement in writing, may vary the procedures set forth in these Supplementary Procedures.

b. The Supplementary Procedures are supplemental to the AAA's Commercial Dispute Resolution Procedures, or any other set of applicable AAA rules, which shall remain applicable except where modified by the Supplementary Procedures.

c. The AAA may decide that an arbitration shall not be conducted under the Supplementary Procedures where a party lacks the capacity to participate in the arbitration in accordance with these Procedures, or where the AAA otherwise finds, in its discretion, that an arbitration should not be conducted under these Procedures. In the event that the AAA makes such a determination, the arbitration shall be conducted in accordance with the Commercial Dispute Resolution Procedures or other applicable AAA rules.

d. By agreeing to the Supplementary Procedures, the parties also agree to the Portal Terms in effect at the time of commencement of the arbitration.

e. When the parties agree to arbitrate under the Supplementary Procedures, they thereby authorize the AAA to administer the arbitration.

2.   Serving of Notices and Calculation of Time Periods

a. Except as otherwise agreed by the parties and approved by the Arbitrator, all submissions provided for under the Supplementary Procedures shall be deemed to have been made when received at the Case Site. The date and time of receipt shall be that stated in the confirmatory e-mail sent from the Case Site to the party making the submission.

b. For the purposes of calculating a period of time under the Supplementary Procedures, such period shall begin to run from the date of receipt at the Case Cite.

3.   The Claim in Arbitration a. The Claimant shall initiate the arbitration by submitting to the Administrative Site a claim in arbitration (the "Claim"), which shall include: the parties' arbitration agreement; any agreement between the parties regarding the number, identity, qualifications, and/or the manner of selection of the Arbitrator; basic documents insofar as reasonably susceptible to electronic transmittal; and a statement of the nature of the dispute, the legal arguments which support the Claim, the amount involved, if any, and the remedy sought.

b. In addition to the foregoing, the Claim shall provide the following information:

> (1) the e-mail address at which the Claimant will receive e-mail communications from the Case Site;
>
> (2) the last known valid e-mail address of the Respondent; and
>
> (3) the names, postal addresses, and telephone and facsimile numbers of the parties.

c. The Claimant shall pay the appropriate filing fee within five days of submitting the Claim to the Administrative Site. Such fee may be paid electronically or by any other method prescribed by the AAA.

4.   Notification of Complaint a. Upon receipt of the appropriate filing fee from the Claimant, the AAA shall review the Claim to ascertain whether it complies with Section 3. Once the AAA has satisfied itself of the foregoing, the AAA shall, within five business days, establish a Case Site upon which the Claim shall immediately be made available. The AAA shall notify the parties by e-mail of the Internet address for the Case Site. The arbitration shall be deemed commenced on the date upon which the Case Site was established, as reflected in the confirmatory e-mails sent by the AAA to the parties.

b. If the AAA finds that notification to the Respondent via e-mail is not possible, the AAA may decide that the Supplementary Procedures should not apply.

c. If the AAA determines that the Claim is administratively deficient, the AAA shall not create a Case Site and shall promptly notify the Claimant of the deficiencies identified.

5.   Response to Claim Within thirty calendar days following the establishment of the Case Site, the Respondent shall submit to the Case Site a response, which shall include:

> (1) the response to the Claim, together with the facts, documents, and legal arguments supporting such response;

(2) any objection to the jurisdiction of the Arbitrator, to the number, identity, qualifications, and/or manner of selection of the Arbitrator, or to the applicability of the Supplementary Procedures;

(3) the e-mail address at which the Respondent will receive e-mail communications from the Case Site; and

(4) if the Respondent has a counterclaim, a submission satisfying the requirements for a Claim set out in Section 3.

6.   Response to Counterclaim Where the Respondent has submitted a counterclaim, the Claimant shall submit to the Case Site a response within thirty calendar days from the date upon which the Respondent's counterclaim was submitted to the Case Site. The response shall include the information sufficient to meet the requirements of a response to a Claim set out in Section 5.

7.   Extensions of Time The AAA or the Arbitrator may, for good cause shown, extend the period of time for the Respondent to submit its response to the Claim or for the Claimant to submit its response to any counterclaim. Any such request made to the Arbitrator shall be submitted to the Case Site. Any such request made to the AAA shall be both submitted to the Case Site and sent by e-mail to the AAA as provided in Section 12(b).

8.   Language of the Arbitration Unless otherwise agreed by the parties, the language of the arbitration shall be that of the document(s) containing the arbitration agreement, subject to the power of the Arbitrator to determine otherwise.

9.   Hearings a. Unless either party requests and the Arbitrator agrees to a Hearing, the Arbitrator will make the award based on the submissions. In the absence of a request for a Hearing, the Arbitrator will render the award within thirty days of the closing of the proceeding.

b. At a Hearing, witness testimony may be received, cross-examination of witnesses may be conducted, and additional documentary evidence may be received as approved by the Arbitrator.

10.   Place of Award The parties may agree in writing upon the place of the award, and the Arbitrator shall designate this as the place of the award in the award. In the absence of such an agreement between the parties, the Arbitrator shall decide and shall designate the place of the award in the award.

11.   Communication of the Award to the Parties The Arbitrator shall submit the award to the Case Site. The award shall be deemed to have been made when submitted, which date shall be stated in the confirmatory e-mail sent from the Case Site to the parties notifying them that the award has been submitted.

The Case Site shall remain available to the parties for thirty days from the date upon which the award was submitted.

12.   Additional Methods of Communication a. The Arbitrator may authorize a method of communicating with the Arbitrator other than the above-described use of the Case Site.

b. The AAA shall provide to the parties and to the Arbitrator an e-mail address for those communications between the parties and the AAA or between the Arbitrator and the AAA which are not to be made available to all parties and the Arbitrator through submission to the Case Site (e.g., administrative queries).

◆ APPENDIX Q ◆

SUPPLEMENTARY RULES OF THE E-ARBITRATION-TRIBUNAL
January, 2003

CUATRECASAS

SUMMARY

SUPPLEMENTARY RULES

Introduction

The Supplementary Rules are aimed to permit that users and well-established organizations can offer the EAT technology without modifying their Rules. TERMS TO ARBITRATE ONLINE should be available in the organization's Web site and the parties will be asked to accept it by double click as soon as they provide the organization with their e-mail address. The terms to arbitrate online could also be accepted by reference (e.g., using links to the organization's Web site). Therefore, it is proposed that the agreement takes the following form:

Asking To Arbitrate Online

To be included in the e-mail sent by the organization or to be available at its Web site.

> #### *Online Arbitration:*
> Thanks to the EAT Technology ©, the organization also offers the possibility of submitting your disputes to online arbitration. To arbitrate online, you only need to have internet access and one e-mail address. By submitting this form you indicate that you have read and understand the TERMS TO ARBITRATE ONLINE and that you agree to them if the other party/parties to the dispute agree to the same. Your submission of this form will constitute your consent to the TERMS TO ARBITRATE ONLINE. For further information about EAT Technology ©, you can log onto www.earbitrationt.com

Terms to Arbitrate Online

1. Use of Electronic Documents

All documents, including pleadings, requests, petitions or briefs, shall be filed from and through the EAT Web site in an electronic format. Except for documents filed with their first communications to the Tribunal, the parties will have to convert non electronic docu-ments into electronic formats. Documents may be computer files or output, scanned im-ages, sound or video must be submitted in one of the format currently listed on the EAT Web site (i.e., TIFF, GIF, or JPEG and word processor output in RTF.

2. *The Parties' Responsibility*

The parties are liable for diligently using and safeguarding their respective passwords to the server, which shall be exclusively disclosed to EAT, the party and its representative. The parties are obliged to act with diligence and periodically log onto the EAT server to preserve their rights and undertake to reply to the communications or notices that are sent to them in the due time limit and in the proper form.

The organization shall establish a mechanism to settle any potential incompatibilities that may arise in relation to the format of the documents filed by the parties. However, each 1 E-Arbitration-T© IST-2000-25464/11/CAL/3022/DD/1 party shall be obliged to notify EAT of the existence of any circumstance that prevents it from gaining access to notices or files registered in the server.

3. *Communications and Notices*

All of the communications between the parties or between the parties and EAT or the Tri-bunal shall be made in and from the EAT web. The parties, however, will have available a private forum where to exchange private information for settlement purposes. EAT shall receive and file all communications made, notify the Tribunal and the other parties at the earliest opportunity and simultaneously thereof, and ensure that the dispatch and delivery of the same is duly recorded.

EAT shall send a message by e-mail to alert the parties that a new communication has been sent to them. If the message is returned, the organization shall resend it twice. If a technical fault is detected, EAT would contact the affected party. Should seven days elapse as of the date on which the notice is made and the party in question fails to connect to the server, confirmation of the aforementioned communications or notices shall be sent by fax or regu-lar mail.

4. *Address for Notification Purposes*

The parties shall exclusively be responsible for ensuring that the respective addresses and identification details published in the EAT server are accurate and complete. Only the ad-dress and identification data recorded in the server shall be deemed as valid for notification purposes.

The parties may modify its address and identification data by notifying EAT server of such change, so that EAT may register it and notify the Tribunal and the other parties thereof. Otherwise, the party's last recorded address shall continue to be deemed as the correct address for notification purposes.

5. *Calculation of Time Limits*

Time limits shall be calculated in calendar days from the day after the notice is delivered. It shall be deemed that the notice is delivered when the first Message Transfer Agent or the MTA designated by each party, if any, accepts the e-mail from the E-Arbitration-T server.

The time limit commences at 00:01 hours the day after the date of the notice and expires at 23:59 hours on the last calendar day, including holidays, in the place where the arbitration is held.

6. *Virtual Hearings*

EAT provides for a documents – only proceedings. However, a virtual hearing is available at the parties request. In that case, the parties waive their right to have physical meetings and agree that either preliminary hearings or any other hearings will take place through the technologies currently listed in the EAT Web site, which provide a range of services running from simple text chat to videoconferencing. 2 E-Arbitration-T© IST-2000-25464/11/CAL/3022/DD/1 3 E-Arbitration-T© IST-2000-25464/11/CAL/3022/DD/1

In any event, the selected technology shall allow the parties, the Tribunal, the witnesses, experts and any other participants of the hearing to connect simultaneously to the com-puter network and to have the same coverage along the hearing. When the connection is established, the arbitrators shall be responsible for verifying that all of the participants are present.

7. *The Electronic Award*

The award shall be made in an electronic format and shall be digitally signed by the major-ity of the arbitrators. If one of the arbitrators does not sign the award, he/she must state the reason for the same. The award shall be reasoned. The date and place of arbitration shall be set out therein. The award may rule on costs and, if appropriate, on the penalties to be applied.

The electronic award shall be notified to the parties electronically. If deposit or notarization is required, EAT may comply with such formalities at the request of either party. If either party so requests, EAT shall send them a certified copy of the hardcopy of the award through any medium which keeps record of it.

8. *Deposits and Other Electronic Money Transfers*

All deposits and payments required by the organization shall be electronically made. EAT guarantees that electronic payments shall occur within a secure environment and shall provide [name of the security provider e.g., verysign] adequate certificates thereof.

◆ APPENDIX R ◆

1958 NEW YORK CONVENTION ON THE RECOGNITION AND ENFORCEMENT OF FOREIGN ARBITRAL AWARDS

The Convention on the Recognition and Enforcement of Foreign Arbitral Awards was signed at the United Nations Conference on International Commercial Arbitration held in New York in June 1958.

The complete text of the Convention is given below for information. Attention is however particularly drawn to Articles I to VII, which contain the essential substance of the Convention. The remaining articles are primarily concerned with procedural matters.

Article 1

1. This Convention shall apply to the recognition and enforcement of arbitral awards made in the territory of a State other than the State where the recognition and enforcement of such awards are sought, and arising out of differences between persons, whether physical or legal. It shall also apply to arbitral awards not considered as domestic awards in the State where their recognition and enforcement are sought.

2. The term "arbitral awards" shall include not only awards made by arbitrators appointed for

each case but also those made by permanent arbitral bodies to which the parties have submitted.

3. When signing, ratifying or acceding to this Convention, or notifying extension under Article X hereof, any State may on the basis of reciprocity declare that it will apply the Convention to the recognition and enforcement of awards made only in the territory of another Contracting State. It may also declare that it will apply the Convention only to differences arising out of legal relationships, whether contractual or not, which are considered as commercial under the national law of the State making such declaration.

Article II

1. Each Contracting State shall recognize an agreement in writing under which the parties undertake to submit to arbitration all or any differences which have arisen or which may arise between them in respect of a defined legal relationship, whether contractual or not, concerning a subject matter capable of settlement of arbitration.

2. The term "agreement in writing" shall include an arbitral clause in a contract or an arbitration agreement, signed by the parties or contained in an exchange of letters or telegrams.

3. The court of a Contracting State, when seized of an action in a matter in respect of which the parties have made an agreement within the meaning of this article, shall, at the request of one of the parties, refer the parties to arbitration, unless it finds that the said agreement is null and void, inoperative or incapable of being performed.

Article III

Each Contracting State shall recognize arbitral awards as binding and enforce them in accordance with the rules of procedure of the territory where the award is relied upon, under the conditions laid down in the following articles. There shall not be imposed substantially more onerous conditions or higher fees or charges on the recognition or enforcement of arbitral awards to which this Convention applies than are imposed on the recognition or enforcement of domestic arbitral awards.

Article IV

1. To obtain the recognition and enforcement mentioned in the preceding article, the party applying for recognition and enforcement shall, at the time of the application, supply:

(a) the duly authenticated original award or a duly certified copy thereof;

(b) the original agreement referred to in Article II or a duly certified copy thereof.

2. If the said award or agreement is not made in an official language of the country in which the award is relied upon, the party applying for recognition and enforcement of the award shall produce a translation of these documents into such language. The translation shall be certified by an official or sworn translator or by a diplomatic or consular agent.

Article V

1. Recognition and enforcement of the award may be refused, at the request of the party against whom it is invoked, only if that party furnishes to the competent authority where the recognition and enforcement is sought, proof that: (a) the parties to the agreement referred to in Article II were, under the law applicable to them, under some incapacity, or the said agreement is not valid under the law to which the parties have subjected it or, failing any indication thereon, under the law of the country where the award was made; or

(b) the party against whom the award is invoked was not given proper notice of the appointment of the arbitrator or of the arbitration proceedings or was otherwise unable to present his case; or

(c) the award deals with a difference not contemplated by or not falling within the terms of the submission to arbitration, or it contains decisions on matters beyond the scope of the submission to arbitration, provided that, if the decision on matters submitted to arbitration can be separated from those not so submitted, that part of the award which contains decisions on matters submitted to arbitration may be recognized and enforced: or

(d) the composition of the arbitral authority or the arbitral procedure was not in accordance with the agreement of the parties, or, failing such agreement, was not in accordance with the law of the country where the arbitration took place; or

(e) the award has not yet become binding on the parties, or has been set aside or suspended by a competent authority of the country in which, or under the law of which, that award was made.

2. Recognition and enforcement of an arbitral award may also be refused if the competent authority in the country where recognition and enforcement is sought finds that:

(a) the subject matter of the difference is not capable of settlement by arbitration under the law of that country; or

(b) the recognition or enforcement of the award would be contrary to the public policy of that country.

Article VI

If an application for the setting aside or suspension of the award has been made to be a competent authority referred to in Article V paragraph (1) [e], the authority before which the award is sought to be relied upon may, if it considers it proper, adjourn the decision on the enforcement of the award and may also, on the application of the party claiming enforcement of the award, order the other party to give suitable security.

Article VII

1. The provisions of the present Convention shall not affect the validity of multilateral or bilateral agreements concerning the recognition and enforcement of arbitral awards entered into by the Contracting States nor deprive any interested party of any right he may have to avail himself of an arbitral award in the manner and to the extent allowed by the law or the treaties of the country where such award is sought to be relied upon.

2. The Geneva Protocol on Arbitration Clauses of 1923 and the Geneva Convention on the Execution of Foreign Arbitral Awards of 1927 shall cease to have effect between the Contracting States on their becoming bound and to the extent that they become bound, by this Convention.

Article VIII

1. This Convention shall be open until 31 December 1958 for signature on behalf of any Member of the United Nations and also on behalf of any other State which is or hereafter becomes a member of any specialized agency of the United Nations, or which is or hereafter becomes a party to the Statute of the International Court of Justice, or any other State to which an invitation has been addressed by the General Assembly of the United Nations.

2. This Convention shall be ratified and the instrument of ratification shall be deposited with the Secretary General of the United Nations.

Article IX

1. This Convention shall be open for accession to all States referred to in Article VIII.

2. Accession shall be effected by the deposit of an instrument of accession with the Secretary General of the United Nations.

Article X

1. Any State may, at the time of signature, ratification or accession, declare that this Convention shall extend to all or any of their territories for the international relations of which it is responsible. Such a declaration shall take effect when the Convention enters into force for the State concerned.

2. At any time thereafter any such extension shall be made by notification addressed to the Secretary General of the United Nations and shall take effect as from the ninetieth day after the day of receipt by the Secretary General of the United Nations of this notification, or as from the date of entry into force of the Convention for the State concerned, whichever is the later.

3. With respect to those territories to which this Convention is not extended at the time of signature, ratification or accession, each State concerned shall consider the possibility of taking the necessary steps in order to extend the application of this Convention to such territories, subject, where necessary for constitutional reasons, to the consent of the Governments of such territories.

Article XI

1. In the case of a federal or non-unitary State, the following provisions shall apply:

(a)   With respect to those articles of this Convention that come within the legislative jurisdiction of the federal authority, the obligations of the federal Government shall to this extent be the same as those of Contracting States which are not federal States;

(b)   With respect to those articles of this Convention that come within the legislative jurisdiction of constituent states or provinces which are not, under the constitutional system of the federation, bound to take legislative action, the federal Government shall bring such articles with a favourable recommendation to the notice of the appropriate authorities of constituent states or provinces at the earliest possible moment;

(c)   A federal State party to this Convention shall, at the request of any other Contracting State transmitted through the Secretary General of the United Nations, supply a statement of the law and practice of the federation and its constituent units in regard to any particular provision of this Convention, showing the extent to which effect has been given to that provision by legislative or other action.

Article XII

1. This Convention shall come into force on the ninetieth day following the date of deposit of the third instrument of ratification or accession.

2. For each State ratifying or acceding to this Convention after the deposit of the third instrument of ratification or accession, this Convention shall enter into force on the ninetieth day after deposit by such State of its instrument of ratification or accession.

Article XIII

1. Any Contracting State may denounce this Convention by a written notification to the Secretary General of the United Nations. Denunciation shall take effect one year after the date of receipt of the notification by the Secretary General.

2. Any State which has made a declaration or notification under Article X may, at any time thereafter, by notification to the Secretary General of the United Nations, declare that this Convention shall cease to extend to the territory concerned one year after the date of the receipt of the notification by the Secretary General.

3. This Convention shall continue to be applicable to arbitral awards in respect of which recognition or enforcement proceedings have been instituted before the denunciation takes effect.

Article XIV

A Contracting State shall not be entitled to avail itself at the present Convention against other Contracting States except to the extent that it is itself bound to apply the Convention.

Article XV

The Secretary General of the United Nations shall notify the States contemplated in article VIII of the following:

(a)   Signatures and ratifications in accordance with article VIII;

(b)   Accessions in accordance with article IX;

(c)   Declarations and notifications under articles I, X and XI;

(d)   The date upon which this Convention enters into force in accordance with article XII;

(e)   Denunciations and notifications in accordance with article XIII.

Article XVI

1. This Convention, of which the Chinese, English, French, Russian and Spanish texts shall be equally authentic, shall be deposited in the archives of the United Nations.

2. The Secretary General of the United Nations shall transmit a certified copy of this Convention to the States contemplated in article VIII.

◆ APPENDIX S ◆

Arguments to Support Rulings on Various Motions and Objections During Arbitration Proceedings

A. INTRODUCTION.

This Appendix A is an idea generator. Its principal purpose is to provide the arbitration advocate, claimant and respondent alike, with a kaleidoscope of ideas for arguments to advance in order to prevail on various oral motions and objections made during the course of an arbitration. It can also be used by the arbitration advocate as a resource to focus legal research in connection with preparing written motions and responses prior to, during, or after an arbitration hearing. In some situations, a single argument will be sufficient independently to provide support for an arbitrator's ruling on a particular motion or objection; in others, several arguments may be combined to provide such support.

Index of Motions and Objections

1. Motion to Dismiss Based on Failure of Party to Timely Initiate Arbitration.
2. Motion to Dismiss Claim Because of Lack of Arbitrability.
3. Motion to Dismiss for Failure to State a Claim.
4. Motion to Dismiss Based on Res Judicata, Collateral Estoppel, or Waiver.
5. Motion to Dismiss for Failure to Prosecute Claim.
6. Motion for Entry of Default Award for Failure to Defend.
7. Motion to Dismiss or to Join a Party.
8. Motion to Sever Claim or Cause of Action.
9. Motion for More Definite Statement.
10. Motion for Entry of An Award on the Pleadings.
11. Motion to Strike Pleadings.
12. Motion for Summary Judgment.
13. Motion to Compel Discovery.
14. Motions for Restraining Orders or Injunctions.
15. Motion for Continuance.
16. Motion for Bifurcated Discovery and/or Arbitration Hearing.
17. Motion for Disqualification of Attorney.
18. Objection to Opening Statement.
19. Motion for Arbitrator to Take Judicial Notice.
20. Motion to Exclude Evidence on Relevance Grounds.
21. Objection to Character Evidence.

22. Objection to Evidence of Habit, Custom, or Common Practice.

23. Objection to Evidence of Subsequent Remedial Measures.

24. Objection to Evidence Based on Assertion of Privilege.

25. Objection to Scope of Direct Examination.

26. Objection to Scope of Cross-examination.

27. Objection to Scope of Redirect Examination.

28. Objection to Scope of Re-cross-examination.

29. Objection to Questioning Procedure or to Substance of Testimony on Direct Examination.

30. Objection to Questioning Procedure or to Substance of Testimony on Cross-examination.

31. Objection to Expert Testimony.

32. Objection to Hearsay Evidence.

33. Assertion of Exception to Hearsay Rule—Admission of Party.

34. Assertion of Exception to Hearsay Rule—Prior Statement of Witness.

35. Assertion of Exception to Hearsay Rule—Excited Utterance.

36. Assertion of Exception to Hearsay Rule—State of Mind: Emotional or Mental State.

37. Assertion of Exception to Hearsay Rule—Statement of Physical Condition.

38. Assertion of Exception to Hearsay Rule: Private, Published, and Institutional Records.

39. Assertion of Exception to Hearsay Rule—Public Records.

40. Assertion of Exception to Hearsay Rule—Declarant Unavailable.

41. Objection to Evidence Based on Lack of Foundation.

42. Objection to Evidence Based on Best Evidence Rule.

43. Objection Relating to Closing Argument.

44. Motion for Reconsideration or for Order for Additional or Amended Findings.

45. Objection Relating to Interest on Award.

46. Objection Relating to Award of Costs.

47. Objection Relating to An Award of Attorney's Fees.

48. Motion to Reopen Arbitration Hearing.

B. SUPPORT FOR ORDERS AND RULINGS ENTERED PRIOR TO ARBITRATION HEARING.

1. Motion to Dismiss Based on Failure of Party to Timely Initiate Arbitration.

ORDER DENYING DISMISSAL OF ARBITRATION PROCEEDINGS	ORDER GRANTING DISMISSAL OF ARBITRATION PROCEEDINGS
POSSIBLE SUPPORTING ARGUMENTS:	*POSSIBLE SUPPORTING ARGUMENTS:*
1. Tolling of time limits	1. Tolling inapplicable
2. Moving party waived right to object	2. Moving party's waiver of right to object was ineffective
3. Moving party fraudulently concealed evidence breach of agreement	3. Nonmoving party lacked diligence in complying with initiation clause
4. Moving party is estopped to complain because of its prior statements or conduct	4. Moving party's silence did not constitute acquiescence in untimely initiation
5. Moving party relied on wrong clause/statute/rule	5. Nonmoving party relied on wrong clause/statute/rule
6. Sufficient evidence of prior acknowledgment by moving party that initiation was timely	6. Insufficient evidence of moving party's prior acknowledgment of timeliness

2. Motion to Dismiss Claim Because of Lack of Arbitrability.

ORDER DENYING DISMISSAL	ORDER GRANTING DISMISSAL
POSSIBLE SUPPORTING ARGUMENTS	*POSSIBLE SUPPORTING ARGUMENTS:*
1. Arbitrability founded in case law	1. Non-moving party waived right to arbitrate claim
2. Statute/rule permits or requires arbitration of claim	2. Non-moving party is estopped from arbitrating claim
3. Parties agreed to arbitrate claim	3. Parties did not agree to arbitrate claim

3. Motion to Dismiss for Failure to State a Claim.

ORDER DENYING DISMISSAL	ORDER GRANTING DISMISSAL
POSSIBLE SUPPORTING ARGUMENTS:	*POSSIBLE SUPPORTING ARGUMENTS:*
1. Allegations sufficient	1. Allegations insufficient and not remediable
2. Errors in statement of claim correctable	2. Allegations consist of legal conclusions
3. Statement of claim is amendable	3. Uncontradicted evidence of affirmative defense obviates non-moving party's ability to state claim
4. Motion to dismiss is insufficiently specific	4. Statement of claim fails to comply with provisions of the arbitration rules

4. Motion to Dismiss Based on Res Judicata, Collateral Estoppel or Waiver.

ORDER DENYING RES JUDICATA OR COLLATERAL ESTOPPEL EFFECT	ORDER BARRING ACTION OR RELITIGATION OF AN ISSUE
POSSIBLE SUPPORTING ARGUMENTS:	*POSSIBLE SUPPORTING ARGUMENTS:*
1. Lack of final judgment on merits	1. Prerequisites for res judicata met
2. Prior judgment is null and void	2. Prior judgment is valid
3. Lack of identity of parties or privity	3. Matters that could have been litigated are barred by res judicata (not collateral estoppel)
4. Different cause of action	4. Failure to plead compulsory counterclaim constitutes waiver and res judicata doctrine bars later suit on such claim
5. Waiver	5. Collateral estoppel bars claim where party had full and fair opportunity to litigate it in prior action

| 6. Lack of mutuality as required by collateral estoppel doctrine | 6. Negligence in litigating prior action is not a defense to the application of collateral estoppel |
| 7. Lack of full and fair opportunity to litigate as required by collateral estoppel doctrine | 7. Statute or rule provision specifically bars relitigation of cause of action or claim |

5. Motion to Dismiss for Failure to Prosecute Claim.

ORDER DENYING DISMISSAL	ORDER GRANTING DISMISSAL
POSSIBLE SUPPORTING ARGUMENTS:	*POSSIBLE SUPPORTING ARGUMENTS:*
1. No abandonment	1. Prejudice to defendant
2. Complicated nature of case	2. Abuse of process
3. Illness	3. Negligence of complainant or counsel
4. Attorney error	4. Noncompliance with arbitrator's orders
5. Delay due to defendant	5. Complainant's specific intent to delay proceedings

6. Motion for Entry of Default Award for Failure to Defend.

ORDER REFUSING DEFAULT AWARD	ORDER GRANTING DEFAULT AWARD
POSSIBLE SUPPORTING ARGUMENTS:	*POSSIBLE SUPPORTING ARGUMENTS:*
1. Compliance with statutes and rules	1. Mandatory statutory provision
2. Nonarbitrability	2. Mandatory rule provision
3. Sufficient appearance	3. Arbitration clause provision
4. Waiver by moving party	4. Non-moving party waived right to object to entry of default award
5. Moving party's defective pleadings	5. Non-moving party estopped from objecting to entry of default award
6. Improper or inadequate notice	6. Proper notice served on non-moving party

7. Inadequate proof of liability (if jurisdiction requires proof of all elements of claims)	7. Moving party presents adequate proof of liability (if required) and damages
8. Inadequate proof of damages	8. Non-moving party's failure to comply with arbitrator's orders or rulings

7. Motion to Dismiss or to Join a Party.

ORDER DENYING DISMISSAL OF PARTY (OR GRANTING MOTION TO JOIN PARTY)	ORDER GRANTING DISMISSAL OF PARTY (OR DENYING MOTION TO JOIN PARTY)
POSSIBLE SUPPORTING ARGUMENTS:	POSSIBLE SUPPORTING ARGUMENTS:
1. Statutory, rule, or contract provision	1. Statutory or rule provision
2. Untimely motion	2. Not a party to arbitration agreement
3. Other Waiver	3. Party has no interest or involvement in subject matter of arbitration

8. Motion to Sever Claim or Cause of Action.

ORDER DENYING SEVERANCE OF CAUSE OF ACTION	ORDER GRANTING SEVERANCE OF CAUSE OF ACTION
POSSIBLE SUPPORTING ARGUMENTS:	POSSIBLE SUPPORTING ARGUMENTS:
1. Complete relief otherwise unattainable	1. Fairness, convenience, or certain prejudice to moving party if there is a single hearing
2. Causes of action/claims interwoven and covered by arbitration clause	2. Avoidance of confusion
3. Prejudice to defendant who would be required to defend in two separate arbitrations	3. Cause of action or claim not covered by arbitration clause or non-moving party waived right to object to severance

9. Motion for More Definite Statement.

ORDER DENYING MOTION FOR MORE DEFINITE STATEMENT	ORDER GRANTING MOTION FOR MORE DEFINITE STATEMENT
POSSIBLE SUPPORTING ARGUMENTS:	*POSSIBLE SUPPORTING ARGUMENTS:*
1. Pleading is acceptable	1. Ambiguous and/or vague pleadings
2. Moving party is seeking opponent's contentions rather than factual allegations	2. Moving party is unable to formulate a response on the basis of the information provided and will be prejudiced
3. Motion is inadequate, unclear, or incomplete	3. Pleading fails to state a claim for relief

10. Motion for Entry of An Award on the Pleadings.

ORDER DENYING MOTION FOR AWARD ON THE PLEADINGS	ORDER GRANTING MOTION FOR AWARD ON THE PLEADINGS
POSSIBLE SUPPORTING ARGUMENTS:	POSSIBLE SUPPORTING ARGUMENTS:
1. Pleading attacked is not fatally defective and can be amended	1. Pleading is fatally defective and defect cannot be cured
2. Resolving all doubts in favor of the non-movant, there is an issue of fact which requires determination	2. No issues of fact are in dispute and only an issue or issues of law need to be resolved
3. Movant waived right to move for judgment on the pleadings by its conduct	3. Non-moving party elects not to respond to motion, thereby waiving right to object to an award on the pleadings
4. Motion is premature	4. Non-movant admitted allegations of pleadings in answers to requests to admit or in answers to interrogatories

11. Motion to Strike Pleadings.

ORDER DENYING MOTION TO STRIKE PLEADINGS	ORDER GRANTING MOTION TO STRIKE PLEADINGS
POSSIBLE SUPPORTING ARGUMENTS:	*POSSIBLE SUPPORTING ARGUMENTS:*
1. Pleadings are sufficient	1. Pleadings are insufficient and vague

2. Granting motion to strike would leave pleadings ambiguous	2. Pleadings are irrelevant, frivolous, or redundant
3. No prejudice to moving party if motion is denied	3. Pleadings are scandalous, impertinent, or a sham
4. Movant waived right to move to strike by prior conduct	4. Denying motion to strike would materially prejudice movant in presenting case

12. Motion for Summary Judgment.

ORDER DENYING MOTION FOR SUMMARY JUDGMENT	ORDER GRANTING MOTION FOR SUMMARY JUDGMENT
POSSIBLE SUPPORTING ARGUMENTS:	*POSSIBLE SUPPORTING ARGUMENTS:*
1. Fact in issue is genuine	1. No Genuine Issue of Material Fact
2. Fact in issue is material	2. Lack of Counter-Affidavits or other responding materials
3. Movant failed to comply with statute or rule regarding inclusion of affidavits, transcripts, or other supporting materials	3. Movant prevails on the issues of law raised

13. Motion to Compel Discovery.

ORDER DENYING MOTION TO COMPEL DISCOVERY	ORDER GRANTING MOTION TO COMPEL DISCOVERY
POSSIBLE SUPPORTING ARGUMENTS:	*POSSIBLE SUPPORTING ARGUMENTS:*
1. Information sought is privileged or otherwise immune from production	1. Information sought is reasonably calculated to lead to the discovery of admissible evidence
2. Motion is made to embarrass or harass a party, or for purposes of delay	2. Asserted privilege is nonexistent or inapplicable
3. Discovery request is overbroad or burdensome	3. Scope of discovery request is reasonable and procedures can be prescribed which facilitates production and lessens its cost

14. Motions for Restraining Orders or Injunctions

ORDER DENYING MOTION FOR TRO, INJUNCTION, OR OTHER INTERIM RELIEF	ORDER GRANTING MOTION FOR TRO, INJUNCTION, OR OTHER INTERIM RELIEF
POSSIBLE SUPPORTING ARGUMENTS:	*POSSIBLE SUPPORTING ARGUMENTS:*
1. Movant has adequate legal remedy	1. Irreparable injury will occur if interim relief is denied
2. Order granting interim relief would restrain nonmovant from exercising legal or Constitutional rights	2. Movant has no adequate remedy at law
3. Movant lacks clean hands in connection with the matter for which he or she seeks relief	3. Movant is likely to succeed on the merits of his or her claims in the arbitration hearing
4. Movant is guilty of laches or has acquiesced in nonmovant's acts	4. Statute or rule authorizes interim relief to be granted on the specific facts presented
5. Any order entered would be overly broad or vague and incapable of compliance	5. Public will not suffer substantial harm if interim relief is granted
6. Movant will not likely succeed on the merits of his or her claims in the arbitration proceeding	6. Substantial public harm will occur if interim relief is not granted

15. Motion for Continuance.

ORDER DENYING MOTION FOR CONTINUANCE	ORDER GRANTING MOTION FOR CONTINUANCE
POSSIBLE SUPPORTING ARGUMENTS:	*POSSIBLE SUPPORTING ARGUMENTS:*
1. Reasons for continuance are inconsequential, frivolous, or not convincing	1. Movant would suffer significant prejudice in presenting case if motion were denied
2. Movant has shown lack of due diligence	2. Movant has shown due diligence
3. Movant has failed to show that evidence which would be unavailable if continuance is denied is material and not merely cumulative	3. Statute or rule specifically requires a continuance be granted in circumstances presented

16. Motion for Bifurcated Discovery and/or Arbitration Hearing.

ORDER DENYING BIFURCATED DISCOVERY AND/OR TRIAL	ORDER GRANTING BIFURCATED DISCOVERY AND/OR TRIAL
POSSIBLE SUPPORTING ARGUMENTS:	*POSSIBLE SUPPORTING ARGUMENTS:*
1. Issues of liability and damages are intertwined	1. Evidence on liability and damages is significantly different
2. Multiple hearings would be overly duplicative and would require recalling of several witnesses	2. Bifurcation would expedite arbitration proceedings and lessen their overall cost
3. Bifurcation would add time and expense with no counter-balancing advantages	3. Bifurcation would be more convenient for the parties, the arbitrators, and the witnesses
4. Issues in case are relatively simple and straight forward	4. Parties consent to bifurcation

17. Motion for Disqualification of Attorney.

ORDER DENYING DISQUALIFICATION OF ATTORNEY	ORDER GRANTING DISQUALIFICATION OF ATTORNEY
POSSIBLE SUPPORTING ARGUMENTS:	*POSSIBLE SUPPORTING ARGUMENTS:*
1. Attorney's client consents to representation after full disclosure of apparent or actual conflict of interest	1. Attorney's conflict of interest which client has not waived or cannot waive
2. Disqualification would work a substantial hardship to the attorney's client	2. Attorney's representation of a party in a present matter adverse to the interests of a former client if there is a substantial relationship between the subject matters of the present and former representations
3. Moving party failed to promptly object	3. Attorney, or another attorney in his/her law firm will be called as a witness on behalf of the attorney's client
4. Moving party would not be prejudiced if disqualification is denied	4. Attorney is senile, mentally incompetent, or under the influence of drugs or alcohol

B. SUPPORT FOR ORDERS AND RULINGS ENTERED DURING THE COURSE OF ARBITRATION HEARING.

18. Objection to Opening Statement.

ORDER SUSTAINING OBJECTION TO OPENING STATEMENT	ORDER OVERRULING OBJECTION TO OPENING STATEMENT
POSSIBLE SUPPORTING ARGUMENTS:	*POSSIBLE SUPPORTING ARGUMENTS:*
1. Attorney is presenting legal arguments	1. Attorney may refer briefly to applicable statute or rule in opening statement
2. Attorney is presenting personal opinion, touting own credibility, or asserting personal knowledge of facts	2. Attorney is not presenting personal opinion, touting own credibility, or asserting personal knowledge of facts
3. Attorney is raising matters outside scope of pleadings	3. Attorney is referring to matters within scope of pleadings
4. Attorney is discussing excluded or inadmissible evidence	4. No ruling has been made with regard to the challenged evidence
5. Attorney's comments are demeaning to opponent's client or witnesses	5. Attorney's references to opposing party's behavior is within the bounds of permissible comment
6. Attorney is exceeding time limits for opening statement	6. Objecting party may have additional time to respond if it desires

19. Motion for Arbitrator to Take Judicial Notice.

JUDICIAL NOTICE REFUSED	JUDICIAL NOTICE TAKEN
POSSIBLE SUPPORTING ARGUMENTS:	*POSSIBLE SUPPORTING ARGUMENTS:*
1. Facts sought to be judicially noticed are uncertain or doubtful	1. Facts sought to be judicially noticed
2. Facts are known to judge personally, but are not common knowledge	2. Judicial notice of certain facts is required by statute or rule

20. Motion to Exclude Evidence on Relevance Grounds.

ORDER SUSTAINING OBJECTION TO RELEVANCE (EVIDENCE EXCLUDED)	ORDER OVERRULING OBJECTION TO RELEVANCE (EVIDENCE ADMITTED)
POSSIBLE SUPPORTING ARGUMENTS:	*POSSIBLE SUPPORTING ARGUMENTS:*
1. Evidence does not tend to prove or disprove issues in case	1. Evidence tends to prove or disprove issues in case
2. Evidence does not render a fact more or less probable	2. Objection is untimely and right to object is therefore waived
3. Evidence is not logically linked to other evidence to aid arbitrator in determining a fact in issue	3. Evidence that is weak, incomplete, or slightly prejudicial does not require exclusion on ground of irrelevance

21. Objection to Character Evidence.

ORDER SUSTAINING OBJECTION TO EVIDENCE OF CHARACTER (EVIDENCE EXCLUDED)	ORDER OVERRULING OBJECTION TO EVIDENCE OF CHARACTER (EVIDENCE ADMITTED).
POSSIBLE SUPPORTING ARGUMENTS:	*POSSIBLE SUPPORTING ARGUMENTS:*
1. Character of party is not at issue	1. Character of party is at issue
2. Unless witness'scharacter has been attacked, character evidence is inadmissible to enhance witness's credibility	2. Evidence of witness's bad reputation for truthfulness or veracity is admissible for impeachment purposes
3. Improper evidence of character is offered (specific acts or personal opinion of witness instead of general reputation of witness in the community)	3. Evidence of a witness's good character or reputation for truthfulness or honesty is admissible to rebut impeaching evidence

22. Objection to Evidence of Habit, Custom, or Common Practice.

ORDER SUSTAINING OBJECTION TO ADMISSIBILITY (EVIDENCE EXCLUDED)	ORDER OVERRULING OBJECTION TO ADMISSIBILITY (EVIDENCE ADMITTED)
POSSIBLE SUPPORTING ARGUMENTS:	*POSSIBLE SUPPORTING ARGUMENTS:*
1. In some jurisdictions, evidence of habit is not admissible to show that a person acted in a particular way at a particular time	1. Federal Rules of Evidence and some jurisdictions allow evidence of habit to be used to prove an act or a specific occasion, if the habit is sufficiently regular and uniform, particularly if there are no eyewitnesses available to testify
2. Evidence of habit is not sufficiently regular or uniform	2. Evidence of habit or customary practices of business organizations (as opposed to individuals) is routinely admissible
3. Evidence of habit is not sufficiently routine	3. Except in cases of negligence per se, or inherently dangerous activities, or dissimilar circumstances, evidence of habit of normally prudent people in performing an act or using a instrument is admissible to permit the arbitrator to decide if the particular use which caused an injury was or was not negligent under the circumstances of its use.

23. Objection to Evidence of Subsequent Remedial Measures.

ORDER SUSTAINING OBJECTION TO EVIDENCE OF SUBSEQUENT REMEDIAL MEASURES (EVIDENCE EXCLUDED)	ORDER OVERRULING OBJECTION TO EVIDENCE OF SUBSEQUENT REMEDIAL MEASURES (EVIDENCE ADMITTED)
POSSIBLE SUPPORTING ARGUMENTS:	*POSSIBLE SUPPORTING ARGUMENTS:*
1. Evidence of subsequent remedial measures is inadmissible to prove negligence	1. Evidence of subsequent remedial measures is admissible to show that such measures are feasible, if feasibility of remedial measures is an issue in case
2. Control of premises is not an issue in the case	2. Evidence is admissible to show control of premises or object, if control is a matter in dispute
3. Physical condition at time of accident is not an issue in the case	3. Evidence is admissible to establish physical conditions existing at time of accident
4. Evidence is not being offered to impeach credibility of witness	4. Evidence may be admitted to impeach credibility of a witness
5. This is not a strict products liability case	5. Evidence is admissible in strict products liability case

24. Objection to Evidence Based on Assertion of Privilege.

ORDER SUSTAINING OBJECTION BASED ON ASSERTION OF PRIVILEGE (EVIDENCE EXCLUDED)	ORDER OVERRULING OBJECTION BASED ON ASSERTION OF PRIVILEGE (EVIDENCE ADMITTED)
POSSIBLE SUPPORTING ARGUMENTS:	*POSSIBLE SUPPORTING ARGUMENTS:*
1. Communication is privileged on basis of common law	1. No common law privilege exists in jurisdiction
2. Communication is privileged on basis of statute	2. No statutory privilege exists in jurisdiction

3. Communication is privileged by prior agreement of the parties	3. Objector has no right to claim privilege because no requisite privileged relationship existed or because of some other technical noncompliance with case law or statute
4. Privilege was not waived, or if waived, waiver was timely withdrawn	4. Objector waived privilege by word or action, such as failure to timely object, or by voluntary disclosure of privileged matter in discovery or privately to third persons

25. Objection to Scope of Direct Examination.

RULING EXCLUDING TESTIMONY	RULING ALLOWING TESTIMONY
POSSIBLE SUPPORTING ARGUMENTS:	*POSSIBLE SUPPORTING ARGUMENTS:*
1. Evidence is irrelevant	1. Evidence is relevant and material
2. Evidence is immaterial	2. Evidence relates to background of witness

26. Objection to Scope of Cross-examination.

RULING EXCLUDING TESTIMONY	RULING ALLOWING TESTIMONY
POSSIBLE SUPPORTING ARGUMENTS:	*POSSIBLE SUPPORTING ARGUMENTS:*
1. Questions seek evidence beyond scope of direct examination	1. Questions seek evidence within scope of direct examination
2. Cross-examiner is attempting to impeach witness on a collateral matter	2. Questions seek evidence relating to credibility witness

27. Objection to Scope of Redirect Examination.

RULING EXCLUDING TESTIMONY	RULING ALLOWING TESTIMONY
POSSIBLE SUPPORTING ARGUMENTS:	*POSSIBLE SUPPORTING ARGUMENTS:*
1. Questions seek to elicit information unrelated to any issue yet raised by either party	1. Questions seek to elicit testimony clarifying the subject matter of the direct examination or any new matters brought out by cross-examination

2. Questions do not seek information designed to rehabilitate witness	2. Questions seek information designed to rehabilitate witness, by bringing forth matters rebutting or explaining unfavorable inferences raised on cross-examination

28. Objection to Scope of Re-cross-examination.

RULING EXCLUDING TESTIMONY	RULING ALLOWING TESTIMONY
POSSIBLE SUPPORTING ARGUMENTS:	*POSSIBLE SUPPORTING ARGUMENTS:*
1. Questions seek information that is cumulative or not within scope of redirect examination	1. Questions seek information responsive to new matters arising on re-cross-examination

29. Objection to Questioning Procedure or to Substance of Testimony on Direct Examination.

ORDER SUSTAINING OBJECTION (EVIDENCE EXCLUDED)	ORDER OVERRULING OBJECTION (EVIDENCE ADMITTED)
POSSIBLE SUPPORTING ARGUMENTS:	*POSSIBLE SUPPORTING ARGUMENTS:*
1. Examiner has asked a leading question, not satisfying a permitted exception to the rule against leading questions on direct examination	1. Leading question on direct examination is appropriate where witness is hostile or where answers of the witness have surprised direct examiner
2. Questions seek cumulative information or are repetitious	2. Leading questions are addressed to preliminary or background matters not in dispute, or they seek to direct witness to a particular subject
3. Questions seek information not based on witness's first-hand knowledge or opportunity to observe	3. Leading questions are permissible where direct examiner has difficulty obtaining intelligible answers because the witness is a child, is timid or ignorant, or has difficulty understanding English

4. In some jurisdictions, it is improper to allow witness to use a memorandum to refresh past recollection where no past recollection is revived if the memorandum is not made at or about the time the events were fresh in the witness's mind	4. Cumulative questioning is permissible where a witness does not understand the question, or gives unclear testimony, or where the witness's answer is incomplete
5. In some jurisdictions, it is improper for witness to use a writing to refresh recollection if no proper foundation is laid for the use of the writing or if adversary is denied opportunity to inspect the writing	5. Witness must testify from personal knowledge or observation, but the opportunity to observe may be limited, attention may be imprecise, and the recall of witness need not be absolutely certain
6. Traditionally, lay witness may not give opinion testimony, particularly when the opinion will prejudice, confuse, or mislead the fact-finder	6. Most jurisdictions allow witness to refresh memory by use of a written memorandum, whether written by witness, or someone else, and whether the document is an original or a copy.
7. Lay witness may not express an opinion about an ultimate fact or issue or to state how he/she thinks a case ought to be decided	7. Most jurisdictions allow a witness' recollection to be refreshed by a photograph, report, record, an object, any document, or even a leading question
8. Lay witness may not give an opinion on conclusions of law	8. Lay witness may give opinion evidence as a matter of convenience, if it would be difficult or impossible for the witness to actual and accurate details, or if the witness is more knowledgeable about the particular subject than the average fact-finder

30. Objection to Questioning Procedure or to Substance of Testimony on Cross-Examination.

ORDER SUSTAINING OBJECTION TO TESTIMONY ON CROSS-EXAMINATION (EVIDENCE EXCLUDED)	ORDER OVERRULING OBJECTION TO TESTIMONY ON CROSS-EXAMINATION (EVIDENCE ADMITTED)
POSSIBLE SUPPORTING ARGUMENTS:	*POSSIBLE SUPPORTING ARGUMENTS:*
1. Question asked by cross-examiner is improper in that it is insulting, harassing, repetitive, argumentative, or causes undue embarrassment	1. Question seeks information showing that witness made a prior inconsistent statement (or made a prior statement with an omission) that is materially inconsistent with witness's current testimony
2. Question seeks information that is not impeaching in that witness' prior statement is not in fact inconsistent with witness's present testimony	2. Question seeks information showing that witness's credibility is impeached because his or her mind or memory is impaired in such a way that the witness's capacity to perceive, remember, or describe correctly is affected
3. Question seeks to impeach witness by eliciting a witness' prior statement without laying a proper foundation for the prior statement	3. Question seeks information showing that the witness's credibility is impeached because the witness is biased, prejudiced, or has an interest in the outcome of the arbitration
4. In some jurisdictions, questions seeking information that would impeach a witness' testimony only on a collateral matter are improper	4. Question seeks information showing that the witness's credibility is impeached because he or she has been convicted of a crime. (In some jurisdictions, the crime must be punishable by imprisonment of more than one year, involve dishonesty, involve moral turpitude, and the conviction must predate the current testimony by a certain limited time period)
5. Question seeks information regarding an arrest, accusation, or prosecution of witness, where no conviction can be proved	5. Question seeks information that witness's credibility is impeached because of the witness's character or reputation for lack of truthfulness

6. Question seeks information regarding witness's drug use solely for the purpose of showing witness is generally unreliable or lacks truthfulness.	6. Question seeks information to show that witness is currently under the influence of drugs while testifying or that the witness was under the influence of drugs at the time of the occurrence at issue

31. Objection to Expert Testimony.

ORDER SUSTAINING OBJECTION TO EXPERT TESTIMONY (EVIDENCE EXCLUDED)	ORDER OVERRULING OBJECTION TO EXPERT TESTIMONY (EVIDENCE ADMITTED)
POSSIBLE SUPPORTING ARGUMENTS:	*POSSIBLE SUPPORTING ARGUMENTS:*
1. Expert's testimony is not limited to matters within his/her expertise	1. Expert is testifying within area of expertise
2. Witness was not properly qualified as expert	2. Expert opinion may be based, in part, on hearsay evidence
3. In some jurisdictions, expert may not give an opinion on an improper hypothetical question	3. Expert witness is properly qualified to testify on the basis of experience, education, and training
4. In some jurisdictions, an expert may not state an opinion based on facts and data not in evidence	4. Some jurisdictions allow expert to give opinion on an ultimate issue in the case
5. In some jurisdictions, expert may not give opinion testimony when the subject matter of the testimony is within the understanding of the average fact-finder	5. Expert may testify as to the particular hypothetical question asked
6. Ordinarily, an expert may not testify to a conclusion of law	6. Expert's prior relationship with party or counsel is insufficient to render testimony non-probative
7. Expert failed to disclose report prior to hearing	7. Error in expert's list of credentials is insufficient to bar his/her testimony

32. Objection to Hearsay Evidence.

ORDER SUSTAINING OBJECTION TO HEARSAY GENERALLY (EVIDENCE EXCLUDED)	ORDER OVERRULING OBJECTION TO HEARSAY GENERALLY (EVIDENCE ADMITTED)
POSSIBLE SUPPORTING ARGUMENTS:	*POSSIBLE SUPPORTING ARGUMENTS:*
1. The statement is other than one made by the declarant while testifying at a trial or hearing and it is being offered in evidence to prove the truth of the matter asserted	1. Objection is untimely
2. The witness's own previous out-of-arbitration statement may constitute hearsay	2. Statement is not offered to prove the truth of the matter asserted, but rather the effect on the hearer of the statement
3. Conduct which was intended as an assertion may be considered as a "statement" excluded by the rule against hearsay	3. The witness's own prior statement is not hearsay because: it was given under oath and it is inconsistent with the witness's current testimony; or, it is consistent with current testimony and it is offered to rebut a charge of recent fabrication; or, it is a statement of past identification; or, it is an admission against interest and offered against that party as such
4. The statement does not satisfy any exception to the rule against hearsay (see below)	4. The statement satisfies one of the exceptions to the rule against hearsay (see below)

33. Assertion of Exception to Hearsay Rule—Admission of Party.

RULING EXCLUDING EVIDENCE (EXCEPTION DOES NOT APPLY)	RULING ADMITTING EVIDENCE (EXCEPTION APPLIES)
POSSIBLE SUPPORTING ARGUMENTS:	*POSSIBLE SUPPORTING ARGUMENTS:*
1. Person making admission lacks capacity to make an admission	1. A written or oral admission of a party or his/her representative is admissible as substantive evidence of the fact admitted even if it is not against interest when made and even if it is opinion or legal conclusion
2. Inconsistent statements in pleadings or pleadings in the alternative are not considered to be admissions	2. An admission in a pleading can be considered a judicial admission which waives production of evidence and removes the admitted fact from controversy
3. An admission by an agent or employee should not be received into evidence if the employment or agency relationship was terminated before the statement was made; or if the statement was not made within the scope of agency or employment	3. An admission by an agent or employee of a party may constitute the party's admission if the statement was made within the scope of the agent's or employee's duties and if it was made while the agency or employment was still in effect
4. Declarant was not in privity with the party to whom admission is to be attributed	4. An admission can be by conduct or by express adoption of another's statement
5. Silence in face of an oral statement may not be considered an admission if the silent person did not hear or understand it; has physical or emotional impediments to responding; had a relationship with speaker such that a denial was difficult or unlikely; reasonably thought the oral statement did not call for a response	5. Silence can constitute an admission where there is a failure to deny or object to an oral or written statement calling for a response or denial

| 6. Subsequent remedial measures, offers to compromise a claim, or offers to pay medical expenses ordinarily do not constitute admissions | 6. An admission may be received into evidence if made by someone in privity with the party against whom the declaration is offered as long as the declaration relates to the interest in property and is made when the declarant has an interest in the property |

34. Assertion of Exception to Hearsay Rule—Prior Statement of Witness.

RULING EXCLUDING EVIDENCE (EXCEPTION DOES NOT APPLY)	RULING ADMITTING EVIDENCE (EXCEPTION APPLIES)
POSSIBLE SUPPORTING ARGUMENTS:	*POSSIBLE SUPPORTING ARGUMENTS:*
1. In some jurisdictions, prior statements are only admissible for the limited purpose of impeachment and may not be used as substantive evidence unless they fall within another recognized exception to the hearsay rule	1. The witness admits in present testimony that the prior inconsistent statement is true
2. In some jurisdictions, no inconsistency can exist where the witness's present testimony is strictly "I don't remember"	2. "Inconsistent" means any material variation between the prior statement and the present testimony of the witness, including omission from the prior statement of a material fact that the witness includes in present testimony
3. A consistent statement made after the source of bias, interest, influence or incapacity arose is irrelevant and inadmissible	3. A consistent statement made soon after the event testified to transpired is admissible to counter allegation that the witness's memory at trial is impaired or that the present testimony is a recent fabrication

4. Consistent statements cannot be used to counter impeachment by prior inconsistent statements since the inconsistency remains despite any statement to the contrary	4. Some jurisdictions admit prior consistent statements to rebut any form of impeachment, including prior inconsistent statements
5. Assertion of exception to hearsay rule is untimely or was waived	5 Assertion of exception to hearsay rule has not been waived

35. Assertion of Exception to Hearsay Rule—Excited Utterance.

RULING EXCLUDING EVIDENCE (EXCEPTION DOES NOT APPLY)	RULING ADMITTING EVIDENCE (EXCEPTION APPLIES)
POSSIBLE SUPPORTING ARGUMENTS:	*POSSIBLE SUPPORTING ARGUMENTS:*
1. Proponent of evidence failed to put forward sufficient independent evidence to support a finding that a startling event occurred and that the declarant actually witnessed it	1. An excited utterance is admissible regardless of whether the statement explains or illuminates the event which provoked it
2. The utterance was not reasonably contemporaneous with the event to which it relates	2. The only tests of competency applying to a declarant of an excited utterance is the ability to observe and communicate
3. Present sense impression was not contemporaneous with event it describes	3. Declarant's emotional condition compensated for and explained the considerable length of time between the excited utterance and the preceding event to which it related
4. Declarant's statement was self-serving and he/she had time to reflect and fabricate before speaking	4. Even though declarant's statement was not an excited utterance, it qualifies for admission as a present sense impression
5. Assertion of exception to the hearsay rule is untimely or was waived	5. Even though there was a substantial time lapse between the event and the declarant's present sense impression, there is substantial circumstantial evidence corroborating the accuracy of the statement

36. Assertion of Exception to Hearsay Rule—State of Mind: Emotional or Mental State.

RULING EXCLUDING EVIDENCE (EXCEPTION DOES NOT APPLY)	RULING ADMITTING EVIDENCE (EXCEPTION APPLIES)
POSSIBLE SUPPORTING ARGUMENTS:	*POSSIBLE SUPPORTING ARGUMENTS:*
1. Statement of witness's belief is inadmissible to prove a fact	1. Statement of intent to perform a certain act is admissible as circumstantial evidence that the declarant acted according to his/her stated intent
2. Declarant's mental or emotional condition did not exist at the time statement was made	2. In some jurisdictions, a declaration of intent by one person to prove that another person acted accordingly is admissible
3. Statement by one person as to the mental or emotional condition of another is inadmissible under the state of mind exception	3. In some jurisdictions, all statements of a deceased declarant, made in good faith with personal knowledge before the litigation commenced, are admissible
4. A declaration of mental or emotional condition is inadmissible because the declarant's state of mind is not an issue in th ase	4. Mental or emotional condition of the declarant is the key fact on which an element of the case depends

37. Assertion of Exception to Hearsay Rule—Statement of Physical Condition.

RULING EXCLUDING EVIDENCE (EXCEPTION DOES NOT APPLY)	RULING ADMITTING EVIDENCE (EXCEPTION APPLIES)
POSSIBLE SUPPORTING ARGUMENTS:	*POSSIBLE SUPPORTING ARGUMENTS:*
1. Statements of medical history, past pain, symptoms, or causation do not fall within hearsay exception for physical condition	1. In some jurisdictions, a spontaneous statement of physical condition is admissible even though it was made to a nonphysician, and Federal Rules of Evidence extend rule to statements of medical history, past or present symptoms, pain sensations or general causation made for the purpose of medical diagnosis or treatment

2. Statements were made for the purpose of preparing a physician to testify on declarant's behalf	2. Nonspontaneous statement regarding physical condition was made to a physician for the purpose of obtaining his testimony, but the declarant had a significant treatment motive in consulting the physician, and evidence that the declarant followed the physician's advice is highly probative of treatment motive
3. Statements made to physician related to fault and are not admissible under the physical condition exception	3. Under the Federal Rules of Evidence, all statements on which a non-treating physician relied in forming his/her opinion are admissible as substantive evidence
4. Assertion of the exception is untimely or was waived	4. Declaration of someone other than patient is admissible because it was made for the purpose of obtaining medical treatment

38. Assertion of Exception to Hearsay Rule—Private, Published, and Institutional Records.

RULING EXCLUDING EVIDENCE (EXCEPTION DOES NOT APPLY)	RULING ADMITTING EVIDENCE (EXCEPTION APPLIES)
POSSIBLE SUPPORTING ARGUMENTS:	*POSSIBLE SUPPORTING ARGUMENTS:*
1. Proponent of evidence has not shown that the private record was made when the facts were still fresh in the declarant's mind and that the information in the private record was true and accurate when the private record was made	1. Under Federal Rules of Evidence, total loss of memory is not required as a prerequisite to admission of past recollection recorded
2. Business record is inadmissible were the informant had no business duty to report the information to the author	2. "Business record" is liberally construed and "business" consists of almost any regularly conducted, organized activity for purposes of the exception

3. Record was prepared with a view toward litigation and not in the regular course of business	3. Computer printouts, results of psychological tests, desk calendars, notes of conversations, photographs, and short-hand notes have qualified for admissibility under the business records exception
4. Too much time lapse between the event and the recording to allow record to be admitted under the business records exception	4. Party has not waived right to assert the exception

39. Assertion of Exception to Hearsay Rule—Public Records.

RULING EXCLUDING EVIDENCE (EXCEPTION DOES NOT APPLY)	RULING ADMITTING EVIDENCE (EXCEPTION APPLIES)
POSSIBLE SUPPORTING ARGUMENTS:	*POSSIBLE SUPPORTING ARGUMENTS:*
1. Record contains information given to the author by another person, and the informant's statements do not fall within an exception to the hearsay rule	1. Investigatory records of public agencies are admissible if they involve "factual findings," findings of law, and conclusions based on disputed factual information supplied to the author by other persons
2. The broader business records exception cannot be used to justify admissibility of investigatory records of public agencies	2. The public records exception does not exclude investigatory records of a public agency on the ground that they were primarily prepared with a view to litigation
3. Source of information contained in public record lack trustworthiness	3. A report made to a public agency by one with a professional duty is admissible under the public records exception
4. Declarations of remote cause in death certificates, as opposed to immediate cause, are inadmissible because such statements were made to the examining physician by another person	4. Judgment of a foreign court in a criminal matter qualifies for admission under the public records exception if the foreign proceedings were conducted according to standards of civilized jurisprudence

5. Mere fact that report is required by law does not satisfy admissibility requirement that declarant have an official or professional duty to report	5. Evidence of prior conviction is admissible in the present proceeding to prove a fact that was a necessary element of the criminal offense
6. Evidence of a prior conviction is inadmissible to prove facts that were not essential to sustain the judgment	6. Party did not waive right to assert exception to hearsay rule

40. **Assertion of Exception to Hearsay Rule—Declarant Unavailable**.

RULING EXCLUDING EVIDENCE (EXCEPTION DOES NOT APPLY)	RULING ADMITTING EVIDENCE (EXCEPTION APPLIES)
POSSIBLE SUPPORTING ARGUMENTS:	*POSSIBLE SUPPORTING ARGUMENTS:*
1. Advantages of proceeding with hearing without declarant's live testimony do not outweigh need for granting a postponement	1. Declarant's testimony is unavailable when declarant is dead, sick, insane, is beyond reach of process, invokes a privilege against testifying, or refuses to testify
2. Proponent of evidence failed to show that he/she exhausted all reasonable means to obtain the testimony by making a good faith effort to locate missing declarant and by taking all reasonable steps necessary to subpoena declarant to ensure presence at hearing	2. In some jurisdictions, when the declarant is beyond reach of process, proponent need not make an effort to secure declarant's voluntary testimony
3. Prior testimony of unavailable declarant is inadmissible because party against whom the testimony is offered did not have an adequate opportunity and similar motive to examine the declarant when the testimony was taken	3. Prior testimony is admissible because party against whom it is being offered (or predecessor in interest) had an opportunity and similar motive to develop the testimony during the former proceedings
4. Declaration against interest was not against declarant's interest at the time the statement was made	4. Declarations against interest includes statements against proprietary, pecuniary, penal, and social interests.

5. Declaration against interest is inadmissible because, at the time the statement was made, the declarant would not have been competent to testify	5. Unlike an admission, which may only be use against the party who made it or his/her privies in interest, a declaration against interest may be introduced in evidence by or against anyone
6. Assertion of exception to hearsay rule is untimely or was waived	6. Many of the traditional restrictions on use of a dying declaration have been abandoned; it is now usually admissible in civil cases; where declarant believed death was imminent though he/she later recovered, and statements are not necessarily restricted to the cause or circumstances of death.

41. Objection to Evidence Based on Lack of Foundation.

RULING EXCLUDING EVIDENCE (FOUNDATION INADEQUATE)	RULING ADMITTING EVIDENCE (FOUNDATION ADEQUATE)
POSSIBLE SUPPORTING ARGUMENTS:	*POSSIBLE SUPPORTING ARGUMENTS:*
1. Proponent of evidence has not advanced sufficient admissible evidence to support a finding of authenticity	1. Question of whether the proponent of evidence has proved an adequate chain of custody goes to weight rather than to the admissibility of the evidence
2. Lay witness may not authenticate genuineness of handwriting if his/her familiarity with the handwriting by making only a single comparison with another sample for purposes of adversary proceedings	2. Methods of authentication may be used alone or in combination to build a prima facie case of authenticity
3. Fact that telephone caller identified himself is insufficient in itself to authenticate the identity of the caller	3. A privately maintained document is properly authenticated by the testimony of a witness with knowledge of either a direct or circumstantial nature, and answers to interrogatories are properly considered as testimony for purposes of authentication

4. Proponent of evidence failed to authenticate specimen	4. Authenticity may be proven by showing that the document contains information only the purported author was likely to know, that the appearance of the document suggests a single source, that the document was a reply to another authenticated communication, or that the document reflects the special linguistic characteristics of its author
5. Proponent of computer-generated evidence failed to authenticate it by testimony that describes the process or system and proves that it produces accurate results	5. In some jurisdictions, certain documents are presumed authenticate--i.e. are self-authenticating: newspapers, periodicals, trade inscriptions, commercial paper, and certified copies of public documents including judgments of conviction

42. Objection to Evidence Based on Best Evidence Rule.

RULING EXCLUDING SECONDARY EVIDENCE	RULING ADMITTING SECONDARY EVIDENCE
POSSIBLE SUPPORTING ARGUMENTS:	*POSSIBLE SUPPORTING ARGUMENTS:*
1. Secondary evidence is inadmissible where there is an insufficient showing that the original could not be produced	1. Best evidence rule does not apply where a writing is not offered to prove its contents such as instances: where witness testifies about an event that was only incidentally memorialized in writing; where a writing is used to refresh a witness's recollection or to illustrate his/her testimony; or where a witness testifies that records do not contain a particular entry

2. Best evidence rule may be applied to exclude the testimony of a witness concerning the identity, rather than the contents, of a writing if the witness had to take note of the contents in order to make the identification	2. A duplicate is admissible to the same extent as an original unless a genuine question is raised concerning the authenticity of the original or it would be unfair to admit the duplicate in lieu of the original
3. Original of a photograph or recording must be produced to prove its contents	3. Secondary evidence is admissible to prove contents of original if: there is proof that the original was lost or destroyed but not in bad faith; the original is outside the reach of the process; or the writing is collateral to a material issue
4. Photocopies are secondary evidence and inadmissible unless production of the original is excused	4. Secondary evidence is admissible where original was destroyed by accident or mistake or in the ordinary course of business
5. Duplicate document is inadmissible because it is incomplete or illegible, or evidence shows that the original document may have been intentionally destroyed thereby producing an inference of fraud	5. Contents of a public record may be proven by a certified copy
6. Proponent's request to offer secondary evidence is untimely	6. Objector waived right to require best evidence

43. Objection Relating to Closing Argument.

ORDER OVERRULING OBJECTION TO SCOPE AND CONTENT OF CLOSING ARGUMENT	ORDER SUSTAINING OBJECTION TO SCOPE AND CONTENT OF CLOSING ARGUMENT
POSSIBLE SUPPORTING ARGUMENTS:	*POSSIBLE SUPPORTING ARGUMENTS:*
1. Comment on discrepancy between pleading and proof is proper in closing argument	1. Scope of closing argument is properly confined to the record

2. Counsel may argue law in closing argument	2. Counsel refers to facts not in evidence or misstates the evidence in the record
3. Counsel is allowed wide latitude to make emotional argument in closing	3. Counsel's overly emotional appeals are improper
4. Counsel may legitimately comment on failure of opponent to call an available witness	4. Counsel may not express his/her personal belief in the justness of the client's cause or the credibility of the witnesses, nor assert his/her personal knowledge of the facts in issue

D. SUPPORT FOR ORDERS AND RULINGS ENTERED AFTER ARBITRATION HEARING.

44. Motion for Reconsideration or for Order for Additional or Amended Findings.

ORDER DENYING RECONSIDERATION OR ADDITIONAL OR AMENDED FINDINGS	ORDER GRANTING RECONSIDERATION OR ADDITIONAL OR AMENDED FINDINGS
POSSIBLE SUPPORTING ARGUMENTS:	*POSSIBLE SUPPORTING ARGUMENTS:*
1. Movant's request is untimely	1. Case issued after the close of the evidence but before ruling should be considered by the arbitration panel
2. Movant's request for reconsideration is without merit	2. Reconsideration of quality or quantity of evidence pertaining to a critical aspect of claim or defense is proper
3. Movant had access to evidence he/she now wishes to present to the arbitration panel as "newly discovered evidence"	3. Additional findings are necessary to effectuate the arbitration award

45. Objection Relating to Interest on Award.

ORDER REFUSING TO AWARD INTEREST OR REDUCING THE AMOUNT OF INTEREST AWARDED	ORDER AWARDING INTEREST
POSSIBLE SUPPORTING ARGUMENTS:	*POSSIBLE SUPPORTING ARGUMENTS:*
1. Party was not deprived of use of money for the period during which interest was awarded	1. Statute requires award of interest
2. No interest may be imposed where money is not part of award, such as an award in rem	2. Rule requires award of interest
3. Statute does not allow an award of interest	3. Agreement requires award of interest
4. By statute, interest is not due on a lump sum payable in installments	4. Case law requires award of interest
5. Wrong date used to begin interest computation	5. Law permits pre-award interest
6. Improper method used to compute interest	6. Additional interest is awardable because of error in computation

46. Objection Relating to Award of Costs.

ORDER REFUSING TO ALLOW COSTS	ORDER ALLOWING COSTS
POSSIBLE SUPPORTING ARGUMENTS:	*POSSIBLE SUPPORTING ARGUMENTS:*
1. No statute or rule expressly provides for the awarding of costs	1. Statute or rule makes the award of costs mandatory
2. Party requesting costs is not a "prevailing party" within the meaning of the statute or rule	2. Costs may be assessed against a party for misconduct of its attorney such as for filing untrue pleadings, or for unduly delaying proceedings

3. Prevailing plaintiff is not entitled to costs because defendant offered a sum to settle before hearing pursuant to rule, and plaintiff is being awarded an amount less than that sum	3. Defendant offered an amount in judgment prior to arbitration and plaintiff proceeded to trial and recovered less than the amount offered
4. Entity requesting costs is not technically a party to the arbitration	4. Party requesting costs was prevailing party
5. Party failed to submit a bill of costs in accordance with the pertinent statute or rule	5. Party requesting costs is a bonafide party to the arbitration
6. Party's request for costs is premature; it must await outcome of arbitration of consolidated case	6. Party's request for costs is timely
7. Party waived its right to request costs prior to the hearing	7. Party has not waived its right to request costs

47. Objection Relating to An Award of Attorney's Fees.

ORDER REFUSING ATTORNEY'S FEES	ORDER ALLOWING ATTORNEY'S FEES
POSSIBLE SUPPORTING ARGUMENTS:	*POSSIBLE SUPPORTING ARGUMENTS:*
1. No statute, rule, or contract provision provides for an award of attorney's fees	1. Statute or rule specifically provides for an award of attorney's fees
2. Party requesting fees is not a prevailing party	2. Successful litigant sued on behalf of a class and provided a common benefit
3. Party requesting fees did not actually incur the expenses of an attorney	3. Party seeks attorney's fees because opposing party acted in bad faith
4. Prevailing party acted for himself and there is no common benefit	4. Party seeks attorney's fees because opposing party conducted the arbitration vexatiously, oppressively, or unreasonably

5. Prevailing party is not entitled to attorney's fees under the bad faith exception to the rule precluding them when the opposing attorney merely litigates a claim in an unsettled area of the law and loses	5. Party seek attorney's fees because opposing party willfully abused the judicial process
6. Attorney's fees may be reduced if the award is based on an improper method of calculation	6. Party seeks attorney's fees because opposing party perpetrated a fraud on the court
7. Party waived right to request attorney's fees	7. Party did not waive right to request attorney's fees

48. Motion to Reopen Arbitration Hearing.

ORDER REFUSING TO REOPEN ARBITRATION HEARING	ORDER ALLOWING REOPENING OF ARBITRATION HEARING
POSSIBLE SUPPORTING ARGUMENTS:	*POSSIBLE SUPPORTING ARGUMENTS:*
1. Motion to reopen hearing is untimely	1. Motion to reopen hearing is timely made
2. Movant failed to comply with requirements of statute or rule	2. Newly discovered evidence came to light after the arbitration hearing, the party discovering the evidence was not negligent in failing to discover it prior to the hearing, the evidence is material and not merely cumulative, the evidence is such that it is reasonably probable that it would change the result of the arbitration
3. Movant failed to specify grounds for reopening hearing	3. Movant would be greatly prejudiced if hearing were not reopened
4. Offer of proof, if admitted as evidence, would not change arbitrators' decision	4. Arbitrators reopen hearing on their own motion to take additional evidence
5. No just cause exists for reopening hearing	5. Hearing is reopened to permit counsel to argue applicability of recent Supreme Court decision to the facts of this case
6. Movant waived his right to request reopening of hearing	6. Movant did not waive his right to request reopening of hearing

◆INDEX◆